# RANDOM HOUSE WEBSTER'S

# DICTIONARY

## OF THE

# Law

JAMES E. CLAPP
Member of the New York and
District of Columbia Bars

Random House
New York

**Library of Congress Cataloging-in-Publication Data:**

Clapp, James E. (James Edward), 1943-
    Random House Webster's Dictionary of the Law / James E. Clapp.--1st Random House ed.
    p. cm.
  ISBN: 0-375-70239-3
  1. Law--United States--Dictionaries. I. Title: Webster's dictionary of the law. II. Title: Dictionary of the law. III Title.

KF156.C57 2000
349.73'03--dc21                                              00-059098

Visit the Random House Web site at www.randomhouse.com

Typeset and printed in the United States of America.
9 8 7 6 5 4 3

New York   Toronto   London   Sydney   Auckland

*For my mother*
Laura R. Clapp
*and in memory of my father*
Harold L. Clapp

# Contents

# Preface

The law touches every aspect of our lives. It regulates the food we buy, the water we drink, the drugs we take, the air we breathe. It controls whom we can marry and what our sexual and reproductive rights are. It sets the standards for care and education of our children. It governs our business and financial relationships; our rights as consumers; the qualifications we must have to practice trades and professions; our rights if we are injured or cheated; our obligations toward others and the penalties if we fail; what we can read and what we can say; what property we can own, what use we can make of it, and how it may be disposed of when we die. The law determines what country we can live in; our rights and duties as a citizen; how we will be governed; and how we can change the government. International law attempts even to regulate the conduct of entire nations: their rights with respect to each other; their conduct in times of war; their obligations to humanity and the environment.

The language of law is therefore as broad and complex as human experience itself. Defining, refining, debating, interpreting, and applying the words of constitutions and statutes, contracts and wills, judicial opinions and scholarly writings, is a major preoccupation of the law.

It is, in fact, a fundamental preoccupation: to question the meaning of a legal term is to question the scope of the law itself. A complete definition of the legal concept of "murder," for example, would embody an understanding of how contemporary society draws some of its most difficult and important moral lines, distinguishing the most heinous of crimes from an act of self-defense, military heroism, merciful medicine, mental derangement, understandable passion, or simple negligence.

As society evolves, the language of law expands: Ancient terms describing the legal foundations upon which the culture was built, like *fee simple absolute* and *habeas corpus*, are augmented by more modern concepts, such as *freedom of religion* and *antitrust*, in a continuing process that in recent years has added terminology for such contemporary concerns as *soft money, cybersquatting, covenant marriage, civil union, physician-assisted suicide,* and *ethnic cleansing*.

*Random House Webster's Dictionary of the Law* seeks to present the vocabulary of law in a way that provides not just each term's meaning in isolation but also an understanding of its place in the larger legal picture.

To this end, this dictionary features

- groups of related phrases collected and defined together to flesh out the meaning of the main entry term.
- copious cross references to related or contrasting terms that help to place an entry in context and clarify its scope.
- regular use of illustrative phrases and sentences to show how a term is used correctly in legal discourse.
- supplementary notes for extended discussion of such matters as historical background, usage, pronunciation, and "false friends"—those terms whose technical meanings differ substantially from their ordinary meanings, often to the surprise of nonlawyers.
- appendices containing (1) the full text of the Constitution introduced by a guide to orient the user, summarize the principal provisions, and direct attention to the entries in the dictionary where key constitutional terms are discussed; (2) an outline of the principal units and agencies of the United States government and of the United Nations, the European Union, and other international organizations; and (3) a selected list of Internet metasites that can serve as a springboard to legal information available on the World Wide Web.

JEC
New York
April 2000

## Acknowledgments

Many people have been instrumental in bringing this work to fruition. Particular thanks go to my friends and colleagues William H. Roth, Esq.; Baila H. Celedonia, Esq.; Sue E. Spencer; Nancy S. Erickson, Esq.; and Paul E. Merrell, Esq.; all of whom provided essential support, advice, and assistance. Each one's contributions were unique and invaluable; I am very much in their debt.

Everyone associated with Random House Reference and Information Publishing has been exceptionally gracious and helpful. Among them, special thanks go to Charles Levine, the division's Publisher when this project was undertaken, and Wendalyn Nichols, Editorial Director of Dictionaries, both of whom have been unfailingly supportive. I am grateful to Patricia Ehresmann, Lisa Abelman, and Beth Levy for their careful and efficient attention to production details. My appreciation also goes to Paul Hayslett of Cow Bay Software, Helen Langone, and Constance Baboukis, who together provided the computer expertise for the creation, management, and final composition of the Dictionary's complex database of SGML-tagged text. To prepare the electronic manuscript in Standard Generalized Markup Language, I used the XML/SGML and macro capabilities of Corel WordPerfect 8 and 9.

Scholarly research requires access to scholarly resources, and libraries and librarians make it possible. My admiration and appreciation go to the helpful and knowledgeable circulation and reference librarians at three great libraries: the Science, Industry and Business Library of the New York Public Library, the Library of the Association of the Bar of the City of New York, and especially the Arthur W. Diamond Law Library at my alma mater, the Columbia University School of Law.

Above all, I extend my profound gratitude to my editor, Enid Pearsons, for her counsel, encouragement, and hard work throughout. Her guidance and assistance in every aspect of the undertaking made this book possible.

# Guide to the Dictionary

## Main Entries

### Word Order

Main entries, printed in **large bold type,** are alphabetized word by word. For example, the various Latin phrases beginning with the word *per* (such as **per curiam, per se,** and **per stirpes**) are grouped together before such words as **percentage lease, perjury,** and **person.**

Hyphenated entries and entries containing slashes are alphabetized according to whether the underlying form is one word or two. Discrete words joined by hyphens or slashes are alphabetized word by word:

> **buy and bust**
> **buy-sell agreement**
> **buyer**

> **free press**
> **free press/fair trial**
> **free speech**

But if the hyphen or slash merely sets off a prefix or a single letter, the entry is alphabetized as if the punctuation were not there and that part of the term were solid:

> **antilapse statute**
> **anti-spam law**
> **antitrust**

> **eloign**
> **e-mail harassment**
> **emancipation**

> **fault**
>
> **f/b/o**
>
> **fealty**

Periods are disregarded, and ampersands (&) are treated as if spelled out: **J.D.** is alphabetized as "JD"; **E&O insurance** as "E and O insurance." Numerical entries, like **401(k) plan,** are alphabetized as if the first digit were spelled out.

## Parts of Speech

Most entries are given part of speech labels (see abbreviations on p. xx), and definitions are grouped by part of speech:

> **patent** *n.* **1.** the exclusive right to exploit an invention for a number of years . . .
> **2.** a formal document conferring rights, official status, or the like . . .
> —*v.* **3.** to apply for and receive a patent on one's invention.
> —*adj.* **4.** open; public rather than private; intended as a public record . . .
> **5.** obvious; apparent at a glance or upon reasonable inspection . . .

## Terms with Identical Spellings

Certain terms, although spelled alike, are given separate entries (marked by superscript numbers) in order to distinguish between unrelated or easily confused meanings, forms, and uses. For example, the word *acquit* has meanings that are historically related but very different in modern usage. Distinguishing them is important because the related noun forms of the word are different:

> **acquit¹** *v.* . . . to release a criminal defendant from a charge . . .
> —**acquittal** *n.*
>
> **acquit²** *v.* . . . to release a person from a contractual obligation . . .
> —**acquittance** *n.*

## Subentries

Many entries include related terms and phrases of various kinds, shown within the entry in **bold** type:

## Phrases Containing the Main-Entry Term

For ease of comparison, selected phrases containing the main-entry term are defined under that term. These phrases are grouped by part of speech; for example, at **contract,** the noun definitions and the phrases using *contract* as a noun are grouped together, followed by the verb definition:

> **contract** *n.* **1.** broadly, any legally en-
> forceable promise . . .
> **2.** in its usual sense, an agreement
> among two or more persons or entities
> . . .
> **3.** a document embodying such an
> agreement.
> **4. adhesion contract** a preprinted
> contract that is not subject to negotia-
> tion . . .
> **5. aleatory contract** (in civil law, as
> in Louisiana) a contract in which the
> performance of one or both parties, or
> the extent of performance, depends
> upon uncertain future events . . .
> . . .
> **23. unilateral contract** . . .
> **24. yellow-dog contract** . . .
> —*v.* **25.** to enter into a contract . . .

## Alternate Forms

Alternate terms with the same meaning and alternate spellings for the same term
are introduced by such signals as "or," "Also," "Also called," or "Also spelled":

> **treason** *n.* . . . .
> **4. petit** (or **petty**) **treason** in early
> English law, the murder of one (other
> than a royal) to whom one owed alle-
> giance . . .

> **term of art** *n.* a word or phrase having
> a special meaning in a particular field,
> different from or more precise than its
> customary meaning. Also called **word
> of art** or, when referring to a phrase,
> **words of art**.

## Terms Defined in Context

Some terms related to a main-entry term are incorporated into the text of the definition, where their meaning is made clear:

> **demise** *n.* . . . .
> **2.** the leasing of a ship by the owner
> (the **demisor**) to another (the **demi-
> see**) upon terms whereby the owner
> completely relinquishes possession,
> command, and navigation of the vessel
> to the demisee for the duration of the
> contract . . .

> **domicile** *n.* the place where one has one's permanent and primary home . . . One can have many residences, but only one domicile. One whose domicile is in a particular place is said to be **domiciled** there or to be a **domiciliary** of that place . . .

## Run-on Entries

Grammatically related terms whose meanings are easily derivable from the meanings of the main-entry term are given at the end of the definitions. These differ from the main entry in the presence or absence of a standard suffix:

> **usury** *n.* the crime of charging a higher rate of interest for a loan than is allowed by law.
> —**usurer** *n.*
> —**usurious** *adj.*
> —**usuriously** *adv.*

## Inflected Forms

*Nouns*

Nouns that have plurals normally form them by adding -*s* or -*es*: *law, laws; heiress, heiresses.* Unless otherwise indicated, any noun in this dictionary that can be pluralized follows this regular pattern. Plurals of words and phrases that in standard American legal usage are formed in any other way are shown in full:

> **administratrix** *n., pl.* **administratrices**

> **court-martial** *n., pl.* **courts-martial**

Plurals of words and phrases that might be confusing are shown even if formed regularly:

> **subpoena** *n., pl.* **subpoenas**
> [not *subpoenae*]

The plural forms indicated for nouns labeled *Latin* represent the nominative plural (e.g., **jus** *n., pl.* **jura; res** *n., pl.* **res**). Users familiar with Latin will understand that many other singular and plural forms exist (e.g., the forms used in the phrases *de jure* and *in rem*).

*Verbs*

Verbs normally form both the past tense and past participle by adding *-ed,* and the present participle by adding *-ing.* When a verb forms its principal parts in any other way, they are shown in full:

**aver** *v.*, **averred, averring**

**buy** *v.*, **bought, buying**

When the past tense and past participle are different, both are shown:

**take** *v.*, **took, taken, taking**

Occasionally the principal parts of a verb are shown to make it clear that they are formed in the regular way:

**implead** *v.*, **impleaded** . . .
[not *impled*]

## Labels

An italicized label quickly categorizes a term. For example, a label can identify a term as relating to a particular era or area of law (*English Legal History; International Law*) or advise that it is claimed to be proprietary (*Trademark*) or is significantly more casual in tone than is typical of legal discourse (*Informal; Slang; Police Jargon*).

Words and phrases in another language, most frequently *Latin, French,* or *Law French* (a dialect used extensively in English law in the fourteenth and fifteenth centuries and quite distinct from modern French), are so labeled. Unless the current definition is substantially the same as the original meaning, a more literal translation is added in parentheses:

**cy pres** *n. Law French.* (lit. "as near") the doctrine under which a court confronted with a deed or will whose terms cannot be carried out exactly may modify it so as to carry out the intent of the maker as nearly as possible
. . .

**parens patriae** *n. Latin.* (lit. "parent of the country," originally a reference to the King or Queen) a state government in its role as protector of the people, and especially of children and the mentally infirm . . .

## Illustrative Examples

Many definitions include phrases or sentences showing how the term is used. These examples are shown in *italics:*

> **stale** *adj.* rendered ineffective or unen-
> forceable by the passage of time: *stale
> check; stale claim; stale offer.*

> **go to** to bear upon; be relevant to the
> issue of: *That evidence is admissible
> because it goes to the witness's credibil-
> ity. Point 3 of their brief goes to the
> constitutionality of the statute.*

## Case Citations

Quotations from judicial opinions are identified by the name of the case and a citation to the opinion in conventional legal form. For example, the Supreme Court's
landmark decision outlawing racial segregation in public schools, handed down in
1954, is cited: *Brown v. Board of Education,* 347 U.S. 483 (1954), meaning that it is
published in United States Reports, volume 347, at page 483.

## Cross References

References to main entries in another part of the dictionary are printed in SMALL
CAPITALS; references to subentries are printed in *italics.* Such cross references serve
several purposes:

1. Directing the user to the main entry where a term that the user has looked up
   is defined:

> **adhesion contract** *n.* See under CON-
> TRACT.

2. Showing where phrases using a particular entry term are defined:

> **judicial** *adj.* **1.** relating to a court or the
> courts . . .
> **2.** relating to a judge or judges . . .
> . . .
> See also *judicial bond* (under BOND²);
> *judicial day* (under DIES JURIDICUS);
> *judicial discretion* (under DISCRETION);
> . . .

3. Signaling that a key term in a definition is itself defined elsewhere in the dictionary:

> **burden²** *n.* **1.** a restriction upon the uses that an owner may make of a piece of land, resulting from an EASE-MENT, a *covenant running with the land* (see under COVENANT), or the like
> . . .

4. Calling attention to related or contrasting entries that enlarge upon a definition by placing the term in a broader context:

> **freedom of religion** *n.* the freedom to hold and practice one's religious beliefs and freedom from government involvement in religious matters . . . See also SEPARATION OF CHURCH AND STATE.

Sometimes attention is drawn to another subentry under the same main entry, in which case the small-capital reference to the main entry term is omitted. Often the reference is to a contrasting subentry, signaled by "Cf." (meaning "compare"):

> **jurisdiction¹** *n.* **1.** the power and authority of a court or administrative tribunal to decide legal issues and disputes . . .
>
> . . .
>
> **3. appellate jurisdiction** jurisdiction to review orders and judgments of a lower tribunal. Cf. *original jurisdiction.*
>
> . . .
>
> **15. original jurisdiction** jurisdiction to give a case its first hearing and issue a judgment . . . Cf. *appellate jurisdiction.*

## Supplementary Notes

Many entries end with one or more notes containing supplemental information. These may touch upon any aspect of the term or concept under discussion, but the following specific types are the most common:

**Usage** notes discuss preferred spelling or terminology, grammar, technical distinctions, historical vs. modern terminology, and the like. See, for example, the notes at MAKE ("make a check" vs. "draw a check") and PLEAD ("pleaded" vs. "pled").

**History** notes examine the origins or development of a legal term or principle (sometimes ancient, sometimes recent), significant or interesting cases on the subject, and the like. See the notes at IGNORAMUS (discussing how this legal term entered the nonlegal vocabulary) and SEPARATE BUT EQUAL (discussing the concept in the context of recent cases on sex-segregated public education).

**Pronunciation** notes call attention to particular niceties or peculiarities in the pronunciation of specific legal terms. They use "newspaper style" respellings rather than special pronunciation symbols. See the notes at PRECEDENT (distinguishing the noun and adjective pronunciations) and OYEZ (explaining the history of both the traditional pronunciation and the more recent, less authentic one).

**False Friend** notes highlight terms whose legal meanings differ from their ordinary meanings in ways that could be confusing for nonlawyers. See the notes at IN-FANT (not necessarily a baby) and CRIMINAL CONVERSATION (not a crime and not conversation).

## Personal Pronouns

The approach taken in this book to the perennial problem of masculine and feminine pronouns (he/she, him/her, etc.) is to use them interchangeably and randomly. Unless the context clearly indicates otherwise, each should be read as including the other. Obviously, no suggestion should be read into any use of such a term that one sex is more likely than the other to sue or be sued, commit a crime or a tort, be a lawyer or a judge, or the like.

## Abbreviations

| | |
|---|---|
| abbr. | abbreviation |
| adj. | adjective |
| adv. | adverb |
| amend. | amendment |
| art. | article |
| Brit. | British |
| c. | circa |
| cf. | compare (Latin *confer*) |
| cl. | clause |
| conj. | conjunction |
| def., defs. | definition, definitions |
| e.g. | for example (Latin *exempli gratia*) |
| esp. | especially |
| i.e. | that is (Latin *id est*) |
| interj. | interjection |
| lit. | literally |
| n. | noun |
| n.pl. | plural noun |
| pl. | plural |
| prep. | preposition |
| v. | verb; versus (in case names) |
| vs. | versus (other than in case names) |
| § | section |

# A

**a aver et tener** *Law French.* to have and to hold; for having and holding. See HABENDUM CLAUSE and note at TO HAVE AND TO HOLD.

**a fortiori** *adv. Latin.* (lit. "by a stronger [reason]") even more certainly; all the more: used in arguing that one proposition necessarily implies another, especially where the second is included within the first: *The plaintiff never read the prospectus; a fortiori, she was not misled by it.*

**a mensa et thoro** *adj. Latin.* (lit. "from table and bed") from bed and board. See *divorce a mensa et thoro* (under DIVORCE).

**a quo** *adj. Latin.* from which. See also *court a quo* (under COURT); DIES A QUO; *judge a quo* (under JUDGE); TERMINUS A QUO. Cf. AD QUEM.

**a vinculo matrimonii** *adj. Latin.* from the bond of marriage. See *divorce a vinculo matrimonii* (under DIVORCE).

**ab ante** *adv. Latin.* (lit. "from before") in advance.

**ab antiquo** *adv. Latin.* from antiquity.

**ab initio** *adv. Latin.* from the beginning; see, for example, *void ab initio* (under VOID).

**ABA** AMERICAN BAR ASSOCIATION.

**abandon** *v.* **1.** to give up a right, claim, or interest without specifically transferring it to someone else.
**2.** to desert a child or spouse. See also DESERTION.
**3.** *Marine Insurance.* to relinquish to the insurer all rights to a ship or cargo that has been damaged or lost, as a condition of receiving payment upon a claim of total loss under the insurance policy. This enables the insurer to salvage whatever it can in order to reduce its losses. *When the news arrived that the ship had sunk, the owner abandoned the vessel. Finding the insured cargo of fresh fruit to be a complete loss after the delay caused by the typhoon, the shipper elected to abandon.*
—**abandonable** *adj.*
—**abandonment** *n.*

**abandonee** *n.* a party to whom a right or property has been relinquished; especially, an insurer to whom a ship or cargo has been abandoned.

**abate** *v.,* **abated, abating. 1.** to reduce or eliminate: *abate taxes; abate rent; abate a nuisance.*
**2.** to diminish or be extinguished: *The action abated because the plaintiff failed to serve the defendant with a summons.*
—**abatable** *adj.*
—**abatement** *n.*

**abator** *n.* **1.** one who abates a nuisance.
**2.** in old law of real property, one who wrongfully takes over land whose owner has died, before the heir or devisee of the property can take possession.

**abdicate** *v.,* **abdicated, abdicating. 1.** to renounce or relinquish a position, right, duty, or responsibility, especially one conferred by law, and most especially the throne: *The state must not abdicate its trust over property in which the whole people are interested. Within a year after he became king, Edward VIII abdicated.*
**2.** in Roman law, to disown or disinherit: *He abdicated his son.*
—**abdicable** *adj.*
—**abdicative** *adj.*
—**abdication** *n.*
—**abdicator** *n.*

**abduction** *n.* **1.** KIDNAPPING, especially of another's child, ward, or spouse.
**2.** the tort of luring away, carrying off, or concealing another's spouse or child. When no force is involved, also called

**enticement.** The tort has its origins in a man's ownership of his wife and children and his right to compensation for being deprived of their services. The modern scope of the tort varies from state to state.

**abet** *v.*, **abetted, abetting.** to incite, encourage, instigate, or support, especially something bad. In legal contexts, used almost exclusively in, or as short for, the phrase AID AND ABET.
—**abettor, abetter** *n.*

**abeyance** *n.* **1.** a temporary or indefinite state of inactivity; suspension of activity. Often in the phrase 'in abeyance': *Work on the dam is in abeyance while the court considers the motion for an injunction.*
**2.** a gap in ownership of land or occupancy of a position; the status of an estate or a title when there is no person in being in whom it is vested.

**abide** *v.*, **abided** (for 1–5) or **abode** (for 4), **abiding. 1.** to await. For example, see *costs to abide the event* (under COSTS).
**2.** to accept; submit to; adhere to: *to abide the decision of the court.* See also LAW-ABIDING.
**3.** to tolerate: *Our legal system cannot abide jury tampering.*
**4.** to remain; dwell; reside: *While the appeals drag on, the defendant abides in jail.*
**5. abide by** to act in conformity with; to submit to and obey: *Jurors must abide by the judge's instructions.*

**abiding** *adj.* steadfast; unshakeable; permanent (sometimes well-founded, sometimes not): *Our legal system is based upon an abiding belief in the wisdom of the jury.* See also LAW-ABIDING.

**abiding conviction** *n.* a very firm belief; in particular, a sufficiently strong belief in the guilt of a criminal defendant, based upon the evidence in a case, to warrant a guilty verdict. See also ABIDING FAITH; MORAL CERTAINTY.

**abiding faith** *n.* **1.** an unshakeable belief, especially a belief that does not depend upon proof: *The parents withheld consent for surgery on the child because of their abiding faith in God's healing*

*powers.*
**2.** Same as ABIDING CONVICTION.
—**Note.** In some jurisdictions this phrase is used in instructing jurors as to the kind of confidence that they must have in a criminal defendant's guilt in order to convict. For example, jurors may be told that if, after considering the evidence, they have an "abiding faith to a moral certainty in the defendant's guilt," then they may find the defendant guilty BEYOND A REASONABLE DOUBT. The phrase "abiding faith" in this context is singularly misleading, since it suggests that ultimately what is required is not a reasoned conclusion based upon the evidence but a leap of faith. See also note at MORAL CERTAINTY.

**abjuration** *n.* **1.** renunciation of allegiance, upon oath.
**2.** any act of abjuring.
Cf. ADJURATION.

**abjure** *v.*, **abjured, abjuring. 1.** to renounce or give up under oath; forswear: *To become a naturalized citizen one must abjure allegiance to foreign powers.*
**2.** to renounce, repudiate, retract, or recant, especially under oath or with formal solemnity: *On the stand, the defendant abjured his signed confession.*
**3.** to avoid or shun: *My client abjures alcohol.*
Cf. ADJURE.
—**abjuratory** *adj.*
—**abjurer** *n.*

**able buyer** *n.* See under BUYER.

**abnegate** *v.*, **abnegated, abnegating.** to reject, renounce, or relinquish, as a right, privilege, duty, or belief.
—**abnegation** *n.*
—**abnegator** *n.*

**abnormally dangerous activity** *n.* an activity, such as blasting, that is regarded as so inherently dangerous that anyone who engages in it should be held strictly liable for any damage it causes to person or property. Also called **ultrahazardous activity.** See also *strict liability* (under LIABILITY).

**abode¹** *n.* dwelling; the place in which a person resides: *For several weeks the* *family's only abode was a beat-up automobile.* Also called **place of abode.**

**abode²** *v.* a past tense and past participle of ABIDE.

**abolish** *v.* to do away with; put an end to; annul; repeal: *Lincoln's Emancipation Proclamation abolished slavery in those states or parts of states then in rebellion against the United States.*
—**abolishable** *adj.*
—**abolisher** *n.*

**abolition** *n.* **1.** the act of abolishing. **2.** the state of being abolished; annulment; abrogation. **3.** the legal prohibition and ending of slavery, especially the slavery of blacks in the United States.
—**abolitionary** *adj.*

**abolitionism** *n.* **1.** the principle or policy of abolition, especially of slavery of blacks in the United States. **2.** the nineteenth century movement to abolish slavery in the United States.
—**abolitionist** *n.*

**abortifacient** *adj.* **1.** capable of causing abortion.
—*n.* **2.** a drug or device that causes abortion.

**abortion** *n.* the intentional termination of a pregnancy other than by live birth. A limited right of a woman to decide for herself whether to seek an abortion is included in the RIGHT TO PRIVACY protected by *substantive due process* (see under DUE PROCESS).

**about** *adv.* See ON OR ABOUT.

**above** *adv.* previously in the same document: *the authorities cited above.* See also SUPRA.

**abridge** *v.*, **abridged, abridging.** to restrict or diminish a legal right: *The First Amendment prohibits Congress from abridging freedom of speech.*
—**abridgment** *n.*

**abrogate** *v.*, **abrogated, abrogating.** to annul, repeal, overturn, supersede, or cancel by some legally effective means: *to abrogate a statute, an order, a contract, a will.*
—**abrogation** *n.*

**abs. re.** ABSENTE REO.

**abscond** *v.* to depart from a jurisdiction or secrete oneself in order to avoid arrest, service of a summons or other process, or action by creditors: *He absconded with the stolen stock certificates.*
—**absconding, abscondence** *n.*

**absence without leave (AWOL)** *n.* in military law, the offense of being away from one's post without permission, but without the intention of deserting. Cf. DESERTION (def. 2).

**absent without leave (AWOL)** *adj.* away from one's military duties without permission, but without the intention of deserting.

**absente** *Latin.* (lit. "being absent") being absent; in the absence of. Used in old case reports to refer to a judge who did not participate in a particular action: *per curiam (Nevius, J., absente). The court en banc (absente Smith, J.) affirmed the decision.*

**absente reo (abs. re.)** *Latin.* (lit. "the defendant being absent") the defendant being absent; in the absence of the defendant: *When the defendant refused to leave his jail cell to appear in court the judge issued a contempt citation absente reo.*

**absentee** *n.* a person who is absent from a place where one would normally expect to find him, such as school or work or the state where he is domiciled or the place where an official duty is to be performed.

**absentee ballot** *n.* a paper ballot for use by an ABSENTEE VOTER, which may be cast by mail.

**absentee landlord** *n.* a LANDLORD who does not reside near the leased premises and is not readily available to deal with problems concerning the property.

**absentee voter** *n.* a citizen who is permitted to vote by mail because she expects to be absent from her voting district or unable to get to the polls on election day.

**absenteeism** *n.* **1.** the collective repeated absence of employees from a

place of business, students from a school, or the like: *Legislators' need to spend time fund-raising contributes to absenteeism in the Legislature.*
**2.** frequent absence from a place of duty by a particular individual: *The employee was fired for unexplained absenteeism.*
**3.** The practice of being an absentee landlord.

**absentia** *n.* See IN ABSENTIA.

**absolute** *adj.* unrestricted; unencumbered; unconditional. A term used to distinguish an unqualified right, interest, duty, privilege, order, transaction, document, or the like from one that is qualified in some way. See, for example, *absolute discretion* (under DISCRETION); *absolute divorce* (under DIVORCE); *absolute immunity* (under IMMUNITY); *absolute privilege* (under PRIVILEGE); *decree absolute* (under DECREE); *fee simple absolute* (under FEE[1]); *judgment absolute* (under JUDGMENT); *rule absolute* (under RULE).

**absolute law** *n.* Same as NATURAL LAW.

**absolution** *n.* **1.** in canon law, the act by which the clergy declare that a penitent's sins are forgiven.
**2.** in ancient civil law, an acquittal; a judicial declaration that the accused is innocent of the crime charged.
**3.** the state of being absolved.

**absolutism** *n.* **1.** the principle or practice of government through exercise of complete and unrestricted power over the people governed, as by a dictator, absolute monarch, or military junta.
**2.** any theory holding that values or principles are absolute and not relative, dependent, or changeable.
—**absolutist** *n.*

**absolve** *v.,* **absolved, absolving. 1.** to grant ABSOLUTION.
**2.** to free of guilt or suspicion: *The suspect was absolved by the DNA evidence.*
**3.** to free from a duty, responsibility, or obligation: *The first clause of the will absolved the decedent's brother from his debts to the decedent.*

**abstain** *v.* **1.** to hold oneself back voluntarily, especially from something regarded as improper or unhealthy.
**2.** to refrain from casting a vote or participating in deliberations, especially because of a conflict of interest or as a matter of principle.
**3.** of a court, to refuse to decide a case within its jurisdiction out of deference to another tribunal.

**abstention** *n.* **1.** any act of abstaining.
**2.** especially, the act of a federal court in refusing to exercise its jurisdiction over a case on the ground that the issues would be better dealt with by a state court or an administrative agency.
**3. abstention doctrine a.** the doctrine that federal courts should abstain from exercising their jurisdiction in some situations. **b.** any of several rationales for federal court absention in different kinds of cases. These are typically associated with the name of the United States Supreme Court decision in which the doctrine was first applied.
**4. Burford absention** absention by a federal court from considering challenges to state administrative regulations and proceedings when federal review would disrupt state efforts to establish a coherent policy in a matter of substantial public concern. Named after *Burford v. Sun Oil Co.,* 319 U.S. 315 (1943).
**5. equitable abstention a.** refusal by a court to enjoin or interfere with proceedings in another tribunal when the party seeking relief has not shown that he lacks an adequate remedy in the other proceeding; particularly, *Younger abstention.* **b.** broadly, any refusal by a court to exercise its jurisdiction over a case out of deference to another tribunal. See also COMITY; FORUM NON CONVENIENS.
**6. Pullman abstention** abstention by a federal court from deciding a constitutional question that depends upon interpretation of a state law, to await interpretation of the law by the courts of that state. Named after *Railroad Commission of Texas v. Pullman Co.,* 312 U.S. 496 (1941).

**7. Rooker-Feldman abstention** abstention by a lower federal court from considering a challenge to a state court judgment on the ground that the judgment itself violates federal rights. The proper avenue for such a challenge is appeal through the state court system. Named after *Rooker v. Fidelity Trust Co.*, 263 U.S. 413 (1923), and *District of Columbia Court of Appeals v. Feldman*, 460 U.S. 462 (1983).

**8. Thibodaux abstention** abstention by a federal court from intervening in eminent domain proceedings involving unsettled questions of state law. Named after *Louisiana Power & Light Co. v. City of Thibodaux*, 360 U.S. 25 (1959).

**9. Younger abstention** abstention by a federal court from enjoining or interfering with state proceedings, especially state criminal proceedings, out of faith that the arguments of the party seeking federal intervention can be raised and fairly determined in the state forum. Named after *Younger v. Harris*, 401 U.S. 37 (1971).
See also OUR FEDERALISM.

**abstract** *n.* **1.** a very concise digest or summary that captures the essence of the original.
**2.** an excerpt or set of excerpts containing the essential elements of the original.
—*v.* **3.** to make an abstract of; summarize.
**4.** to withdraw; take out; take away.
**5.** to remove wrongfully or by stealth; to steal.
—**abstracter** *n.*

**abstract of record** *n.* a concise digest of the RECORD of a case prepared by the attorneys for the benefit of the appellate court, summarizing all steps in the case so far and showing how the issues on appeal were raised and decided in the courts below.

**abstract of title** *n.* a summary of the history of ownership of a parcel of land, with a list of encumbrances on the land. An abstract of title is typically prepared in connection with a proposed sale of land, by a company in the business of ferreting out such information from public records.

**abstraction** *n.* **1.** the act of taking away or separating; withdrawal.
**2.** Also called **wrongful abstraction.** unauthorized withdrawal of funds or financial instruments with intent to misappropriate them.

**abuse** *n., v.,* **abused, abusing.** —*n.* **1.** mistreatment of a person: *physical abuse; psychological abuse.* See also CHILD ABUSE; SPOUSAL ABUSE.
**2.** wrongful or unwarranted exercise of a right or power. See, e.g., ABUSE OF DISCRETION; ABUSE OF PROCESS.
—*v.* **3.** to mistreat or use wrongfully.

**abuse excuse** *n. Informal.* **1.** the legal tactic in which a criminal defendant offers evidence of a history of physical or psychological mistreatment as an explanation for the conduct with which the defendant is charged, especially in cases involving violent retaliation against the alleged abuser.
**2.** Any specific excuse of that nature.
—**Usage.** The phrase is employed almost exclusively to disparage: Those who are sympathetic to the defendant refer to his "history of victimization"; those who are not deride his "abuse excuse."

**abuse of discretion** *n.* an unsound or illogical ruling by a court or administrative body on a matter within its DISCRETION. A discretionary ruling will not be reversed simply because the reviewing court would have decided the matter differently, but only if the decision is found to be so unreasonable as to constitute an "abuse of discretion." The phrase does not imply wrongdoing; it simply indicates that the tribunal committed an error. Also called **improvident exercise of discretion.**

**abuse of process** *n.* the tort of instituting a judicial proceeding or otherwise using judicial PROCESS for an improper purpose. Essentially it is the use of an otherwise justifiable judicial procedure as a form of extortion to gain some advantage or benefit unrelated to the legitimate objective of the judicial proceeding. This tort differs from MALICIOUS PROSECUTION in that there may have been a legally sufficient basis for instituting such a proceeding, but the actual purpose to which the proceeding is put is wrongful.

**abut** *v.*, **abutted, abutting.** to border on; to touch (said of a parcel of land).

**abuttals** *n.pl.* the boundaries of a piece of land as viewed in relation to adjoining lands and features.

**abutter** *n.* one who owns adjacent land.

**academic degree** *n.* See under DE-GREE.

**academic freedom** *n.* **1.** freedom of a teacher or student to discuss or investigate any issue, or express any opinion, without interference or penalty from the school or the state.
**2.** freedom of a school from governmental control over its policies.
**——Note.** The extent to which academic freedom is legally recognized and protected depends upon many factors, including whether the school involved is at the primary, secondary, or university level and whether the school is public or private.

**accede** *v.*, **acceded, acceding. 1.** to give consent, approval, or adherence, especially when it involves yielding a position of one's own: *The Senate acceded to the House amendment.*
**2.** to become a party to an international treaty by way of ACCESSION.
**3.** to assume an office or title: *When Edward VIII abdicated in 1936, his brother acceded to the throne.*

**accelerate** *v.*, **accelerated, accelerating. 1.** to cause a legal right, duty, or interest that was to arise or vest in the future to arise or vest immediately.
**2.** in particular, to cause a debt that was to be repaid in the future to become immediately due: *Under the terms of the automobile loan, his failure to pay one installment accelerated the entire debt.*
**—acceleration** *n.*

**acceleration clause** *n.* a clause in a credit agreement providing that upon the occurrence of specified events the party extending credit may declare the entire outstanding balance immediately due. The purpose of such clauses is to enable the creditor to take immediate legal action to recover the amount loaned if it appears that the debtor is in financial difficulty.

**accept** *v.* to manifest satisfaction with or assent to a transaction, proposal, or state of affairs, thereby becoming legally bound. For example: **a.** in property law, to take delivery of property or otherwise give formal assent to becoming the owner. **b.** in contract law, to agree to an offer. This is the final step in forming a legally binding contract. **c.** in the case of a bank or other entity upon which a check or other draft is drawn, to indicate on the instrument that it will be paid; for example, to certify a check.
**—acceptance** *n.*
**—acceptor** *n.*

**access** *n.* **1.** the ability, right, or permission to approach, enter, speak with, use, or view; admittance.
**2.** Also called **easement of access.** the right of the owner of land that abuts a public highway use the highway to enter and leave the land. See also *easement of access* (under EASEMENT).
**3.** Also called **parental access.** VISITATION by a parent with a child of whom the parent does not have custody.
**4.** in paternity cases, **a.** circumstances that could afford the putative father an opportunity for sexual intercourse with the mother. **b.** sexual intercourse in such circumstances. See note below.
**5. multiple access** the defense in a paternity action that other men also had, or could have had, sexual relationships with the mother at the relevant time. See note below.
**6. public access** a right of access available to the public at large.
**——History.** DNA technology has virtually eliminated the issue of "access" in paternity actions. There is no longer any need or excuse for the unseemly spectacle of a mother and putative father arguing about whether they had sexual intercourse at the relevant time, or whether there are other men who could have fathered the child in question. These unnecessary dramas are still played out, but they have moved from

the courtroom to a different forum—the daytime television talk show.

**accessary** n., pl. **accessaries.** Variant of ACCESSORY.
—**accessarily** adv.
——**Usage.** This was a common spelling until well into the twentieth century, but it has now largely given way to the -o- spelling.

**accession** n. **1.** increase or enlargement by something added, as by the addition of territory to a country: *the accession of East Germany by the Federal Republic of Germany after the fall of the Berlin Wall.*
**2. a.** addition to property by growth or improvement, as by a receding water line or construction of buildings. **b.** the principle that the owner of anything becomes the owner of anything produced by the property or added to it.
**3.** consent or agreement, especially when it involves some yielding of one's own position.
**4.** in international law, formal assent by one nation to a treaty already concluded between other nations, by which the nation acceding to the treaty becomes a party to it.
**5.** the act of acceding to an office or title.

**accessory** n., pl. **accessories. 1.** one who assists a criminal in connection with a crime, especially a felony, without being present when the crime is committed.
**2. accessory after the fact** one who knowingly assists a person who has committed a felony to avoid or hinder capture, prosecution, conviction, or punishment. This conduct is usually treated as an offense of less severity than the felony itself, often under the name HINDERING PROSECUTION. See also OBSTRUCTION OF JUSTICE.
**3. accessory before the fact** one who encourages or assists in the planning or commission of a felony without being present. An accessory before the fact is an *aider and abettor* (see under AID AND ABET) and is ordinarily regarded by the law as equally culpable with the person who directly commits the felony.

—**accessorial** adj.
—**accessorily** adv.

**accident** n. **1.** an undesirable or unfortunate happening that occurs unintentionally, especially one that results in harm, injury, damage, or loss.
**2.** an event, especially an undesirable or harmful event, that is unusual in the circumstances in which it occurred and unexpected by the person to whom it happens.
**3. unavoidable accident** an accident that occurs without any intention, negligence, or other fault on the part of anyone involved. Also called **inevitable accident.**
—**accidental** adj.
—**accidentally** adv.

**accident insurance** n. insurance that compensates the insured for losses incurred because of an accident.

**accidental death** n. death resulting from an accident; death resulting from an unusual and unexpected event.
——**False Friend.** In legal usage, a death may be "accidental" even if it is intentional. Insurance policies that provide an ACCIDENTAL DEATH BENEFIT typically pay the benefit if the insured is murdered.

**accidental death and dismemberment insurance** n. insurance that pays the insured or the insured's beneficiary specified amounts for loss of a limb or other specified body parts or functions, or death, resulting from an accident.

**accidental death benefit** n. an extra payment provided for by a life-insurance or accident-insurance policy, to be paid if the insured suffers an ACCIDENTAL DEATH. See also DOUBLE INDEMNITY.

**accommodated party** n. See under ACCOMMODATION PARTY.

**accommodating party** n. Same as ACCOMMODATION PARTY.

**accommodation** n. something done as a favor rather than for consideration, especially acting as a SURETY: *The* *mother signed the car loan as an accommodation to her son.* See also PUBLIC ACCOMMODATION.

**accommodation note** *n.* See under NOTE[1].

**accommodation paper** *n.* a NEGOTIABLE INSTRUMENT signed by one person solely as an ACCOMMODATION to another party to the instrument.

**accommodation party** *n.* a person who adds her signature to a negotiable instrument or credit agreement, and so becomes liable on it, solely as a favor to the signer who really owes the money (the **accommodated party**). This is often done when a person taking the instrument or extending the credit is not satisfied with the creditworthiness of the accommodated party. Also called **accommodating party** or, in the case of one signing a promissory note, **accommodation maker.**

**accomplice** *n.* one who, for the purpose of promoting or facilitating a crime, solicits or encourages another to commit it, assists or attempts to assist in its planning or commission, or in some situations simply fails to make an attempt to prevent it. An accomplice is normally equal in culpability to the person who directly commits the crime.

**accord** *n.* **1.** an agreement to settle a claim for a sum of money to be paid in the future, or occasionally for some other performance.
**2. accord and satisfaction** an accord that has been satisfied by rendering the promised payment or performance. A claim that is the subject of an accord and satisfaction can never again be raised in court.

**account** *n.* **1.** a record of money transactions, especially one of a complete set of such records for the various financial dealings of a business, kept in accordance with standard bookkeeping principles. See also *book of account* and *books of account* (under BOOK), MONEY OF ACCOUNT.
**2.** a list of financial transactions between two parties, typically a buyer and seller of goods or services, showing amounts of money paid and to be paid

as a result of their business with each other.
**3.** the balance remaining to be paid, or credit balance to be refunded, shown by such an account.
**4.** in Article 9 of the Uniform Commercial Code, a right to payment for goods sold or leased or for services rendered which is not evidenced by a negotiable instrument or chattel paper.
**5.** a business relationship involving management of money or extension of credit: *brokerage account; charge account.*
**6.** Same as ACCOUNTING (defs. 1, 2).
**7.** a common law FORM OF ACTION or writ to compel a person to account for money or property; superseded by the equitable proceeding for an ACCOUNTING.
**8.** Also called **bank account.** a deposit of money in a bank, pursuant to an agreement with the bank as to services it will provide (such as payment of checks), interest to be paid by the bank for the use of the money, and fees to be paid by the depositor.
**9. deposit account** any account with a bank, credit union, or similar financial institution in which money is deposited, other than an account evidenced by a certificate of deposit.
**10. individual account** a bank account held by one person only.
**11. joint account** a bank account held by two or more people, each of whom may withdraw funds without the consent of the other. Such an account usually entails a RIGHT OF SURVIVORSHIP, so that any balance in the account when one holder dies becomes the property of the surviving holders. See also *Totten trust* (under TRUST).
**12. open account a.** an account showing a balance that has not yet been paid. **b.** Also called **running account.** an account for transactions in an ongoing business relationship.
—*v.* **13.** of a fiduciary, to render an ACCOUNTING (def. 1).

**account creditor** *n.* the person to whom the balance of an ACCOUNT is owed. Cf. ACCOUNT DEBTOR.

**account debtor** *n.* **1.** the person who

owes the balance of an ACCOUNT, typically a purchaser of goods or services on credit. Cf. ACCOUNT CREDITOR.

**2.** in Article 9 of the Uniform Commercial Code, the person who is obligated on an account, CHATTEL PAPER, or certain intangible property.

**account payable** *n., pl.* **accounts payable. 1.** an ACCOUNT showing a balance owed to another person or entity. **2.** the balance owed as shown by such an account. Often referred to somewhat less formally as a **payable.** Cf. ACCOUNT RECEIVABLE.

**account receivable** *n., pl.* **accounts receivable. 1.** an ACCOUNT showing a balance owed to the account holder by another person or entity. **2.** The balance that the account holder is owed as shown by such an account. Often referred to somewhat less formally as a **receivable.** Cf. ACCOUNT PAYABLE.

**account rendered** *n., pl.* **accounts rendered.** a statement of account presented by the ACCOUNT CREDITOR to the ACCOUNT DEBTOR.

**account stated** *n., pl.* **accounts stated. 1.** a statement of account upon which the parties agree; typically it is prepared by the party to whom money is owed and submitted to the debtor, who indicates assent. **2.** a common law action for the balance due upon such an account. See also COMMON COUNTS.

**accountability** *n.* **1.** the state of being accountable, liable, or answerable. **2.** a policy or practice of holding people responsible their acts or for the success or failure of projects or institutions under their supervision or control.

**accountable** *adj.* subject to the obligation to report, explain, or justify something; responsible; answerable.

**accountancy** *n.* the profession of an ACCOUNTANT.

**accountant** *n.* **1.** a person whose profession is accounting. **2. public accountant** an accountant who offers accounting services to the public for a fee, and exercises independent judgment in performing such services. Also called **independent public accountant.** See also CERTIFIED PUBLIC ACCOUNTANT.

**accountant-client privilege** *n.* an *evidentiary privilege* (see under PRIVILEGE), adopted in some states, shielding confidential information provided by a client to an accountant from discovery. Also called **accountant's privilege.**

**accountant's privilege** *n.* Same as ACCOUNTANT-CLIENT PRIVILEGE.

**accounting** *n.* **1.** a detailed description of how the assets in an estate or trust fund have been managed and disposed of. **2.** a proceeding, which originated in courts of equity, to compel a FIDUCIARY or a *constructive trustee* (see under TRUSTEE) to account for all assets handled in a fiduciary capacity and to turn over any profits received. **3.** the theory and practice of setting up, maintaining, auditing, and analyzing the financial records of a firm. For defs. 1, 2, also called **account.**

**accounting method** or **method of accounting** *n.* **1.** a consistent and accepted method of calculating the income and expenses of an individual or enterprise and allocating them to a particular ACCOUNTING PERIOD for financial statement or tax purposes. **2. accrual method** an accounting method in which income is reported when earned rather than when received, and expenses are reported when incurred rather than when paid. **3. cash method** an accounting method in which income is reported when received and expenses are reported when paid. **4. completed contract method** an accounting method in which income and expenses associated with a long-term project are not reported until the project is completed. **5. percentage of completion method** an accounting method in which income and expenses associated with a long-term project are reported periodically in proportion to the percentage of the project completed so far.

**accounting period** *n.* a regular span of time, such as three months or one year, covered by a single set of financial statements or tax returns for an individual or entity.

**accredit** *v.* **1.** to acknowledge or certify as possessing necessary credentials or qualifications.
**2.** to certify that a school, college, or the like meets certain minimum educational standards. See also *accredited law school* (under LAW SCHOOL).
**3.** in international law, to bestow or acknowledge status as a diplomat; to send or receive an envoy or ambassador.
—**accreditation** *n.*

**accrete** *v.* accreted, accreting. to grow or add to by ACCRETION.

**accretion** *n.* **1.** gradual increase in land belonging to a property owner or a state or nation through natural processes such as gradual change in the course of a river or gradual receding of a water line.
**2.** the land added by such a process. See also ALLUVION; RELICTION.
—**accretive, accretionary** *adj.*
——**Note.** Land added to the property of an individual or a political jurisdiction by accretion becomes legally a part of that property. For example, if the action of water in a river gradually erodes soil from one bank and deposits it downstream on the other bank, the property of the landowner on the first bank gradually gets smaller and the property of the landowner on the second bank gradually gets larger. Cf. AVULSION.

**accrual method** *n.* See under ACCOUNTING METHOD.

**accrue** *v.,* accrued, accruing. **1.** (of a financial right or obligation) to come into existence, mature, or accumulate: *accrued interest.*
**2.** (of a legal claim) to arise; to come into existence or mature so that it can be sued upon: *The statute of limitations begins to run when the cause of action accrues.*
—**accrual** *n.*

**accumulation trust** *n.* See under TRUST.

**accusatorial system** *n.* the Anglo-American system of criminal prosecution, in which the government, having accused the defendant, must prove its allegations by the adversary process, with the judge acting only as a neutral referee. Same as ADVERSARY SYSTEM, except that the latter term applies to both civil and criminal cases. Cf. INQUISITORIAL SYSTEM.

**accusatory instrument** *n.* a formal document accusing a person of a crime and initiating a criminal prosecution, such as an INFORMATION or INDICTMENT.

**accused** *n.sing. or pl.* a person or persons arrested, indicted, or otherwise formally charged with a crime; the defendant(s) or prospective defendant(s) in a criminal case: *The Sixth Amendment guarantees the accused the right to a speedy and public trial.*

**acknowledgment** *n.* **1.** an admission of the truth of a fact or the existence of an obligation, by which one accepts civil legal responsibility. This may be by words ("I am the father of that child") or by action (e.g., signifying acknowledgment of a debt by making a partial payment).
**2.** an individual's declaration that she is the one who executed a particular deed or other instrument, and that she did so for the purposes stated in the instrument. Such an acknowledgment is made before a notary public or similar officer, who is responsible for confirming the individual's identity, and who puts a formal notation of the acknowledgment on the instrument.
Also, esp. Brit., **acknowledgement.**
—**acknowledge** *v.,* acknowledged, acknowledging.
—**acknowledger** *n.*

**acquaintance rape** *n.* See under RAPE.

**acquest** *n.* **1.** in civil law, an item of property acquired other than by inheritance.

**2. acquests and gains** noninherited property and income added to the COMMUNITY PROPERTY of a married couple in a *community property state* (see under COMMUNITY PROPERTY).
**3. community** (or **partnership**) **of acquests and gains** in community property states, **a.** a married couple viewed in relation to its community property. **b.** the marital relationship viewed as a regime of property ownership.
See also ACQUET.

**acquet** *n. Louisiana Law.* ACQUEST.
——**Usage.** Although the English spelling *acquest* is sometimes seen in Louisiana, especially in older cases, the preferred term in that state is *acquet,* from the French *acquêt.* Since Louisiana is the only state that still uses this terminology other than in historical contexts, in modern American cases one is more likely to see **acquet, aquets and gains, community of aquets and gains,** or **partnership of aquets and gains** than the more widely applicable but now less-used forms defined at ACQUEST.

**acquit¹** *v.,* **acquitted, acquitting.** to release a criminal defendant from a charge, either upon a finding of NOT GUILTY by the jury or because the court or the prosecution determined that the case should not go forward after the trial was commenced. See also AUTREFOIS ACQUIT; DOUBLE JEOPARDY.
——**acquittal** *n.*

**acquit²** *v.,* **acquitted, acquitting.** to release a person from a contractual obligation (especially an obligation to pay money) or acknowledge that the obligation has been fulfilled, as by giving a receipt.
——**acquittance** *n.*

**act** *n.* **1.** a statute: *act of Congress; legislative act; the Civil Rights Act of 1964.* See also *private act* (under PRIVATE LAW); *public act* (under PUBLIC LAW).
**2.** something done (an **affirmative act** or **act of commission**) or under some circumstances not done (a **negative act** or **act of omission**) by a person. See also ACTUS REUS; AUTHENTIC ACT;

OMISSION; OVERT ACT; VERBAL ACT.
——**actor** *n.*

**act of bankruptcy** *n.* under former bankruptcy law, any of a number of specific acts that could subject one to being proceeded against as a BANKRUPT.

**act of God** *n.* a natural event such as lightning, a hurricane, an earthquake, or some other natural catastrophe beyond human causation or control. Sometimes such events provide an excuse for nonperformance of an obligation, either because a contract specifically so provides or as a matter of law.

**act of insolvency** *n.* an act indicating that an individual or entity is INSOLVENT, and subjecting the party to INSOLVENCY PROCEEDINGS.

**act of state** *n.* an official act of a foreign government. Under the relevant doctrine (the **act of state doctrine**), American courts will not question the validity of such an act (for example, the expropriation of American property) by a recognized foreign government within its own territory.

**act of war** *n.* an act of aggression by a country against another with which it is nominally at peace.

**act or omission** *n.* any act or failure to act: *Employers are liable for injuries caused by the negligent acts or omissions of employees within the scope of their employment.*

**acta** *n.pl.* See ACTUM.

**acta publica** *n.pl. Latin.* (lit. "public acts") **1.** matters of general knowledge and concern.
**2.** transactions before public officers.

**actio** *n., pl.* **actiones.** *Latin.* (lit. "action") *Civil Law.* **1.** an action to obtain a legal remedy.
**2.** the right to a obtain a remedy by means of legal action.
**3. actio in personam** (lit. "action against the person") action to obtain a remedy for breach of an obligation.
**4. actio in rem** (lit. "action against the thing") action to recover property.
——**False Friend.** The civil law concepts

of *actio in personam* and *actio in rem* are similar but not identical to the common law concepts of *action in personam* and *action in rem* (see both under ACTION). For example, an action to recover property from a specific person would be classified as an action against the person in the common law system but an action against the property in the civil law system.

**actio in personam** *n., pl.* **actiones in personam.** See under ACTIO.

**actio in rem** *n., pl.* **actiones in rem.** See under ACTIO.

**action** *n.* **1.** any conduct; an act or series of acts by a person or entity. See also STATE ACTION.
**2.** a court case, especially a civil case; the procedure by which a legal dispute, claim, or accusation is resolved.
**3. civil action** an action brought for any purpose other than punishment of a crime. This is the usual meaning of the word "action."
**4. class action** an action brought on behalf of, or occasionally against, a class of persons having a common interest but too numerous to be conveniently joined as individual parties in the case.
**5. criminal action** a case brought by the government to punish a person or entity for a crime; more often called a criminal case, a criminal proceeding, or a prosecution.
**6. damage action** See under DAMAGES.
**7. derivative action** an action brought on behalf of a corporation by one of its shareholders, to protect a right of the corporation. Also called **shareholder derivative action** or **stockholder derivative action.**
**8. equitable action** an action of a type traditionally maintainable only in courts of EQUITY. Also called **action in equity** or, especially historically, *suit in equity* (see under SUIT).
**9. in personam action** or **action in personam** an action in which the plaintiff seeks damages or other relief against a specific person or entity. It must be based upon *in personam jurisdiction* (see under JURISDICTION¹) over

the defendant. Most lawsuits are of this type. See also IN PERSONAM. Cf. *in rem action; quasi in rem action.*
**10. in rem action** or **action in rem** an action in which the plaintiff seeks judgment declaring the status or disposition of property or of a relationship within the jurisdiction of the court. For examples, see *in rem jurisdiction* (under JURISDICTION¹) and CYBERSQUATTING. See also IN REM. Cf. *in personam action; quasi in rem action.*
**11. legal action a.** broadly, any court case. **b.** Also called **common law action** or **action at law.** an action of a type traditionally maintained in courts of LAW as distinguished from courts of EQUITY. See also FORM OF ACTION, CAUSE OF ACTION, EX CONTRACTU, EX DELICTO, and MERGER OF LAW AND EQUITY.
**12. quasi in rem action** or **action quasi in rem** an action against an out-of-state defendant, typically commenced by ATTACHMENT of property of the defendant located within the state, in which the plaintiff seeks judgment on a claim unrelated to the property and seeks to use the seized property to satisfy that judgment if payment is not made. This was formerly a device by which a claim could be litigated against a defendant who was not personally subject to the jurisdiction of the court, but the modern view is that the court must have *in personam jurisdiction,* not just *quasi in rem jurisdiction* (see both under JURISDICTION¹), to render such a judgment. See also QUASI IN REM. Cf. *in personam action; in rem action.*
**13. third-party action** See THIRD-PARTY ACTION.

**action over** *n., pl.* **actions over.** Same as THIRD-PARTY ACTION.

**actionable** *adj.* **1.** furnishing grounds for a lawsuit; of such a character that an action on account of it will lie: *The driver's failure to slow down before entering the main road was actionable negligence. A misrepresentation is not actionable as fraud if it is not relied upon.*
**2.** defamatory: *The speech contained several statements that were actionable.*

**3. actionable per quod** amounting to *slander per quod* (see under SLANDER) or *libel per quod* (see under LIBEL[1]). See also PER QUOD.

**4. actionable per se  a.** actionable on its face; needing nothing more to constitute a cause of action. **b.** amounting to *slander per se* (see under SLANDER) or *libel per se* (see under LIBEL[1]). See also PER SE.
—**actionability** *n.*
—**actionably** *adv.*

**actionable words** *n.pl.* words for which an action for libel or slander could be brought, more specifically referred to as **words actionable per quod** or **words actionable per se** (also called **words actionable in themselves**) depending upon the specific nature of the potential defamation action. See details at ACTIONABLE; LIBEL[1]; SLANDER.

**active judge** *n.* See under JUDGE.

**active trust** *n.* See under TRUST.

**actual** *adj.* real; existing in fact: a word used to distinguish something known to have happened or to exist from something that the law simply deems to have happened or to exist. The opposite of CONSTRUCTIVE, IMPUTED, APPARENT, and *implied in law* (see under IMPLIED). See *actual authority* (under AUTHORITY[1]); *actual damages* (under DAMAGES); *actual eviction* (under EVICTION); *actual fraud* (under FRAUD); *actual knowledge* (under KNOWLEDGE); *actual malice* (under MALICE); *actual notice* (under NOTICE).

**actum** *n., pl.* **acta** *Latin.* (lit. "a thing done") a thing done; especially, a thing done by words as distinguished from actions. Usually used in the plural. See, e.g., ACTA PUBLICA. Cf. ACTUS; GESTUM.

**actus** *n., pl.* **actus** *Latin.* (lit. "motion; the doing of a physical act") **1.** the performance of an act. The term appears in many maxims, such as "Actus me invito factus, non est meus actus": An act done by me against my will is not my act. Cf. ACTUM.
**2.** in old English usage, an act of Parliament; the enactment of a statute.

**actus reus** *Latin.* (lit. "guilty act") a voluntary act or omission to which criminal responsibility can attach. Without such an act there can be no crime, for a fundamental principle of Anglo-American law is that one cannot be punished for bad thoughts alone. See also MENS REA.

**ad audiendum judicium** *Latin.* for the purpose of hearing judgment. See *capias ad audiendum judicium* (under CAPIAS).

**ad damnum** *n.* *Latin.* (lit. "to the loss") the amount of money sought as damages in a complaint. The **ad damnum clause** is the part of a complaint in which that amount is specified. If judgment is obtained by default, it cannot exceed that amount; if the defendant does not default, then the judgment will be for whatever amount of damages the plaintiff proves at trial, whether higher or lower than the ad damnum.

**ad deliberandum** *Latin.* for the purpose of deliberating. See *habeas corpus ad deliberandum et recipiendum* (under HABEAS CORPUS).

**ad faciendum** *Latin.* for the purpose of doing. See *habeas corpus ad faciendum et recipiendum* (under HABEAS CORPUS).

**ad hominem** *adj.* *Latin.* (lit. "directed at the person") attacking an opponent's character rather than answering his argument: *The jury was instructed to disregard the attorney's ad hominem statements.*

**ad idem** *Latin.* (lit. "to the same") to the same point or effect.

**ad initium (ad init.)** *Latin.* at the beginning.

**ad interim (ad int.)** *Latin.* (lit. "for the intervening time") —*adv.* **1.** meanwhile; in the meantime; for the time being: *Since the chairperson has been delayed, the vice-chair will preside ad interim.*
—*adj.* **2.** temporary, interim: *an ad interim appointment; the chargé d'affaires ad int.*

**ad litem** *adj.* *Latin.* (lit. "for the case")

for purposes of a particular case. Used primarily in the phrase *guardian ad litem* (see under GUARDIAN). See also ADMINISTRATOR AD LITEM.

**ad prosequendum** *Latin.* for the purpose of prosecuting. See *habeas corpus ad prosequendum* (under HABEAS CORPUS).

**ad quem** *adj. Latin.* to which. See also *court ad quem* (under COURT); DIES AD QUEM; TERMINUS AD QUEM. Cf. A QUO.

**ad recipiendum** *Latin.* for the purpose of receiving. See *habeas corpus ad subjiciendum et recipiendum, habeas corpus ad deliberandum et recipiendum,* and *habeas corpus ad faciendum et recipiendum* (all under HABEAS CORPUS).

**ad respondendum** *Latin.* for the purpose of answering. See *capias ad respondendum* (under CAPIAS); *habeas corpus ad respondendum* (under HABEAS CORPUS).

**ad satisfaciendum** *Latin.* for the purpose of giving satisfaction. See *capias ad satisfaciendum* (under CAPIAS); *habeas corpus ad satisfaciendum* (under HABEAS CORPUS).

**ad sectam (ads.)** *Latin.* **1.** at the suit of. The abbreviation was formerly commonly used in indexing of cases, and occasionally in court papers, to put the defendant's name first, so that the case of Able, plaintiff, against Zabel, defendant, could be found either as *Able v. Zabel* or as *Zabel ads. Able.* **2. ad sectam index** a separate index or docket of cases, judgments, or the like by defendant's name rather than plaintiff's name.
—**History.** See note at SECTA.

**ad subjiciendum** *Latin.* for the purpose of submitting. See *habeas corpus ad subjiciendum* and *habeas corpus ad subjiciendum et recipiendum* (under HABEAS CORPUS).

**ad testificandum** *Latin.* for the purpose of testifying. See *habeas corpus ad testificandum* (under HABEAS CORPUS); *subpoena ad testificandum* (under SUBPOENA).

**ad valorem** *adj. Latin.* (lit. "according to the worth") **1.** in proportion to the value of something. **2. ad valorem tax** a tax or duty calculated as a percentage of the stated or assessed value of the thing taxed.

**additur** *n. Latin.* (lit. "it is added") an order increasing the amount of damages awarded by a jury. The defendant must either agree to the higher figure or submit to a new trial. Cf. REMITTITUR.

**ademption** *n.* the reduction or extinguishment of a legacy because, by the time of the testator's death, some or all of the money or property needed to satisfy the legacy has been destroyed, disposed of, or already given to the legatee. Cf. ADVANCEMENT.
—**adeem** *v.*

**adequate protection** *n.* measures or conditions deemed reasonably sufficient to prevent deterioration of the value of a secured creditor's interest in the estate of a bankrupt during bankruptcy proceedings.

**adequate remedy at law** *n.* See under REMEDY.

**adhesion contract** *n.* See under CONTRACT.

**adjacent** *adj.* of land, lying near; close, but not necessarily bordering upon. Cf. ADJOINING.
—**adjacency, adjacence** *n.*
—**adjacently** *adv.*

**adjective law** *n.* Same as PROCEDURE (def. 2).

**adjoining** *adj.* of land, bordering upon; touching; abutting. Cf. ADJACENT.
—**adjoin** *v.*

**adjourn** *v.* to suspend or postpone a proceeding, either temporarily or indefinitely.
—**adjournment** *n.*

**adjudge** *v.,* **adjudged, adjudging.** to render a judicial decision or judgment to a certain effect: *The will was adjudged void. It is adjudged that the plaintiff shall recover the sum of $3,500.*

**adjudicate** *v.,* **adjudicated, adjudicating.** to hear and resolve a case in a court or administrative agency: *The*

*matter was adjudicated in the Court of Common Pleas.*
—**adjudication** *n.*
—**adjudicator** *n.*
—**adjudicative, adjudicatory** *adj.*

**adjudicated** *adj.* determined by adjudication: *an adjudicated incompetent; an adjudicated matter.*

**adjuration** *n.* **1.** a swearing or binding upon oath.
**2.** an earnest request; entreaty.
Cf. ABJURATION.

**adjure** *v.*, **adjured, adjuring. 1.** to charge, bind, or command earnestly and solemnly, often under oath or the threat of a penalty: *The jurors were adjured to consider only the evidence admitted by the judge.*
**2.** to entreat or request earnestly or solemnly: *The mayor adjured the citizens to conserve water during the drought.*
Cf. ABJURE.
—**adjuratory** *adj.*
—**adjurer, adjuror** *n.*

**adjust** *v.* **1.** to settle; to bring to a mutually satisfactory state: *The parties adjusted their differences out of court.*
**2.** in tax law, to modify a sum of money that enters into tax calculations by addition or subtraction of certain legally required or permitted amounts. See, for example, *adjusted basis* (under BASIS).
**3.** to determine the amount that an insurance company will agree or offer to pay on a claim for property damage or loss covered by an insurance policy issued by the company.
—**adjustment** *n.*

**adjustable** *adj.* **1.** (of loans, mortgages, etc.) having a flexible rate, as one based on money market interest rates or on the rate of inflation or cost of living.
**2.** (esp. of life insurance) having flexible premiums and coverage, based on the insuree's current needs and ability to pay.
—**adjustability** *n.*
—**adjustably** *adv.*

**adjusted basis** *n.* See under BASIS.

**adjuster** *n.* **1.** an insurance company representative who investigates claims and makes settlement recommendations based on an evaluation or estimate of the damages and the company's liability.
**2. public adjuster** a person who offers services to the public at large in evaluating, presenting, and adjusting their claims under insurance policies for property damage and loss.
Also called **claims adjuster** (or, very rarely, **claim adjuster**); **insurance adjuster.**

**administer** *v.* to take charge of the estate of a decedent, marshal and manage the assets, see to the paying of the estate's debts and taxes, and distribute whatever is left in accordance with the terms of the will or, if there is no will, the laws of INTESTATE SUCCESSION. See also ADMINISTRATOR; EXECUTOR; PERSONAL REPRESENTATIVE.
—**administration** *n.*

**administrative** *adj.* pertaining to an ADMINISTRATIVE AGENCY or to the work of such agencies in general: *administrative officer; administrative order; administrative function.* See also *administrative procedure* (under PROCEDURE); *administrative review* (under REVIEW).
—**administratively** *adv.*

**administrative agency** *n.* a federal, state, or local governmental unit with responsibility for administering and enforcing a particular body of law; for example, the Internal Revenue Service, a state power commission, or a city human rights department. Also called **agency.** See also REGULATORY AGENCY.

**administrative law** *n.* **1.** the body of law that deals with the duties and operations of administrative agencies.
**2.** a body of law on a particular subject created by an administrative agency through its regulations and decisions.

**administrative law judge (ALJ)** *n.* an official of an administrative agency who hears, weighs, and decides on evidence in administrative proceedings. In some states called a **hearing examiner** or **hearing officer.**

**administrator** *n.* **1.** a person appointed by a court to ADMINISTER all or part of a decedent's estate in the absence of an EXECUTOR, as when the decedent left no will, or the will failed to designate an executor or failed to dispose of the entire estate, or the designated executor is unwilling or unable to serve. The quaint term ADMINISTRATRIX is still generally used to refer to an administrator who is a woman.

**2. ancillary administrator** an administrator appointed by a court in a state other than the one where the decedent was domiciled, for the purpose of administering only those assets located in that state as an adjunct to the administration of the estate as a whole by the administrator appointed in the state where the decedent was domiciled. —**administratorship** n.

**administrator ad litem** n., pl. **administrators ad litem.** a person appointed by a court to represent the interests of a decedent's estate in a case. See also AD LITEM.

**administrator cum testamento annexo** or **administrator c.t.a.** n., pl. **administrators cum testamento annexo** or **administrators c.t.a.** a person appointed to ADMINISTER the estate of a decedent who left a will but did not appoint an executor, or whose designated executor refused or was incapable of serving. Also called **administrator with will annexed** or **administrator with the will annexed**. See also CUM TESTAMENTO ANNEXO.

——**False Friend.** It is difficult to read of an "administrator with will annexed" without visualizing a person plastered with paper—rather like a blue-suited lawyer on whose back a practical joker has slapped a sign that says "Kick me!" In actuality the will is attached, not to the administrator, but to the court's order of appointment. See more at CUM TESTAMENTO ANNEXO.

**administrator de bonis non** or **administrator d.b.n.** n., pl. **administrators de bonis non** or **administrators d.b.n.** a person appointed to ADMINISTER the undistributed assets remaining in a decedent's estate when the previous administrator ceases to serve. See also DE BONIS NON.

**administrator de bonis non cum testamento annexo** or **administrator d.b.n.c.t.a.** n., pl. **administrators de bonis non cum testamento annexo** or **administrators d.b.n.c.t.a.** a person appointed to ADMINISTER assets remaining to be distributed under a will when the executor named in the will ceases to serve. Also called **administrator de bonis non with will annexed** or **administrator de bonis non with the will annexed.** See also DE BONIS NON; CUM TESTAMENTO ANNEXO.

**administratrix** n., pl. **administratrices.** See under ADMINISTRATOR.

**admiralty** n., adj. See under MARITIME.

**admissible** adj. **1.** (of evidence) permitted by the rules of evidence to be considered by the judge or jury in a case. Evidence that is admissible may nevertheless not be admitted by the judge if, for example, it is CUMULATIVE or unduly inflammatory. See also PREJUDICIAL EFFECT.

**2. admissible for a limited purpose** describing evidence that may be considered for one purpose or on one issue, but not another. —**admissibility** n. —**admissibly** adv.

**admission** n. **1.** any words or acts of a party to a case offered as evidence by that party's opponent. Admissions are usually allowed into evidence as an exception to the *hearsay rule* (see under HEARSAY) on the ground that the party whose admission is being offered can take the stand and explain or dispute it if it is misleading.

**2.** a defendant's failure to deny an allegation in a complaint, counterclaim, or *request for admissions*. The usual consequence is that the allegation in question is deemed true and may no longer be contested in the case.

**3.** the act of a judge in allowing proffered evidence to be considered by the jury. See also RECEIVE. Cf. EXCLUSION.

**4. admission to the bar** the granting or obtaining of a license from the state, or permission from a court, to practice law in that state or before that court.

When an out-of-state lawyer, or a lawyer not admitted to the bar of a particular court, is given special permission to appear in a particular case, that is called **admission pro hac vice**. See also PRO HAC VICE; BAR EXAMINATION; RECIPROCITY.
**5. request for admissions** a paper served by one party upon another in a case, demanding that an adversary admit or deny certain facts; often served shortly before a trial to narrow the issues and eliminate the need to spend court time proving things that are not in dispute.
—**admit** *v.*, **admitted, admitting.**

**admonition** *n.* a judge's courtroom direction, advice, or warning to a jury, witness, lawyer, or even spectator, regarding any matter arising during a proceeding.
—**admonish** *v.*
—**admonitory** *adj.*
—**admonitorily** *adv.*

**adopt** *v.* **1.** to take on the status of a parent with respect to another's child through the legal process of ADOPTION.
**2.** to accept legal responsibility for the act of another; treat as one's own act; RATIFY.
**3.** to vote to accept: *The house adopted the report.*
—**adopter** *n.*

**adoptable** *adj.* capable of being adopted; suitable or eligible for adoption: *an adoptable child.*
—**adoptability** *n.*

**adoptee** *n.* a person who is adopted.

**adoption** *n.* **1.** the legal procedure by which an adult acquires the rights, duties, and status of a parent with respect to a child who is not the adult's natural offspring.
**2.** the act of adopting.
**3.** the state of being adopted.
**4. open adoption** an adoption of a child in which the natural parent or parents meet with the adoptive parent or parents, select or participate in the selection of the adoptive parents, and, though relinquishing all parental rights, retain the right or expectation of continuing contact with the child and knowledge of the child's whereabouts and welfare.

**adoptive** *adj.* **1.** acquired or related by adoption: *adoptive parent; adoptive child.*
**2.** of or involving adoption of any kind: *adoptive conduct.*
—**adoptively** *adv.*
——**Usage.** Although *adoptive* in the sense "acquired or related by adoption" can refer to either the parent or the child in such a relationship, *adoptive* is customarily applied to the parent (*her adoptive mother*) and *adopted* to the child (*their adopted son*).

**adquate** *adj.* sufficient in the eyes of the law; objectively reasonable under the circumstances: *adquate grounds for suit; adequate care.*
—**adequately** *adv.*
—**adequacy** *n.*

**ADR** ALTERNATIVE DISPUTE RESOLUTION.

**ads.** AD SECTAM.

**adult offender** *n.* See under OFFENDER.

**adulterant** *n.* a substance that adulterates.

**adulterate** *v.*, **adulterated, adulterating. 1.** to debase or make impure by adding cheaper, inferior, or dangerous elements or ingredients: *adulterated food; adulterated heroin.*
**2.** under the federal Food, Drug, and Cosmetic Act, to engage in virtually any conduct that causes a regulated product to be substandard or potentially dangerous: *to adulterate a medical device by marketing it without obtaining the legally required approval of the Food and Drug Administration.*
—**adulteration** *n.*
—**adulterator** *n.*

**adulterer** *n.* a person who commits ADULTERY. In older usage, a woman who committed adultery was referred to as an **adulteress**.

**adulteress** *n.* See under ADULTERER.

**adultery** *n.* voluntary sexual intercourse by a married person with someone

other than that person's spouse. Adultery is traditionally regarded by the law both as a crime and as a ground for divorce. Many states have abolished the crime and eliminated the requirement of an accusation of wrongdoing in order to obtain a divorce.
—**adulterous** adj.
—**adulterously** adv.
——**Usage.** In a strict sense, only a married person can commit adultery. In traditional analysis, an unmarried person voluntarily having sexual intercourse with a married person would not be committing the crime of adultery, but rather the crime of FORNICATION and the tort of CRIMINAL CONVERSATION. But in the many states where adultery is still a crime, the statutes now generally provide that both participants may be charged with the offense.

**adustable-rate mortgage (ARM)** n. See under MORTGAGE.

**advance directive** n. a LIVING WILL, a HEALTH CARE PROXY, or a combination of the two.

**advance parole** n. See under PAROLE.

**advancement** n. an advance payment or transfer of a portion of one's estate to an heir (usually a child) while one is still alive, with the understanding that this is in place of a share of the estate after death. The effect is to extinguish, to the extent of the advancement, that heir's claim to a share of the estate under the laws of INTESTATE SUCCESSION. Cf. ADEMPTION.

**adventure** n. **1.** a commercial or financial speculation of any kind; venture.
**2.** in marine insurance, **a.** an insured voyage. **b.** any of the risks and perils insured against.
**3. joint adventure** Same as JOINT VENTURE.
—**adventurer** n.

**adversary** n., pl. **adversaries,** adj. —n.
**1.** an opponent; especially the opposing party or attorney in a court case.
—adj. Also **adversarial. 2.** pertaining to an adversary or involving adversaries.

**adversary proceeding** n. a proceeding brought in Bankruptcy Court to resolve a dispute relating to the assets of a BANKRUPT.

**adversary system** n. the Anglo-American method of adjudication, in which the responsibility for ferreting out the truth in a case rests almost exclusively on the opposing parties and their lawyers, through examination and cross-examination of witnesses of their choosing. With reference to criminal cases, also called ACCUSATORIAL SYSTEM. Cf. INQUISITORIAL SYSTEM.

**adverse possession** n. a method of acquiring title to real estate, accomplished by openly occupying the property to the exclusion of others and in defiance of the rights of the real owner for a period of time set by statute, typically ten to twenty years. If the owner fails to take appropriate action to oust the adverse possessor from the land within the statutorily prescribed time, the adverse possessor acquires title to the land.
——**Note.** In a minority of states, adverse possession does not confer title unless the adverse possessor was acting pursuant to a good faith belief that the land is actually his.

**adverse witness** n. Same as hostile witness (see under WITNESS).

**advice** n. **1.** an opinion or recommendation offered as a guide to action or conduct.
**2.** a notification, especially of a formal or official nature.

**advice and consent** n. the phrase used in the United States Constitution to describe the role of the Senate with respect to treaties negotiated by the President and the President's appointment of ambassadors, judges, and other officers of the United States. The "consent" part of this role takes the form of a vote (which in the case of treaties must be a two-thirds vote); the "advice" part is not formalized, but Senators have no difficulty making it clear to the President which potential nominees and treaty terms they regard as acceptable.

**advise** *v.*, **advised, advising. 1.** to give counsel to; recommend a course of action to; render a professional opinion to: *Her lawyer advised her to accept the plea bargain.*
**2.** to render professional advice and counsel generally: *The firm advises on patent, copyright, and trademark matters.*
**3.** to notify: *The warden was advised of the clemency order five minutes before the execution was to take place.*
—**advisory** *adj.*

**adviser** or **advisor** *n.* One who gives advice; particularly one who renders advice in a particular field as a profession. See also INVESTMENT ADVISER.
—**Usage.** Although *adviser* is the usual and more conservative spelling, *advisor* is very common, especially as a professional title, perhaps because it is evocative of words like *doctor* and *counselor.* But see note at INVESTMENT ADVISER.

**advisory opinion** *n.* an opinion by a court on a hypothetical legal question posed by a legislative or executive body or official, as distinguished from a question arising in an actual case; for example, a question about the constitutionality of a proposed law or the legality of a proposed transaction. The Constitution bars federal courts from issuing advisory opinions, but some state courts are authorized to render such advice in certain circumstances.

**advocacy** *n.* the act of pleading for a cause or person; supporting a cause or person by argument.

**advocate** *n.*, *v.*, **advocated, advocating. —***n.* **1.** one who actively supports a cause or a person; one who writes and speaks for or in behalf of another.
**2.** a lawyer, particularly one who represents clients in judicial proceedings and similar matters.
—*v.* **3.** to speak or write in favor of; support by argument.

**advowson** *n.* (in old English law) the right to present a candidate for appointment to fill a vacant position as parson of a church.
—**History.** The right of advowson originally belonged to the lord of the manor on whose property the church sat, but came to be a property right that could be transferred or inherited independently of the land itself. The bishop could refuse to appoint the candidate presented only for very limited reasons. See also DARREIN PRESENTMENT.

**aff'd** AFFIRMED.
—**Usage.** The abbreviation is used in citations to indicate that the decision just cited was upheld on appeal in the decision whose citation follows immediately: *Goesaert v. Cleary,* 74 F. Supp. 735 (E.D. Mich. 1947), *aff'd,* 335 U.S. 464 (1948). Cf. AFF'G; REV'D.

**aff'g** AFFIRMING.
—**Usage.** The abbreviation is used in citations to indicate that the decision just cited was an affirmance of the decision whose citation follows immediately: *Goesaert v. Cleary,* 335 U.S. 464 (1948), *aff'g* 74 F. Supp. 735 (E.D. Mich. 1947). Cf. AFF'D; REV'G.

**affiant** *n.* the person who makes an AFFIDAVIT.

**affidavit** *n.* **1.** a formal written statement affirming or swearing to the truth of the facts stated, signed before a notary public or similar officer. Dishonesty in an affidavit is FALSE SWEARING or PERJURY. In a narrow sense, "affidavit" refers to a sworn statement (see SWEAR) and so is distinguished from AFFIRMATION (def. 2); in a broader sense it includes affirmations.
**2. affidavit** (or **affirmation**) **of service** an affidavit or affirmation stating the time and manner in which a summons or other process or court paper was served in a case. See also PROOF OF SERVICE; RETURN OF SERVICE.

**affiliate¹** *n.* **1.** a person or entity having a formal relationship with another entity.
**2.** especially, a corporation that is the PARENT COMPANY or SUBSIDIARY of another corporation, or under common ownership with another corporation, as in the case of *sister corporations* (see under CORPORATION).

**affiliate²** *v.*, **affiliated, affiliating. 1.** to

become an affiliate or bring others together so as to make them affiliates.
**2.** Same as FILIATE.

**affiliation** *n.* **1.** the act of affiliating or the state of being affiliated.
**2.** Same as FILIATION.

**affiliation order** *n.* See under FILIATION.

**affiliation proceeding** *n.* See under FILIATION.

**affinity** *n.* **1.** relationship by marriage. Cf. CONSANGUINITY.
**2.** relationship by marriage within a legally specified degree; relationship between close in-laws.

**affirm¹** *v.* **1.** to declare solemnly that certain statements are true, or that one will testify truthfully. Such an affirmation has the effect of an oath for purposes of the laws against PERJURY and FALSE SWEARING.
**2.** to make a solemn promise, particularly to carry out one's duties as a citizen or officeholder and to obey or uphold the law.
See also SWEAR; SWEAR OR AFFIRM; OATH; OATH OR AFFIRMATION.
—**affirmation** *n.*

**affirm²** *v.* to uphold the judgment of a lower tribunal in a case that has been appealed. Cf. REVERSE; REMAND; VACATE.
—**affirmance** *n.*

**affirmant** *n.* one who formally affirms; the maker of an affirmation.

**affirmation** *n.* **1.** the act of affirming something (see AFFIRM¹), or the words recited in doing so. An affirmation has exactly the same legal effect as an OATH.
**2.** a formal written statement affirming certain facts subject to the penalties for false swearing and perjury, sometimes required to be executed before a notary public and sometimes not. This is substantially the same in form, and exactly the same in legal effect, as an AFFIDAVIT.
See also *affirmation of service* (under AFFIDAVIT); OATH; OATH OR AFFIRMATION.

**affirmative act** *n.* See under ACT.

**affirmative action** *n.* any step by a public or private employer, school, institution, or program, beyond the mere cessation of intentional discrimination, to promote diversity, provide opportunities, and alleviate the effects of past discrimination on the basis of race, sex, national origin, or disability.

**affirmative defense** *n.* See under DEFENSE.

**affirmative easement** *n.* See under EASEMENT.

**affirmative relief** *n.* See under RELIEF.

**affirmative warranty** *n.* See under WARRANTY.

**affirmed (aff'd)** upheld on appeal. See AFF'D for usage.

**affirming (aff'g)** upholding on appeal. See AFF'G for usage.

**affray** *n.* the offense of voluntary fighting by two or more people in a public place to the terror of public or disturbance of public tranquility.

**affrayer** *n.* one who engages in an affray.

**affreighter** *n.* one who hires a ship to carry freight.

**affreightment** *n.* the hiring of a ship to carry freight.

**aforementioned** *adj.* previously cited or mentioned.

**aforesaid** *adj.* Same as SAID.

**aforethought** *adj.* thought of previously; considered in advance. See also *malice aforethought* (under MALICE).

**after-acquired property** *n.* property acquired by a debtor after the debtor's existing property has been pledged as collateral for a loan. The security agreement with the lender may provide that any after-acquired property will automatically become part of the collateral.

**after-born child** *n.* a child born after a legally significant cut-off date, usually the date that a will is executed, a testator dies, or a gift to a class of which the child would have been a part takes effect.

**A.G.** ATTORNEY GENERAL.

**against the weight of the evidence** See *verdict against the weight of the evidence* (under VERDICT).

**age** *n.* **1. age of consent a.** the age below which one may not get married without a parent's consent. **b.** the age below which a person is deemed incapable of consenting to sexual intercourse. Sexual intercourse with a person below that age is *statutory rape* (see under RAPE). In many states the age of consent depends upon the age of the other party to the sexual act; for example, a fourteen-year-old might be regarded by the law as capable of consenting to intercourse with a seventeen-year-old but not with an eighteen-year-old.
**2. age of majority** the age at which an otherwise competent person acquires the power to make binding contracts, along with most of the other legal rights and responsibilities of adulthood. Traditionally twenty-one, the age of majority has generally been reduced to eighteen in the wake of ratification of the Twenty-Sixth Amendment (see Appendix). Also called **majority; full age.** See also *legal age.*
**3. age of reason** the age below which a child cannot be found guilty of a crime or, in some states, liable for a tort; most commonly, the age of seven.
**4. legal age** the age at which a person becomes legally capable of exercising certain rights or assuming certain responsibilities. For most purposes, same as *age of majority;* but it may be younger (e.g., driving age) or older (e.g., drinking age).
See also UNDERAGE.

**age discrimination** *n.* discrimination on the basis of a person's age. Federal law protects most workers between the ages of forty and seventy from age discrimination in employment; other federal and local laws provide varying degrees of protection from age discrimination in such areas as credit, housing, and public accommodations. See also BONA FIDE OCCUPATIONAL QUALIFICATION; SENIORITY SYSTEM.

**agency** *n., pl.* **agencies. 1.** a relationship between two people or entities whereby one (the AGENT) is authorized to act on behalf of the other (the PRINCIPAL). For legal purposes, the acts of the agent within the SCOPE OF AUTHORITY are generally deemed to be acts of the principal, and the agent is a FIDUCIARY of the principal.
**2.** Short for ADMINISTRATIVE AGENCY.

**agency shop** *n.* See under SHOP.

**agent** *n.* **1.** a person or entity authorized to act on behalf of another in some matter or range of matters. For example, an insurance agent is authorized by one or more insurance companies to sell their insurance; an ATTORNEY IN FACT is an agent. See also AGENCY; ESCROW AGENT.
**2. del credere agent** an agent who guarantees the performance, payment, or solvency of the principal, and ordinarily receives higher commissions for doing so. See also DEL CREDERE.

**Aggadah** *n. Jewish Law.* the nonlegal or narrative material, as parables, maxims, or anecdotes, in the Talmud and other rabbinical literature, serving to illustrate the meaning or purpose of the law or other matter being discussed. Also called **Haggadah.**

**aggravate** *v.,* **aggravated, aggravating.** to make worse: *The doctor's malpractice aggravated the injury.*
—**aggravation** *n.*

**aggravated** *adj.* **1.** (of a crime) characterized by some element that makes the crime more serious, such as the use of a deadly weapon, the seriousness of the injury caused or intended, or the youthfulness of the victim: *aggravated assault, aggravated rape.* Aggravated offenses are subject to more serious penalties than unaggravated forms of the same offense.
**2.** (of a tort) characterized by conduct, such as willfulness or malice, that justifies the imposition of *punitive damages* (see under DAMAGES).
—**Note.** The precise circumstances that elevate an offense to the status of an aggravated offense vary from state to state. The Indiana Supreme Court

made this point in unusually colorful terms when it said, "it will be noted that there are two basic forms of aggravated assault statutes. In the first type...the 'aggravating' circumstance is the particular state of mind of the actor, specifically, to do great bodily harm to the victim.... Under the second type statute, the 'aggravating' circumstance is not the actor's wicked intent, but, rather, the seriousness of the unpermitted touching.... Our statute requires that great bodily harm or disfigurement be inflicted. One who merely intends to tie up his victim and pound him about the head with a meat tenderizing tool has not committed the crime of aggravated assault in Indiana. On the other hand, if one throws a piece of chalk at the legendary victim with an EGGSHELL SKULL, and the chalk strikes the victim and fractures his skull, the perpetrator would be guilty under our statute...." *Defries v. State,* 264 Ind. 233 (1976).

**aggravating circumstance** *n.* **1.** an element or circumstance involved in the commission of a tort or crime that elevates its seriousness in the eyes of the law; a fact justifying more than the usual measure of damages or punishment. See also note at AGGRAVATED.
**2.** especially, a circumstance in a murder case that makes the death penalty available as a punishment.
Also called **aggravating factor**. See also SPECIAL CIRCUMSTANCES.

**aggression** *n. International Law.* the use of armed force by a state against the sovereignty, territorial integrity, or political independence of another state, or in any other manner inconsistent with the Charter of the United Nations.
**——History.** One of the principal purposes for the founding of the United Nations—in fact the first one mentioned in Article 1 of the UN Charter—is the maintenance of international peace and security through the taking of collective measures to remove threats to peace and suppress acts of aggression. The hope was that aggression could be prevented or defeated by collective international diplomatic and military action. This principle has proved easier to state

than to implement. The Charter gives the Security Council ultimate authority to determine whether an act of aggression calling for United Nations action has occurred, and since any action by the Security Council requires a unanimous vote, such findings are seldom made. In 1998, the diplomatic conference that established the framework for the INTERNATIONAL CRIMINAL COURT reached general agreement that individuals responsible for state aggression should be subject to sanction in the court. That principle, however, turned out to be extremely difficult even to state, let alone implement; in the end, the statute that the conference adopted to establish the court could only say: "The Court shall exercise jurisdiction over the crime of aggression once a provision is adopted...defining the crime and setting out the conditions under which the Court shall exercise jurisdiction with respect to this crime."

**aggrieved** *adj.* adversely affected by an act or a situation, or perceiving oneself to be so affected: *A party aggrieved by a trial court's judgment may appeal.*

**agrarian law** *n.* **1.** Usually, **agrarian laws. a.** *Roman Law.* a set of laws regulating use of public land by individuals, and particularly providing for disposition of lands in conquered territories and limiting the amount of land any one individual could hold. **b.** any law or set of laws limiting the size of individual landholdings as a means of spreading wealth and reducing disparities in economic power.
**2.** law relating to land, land tenure, or the division of landed property generally.

**agreed case** *n.* See under CASE¹.

**agreement** *n.* **1.** a manifestation of assent by two or more people to a course of action. An agreement is normally enforceable only if it meets the requirements of a CONTRACT, in which case the terms "agreement" and "contract" are interchangeable.
**2. agreement to agree** a preliminary agreement that the parties will enter into a contract along certain lines, the

exact terms of which have not yet been entirely worked out. Whether the agreement to agree is itself a contract, and thus enforceable, depends upon how definite or INDEFINITE it is.

See also *collective bargaining agreement* (under COLLECTIVE BARGAINING); DIVORCE AGEEMENT; GENTLEMEN'S AGREEMENT; PRENUPTIAL AGREEMENT; SEPARATION AGREEMENT.

**agricultural disparagement** *n.* Same as FOOD DISPARAGEMENT.

**aid and abet** *v.,* **aided and abetted, aiding and abetting. 1.** to order, encourage, or knowingly assist or attempt to assist a person who commits a crime. Aiding and abetting a crime is normally punishable to the same extent as committing the crime directly.
**2.** to assist another in the commission of a tort. Ordinarily this results in joint liability with the primary actor.
See also *joint tortfeasor* (under TORTFEASOR).
—**aider and abettor** (or **abetter**), *n.*
—**aiding and abetting** *n.*
——**Note.** On redundancy in such expressions as this, see note at TO HAVE AND TO HOLD.

**aider by verdict** *n.* (in older practice) the effect of a verdict in curing defects in the initial pleadings.
——**History.** In the days before *notice pleading* (see under PLEADING), when much could be made of minor errors or omissions in pleadings, the doctrine of aider by verdict overcame some of the legal pettiness by presuming that the elements necessary to support a verdict must have been established at trial even if they had not been precisely specified in the pleadings. This reduced or eliminated argument over the wording of the initial pleadings after a case had proceeded through trial to a verdict. See also note at DEMURRER regarding etymology.

**aiel** *n. Law French.* **1.** grandfather.
**2. writ of aiel** an ancient writ by which a grandchild who inherited a possessory interest in land from a grandfather or grandmother could gain possession of the land from another

person who had taken possession. See also note at MORT D'ANCESTOR.
Also spelled **ayel** and in many other variations.

**air piracy** *n.* See under PIRACY.

**air waybill** *n.* Same as AIRBILL.

**airbill** *n.* a BILL OF LADING for shipment of goods by air. Also called **air waybill**.

**a.k.a.** ALSO KNOWN AS.

**alderman** *n., pl.* **aldermen.** a member of a municipal legislative body similar to a city council. Also called **alderperson.** A female member may also be called **alderwoman.**
—**aldermancy** *n.*
—**aldermanic** *adj.*

**alderperson** *n., pl.* **alderpersons.** Same as ALDERMAN.

**alderwoman** *n., pl.* **alderwomen.** a female member of a municipal legislative body similar to a city council. See also ALDERMAN.

**aleatory** *adj.* **1.** contingent; subject to uncertainties. See also *aleatory contract* (under CONTRACT).
**2.** of or pertaining to accidental causes; of luck or chance; unpredictable: *an aleatory element.*

**Alford plea** *n.* a guilty plea by a criminal defendant who denies having committed the crime, entered in order to take advantage of a PLEA BARGAIN.
——**History.** The Alford plea is named after the case of *North Carolina v. Alford,* 400 U.S. 25 (1970), in which the United States Supreme Court held that such a plea may be accepted in the federal courts when there is evidence indicating that the defendant is actually guilty.

**ALI** AMERICAN LAW INSTITUTE.

**alias** *adv., n., pl.* **aliases,** *adj.* —*adv.* **1.** at another time; in another place; in other circumstances; otherwise: "Jones, *alias* Smith" means that Jones in other circumstances has called himself Smith.
—*n.* **2.** a name assumed to conceal one's identity, especially for a nefarious purpose: *Jones used the alias "Smith" when he rented the truck to transport*

*the bomb.*

**3.** a writ or other process issued to replace a previous one that proved ineffective; especially the first such replacement, the next being called the PLURIES. —*adj.* **4.** describing such a replacement; see for example *alias summons* (under SUMMONS); *alias writ* (under WRIT).

——**False Friend.** The "alias" in defs. 3 and 4 has nothing to do with false names or concealment. It comes from the original Latin wording of such writs, which stated, "We command you, *as before* [in Latin, *sicut alias*]...."

**alibi** *n., pl.* **alibis.** in a criminal case, a defense that the accused was somewhere else when the crime was committed. In the federal and most state systems, the defendant must notify the prosecution in advance if she intends to use such a defense. See also *alibi witness* (under WITNESS).

**alien**[1] *n.* **1. a.** a person who is not a citizen or subject or national of a particular country. **b.** in United States law, a person who is not a citizen or national of the United States. This is the sense in which the word *alien* is generally used in this dictionary.

**2. deportable alien** an alien who may be deported, either because the person was an *inadmissible alien* in the first place or for any of a large number of other reasons relating to failure to obey immigration regulations, commission of a crime, posing a security risk to the country, or requiring public financial assistance.

**3. inadmissible alien** an alien who cannot legally enter the United States. The rules on excludability of aliens are detailed, complex, and very wide-ranging; general grounds for exclusion include health grounds (such as being infected with the AIDS virus), criminal involvement, national security concerns, likelihood of becoming a public charge, entering the country to seek work in a field that has a sufficient labor pool of people already in the country, failure to adhere to immigration rules, prior deportation, ineligibility for citizenship, history of evasion of the draft in the United States, and being a

practicing polygamist. Also called **excludable alien.**

**4. nonresident alien** an alien whose permanent residence is in another country; for example, a tourist or seasonal worker.

**5. resident alien** an alien who has lawfully established a permanent residence in the United States. Such persons are entitled to full constitutional protection, and may not be discriminated against in employment on the basis of citizenship. See also ALIENAGE.

**6. undocumented alien** an alien who has entered or remained in the United States without government authorization. Also called **illegal alien.** Although it is illegal for an employer to hire such a person, the Supreme Court has held that the public schools may not exclude children for being undocumented.

—*adj.* **7.** belonging or pertaining to an alien or to aliens generally.

See also *alien enemy* or *enemy alien* (under ENEMY); *alien property* (under PROPERTY).

**alien**[2] *v.* to transfer ownership of; ALIENATE (property).

**alienable** *adj.* (of property or an interest in property) capable of being transferred; capable of being alienated. —**alienability** *n.*

**alienage** *n.* the state of being an alien. For EQUAL PROTECTION purposes, alienage is a SUSPECT CLASSIFICATION, so that laws and public policies discriminating between citizens and *resident aliens* (see under ALIEN) are subject to STRICT SCRUTINY.

**alienate** *v.,* **alienated, alienating.** to transfer property to another by gift, sale, or will. See also RESTRAINT ON ALIENATION. —**alienation** *n.*

**alienation of affections** *n.* a tort consisting of conduct by a third party intentionally causing one spouse in a married couple to become disaffected with the other. The tort has been abolished in many states.

**alienee** *n.* transferee; a person to whom property is alienated.

**alieni juris** *adj. Latin.* (lit. "of the right of another") *Roman Law.* subject to the authority of another; not possessing legal capacity, as a child, wife, or slave. Cf. SUI JURIS.

**alimony** *n.* money that one divorced spouse must pay to the other for support during or after the divorce, pursuant to a court order or an agreement between the parties. Also called **maintenance**; **spousal support.**

**aliquot** *adj.* **1.** fractional, resulting from division into equal portions: *Each of the joint owners will receive an aliquot part of the proceeds from the sale of the property.*
—*n.* **2.** an equal fractional share.

**aliter** *adv. Latin.* (lit. "otherwise; else") otherwise; it is otherwise: *The case was properly dismissed as against the employer; aliter as to the employee. The insurance policy covers the policy owner's partner if they are married; aliter if they are not.*

**aliunde** *adv., adj. Latin.* (lit. "from a different direction; from elsewhere") from another place, person, or source. Used chiefly in regard to evidence or proof: outside evidence is *evidence aliunde.*

**ALJ** ADMINISTRATIVE LAW JUDGE.

**all fours** See ON ALL FOURS.

**all-points bulletin (APB)** *n.* a broadcast alert from one police station to all others in an area, state, etc., as with instructions to arrest a particular suspect or suspects.

**all-purpose public figure** *n.* See under PUBLIC FIGURE.

**all the world** *n.* everyone in the world. Often referred to simply as **the world.** Whereas an IN PERSONAM action normally determines only the relative rights of the particular parties before the court, an IN REM action, being directed at a piece of property rather than a particular person, typically seeks to establish the plaintiff's rights with respect to that property as against "(all) the world."

**allegation** *n.* **1. a.** an assertion that one intends to prove at trial, especially such an assertion as set forth formally in a complaint, indictment, or the like. **b.** any assertion made without giving proof, especially an assertion of wrongdoing.
**2.** the act of making such an assertion.

**allege** *v.*, **alleged, alleging.** to assert without giving proof; especially, to assert as fact that which one intends to prove at a trial.
—**allegeable** *adj.*

**alleged** *adj.* **1.** asserted as a fact that would be an issue at trial: *the alleged murderer; the alleged breach of contract.* **2.** purported; asserted but doubtful: *the alleged cure-all.*
—**allegedly** *adv.*

**Allen charge** *n.* See under CHARGE.

**allocatur** *n. Latin.* (lit. "it is allowed") allowance; permission; an order allowing something or granting a request, as an order awarding costs or granting permission to appeal.

**allocute** *v.*, **allocuted, allocuting.** to make an ALLOCUTION: *The guilty plea was not entered because the defendant refused to allocute.*

**allocution** *n.* **1.** the process by which a guilty plea is made and accepted in a criminal case, typically involving a series of questions and answers through which the judge seeks assurance that the defendant understands the charges, understands the consequences of the plea and the rights that are being given up, and is pleading guilty of his own free will.
**2.** the procedure by which a criminal defendant who is about to be sentenced is given an opportunity to make a personal statement to the judge. Typically, the judge, having heard argument from both the prosecution and the defendant's lawyer, addresses the defendant by name and says, "Is there anything that you would like to say before I pronounce sentence?"
**3.** a similar procedure by which the victim of a crime is sometimes given an opportunity to address the court personally before sentence is pronounced on the person convicted of the crime.

**allodium** or **alodium** *n., pl.* **allodia** or **alodia.** an estate owned absolutely and not subject to a feudal overlord.
—**allodial, alodial** *adj.*
—**allodially, alodially** *adv.*
——**History.** The feudal property system instituted in England after the Norman Conquest eliminated allodial ownership and subjected all tenancy of land to feudal duties to lords, with the king at the top of the pyramid as lord of the realm. Instead of an allodium, a landowner held only a feud (see FEUD[1]). Technically, even today there is no allodial property in England, since all land is theoretically held of the king or queen. Property ownership in the United States is allodial, but most of the law relating to real property in the United States has its origins in the early feudal system in England; consequently we still speak of landlords and tenants, fee simple and life estate, inheritable interests and escheat.

**allonge** *n.* a paper annexed to a negotiable instrument, for endorsements too numerous or lengthy to be contained in the original.

**allow** *v.* **1.** to permit: *The judge overruled the objection and allowed the question.*
**2.** to receive or admit into evidence: *The exhibit is allowed.*
**3.** to rule favorably upon: *The agency allowed the claim.*
**4.** to grant or award: *The plaintiff's costs are allowed in the amount of $500.*
See also DEPLETION ALLOWANCE.
—**allowable** *adj.*
—**allowability** *n.*
—**allowance** *n.*

**alluvial** *adj.* pertaining to or resulting from alluvion or alluvium.

**alluvion** *n.* **1.** gradual depositing of land by water. See also ACCRETION.
**2.** in older usage, sometimes same as ALLUVIUM.
Cf. RELICTION.

**alluvium** *n.* land deposited by water. Cf. ALLUVION.

**alodium** *n., pl.* **alodia.** See ALLODIUM.

**also known as (a.k.a.)** phrase or abbreviation used to introduce another name or a list of other names used by a named individual so as to avoid mistake about the individual's identity.

**alter ego** *n. Latin.* (lit. "the other I") **1.** a substitute acting on one's behalf, and for whose acts one is therefore responsible; a deputy or agent.
**2.** a sham corporation acting for its owner.
See *corporate veil* (under CORPORATE).

**alternate valuation** *n.* the setting of the value of a decedent's estate for tax purposes as of the date six months after death (the **alternate valuation date**) rather than the date of death, as permitted by the Internal Revenue Code.

**alternative dispute resolution (ADR)** *n.* **1.** any formal procedure for obtaining a final determination of a legal dispute without a full trial in state or federal court. The parties to such a proceeding must agree to be bound by the result; such an agreement may be entered into either before any dispute arises or specifically in connection with a particular dispute. Examples include ARBITRATION; PRIVATE JUDGING; and MINITRIAL.
**2.** more broadly, any procedure for resolving a dispute without a court trial, including MEDIATION and CONCILIATION.

**alternative minimum tax (AMT)** *n.* a tax that some high-income or corporate taxpayers are required to pay to avoid excessive reduction of their total tax liability through exemptions, deductions, and credits.

**alternative pleading** *n.* See under PLEADING.

**ambulance chasing** *n.* the solicitation of legal business, particularly for the bringing of a personal injury or wrongful death action, from an accident victim or the the relatives of an accident victim, particularly as a regular or frequent practice.
—**ambulance chaser** *n.*

**ameliorating waste** *n.* See under WASTE.

**amenable** *adj.* **1.** legally required to respond; legally subject to: *amenable to suit; amenable to the jurisdiction of the district court.*
**2.** capable of; susceptible to; disposed toward; subject to: *The parties are amenable to settling out of court. The concept is not amenable to precise definition.*
—**amenability** *n.*

**amend** *v.* to revise, correct, add to, or subtract from a document of legal significance such as a constitution, a legislative bill, an executive order, a tax return, or a corporation's bylaws. Virtually any paper submitted to or issued by a court may be amended if prompt action is taken and no undue prejudice results: *amended complaint; amended offer of proof; amended reply; amended order.* Cf. EMEND.
—**amendable** *adj.*
—**amendatory** *adj.*

**amendment** *n.* **1.** the act or process of amending something.
**2.** the words added to, or other changes made in, a document that has been amended; especially, an addition to the Constitution of the United States. The term is usually capitalized when referring to a specific amendment to the Constitution: *the Fifth Amendment; the Prohibition Amendment.* For a summary of all U.S. constitutional amendments to date, see Appendix.
See also NONGERMANE AMENDMENT. Cf. EMENDATION.

**amerce** *v.,* **amerced, amercing. 1.** in old English law, to impose a financial penalty in an amount not fixed by statute, especially a relatively mild fine for a relatively minor offense.
**2.** to impose any discretionary punishment.
—**amerceable** *adj.*
—**amercer** *n.*

**amercement** *n.* **1.** an amercing; the imposition of a discretionary fine or penalty.
**2.** the fine or punishment so inflicted.

**American Bar Association (ABA)** *n.* The largest national organization of lawyers in the United States, open to all lawyers. See also note at LAW SCHOOL.

**American Law Institute (ALI)** a national organization of judges, lawyers, and law teachers founded in 1923 to promote clarification, simplification, and improvement in the law. Membership is by election. The ALI has exercised great influence in American law through such projects as the RESTATEMENTS OF THE LAW and the MODEL PENAL CODE, among many others.

**amicus curiae** *n., pl.* **amici curiae.** *Latin.* (lit. "friend of the court") a nonparty that volunteers or is invited by the court to submit its views on the issues presented in a case, because it has an interest in or perspective on the matter that may not be adequately represented by the parties. Usually the amicus curiae (or **amicus** for short) only submits a BRIEF (called a **brief amicus curiae** or **amicus brief**), but sometimes the amicus is also allowed to participate in oral argument. Also called **friend of the court.**

**amnesty** *n., pl.* **amnesties.** a government's forgiveness of past offenses for a class of people, as when a state or city declares that for a period of time anyone who turns in an illegal weapon will not be prosecuted for illegal possession, or when President Ford declared an amnesty for Vietnam War deserters and draft evaders on the condition that they perform alternative public service. Amnesties may be granted either by executive decree or by legislative act, and have the effect of a PARDON for each individual covered. Cf. COMMUTE; REPRIEVE. See also CLEMENCY.

**amortize** *v.,* **amortized, amortizing. 1.** to pay off a debt in regular installments over a specific period of time.
**2.** to write off or deduct for income tax purposes a portion of the cost of an intangible asset each year until the entire cost has been used up.
—**amortization** *n.*
—**amortizable** *adj.*

**amount** *n.* See JURISDICTIONAL AMOUNT.

**AMT** ALTERNATIVE MINIMUM TAX.

**analogous art** *n.* See under ART.

**ancestor** *n.* **1.** Also called **ascendant.** one who precedes another in the line of descent; a parent, grandparent, great-grandparent, etc.
**2.** any relative from whom property is inherited by intestate succession.
——**False Friend.** In nonlegal contexts, *ancestor* typically refers to generations long gone. In legal usage the term often refers to the immediately preceding generation, and can even refer to a sibling or cousin from whom property is inherited by intestate succession.

**ancient document** *n.* **1.** a DOCUMENT offered as evidence, which because of its age might be difficult to AUTHENTICATE by means of a witness who could testify as to the circumtances of its making. At common law a document thirty years old was "ancient"; under the Federal Rules of Evidence the age is set at twenty years.
**2. ancient document rule** or **ancient documents rule** the rule of evidence that a document may be admitted into evidence without further authentication if there is evidence that it is at least twenty or thirty years old (depending upon the jurisdiction), was found in a place where such a document would likely be, and is in such condition as to create no suspicion concerning its authenticity.

**ancillary** *adj.* auxiliary; subordinate; supplementary. See for example *ancillary administrator* (under ADMINISTRATOR); *ancillary jurisdiction* (under JURISDICTION[1]).

**and his heirs** See under HEIRS.

**animo** *Latin.* **1.** with intent; with the intention.
**2. animo donandi** with the intention of giving.
**3. animo furandi** with the intention of stealing.
**4. animo malo** with evil intent.
**5. animo testandi** with testamentary intent.

**animus¹** *n.* **1.** strong dislike; hostility; animosity; strongly negative prejudice;

hate. Animus toward a particular group is the component that distinguishes a HATE CRIME from an identical crime not so labeled.
**2. racial animus** hate based upon race.

**animus²** *n. Latin.* (lit. "character; disposition; inclination") **1.** intent; the intention with which an act is done.
**2. animus donandi** the intention of giving; donative intent.
**3. animus furandi** the intention of stealing. This is an essential element of the common law crime of LARCENY.
**4. animus malus** evil intent.
**5. animus testandi** the intention of making a will; testamentary intent.

**annotated** *adj.* describing a compilation of statutes to which ANNOTATIONS have been added for the benefit of legal researchers; a typical title is *United States Code Annotated.* Cf. UNITED STATES CODE.

**annotation** *n.* **1.** Also called **case note.** a one-paragraph summary of the holding of a case applying or interpreting a particular statutory provision, appended to the statute in question by the editors of a set of ANNOTATED statutes. An important statute may have hundreds, even thousands, of annotations in such a book.
**2.** a COMMENT.

**annual percentage rate (APR)** *n.* the interest rate charged for a loan or credit arrangement expressed as a percentage on an annualized basis, as calculated in accordance with standardized methods prescribed by consumer protection statutes and regulations.

**annual percentage yield (APY)** *n.* the total amount of interest or income that would be received on a deposit or investment held for one year, expressed as a percentage and calculated in accordance with standardized methods prescribed by consumer protection statutes and regulations.

**annuity** *n., pl.* **annuities. 1.** a regular income paid out at fixed intervals for a certain period of time, often beginning at a certain age and continuing for the life of the recipient (the **annuitant**), usually in consideration of a PREMIUM paid by the annuitant either in a lump sum or in installments.

**2.** the right to receive such income.

**3.** a contract or other arrangement providing for such payments.

**4. annuity certain** an annuity payable over a specified period even if the annuitant dies.

**5. annuity due** an annuity under which a payment is made at the beginning rather than the end of each payment period.

**6. contingent annuity** an annuity to be paid over a period of time whose beginning, end, or duration depends upon uncertain future events.

**7. deferred annuity** an annuity under which payments are to begin at a future date. Cf. *immediate annuity.*

**8. fixed annuity** an annuity providing for payments in a fixed amount. Cf. *variable annuity.*

**9. group annuity** an annuity contract covering all members of a group, normally employees under a PENSION PLAN.

**10. immediate annuity** an annuity paid for in a lump sum and commencing at once. Cf. *deferred annuity.*

**11. individual retirement annuity** See INDIVIDUAL RETIREMENT ANNUITY.

**12. joint and survivor annuity** an annuity payable to two or more annuitants (typically a husband and wife) so long as any one of them remains alive. Cf. *joint annuity.*

**13. joint annuity** or **joint life annuity** an annuity payable to two or more annuitants jointly (typically a husband and wife), but only so long as they all remain alive. Cf. *joint and survivor annuity.*

**14. life annuity** an annuity payable for the life of the annuitant.

**15. reverse annuity mortgage** See under MORTGAGE.

**16. survivorship annuity** an annuity payable for the life of the annuitant and then to a specified survivor (typically the spouse) for the life of the survivor.

**17. variable annuity** an annuity whose payments vary in amount according to the value of the investments made with the funds paid by all the annuitants or employers who have purchased the same type of annuity. Cf. *fixed annuity.*

**annuity certain** *n., pl.* **annuities certain.** See under ANNUITY (def. 4).

**annuity due** *n., pl.* **annuities due.** See under ANNUITY (def. 5).

**annul** *v.,* **annulled, annulling. 1.** to render void or ineffective; cancel; invalidate.

**2.** to declare judicially that something is legally VOID, either as of the date of the decree or AB INITIO.

**3.** in particular, to decree that a marriage is void because of some defect dating back to the time of the marriage, such as the fact that one of the partners was already married.

—**annullable** *adj.*

**annulment** *n.* **1.** the act of annulling or state of being annulled.

**2.** a judicial decree declaring that something, particularly a marriage, is annulled.

**anonymous work** *n.* See under WORK.

**answer** *v.* **1.** to respond to a summons, complaint, subpoena, motion, discovery request, or other judicial process or procedural step in a case.

**2.** to account for one's actions; put up a defense: *We will answer the allegations in court.*

**3.** to assume responsibility or liability: *Under the statute of frauds, an agreement to answer for the debt of another is not enforceable unless it is in writing.*

**4.** to suffer the consequences: *The murderer will answer for his crime.*

**5.** to respond to a question: *The witness is directed to answer.*

—*n.* **6.** a response to a question. See also RESPONSIVE ANSWER; UNRESPONSIVE ANSWER.

**7.** a response to a procedural step, allegation, judicial process, or the like: *Our answer to the motion will be filed on Friday.*

**8.** in particular, the pleading filed in a civil case in response to the COMPLAINT. In the answer, the defendant must admit or deny each allegation in the complaint except for those as to

which she lacks sufficient information to respond. The answer must also contain any *affirmative defense* (see under DEFENSE) that the defendant wishes to raise, and may contain COUNTER-CLAIMS, to which the plaintiff must then file a REPLY.
—**answerable** *adj.*
—**answerability** *n.*

**answering brief** *n.* See under BRIEF.

**ante** *prep. Latin.* before.

**ante litem** *Latin.* before suit: *The rules provide for ante litem notice.*

**ante litem motam** *Latin.* (lit. "before suit having been set in motion") before the prospect of suit; before the lawsuit would have been anticipated (and thus, by implication, before there was a motive to lie about the underlying facts).
——**Usage.** This phrase was traditionally used solely in discussions of whether a relevant statement made before a suit was filed could have been colored by the prospect of such a suit: Might the statement have been made with an eye to the suit, or was it made *ante litem motam*, that is, before the foreseeability of suit gave rise to a motive to lie? To the extent that the phrase is still used today, that is still what it means; occasionally, however, a court confuses it with ANTE LITEM and uses it simply to mean "before suit" in a context having nothing to do with motive to lie.

**ante mortem** *Latin.* before death.

**antecedent** *adj.* preceding; preexisting; prior.
—**antecendently** *adv.*
—**antecedence** *n.*

**antecessor** *n., pl.* **antecessores** *Latin.* (lit. "predecessor; ancestor") **1.** ancestor; individual from whom one is descended.
**2.** a relative from whom one inherits an interest in land.
See also *assisa de morte antecessoris* or *assisa mortis antecessoris* (under AS-SISA).

**antenuptial agreement** *n.* Same as PRENUPTIAL AGREEMENT.

**antichresis** *n., pl.* **antichreses.** (in civil law and Louisiana law) a pledge of immovable property as security for payment of a debt, under which the creditor takes possession of the property and assumes responsibility for maintaining it, and applies income from the property to the debt.
—**antichretic** *adj.*

**anticipation** *n.* **1.** the doing of something in advance; often in a negative sense of doing of something before the proper time.
**2.** a premature withdrawal or assignment of money from a trust estate; payment or commitment of trust income before it has been earned.
**3.** in patent law, the prior existence of substantially the same invention as one for which a patent is sought, or the existence of *prior art* (see under ART) which would make the invention obvious to people of ordinary skill in that field. An invention that has been "anticipated" in this sense cannot be patented, because it is not really new.
—**anticipate** *v.*, **anticipated, anticipating.**

**anticipatory** *adj.* in the nature of or characterized by ANTICIPATION; premature; preliminary. See also *anticipatory breach* or *anticipatory repudiation* (under BREACH); *anticipatory crime* or *anticipatory offense* (under CRIME).
—**anticipatorily** *adv.*

**antidumping** *adj.* **1.** designed or intended to counteract the export of products from other countries into the United States market at unfairly low prices. See also DUMPING.
**2. antidumping duty** a duty (see DUTY[2]) imposed on a product imported into the United States when it is determined that the product is being sold or is likely to be sold at less than fair value to the material detriment of American industry. The duty is imposed in an amount sufficient to raise the price of the product to what is regarded as a normal value.
**3. antidumping law** a statute intended to counteract exports of products to the United States at unfairly low

prices to the detriment of American industry.

**anti-heart-balm statute** *n.* Same as HEART BALM STATUTE.

**antilapse statute** *n.* a statute that protects the family of a person named in a will from losing the legacy if that person dies before the will takes effect. For example, if a testator names his sister in his will but then the sister dies before the testator, at common law the bequest to the sister would LAPSE and the sister's family might end up with nothing. Under antilapse statutes in most states, the bequest to the sister would remain valid and be distributed to her own heirs.

**antimarital fact privilege** *n.* See under MARITAL PRIVILEGE.

**anti-SLAPP statute** *n.* a state statute designed to protect people against SLAPP suits by various means, such as providing immunity from suit for information communicated to public agencies about matters within their purview, providing expedited procedures for dismissal of frivolous claims based upon such communications, or permitting awards of attorneys fees to the defendants in such suits. Also called **anti-SLAPP law.**

**anti-spam** (or **anti-spamming**) **law** *n.* any actual or proposed law intended to criminalize or control the sending of unsolicited commercial bulk e-mail (SPAM).
——**Note.** Although spamming is widely (though by no means universally) viewed as a problem—primarily because of the costs and burdens it imposes on the Internet system—the workability, desirability, and constitutionality of various proposed legislative approaches to the problem are in dispute and will take some years to work out.

**antitrust** *adj.* relating to the body of law—primarily federal law—intended to foster vigorous competition among businesses by outlawing such practices as price fixing and monopolization. The principal antitrust laws are the SHERMAN ANTITRUST ACT and the CLAYTON ACT. See also TRADE REGULATION.

**apartheid** *n.* **1.** a pervasive policy, system, or practice of rigid segregation of people according to race, class, or the like; especially the institutionalized policy of dominance by the white minority and separation of whites from the nonwhite majority that prevailed in South Africa from 1950 until 1994. See also SEPARATE BUT EQUAL.
**2.** *International Law.* as defined in the 1998 agreement to establish the INTERNATIONAL CRIMINAL COURT, inhumane acts committed in the context of an institutionalized regime of systematic oppression and domination by one racial group over any other racial group or groups and committed with the intention of maintaining that regime. Apartheid, as so defined, is classified as a CRIME AGAINST HUMANITY within the jurisdiction of that court.

**APB** ALL-POINTS BULLETIN.

**apostille** *n.* *French.* (lit. "footnote; recommendatory note") *International Law.* a certificate by which officials of one country authenticate a document for use in another country.

**apparent** *adj.* **1.** obvious, or at least deducible from the facts available: *It is apparent from the record that the defendant failed to exercise due care.*
**2.** seeming, but not ACTUAL; for example, see *apparent authority* (under AUTHORITY[1]).

**apparent defect** *n.* See under DEFECT[2].

**apparent heir** *n.* See under HEIR.

**appeal** *n.* **1.** the process by which one obtains review of a judicial decision by a higher court, or of an administrative decision by a court or by a higher authority within the administrative agency: *The case is on appeal.*
**2. appeal as of right a.** an appeal that the higher tribunal is required by law to consider. **b.** to file or pursue such an appeal: *The defendant appealed as of right to this court.*
**3. appeal by permission a.** Also called **discretionary appeal.** an appeal

that may be pursued only if specific permission is granted by a court. **b.** to file or pursue such an appeal.

**4. consolidated appeal** an appeal in which two or more cases raising related issues but tried separately—often in different courts and with different results—are briefed, argued, and decided together.

**5. interlocutory appeal** an appeal from an interim order in a case that is still proceeding in the lower tribunal. Most jurisdictions permit interlocutory appeals only under limited circumstances.

—*v.* **6.** to seek or pursue review by a higher authority: *If we lose, we will appeal. They are appealing the order.* —**appealable** *adj.* —**appealability** *n.*

**appeal bond** *n.* See under BOND[2].

**appealable order** *n.* See under ORDER[1].

**appear** *v.* **1.** (of a person) to come before a court or file a formal paper announcing that one will participate in a case: *The defendant appeared voluntarily; the attorney appeared on behalf of the defendant; the witness appeared pursuant to subpoena.* For many purposes a party need not appear personally but may send a lawyer instead **(appear by counsel).**
**2.** (of a fact) to be found in or deducible from the record in a case, so that it can be considered by an appellate court: *The victim's age does not appear in the record.*

**appearance** *n.* **1.** the act of coming before a court or of formally notifying the court that one will participate in a case as a party, lawyer, or witness.
**2. general appearance** an appearance in which a party consents to the court's jurisdiction and agrees to participate in a case for all purposes.
**3. special appearance** an appearance for the limited purpose of contesting the court's jurisdiction. Also called **limited appearance.**

**appellant** *n.* the party who files an appeal.

**appellate** *adj.* relating to appeals or an appeal: *appellate judge; appellate decision.* See also *appellate brief* (under BRIEF); *appellate jurisdiction* (under JURISDICTION[1]); *appellate review* (under REVIEW).

**appellate court** *n.* See under COURT.

**appellate defender** *n.* See under DEFENDER.

**appellate judge** *n.* See under JUDGE.

**appellee** *n.* the adversary of the party who files an appeal.

**applicable** *adj.* applying or capable of being applied; relevant; suitable; appropriate.
—**applicability** *n.*
—**applicably** *adv.*

**applicant** *n.* a person who applies for something; one who requests; a candidate.

**application** *n.* **1.** the act of applying.
**2.** a formal request or petition, either oral or written: *The attorney made her application for judgment notwithstanding the verdict immediately after the verdict was rendered, and filed her application for leave to appeal within thirty days.*
**3.** the use or purpose to which something is put.

**apply** *v.,* **applied, applying. 1.** to request formally of a court; petition; seek: *apply for relief from an injunction.*
**2.** to make a request; to seek acceptance or admission: *apply for a vacant position; apply to law school.*
**3.** to be pertinent or instructive: *The case cited by the appellants does not apply here.*
**4.** to use for or assign to a specific purpose: *Each payment is applied first to interest due and then to the outstanding balance.*

**appoint** *v.* **1.** to designate a person to fill a position or perform a task: *The president appoints federal judges.*
**2.** to designate who shall receive property that is the subject of a POWER OF APPOINTMENT.

**appointee** *n.* **1.** a person who is appointed or assigned to a position or task.

**2.** the person appointed to receive property pursuant to a POWER OF APPOINTMENT.

**appointment** *n.* **1.** the act of appointing, designating, or placing in office: *to fill a vacancy by appointment.*
**2.** an office, position, or the like, to which a person is appointed: *He received an appointment as ambassador to Italy.*
**3.** the exercise of a POWER OF APPOINTMENT; the act of designating who shall receive property that is the subject of the power.

**apportionment** *n.* **1.** division, allocation, or distribution of something, as money or liability for taxes, according to a rule of proportionality.
**2.** Also called **legislative apportionment.** allocation of seats in a legislative body in proportion to population; the drawing of voting district lines so as to equalize population and voting power among the districts.
**3.** Also called **congressional apportionment.** legislative apportionment as applied to the United States House of Representatives; the fixing of the number of representatives allocated to each state and the drawing of congressional district lines within each state.
See also GERRYMANDER; ONE PERSON, ONE VOTE; REAPPORTIONMENT.
—**apportion** *v.*
—**apportionable** *adj.*
—**apportionability** *n.*

**apposite** *adj.* (of a precedent) pertinent; similar to the present case in ways that make it instructive with respect to the issue under consideration.
—**appositely** *adv.*
—**appositeness** *n.*

**appraisal rights** *n.pl.* the rights of corporate shareholders, granted by statutes which vary from state to state, to dissent from certain extraordinary corporate actions such as a merger, have the value of their stock prior to such an action appraised in a judicial proceeding, and compel the corporation to buy the stock back at the appraised value.

**appraise** *v.*, **appraised, appraising.** to determine the MARKET VALUE of something. Cf. ASSESS.
—**appraisal** *n.*

**appraiser** *n.* **1.** one who appraises.
**2.** especially, a person in the business of appraising; a person with particular training or experience in determining the value of a particular class of property: *art appraiser; real estate appraiser.*

**appreciate** *v.*, **appreciated, appreciating.** to rise in market value; to become more valuable.
—**appreciation** *n.*

**approach** *v.* **1.** to draw closer; especially, to draw closer to the judge or a witness in a courtroom proceeding.
**2. approach the bench** to draw closer to the judge, as to hand up a document or for a SIDEBAR CONFERENCE.
——**Usage.** Since attorneys must receive permission from the judge before approaching either the judge or a witness in the courtroom, every such approach is preceded by a little dialog, in which "approach the bench" and "approach the witness" are very often shortened to just "approach": *May I approach? Will counsel please approach?*

**appropriation** *n.* **1.** the taking of anything; for example, the government's TAKING of private property for public use: *appropriation of land for construction of a school.*
**2.** the act of a legislative body in setting aside a sum of money from public funds for a particular use: *appropriation of $1,000,000 for construction of a school.*
—**appropriate** *v.*, **appropriated, appropriating.**

**approximation of laws** *n.* harmonization of laws among member states of the European Community on matters relevant to the functioning of the Common Market.

**appurtenant** *adj.* describing a right or thing attached to or associated with a parcel of land in such a way that it normally passes with title to the land. For example, buildings on land are appurtenant to it, and an easement to pass over a neighbor's land to reach one's own land is appurtenant to one's own

land. See also *easement appurtenant* (under EASEMENT).
—**appurtenance** *n.*

**APR** ANNUAL PERCENTAGE RATE.

**APY** ANNUAL PERCENTAGE YIELD.

**arbitrary** *adj.* completely unreasonable; lacking a rational basis. Often used in the phrase **arbitrary and capricious,** which means the same thing.

**arbitration** *n.* **1.** a process for resolution of disputes without resort to the courts, through submission of the dispute to a private individual (the **arbitrator**), or a panel of arbitrators, selected jointly by the parties. Arbitration can sometimes be cheaper and quicker than litigation and have the advantage of utilizing arbitrators who are specialists in the field involved in the dispute. It can also be amazingly expensive and time-consuming, and result in decisions biased in favor of the industry with which the specialist arbitrators are associated. Cf. MEDIATION.
**2. arbitration clause** a clause in a contract providing that the parties will submit any dispute arising from the contract to arbitration rather than litigation in court.
**3. compulsory arbitration** arbitration required by law, rather than submitted to by mutual agreement.
—**arbitrable** *adj.*
—**arbitrate** *v.,* **arbitrated, arbitrating.**

**arguable** *adj.* capable of being supported by respectable argument, though not necessarily a winning argument.
—**arguably** *adv.*
——**False Friend.** Outside legal circles a common meaning of *arguable* is "susceptible to debate, challenge, or doubt; questionable." That sense of the word is virtually nonexistent in legal discourse.

**argue** *v.,* **argued, arguing.** to present an ARGUMENT on a matter: *argue the motion; argue the appeal; argue the issue;* or simply *argue.*

**arguendo** *adv.* Latin. (lit. "in arguing") hypothetically; for purposes of argument; a term used in assuming a fact for the purpose of argument without waiving the right to question its truth later: *Assuming arguendo that the plaintiff's allegations are true, the complaint nevertheless fails to state a claim.*

**argument** *n.* **1.** the reasons supporting a conclusion or proposed conclusion, or the formal presentation of such reasons to a person or body that one hopes to convince.
**2.** the section of a BRIEF in which a party presents its analysis of the law pertaining to a motion or appeal. This follows a section in which the pertinent facts are outlined, and explains why the party contends that, upon those facts, the law requires a particular decision.
**3.** Also called **oral argument. a.** an oral presentation to a court of the reasons—both legal and factual—why a party contends that the court should reach a particular conclusion or take a particular action. **b.** the procedure in which a court hears such arguments from both sides on a motion or appeal, often questioning the lawyers on various details as they argue. Cf. *take on submission* (under SUBMIT).
**4.** Also called **closing argument.** a SUMMATION.

**argumentative** *adj.* (of a statement or question) suggesting that the facts support a particular inference or conclusion. See also *argumentative question* (under QUESTION).
—**argumentatively** *adv.*
—**argumentativeness** *n.*

**ARM** *n.,* *pl.* **ARMs, ARM's.** *adjustable-rate mortgage* (see under MORTGAGE).

**armed robbery** *n.* See under ROBBERY.

**arm's length** *n.* referring to dealings between unrelated parties, each motivated solely by its own self-interest: *The parties dealt at arm's length. It was an arm's-length transaction.* See also MARKET VALUE.

**arraignment** *n.* the proceeding in which a criminal defendant is brought before the court, formally advised of the charges, and required to enter a PLEA.
—**arraign** *v.*

**array** *n.* Same as VENIRE.

**arrear** *n.* **1.** Usually, **arrears.** the state of being behind or late in the performance of an obligation, especially a financial obligation. The term in this sense occurs almost exclusively in the phrase **in arrear** or **in arrears:** *He is in arrears in his child support obligation. The rent is in arrear.*
**2.** Usually, **arrears.** (used with either a *sing.* or *pl.* verb) an overdue debt or obligation; an amount overdue; outstanding debts collectively: *She owes an arrear of one month's rent. How much was the arrears as of the end of last month? The arrears total over five thousand dollars.*

**arrearage** *n.* **1.** an overdue debt; an amount overdue.
**2.** Often, **arrearages.** amounts overdue or the total of such amounts; overdue debts collectively.
**3.** the state or condition of being in arrears.

**arrest** *n.* **1.** any significant deprivation of an individual's freedom of action, especially the taking of an individual into custody for the purpose of transporting him to a police station and charging him with a crime. Cf. STOP.
**2. citizen's arrest** an arrest made by a private citizen rather than a law enforcement officer, as when bystanders tackle a purse-snatcher. Such arrests are lawful only under narrow circumstances.
**3. false arrest** See under FALSE IMPRISONMENT.
**4. pretextual arrest** a valid arrest for a minor offense, made for the actual purpose of seeking evidence to support an arrest for a more significant crime of which the arrestee is suspected, but for which there is as yet no probable cause to arrest. Also called **pretext arrest.**
**5. warrantless arrest** an arrest made without a warrant (see WARRANT[1]). As a general rule, a police officer may arrest a person for a felony without a warrant if she has PROBABLE CAUSE and the arrest is made in a public place, but a warrant is required to enter a person's home.
—*v.* **6.** to make an arrest of a person.
—**arrestable** *adj.*

—**arrester, arrestor** *n.*
—**arrestee** *n.*

**arrest of judgment** *n.* (at common law) the action of a judge in stopping a judgment from being entered on a verdict because of a defect or error in the proceedings, or because the judgment is not supported by the evidence.

**arrest warrant** *n.* See under WARRANT[1].

**arson** *n.* the crime of intentionally causing a dangerous fire or explosion, especially for the purpose of destroying a building of another or of damaging property in order to collect insurance.

**art** *n.* **1.** (in patent law) a process, technique, or method for accomplishing a useful result; particularly the process involved in an invention for which a patent is sought or has previously been granted.
**2. analogous art** any existing process or method for accomplishing the same result as that accomplished by an invention for which a patent is sought.
**3. prior art** any process, method, or invention already in existence before the invention for which a patent is sought and reasonably knowable to people in the field, including anything covered by prior patents or described in printed scientific publications. See also TERM OF ART.

**ART** Abbreviation for ASSISTED REPRODUCTIVE TECHNOLOGY.

**art.** ARTICLE.

**artful pleading** *n.* **1.** the drafting of a complaint so as to characterize the cause of action as falling under a body of law that would be favorable to the plaintiff, rather than an arguably applicable body of law that would be unfavorable.
**2.** the drafting of a pleading in such a way as to favor the client's position more than might have seemed possible without actually lying.
——**Usage.** The word "artful" in reference to pleadings usually reflects a mixture of disparagement for the lawyer's attempt to circumvent the applicable law or facts and grudging admiration

for the cleverness of the attempt: *The plaintiff cannot be allowed to circumvent the arbitration clause, no matter how artful the pleading. An examination of the answer indicates that by artful pleading, no damaging statements were actually denied, although at first glance it might appear otherwise.*

**article** *n., v.,* **articled, articling.** —*n.* **1.** (abbreviated **art.**) a subdivision of a written instrument; particularly **a.** a subdivision of a statute or constitution, usually further subdivided into SECTIONS. **b.** one of the items or clauses in a contract, treaty, or other agreement. **2. articles** a written instrument, especially a contract, consisting of several items each of which is designated as an article. —*v.* **3.** to set forth in articles; charge or accuse specifically: *They articled his alleged crimes.* **4.** to bind as a apprentice (under what were called "articles of apprenticeship"): *He was articled to a London solicitor in 1820.*

**Article I court** *n.* See under COURT.

**Article I judge** *n.* See under JUDGE.

**Article III court** *n.* See under COURT.

**Article III judge** *n.* See under JUDGE.

**articled clerk** *n.* See under CLERK.

**articles of association** *n.* an agreement by which an ASSOCIATION is formed, setting forth the purpose and rules of the organization.

**Articles of Confederation** *n.* the first constitution of the thirteen American states, ratified in 1781 and replaced in 1789 by the Constitution of the United States.

**articles of impeachment** *n.pl.* the formal written instrument that forms the basis for an IMPEACHMENT proceeding against a public officer, listing the charges against the officer.

**articles of incorporation** *n.pl.* a document setting forth the basic structure of a corporation, including its name and purposes and the number of shares of stock that it will be authorized to issue, which must be filed with a state

government in order to bring the corporation into existence. See also CERTIFICATE OF INCORPORATION; CHARTER[1].

**articles of war** *n.* **1.** military law; regulations for the government of military forces. **2. Articles of War** (in the United States) the body of laws and legal procedures of the U.S. Army and Air Force prior to the adoption of the Uniform Code of Military Justice in 1951.

**artificial person** *n.* See under PERSON.

**as a matter of law** (of a legal conclusion) compelled by principles of law and justice; said particularly of factual findings that a court takes out of the hands of the jury: *The judge directed a verdict for the defendant in the personal injury case because the plaintiff deliberately ignored a warning sign and therefore assumed the risk of injury as a matter of law.* See also BY OPERATION OF LAW; IN LAW.

**as applied** *adv.* See *unconstitutional* (or *invalid*) *as applied* (under UNCONSTITUTIONAL).

**as is** *adv.* without any express or implied warranty. The words "as is," "with all faults," or the like in a contract for sale of goods mean that the buyer assumes the risk of any defects or malfunctions.

**ascendant** *n.* Same as ANCESTOR (def. 1).

**asportation** *n.* carrying away; moving, if only a slight distance; exercising control over. Asportation is an essential element of the common law crime of LARCENY. —**asport** *v.*

**assault** *n.* **1.** in tort law, an act putting another person in apprehension of imminent BATTERY, done either with intent actually to cause a battery (as by taking a swing at someone) or simply with intent to cause the apprehension (as by shaking one's fist under someone's nose). If in either case the act results in physical contact, then there has been both an assault and a battery. **2.** in criminal law, a term used in different states to mean one or more of the following crimes: **a.** BATTERY. **b.** attempted battery. **c.** conduct inducing a reasonable fear of battery or immediate bodily harm. See also note at AGGRAVATED.

**3. assault and battery** another term for the crime of battery. See also *trespass in assault and battery* (under TRESPASS²).

**4. atrocious assault** or **atrocious assault and battery** a criminal assault involving actual wounding, or particularly severe wounding or maiming.

**5. sexual assault** the crime of intentionally touching another person in a sexual way without that person's consent, or when that person lacks the capacity to give legally effective consent. Also called **indecent assault.**
—**assaulter** *n.*
—**assaultive** *adj.*
—**assaultively** *adv.*

**assembly** *n., pl.* **assemblies. 1.** a gathering or coming together of a number of people, usually for a particular purpose.
**2.** the group of persons so assembled.
**3.** Often, **Assembly.** a legislative body, especially the lower house of the legislature in certain states of the United States.
See also FREEDOM OF ASSEMBLY; UNLAWFUL ASSEMBLY.

**assemblyman** *n., pl.* **assemblymen.** a member of a state legislative assembly. Also called **assemblyperson.** A female member may also be called **assemblywoman.**

**assemblyperson** *n., pl.* **assemblypersons.** a member of a state legislative assembly.

**assemblywoman** *n., pl.* **assemblywomen.** a female member of a state legislative assembly.

**assess** *v.* **1.** to set the amount of, and impose, a tax, fine, or damages: *Damages were assessed at $1.5 million. The Liquor Authority assessed a fine of $10,000.*
**2.** to establish the value of real estate for property tax purposes (the **assessed value**). Typically the assessed value is lower than the MARKET VALUE. Cf. APPRAISE.
**3.** to require stockholders to make additional contributions to the corporation, or partners to make additional contributions to the partnership, to fill a need for additional capital. See also *assessable stock* and *nonassessable stock* (under STOCK).
—**assessable** *adj.*
—**assessment** *n.*
—**assessor** *n.*

**assessable stock** *n.* See under STOCK.

**asset** *n.* **1.** any property or right of a person or entity that has monetary value, such as land, an automobile, stock, a copyright, money, or a right to payment for goods sold (if payment is a realistic possibility). Cf. LIABILITY (def. 3).
**2. assets** all such property and rights collectively, or their total value; the total resources of a person, estate, business, etc. If assets exceed liabilities, the excess is the entity's **net assets:** *The company has assets of $1,000,000, liabilities of $900,000, and net assets of $100,000.*
**3. intangible asset** an asset that is not a physical thing; for example, a patent, a right to payment, or GOODWILL.
**4. capital asset** for income tax purposes, virtually all property of a taxpayer except certain business assets and certain other property excluded by the Internal Revenue Code. The tax treatment of a sale or exchange of property depends in part upon whether the property was a capital asset.
**5. fixed asset** a tangible, long-term asset of a business, such as a building, land, furniture, or manufacturing equipment.
**6. liquid asset** an asset readily convertible into cash, such as shares of publicly traded stock.
**7. tangible asset** a physical asset, such as land, equipment, or salable inventory.

**asset forfeiture law** *n.* a law providing for FORFEITURE of property, particularly property used in a crime or derived from a crime.
——**History.** Asset forfeiture laws have

been criticized by some—and are supported by others—for their harshness, since they can result in severe punishment for a relatively minor offense, such as the forfeiture of a house because the owner grew some marijuana plants in it. Their effect on innocent parties can also be severe, as a woman in Michigan found out when the Detroit police spied her husband using their car for an assignation with a prostitute. The state took away the car, of which she was a joint owner, and refused to compensate her for her half interest in the car even though she had most assuredly not participated in the crime. The United States Supreme Court upheld the state's punishment of the innocent spouse: by a vote of five to four, with both wives on the court voting in the majority, it held that she was not deprived of property without DUE PROCESS in violation of the Fourteenth Amendment, nor was her property taken without JUST COMPENSATION in violation of the Fifth Amendment. *Bennis v. Michigan,* 516 U.S. 442 (1996).

**assign** *v.* **1.** to transfer an interest, right, or duty; to substitute another person for oneself in a contract: *The company assigned its accounts receivable to the bank. I assigned my lease to someone else and moved to San Francisco.* **2.** to appoint: *The judge assigned counsel for the defendant.* **3.** to identify, point out: *The appellant assigns numerous alleged errors by the trial judge.* —*n.* **4. assigns** persons to whom an interest, right, or duty might be assigned. Used principally in the phrase *heirs and assigns* (see under HEIR); in most other contexts, and whenever the singular is called for, the term used is ASSIGNEE. —**assignment** *n.*

**assignable** *adj.* capable of being assigned. Some rights and most duties are not assignable, at least without the permission of other parties involved; for example, an opera star cannot unilaterally assign her contract to sing in an opera to an inferior performer. But a right to receive a payment is normally freely assignable. —**assignability** *n.*

**assigned counsel** *n.* See under COUNSEL.

**assigned risk** *n.* a risk that, under state law, is assigned to an insurer chosen from a pool of insurers who otherwise would not accept it.

**assignee** *n.* the person or entity to which an interest, right, or duty is assigned.

**assignment for the benefit of creditors** *n.* an assignment, by an entity overwhelmed with debts, of substantially all of its assets to a trustee, to be liquidated and used to satisfy the debts to the extent possible.

**assignment of error** *n.* a specification, in appellate papers, of a ruling by the court below that the appellant contends was improper and requires reversal.

**assignor** *n.* the person or entity that assigns an interest, right, or duty to another.

**assise** *n. Law French.* (lit. "sitting; seated; a sitting; an assessment") Same as ASSIZE.

**assissa** *n., pl.* **assissae.** *Latin.* **1.** ASSIZE. **2. assisa de morte antecessoris** or **assisa mortis antecessoris** the *assize of mort d'ancestor* (see under MORT D'ANCESTOR). **3. assisa novae disseisinae** the *assize of novel disseisin* (see under NOVEL DISSEISIN). **4. assisa ultimae praesentationis** the *assize of darrein presentment* (see under DARREIN PRESENTMENT). **5. assisa utrum** or **assisa de utrum** the *assize utrum* or *assize of utrum* (see under UTRUM).

**Assistant United States Attorney (AUSA)** *n.* See under UNITED STATES ATTORNEY.

**assisted reproductive technology (ART)** *n.* any technique for assisting in human reproduction that involves laboratory handling of eggs, sperm, or the early products of fertilization.

**assisted suicide** *n.* See under SUICIDE.

**assize** *n. English Legal History.* **1.** an edict, ordinance, or decree made at a sitting of the king's council or, later, another legislative body, usually named after the place where it occurred or the subject matter covered: *Assize of Northampton* (1176); *Assize of Bread and Ale* (1266).
**2.** Also called **recognition.** an early form of judicial inquest or investigation regarding rights to land, held locally with a panel of sworn RECOGNITORS.
**3.** a trial, especially one held by a traveling judge in the county where the land involved is located or the crime occurred or the dispute arose.
**4.** the jury at such a trial or inquest. See also RECOGNITOR.
**5.** a cause of action; a case, particularly of certain types relating to possession or ownership of land.
**6.** Also called **writ of assize.** the writ by which such an action was commenced. The writ directed the sheriff of the county to summon a jury to decide the matter.
**7.** Usually, **assizes.** a session or term of court held in the countryside by a traveling judge, or the period during which such a session is held—typically a fixed period one or more times each year.
**8. grand assize** the action, trial, or jury in a case brought by WRIT OF RIGHT to determine ownership of land.
**9. petty assize** the cause of action, trial, jury, or writ in any of four specific types of action over rights to possession of land and similar interests: DARREIN PRESENTMENT; MORT D'ANCESTOR; NOVEL DISSEISIN; UTRUM. See those terms for specific phrases with the word *assize.*
——**History.** The grand assize and the four petty assizes were established in the twelfth century by Henry II. The grand assize involved the selection by the sheriff of four knights, who in turn selected twelve more, making a panel of sixteen "recognitors" who were to decide the legal and factual issue of who had the ultimate right to the land on the basis of their own knowledge of the circumstances of the case. This represented a considerable change from prior practice, in which the established method for resolving an issue of ownership was trial by battle. Under the new procedure, however, the challenger still had to offer trial by battle; the option of battle or grand assize rested with the person in possession of the land. One of the concessions that the barons obtained from King John in the MAGNA CARTA in 1215 was that the king would send justices around to each county four times a year to hold petty assizes so that knights serving as recognitors would not have to travel to Westminster to perform their duties as jurors; this established the association of assizes with local trials by itinerant judges (def. 3 above). These assizes lasted in England until 1971. See also note at MORT D'ANCESTOR.

**associate** *n.* the usual title for an attorney in a law firm who works on salary but does not share in the firm's profits. Most attorneys in large law firms are associates rather than partners or owners.

**associate judge** *n.* See under JUDGE.

**association** *n.* **1.** Also called **unincorporated association.** any group of people organized for a common purpose and not formed as a corporation.
**2.** for income tax purposes, an unincorporated organization having characteristics that make it more like a corporation than like a partnership or trust. Such an association is taxed as a corporation.
**3. joint stock association** The name used in some states for *joint stock company* (see under COMPANY).
**4. professional association** The name used in some states for *professional corporation* (see under CORPORATION).
See also ARTICLES OF ASSOCIATION; *cooperative association* (under COOPERATIVE).

**Association of American Law Schools (AALS)** *n.* a national organization of law schools. A law school cannot apply for membership until it has offered five years of instruction and graduated three classes; it must then be voted into membership upon a determination that it meets the association's educational standards. See also note at LAW SCHOOL.

**assume** *v.*, **assumed, assuming.** to take on or accept responsibility for; especially, to take over an obligation of another. For example, the purchaser of a house with a mortgage may assume the mortgage; the purchaser of a business may assume the debts of the business. —**assumption** *n.*

**assumpsit** *n. Latin.* (lit. "he has undertaken; he has taken upon himself") **1.** (at common law) an enforceable promise or undertaking not under seal, either made orally or in writing **(express assumpsit)** or presumed in law from an individual's conduct or the circumstances of the case **(implied assumpsit).** **2.** the common law FORM OF ACTION to recover damages for breach of a contract not under seal. **a. general assumpsit** the action upon an implied promise. Also called **common assumpsit, indebitatus assumpsit. b. special assumpsit** the action upon an express promise. See also INDEBITATUS ASSUMPSIT; COMMON COUNTS. Cf. COVENANT.

**assumption of risk** *n.* the doctrine that one who voluntarily enters into a situation known to be dangerous may not recover from someone else for any resulting injury; the injured party is said to have "assumed the risk" of being injured. The defense of assumption of risk has been modified or abolished in many states. Cf. *comparative negligence* (under NEGLIGENCE).

**assure** *v.*, **assured, assuring.** to provide INSURANCE, act as a SURETY, or put up collateral (see COLLATERAL¹). —**assurance** *n.* —**assured** *adj., n.* —**assurer** *n.*

**astroturf** *adj. Informal.* **1.** (of political activity) fake grass-roots; planned, financed, and managed by big business or moneyed interests but carried out in such a way as to look like a spontaneous outpouring of sentiment among ordinary people: *an "astroturf" paid signature campaign.*

**2. astroturf lobbying** a fake grass-roots campaign of support or opposition to specific legislation. —*n.* **3.** an astroturf campaign, or a feature or product of such a campaign: *The aide stated that of the calls the Senator has received on the issue, about half are astroturf and half are real.* ——**Usage.** *AstroTurf*—originally called *ChemGrass*—is the name of a brand of synthetic turf and a registered trademark. In the political sense of the word, newspapers generally write it *Astroturf* and law reviews generally write it *astroturf*, usually in quotation marks. Either way is acceptable.

**asylum** *n.* **1.** *International Law.* Also called **political asylum. a.** legal permission to live in a country given by its government to a person from another country when that person is unable or unwilling to return to his country of nationality because of persecution or a well-founded fear of persecution on account of race, religion, nationality, membership in a particular social group, or political opinion. **b.** temporary refuge granted, especially to political offenders, in a foreign embassy within their own national boundaries. **2.** (esp. formerly) an institution for the maintenance and care of the mentally ill, orphans, or other persons requiring specialized assistance.

**at** *prep.* **1.** the word customarily used instead of "in," "under," "by," or the like in referring to modern or ancient COMMON LAW (often shortened to "law"): *Commercial bribery was not a crime at common law, but is a crime under modern criminal statutes.* See also AT LAW. **2.** the word usually used by lawyers to refer to a page number: *You'll find the citation at page 33, Your Honor, and the discussion begins at 35.*

**at bar** *adj.* See under BAR³.

**at large** **1.** free from restraint or confinement; at liberty: *The murderer is still at large.* **2.** Also, **at-large.** representing the whole of a state, district, or body rather than one division or part of it: *a delegate at large; an at-large delegate.*

**at law** under or pursuant to principles of law; concerned with law; before a court of law. See also *action at law* (under ACTION); *adequate remedy at law* (under REMEDY); AT; ATTORNEY AT LAW; *heir at law* (under HEIR); *remedy at law* (under REMEDY). Cf. IN EQUITY; IN LAW.
——**Usage.** In most contexts, this phrase refers not to law in a general sense, but to "law" as distinguished from EQUITY: *We are seeking relief in equity because we do not have an adequate remedy at law.* See LAW (def. 4); see also COMMON LAW (def. 3).

**at will** describing or referring to a status or relationship that can be terminated at any time for any reason: *tenancy (or estate) at will* (see under TENANCY); *employee at will.*

**atrocious assault** or **atrocious assault and battery** *n.* See under ASSAULT.

**attach** *v.* **1.** to effect an ATTACHMENT of: *The plaintiff attached the defendant's car and bank account.*
**2.** to arise or become legally effective; to take legal effect in connection with something: *The obligation attaches when the contract is signed.*
—**attachable** *adj.*

**attaché** *n.* **1.** a diplomatic official attached to an embassy or legation, especially in a technical capacity: *a commercial attaché; a cultural attaché.*
**2.** a military officer who is assigned to a diplomatic post in a foreign country.

**attachment** *n.* **1.** the seizing or freezing of property by court order in order to subject the property to the jurisdiction of the court, either so that a dispute as to ownership of it can be resolved or so that it will be available to satisfy a judgment against the owner.
**2.** the writ or other document authorizing or effecting such a seizure.

**attachment bond** *n.* See under BOND[2].

**attack** *v.* **1.** to assail physically.
**2.** to attempt to defeat, destroy, or undermine by argument; especially, to seek to overturn a judgment or other court order.

—*n.* **3.** the act of attacking; an attempt to defeat or overturn.
See also *direct attack* (under DIRECT[1]); *collateral attack* (under COLLATERAL[2]).
—**attackable** *adj.*
—**attacker** *n.*

**attainder** *n.* **1.** in early English law, the CIVIL DEATH and CORRUPTION OF BLOOD that attached automatically upon pronouncement or enactment of a sentence of death, or declaration of outlawry, for felony or treason.
**2.** the act of subjecting a person to attainder, or the instrument by which this was effected.
See also BILL OF ATTAINDER.

**attaint** *English Legal History.* —*v.* **1.** in very early law, to convict a jury of having rendered a false verdict, or to bring an action to overturn a verdict in this manner.
**2.** to condemn by a sentence, bill, or act of ATTAINDER. See also AUTREFOIS ATTAINT.
—*n.* **3.** the conviction of a jury for rendering a false verdict.
**4.** a proceeding or writ **(writ of attaint)** to overturn a verdict and convict the jurors.
——**History.** The jury system originated as a mechanism whereby people in the neighborhood where a crime occurred or a dispute arose were called upon, under oath, to determine the facts on the basis of their personal knowledge. The verdict of a jury of twelve could be overturned only by a jury of twenty-four; since this amounted to a finding that the original jurors had been dishonest, the attainted jurors were severely punished.

**attempt** *n.* the taking of a substantial step toward the commission of a crime, beyond mere preparation. Attempt is itself a crime, sometimes punishable to the same extent as the crime that was attempted, sometimes (especially in the case of more serious crimes such as murder) treated as a slightly lower grade of offense. In a prosecution for attempt, it does not matter whether the attempt was successful or not.
—**attempted** *adj.*

**attest** *v.* **1.** to sign a document as a witness to its execution by someone else. **2.** to CERTIFY the authenticity of a document or the accuracy of a copy. **3. attested copy** Same as *certified copy* (see under CERTIFY). —**attester, attestor** *n.* —**attestation** *n.*

**attesting witness** *n.* See under WITNESS.

**attorn** *v.* **1.** to turn over to another; to transfer. **2.** (of a tenant) to acknowledge the status of a successor landlord, as by paying rent to a mortgagee who has acquired the property by foreclosure. —**attornment** *n.*

**attorney** *n., pl.* **attorneys. 1.** Also called **attorney at law.** Same as LAWYER. **2.** Also called **attorney in fact.** a person who acts on behalf of another pursuant to a POWER OF ATTORNEY.

**attorney at law** *n., pl.* **attorneys at law.** ATTORNEY (def. 1).

**attorney-client privilege** *n.* the *evidentiary privilege* (see under PRIVILEGE) possessed by the client in an attorney-client relationship, to prevent disclosure of any confidential communication made to her lawyer for the purpose of obtaining legal advice or assisting in legal representation. Also called **lawyer-client privilege.**

**Attorney General (A.G.)** *n., pl.* **Attorneys General, Attorney Generals. 1.** the chief legal officer of the federal government or of a state; the head of the United States Department of Justice or of a state's legal department. Cf. SOLICITOR GENERAL; UNITED STATES ATTORNEY. **2. private attorney general** *Informal.* a private person who brings a civil case to draw attention to unlawful conduct and force compliance or punish non-compliance with a law, not only for personal satisfaction or compensation but also in the hope that the public at large will ultimately benefit. The term is rather subjective; what one person

might hail as the action of a private attorney general another might condemn as a *strike suit* (see under SUIT).

**attorney in fact** *n., pl.* **attorneys in fact.** ATTORNEY (def. 2).

**attorney of record** *n., pl.* **attorneys of record.** the attorney or law firm listed in court records as representing a particular party in a case. All papers and communications in a case intended for that party must go to the attorney of record. Cf. PRO SE.

**attorney pro hac vice** *n., pl.* **attorneys pro hac vice.** Same as *counsel pro hac vice* (under COUNSEL).

**attorney work product** *n.* Same as WORK PRODUCT.

**attorney's lien** *n.* See under LIEN.

**attractive nuisance** *n.* a condition existing on private property, but in a place where children are likely to trespass, that poses an unreasonable danger to such children. —**Note.** In general, property owners will be held liable in tort to children injured by such conditions if the danger could have been prevented by reasonable measures. For example, a homeowner would be expected to take strong precautionary measures to make sure that children cannot get in and play near an uncovered swimming pool without supervision.

**AUSA** Abbreviation for *Assistant United States Attorney* (see under UNITED STATES ATTORNEY).

**authentic act** *n. Civil Law.* a writing executed with certain formalities before a public officer such as a notary public.

**authenticate** *v.,* **authenticated, authenticating. 1.** to show, or to introduce evidence tending to show, that a document or other item offered as evidence in a case is in fact what the proponent claims it to be. Some authenticating evidence is ordinarily required before an exhibit can be admitted into evidence. **2.** to signify by some mark that a written document is authentic, valid, effective, intended as the expression of its author, or the like, as by signing, stamping, or certifying it.

**3. self-authenticating** showing on its face that it is authentic, or otherwise presumed to be authentic, so that no other authenticating evidence is required unless the authenticity of the item is called into question; for example, a certified copy of a public document.

—**authentication** *n.*

**author** *n. Copyright Law.* the creator of a copyrightable work.

—**authorship** *n.*

——**False Friend.** The Constitution grants Congress the power to adopt copyright and patent laws giving "Authors and Inventors the exclusive Right [for a limited time] to their respective Writings and Discoveries." A nonlawyer could be forgiven for concluding from this language that the drafters of the Constitution were using *author* in its usual sense of "writer." The drafters do not appear to have contemplated that copyright protection would extend, for example, to sculptors and architects, and they certainly did not foresee the need to protect film makers and recording artists. But this has never troubled either Congress or the Supreme Court; all of these categories of people and more are now treated by the copyright laws as "authors" within the meaning of the Constitution. See *original work of authorship* (under WORK).

**authority**[1] *n.* **1.** the legal power of a public official or body to act in an official capacity.

**2.** the power to act on behalf of another and bind the other by such actions; the power of an AGENT to act on behalf of the PRINCIPAL. See also SCOPE OF AUTHORITY.

**3. actual authority** authority intentionally granted by a principal to an agent. Such authority may be granted explicitly **(express authority)** or simply understood as necessary or proper in order to carry out expressly authorized tasks **(implied authority).**

**4. apparent authority** authority of an agent reasonably inferred from conduct of the principal, even if the principal did not intend the agent to have such authority.

**authority**[2] *n., pl.* **authorities. 1.** a source of information or insight on how to interpret and apply the law in a particular situation. The term includes judicial decisions, legislative history, and scholarly writing.

**2. binding authority** with respect to an issue in a court case, a clearly applicable HOLDING by a higher court in the same jurisdiction. The lower court is required to adhere to such a precedent. Also called **controlling authority.**

**3. persuasive authority** authority that carries weight in the consideration of an issue because of the strength of its reasoning or because it represents a widely held view, but that a court is not required to follow; for example, decisions of other courts at the same level, decisions of higher courts in other jurisdictions, or scholarly writing.

**4. primary authority** records of the law-making process itself: judicial opinions and other court records and legislative records.

**5. secondary authority** writing and analysis about the law, such as law review articles and legal treatises.

**auto-da-fé** *n., pl.* **autos-da-fé.** *Portuguese.* (lit. "act of the faith") the public declaration of the judgment passed on persons tried in the courts of the the Spanish Inquisition, followed by the execution by the civil authorities of the sentences imposed, especially the burning of condemned heretics at the stake.

**automatic stay** *n.* See under STAY.

**automobile guest statute** *n.* a statute providing that a nonpaying passenger in an automobile (a "guest" of the driver) who is injured in an accident caused by the driver's negligence may not recover damages from the driver, and hence from the driver's insurance company, unless the driver's negligence was extreme. At one time over half the states had such statutes, largely as a result of insurance industry lobbying. In recent years the tide has turned, and now only a few states still have such statutes.

**autoptic** *adj.* characterized by or based upon personal observation: *autoptic testimony; an autoptic witness.*

**autoptic evidence** *n.* Same as *demonstrative evidence* (see under EVIDENCE).

**autre** or **auter** *adj. Law French.* other; another. See also PUR AUTRE VIE.

**autrefois** *adv. Law French.* at another time; formerly; heretofore.

**autrefois acquit** *Law French.* (lit. "formerly acquitted") at common law, a plea made by a defendant indicted for a crime, that he has already been tried and acquitted of that very crime. See also DOUBLE JEOPARDY.

**autrefois attaint** *Law French.* (lit. "formerly attainted") in old English law, a plea that the defendant has been attainted for one felony, and therefore cannot be criminally prosecuted for another. See also ATTAINT; ATTAINDER.

**autrefois convict** *Law French.* (lit. "formerly convicted") at common law, a plea made by a defendant indicted for a crime, that he has already been convicted of that very crime. See also DOUBLE JEOPARDY.

**aver** *v.,* **averred, averring.** to assert as a fact; allege.

**aver et tener** *Law French.* (lit. "to have and to hold; having and holding") See A AVER ET TENER.

**average** *n.* **1.** expense or loss resulting from damage to a ship or cargo at sea, where there is not a total loss of the vessel.
**2.** the apportionment of such expense or loss to the parties involved. The parties involved are invariably insured, so determination of average is primarily an issue in the law and practice of marine insurance.
**3. general average** loss incurred, or the apportionment of loss incurred, as a result of deliberate action intended to save as much of the ship and cargo as possible, as by jettisoning equipment or cargo in order to stay afloat. The loss in such a case was incurred for the benefit of all and so is shared by all.

**4. particular average** loss incurred through unavoidable accident affecting the ship or certain cargo. Those losses are borne by the specific parties whose property was damaged.

**average basis** *n.* See under BASIS.

**averment** *n.* **1.** the act of averring. **2.** a positive statement; allegation.

**avoid** *v.* **1.** to nullify, upon some legal ground, an obligation or transaction to which one is a party; especially, in a situation where one party to a contract lacked the capacity to contract (e.g., because of infancy), to render the contract void by disaffirming it. See also VOIDABLE. Cf. RATIFY.
**2.** to keep away from; prevent. See also TAX AVOIDANCE.
—**avoidable** *adj.*
—**avoidance** *n.*

**avulsion** *n.* **1.** the sudden removal or severing of land from the property or jurisdiction of which it had been a part, through a natural force such as a flood or a sudden change of course of a river that had served as a boundary line.
**2.** the land severed or moved in this way.
—**Note.** Land that is severed by avulsion remains legally a part of the property or political jurisdiction to which it was originally attached. A close look at a good map of the western boundary of the state of Mississippi, along the meandering Mississippi River, will show many examples. Cf. ACCRETION.

**award** *n.* **1.** a grant of damages or other relief by a court, jury, or administrative tribunal.
—*v.* **2.** to grant such relief: *The plaintiff was awarded $5,000.*
—**awardability** *adv.*
—**awardable** *adj.*

**AWOL** *adj.* **1.** Abbreviation for ABSENT WITHOUT LEAVE.
—*n.* **2.** Abbreviation for ABSENCE WITHOUT LEAVE.
**3.** a soldier or other military person who is absent from duty without leave.

**ayel** *n.* Same as AIEL.

# B

**baby act** *n. Slang.* **1.** the conduct of one who is acting like a baby.
**2.** any statute or hypothetical statute providing that minors or children under a particular age cannot be held civilly liable or criminally responsible for acts of a certain kind; for example, a statute declaring that minors lack the legal capacity to enter into a binding contract.
**3. plead the baby act  a.** to enter a plea or raise a defense of incapacity due to youth. **b.** to point to one's youthfulness as an excuse or in mitigation of wrongful or unwise behavior.
——**Usage.** It would be difficult if not impossible to find a legal citation in which a statute was actually referred to as a "baby act," or a case in which a defendant who had a genuine defense of NONAGE or INCAPACITY was said to be "pleading the baby act." The real use of these phrases is to deride defendants or others who were old enough to be held responsible for their conduct but try to minimize its significance by characterizing it as a youthful indiscretion.

**BAC** Abbreviation for *blood alcohol concentration* or *blood alcohol content* (see BLOOD ALCOHOL CONCENTRATION).

**Bachelor of Laws (LL.B.)** *n.* See LL.B.

**bad** *adj.* generally, not favored by the law or acceptable in the marketplace. The specific legal meaning varies from phrase to phrase; see the entries directly below and *bad check* (under CHECK); *bad debt* (under DEBT); *bad title* (under TITLE).
—**badness** *n.*

**bad faith** *n.* absence of GOOD FAITH; lack of overall fairness and honesty in a transaction; especially, an intent to deceive others or to evade one's own obligations.

**bad law** *n.* **1.** a judicial opinion or decision that misconstrues or misapplies a legal principle, producing erroneous or misleading results.
**2.** any statute or ruling regarded by the speaker as unwise.
Cf. GOOD LAW.

**badge of slavery** *n.* **1.** a legal disability characteristic of slavery, such as inability to vote or make a contract.
**2.** a vestige of slavery, such as racial discrimination in real estate sales.

**bail**[1] *n.* **1.** money or other property pledged to a court by or on behalf of a person accused of a crime to assure her appearance in court. Cf. PREVENTIVE DETENTION; RELEASE ON OWN RECOGNIZANCE.
**2. bail bond** the document in which bail is pledged by the accused. Typically a third party acceptable to the court (called a **bail bondsman** or **bail bondswoman**) must also sign as a SURETY, so that the court will not have to try to collect forfeited bail from a missing defendant.
**3. cash bail** bail posted entirely in cash. If the accused satisfies all bail conditions, the cash is eventually returned.
**4. excessive bail** bail set in an amount higher than is reasonably necessary to secure the defendant's presence at trial. The Eighth Amendment (see Appendix) prohibits the government from demanding excessive bail and thereby keeping people not convicted of a crime in jail unnecessarily.
**5. jump bail** to flee or go into hiding while free on bail; to fail to make a required court appearance while out on bail.
**6. make bail** to secure one's own release from custody by posting the required bail or having someone else do so.

**7. on bail** or **out on bail**   free from custody because bail has been posted.

**8. post bail**   to provide the required cash or bond for bail, either for oneself or for someone else.

**9. stand bail**   to post bail for someone else.

—*v.* **10.** to secure the release of a person by posting bail (usually followed by *out*): *My sister bailed me out.*

—**bailable** *adj.*

**bail²** *v.* to transfer possession of personal property temporarily.   See also BAILMENT.

**bail bondsman** *n., pl.* **bail bondsmen.** See under BAIL¹.

**bail jumper** *n.* a person who jumps bail. See *jump bail* (under BAIL¹).

—**bail jumping** *n.*

**bailable offense** *n.* a charged offense for which the accused may be released on bail. Cf. PREVENTIVE DETENTION.

**bailee** *n.* See under BAILMENT.

**bailer** *n.* Same as BAILSMAN.

**bailiff** *n.* a court officer charged with managing the courtroom and taking care of the jury.

**bailment** *n.* an arrangement in which one person (the **bailor**) transfers possession (but not ownership) of personal property to another (the **bailee**)for storage, use, or some other temporary purpose. The legal rights and duties of the parties depend upon the purpose and terms of the bailment. The bailee may be storing the bailor's goods for a fee **(bailment for hire),** or working on them, as in the case of a car in a repair shop **(bailment for mutual benefit),** or simply borrowing them **(gratuitous bailment);** in each case, the bailor and bailee may be referred to according to type of bailment: *gratuitous bailee, bailor for mutual benefit,* etc. See also BAIL².

—**Usage.** If one person is renting property from the other, the arrangement is usually referred to as a LEASE rather than a bailment.

**bailor** *n.* See under BAILMENT.

**bailsman** *n., pl.* **bailsmen.** one who posts bail for another. See BAIL¹.

**bait and switch** *n.* the practice of drawing customers into a store by advertising a product at a low price and then inducing them to purchase a more expensive product by disparaging the advertised product or saying that it is not available. This is usually a crime. See also FALSE ADVERTISING.

**balance** *v.,* **balanced, balancing,** *n.*

—*v.* **1.** to estimate the relative weight or importance of; compare: *to balance the risks and the benefits a proposed course of action.*

**2.** to add up credits and debits and determine the difference: *to balance a checkbook.*

—*n.* **3.** the result of balancing: *On balance, the risks outweigh the benefits. The unpaid balance is one thousand dollars.*

**balancing of the equities** *n.* a court's weighing of all factors favoring each side in order to determine the overall fairness of granting or denying an injunction or other equitable relief. Also called **balancing of the hardships.**

**balancing test** *n.* any decision-making process that involves the weighing of competing values and interests.

**balloon** *adj.* **1.** (of a loan, mortgage, or the like) having a payment at the end of the term that is much bigger than previous ones. See for example *balloon mortgage* (under MORTGAGE).

—*n.* **2.** Also called **balloon payment.** the amount of the final payment of a balloon loan: *Repayment is to be made at the rate of five hundred dollars per month for five years with a balloon of five thousand dollars.*

—*v.* **3.** to increase suddenly.

**4.** (of a loan) to have the balloon payment come due: *The loan balloons after five years.*

**ballot** *n., v.* **balloted, balloting.** —*n.* **1.** the sheet of paper upon which a voter marks a vote. See also ABSENTEE BALLOT.

**2.** an election or a round of voting.

**3.** the right to vote.

**4. secret ballot** a vote in which the confidentiality of how one votes is safeguarded.
—*v.* **5.** to vote by ballot.

**ban** *v.*, **banned, banning,** *n.* —*v.* **1.** to prohibit.
—*n.* **2.** the act of prohibiting; a prohibition.
**3.** in ancient usage, **a.** a public proclamation. **b.** a sentence of BANISHMENT.
—**bannable** *adj.*

**banc** *n.* See EN BANC.

**banish** *v.* **1.** in very early English law, to OUTLAW; to declare to be an outlaw.
**2.** to expel from a region; condemn to exile.

**banishment** *n.* **1.** the act of banishing, or the sentence or decree by which one is banished.
**2.** the state of being banished.
See also note at TRANSPORTATION.

**bank account** *n.* See under ACCOUNT.

**bank check** *n.* See under CHECK.

**bankrupt** *n.* a person or entity that is the subject of BANKRUPTCY proceedings.

**bankruptcy** *n.*, *pl.* **bankruptcies. 1.** a judicial proceeding under federal law (the **Bankruptcy Code**) by which a person or corporation unable to pay its debts can have the debts adjusted and get a fresh start. The entity that is the subject of such proceedings is referred to as the DEBTOR or the BANKRUPT, and is said to be "in bankruptcy." The proceedings are often identified by the chapter of the Bankruptcy Code under which they are brought: **Chapter 7 bankruptcy** (also called **straight bankruptcy**), in which most of the debtor's remaining assets are sold outright, the court distributes the proceeds among the creditors, and the debts are extinguished; **Chapter 11 bankruptcy** (also called **reorganization**), in which the debtor, usually a corporation, is allowed to continue operating its business in the hope of making more money with which to pay creditors, and a plan **(reorganization plan** or **plan of reorganization)** is worked out under which creditors agree to reduce the

amount of the debts or extend the payment schedule; **Chapter 12 bankruptcy,** a proceeding analogous to Chapter 11, designed specifically for farmers going through hard times to enable them to keep their farms and keep farming; **Chapter 13 bankruptcy** (also called REHABILITATION), a proceeding analogous to Chapter 11, designed specifically for individuals with a steady income and involving a plan **(wage earner's plan)** under which they agree to pay off at least a specified portion of their debts over time.
**2. involuntary bankruptcy** a bankruptcy proceeding initiated by a creditor.
**3. prepackaged bankruptcy** a bankruptcy in which the debtor and the principal creditors work out in advance the arrangement that they would like to see the court order, and then file the action seeking the court's approval. Also called (*slang*) a **prepack.**
**4. voluntary bankruptcy** a bankruptcy proceeding initiated by the debtor.
See also *bankruptcy estate* (under ESTATE[2]); *bankruptcy trustee* (under TRUSTEE); *discharge in bankruptcy* (under DISCHARGE).

**bar¹** *n.*, *v.*, **barred, barring.** —*n.* **1.** a legal impediment or barrier, especially to the formation of a valid contract or the pursuit or defense of a case.
**2. in bar** as a bar to an action: *Because the defendant in the contract action was a minor when she signed the contract, she pleaded legal incapacity in bar.*
—*v.* **3.** to prohibit or act as a bar to: *The statute of limitations bars the action.*
See also TIME-BARRED.
—**barrable** *adj.*

**bar²** *n.* **1.** the legal profession generally; practicing lawyers collectively, as distinguished from judges. See also *admission to the bar* (under ADMISSION); DISBAR. Cf. BENCH.
**2.** all lawyers who are admitted to practice in a particular jurisdiction or a particular court: *the Illinois bar; the Tax Court bar.*

**3.** a group of lawyers whose practices share a common element: *the Houston bar; the plaintiffs' bar; the patent bar.*

**4.** a BAR ASSOCIATION, especially one with compulsory membership (see *integrated bar*): *the District of Columbia Bar; the State Bar of Michigan.*

**5. integrated bar** a bar association to which all lawyers practicing in a state or similar jurisdiction are required to belong. Also called **unified bar, mandatory bar, compulsory bar.**

**6. voluntary bar** a bar association in which membership is optional.

**bar³** *n.* **1.** a court, or the nonpublic portion of a courtroom in the immediate vicinity of the judge: *The criminal got his just deserts at the bar of justice.*

**2. at bar** currently before the court: *the case at bar; the plaintiff at bar.*

**3. side bar** the side of the judge's bench that is away from the jury, or the area immediately adjacent to it, where brief conferences between the judge and the lawyers can be held out of the hearing of the jury: *Will counsel please approach the side bar.* See also SIDEBAR; SIDEBAR CONFERENCE.

**bar association** *n.* a professional organization of lawyers, organized either geographically or according to a common interest. Sometimes also called **bar** (see BAR², defs. 4–6.) See also AMERICAN BAR ASSOCIATION.

**bar examination** *n.* an examination administered to individuals seeking *admission to the bar* (see under ADMISSION). Referred to informally as the **bar exam.**

**——Note.** Each state has its own bar examination, typically extending over two or more days and including some components testing general legal knowledge and other components specific to the law of the particular state. In most states, the components testing general legal knowledge include the MULTISTATE BAR EXAMINATION and the MULTISTATE PROFESSIONAL RESPONSIBILITY EXAMINATION; some also include the MULTISTATE ESSAY EXAMINATION or the MULTISTATE PERFORMANCE TEST. See also RECIPROCITY.

**bare** *adj.* Same as NAKED.

**bare licensee** *n.* See under LICENSEE.

**bareboat charter** *n.* See under CHARTER².

**bargain** *v.* **1.** to negotiate terms of a contract; haggle.

**—***n.* **2.** a negotiated contract. Cf. *adhesion contract* (under CONTRACT).

**—bargainable** *adj.*

**bargain and sale** *n.* in old English law, a sale of land by means of a written contract in which the seller (the **bargainor**), for valuable consideration the receipt of which was recited in the contract, agreed to sell the land to the buyer (the **bargainee**).

**——History.** Before the enactment of the STATUTE OF USES in 1535, the bargain and sale gave the buyer an equitable interest in the land but legal title stayed in the seller unless there was also LIVERY OF SEISIN. After enactment of the Statute of Uses, the bargain and sale was deemed to convey legal title to the land.

**bargained for** *adj.* **1.** describing a contract term that was subject to negotiation or for which some concession or return benefit is deemed to have been given. If placed before the noun, requires a hyphen: *The term was bargained for; a bargained-for term.* Cf. BOILERPLATE.

**2. bargained-for exchange** a classic definition of CONTRACT, reflecting the ideal that a contract represents a mutually satisfactory exchange of benefits resulting from genuine bargaining between parties of equal BARGAINING POWER. The reality is often very different. Cf. *adhesion contract* (under CONTRACT).

**bargainee** *n.* the buyer of land in a BARGAIN AND SALE.

**bargainer** *n.* one who bargains; a negotiator; a haggler. Cf. BARGAINOR.

**bargaining** *n.* See COLLECTIVE BARGAINING.

**bargaining power** *n.* the ability of a party to a proposed contract to influence the terms of the contract. Two successful corporations negotiating a joint venture typically have equal bargaining power; an individual seeking coverage from an insurance company typically has no bargaining power at all.

**bargaining unit** *n.* a group of employees within a company or an industry that may be represented by a single union. Also called **collective bargaining unit**.

**bargainor** *n.* the seller of land in a BARGAIN AND SALE. Cf. BARGAINER.

**barrator** *n.* one who stirs up litigation or quarrels; one who commits barratry. Also called **common barrator**.

**barratry** *n.* persistently stirring up litigation or quarrels. This was an offense at common law. Initiating or provoking groundless litigation is still a statutory offense in some states. Also called **common barratry**. See also CHAMPERTY; MAINTENANCE; ABUSE OF PROCESS; MALICIOUS PROSECUTION.
—**barratrous** *adj.*
—**barratrously** *adv.*

**barrister** *n.* **1.** in England, a lawyer who is a courtroom advocate. Cf. SOLICITOR.
**2.** in America, occasionally and informally, another word for lawyer.
—**barristerial** *adj.*
—**barristership** *n.*

**barter** *n.* **1.** an exchange of goods or services without using money. Such transactions are normally subject to the same income and sales taxes as money transactions, but are sometimes employed to evade taxes because they are difficult to trace.
—*v.* **2.** to effect or engage in a barter.
—**barterer** *n.*

**basis** *n., pl.* **bases. 1.** the amount of one's investment in a piece of property as measured for tax purposes. One's gain or loss on sale of the property is the amount by which the value received for the property exceeds or falls short of the basis.
**2. adjusted basis** a taxpayer's basis in a piece of property after making certain additions or subtractions to reflect changes that have occurred since the property was first acquired, such as improvements or depreciation.
**3. average basis** a taxpayer's basis per share of a mutual fund as calculated by dividing her total basis in the category of fund shares under consideration by the number of such shares held. See also SINGLE-CATEGORY METHOD; DOUBLE-CATEGORY METHOD.
**4. carryover basis** in certain transfers of property, the previous owner's basis at the time of the transfer, deemed to be the new owner's original basis. Under current law, property acquired by gift generally has a carryover basis.
**5. cost basis** the amount paid for an item of property, including the value of money, property, and services given in exchange, the amount of debt assumed, and other amounts paid in connection with the acquisition such as transfer taxes and broker's fees.
**6. stepped-up basis** in certain transfers of property, the fair market value of the property at the time of the transfer, deemed to be the new owner's original basis. (In cases where the value of the property declined in the previous owner's hands, this may be referred to as a **stepped-down basis**.) Under current law, property received by inheritance generally has a stepped-up basis.
**7. unrecovered basis** the portion of one's original basis in a piece of property that has not yet been recovered (see RECOVER def. 3), as through depreciation allowances or tax credits associated with the property.

**bastard** *n.* an illegitimate child; a child born out of wedlock or, sometimes, a child born to a woman married to someone other than the child's biological father.
—**Usage.** Although this has been a standard legal term for centuries, and is still found in statutes and occasional judicial decisions, it is now regarded as disparaging and inappropriate for most purposes. Indeed, even the term ILLEGITIMATE is now often avoided, in favor of phrases such as "born out of wedlock." In isolated cases, however, the

term can be used in a negative sense for rhetorical effect: *This court will not tolerate a stipulation between the divorcing parties that would make a bastard of their child.* The same principles apply to related terms such as BASTARDIZE.

**bastard eigne** *n. Old English Law.* the firstborn illegitimate son of parents who subsequently married and had a legitimate son. See also EIGNE. Cf. MULIER PUISNE.

**bastardize** *v.*, **bastardized, bastardizing.** to confer the status of an illegitimate child upon one seemingly legitimate, as by a husband's disavowal of paternity. But see PRESUMPTION OF PATERNITY. See note at BASTARD.
—**bastardization** *n.*

**bastardy** *n.* **1.** the act of begetting an illegitimate child. See also BASTARDY ACTION.
**2.** the state or condition of being a bastard; illegitimacy.

**bastardy action** (or **bastardy proceeding**) *n.* an older legal term for a PATERNITY SUIT.

**battered person syndrome** *n.* a psychological condition said to result from persistent physical abuse, invoked in recent years as a proposed JUSTIFICATION for homicide. The argument has had a mixed reception from courts and scholars, but often finds favor with juries. Also called **battered woman syndrome, battered child syndrome,** etc., according to the circumstances.

**battery** *n., pl.* **batteries.** harmful or offensive touching of another person, either intentionally or as a by-product of some other intentional wrong. The touching may be either direct or indirect, as by grabbing clothes, using a stick, or launching a projectile. Battery is usually both a tort and a crime. Cf. ASSAULT. See also *trespass in assault and battery* (under TRESPASS²).
—**batter** *v.*
—**batterer** *n.*

**battle of the experts** *n. Informal.* a trial whose outcome depends in large part on a choice between the conflicting opinions of expert witnesses hired by the opposing sides. In the federal courts and in most states the court can appoint a neutral expert, but this is seldom done.

**battle of the forms** *n. Informal.* the exchange of different preprinted forms with incompatible terms by a buyer and seller who are arranging a transaction.

**bawdy house** or **bawdyhouse** *n.* a house of prostitution; brothel.

**bearer** *n.* a person in possession of a negotiable instrument or other document, especially an instrument or document made out or indorsed to "bearer" or in some other way that does not designate a specific payee or person entitled to enforce it, such as a check made out to "cash" or indorsed IN BLANK. Such a document is called a **bearer instrument, bearer bond,** or the like, depending upon its nature; and if it is an instrument for the payment of money, such as a check or note, it is **payable to bearer.** Bearer paper must be carefully safeguarded, since anyone who comes into possession of it may NEGOTIATE it. Cf. *order instrument* (under ORDER²).

**belligerent** *adj.* **1.** waging war; engaged in war.
**2.** hostile; warlike.
—*n.* **3.** a state or nation at war.
**4.** a member of the military forces of such a state.
—**belligerency** *n.*
—**belligerently** *adv.*

**below** *adv.* **1.** in the lower court from which an appeal was taken (the **court below**): *The decision below should be affirmed.*
**2.** later on in the same document: *As we will explain below, the decision should be affirmed.* See also INFRA.

**bench** *n.* **1.** the judge's seat and desk in a courtroom: *Instead of issuing a written opinion, the judge ruled from the bench.* See also *approach the bench* (under APPROACH).
**2.** the judicial profession; judges collectively, as distinguished from practicing

lawyers: *The conference provided an opportunity for the bench and the bar to meet informally.* Cf. BAR[2].

**bench conference** *n.* Same as SIDEBAR CONFERENCE.

**bench memo** *n. Informal.* Same as BENCH MEMORANDUM.

**bench memorandum** *n.* **1.** a memorandum summarizing the facts, issues, and arguments in a case, prepared by a judge's law clerk for the judge to refer to while on the bench.
**2.** a short memorandum on an issue in a case prepared by a lawyer and provided to the judge, typically by handing it up in court.
**3.** a short memorandum written by a judge while on the bench or shortly thereafter, explaining a decision.
In all senses, the phrase is often shortened informally to **bench memo**.

**bench trial** *n.* See under TRIAL.

**bench warrant** *n.* See under WARRANT[1].

**beneficial** *adj.* referring to rights that derive from something other than legal title to property, particularly rights of a trust beneficiary. See *beneficial estate* (under ESTATE[1]); *beneficial interest* (under INTEREST[1]); *beneficial owner* (under OWNER). See also EQUITABLE.

**beneficiary** *n., pl.* **beneficiaries. 1.** a person for whose benefit a trust is established, and for whose benefit the trustee must manage the trust property.
**2.** the person to whom benefits are to be paid under an insurance policy.
**3. incidental beneficary** a person who happens to benefit from a contract or trust, but who is neither a party to the contract or trust nor a person for whose specific benefit it was entered into. An incidental beneficiary has no legally enforceable interest in the contract or trust.
**4. third-party beneficiary** See under CONTRACT.
See also DONEE BENEFICIARY; RECIPROCAL BENEFICIARY.

**benefit** *n.* See FOR THE BENEFIT OF; *for the use and benefit of* (under FOR THE USE OF).

**benefit of clergy** *n.* **1.** in old law, exemption from criminal trial or punishment by reason of being a member of the clergy or able to read. See also NECK-VERSE.
**2.** *Informal.* **a.** formal marriage: *They lived together for three years without benefit of clergy.* **b.** the rites or sanctions of a church: *He was buried without benefit of clergy.*
——**History.** In ancient English law, the king's courts had no jurisdiction to try ordained clergymen for felonies. A clergyman accused of such a crime could claim "benefit of clergy" and so be remanded to ecclesiastical courts, where the punishment of death was not available. Over the centuries, benefit of clergy evolved into a plea by which any man capable of reading—originally a skill possessed only by members of the clergy—could escape the hangman's noose. Peers and peeresses could claim benefit of clergy repeatedly. Male commoners who could read—or who could fake it (see note at NECK-VERSE)—could claim benefit of clergy once, but were branded on the hand so that any effort to escape hanging for a second felony would be detected. Female commoners were not entitled to benefit of clergy. The United States Congress abolished the exemption for federal crimes punishable by death in 1790; the remnants of benefit of clergy were abolished in England in 1827.

**bequeath** *v.* **1.** to give personal property by will. Cf. DEVISE.
**2.** broadly, to give any property by will.
—**bequeathable** *adj.*

**bequest** *n.* **1.** a gift of personal property by will, or the property so given. Also called **legacy,** especially in reference to gifts of money. Cf. DEVISE.
**2.** broadly, any testamentary gift of property, whether real or personal. *Legacy* is also used in this broad sense.
**3. general bequest** (or **legacy**) a bequest to be paid out of the general assets of the estate, that is, out of whatever is left after payment of debts and expenses and distribution of specific bequests.
**4. residuary bequest** (or **legacy**) the

final bequest in a typical will, disposing of any assets left over after payment of all debts and expenses and satisfaction of all other bequests.

**5. specific bequest** (or **legacy**) a bequest of a specific item or items of property.

**besaiel** *n. Law French.* **1.** great-grandfather.

**2. writ of besaiel** an ancient writ by which a great-grandchild who inherited a possessory interest in land from a great-grandparent could gain possession of the land from another person who had taken possession. See also note at MORT D'ANCESTOR.

Also spelled **besaile** and in many other variations.

**best efforts** *n.pl.* **1.** diligence going beyond a mere GOOD FAITH effort.

**2. best efforts underwriting** distribution of a new issue of securities on behalf of the issuer under an agreement whereby the underwriter agrees to use best efforts to find buyers for the securities but does not promise that all shares will be sold and does not agree to buy up any unsold shares. Cf. UNDERWRITE.

**best evidence rule** *n.* the principle that in order to prove the contents of a writing, photograph, or the like, one must produce the original unless it is unavailable through no serious fault of one's own. Modern evidence rules, however, permit the use of a duplicate, such as a photocopy, in most circumstances.

**best interests of the child** *n.pl.* the test used in child custody disputes and many other types of cases involving children, in which the preferences of parents are subordinated to concerns for the welfare of the child.

**best use** or **best and highest use** *n.* See under USE.

**bestiality** *n.* sexual contact between a human being and an animal.

**better law** (or **better rule**) **approach** *n.* an approach to CONFLICT OF LAWS issues used in some states, under which a number of legal objectives are considered and weighed in reaching a decision as to which of two conflicting bodies of law to apply to an issue in a case that involves two or more states or nations. Rather than use a mechanical test for choosing which law to apply, the court chooses whichever law seems best suited to serve the overall objectives of law in light of the individual facts of the case. The chosen rule is referred to as the **better law** or the **better rule** or, often, the **better rule of law**.

**betterment** *n.* **1.** a public improvement that increases the value of specific private property; for example, the extension of a sewer line or the paving of a road.

**2.** any IMPROVEMENT to real property.

**betterment tax** *n.* a tax adopted in order to raise revenue to pay for a BETTERMENT; especially one that is imposed only upon the property owners whose property is benefited by the betterment.

**beyond a reasonable doubt** the highest STANDARD OF PROOF; the degree of certainty necessary to convict a defendant of a crime. It does not mean beyond all possible doubt, but beyond any doubt based upon reason and common sense.

**beyond the scope** Short for **beyond the scope of the direct (cross, redirect, recross) examination.** The objection raised at a trial or hearing when a person examining a witness (other than on direct examination) attempts to delve into matters that were not asked about in the immediately preceding examination. See also EXAMINATION; SCOPE OF EXAMINATION; OPEN THE DOOR. Cf. SCOPE OF EXPERTISE.

**BFOQ** See BONA FIDE OCCUPATIONAL QUALIFICATION.

**bias crime** *n.* Same as HATE CRIME.

**bid** *v.*, **bid, bidding,** *n.* —*v.* **1.** to offer to pay a specific sum of money for something: *The Smiths bid $110,000 for the house.*

**2.** to offer to accept a specific sum of money for certain work or materials:

*The company bid $3 million for the contract to repair the bridge.*
—*n.* **3.** an act or instance of bidding.
**4.** the amount offered by the person bidding: *a $110,000 bid; a bid of $3,000,000.*
**5. open bidding** a process of competitive bidding in which each bid is announced as it is made and bidders may revise their bids repeatedly.
**6. sealed bidding** a process of competitive bidding in which all bids are kept secret until the winning bid is announced. Each bid is submitted in writing and is referred to as a **sealed bid**.
—**bidder** *n.*

**bid rigging** or **bid-rigging** *n.* **1.** collusion among people or companies that otherwise would be competitors with respect to bidding for a project.
**2.** any collusion among bidders, auctioneers, or others involved in a competitive bidding situation whereby certain bidders or other participants in the process are given an unfair advantage.

**bigamy** *n.* **1.** the crime of marrying, or purportedly marrying, another person with knowledge that one party or the other is already married to someone else.
**2.** sometimes, the crime of cohabiting with a person with knowledge that one or the other of the cohabiting parties is married to someone else.
See also note at POLYGAMY.
—**bigamist** *n.*
—**bigamous** *adj.*
—**bigamously** *adv.*

**bilateral contract** *n.* See under CONTRACT.

**bill** *n.* **1.** a formal document, often one containing a list of items.
**2.** a proposed statute filed in Congress or a state or local legislature by one or more members for consideration by the whole body. See also ENGROSSED BILL; ENROLLED BILL; OMNIBUS BILL; PRIVATE BILL; PUBLIC BILL.
**3.** the initial pleading in courts of EQUITY. In modern practice this has been replaced by the COMPLAINT.
**4.** a statement of money owed for goods or services with a request for payment.
**5. no bill** or **no true bill** words endorsed on a proposed indictment to indicate that the grand jury has refused to issue it. See also IGNORAMUS.
**6. true bill** words endorsed on a proposed indictment to indicate that the grand jury has approved of it; hence, an INDICTMENT.
—*v.* **7.** to render a request for payment for goods or services; to send a bill to.

**bill of attainder** *n., pl.* **bills of attainder. 1.** in old English law, a bill or act in Parliament imposing a sentence of death and ATTAINDER upon one or more individuals, usually for threatening or attempting to overthrow the government. No trial or judicial proceeding was required. During the American Revolution, state legislatures enacted bills of attainder directed at Tories. Cf. BILL OF PAINS AND PENALTIES.
**2.** in the constitutional law of the United States, any bill or law that punishes specific individuals or groups or deprives them of civil or political rights. Bills of attainder, construed in this broad sense, are prohibited by the Constitution.
—**History.** Attainder was not a purely British phenomenon: During the American Revolution, state legislatures passed many bills of attainder and bills of pains and penalties directed at British loyalists.

**bill of costs** *n.* an itemized and verified list of the COSTS incurred by the winning party in a court case, submitted to the court as proof if the amount that should be taxed to the losing party.

**bill of exchange** *n.* Same as DRAFT.

**bill of goods** *n.* **1.** a quantity or consignment of salable items; a list of items included in a shipment, order, or the like.
**2.** *Informal.* something fraudulent, deceptive, defective, exaggerated, not to be trusted: *The representation that the car had been driven only 27,000 miles was a bill of goods.*
—**Usage.** There is nothing inherently bad about a "bill of goods" in the literal

sense of def. 1, which is still occasionally seen in legal contexts. But someone long ago—or perhaps a good many people—must have been cheated by a fraudulent bill of goods. Perhaps they paid for a shipment after checking the bill of goods to make sure that everything was in order, only to find upon opening the box that the goods were not there: They had been sold nothing but a bill of goods. Whatever its exact origins, the phrase has come to be used almost exclusively in the negative and figurative sense of def. 2.

**bill of health** *n.* **1.** a certificate, carried by a ship, attesting to the presence or absence of infectious diseases among the ship's crew and at the port from which it has come, certifying to the sanitary history and condition of the vessel, and the like, to be presented to authorities at ports of call.
**2.** a document certifying the health —good or bad—of an individual or animal.
**3. clean bill of health** a bill of health showing that there is no evidence of infectious diseases or other unhealthy conditions on a vessel, or that a person or animal is healthy.

**bill of indictment** *n.* **1.** a proposed IN-DICTMENT itemizing the accusations against a person, presented to a *grand jury* (see under JURY) to approve or disapprove.
**2.** the indictment as approved by the grand jury.
See also *no bill* and *true bill* (under BILL).

**bill of lading** *n.* **1.** a document issued by a person or entity in the business of transporting or forwarding goods, identifying goods received for shipment and designating who is entitled to delivery of them.
**2. clean bill of lading** or **clean bill** a bill of lading with no added notations qualifying its terms.
**3. order bill of lading** or **order bill** a bill of lading stating that the goods are to be delivered to the order of a named party. This is a *negotiable document of title* (see under DOCUMENT OF TITLE).
**4. straight bill of lading** or **straight**

**bill** a bill of lading stating that the goods are to be delivered to a specific named party. This is a *nonnegotiable document of title* (see under DOCUMENT OF TITLE).
**5. through bill of lading** or **through bill** a bill of lading issued by the first of a series of connecting carriers, assuming responsibility for the entire shipment.

**bill of pains and penalties** *n., pl.* **bills of pains and penalties.** a legislative enactment similar to a BILL OF ATTAINDER but imposing a sentence less than death. The United States Constitution's proscription of bills of attainder is construed as including bills of pains and penalties.

**bill of particulars** *n.* a written statement setting forth the details of a civil claim or a criminal charge.

**Bill of Rights** *n.* **1.** the first ten amendments to the Constitution, added to the Constitution shortly after its adoption as a formal statement of fundamental rights of Americans. See Appendix for summary. Originally intended only as a limitation on the powers of the federal government (not state governments), most of the Bill of Rights has now been extended to the states, so that, for example, a law restricting freedom of speech would be unconstitutional whether adopted by Congress or by a state legislature. See INCORPORATION DOCTRINE.
**2.** Sometimes, **bill of rights.** by extension, a name given to any formal list of rights of a group, enacted as a law or adopted by an organization or institution: *patients' bill of rights; victim's bill of rights; consumer bill of rights.*

**bill of sale** *n.* a document transferring title in personal property from seller to buyer.

**billable** *adj.* **1.** worthy of being billed; qualifying as work for which payment should be expected.
**2. billable hours** person-hours of work by an individual or a firm spent in such a way that one could expect the

client to be billed for the work: *We ex-*
*pect our associates to work 2,200 billa-*
*ble hours per year, and spend an addi-*
*tional 500 hours on administrative*
*tasks, continuing legal education, and*
*client entertainment.*

**bind** *v.*, **bound, binding.** to put under a
legal obligation. See also *binding au-*
*thority* (under AUTHORITY²).

**bind over** *v.*, **bound over, binding**
**over.** to order that a person accused of
a crime be subjected to a trial, as a result of a finding of PROBABLE CAUSE at
a *bindover hearing* (see under HEAR-
ING): *The defendant was bound over to*
*the Superior Court for trial.*

**binder** *n.* a document granting a person
who has applied for an insurance policy temporary coverage until the policy
is issued or the application is rejected.

**biological** *adj.* **1.** genetically related; related by genetic descent.
**2. biological mother** or **father** or **par-**
**ent**    a parent whose egg or sperm
gave rise to a specified child. Also
called **genetic mother** or **father** or
**parent.** See note at BIRTH MOTHER.
**3. biological child**   a child genetically
descended from a specified parent. Also
called **genetic child.**

**birth mother** *n.* the woman who gave
birth to a particular child.   Also called
**gestational mother.**
—**Usage.** These terms are usually
used to distinguish a child's natural
mother from a woman who subsequently takes on a maternal or quasi-
maternal role, such as an adoptive
mother, stepmother, or foster mother.
But in rare cases of pregnancy resulting
from implantation of the product of in
vitro fertilization with a donated ovum,
the term *birth mother* or *gestational*
*mother* could be used in contrast to *ge-*
*netic mother* or *biological mother* (see
under BIOLOGICAL). See also SURRO-
GATE MOTHER; GESTATIONAL SURRO-
GATE.

**black codes** *n.pl.* collective name for
statutes adopted throughout the former
Confederacy in the wake of the Civil
War, designed to perpetuate to the extent possible the separate and subordinate status of blacks.
—**History.** Congress, both in the CIVIL
WAR AMENDMENTS to the Constitution
and in subsequent civil rights legislation, attempted to override some aspects of the black codes; but the United
States Supreme Court, in the ironically
named *Civil Rights Cases,* 109 U.S. 3
(1883), and in such cases as *Plessy v.*
*Ferguson* (see SEPARATE BUT EQUAL), interpreted the amendments narrowly
and overturned the legislation, locking
into place for many generations to
come the institutionalized and govern-
ment-mandated racism of the black
codes.

**black letter law** *n.* Same as HORN-
BOOK LAW.

**black market** *n.* a MARKET in which
forbidden goods or services are bought
and sold, or restricted goods are sold
without restriction: *Prescription narcot-*
*ics are sometimes available on the black*
*market.* Cf. GRAY MARKET.

**black-market** *adj.* traded in or characteristic of a black market. —*v.* to sell
something in a black market.

**Blackacre** *n.* the conventional name for
a hypothetical tract of land used in discussing basic concepts and issues of
property law: *A conveys Blackacre to B*
*for life, then to C and his heirs.* In hypotheticals involving two tracts of land,
the second is usually **Whiteacre.** Blackacre and Whiteacre are to hypotheticals
about land what Doe and Roe or Smith
and Jones are to hypotheticals about
people.

**blackmail** *n.* **1.** EXTORTION, especially
extortion by means of threats to reveal
injurious truths about a person.
—*v.* **2.** to extort money from a person,
especially by threatening to reveal an
injurious truth.
—**blackmailer** *n.*

**blank indorsement** *n.* See under IN-
DORSEMENT.

**blanket bond** *n.* See under BOND².

**blaspheme** *v.,* **blasphemed, blaspheming. 1.** to speak or act blasphemously; to utter a blasphemy.
**2.** to speak blasphemously of; utter a blasphemy with respect to.
—**blasphemer** *n.*

**blasphemy** *n., pl.* **blasphemies. 1.** impious or irreverant words or conduct, especially if directed at Christian religious figures.
**2.** the common law crime, and still in several states the statutory crime, of uttering blasphemous words or engaging in blasphemous conduct.
—**blasphemous** *adj.*
—**blasphemously** *adv.*
——**Note.** Few today would argue that blasphemy laws could withstand constitutional scrutiny, but in the states where they remain on the books apparently few would dare try to remove them. For example, a Maryland law calling for up to six months' imprisonment for anyone who "shall blaspheme or curse God, or shall write or utter any profane words of and concerning our Saviour Jesus Christ, or of and concerning the Trinity, or any of the persons thereof," was declared unconstitutional by an appellate court in 1970 on the appeal of a person convicted of the crime, but was left on the books into the twenty-first century nonetheless.

**blind trust** *n.* See under TRUST.

**blockbusting** *n.* inducing people to sell their homes by spreading stories about ethnic minorities moving into the neighborhood. This once-common device used by real estate agents to induce panic selling by white homeowners—generating commissions for the agents—was outlawed in 1968 by the federal Fair Housing Act.
—**blockbuster** *n.*

**blood alcohol concentration** or **blood alcohol content (BAC)** *n.* the concentration of alcohol in a person's blood expressed as a percentage. State laws on drunk driving are now often expressed in terms of permissible and impermissible blood alcohol concentration levels.

**blue law** *n.* a law of Puritan origin or inspiration regulating conduct for essentially religious reasons, especially a SUNDAY CLOSING LAW.

**blue sky law** *n.* any of the state statutes, which exist in all fifty states, regulating the issuance of securities within the state; the state counterparts of the federal SECURITIES ACTS.

**blue wall of silence** *n.* the long tradition among police officers of not reporting, and sometimes of helping to cover up, wrongdoing by fellow officers. Also called **blue wall,** or **wall of silence.**

**Bluebook, The** *n.* the most commonly used reference work on how cases, statutes, and other authorities are cited in legal writing. Formerly titled, and now subtitled, **A Uniform System of Citation.**

**board** *n.* an official group of persons who direct or supervise some activity.

**board of directors** *n.* the governing body of a corporation, elected by the shareholders to set policy, select officers to carry it out, monitor the corporation's operations, and make major decisions regarding the corporation's business and finances.

**board of education** *n.* a public body responsible for running the public schools in a city or region.

**board of election** or **board of elections** *n.* a public body responsible for registering voters and managing elections.

**board of equalization** *n.* a public body responsible for spreading the property tax burden fairly among property owners in a region or among regions in a state. Also called **equalization board.**

**board of pardons** *n.* a state body authorized to grant pardons and commutations of sentence to convicted criminals. Also called **pardon board.**

**board of parole** *n.* Same as PAROLE BOARD.

**bodily heir** *n.* Same as *heir of the body* (under HEIR).

**bodily injury** *n.* See under INJURY.

**body corporate** *n.* a CORPORATION.

**body of the crime** *n.* See CORPUS DE-LICTI.

**body politic** *n.* **1.** in early English law, a CORPORATION.
**2.** a people regarded as a political body under an organized government; the people of a state or nation viewed collectively.

**boiler room sales** *n.pl.* high-pressure selling of securities by telephone.

**boilerplate** *n.* standardized language usually included in legal documents of a certain type, such as contracts, wills, or deeds, or in a particular class of such documents, such as apartment leases or bank loan agreements. In a printed contract, boilerplate often appears in FINE PRINT and represents terms that are either noncontroversial (such as a clause specifying which state's law governs the contract) or nonnegotiable. See also *adhesion contract* (under CONTRACT).

**bona** *Latin.* —*n.pl.* **1.** goods; things; property.
—*adj.* **2.** a form of *bonus,* 'good'.

**bona et catalla** *n.pl. Latin.* goods and chattels; personal property of every kind.

**bona fide¹** *adv. Latin.* in good faith; with good faith.

**bona fide²** *adj.* **1.** describing a thing done or a person acting in GOOD FAITH: *bona fide efforts to settle the case; bona fide purchaser.*
**2.** genuine: *bona fide occupational qualification.*

**bona fide occupational qualification (BFOQ)** *n.* a qualification reasonably necessary to the normal operation of a particular business or enterprise.
—**Note.** The federal civil rights laws outlawing discrimination in employment provide exceptions for situations in which a particular religion, sex, national origin, or age range (but not race or color) is a bona fide occupational qualification. In addition, a special exception allows religious organizations and schools to discriminate on the basis of religion even when hiring people for positions for which religion is not a bona fide occupational qualification, such as janitor in a church-owned building in which no religious activities take place.

**bona fide purchaser** or **bona fide purchaser for value** *n.* Same as GOOD FAITH PURCHASER.

**bona fides¹** *n. Latin.* good faith; absence of fraud or deceit; the state of being exactly as claims or appearances indicate: *The bona fides of this contract is open to question. His bona fides was proved at trial.*
—**Usage.** Because the ending *s* in this Latin phrase makes it look like an English plural, one occasionally sees it used erroneously with a plural verb (*His bona fides were proved...*); more often the phrase is used in a way that avoids the issue: *He proved his bona fides.* More often still, in modern legal writing, the expression is rejected entirely in favor of the English GOOD FAITH.

**bona fides²** *n.pl.* **1.** credentials; documents or other evidence of good faith, trustworthiness, authenticity, or the like: *Her bona fides as a banker provided cover for her spying activities.*
**2.** official documents that prove authenticity, legitimacy, etc., as of a person or enterprise: *Our bona fides as a corporation are on file with the Secretary of State.*
—**False Friend.** This is a relatively new use of the phrase *bona fides,* and one that could be troublesome in legal contexts because of the potential for confusion with the traditional legal meaning of the term. "Bona fides" in the sense of "circumstances indicating trustworthiness" can be false and misleading; "bona fides" in the traditional sense of "good faith" is by definition true and reliable.

**bona immobilia** *n.pl. Latin.* (lit. "immovable goods") Same as *immovable property* (see under PROPERTY).

**bona mobilia** *n.pl. Latin.* (lit. "movable goods") Same as *movable property* (see under PROPERTY).

**bona vacantia** *n.pl. Latin.* (lit. "ownerless goods") property with no owner, such as shipwrecks, fish, or land formerly owned by a decedent who left no will and no heirs. In some situations such property can be claimed by anyone who finds it; in other situations it escheats to the state.

**bond¹** *n.* **1.** a kind of security (see SECURITY²) issued by a corporation or governmental body in order to borrow money from the public. It is in the form of a certificate evidencing the issuer's obligation to repay the debt in full on or by a specific date, and usually to make regular interest payments until then. Unlike a stockholder, the owner of a bond (the **bondholder**) has no ownership interest in the issuing corporation, but is simply a CREDITOR of the issuer. See also DEBENTURE.
**2. bearer bond** See under BEARER.
**3. convertible bond** a bond that may be exchanged for shares of stock in the issuer under specified conditions.
**4. general obligation bond** a government bond under which payment is to be made out of general tax revenues rather than a special fund. Cf. *revenue bond.*
**5. guaranteed bond** a bond under which payment is guaranteed by an entity other than the issuer.
**6. junk bond** *Informal.* a high-risk corporate bond. Junk bonds carry high rates of interest to induce investors to take the risk of lending money to a company that might end up in bankruptcy. Many unsophisticated investors have lost large amounts of money on such bonds because they were attracted by the high interest rates and did not understand the risks involved.
**7. municipal bond** a bond issued by, or sometimes guaranteed by, a state or local government or governmental agency.
**8. revenue bond** a bond issued to raise money for a specific project and payable only from the proceeds from that project. Cf. *general obligation bond.*
**9. zero-coupon bond** a bond under which no interest is paid during the term of the bond. It is purchased at a discount from the face value, and redeemed at maturity for the face value.

**bond²** *n.* **1.** a written obligation to pay or forfeit a sum of money, or occasionally to perform some other act, upon the occurrence of a specified event—particularly some default by the person or entity by or for which the bond is issued. The bond may be issued by the person or entity whose default is being guarded against **(personal bond),** but in most situations it is provided—for a fee—by a third party such as an insurance company **(surety bond** or **suretyship bond).** See also SURETY; SURETYSHIP.
**2. appeal bond** a bond required of a losing party in a civil case who wishes to appeal, to assure that the winning party's costs will be paid if the appeal is dropped or is unsuccessful.
**3. attachment bond** a bond posted by a person whose property has been attached, as a substitute for the attached property. This frees the property while providing the same protection for the attacher. See also ATTACH; ATTACHMENT.
**4. bail bond** See under BAIL¹.
**5. blanket bond** a bond covering an entire group or class of people; especially, a fidelity bond covering all of a company's employees or all of a company's employees in a particular job category. For example, a messenger service might obtain a blanket bond to insure against theft of clients' packages by any of its messengers.
**6. completion bond** a bond posted to provide money to complete a construction project if the construction contractor fails to do so in accordance with the terms of the contract. Also called **performance bond.**
**7. fidelity bond** insurance against loss due to embezzlement or other dishonest conduct by an employee, particularly one whose position deals with the employer's financial affairs.
**8. fiduciary bond** a bond issued to

protect against misappropriation or misapplication of property under the control of a FIDUCIARY such as a trustee, a guardian, or the executor or administrator of an estate.

**9. in bond**  stored in a *bonded warehouse* (see under WAREHOUSE).

**10. indemnity bond**  a bond to provide compensation for damage or loss for which the covered person or entity is responsible.

**11. judicial bond**  any bond required in a court proceeding, such as an *appeal bond, attachment bond,* or *supersedeas bond.*

**12. payment bond**  a bond issued to guarantee that funds will be available to pay workers, subcontractors, and suppliers of materials for a construction project if the general contractor fails to pay them, so that their claims will not be a lien on the property.

**13. penal bond**  a bond guaranteeing payment of a contractually required penalty if the party covered by the bond fails to meet a deadline or other requirement of the contract. Also called **penalty bond.**

**14. supersedeas bond**  a bond required of a losing party in a case as a condition for obtaining a delay in execution of the judgment while the judgment is appealed. The purpose is to assure that there will be money available to satisfy the judgment if the appeal is unsuccessful. See also SUPERSEDEAS.

—*v.* **15.** to issue or obtain a bond for: *Our cashiers are bonded by a national insurance company. We bond all our cashiers.*

—**bondable** *adj.*
—**bondability** *n.*
—**bonder** *n.*

**bond³** *adj.* in slavery or serfdom; in bondage; unfree.

**bonded** *adj.* **1.** protected or secured by a bond (see BOND²): *bonded debt; bonded employees.*

**2.** placed or maintained in a *bonded warehouse* (see under WAREHOUSE): *bonded whiskey.*

**bondholder** *n.* See under BOND¹.

**bondman** *n., pl.* **bondmen.** a male serf or slave; a man bound to service without wages. Also called **bondsman.**

—**Usage.** Although human bondage has by no means disappeared from the earth, the term *bondman* is used almost exclusively in historical contexts. In old writings the term *bondsman* is sometimes seen as a variant; but since the latter term has a modern meaning and use that is completely different (see BONDSMAN¹) in modern writing only the spelling without the *s* should be used in reference to a person in bondage.

**bondsman¹** *n., pl.* **bondsmen. 1.** one who gives a bond to guarantee the performance of another (see BOND²); a SURETY.

**2.** especially, a *bail bondsman* (see under BAIL¹).

—**Usage.** One occasionally sees a bail bondsman referred to as a "bondman." This is an ironic mistake since, as between the bondsman and accused person for whom the bondsman puts up bail, it is the latter who is in a sort of bondage, and who can be hunted down and brought back in chains if he attempts to evade his obligations. See BONDMAN; BOUNTY HUNTER.

**bondsman²** *n., pl.* **bondsmen.** BONDMAN. See note at BONDMAN.

**bondswoman¹** *n., pl.* **bondswomen. 1.** a woman who gives a bond to guarantee the performance of another (see BOND²); a woman who is a SURETY.

**2.** especially, a *bail bondswoman* (see under BAIL¹).

See note at BONDSMAN.

**bondswoman²** *n., pl.* **bondswomen.** BONDWOMAN. See note at BONDMAN.

**bondwoman** *n., pl.* **bondwomen.** a female serf or slave; a woman bound to service without wages.  Also called **bondswoman.** See note at BONDMAN.

**bonus** *n., pl.* **bonuses. 1.** compensation paid to an employee in addition to regular pay, in recognition of work especially well done or for other reasons, not as a gratuity but beyond what was technically required by the terms of employment.

**2.** anything given or paid beyond what

is due or legally required.

**3.** something free, as extra shares of stock, given by a corporation to a purchaser of its securities.

**4.** a premium paid for a loan, contract, etc.

**5.** an extra advantage or benefit attached to any action, condition, status, or the like. See, e.g., MARRIAGE BONUS.

**book** *n.* **1.** a register in which entries are made in order to preserve a systematic record of transactions or events of a particular kind, such as the financial transactions of a business, the arrests made by a police precinct, or the bets taken in a gambling operation.

**2. book of account** any journal or ledger included in a system of original records of financial transactions by a company or organization.

**3. books** the system of journals and ledgers in which the financial transactions of a company or organization are recorded as they occur. Also called **books of account.**

**4. books and records** all financial and other records of a person or entity. Also called **books and papers.**

**5. make book** to accept or place the bets of others, as on horse races or sports, especially as a business.

—*v.* **6.** to enter in a book or list; record; register.

**7.** to enter the name of a person arrested, the charge, and other details of the arrest in a log maintained at a police station for that purpose.

**8.** to process an arrest at a police station, including fingerprinting and photographing the defendant as well as logging the arrest in a book.

**book value** *n.* the value of an asset as shown on a company's books. This may be very different from the current MARKET VALUE since entries in books are based upon past transactions rather than current conditions.

**bookie** *n. Slang.* BOOKMAKER.

**bookmaker** *n.* a person who makes a business of accepting the bets of others on the outcome of sports contests, horse races, and the like.

—**bookmaking** *n.*

**boot** *n.* **1.** money or property given or received in addition to the basic thing bargained for in order to equalize a transaction.

**2.** especially, an extra sum of money or unrelated property included in an otherwise tax-free exchange of LIKE-KIND PROPERTY. The boot is treated as taxable income to the recipient.

**bootleg** *v.,* **bootlegged, bootlegging,** *adj., n.* —*v.* **1.** to make, transport, or sell something, especially liquor, illegally or without registration or payment of taxes.

—*adj.* **2.** made, sold, or transported unlawfully; illegal or clandestine.

—*n.* **3.** something made, transported, or sold illegally.

—**bootlegger** *n.*

—**bootlegging** *n.*

**border search** *n.* See under SEARCH.

**borough-English** or **borough English** *n.* (formerly, in some parts of England) a custom by which the youngest son inherited the entire estate upon the death of his father. Also called **postremogeniture, ultimogeniture.** Cf. GAVELKIND; PRIMOGENITURE.

——**False Friend.** "Borough-English" is neither a borough nor a form of English. The term has its origins in a famous case reported in the year 1327, in which it was observed that two neighboring towns in the region of Nottingham—one settled by the English and the other by the French—had different customs regarding descent of land: In the French town the land descended to the eldest son; in the English town (*Burgh Engloys* in the Law French of the decision) land descended to the youngest son. It was natural thereafter to refer to descent to the youngest son by phrases (in Law French) along the lines of "the custom of the English town" or "tenure as in the English town." Over time *Burgh Engloys* was Anglicized to "borough-English" and the preliminary phrases were dropped.

**borrowed servant** *n.* an employee of one employer temporarily working under the supervision and control of another employer, with the permission of the first. Also called **borrowed employee**. See note at MASTER AND SERVANT.

**borrowed servant doctrine** or **borrowed servant rule** *n.* the common law principle that the employer with temporary control over a BORROWED SERVANT is liable for the employee's conduct during that period rather than the employee's regular employer. Also called **borrowed employee doctrine** or **borrowed employee rule**. See also RESPONDEAT SUPERIOR.

**borrowing statute** *n.* a state statute that requires the courts of the state to apply ("borrow") the STATUTE OF LIMITATIONS of the state where a cause of action arose to any action brought in the state. The purpose of such statutes is to discourage forum-shopping by making the same statute of limitations apply wherever the action is brought. Actions brought by citizens of the state, however, are sometimes exempt from the borrowing statutes.

**bounty** *n., pl.* **bounties. 1.** a premium or reward, especially one offered by a government: *a bounty for information leading to the arrest of the escapee; a bounty for dead coyotes.*
**2.** generosity in giving: *The estranged daughter was excluded from the testator's bounty.*

**bounty hunter** *n.* **1.** a person who hunts outlaws or wild animals for the bounty offered for capturing or killing them.
**2.** in particular, one who hunts for and captures BAIL JUMPERS for a reward offered by the bondsman who posted bail.
—**bounty hunting** *n.*

**boycott** *n.* **1.** concerted action by two or more people or entities not to buy from, sell to, work for, or in some other way deal with a company, or an effort to induce others to engage in such conduct. The legality of a boycott depends upon the circumstances.
**2. group boycott** concerted action by a group of business competitors to boycott a business that they otherwise might do business with, for example a

boycott of a supplier to pressure it into lowering its prices. Group boycotts are a violation of the SHERMAN ANTITRUST ACT.
**3. primary boycott** a union-organized boycott of an employer with which the union is engaged in a labor dispute; for example, urging shippers to refuse to ship the employer's goods or consumers not to buy them. Primary boycotts are permitted by the National Labor Relations Act.
**4. secondary boycott** a boycott or other coercive tactics directed at an employer other than the one with which a union has a grievance, for the purpose of inducing that employer to refrain from dealing with the one with which the union does have a grievance. Secondary boycotts are forbidden by federal law.
—*v.* **5.** to engage in a boycott directed against a particular company, group of companies, or product: *to boycott a store; to boycott grapes.*
—**boycotter** *n.*

**Brady material** *n.* any evidence known to the prosecution that is favorable to the defendant in a criminal case. Under a rule laid down by the Supreme Court *Brady v. Maryland,* 373 U.S. 83 (1963) (the **Brady rule**), such evidence must be disclosed to the defendant if requested. A later modification of the rule requires such material to be disclosed even if not requested, if it is obviously helpful to the defendant's case.

**brain death** *n.* irreversible cessation of brain functioning. In an age when heart and lung functioning can often be maintained indefinitely by machines, this is increasingly used as the legal definition of death, though the details of the definition vary from state to state.
—**brain-dead, brain dead** *adj.*

**brand name** *n.* a name used by a manufacturer or merchant to identify its products; a name that is a TRADEMARK. Cf. GENERIC NAME; TRADE NAME.

**Brandeis brief** *n.* a BRIEF bringing extensive sociological, economic, or other scientific and statistical evidence to bear on the legal issues in a case.

——**History.** This approach to briefing gets its name from Louis D. Brandeis, who pioneered the technique with a successful brief to the Supreme Court in support of a law limiting the working hours of female laundry workers to ten hours per day. *Muller v. Oregon,* 208 U.S. 412 (1908). Brandeis subsequently ascended to the Supreme Court bench himself, and served as a justice of that court from 1916 to 1939.

**breach** *n.* **1.** a violation of a legal duty. Usually the term refers to wrongful conduct viewed as the basis for a civil remedy rather than a criminal penalty: *Embezzlement is both a crime and a breach of the employee's duty of loyalty to the employer.*
**2. anticipatory breach** a statement or action showing that a party to a contract does not intend or will not be able to perform when the time comes to do so. Most jurisdictions allow the other party to treat that as a *breach of contract* even though, technically, no obligation has yet been breached because the performance is not yet due. Also called **anticipatory repudiation.** See also REPUDIATION.
**3. breach of fiduciary duty** an intentional or unintentional failure by a FIDUCIARY to live up to the duty of utmost care and loyalty in dealing with matters that are the subject of a FIDUCIARY RELATIONSHIP. See also FIDUCIARY DUTY.
**4. breach of contract** any failure, without legal justification, to perform as promised in a contract, or any act hindering another party from performing as promised; for example, after contracting for certain repairs to one's house, not allowing the contractor in to do the work.
**5. breach of promise** Short for **breach of promise of marriage** or **breach of promise to marry;** the breaking off of an engagement to be married. The common law action for damages for breach of promise has been abolished in many states.
**6. breach of the peace a.** broadly,

any conduct, especially criminal conduct, tending to provoke violence or disrupt public tranquility. **b.** in some jurisdictions, a specifically defined offense; see under DISORDERLY CONDUCT.
**7. breach of trust** a *breach of fiduciary duty,* especially by a TRUSTEE and especially if it is intentional: *It was a breach of trust for the guardian of the child's property to borrow money from the child's bank account to pay a personal debt.*
**8. breach of warranty** any falsehood in a WARRANTY; any failure of a product, instrument, or transaction to conform to a warranty made with respect to it.
**9. immaterial** (or **partial**) **breach** a minor breach of contract, entitling the aggrieved party to damages or some other appropriate remedy, but not entitling that party to cancel the contract.
**10. material** (or **total**) **breach** a breach of contract so serious that it destroys the value of the contract for the other party, entitling that party to call off the deal and refuse any further performance of its own obligations under the contract.
——*v.* **11.** to violate a legal duty: *By driving when he was too tired, he breached the duty of due care.*

**breakdown of the marriage** (or **of the marriage relationship**) *n.* the stated ground for divorce in many NO-FAULT DIVORCE statutes. The statutes typically provide that divorce may be granted if the court finds so severe a breakdown "that the objects of matrimony have been destroyed and there remains no reasonable likelihood that the marriage can be preserved." Variations on this phrase in various states include **irretrievable breakdown of the marriage, irretrievable breakdown of the marriage relationship,** and **irremediable breakdown of the marriage.** See also IRRECONCILABLE DIFFERENCES.

**breaking and entering** *n.* two of the elements of the crime of BURGLARY. At common law, breaking and entering required forcible entry into the premises of another; under modern statutes, it is usually enough simply to enter or remain without authorization, as by crawling in through an open window or hiding in a store until it closes. See also *criminal trespass* (under TRESPASS).

**breath analyzer** *n.* any device for measuring the level of alcohol in a person's body by analyzing the person's breath. See also BREATHALYZER.

**Breathalyzer** *n. Trademark.* **1.** a brand of BREATH ANALYZER.
**2. breathalyzer.** any breath analyzer.
—**Usage.** It might not please the owners of the *Breathalyzer* trademark, but "breathalyzer" has become an extremely common generic term for breath analyzers among writers of statutes and judicial opinions: *"Trooper McNair...gave Petitioner a breathalyzer test on a Data Master breath analyzer machine." Wisdom v. Director of Revenue,* 988 S.W.2d 127 (Mo. Ct. App. 1999).

**brethren** *n.pl.* a plural of BROTHER. See note at that entry.

**breve** *n., pl.* **brevia.** *Latin.* (lit. "a concise writing") writ; especially, an *original writ* (see under WRIT).

**bribe** *n., v.,* **bribed, bribing.** —*n.* **1.** money or any other valuable consideration given or promised with a view to corrupting the behavior of a person, especially in that person's performance as a public official, juror, athlete, or other capacity in which the public has an interest.
—*v.* **2.** to give or promise a bribe to.
**3.** to influence or corrupt by a bribe.
—**bribable, bribeable** *adj.*
—**bribability, bribeability** *n.*
—**bribee** *n.*
—**briber** *n.*

**bribery** *n., pl.* **briberies. 1.** the act or practice of giving or accepting a BRIBE.
**2.** the crime of giving or receiving, or offering or soliciting, something of value to influence the official conduct of a public official.
**3.** Also called **commercial bribery.** the giving or receiving of something of value to influence the business conduct of an employee or agent of a company. This is usually both a crime and a tort against the company, as well as a form

of UNFAIR COMPETITION. See also COMPOUNDING A CRIME; KICKBACK.
**4.** Also called **sports bribery.** bribery intended to influence the outcome of a sporting event. This has been made a specific crime in several states.

**bridge loan** *n.* See under LOAN.

**brief** *n.* **1.** a written argument submitted to a court, outlining the facts and presenting the legal authorities upon which a party relies in a case. In addition to briefs stating the parties' overall positions on a case, submitted at major stages (**trial brief,** often submitted just before a trial; **appellate brief,** submitted when the case is on appeal), briefs are submitted in connection with motions, evidentiary issues, and other matters as they arise during the course of a case. On most motions and on appeal, three briefs are normally submitted: a **brief in support** or **main brief** by the party making the motion or taking the appeal; a **brief in opposition** or **answering brief** by the opposing party; and a **reply brief** by the first party. Occasionally a court will give special permission for the opposing party to put in a **surreply brief** responding to new arguments made in the reply brief. In some courts, a brief is customarily referred to as a **memorandum of law, memorandum of points and authorities,** or simply **memorandum.** See also *brief amicus curiae* (under AMICUS CURIAE).
**2.** a digest of a judicial opinion, usually prepared by a law student or junior lawyer.
—*v.* **3.** to prepare or submit a brief on a matter: *The judge asked us to brief the issue* (or *brief her on the issue*) *of the plaintiff's standing to sue. Beginning law students are required to brief each case they read.*

**bring** *v.,* **brought, bringing. 1.** to initiate; file in court: *to bring suit; bring a complaint; bring a motion.*
**2. bring on** to call a case or motion for trial, hearing, or argument, or cause it to be called: *The motion for a preliminary injunction was brought on by order to show cause. After several months*

*of discovery, the case was brought on for trial.*

**broad construction** *n.* See under CONSTRUCTION.

**broker** *n.* a middleman; a person or entity that puts together a buyer and seller of property or services, acting as an AGENT for one or both of the parties and taking a COMMISSION on the transaction. Examples include a broker who arranges insurance coverage for people or companies **(insurance broker),** a broker who arranges sales of real property **(real estate broker),** and a broker who arranges purchases and sales of stocks and bonds **(securities broker)** or **(stockbroker).**

**broker-dealer** *n.* a company that acts both as a securities broker, taking commissions on securities transactions in which it is merely a middleman, and as a securites dealer, buying and selling securities in its own name and taking a profit, or occasionally a loss, on the change in price.

**brokerage** *n.* **1.** the business of a broker.
**2.** a broker's commission.

**brother** *n., pl.* **brothers, brethren. 1.** traditionally, a fellow member of trade union, fraternal organization, profession, etc.
**2.** in particular, a traditional term of respect and collegiality by which one lawyer or judge refers to another.
——**Usage.** As the ranks of lawyers and judges have opened to women, the use of the term *brother* to refer to fellow lawyers or judges generally (e.g., *Most lawyers are very reluctant to sue a brother lawyer for malpractice.*) has diminished, although the term is still often used in reference to a specific colleague—especially a fellow judge—who is male. For the plural, *brothers* and *brethren* are both seen, the former being more usual when referring to a small number of specific individuals, especially by name (*I respectfully disagree with my brothers Smith and Jones as to the applicability of the parol evidence rule in this case.*), and the latter

in reference to larger groups of colleagues or to fellow lawyers or judges generally. Today the usual practice in referring to a group that may include women is to use a more sex-neutral term such as *fellow judges* or *colleagues,* although phrases such as *brothers and sisters* or *brother and sister judges* are also used. See also note at SISTER.

**burden¹** *n.* **1.** an obligation to take some action to protect one's own rights: *The burden was on the insurance company, as drafter of the policy, to make sure that the language was unambiguous; therefore the ambiguous clause will be construed against the company.*
**2. burden of persuasion** the requirement that a party to a case introduce sufficient evidence of a fact to persuade the jury (or judge in a bench trial) of it by the applicable STANDARD OF PROOF. Also called **risk of nonpersuasion.** See also *burden of proof.*
**3. burden of pleading** the requirement that a party seeking to raise a particular issue in a case include allegations about it in the pleadings.
**4. burden of producing evidence** the requirement that a party to a case introduce evidence to support a claim or defense in order to have that issue considered by the judge or jury. Also called **burden of going forward (with evidence), burden of introducing evidence, burden of proceeding, burden of production.** See also *burden of proof;* PRIMA FACIE CASE.
**5. burden of proof a.** usually, same as *burden of persuasion.* **b.** occasionally, same as *burden of producing evidence.* In most situations, the same party will have both the initial burden of producing evidence and the ultimate burden of persuasion on a particular issue, so that *burden of proof* can be used to refer to both simultaneously.
**6. burden shifting** the shifting of the *burden of producing evidence* on a particular issue from one party to another as the evidence unfolds at trial.
See also *affirmative defense* (under DEFENSE) (for defs. 2–5).

**burden²** *n.* **1.** a restriction upon the

uses that an owner may make of a piece of land, resulting from an EASEMENT, a *covenant running with the land* (see under COVENANT), or the like. It is not the owner, but the land itself, that is said to be under a burden.
—*v.* **2.** to impose or constitute a burden upon a piece of land; for example, if Jones has an easement to walk across Smith's land in order to reach his own land, Smith's land is "burdened" by the easement.

**Burford abstention** *n.* See under ABSTENTION.

**burglar** *n.* a person who commits burglary.

**burglarize** *v.,* **burglarized, burglarizing.** to commit burglary.

**burglary** *n., pl.* **burglaries.** the crime of BREAKING AND ENTERING with intent to commit a crime in the place entered.
—**burglarious** *adj.*
—**burglariously** *adv.*

**burgle** *v.,* **burgled, burgling.** to burglarize.

**business** *n.* See DOING BUSINESS; TRANSACTION OF BUSINESS.

**business compulsion** *n.* Same as ECONOMIC DURESS.

**business corporation** *n.* See under CORPORATION.

**business judgment rule** *n.* the rule of corporate law that directors and officers cannot be held liable to investors for business decisions that turn out to have been bad for the corporation, so long as the decisions were within their power to make, were made in good faith, and had a reasonable basis.

**business record** *n.* See under RECORD.

**business trust** *n.* See under TRUST.

**but-for cause** *n.* an action or event without which a particular result would not have occurred.
——**Note.** To hold a person liable for damages in a tort case, it is not ordinarily sufficient to show that that person's conduct was a but-for cause of the injury. If A lends a car to B, who is struck and injured by drunk driver C,

no one would say that A is responsible for the injury even though if A had not loaned the car B would not have been injured. Cf. PROXIMATE CAUSE.

**buy** *v.,* **bought, buying,** *n.* —*v.* **1.** to acquire rights or property, or an interest in property, by promising or giving something of value, usually money, in exchange.
—*n.* **2.** an act or instance of buying.
See also *reverse buy* (under STING).

**buy and bust** *n. Police Jargon.* a law enforcement operation in which an undercover officer purchases drugs or other contraband and then arrests the seller. Also called **buy-bust.**

**buy-sell agreement** *n.* an agreement among shareholders in a *close corporation* (see under CORPORATION) that if any one of them leaves the business or dies, her shares will be sold to, and bought by, the remaining shareholders or the corporation itself, so as to keep the business in the hands of the original group.

**buyer** *n.* **1.** a person who buys or contracts to buy goods or other property.
**2.** a potential buyer.
**3. able buyer a.** a potential buyer who has both the legal capacity and the financial ability to make a particular purchase. **b.** Same as *ready, willing, and able buyer.*
**4. buyer in the ordinary course of business** a buyer of some product who buys it in the normal way from a person in the business of selling goods of that kind and buys it in good faith, without knowledge that the sale is a violation of someone else's rights in the goods. Such a buyer will get good title to the thing bought even if the thing was in fact pledged to a lender as security for a loan.
**5. ready, willing, and able buyer** a potential buyer who is has both the ability and the disposition to make a particular purchase. A real estate agent retained to assist in selling a property normally earns her commission by producing a ready, willing, and able buyer, even if the seller decides not to go through with the sale.

**6. straw buyer** See STRAW PUR-CHASER.

**by operation of law** as a result of application of legal rules, rather than the action or intent of a person: *Upon her death, the property that she did not dispose of by will went to her children by operation of law.* See also AS A MATTER OF LAW; IN LAW.

**by the entirety** words used to describe ownership of an interest in real property granted to a married couple as a unit, with each spouse having RIGHT OF SURVIVORSHIP: *estate by the entirety; ownership by the entirety; tenants by the entirety.* Also, **by the entireties.**

See also *four unities* and *unity of person* (both under UNITY). Cf. COMMUNITY PROPERTY; JOINT; IN COMMON; IN SEVERALTY.
——**History.** At common law the husband had exclusive control over all property held by the entirety so long as he lived, on the theory often characterized as "the husband and wife are one, and that one is the husband." This form of ownership has been abolished in the majority of states; where it still exists, the husband and wife now have equal rights with respect to the property, making ownership by the entirety substantially identical to joint ownership.

# C

© copyright; a symbol giving notice that COPYRIGHT protection is claimed for the work upon which it appears. If the copyright is valid, the work may not be copied without permission of the copyright owner, whose name ordinarily appears with this symbol, along with the year from which the copyright runs.

**C. & F.** or **C.F.** cost and freight. In the price term of an offer or contract for sale of goods, this means that the quoted price includes both the cost of the goods and freight to the named destination.

**C corporation** *n.* See under CORPORATION.

**ca. resp.** Abbreviation for *capias ad respondendum* (see under CAPIAS).

**ca. sa.** Abbreviation for *capias ad satisfaciendum* (see under CAPIAS).

**cabotage** *n.* **1.** trade and transport by sea among different ports within the same country, especially among ports along the same coastline.
**2.** air transport between points within the same country, or the right to engage in such transport, or a country's restriction of that right to domestic carriers.

**cadastre** or **cadaster** *n.* an official register of real property, usually indicating boundaries, ownership, and value for tax purposes.

**calendar** *n.* **1.** a court's list of cases scheduled for argument, hearing, or trial on a particular day or over a certain time period. Sometimes called a DOCKET.
**2. calendar call** a courtroom procedure in which a court officer calls out the names of cases on the calendar and lawyers or litigants respond by saying whether they are ready to proceed or desire an adjournment. The officer is said to **call the calendar.**

**call** *n.* **1.** a demand for payment, or for delivery of a bond (see BOND[1]) or other instrument in exchange for payment, by one having a right to make such a demand.
—*v.* **2. call the calendar** See under CALENDAR.

**callable security** *n.* Same as *redeemable security* (see under SECURITY[2]).

**calumniate** *v.,* **calumniated, calumniating.** to make false and malicious statements about; to utter calumnies.
—**calumniation** *n.*
—**calumniator** *n.*

**calumnious** *adj.* of, involving, or using calumny; defamatory.
—**calumniously** *adv.*

**calumny** *n., pl.* **calumnies. 1.** a false and malicious statement designed to injure the reputation of someone or something; a false charge.
**2.** the act of uttering calumnies; defamation.
**3.** in old law, the unjust prosecution or defense of a suit.

**camera** *n., pl.* **camerae.** *Latin.* chamber. See also IN CAMERA.

**cancel** *v.,* **canceled, canceling** or (*esp. Brit.*) **cancelled, cancelling. 1.** to mark, perforate, or otherwise physically alter a writing to render it invalid: *She canceled her will by tearing it up.* See also *canceled check* (under CHECK).
**2.** to revoke; annul; call off; withdraw: *They canceled their order. The contract may be canceled by either party upon ninety days' written notice to the other.*
—**cancelable;** *esp. Brit.,* **cancellable** *adj.*
—**canceler;** *esp. Brit.,* **canceller** *n.*

**cancellation** *n.* **1.** an act of canceling.
**2.** the marks or perforations made in canceling.
Also, **cancelation.**

**cane** *n., v.,* **caned, caning.** —*n.* **1.** the stem of a woody vine, soaked in water for use as a whip.
—*v.* **2.** to flog with a cane.

**caning** *n.* flogging with a rattan cane as a form of punishment.
——**History.** Caning is still an officially authorized punishment in a number of countries. It became briefly a cause célèbre in the United States in 1994 when 18-year-old Michael Fay, from suburban Dayton, Ohio, was sentenced on a vandalism charge in Singapore to four months in jail, a $2,230 fine, and six strokes of the cane, subsequently reduced to four. Surveys found public opinion in the United States evenly divided on sentence. It is not known to what extent the supporters understood that caning as practiced in Singapore and elsewhere systematically flays the skin from the victims, leaving them in shock from the pain and massively scarred.

**canon** *n.* a rule or principle, particularly one regarded as fundamental: *a canon of the law of wills; the canons of judicial ethics.*

**canon law** *n.* the body of internal rules of the Roman Catholic Church, or a similar body of religious rules in certain other Christian denominations.

**canon lawyer** *n.* Same as CANONIST.

**canon of construction** *n.* any of the numerous maxims and principles developed by the common law to help in construing statutes, contracts, or other writings whose meaning is in dispute: *Because the contract could be read either way, the judge applied the canon of construction that calls for an ambiguous contract to be construed against the party who drafted it.*
——**Note.** Canons of construction are not firm, codified rules, but rather general principles that courts apply flexibly in an effort to reach the most reasonable result in each individual case—or cite to add weight to a conclusion already reached on other grounds. Often a canon can be found to support either possible outcome.

**canonical** *adj.* **1.** pertaining to CANON LAW.
**2.** pertaining to, established by, or conforming to a canon or canons.
—**canonically** *adv.*

**canonical disability** *n.* a circumstance or condition that renders a marriage voidable under canon law, including CONSANGUINITY, AFFINITY, and inability to engage in sexual intercourse. Cf. CIVIL DISABILITY.

**canonist** *n.* a scholar or practitioner of CANON LAW. Also called **canon lawyer.**
—**canonistic** *adj.*

**capable of repetition, yet evading review** *adj.* (of a legal issue or controversy) of a type likely to recur but of such short duration by nature that no specific case will remain a live controversy long enough to work its way through all levels of judicial review.
——**Note.** Ordinarily, court cases are dismissed if they become MOOT; but an exception can be made for cases involving a recurring legal question that otherwise might never be definitively resolved, and this phrase from a 1911 Supreme Court case is the conventional language used to describe such questions. For example, "Jane Roe" was pregnant in March of 1970 when she sued, on behalf of herself and others similarly situated, for the right to have an abortion. Although her challenge to the Texas abortion law moved through the courts with considerable dispatch, when it reached the Supreme Court the state suggested that "Roe's case must now be moot because she and all other members of her class are no longer subject to any 1970 pregnancy." The Court responded: "[W]hen, as here, pregnancy is a significant fact in the litigation, the normal 266-day human gestation period is so short that the pregnancy will come to term before the usual appellate process is complete.... Pregnancy provides a classic justification for a conclusion of nonmootness. It truly could be 'capable of repetition, yet evading review.'" Having refused to dismiss the case on the ground of mootness, the Court went on to issue

one of the most significant and controversial decisions in its history, declaring laws prohibiting most abortions to be unconstitutional: *Roe v. Wade,* 410 U.S. 113 (1973).

**capacity** *n., pl.* **capacities. 1.** Also called **legal capacity.** the legal ability or qualification to perform an act having legal consequences, such as entering into a contract, making a will, suing or being sued, committing a crime, or getting married. See also DIMINISHED CAPACITY.
**2.** position; function; role: *She was named as a defendant in her capacity as a director of the corporation.*
**3. individual capacity**  one's role as a private individual: *The company should not be held liable for defamatory remarks made by its president in his individual capacity.* Also called **private capacity.**
**4. official capacity**  one's role in an organization; one's position in private or public office: *The actions of a trustee in her official capacity are judged by a very high legal standard.*
**5. public capacity a.** the role of a public official in carrying out the duties of his office. **b.** the role of any individual in matters with respect to which the individual has sought public prominence.

**capax doli** *adj.* Same as DOLI CAPAX.

**capax negotii** *adj. Latin.* (lit. "capable of carrying on business") legal capacity to enter into a contract.

**capias** *n. Latin.* (lit. "may you seize") **1.** any of a class of writs (each of which can be called a **writ of capias**) formerly issued in civil cases to command the sheriff to take a defendant into custody. The purpose for which the defendant was to be seized was specified in the name of the particular form of writ employed by the court, as in the examples that follow.
**2. capias ad audiendum judicium** (lit. "...to hear judgment") a writ issued to bring a misdemeanant who has appeared and been found guilty into court for pronouncement of judgment.
**3. capias ad respondendum (ca.**

**resp.)** (lit. "...for the purpose of answering") a writ issued to have the defendant in a civil case held until the return date and then produced in court to answer.
**4. capias ad satisfaciendum (ca. sa.)** (lit. "...to give satisfaction") a writ ordering that a judgment debtor be seized and held to be produced in court to satisfy the judgment, or held until the judgment is paid or otherwise discharged.
**5. capias pro fine** (lit. "...for the fine") in certain kinds of cases in which a defendant might be ordered to pay both damages and a fine, a writ ordering the defendant to be held until payment of the fine.

**capita** *n.* See PER CAPITA.

**capital**[1] *n.* **1.** broadly, any form of wealth used or capable of being used for the production of more wealth.
**2.** money and property owned or employed in business by a corporation or other enterprise. Sometimes refers to a company's total *assets,* sometimes to *net assets* (see both under ASSET). See also *capital stock* (under STOCK).
**3. capital gain** (or **loss**)  the GAIN or LOSS incurred by a taxpayer upon the sale or exchange of a *capital asset* (see under ASSET).
**4. capital gains tax**  income tax on a capital gain, such as an investor's profit on sale of stock; often this is taxed at lower rates than wages and other ordinary income. See also HOLDING PERIOD.

**capital**[2] *adj.* punishable by death, or involving the death penalty: *capital case; capital crime.*

**capital asset** *n.* See under ASSET.

**capital defender** *n.* See under DEFENDER.

**capital punishment** *n.* the killing of a person by the government as punishment for a crime.  Also called **death penalty.**

**capital stock** *n.* See under STOCK.

**capitalism** *n.* an economic system in which the means of production, distribution, and exchange of wealth are owned and controlled chiefly by private individuals or corporations, in contrast to systems characterized predominantly by cooperatively owned or state-owned means of wealth.

**capitalist** *n.* **1.** a person who has capital, especially extensive capital, invested in business enterprises.
**2.** an advocate of capitalism.

**capitalistic** *adj.* pertaining to capital, capitalism, or capitalists; founded on or believing in capitalism.
—**capitalistically** *adv.*

**capitation** *n.* **1.** a POLL TAX or other fee or payment of a fixed amount from each person: *Student activities at the university are supported by a capitation of $150 per student each semester.*
**2.** the imposition of such a tax or fee.

**capitation tax** *n.* Same as POLL TAX.

**capricious** *adj.* arbitrary; unreasonable. Usually used in the phrase *arbitrary and capricious* (see under ARBITRARY).

**caption** *n.* **1.** the heading on a court paper, containing such information as the name and number of the case, the name of the court, and the nature of the paper. The exact form of the caption in each court is a matter of local custom. See also note at VERSUS.
**2.** (in old law) arrest; the seizing of a person pursuant to judicial process.

**care** *n.* **1.** the exercise of caution and prudence in one's conduct so as to avoid causing injury or loss.
**2. ordinary care** the degree of care that a person of ordinary intelligence and prudence would exercise under the given circumstances. This is the standard of care expected of virtually everyone at all times; a failure to exercise ordinary care is NEGLIGENCE. Also called **due care** or **reasonable care**. See also MALPRACTICE.
**3. utmost care** the standard of care that must be exercised by a trustee or other FIDUCIARY in matters relating to her fiduciary responsibilities; also called **extraordinary care** or **highest degree of care**. A fiduciary's failure to exercise such care is a *breach of fiduciary duty* (see under BREACH).

**career criminal** *n.* See under CRIMINAL.

**carjacking** *n.* theft of a car by means of violence or intimidation of the driver or passengers.
—**carjacker** *n.*

**carnal abuse** *n.* Same as SEXUAL ABUSE.

**carnal knowledge** *n.* an old term for sexual intercourse.

**carrier** *n.* See COMMON CARRIER.

**carry** *v.*, **carried, carrying. 1.** to transport (people, goods, or information). See COMMON CARRIER.
**2.** to sustain; maintain. See CARRYING CHARGE.
**3.** to allocate for tax purposes. See *carry back* (under CARRYBACK); *carry over* and *carry forward* (under CARRYOVER). See also *carryover basis* (under BASIS).

**carryback** *n.* a portion of an income tax credit or deduction that cannot be claimed in the period during which it was earned or incurred, but that the taxpayer may allocate **(carry back)** to one or more previous periods.

**carryforward** *n.* Same as CARRYOVER.

**carrying charge** *n.* **1.** a charge made by a creditor for carrying an account.
**2.** the basic, ongoing cost of keeping and maintaining an item of property, expressed as a periodic figure; for example, the lease payments for a machine, or the mortgage, tax, and utility payments for real property.

**carryover** *n.* **1.** a portion of an income tax credit or deduction that cannot be claimed in the period during which it was earned or incurred, but that the taxpayer may allocate **(carry over** or **carry forward)** to one or more subsequent periods. Also called **carryforward.**
—*adj.* **2.** carried over; transferred to or received from another person. See *carryover basis* (under BASIS).

**carryover basis** *n.* See under BASIS.

**cartel** *n.* **1.** a group of participants in an industry who have joined together to reduce or prevent competition among themselves by establishing prices and regulating output of a product or service.

**2.** the agreement among members of such a group regarding prices, output, and organization.

**3.** *International Law.* a written agreement between belligerents, especially for the exchange of prisoners.

**cartelize** *v.,* **cartelized, cartelizing. 1.** to organize (an industry) into a cartel.
**2.** to become a cartel or to become dominated by one or more cartels.
—**cartelization** *n.*

**cas fortuit** *n., pl.* **cas fortuits.** *French.* (lit. "chance event; accident") (in marine insurance) an unavoidable accident.

**case¹** *n.* **1.** all proceedings with respect to a charge, claim, or dispute filed with a court: *criminal case; civil case; contract case.*
**2. agreed case** a civil case in which the parties stipulate to the facts and submit them to the judge for a ruling upon their legal effect instead of having a trial. Also called **case stated.**
**3. case in point** a previously decided case involving facts or issues that are similar or analogous to those currently under consideration, cited as a precedent.
**4. case of first impression** a case raising a significant legal issue that has not previously been ruled upon by any court.
**5. companion case** one of a pair or group of separate cases raising related issues, dealt with at the same time by a court, especially the Supreme Court.
**6. consolidated case** two or more separately filed cases involving common issues, combined into a single case for efficient treatment.
**7. diversity case** a federal civil suit between citizens of different states. See also *diversity jurisdiction* (under JURISDICTION¹).
**8. federal case** a case filed in federal court, especially one involving FEDERAL LAW. A federal case is not necessarily big or important, and you cannot "make a federal case out of" a case that does not fall within the *limited jurisdiction* (see under JURISDICTION¹) of the federal courts.
**9. landmark case** a case whose decision established a new legal principle of historic importance; a case viewed as representing a great stride forward for the law. For example, *Marbury v. Madison* (the 1803 decision establishing the doctrine that courts may strike down laws as unconstitutional) or *Brown v. Board of Education* (the 1954 decision outlawing racial segregation in public schools).
**10. leading case** a case that is generally regarded as the first example of a particular legal principle, or whose decision is an especially influential early exposition of a principle; for example, the 1863 English case of *Byrne v. Boadle,* in which the phrase RES IPSA LOQUITUR was first used.
**11. test case** a case instituted or continued for the purpose of testing the constitutionality of a law or establishing a new legal principle.

**case²** *n.* the totality of evidence presented by a party in support of its position in a case: *plaintiff's case; defendant's case; prosecution case.* In a typical trial, the plaintiff or prosecution first presents what it regards as sufficient evidence to prove its claims (the **case in chief**), then the defendant puts on its case, then the plaintiff or prosecutor responds with further evidence (the **rebuttal case,** or simply **rebuttal**). Sometimes the defendant then puts in still more evidence (a **surrebuttal case,** or **surrebuttal**) to rebut the rebuttal, but the alternation seldom goes beyond this. The party that ultimately prevails is said to have "proved (or sustained) its case." See also *prima facie case* (under PRIMA FACIE).

**case³** *n.* Same as *trespass on the case* (see under TRESPASS²).

**case⁴** *v.,* **cased, casing.** *Slang.* to examine or survey (a house, bank, etc.) in planning a crime.

**case law** *n.* **1.** law created by judicial decision rather than by statute, including decisions interpreting statutes.
**2.** the body of published judicial opinions in cases dealing with a particular

point or kind of issue: *The case law under this statute generally adopts a narrow construction.*
Also called **decisional law.**

**case method** (or **system**) *n.* the general method by which most legal subjects are taught in most law schools today, in which students' primary reading material consists of judicial opinions in actual cases, which are analyzed in class by use of the SOCRATIC METHOD. See also CASEBOOK.

**case note** *n.* Same as ANNOTATION (def. 1).

**case or controversy** *n.* an actual dispute over legal rights. Under the Constitution, the federal courts may consider only cases or controversies, not hypothetical questions. See also ADVISORY OPINION.

**casebook** *n.* a collection of judicial opinions in a particular area of law, edited, organized, and supplemented with questions and commentary for use in the CASE METHOD of legal instruction.

**cash bail** *n.* See under BAIL¹.

**cashier's check** *n.* See under CHECK.

**castration** *n.* removal of testicles. See also CHEMICAL CASTRATION.
—**castrate** *v.,* **castrated, castrating.**

**casual** *adj.* occasional; irregular; out of the ordinary: *casual employee; casual sale.*

**casual ejector** *n.* See under EJECTOR.

**casualty** *n., pl.* **casualties.** harm to person or property caused by a sudden, unexpected, or unusual event such as an automobile accident or a natural disaster.

**casualty insurance** *n.* insurance that compensates the insured for loss resulting from a casualty. The types of casualty covered by a particular policy are spelled out in the policy.

**catalla** *n.pl. Latin.* chattels. The term appears in various ancient maxims and writs. The singular form of the word **(catallum)** was rarely used. See also BONA ET CATALLA.

**caucus** *n., pl.* **caucuses,** *v.,* **caucused,**

**caucusing. 1.** *U.S. Politics.* **a.** a meeting of party leaders to select candidates, elect convention delegates, etc. **b.** a meeting of party members within a legislative body to select leaders and determine strategy. **c.** Often, **Caucus.** a faction within a legislative body that pursues its interests through the legislative process: *the Women's Caucus; the Black Caucus.*
**2.** any group or meeting organized to further a special interest or cause.
—*v.* **3.** to hold or meet in a caucus.

**causa** *n., pl.* **causae.** *Latin.* (lit. "cause; case") **1.** cause; reason; that which brings about a result.
**2.** suit; action; cause of action.
**3.** *Civil Law.* **a.** consideration for a contract or obligation. **b.** property; thing.

**causa causans** *n. Latin.* (lit. "the causing cause") **1.** the primary cause; the principal cause.
**2.** the original cause; the precipitating event in a chain of causation.
**3.** the immediate cause; the last link in a chain of causation.

**causa mortis** *adj. Latin.* (lit. "because of [impending] death") describing something done by a person in the belief that she is about to die. See also *gift causa mortis* (under GIFT).

**causa proxima** *n. Latin.* (lit. "the nearest cause; the most recent cause") immediate cause; PROXIMATE CAUSE.

**causa remota** *n. Latin.* (lit. "a distant cause") a remote cause; an indirect cause.

**causa sine qua non** *n. Latin.* (lit. "a cause without which not") Same as BUT-FOR CAUSE.

**causation** *n.* the fact that a certain action or event produced a certain result. This is an essential element to be proved in many kinds of cases; for example, to convict a defendant of murder the prosecution must prove that the victim's death actually resulted from the defendant's conduct; to recover damages in a tort or contract action the plaintiff must prove that the claimed loss was actually caused by defendant's wrongful conduct **(causation of loss** or **loss causation).**

**cause** *n., v.,* **caused, causing.** —*n.* **1.** an action or event that brings about or contributes to a particular outcome. See also BUT-FOR CAUSE; *efficient cause* (under PROXIMATE CAUSE); INTERVENING CAUSE; *legal cause* (under PROXIMATE CAUSE); PROCURING CAUSE; PROXIMATE CAUSE; REMOTE CAUSE.
**2.** a reason for taking certain action, especially a good or legally sufficient reason. See also FOR CAUSE; GOOD CAUSE; INSUFFICIENT CAUSE; PROBABLE CAUSE.
**3.** a cause of action; civil case: *The cause was tried in Superior Court, County of Los Angeles.*
—*v.* **4.** to be the cause of; bring about.

**cause of action** *n.* **1.** facts which, if proved, would entitle a party to relief in a lawsuit on some legal theory: *The complaint was dismissed for failure to state a cause of action.* In the federal courts and many states, this terminology has been replaced for many purposes by **claim for relief** (see CLAIM, def. 2).
**2.** a right of recovery arising from such facts: *The seller has a cause of action for breach of contract against the purchaser, who failed to pay for the goods.*

**cautionary instruction** *n.* See under INSTRUCTION.

**caveat** *n.* **1.** a warning or caution; admonition.
**2.** in certain legal contexts, a formal notice of interest in a matter or property; for example, a notice to a court or public officer to suspend a certain proceeding until the notifier is given a hearing: *a caveat filed against the probate of a will.*

**caveat emptor** *Latin.* let the buyer beware: the principle that the seller of a product cannot be held responsible for its quality unless it is guaranteed in a warranty. This principle has been largely supplanted by *implied warranties* (see under WARRANTY) and the law of PRODUCTS LIABILITY.

**caveatee** *n.* one whose interest in a matter is adverse to that of the caveator.

**caveator** *n.* one who files a caveat.

**CD** CERTIFICATE OF DEPOSIT.

**cease and desist order** *n.* an order of an administrative agency directing a person or entity to refrain from specified unlawful conduct.
—**Usage.** If issued by a court, such an order is more often called an INJUNCTION.

**cede** *v.,* **ceded, ceding. 1.** to surrender; transfer; assign.
**2.** *International Law.* to formally yield territory to another country.
**3.** *Insurance Law.* to assign or transfer risk to another insurance company through REINSURANCE.
—**ceder** *n.*

**censor** *n.* **1.** an official who examines books, plays, news reports, motion pictures, radio and television programs, letters, cablegrams, etc., for the purpose of suppressing parts deemed objectionable on moral, political, military, or other grounds.
**2.** (in the ancient Roman republic) either of two officials who kept the register or census of the citizens, awarded public contracts, and supervised manners and morals.
—*v.* **3.** to examine and act upon as a censor.
—**censorable** *adj.*
—**censorial** *adj.*
—**censorship** *n.*

**censurable** *adj.* deserving of censure.

**censure** *n., v.,* **censured, censuring.** —*n.* **1.** a formal statement issued by a body such as a legislature or a bar disciplinary committee condemning the behavior of one of its own members or a member of a group whose conduct it is legally charged with monitoring.
—*v.* **2.** to issue such a statement.
—**censurable** *adj.*
—**censurableness, censurability** *n.*
—**censurably** *adv.*
—**Pronunciation.** The *s* in *censure* and related words is the same as the *s* in *sure.* During debates regarding the impeachment of President Clinton, several members of Congress who did not know this spoke (both pro and con) of

the possibility of "censoring" the President instead of removing him from office. What they were trying to say was "censuring."

**census** *n., pl.* **censuses. 1.** a counting of people in a population.

**2. decennial census** a census taken once every ten years; specifically, the official counting of people in the United States that takes place once every decade.

**—History.** The Constitution requires a decennial census for the purpose of apportionment of seats in the House of Representatives. The Supreme Court has acknowledged that the census methods handed down for two hundred years—simply counting the people the census takers can contact and ignoring the rest—result in a substantially disproportionate undercount of some identifiable groups, including certain minorities, children, and renters. In the 1990's, three boards of the National Academy of Sciences studied the problem at the behest of Congress and concluded that traditional census techniques should be augmented by modern scientific and statistical techniques in order to obtain the best possible count. But in 1999 the Supreme Court rejected a Census Bureau plan to use these techniques to make the Year 2000 census more fair and accurate. By a vote of 5–4, the Court held that modern counting techniques could not be used because Congress—which had an obvious interest in perpetuating the malapportionment by which it had been elected and which had in fact sued to stop the plan—had not authorized such methods. *Department of Commerce v. United States House of Representatives,* 525 U.S. 316 (1999).

**cert.** See under CERTIORARI.

**certifiable** *adj.* **1.** capable of being certified.
**2.** legally committable to a mental institution.
—**certifiability** *n.*
—**certifiably** *adv.*

**certificate** *n.* **1.** a formal document, typically a single sheet of paper, evidencing some right, interest, or permission granted to the person or entity to which it was issued.
**2.** Also called **certification.** a written statement confirming that certain facts are true, that certain acts have been performed, or that something is authentic.

**certificate of convenience and necessity** *n.* a certificate from a regulatory agency certifying that a public need exists for a certain type of service, such as a utility or transportation service, and authorizing a private company to provide that service. Also called **certificate of public convenience and necessity**.

**certificate of deposit (CD)** *n.* an acknowledgment by a bank of receipt of money with a promise to repay it upon specified terms as to interest rate and time of repayment.

**certificate of incorporation** *n.* **1.** in some states, same as ARTICLES OF INCORPORATION.
**2.** in most states, a document issued by the state certifying that articles of incorporation have been filed and the named corporation has come into existence; essentially a fancy receipt for the articles and the filing fee.

**certificate of insurance** *n.* a certificate from an insurance company verifying that an insurance policy of a certain type has been issued to a certain person.

**certificate of mailing** *n.* a certificate provided by the post office certifying that an item was mailed.

**certificate of need** *n.* a certificate from an administrative agency certifying that there is a need for additional health facilities in a region and authorizing a provider to expand its facilities.

**certificate of occupancy** *n.* a certificate from a public agency certifying that a building complies with building codes and may be occupied.

**certificate of origin** *n.* a document certifying the country of origin of a product.

**certificate of participation** *n.* a certificate evidencing the holder's percentage interest in an investment.

**certificate of title** *n.* **1.** an official certificate that a certain person is the owner of a particular motor vehicle. **2.** in jurisdictions with a TITLE REGISTRATION SYSTEM for land, a certificate issued by the state or local government identifying the owner or owners of interests in specified real estate and listing any easements, mortgages, covenants, or other encumbrances on the property. **3.** a certificate issued by a title insurance company expressing its professional opinion, after diligent examination, that a person has good title to certain land, except as specifically noted. This does not constitute a guarantee or insurance of good title.

**certification** *n.* **1.** the act of certifying or issuing a certificate. **2.** the fact or state of being certified. **3.** CERTIFICATE (def. 2). **4.** the word for CERTIORARI in some state court systems.

**certification mark** *n.* **1.** a name, symbol, or other MARK used to certify that goods or services provided by others meet certain standards or requirements established by the owner of the mark. For example, the mark might certify that a product such as cheese or wine comes from a specific geographic region, or that a product such as bedding or clothing is made entirely of certain material, or that a product such as electronic goods meets certain safety standards, or that a product was made by members of a particular union. **2. registered certification mark** a certification mark that is a *registered mark* (see under MARK). See also ®.

**certified public accountant (CPA)** *n.* a *public accountant* (see under ACCOUNTANT) who has satisfied all state licensing requirements for practice as a public accountant and thus is authorized to express an audit opinion on the fairness of corporate financial statements and to perform other accounting work for which a license is required.

**certify** *v.*, **certified, certifying. 1.** to make a written representation or guarantee that something is authentic, acceptable, or true, or that certain acts have been or will be performed. **2.** to issue a CERTIFICATE. **3.** used in reference to certain kinds of judicial determination; as **a.** to determine that a person is INCOMPETENT: *to certify that a person is incompetent; to certify a person.* **b.** to determine that a group of individuals or entities satisfies the criteria for proceeding with a case as a *class action* (see under ACTION): *to certify a class.* **4. certified check** See under CHECK. **5. certified copy** a copy of a document to which a statement has been affixed swearing or affirming that it has been compared with the original and is a true copy. Also called **verified copy** or **attested copy.** **6. certified mail** a form of domestic mail delivery within the United States in which the sender is given a mailing receipt and a record of the delivery is kept at the recipient's post office. For an additional fee the sender may also request proof of delivery in the form of a card signed by the recipient at the time of delivery **(return receipt),** in which case the mail is referred to as **certified mail, return receipt requested.** This is often used for sending legal notices. See also CERTIFICATE OF MAILING; RECORDED DELIVERY; REGISTERED MAIL. **7. certified question** under procedures permitted in some jurisdictions, a question of law posed by a lower court to a higher court, or a question of state law posed by a federal court to the appropriate state court, so that the answer can be applied in resolving a pending case. **8. certify the record** to transmit documents constituting the record in a case to a higher court for appellate review, with a certification that this is in fact the record.

**certiorari** *n. Latin.* (lit. "to be informed," "to be assured") a writ issued by an appellate court as a matter of discretion, directing a lower court to *certify the record* (see under **CERTIFY**) in a case that was not appealable as of right. The usual route by which a case reaches the Supreme Court of the United States is by a petition for certiorari from the party on the losing end of a decision of a United States Court of Appeals or a state's highest court; the Supreme Court grants only about one percent of such petitions. In informal speech, certiorari is typically referred to by its abbreviation: **cert.**

**cession** *n.* **1.** act of ceding, as by treaty. **2.** something that is ceded, as territory.

**cestui** *n., pl.* **cestuis.** *Law French.* (lit. "the one who; the one whose; the one to whom; the one for whom") the beneficiary of a trust; short for **CESTUI QUE TRUST.**
——**History.** The plural form shows that despite its Law French origins, this term has long been fully anglicized: In actual Law French writing the plural would have been *ceux.*

**cestui que trust** *n., pl.* **cestuis que trust** or **cestuis que trustent.** *Law French.* the beneficiary of a trust.
——**Usage.** Like much Law French, this term is a mixture of Norman French (*cestui que*) and English (*trust*). The phrase is generally thought to be a shortening of something along the lines of "the one for whose [use] the trust [was created]." But a rich vein of history treats the word *trust* in this phrase as a verb ("the one who trusts"), and this with a plural verb ending seen not only in modern French but also on verbs in ancient Law French texts produces the plural form *cestuis que trustent.* Although *trustent* has been criticized as based upon a misunderstanding of the phrase, it has been heavily used in the United States for at least two centuries. Legal writers today, however, generally avoid the dilemma: They just say "beneficiaries."

**cestui que use** *n., pl.* **cestuis que use** *Law French.* (lit. "the one for whose use") in old English law, a person for whose benefit another held title to

land; the one having the right to take the profits from the land. Cf. **FEOFFEE TO USES**; see also **STATUTE OF USES**.

**cestui que vie** *n. Law French.* (lit. "the one for whose life") the person for whose life another is entitled to the use of certain property; the person whose life is the **MEASURING LIFE** of an *estate pur autre vie* (see under **ESTATE**[1]).

**C.F.** Same as C. & F.

**cf.** compare (abbreviation of Latin *confer*).
——**Usage.** In nonlegal contexts, *cf.* —like the Latin word for which it is the abbreviation—means "compare." In legal citations that follow **BLUEBOOK** style, *cf.* is supposed to signify that the cited authority "supports a proposition different from the stated proposition but sufficiently analogous to lend support," and *but cf.* is supposed to introduce authority that "supports a proposition analogous to the contrary of the main proposition." Except in carefully edited law reviews, however, when most legal writers write "cf." they just mean "compare."

**CFR** CODE OF FEDERAL REGULATIONS.

**chain gang** *n.* a crew of convicts chained together while working outside the prison.

**chain letter** *n.* **1.** a letter sent to a number of people, each of whom is asked to send copies to other people who are to do likewise, as for the purpose of spreading a message or fundraising.
**2.** especially, such a letter when used as part of an illegal scheme whereby new recipients are supposed to send money to previous recipients several levels back in the chain, in the hope of profiting themselves from continuation of the chain.
——**Note.** Chain letter schemes only profit those who initiate them, since the process can never be continued far enough to profit those farther along in the chain. For example, a chain letter sent by each recipient to ten new recipients would cover all the people in the world before the tenth step could be completed.

**chain of causation** *n.* a series of events in which each is a cause of the next.

**chain of custody** *n.* the sequence of places where, and persons with whom, a piece of physical evidence was located from the time of its gathering to its introduction at a trial. Establishing the chain of custody is essential to proof of authenticity of the evidence.

**chain of evidence** *n.* **1.** a series of connections and inferences that leads an investigator from one piece of evidence to another: *The privilege against self-incrimination applies when the answers elicited might furnish a link in the chain of evidence leading to a conviction.*
**2.** Same as CHAIN OF CUSTODY.

**chain of title** *n.* the sequence of owners and transfers of a parcel of real property. Any gap in the recorded chain of title casts doubt upon the validity of a present claim of title to the property.

**chairman's mark** *n.* See under MARK.

**challenge** *n.* **1.** a party's rejection of a potential juror, either because of an evident bias or interest in the case **(challenge for cause)** or simply because of a belief that the juror may not be receptive to that party's arguments **(peremptory challenge)**. In selecting a jury, each party is allowed unlimited challenges for cause and a limited number of peremptory challenges.
**2. challenge to the array** a party's objection to the manner in which the entire array of potential jurors was selected from the population at large.
—**challenge** *v.,* **challenged, challenging.**
—**challengeable** *adj.*

**chambers** *n.pl.* a judge's office. Depending upon the court, it may be a single room or a suite of two or three rooms for the judge, one or more law clerks, and a secretary. See also ROBING ROOM.

**champerty** *n.* agreeing to finance someone else's lawsuit in return for a share of the proceeds. Prohibitions on champerty are the reason that lawyers working for a *contingency fee* (see under CONTINGENCY) usually insist that filing fees and other expenses of a suit be paid by the client. See also MAINTENANCE; BARRATRY.
—**champertor** *n.*
—**champertous** *adj.*
—**champertously** *adv.*

**chance-medley** *n.* **1.** killing in self-defense in a sudden fight.
**2.** Also called **manslaughter by chance-medley.** a killing other than in self-defense that occurs during a sudden and unpredicted encounter that gets out of hand.
**3.** a sudden and unexpected fight; sudden affray; sudden brawl; especially one in which a participant is killed.

**chance verdict** *n.* See under VERDICT.

**Chancellor** *n.* the traditional title of judges in courts of EQUITY or CHANCERY.

**chancery** *n.* the traditional name for a court of EQUITY. Also called **chancery court** or **court of chancery.**

**change of venue** *n.* the transfer of a case from the court in which it was commenced to a court located elsewhere for reasons of fairness or convenience; for example, the moving of a sensational criminal case to a county where the jury pool might be less biased, or the transfer of a civil case to a court closer to most of the evidence and witnesses. See also VENUE.

**chapter** *n.* **1.** a main division of a code or statute containing many sections.
**2.** a local branch of an organization.

**Chapter 7, 11, 12,** or **13** *n.* See under BANKRUPTCY.

**character** *n.* the general disposition of a person, particularly with respect to some trait that is relevant in a case, such as honesty or propensity for violence. See also *character evidence* (under EVIDENCE); *character witness* (under WITNESS).

**charge** *n., v.,* **charged, charging.** —*n.*
**1.** a formal allegation that a person has

violated a specific criminal law; a COUNT in an indictment or information.
**2.** a judge's INSTRUCTION to the jury on a particular point of law, or her *instructions* collectively (see under INSTRUCTION).
**3.** a lien or debt to be satisfied out of particular property: *The estate tax is a charge upon the estate.*
**4. Allen charge** a charge to a jury that has declared itself unable to reach a verdict, urging it to try harder. The Allen charge is prohibited in some states because of its tendency to coerce holdout jurors to go along with the majority despite genuine doubts. The usual name for the charge comes from the case in which it was approved by the United States Supreme Court, *Allen v. United States,* 164 U.S. 492 (1896). But it is also referred to informally by a host of names alluding to its potential impact on the jury, such as **depth charge** and **dynamite charge.**
**5. requests to charge** Same as REQUESTS FOR INSTRUCTIONS.
—*v.* **6.** to make, impose, or deliver a charge.
—**chargeable** *adj.*

**charge conference** *n.* a conference among the judge and counsel for all parties in a case, held prior to the charging of the jury, in which the judge outlines the instructions that she intends to give to the jury and gives counsel an opportunity to state any legal objections that they have to any particular instructions. Also called **charging conference.**
—**Note.** Attorneys who are informed that a particular charge will or will not be given and fail to point out why that would be improper will ordinarily not be allowed to argue on appeal that the jury was improperly instructed.

**charitable contribution** *n.* a contribution of money or property to a qualified CHARITABLE ORANIZATION that is made voluntarily and without getting or expecting to get anything of equal value in return. Charitable contributions are generally deductible for income tax purposes.

**charitable deduction** *n.* an income tax DEDUCTION in the amount of a CHARITABLE CONTRIBUTION.

**charitable organization** *n.* for tax purposes, an organization that is qualified under section 501(c)(3) of the Internal Revenue Code to receive tax deductible charitable contributions.
—**Note.** In general, in order to qualify under the Internal Revenue Code the organization must be organized under United States law and operated for charitable, religious, scientific, literary, or educational purposes, or for the prevention of cruelty to children or animals. Veterans' organizations, fraternal societies, and nonprofit cemetary companies are also included, as are United States and state governmental entities, Indian tribal governments, and certain organizations that foster national or international sports competition.

**charitable remainder trust** *n.* See under TRUST.

**charitable trust** *n.* See under TRUST.

**charter**[1] *n.* **1.** a formal grant of rights and powers from a sovereign, or the document embodying such a grant; for example, the MAGNA CARTA, or **Great Charter.**
**2.** the basic set of governing principles of an organization: the *United Nations Charter.*
**3.** Also called **corporate charter. a.** a legislative act establishing a corporation and setting forth its purposes and basic structure. **b.** a CERTIFICATE OF INCORPORATION or other document issued by the state granting corporate status to an entity. **c.** a corporation's ARTICLES OF INCORPORATION.
—*v.* **4.** to establish by adopting a charter: *The United Nations was chartered in 1945.*
**5.** to grant a charter to or for: *The corporation was chartered by act of Congress.*
—**charterable** *adj.*

**charter**[2] *n.* **1.** the rental of a ship, airplane, or bus.
**2.** Also called **charter party.** a written contract for the hire of such a vessel, especially a ship.
**3. bareboat charter** the charter of a

ship only, usually with no crew. The charterer takes command of the vessel and takes full responsibility for it, and for any damage caused by it, for the duration of the charter. Also called **demise charter.** See also DEMISE.

**4. time charter** the charter of a ship for a specified period of time, with the shipowner providing the crew and retaining command and responsibility for the vessel.

**5. voyage charter** the charter of a ship for a specific voyage, with the shipowner providing the crew and retaining command and responsibility for the vessel.

—*v.* **6.** to rent a ship, airplane, or bus from someone: *We chartered a bus for the company picnic.*

—**charterable** *adj.*

——**False Friend.** Although *charter party* sounds like an afternoon of fun in a rented boat, it is actually a very dry document filled with an ocean of fine print. The "party" part of the phrase comes from the French *partie,* meaning "parted; separated; divided into parts." The term derives from the ancient practice of writing ship charters in duplicate and then separating the two parts in such a way that each would fit back together only with the other, so that the shipowner and the charterer could each keep one part of the contract and its authenticity could easily be verified.

**charterer** *n.* one who hires a ship, airplane, or bus.

**chattel** *n.* **1.** an item of *personal property* (see under PROPERTY), especially movable property.

**2. chattel personal** movable property; tangible personal property. Also called **personal chattel.**

**3. chattel real** an interest in land which is less than a FREEHOLD, most often a lease for a term of years. Also called **real chattel.**

**chattel mortgage** *n.* See under MORTGAGE.

**chattel paper** *n.* a writing or group of writings evidencing both a monetary obligation and a security interest in or a lease of specific goods; for example, the papers evidencing a *chattel mortgage* (see under MORTGAGE). Chattel paper is governed by Article 9 of the Uniform Commercial Code.

**chattel personal** *n., pl.* **chattels personal.** See under CHATTEL.

**chattel real** *n., pl.* **chattels real.** See under CHATTEL.

**check** *n.* **1.** an instrument by which a person (the drawer) directs a bank (the drawee) to pay a specified sum of money to the order of another person (the payee), or to the bearer of the instrument, upon demand. Normally the payment is made out of funds that the drawer has on deposit with the bank. A check is a special kind of DRAFT.

**2. bank check** a check drawn by a bank upon another bank.

**3. bad check** a check that is forged, drawn upon insufficient funds, or in some other way defective, so that payment is properly refused by the drawee bank.

**4. canceled check** or **cancelled check** a check stamped "paid" or containing some similar marking by the bank on which it was drawn to indicate that it has been paid and so may not be reused.

**5. cashier's check** a check drawn by a bank on itself; it amounts to a promise to pay if the payee makes a proper demand.

**6. certified check** a check on which the bank has written a notice (usually just the word "certified") signifying that the funds necessary to pay it have been set aside so that payment will definitely be made upon proper demand by the payee.

**7. NSF check** a check that the drawee bank may refuse to pay because the drawer does not have sufficient funds on deposit to cover it when it is presented to the bank for payment. NSF stands for "not sufficient funds" or "non-sufficient funds." See also KITE.

**8. paid check** a check upon which the drawee bank has made payment.

**checkoff** *n.* **1.** Also called **dues checkoff.** a system whereby union dues for employees in a company are paid by means of a regular deduction from their paychecks.

**2.** an item in an income tax form providing taxpayers an opportunity to make a small contribution to a specific fund, such as a campaign fund or a fund for conservation purposes, to be paid either out of their income tax or on top of their income tax.

**chemical castration** *n.* administration of drugs or hormones to a man to temporarily reduce or counteract the production or effect of male hormones in his body.
——**Note.** The purpose of chemical castration is to reduce sex drive or sexually incapacitate a sex offender who appears to be incapable of controlling his behavior. Whether this really works, and whether it may be imposed as a condition of parole or even voluntarily submitted to in order to obtain release from custody, are questions that remain open.

**chief judge** *n.* See under JUDGE.

**Chief Justice of the United States** *n.* the formal title of the chief justice of the Supreme Court of the United States.
——**Note.** The Chief Justice has but one constitutional duty: to preside at trials of presidential IMPEACHMENT. By statute, the Chief Justice also has the considerable responsibility of overseeing the entire administration of the Supreme Court; and by custom the Chief Justice swears in each new president of the United States. As a judge, the Chief Justice is regarded as "first among equals": He or she has but one vote, but can exercise considerable persuasive influence in both formal and informal conferences with the other justices. See also PRIMUS INTER PARES.

**child** *n.* **1.** a person deemed by the law to require special protection or treatment because of youth. The age below which one is regarded as a child depends upon the particular statute or legal doctrine at issue.
**2.** an offspring or a person treated as such. Depending upon the context, the term may or may not include an illegitimate child or a stepchild, but would almost always include an adopted child.

**child custody** *n.* See under CUSTODY.

**child molestation** *n.* any crime involving sexual advances upon or sexual contact with a child.
—**child molester** *n.*

**child neglect** *n.* See under NEGLECT.

**child offender** *n.* See under OFFENDER.

**child pornography** *n.* See under PORNOGRAPHY.

**child support** *n.* **1.** the legal obligation to support one's children financially until they reach the age of majority.
**2.** payments made by a parent to help support minor children, either voluntarily or pursuant to court order, in the case of divorce or separation of the parents. Typically the noncustodial parent makes payments to the custodial parent or directly to third parties for certain expenses such as tuition.
**3. decretal child support** a requirement of child support payments included in a divorce decree. Also called **decretory child support.**

**chilling effect** *n.* a tendency to inhibit the exercise of constitutional rights, especially those protected by the First Amendment (see Appendix). Statutes that unnecessarily create such an effect are often held unconstitutional.

**Chinese wall** or **Chinese Wall** *n.* **1.** Also called **ethical wall.** a system established within a law firm intended to prevent a particular lawyer or set of lawyers from having any involvement in a matter or any access to confidential information about the matter, or sharing any relevant information with those involved in the matter, in order to avoid a CONFLICT OF INTEREST. A Chinese wall might be set up, for example, if a lawyer who once worked for a firm that represented company A goes to work for a firm that represents someone who is now suing company A.
**2.** any policy barring communication on certain subjects between one person, department, or entity and another: *The*

*newspaper erected a Chinese wall between the advertising and the editorial staffs to prevent advertisers from influencing how news affecting their industry is covered.*

—**Usage.** Occasionally a court expresses discomfort with this allusion to the Great Wall of China as a metaphor for an impenetrable barrier, and in a few decisions the phrase has been consciously avoided out of concern that it might sound like a gratuitous ethnic reference. Other courts have expressed the view that this concern is misguided. If the customary phrase were "Great Wall," or even "Great Wall of China," the issue would presumably not arise. Whatever the merits of the debate, at present the usual term for a set of policies and practices intended to prevent improper exchanges of confidential information within a firm is still "Chinese wall" or "Chinese Wall" (usually written in quotation marks); "ethical wall" (often in quotation marks) runs a very distant second, but has the advantage of avoiding any risk of offense.

**choice of evils** *n.* Same as NECESSITY.

**choice of forum clause** or **choice-of-forum clause** *n.* a contract clause in which the parties agree that any lawsuit arising from the contract will be brought in a particular court or a particular jurisdiction. The parties cannot confer jurisdiction upon a court, but if the chosen court has jurisdiction this clause would make it difficult for either party to argue that it would be an inconvenient forum. Also called **forum selection clause.**

**choice of law** *n.* the problem of deciding which law to apply when an action involves events that took place or have an impact in two or more jurisdictions having different laws. This is the central concern of the field of CONFLICT OF LAWS.

**choice of law clause** or **choice-of-law clause** *n.* a contract clause in which the parties agree that any dispute arising under the contract should be resolved in accordance with the law of a particular state or nation. The parties' choice is not binding upon the courts, but in the absence of strong countervailing considerations it will normally be honored.

**chop shop** *n. Informal.* a garage where stolen cars are dismantled so that their parts can be sold separately.

**chose** *n., pl.* **choses.** *Law French.* (lit. "thing") **1.** a thing; an item of personal property, whether tangible or intangible.
**2. chose in action** a right to obtain money or personal property by bringing a legal action; a claim for such a thing; for example, a right to recover a debt. Also called **thing in action.**
**3. chose in possession** an item of movable property that is in the possession of its owner. Also called **thing in possession.**

**churning** *n.* a stockbroker's excessive and inappropriate trading of securities in a customer's account for the purpose of generating extra commissions for the broker. This is made illegal by the securities laws.

**C.I.F.** cost, insurance, and freight. In the price term of an offer or contract for sale of goods, this means that the quoted price includes not only the cost of the goods but also insurance and freight to the named destination.

**circuit** *n.* **1.** historically, the itinerary of a traveling judge who went from town to town hearing cases that had accumulated since his last visit; hence, the fairly broad but contiguous geographic area for which such a judge had responsibility.
**2.** a geographic division established by some states for purposes of judicial administration, with one or more courts in each circuit having jurisdiction with respect to cases in that circuit.
**3.** one of the divisions into which the federal judicial system of the United States is divided for appellate purposes. The United States is divided geographically into twelve circuits, with the UNITED STATES COURT OF APPEALS for each such circuit handling appeals from all federal district courts within its area.

In addition, in 1982 Congress established a special circuit covering the entire country, called the **Federal Circuit,** in order to funnel all appeals on a number of specific subjects, such as patents and international trade, to a single specialized court, the **United States Court of Appeals for the Federal Circuit.**
See also *circuit court* (under COURT); *circuit judge* (under JUDGE); *Circuit Justice* (under JUSTICE²). Cf. DISTRICT.

**circular sting** *n.* See under STING.

**circumstance** *n.* See AGGRAVATING CIRCUMSTANCE; MITIGATING CIRCUMSTANCE; SPECIAL CIRCUMSTANCES.

**circumstantial** *adj.* **1.** pertaining to or derived from the surrounding circumstances: *circumstantial guarantees of trustworthiness.*
**2.** relating to or derived from *circumstantial evidence* (see under EVIDENCE): *circumstantial case; circumstantial proof.*
—**circumstantially** *adv.*

**circumstantial evidence** *n.* See under EVIDENCE.

**citation** *n.* **1.** a written notice to appear in court (or sometimes to respond by mail) to answer a charge; for example, a traffic ticket. Citations are a substitute for arrest in minor offenses.
**2.** an oral or written declaration by a judge or legislative body that a person is in CONTEMPT.
**3.** a reference to a statute, previous judicial decision, or other writing as authority for a fact or legal proposition. Standard abbreviations and formats for citing common sources minimize the space required and are recognized by all lawyers.
See also BLUEBOOK.

**citator** *n.* a book or electronic database in which one can look up cases or statutes to see if they have been cited in subsequent cases, and obtain citations to the later cases. Citators also show whether the particular decision one is looking up was affirmed, reversed, or otherwise dealt with by any later decision in the same case.

**cite** *v.*, **cited, citing,** *n.* —*v.* **1.** to issue a

CITATION: *The sanitation department cited him for failing to bag recyclable trash separately. She was cited for contempt for her outburst in court.*
**2.** to provide a citation to a source or precedent: *The attorney cited a Supreme Court decision from 1823.* —*n. Informal.* **3.** a citation to a source or precedent: *Counselor, do you have a cite for that proposition?*
—**citable** *adj.*

**cite-check** *v.,* **cite-checked, cite-checking,** *n.* —*v.* **1.** to check all the quotations and citations in a brief or other legal writing to make sure that the quotations are accurate and that the citations are complete, accurate, and in proper form. See also SHEPARDIZE.
—*n.* **2.** an instance of this: *Have you finished the cite-check on our reply brief?*
**3. substantive cite-check** a cite-check in which the quotations and citations are not only checked for mechanical accuracy, but also evaluated to make sure that the quotations are not taken out of context and that the cited authorities genuinely support the propositions for which they are cited.

**citizen** *n.* **1.** a person who owes allegiance to a government and is entitled to its protection. Under the Fourteenth Amendment (see Appendix), virtually all persons born or naturalized in the United States are citizens of the United States and of the state where they reside. In addition, by statute, persons born in Puerto Rico, the U.S. Virgin Islands, Guam, and the Northern Mariana Islands are citizens of the United States. See also NATIONAL; NATURALIZE.
**2.** for purposes of determining whether a suit by or against a corporation or a resident alien falls within the *diversity jurisdiction* (see under JURISDICTION¹) of the federal courts, an alien admitted to the United States for permanent residence is deemed to be a "citizen" of the state where the alien is domiciled, and a corporation is deemed to be a "citizen" both of the state where it was incorporated and of the state where it has its principal place of business.
—**citizenship** *n.*

**citizenry** *n.* the citizens of a nation or region collectively.

**citizen's arrest** *n.* See under ARREST.

**civil** *adj.* **1.** pertaining to all aspects of law other than those dealing with criminal or military matters: *civil court; civil case.* See also *civil* ACTION, COMMITMENT, CONTEMPT, LIABILITY, PENALTY, PROCEDURE, PROSECUTION, under those words. Cf. CIVIL LAW.
**2.** secular; pertaining to law other than ecclesiastical or canon law, or to secular rather than religious matters: *They were married in a civil ceremony at the city hall.* See also CIVIL DISABILITY.
**3.** pertaining generally to the rights, duties, and status of people as members of society. See CIVIL RIGHTS, CIVIL DISOBEDIENCE.

**civil code** *n.* **1.** a CODE setting forth general laws of a civil, as distinguished from penal, nature, particularly laws regarding personal relationships and property rights.
**2. Civil Code** a specific civil code, especially the CODE NAPOLÉON or one based on it, such as the Civil Code of Louisiana.

**civil death** *n.* **1.** historically, the loss of all civil rights upon sentence of death or outlawry, including the right to contract, the right to sue, the right to inherit, even the right to legal protection; the state of being as good as dead so far as the law was concerned. See also ATTAINDER; OUTLAW.
**2.** in modern usage, the loss of certain civil rights, such as the right to vote, upon conviction of a felony or upon sentencing to life imprisonment. The rights lost and the nature of the crime or sentence that causes them to be lost vary from state to state. See also CRIMINAL DISENFRANCHISEMENT.
—**civilly dead** *adj.*

**civil disability** *n.* **1.** legal restriction of civil rights: *The civil disabilities of Roman Catholics under English law were removed by the Catholic Emancipation Act of 1829.*
**2.** a circumstance or condition barring marriage under legal principles that evolved in the civil law as distinguished from canon law, such as a pre-existing marriage or want of age on the part of one of the parties. Cf. CANONICAL DISABILITY.

**civil disobedience** *n.* open and nonviolent refusal to obey certain laws, and acceptance of punishment, for the purpose of influencing public opinion, legislation, or governmental policy.

**civil law** *n.* the prevailing system of law in continental Europe, derived from Roman law. In contrast to the traditional COMMON LAW system of England and America, the basic source of law in the civil law system is organized codes rather than case-by-case judicial decisions. In the United States, Louisiana stands out as the state whose law is most heavily influenced by civil law, because of its origins as a French territory. See also COMMUNITY PROPERTY; INQUISITORIAL SYSTEM; and note at CODE NAPOLÉON.

**civil lawyer** *n.* See CIVILIAN.

**civil liberties** *n.pl.* See under CIVIL RIGHTS.

**civil rights** *n.pl.* **1.** Also called **civil liberties.** governmentally recognized and legally protected rights and liberties of people in areas of personal autonomy, personal welfare, and participation in the political, business, and social life of the nation. In the United States, these include political and personal liberties protected by the Constitution (see FUNDAMENTAL RIGHT) and freedom from private and governmental discrimination on the basis of characteristics such as race, sex, religion, or disability.
**2.** more narrowly, the phrase "civil rights" is sometimes distinguished from "civil liberties," with the former phrase referring to freedom from discrimination, especially on the basis of race, and the latter referring to rights of personal autonomy and political expression and participation.

**civil union** *n.* in Vermont, a legally recognized relationship between members of the same sex having all the attributes of marriage for purposes of state law, but not constituting marriage for purposes of federal law or of the marriage laws of other states. Cf. DOMESTIC PARTNERSHIP; MARRIAGE; RECIPROCAL BENEFICIARY.

——**History.** On December 20, 1999, the Supreme Court of Vermont ruled that, under the state constitution, same-sex couples may not be denied the legal benefits and protections available to married couples under state law. *Baker v. State,* 744 A.2d 864 (Vt. 1999). The state legislature immediately went to work on the problem, and just four months later gave final approval to a comprehensive statute responding to the court's decision. Under this law, certificates of civil union are available to same-sex couples in the same way and under the same circumstances as certificates of marriage to opposite-sex couples, and confer upon the couples the same benefits, protections, and responsibilities as marriage for purposes of state law. Parties to a civil union are thus treated the same as spouses for such purposes as (1) property law, including the fact that they satisfy the requirement of *unity of person* (see under UNITY) for purposes of tenancy BY THE ENTIRETY; (2) causes of action related to marital status, such as WRONGFUL DEATH and *loss of consortium* (see CONSORTIUM[1]); (3) probate law; (4) adoption law; (5) insurance law and group insurance for state employees; (6) workers' compensation benefits; (7) spouse abuse programs; (8) laws prohibiting discrimination on the basis of marital status; (9) laws relating to hospital visitation and health care decision-making; (10) public assistance programs; (11) the MARITAL PRIVILEGE; and (12) state income tax laws, including any MARRIAGE BONUS or MARRIAGE PENALTY.

**civil war** *n.* See under WAR.

**Civil War amendments** *n.pl.* the Thirteenth, Fourteenth, and Fifteenth Amendments to the Constitution (see Appendix), adopted in the wake of the Civil War to bring a permanent end to slavery and extend basic rights of citizenship and equal treatment to people of color. Also called **Reconstruction amendments.**

——**History.** In the succeeding decades the Supreme Court substantially defeated the purpose of these amendments by construing them so narrowly that legally endorsed public and private discrimination were permitted to continue for almost a century after the Civil War, and became so entrenched that the nation is still struggling with the consequences. See SEPARATE BUT EQUAL and note at BLACK CODES.

**civilian** *n.* **1.** a person who is not on active duty with a military, naval, police, or fire fighting organization.
**2.** Also called **civil lawyer.** a person versed in Roman law or CIVIL LAW; a scholar, judge, or practitioner of civil law. Cf. COMMON LAWYER.

——**False Friend.** Even in the United States one occasionally encounters in legal writing a reference to one or another "great civilian," "eminent civilian," or the like. This is not a comment on the person's military record or lack thereof, but an acknowledgement of the person's influential role in expounding and advancing the civil law.

**claim** *n.* **1.** an assertion that one is entitled to something.
**2.** Also called **claim for relief.** in the federal courts and many states, an assertion of facts that, if true, would legally entitle the claimant to judgment in a civil case. A plaintiff's complaint must allege such facts or suffer dismissal for "failure to state a claim." See also CAUSE OF ACTION.
**3.** an apparent or actual right to receive something by way of a lawsuit: *The person injured in the automobile accident has a tort claim against the negligent driver.*

**claim adjuster** or **claims adjuster** *n.* See ADJUSTER.

**claim joinder** *n.* See under JOINDER.

**claim preclusion** *n.* Same as RES JUDICATA. Cf. *issue preclusion* (under ESTOPPEL).

**claimant** *n.* one who has a claim; one who asserts a claim.

**class** *n.* **1. a.** an identifiable group of people treated or affected differently from others by a regulation or statute. See also CLASSIFICATION. **b. suspect class** such a class identified by race, ethnicity, national origin, or alienage. Also called **protected class.** See also SUSPECT CLASSIFICATION; STRICT SCRUTINY.
**2.** a large group of persons having a common interest in the subject of a lawsuit, such as people who were all injured by the same product, who seek to participate collectively in a *class action* (see under ACTION).
**3.** a group named collectively in a will or instrument of gift, as when the testator leaves a certain sum of money to "my children" or "my heirs." See also *class gift* (under GIFT).
**4.** a category of stock or other security of an issuer, all shares of which have the same characteristics and carry the same rights. See SECURITY².

**class action** *n.* See under ACTION.

**classification** *n.* **1.** in a regulation or statute, a division of people into different classes subject to different legal treatment. This may occur intentionally and explicitly, as when a legislature decrees that only citizens (not aliens) shall receive certain benefits, or simply as a practical consequence of application of the law, as when a fee requirement effectively excludes the poor (but not the wealthy) from some opportunity. For the purpose of assessing the constitutionality of such laws under the EQUAL PROTECTION clause, the Supreme Court has created two special categories of classifications, known as SUSPECT CLASSIFICATION and QUASI-SUSPECT CLASSIFICATION.
**2.** in modern criminal codes, the categorizing of offenses according to severity, with a specified range of punishments for each class of offense.

**Clayton Act** *n.* a federal ANTITRUST law prohibiting a range of business activities that may substantially lessen competition, such as a corporate merger between two dominant companies in the same business whose effect would be to eliminate competition between them and enable them to use their combined strength against smaller competitors.

**CLE** CONTINUING LEGAL EDUCATION.

**clean bill of health** *n.* See under BILL OF HEALTH.

**clean bill of lading** *n.* See under BILL OF LADING.

**clean hands** *n.* the quality of having acted fairly and properly in a matter over which one is suing someone else. Cf. UNCLEAN HANDS; see also *clean hands doctrine* and *clean hands defense* (under UNCLEAN HANDS).

**clear and convincing evidence** *n.* an intermediate STANDARD OF PROOF, more stringent than PREPONDERANCE OF THE EVIDENCE but less than BEYOND A REASONABLE DOUBT. It requires that the factfinder be persuaded that the fact to be proved is highly probable. This standard is used in various types of noncriminal proceeding in which public policy requires an extra level of proof, such as a deportation hearing.

**clear and present danger** *n.* an imminent risk of harm of a type that the government may legitimately protect against; a phrase sometimes used to describe the circumstances under which the government may prohibit or punish SPEECH.

**clear title** *n.* Same as *marketable title* (see under TITLE).

**clearly erroneous** *adj.* indicating the STANDARD OF REVIEW by which a trial judge's findings of fact are normally tested in the appeal of a civil case that was tried without a jury. The appellate court may not reverse simply because it would have reached a different conclusion on the same evidence in a close case; but it may overturn a judge's findings if it regards them as "clearly erroneous," even if there is some evidence to support them. Cf. note at STANDARD OF REVIEW (describing the more deferential standard applicable to jury verdicts).

**clemency** *n.* the exercise by a president or governor of the power to grant an AMNESTY, PARDON, or REPRIEVE, or to

COMMUTE a sentence. Also called **executive clemency.**

**clergy** *n.* See BENEFIT OF CLERGY.

**clergy-communicant privilege** *n.* an *evidentiary privilege* (see under PRIVILEGE) protecting from disclosure confidential communications between an individual and the individual's spiritual advisor. Also called **clergyman-penitent privilege, priest-penitent privilege.**

**clergyman-penitent privilege** *n.* Same as CLERGY-COMMUNICANT PRIVILEGE.

**clerk** *n.* **1.** Also called **court clerk.** a court official charged with the overall administration of the court's operations or with some aspect of administration, particularly the processing and maintenance of court papers and records.
**2.** Also called **law clerk.** a recent law graduate employed as an assistant to a judge for one or two years.
**3.** *Chiefly Brit.* a member of the clergy; a cleric.
**4. articled clerk** *Brit.* in earlier times, an apprentice to an attorney, working as an assistant in return for the opportunity to learn the law.
—*v.* **5.** to serve as a law clerk.
—**clerkship** *n.*

**close¹** *v.,* **closed, closing,** *n.* —*v.* **1.** to consummate a negotiation or transaction. See also CLOSING.
**2.** to bring to an end; bring to a final status; wrap up: *case closed.*
—*n.* **3.** the act of closing.

**close²** *n.* **1.** an enclosed parcel of land, or the fence, wall, hedge, or the like enclosing it.
**2.** the invisible boundary around any otherwise unenclosed parcel of private property, which the law presumes to be "broken" if anyone sets foot on the land without permission or invitation. See *trespass quare clausum fregit* (under TRESPASS²).
——**Pronunciation.** The word *close* in this sense is not pronounced like the verb *close* (as in "close the door"), but rather like the adjective *close* (as in "a close call").

**close** (or **closely held**) **corporation** *n.* See under CORPORATION.

**closed corporation** *n.* See under CORPORATION.

**closed session** *n.* See under SESSION.

**closed shop** *n.* See under SHOP.

**closing** *n.* **1.** the completion of a transaction, especially a real estate transaction or major corporate transaction, usually at a meeting attended by counsel for all parties. A detailed written summary of the financial aspects of the transaction being closed is called a **closing statement.**
**2.** Also called **closing statement** or **closing argument.** a SUMMATION.

**closing costs** *n.pl.* fees and expenses associated with a purchase of real estate beyond the purchase price of the property, such as bank fees and legal fees, which must be paid at the closing.

**cloud on title** *n.* a claim with respect to land that casts doubt on the validity or completeness of the owner's title to the land. The legal mechanism for removing such a cloud is an action to QUIET TITLE.

**CLS** CRITICAL LEGAL STUDIES.

**COBRA** *n.* a federal statute providing that employees who were covered by a group health insurance plan at their place of work may continue that coverage for a specified period of time if their employer terminates them, provided that they pay the entire insurance premium themselves. "COBRA" is an acronym for **Consolidated Omnibus Budget Reconciliation Act of 1985.**

**co-conspirator** *n.* one of the persons who together have formed a CONSPIRACY. Also spelled **coconspirator.** Also called **conspirator.** See also UNINDICTED CO-CONSPIRATOR.
——**Usage.** *Co-conspirator* is more common than *coconspirator,* and is preferable because it makes the pronunciation more obvious. *Co-conspirator* is also more common than *conspirator,* but not for any particular reason. The words mean exactly the same thing and are equally acceptable.

**COD** COLLECT ON DELIVERY.

**code** *n.* **1.** an organized compilation of statutes or rules: CODE OF FEDERAL REGULATIONS; UNITED STATES CODE.
**2.** a coherent and comprehensive statute dealing with a major area of law: INTERNAL REVENUE CODE; UNIFORM COMMERCIAL CODE.

**Code Civil** *n.* See CODE NAPOLÉON.

**Code Napoléon** *n.* the CIVIL CODE of France, governing personal rights and relationships and property ownership and transfer. Also called (in French) **Code Civil,** (in English) **Civil Code, Napoleonic Code.**
——**History.** The *Code Civil* was the first of five legal codes (sometimes referred to collectively as the **Napoleonic Codes**) drawn up under Napoleon's guidance and enacted during the period 1803–1811. Although based in part upon Roman law, it represented a thorough rethinking of legal rights and relationships in the wake of the French Revolution and the overthrow of monarchy. It was hugely influential, spreading to other parts of Europe and Latin America at first through Napoleon's conquests in Europe, and later through voluntary adoption. It was a strong influence in the former French territory of Louisiana, which adopted its own civil code—which has been central to Louisiana law ever since—even though Louisiana had been purchased by the United States in 1803 and admitted as a state in 1812. Early in the twentieth century, Germany and Switzerland adopted substantially different civil codes that have competed with the Code Napoléon for influence; some other countries since then have adopted codes that take ideas from all three.

**Code of Federal Regulations (CFR)** *n.* The official compilation of rules and regulations of all agencies of the government of the United States.

**Code of Hammurabi** *n.* a collection of legal decisions by Hammurabi, king of Babylonia in the eighteenth century B.C., covering a wide range of civil and criminal matters. It is noted both for being the earliest written code of laws that still exists, and for being in many ways quite advanced in its legal thinking.

**codicil** *n.* an addition to or amendment of an existing will. To be valid it must be executed with all the formalities of a will.

**codify** *v.,* **codified, codifying. 1.** to enact a statute embodying a principle of common law or a particular judicial interpretation of the law.
**2.** to organize existing statutes or an existing body of law into a CODE.
—**codification** *n.*

**CODIS** COMBINED DNA INDEX SYSTEM.

**coercion** *n.* Same as DURESS.

**cognizable** *adj.* **1.** within the jurisdiction of a court; capable of being considered: *Divorce actions are not cognizable in federal court.*
**2.** describing a claim for which a court could provide relief: *Mere disagreement by a taxpayer with the way tax revenues are spent does not give rise to a cognizable claim.*

**cognovit** *n. Latin.* (lit. "he has recognized") an instrument containing a CONFESSION OF JUDGMENT. See also *cognovit note* (under NOTE[1]).

**cohabit** *v.* **1.** of unmarried couples, to live together in an intimate relationship similar to that of husband and wife. Viewed until recently as a crime or at least evidence of a crime (see FORNICATION), cohabitation has begun to emerge as a legally protected relationship (see PALIMONY). See also DOMESTIC PARTNERSHIP; CIVIL UNION; BIGAMY. Cf. *common law marriage* (under MARRIAGE).
**2.** of unrelated people generally, to live together. Zoning ordinances may restrict the number of unrelated people who can cohabit in single-family residential areas.
—**cohabitation** *n.*

**coinsurance** *n.* a form of insurance in which the insurance company pays only a certain percentage of any loss, the balance being paid by the policyholder personally or by other insurance

purchased by the policyholder; for example, medical insurance under which the insurer pays 80% of covered expenses and the policyholder pays 20%.
—**coinsurer** *n.*

**cold hit** *n. Informal.* identification of a suspect by scientific analysis of evidence from a crime when no suspect had been previously identified, as by DNA analysis of a semen stain. See also COMBINED DNA INDEX SYSTEM.

**collar** *Police Slang.* —*v.* **1.** to arrest.
—*n.* **2.** an arrest.
**3.** the person arrested.

**collateral¹** *n.* property in which someone has a *security interest* (see under INTEREST¹), especially property pledged as security for a loan (see PLEDGE).

**collateral²** *adj.* **1.** indirect; off to the side. Often used in contrast to DIRECT¹.
**2. collateral attack** an attack on a judgment or judicial proceeding that is made in a different proceeding. For example, if A obtains a default judgment against B in New York and then attempts to seize B's property in California to satisfy the judgment, B might attack the New York judgment in California on the ground that the New York court did not have jurisdiction over him. Cf. *direct attack* (under DIRECT¹).
**3. collateral estoppel** See under ESTOPPEL.
**4. collateral heir** an heir who is not a direct ancestor or descendant of the deceased, but is descended from a common ancestor; for example, a sister, cousin, uncle, or nephew. Cf. *direct heir* (under DIRECT¹).
**5. collateral source rule** the principle of tort law that compensation for an injured party from a source other than the tortfeasor (e.g., from the injured party's insurance company) does not reduce the amount that can be collected from the wrongdoer. See also SUBROGATE.

**collect on delivery (COD)** a form of mail delivery within the United States in which payment for merchandise can be collected by the postal carrier or post office at the time that the merchandise is delivered.

**collective bargaining** *n.* **1.** negotiation between an employer and a union representing employees with regard to wages and other conditions of employment.
**2. collective bargaining agreement** a contract between an employer and a union representing employees with regard to the terms and conditions of employment.

**collective bargaining unit** *n.* Same as BARGAINING UNIT.

**collective mark** *n.* **1.** a TRADEMARK or SERVICE MARK used by members of a group or organization to identify themselves or to identify and distinguish their products or services. For example, see REALTOR.
**2. collective membership mark** a collective mark used to indicate membership in a particular organization, such as a club or union.

**collective work** *n.* See under WORK.

**colloquium** *n., pl.* **colloquia, colloquiums. 1.** in a complaint for libel or slander, especially in traditional common law pleading, **a.** the allegation that the words complained of referred to the plaintiff. **b.** broadly, all introductory matter setting forth the context of the words and the fact that they were spoken of the plaintiff; the INDUCEMENT together with the colloquium proper. Cf. INNUENDO².
**2.** a conference at which scholars or other experts present papers on, analyze, and discuss a specific topic.

**colloquy** *n., pl.* **colloquies.** discussion among lawyers, or between the lawyers and the judge, in the course of a judicial proceeding.

**collude** *v.,* **colluded, colluding.** to engage in COLLUSION; to act together through a secret understanding, especially with harmful intent.
—**colluder** *n.*

**collusion** *n.* **1.** a secret agreement or understanding between two or more persons to act together, especially to gain or achieve something fraudulently or unlawfully.

**2.** in traditional divorce law, an agreement between a husband and wife that one of them will commit an act, or that they will make it appear that one of them has committed an act, constituting a ground for divorce, so that the other can obtain a divorce.

—**collusive** *adj.*

——**Note.** Under the traditional law of divorce still in effect in some states, collusion—evidence of a mutual conviction that the parties would be better off apart and a shared desire to end the marriage—is a bar to divorce. See also CONNIVANCE; RECRIMINATION.

**collusive suit** *n.* See under SUIT.

**color** *n.* **1.** appearance; especially, appearance without reality: *color of authority; color of title.* See also UNDER COLOR OF LAW.
**2.** skin complexion. Constitutional provisions and civil rights statutes prohibiting discrimination on the basis of RACE customarily add "color" as well, to eliminate legalistic arguments over the exact basis upon which someone is wrongfully discriminating.

**color of law** *n.* See UNDER COLOR OF LAW.

**colorable** *adj.* **1.** superficially, and perhaps actually, valid; possibly valid.
**2.** seemingly, but not actually, valid or authentic; deceptive.

**combat zone** *n.* See under ZONE.

**Combined DNA Index System (CODIS)** *n.* a national computerized database of *DNA profiles* (see under DNA PROFILING) maintained by the Federal Bureau of Investigation. A federal statute enacted in 1994 authorizes the FBI to establish DNA indexes for persons convicted of crimes, samples recovered from crime scenes, and unidentified human remains. See also COLD HIT.

**comfort letter** *n.* a letter giving reassurance on some point relevant to a proposed transaction.
——**Note.** Comfort letters typically come into being because one party to a proposed transaction demands that the other party provide such a letter—often from a third party—before closing on the deal. For example, a party might insist on receiving an attorney's letter expressing a legal opinion that the transaction will qualify for certain tax benefits, or a letter from the other party's accountant stating that although the party's most recent financial statements have not been audited, the accountant is not aware of any facts that would require them to be changed. A comfort letter is usually not a guarantee, but could give rise to a cause of action if fraudulently or negligently prepared.

**comitatus** *n., pl.* **comitatus.** *Latin.* county. See POSSE COMITATUS.

**comity** *n.* the principle under which the courts of one jurisdiction will recognize and defer to the decisions, proceedings, and laws of another jurisdiction, not out of obligation but out of mutual respect. For example, American courts will ordinarily extend comity to a decision of a court in another country if it is convinced that the procedures in the other country were fundamentally fair. Cf. FULL FAITH AND CREDIT.

**comment** *n.* an article, usually written by a student and published in a law review, analyzing a particular judicial decision and placing it in a larger legal context. Sometimes called an **annotation.** Cf. NOTE[2].

**commerce** *n.* trade, business, and travel, especially across state lines **(interstate commerce)** or between the United States and other countries **(foreign commerce).** The powerlessness of America's new national government to prevent trade wars between the states following independence from Britain was a principal motivating factor behind the adoption of the Constitution, with a clause (the **Commerce Clause**) giving Congress the power to regulate interstate and foreign commerce (the **commerce power**). This power forged the United States into a powerful economic unit and has also enabled Congress to adopt laws in such diverse fields as guaranteeing civil rights, protecting the environment, and attacking organized crime, since these are matters seen as affecting interstate commerce.

**commercial bribery** *n.* See under BRIBERY.

**commercial frustration** *n.* See FRUSTRATION.

**commercial impracticability** *n.* See IMPRACTICABILITY.

**commercial name** *n.* Same as TRADE NAME.

**commercial paper** *n.* NEGOTIABLE INSTRUMENTS, especially short-term promissory notes (see NOTE[1]) issued by corporations to investors and traded among investors as securities. Also called **paper.**

**commercial speech** *n.* See under SPEECH.

**commission** *n.* **1.** formal written authority to hold an appointive office or perform delegated duties. For example, officers appointed by the President of the United States must receive a commission before they can act.
**2.** compensation for services rendered in facilitating a transaction, or for acting as a trustee, executor, or the like, calculated as a percentage of the value of the transaction or of the property involved. See also KICKBACK.
**3.** the act of committing a crime.
**4.** a name sometimes given to an administrative agency: *Interstate Commerce Commission.*
**—***v.* **5.** to authorize; give a commission to.

**commission of gaol delivery** or **commission of jail delivery** *n.* See under JAIL DELIVERY.

**commission of general gaol delivery** or **commission of general jail delivery** *n.* See under JAIL DELIVERY.

**commission of oyer and terminer** *n.* See under OYER AND TERMINER.

**commissive waste** *n.* See under WASTE.

**commit** *v.,* **committed, committing.**

**1.** to do something wrong: *The witness committed perjury. The judge committed error by admitting hearsay testimony.*
**2.** to place a person in a prison, hospital, or other institution, especially by court order.
**—commitable** *adj.*
**——Usage.** For sense 1, the noun form is COMMISSION; for sense 2, the noun form is COMMITMENT.

**commitment 1.** imprisonment or institutionalization of a person, especially by order of a court.
**2. civil commitment a.** commitment of a person to a mental hospital or other treatment facility upon a court's finding that the person poses a danger to himself or others. **b.** the jailing of a person for *civil contempt* (see under CONTEMPT) to induce compliance with a court order.
**3. voluntary commitment** commitment to a treatment facility upon the request or with the consent of the person in need of care.

**commitment fee** *n.* a fee paid to a bank or other entity that has offered to make a loan upon certain terms, particularly at a certain interest rate, to keep the offer open upon the same terms for a specified period of time.

**committee** *n.* **1.** a small group of members of a larger organization, established to carry out specific duties delegated ("committed") to it by the organization. Virtually all bills in Congress or a state legislature are considered by a committee before being voted on by the entire legislative body.
**2.** the word used in some states for a GUARDIAN of an incompetent adult (the person into whose care the incompetent is committed). See also CONSERVATOR.

**common** *n.* **1.** Also, **right of common.** the right or liberty, in common with other persons, to take profit from the land or waters of another, as by pasturing animals on another's land **(common of pasturage)** or fishing in another's waters **(common of piscary).**
**2.** Also, **commons.** (*used with a sing. v.*) **a.** a tract of land in which people other than the owner have a right of

common. **b.** a tract of land owned and used jointly by the residents of a community, as for a common pasturage or a town square.

See also IN COMMON.

**common assumpsit** *n.* See under AS-SUMPSIT.

**common carrier** *n.* a company in the business of transporting people or goods, or sometimes messages or information, and offering this service to the public at large.

**common counts** *n.pl.* in old common law pleading, a set of standard allegations pleaded in actions of ASSUMPSIT to recover money due.

——**Note.** The function of the common counts was to guard against defeat of a just claim because of some minor variance of the evidence from the theory of the case put forth in the complaint. The common counts recited, in a general and formulaic manner without any reference to the specific facts of the case, the elements of the different legal theories that might apply to such a case; typically, these were INDEBITATUS AS-SUMPSIT, QUANTUM MERUIT, QUANTUM VALEBAT or QUANTUM VALEBANT, and ACCOUNT STATED.

**common defense rule** *n.* Same as JOINT DEFENSE PRIVILEGE.

**common interest rule** *n.* Same as JOINT DEFENSE PRIVILEGE.

**common law** *n.* **1.** the legal system that evolved over many centuries in England and is the foundation of law in Great Britain and many of its former possessions, including the United States. In contrast to the CIVIL LAW system of continental Europe, the basic source of common law is judicial decisions rather than codes, with judges seeking in each new case to adapt the principles worked out in previous cases to new facts and circumstances in such a way as to achieve justice. See also ADVERSARY SYSTEM.
**2.** judge-made law, as distinguished from STATUTORY law. Although large areas of earlier common law have now been codified, including criminal law and commercial law, there remain other large areas, notably tort law, contract law, and property law, that are still predominantly governed by common law rather than statutes. See also *common law crime* (under CRIME).
**3.** Often simply **law.** legal principles that originated in the procedures and decisions of England's law courts (see LAW, def. 4) as distinguished from its courts of EQUITY: *Damages are a common law remedy* (or *remedy at law*), *whereas the injunction is a form of equitable relief.* See also AT, AT LAW; MERGER OF LAW AND EQUITY.
**4.** all of the law of England at the time when America achieved its independence. That law, whether judge-made or statutory, was generally regarded as the common law of the United States after independence.
**5. federal common law** law made by federal court judges with respect to subjects of uniquely federal concern under the Constitution, such as admiralty law and law pertaining to rights of action under the Constitution. With respect to matters of general law traditionally regulated by the states, such as torts and contracts, the federal courts may not develop a uniform national body of common law, but instead must follow state law. See also FEDERAL LAW.
—*adj.* **6.** Also, **common-law.** pertaining to or arising under the common law.

——**Usage.** When the phrase *common law* is used as a modifier (*common law action; common law doctrine*) it is often hyphenated (*common-law action; common-law doctrine*). This is actually clearer since it cannot be misread as referring to a common type of "law action," "law doctrine," or the like, and is especially desirable in writing intended for nonlawyers. In writing intended for lawyers—among whom the phrase "common law" is so familiar that it is normally read as a unit anyway—the more common practice is to omit the hyphen except in particularly unusual or confusing phrases, such as *common-law lawyer.* See also note at COMMON LAWYER.

**common law action** *n.* See under AC-TION.

**common law crime** *n.* See under CRIME.

**common law lawyer** or **common-law lawyer** *n.* Same as COMMON LAWYER.

**common law marriage** *n.* See under MARRIAGE.

**common law state** *n.* a state whose system of rules for ownership of property within marriage is derived from English common law; any state except a COMMUNITY PROPERTY STATE. The basic principle of property ownership in a common law state is that each spouse is viewed as an individual with the right to control his or her own income or property. This principle is subject to many qualifications, however, such as the right of a surviving spouse to an ELECTIVE SHARE of the decedent's estate, and in most states the right of a divorcing spouse to EQUITABLE DISTRIBUTION of marital property. Also called **common law property state, separate property state.**

**common lawyer** *n.* a person versed in the common law; specifically, **a.** a scholar, judge, or practitioner of law in the English tradition as distinguished from the CIVIL LAW. See COMMON LAW (def. 1); cf. CIVILIAN. **b.** within the English tradition itself, a scholar, judge, or practitioner of law (see LAW, def. 4) as distinguished from EQUITY or ECCLESIASTICAL LAW. See COMMON LAW (def. 3). Also called **common law lawyer** or **common-law lawyer.**
——**False Friend.** When a legal writer refers to someone as a *common lawyer,* it is usually for the purpose of emphasizing the person's *un*common expertise and influence in the law. In fact, as often as not the term appears as part of a three-word phrase beginning with "eminent," "able," "distinguished," "great," or the like. Perhaps out of insecurity over the possibility that *common lawyer* could be misunderstood as meaning "run-of-the-mill lawyer," some writers use the phrase *common law lawyer* instead; and because that can also be misread, they often clarify the phrase by writing it as *common-law*

*lawyer.* But secure writers use the term that has been in use since at least the sixteenth century, and that the greats who developed the foundations of our current legal system would have applied to themselves: *common lawyer.*

**common stock** *n.* See under STOCK.

**communication** *n.* **1.** the imparting, interchange, or transmission of information, thoughts, or opinions by any means, as by speech, writing, gestures, or electronic transfer of data.
**2.** that which is imparted or transmitted in a communication.
**3.** the act or process of imparting or transmitting information, thoughts, or opinions.
See also PRIVILEGED COMMUNICATION; UNPRIVILEGED COMMUNICATION.

**community** *n., pl.* **communities. 1.** the people living in a locality, as a village or town and its environs.
**2.** a group of people sharing a cultural, ethnic, religious, or other interest or identification.
**3.** a group of nations united to pursue common goals, especially in trade and economic matters.
**4.** Also called **marital community.** in community property states, a married couple viewed as a unit in relation to its community property.

**community notification law** *n.* a state law providing for continued registration and monitoring of the whereabouts of sexual offenders after they have served their sentences, and official notification of police or residents of any community where they take up residence. Often referred to as MEGAN'S LAW.

**community of acquests** (or **aquets**) **and gains** *n.* See under ACQUEST and ACQUET.

**community of interest** *n.* a shared interest or similarity of position among a group of people with respect to a matter, justifying treating them as a single class for some legal purpose, as for a *class action* (see under ACTION).

**community property** *n.* **1.** a system of property ownership and distribution for married couples, derived from Spanish civil law and followed in California and a few other states, mostly in the West and Southwest. (See COMMUNITY PROPERTY STATE.)

**2.** in a community property state, any income or property obtained by either spouse during a marriage other than by gift or inheritance. All such property is deemed to belong to the *marital community* (see under COMMUNITY); each spouse has an undivided one-half interest in the property. Each spouse may distribute half of the community property by will; in the event of divorce, the community property is divided either equitably (in certain community property states) or equally (in certain community property states, including California).

See also *community of acquests and gains* (under ACQUEST); *community of acquets and gains* (see under ACQUET); EQUITABLE DISTRIBUTION; MARITAL PROPERTY. Cf. BY THE ENTIRETY; SEPARATE PROPERTY.

**community property state** *n.* a state that adheres to the COMMUNITY PROPERTY system of property ownership and distribution for married couples. There are nine such states: Arizona, California, Idaho, Louisiana, Nevada, New Mexico, Texas, Washington, and Wisconsin. Cf. COMMON LAW STATE.

**commutative justice** *n.* See under JUSTICE[1].

**commute** *v.,* **commuted, commuting.** to reduce a convicted criminal's sentence by executive action: *The governor commuted the death sentence to life imprisonment.* Cf. PARDON, REPRIEVE. See also CLEMENCY.
—**commutable** *adj.*
—**commutability** *n.*
—**commutation** *n.*

**compact** *n.* a contract or treaty, especially an agreement between two states **(interstate compact)** to resolve a dispute or cooperate in a matter of mutual concern.

**companion case** *n.* See under CASE[1].

**company** *n., pl.* **companies. 1.** a business enterprise, especially one owned or carried on by a group of people; an association, partnership, or corporation. **2. holding company** a company, usually a corporation, formed to hold stock in other companies, and often to control those other companies through ownership of large amounts of their stock. **3. joint stock company** an unincorporated company with ownership interests represented by shares of stock, in which owners share the profits in proportion to their holdings of stock but, unlike corporate stockholders, are personally liable to the company's creditors if the company's assets prove insufficient to pay its debts. Also called **stock association** or **joint stock association**.

See also PARENT COMPANY.

**comparative negligence** *n.* See under NEGLIGENCE.

**compelling interest** *n.* an extremely important governmental interest, important enough to justify a law that limits a FUNDAMENTAL RIGHT or treats people differently on the basis of a SUSPECT CLASSIFICATION. Also called **compelling governmental interest** or, in the case of a state law, **compelling state interest.**

**compensating use tax** *n.* Same as USE TAX.

**compensation** *n.* **1.** payment for services rendered. See also DEFERRED COMPENSATION.
**2.** payment for injury or loss sustained. See also *compensatory damages* (under DAMAGES); JUST COMPENSATION.
—**compensate** *v.,* **compensated, compensating.**
—**compensatory** *adj.*

**competent**[1] *adj.* possessing sufficient mental capacity to make rational decisions about a legal matter and understand the consequences, so that the law will permit one to proceed and will give legal effect to one's actions: *competent to make a will; competent to stand trial; competent to act as one's own lawyer.*
—**competency;** occasionally, **competence** *n.*

**competent²** *adj.* **1.** (of a person) possessing the legal or other qualifications necessary to perform a task. For example, to be competent to serve as a witness to the execution of a will one must ordinarily be over a certain age and not a beneficiary under the will.
**2.** (of a court or other official body) possessing jurisdiction or authority to deal with a matter. Such a court is often referred to as a "court of competent jurisdiction."
**3.** (of evidence or of a witness in a proceeding) admissible, or possessing information that would be admissible. A person whose only knowledge about an issue is hearsay would ordinarily not be competent to testify on that issue.
—**competence;** (for defs. 1, 3) sometimes **competency** *n.*

**competent evidence** *n.* See under EVIDENCE.

**compilation** *n.* (in copyright law) a work, such as a *collective work* (see under WORK), formed by collecting and assembling preexisting materials or by collecting, coordinating, or arranging data in such a way that the resulting work as a whole constitutes an original work of authorship.

**complain** *v.* to make a complaint.

**complainant** *n.* **1.** one who makes a complaint.
**2.** especially, the person who signs and swears to a *criminal complaint* (see under COMPLAINT).

**complaining witness** *n.* See under WITNESS.

**complaint** *n.* **1.** the initial PLEADING in a civil case, in which the plaintiff states the facts that she contends entitle her to relief and states what relief she seeks. See also *third-party complaint* (under THIRD-PARTY ACTION); *verified complaint* (under VERIFY); WELL-PLEADED COMPLAINT.
**2.** Also called **criminal complaint.** the initial instrument charging a person with a crime, sworn to by a witness or police officer—the COMPLAINANT or *complaining witness* (see under WITNESS)—and describing the alleged crime.

**completed contract method** *n.* See under ACCOUNTING METHOD.

**completely integrated contract** *n.* See under INTEGRATED CONTRACT.

**compos mentis** *adj. Latin.* (lit. "in possession of the mind") sane; competent; in full possession of one's mental faculties. Sometimes shortened to **compos.**

**compose** *v.,* **composed, composing. 1.** to settle; adjust; agree to a settlement of (a dispute or the like).
**2.** especially, to settle a debt through a *composition with creditors* (see under COMPOSITION): *He composed his debts.*

**composition** *n.* **1.** the settlement of a claim or dispute.
**2. composition with creditors** an agreement among a debtor and her creditors that each creditor will take less than the full amount owed so that the debtor will be able to pay at least some portion of the amount due to each creditor.

**compound** *v.* **1.** to agree, for a consideration, not to prosecute or punish a wrongdoer for a crime. See COMPOUNDING A CRIME.
**2.** in older usage, to settle a debt or claim by compromise; to reach a settlement.

**compound question** *n.* See under QUESTION¹.

**compounding a crime** the offense of accepting something of value from a person known to have committed a crime, and agreeing in return not to report or prosecute the crime. If the crime in question is a felony, this offense is also called **compounding a felony**. In some states an exception is made for victims who agree not to prosecute if the criminal restores what was taken or compensates them for their injury or loss. Cf. MISPRISION OF FELONY.

**compromis** *n., pl.* **compromis.** *French.* (lit. "compromise") *International Law.* a formal document, executed in common by nations submitting a dispute to arbitration, that defines the matter at issue, the rules of procedure and the powers of the arbitral tribunal, and the principles for determining the award.

**compromise** *n., v.,* **compromised, compromising.** —*n.* **1.** a settlement of differences by mutual concessions; an agreement to resolve conflicting or opposing claims, principles, etc., by reciprocal modification of demands. —*v.* **2.** to settle by compromise; to make a compromise.

**compromise verdict** *n.* See under VERDICT.

**compulsory arbitration** *n.* See under ARBITRATION.

**compulsory bar** *n.* See under BAR².

**compulsory counterclaim** See under COUNTERCLAIM.

**compulsory joinder** *n.* See under JOINDER.

**computer crime** *n.* **1.** a crime directed at computer equipment or a computer network; for example, intentionally spreading a computer virus. **2.** a crime directed at computerized data or software; for example, breaking into a computerized database to steal proprietary information. **3.** the use of a computer in carrying out or attempting to carry out a crime; for example, using the Internet to promote a phony charity or to lure a child into an illegal sexual encounter. **4.** general criminality of any of the foregoing types: *The Attorney General sought increased funding to combat computer crime.* Also called **cybercrime.** —**computer criminal** *n.*

**computer fraud** *n.* **1.** fraud carried out through the use of computers, especially over the Internet. **2.** the crime of accessing or attempting to access a computer without authorization in order to use it or obtain information from it for fraudulent purposes. **3.** the crime of trafficking in computer passwords or similar information for use in accessing computers without authorization for fraudulent purposes. Also called **cyberfraud.**

**Comstock Law** *n.* **1.** Also called **Comstock Act. a.** the 1873 act of Congress banning the importation, mailing, or distribution in any territory under federal jurisdiction of any obscene or immoral writing or device, including any drug or article for prevention of pregnancy or causing abortion. **b.** any of the modern federal obscenity statutes descended from that act. **2.** a state statute modeled on, or descended from one modeled on, the federal Comstock Law. —**Note.** Anthony Comstock, 1844-1915, had an enormous influence on American social and legal history. Working with the Young Men's Christian Association and his own New York Society for the Suppression of Vice, he lobbied for passage of the first federal anti-obscenity statute—the 1873 "Act for the Suppression of Trade in, and Circulation of, obscene Literature and Articles of immoral Use"—and a tide of similar state statutes banning obscenity, contraception, and abortion. He had himself appointed as a special agent of the United States Post Office so that he could spend his time ferreting out obscene materials and immoral articles to prosecute, and worked at that task, mostly as an unpaid volunteer, until his death more than forty years later. The Comstock laws have proved extremely durable, and have provided generations of business for the courts—sometimes enforcing them, sometimes finding aspects of them unconstitutional.

**Comstockery** *n.* endorsement or enforcement of censorship in regard to sexual expression; moralistic repressiveness.

**con game** *n. Slang.* Same as CONFIDENCE GAME.

**concealed carry** *n.* the carrying of a concealed handgun.

**concealed carry law** *n.* a state statute permitting private individuals to carry loaded handguns concealed on their persons; especially a law that permits such conduct by anyone who is not specifically disqualified by reason of prior criminal record or the like, without a showing on the part of the individual of any particular need to go about armed.

**concealed carry permit** *n.* a permit issued by a state to an individual authorizing the individual to carry a concealed loaded handgun.

**concealed weapon** *n.* See under WEAPON.

**conceptualism** *n.* Same as FORMALISM.
—**conceptualist** *n.*
—**conceptualistic** *adj.*
—**conceptualistically** *adv.*

**conciliation** *n.* **1.** restoration of harmony between adversaries or persons who have had a disagreement, especially with the assistance of a third party.
**2.** a form of ALTERNATIVE DISPUTE RESOLUTION or labor negotiation in which a third party (**conciliator**) assists the disputing parties in reaching a compromise. Sometimes interchangeable with MEDIATION, but sometimes distinguished from mediation in that a mediator might take a more active role than a conciliator in the process of working out a compromise, and a conciliator might not be a neutral party, but rather just a party who wants to see the dispute ended.
**3.** in matrimonial cases, a process in which a third party attempts to help a husband and wife resolve their differences so that they can stay married. In this context, conciliation is quite distinct from mediation, in which a third party attempts to help the spouses reach a mutually agreeable divorce settlement.
—**conciliate** *v.,* **conciliated, conciliating.**
—**conciliatorily** *adv.*
—**conciliatory, conciliative** *adj.*

**conclusion of law** *n.* in a nonjury trial, a judge's decision on a legal issue (e.g., whether the court has jurisdiction or which state's law applies to the case) or conclusion based upon the application of law to the facts (e.g., that the defendant is or is not liable for negligence). Also called **finding of law.**

Cf. FINDING OF FACT; see also FINDINGS OF FACT AND CONCLUSIONS OF LAW.

**conclusive presumption** *n.* See under PRESUMPTION.

**conclusory** *adj.* stating a conclusion without supporting facts: *a conclusory allegation; a conclusory affidavit.*

**concur** *v.,* **concurred, concurring. 1.** (of one or more judges on a panel) to agree with the decision being made by the court; to agree with the conclusion, though not necessarily with all of the reasoning, of the majority or plurality opinion.
**2. concurring in the result** or **concurring in the judgment** a phrase used to emphasize that a particular judge on a panel agrees with the outcome in a case but in no way endorses the reasoning in the majority or plurality opinion.
See also *concurring opinion* (under OPINION).
—**concurrence** *n.*

**concurrent** *adj.* **1.** occurring or existing simultaneously: *concurrent jurisdiction* (see under JURISDICTION[1]); *concurrent sentences* (see under SENTENCE).
**2.** acting together: *concurrent causes; concurrent tortfeasors.*
—**concurrently** *adv.*

**condemn** *v.* **1.** to take property for public use; exercise the power of EMINENT DOMAIN.
**2.** to order something destroyed because it is illegal or poses a hazard to the public.
**3.** to adjudge a person guilty or impose sentence, especially a very severe sentence such as death or life imprisonment.
—**condemnable** *adj.*
—**condemnation** *n.*

**condemnee** *n.* **1.** one whose property is condemned; one whose property is subject to being taken by eminent domain.
**2.** one who claims an interest in property that is being condemned.

**condemnor** or **condemner** *n.* **1.** the governmental instrumentality that has condemned certain property.

**2.** a governmental instrumentality with the power to condemn property.

**condition** *n.* **1.** a circumstance upon which something else is contingent.
**2.** especially, a future event which is possible but not certain, upon the occurrence of which a right, interest, or obligation under a contract, deed, will, or other instrument is made to depend.
**3. condition precedent** (pronounced preSEEdent), a condition that must occur in order for such a right, interest, or obligation to arise.
**4. condition subsequent** a condition whose occurrence extinguishes such a right, interest, or obligation.

**condition of bail** *n.* See under BAIL¹.

**conditional** *adj.* imposing, containing, subject to, or depending on a condition or conditions; not absolute; made or allowed on certain terms: *conditional acceptance.*
—**conditionality** *n.*
—**conditionally** *adv.*

**conditional fee** *n.* Same as **fee simple defeasible** (see under FEE¹).

**conditional privilege** *n.* See under PRIVILEGE.

**conditional sale** *n.* See under SALE.

**condominium** *n.* a form of ownership of real property in which several owners each own a separate residential or commercial unit within the property and all of them together own the common areas, such as lobbies and recreational areas, as tenants in common. Cf. COOPERATIVE (def. 2).

**condonation** *n.* **1.** forgiveness, overlooking, or tacit approval of another's illegal or objectionable behavior.
**2.** in traditional divorce law, behavior by a spouse indicating that conduct by the other spouse that could have been a ground for divorce has been forgiven; especially, a resumption or continuation of sexual relations despite knowledge of the conduct constituting a ground for divorce.
—**condonable** *adj.*
—**condone** *v.,* **condoned, condoning.**
—**condonee** *n.*
—**condoner** *n.*

—**Note.** Under the traditional divorce law still in effect in some states, condonation is an affirmative defense to an action for divorce if the ground upon which the action is based is the conduct that was "condoned." The condonation is voided, however, if the conduct is repeated after the condonation, or if the spouse whose wrongful conduct was purportedly forgiven (the "condonee") thereafter fails to treat the condoning spouse with "conjugal kindness." Cf. CONNIVANCE.

**confession** *n.* **1.** a statement admitting that one has committed a crime.
**2. involuntary confession a.** narrowly, a confession obtained by physical or psychological coercion. **b.** broadly, a confession obtained by such coercion or in violation of the MIRANDA RULE. A confession that is involuntary in this broad sense may not be used in a criminal case against the person who makes it.
**3. voluntary confession** a confession that is not involuntary.

**confession of judgment** *n.* an acknowledgment by a defendant that the plaintiff is right and that judgment should be entered in favor of the plaintiff. See also COGNOVIT.
—**Note.** Transactions in which a party is required to provide such a confession of judgment in advance, so that in the event of any default by that party the other one can go straight into court and get a judgment without allowing any opportunity for presentation of a defense, are restricted or prohibited in many states. For an example, see *cognovit note* (under NOTE¹).

**confidence game** *n.* any swindle in which the swindler, after gaining the confidence of the victim, robs the victim by cheating at a gambling game, appropriating funds entrusted for investment, or the like. Also called **con game.** See also STING.

**confidentiality stipulation** *n.* a STIPULATION by the parties in a case, usually SO ORDERED by the judge (turning it into a **confidentiality order**), that information obtained during pretrial discovery, or the terms of a settlement, will be kept confidential. Sometimes the purpose is to protect legitimate confidential information, such as trade secrets or employee medical records; sometimes it is simply to prevent public access to damaging information that might assist other injured parties in seeking justice.

**confirmation** *n.* an action, declaration, or document confirming something. Examples include: **a.** the action of the United States Senate in consenting to a presidential appointment. See also AD-VICE AND CONSENT. **b.** the conveyance of an interest in real property to one who already has or claims an interest under a previous conveyance, having the effect of curing a defect in the previous conveyance or enlarging or making permanent the interest previously conveyed; especially, a conveyance that makes a voidable estate no longer voidable. The deed by which this is accomplished is called a **deed of confirmation**. **c.** an undertaking, usually by a bank, to honor a LETTER OF CREDIT issued by someone else, and then look to the issuer for reimbursement. **d.** in civil law and Louisiana law, an act or declaration by one who entered into a voidable contract making it not voidable; for example, a person who was too young to enter into an enforceable contract when the contract was signed can confirm it after reaching the age of majority. This is an aspect of what the common law more often calls RATIFICATION. —**confirm** *v.*
—**confirmable** *adj.*

**confirmee** *n.* **1.** one to whom a confirmation is made.
**2.** especially, the recipient of a *deed of confirmation* (see under CONFIRMA-TION).

**confirmer** *n.* one who confirms anything; one who makes a CONFIRMA-TION. Cf. CONFIRMOR.

**confirmor** *n.* one who conveys property, or confirms a conveyance of property, by *deed of confirmation* (see under CONFIRMATION).
—**Usage.** The *-or* spelling of this word has occasionally been used to refer to the maker of a formal confirmation in other legal contexts, particularly to distinguish the giver of a confirmation from the CONFIRMEE. Except in reference to real estate, however, this is extremely rare; the usual spelling in both legal and nonlegal contexts is CONFIR-MER.

**conflict of interest** *n.* **1.** a situation in which one has both a personal interest in a matter and some duty to another, or to the general public, with respect to that same matter, so that one's personal interest could potentially influence the way one carries out the duty. For example, a judge presiding over a suit against a company in which she owns stock, or an office manager asked to hire the best candidate for a position for which his brother is one of the applicants, would have a conflict of interest.
**2.** a situation in which one owes duties to two different people whose interests in a matter may not be compatible, as when an attorney undertakes to represent two different defendants in the same case, or both the husband and the wife in an uncontested divorce. The law tolerates some conflicts of interest if the interested parties are informed of them and have no objection; in other situations, the law requires a person with a conflict of interest to withdraw from the matter.

**conflict of laws** *n.* the field of law that deals with the problems arising from application of the laws of different states or countries to events and transactions affecting two or more jurisdictions. These problems include CHOICE OF LAW and the question whether a judgment rendered in one jurisdiction will be recognized in another. See also COMITY; FULL FAITH AND CREDIT.
—**Note.** In most countries conflict of

laws is primarily a branch of INTERNA-
TIONAL LAW, but because law in the
United States is a patchwork of more
than fifty independent legal systems,
conflict-of-laws problems pervade all
areas of American law. See also FEDER-
ALISM; OUR FEDERALISM; UNIFORM
LAWS.

**conformed copy** *n.* a copy of a document on which changes or insertions
have been made to make it an accurate
copy of the original. When a proposed
order is submitted to a judge, the judge
typically writes in various changes before signing it; then the party who submitted it "conforms" a copy of the proposed order by copying in the judge's
changes and writing the judge's name
on the signature line, and serves that
conformed copy on the person to
whom the order is directed. The original piece of paper signed by the judge
stays on file with the court. See also
/s/.

**conforming use** *n.* See under USE.

**confrontation** *n.* the right of a criminal defendant, under the Sixth Amendment (see Appendix), to be confronted
in open court by the witnesses against
him so that they can be cross-examined
and the jury can evaluate their demeanor. The Supreme Court has held,
however, that a child may be permitted
to testify by closed circuit television
upon a finding that face-to-face confrontation with an alleged abuser would
cause the child serious emotional distress.

**congressional intent** *n.* See under
LEGISLATIVE INTENT.

**conjugal** *adj.* relating to or characteristic of marriage; pertaining to the relation of husband and wife.

**conjugal rights** *n.pl. Informal.* the
rights and privileges conferred on a
husband and wife by marriage; the
privilege a husband and wife enjoy of
having each other's company, and particularly the privilege of engaging in
sexual intercourse.
——**Usage.** Although in many states it is
still true that only married people have
a right to engage in sexual intercourse

(see FORNICATION), the phrase *conjugal
rights* is seldom used in the sense of an
actual legally protected or legally enforceable right. In particular, it never
represents a right of one spouse as
against the other. In England it was formerly possible to bring an action for
"restitution of conjugal rights" against a
spouse who had taken up separate residence without sufficient reason, but
this remedy was never adopted in the
United States: One cannot "insist on his
conjugal rights"; one cannot seek a
court order compelling a spouse to provide companionship, sexual or otherwise. As to rights against third parties,
see ALIENATION OF AFFECTIONS; CON-
SORTIUM.

**conjugal visit** *n.* a visit by one spouse
to another who is institutionalized, as
in a prison or mental health facility,
during which the couple is provided
time and privacy for sexual relations;
usually, an overnight visit.
——**conjugal visitation** *n.*
——**conjugal visitor** *n.*

**connect up** *v.* to introduce evidence
showing that previously offered evidence was admissible. A judge may
permit evidence to be presented to a
jury "subject to connection" or "subject
to connecting up"; if the necessary connection to the case is never shown, the
jury will be instructed to disregard that
evidence.

**connivance** *n.* **1.** tacit encouragement
or assent to the wrongdoing of another.
**2.** in traditional divorce law, the consent of a spouse to conduct by the
other spouse that constitutes a ground
for divorce, especially adultery.
——**connive** *v.,* **connived, conniving.**
——**conniver** *n.*
——**connivery** *n.*
——**connivingly** *adv.*
——**Note.** Connivance differs from CON-
DONATION in that the conniving spouse
knows of the other's conduct in advance or as it is occurring, but either
passively acquiesces or actively con-
trives to bring it about so as to have a
ground for divorce. Under traditional
laws still in effect in some states, the

plaintiff's connivance in conduct constituting a ground for divorce may be raised as a defense to a suit for divorce upon that ground. See also COLLUSION; RECRIMINATION.

**consanguinity** *n.* **1.** relationship by descent from a common ancestor; blood relationship. Cf. AFFINITY.
**2.** blood relationship within a legally specified degree; a sufficiently close blood relationship to bar marriage or fall within laws relating to incest. See also DEGREE OF CONSANGUINITY.
—**consanguineous** *adj.*
—**consanguineously** *adv.*

**conscientious objector** *n.* **1.** a person whose religion or sincere personal belief system forbids participation as a combatant in any war. By statute, conscientious objectors may provide an alternative form of service to the country if drafted in time of war.
**2. selective conscientious objector** a person opposed not to all wars, but only to those he regards as unjust. The law does not give such a person the status of a conscientious objector.

**conscious parallelism** *n.* parallel conduct by two or more competitors in an industry, not pursuant to explicit agreement but each acting with knowledge of the others' actions and without an independent motive to act, having an anticompetitive effect. Conscious parallelism is evidence of a tacit agreement among the participants, and may violate ANTITRUST laws.
—**consciously parallel** *adj.*

**consecutive sentences** *n.* See under SENTENCE.

**consensual sodomy** *n.* See under SODOMY.

**consent** *n.* **1.** acquiescence in a course of action.
**2. age of consent** See under AGE.
**3. informed consent** consent given after receiving sufficient information about the nature, costs, risks, and benefits of a proposed course of action to make an intelligent decision. In the absence of such information, one's "consent" may not be legally valid. For example, surgery upon a person who was not informed of the nature of the procedure may make the surgeon liable for the tort of BATTERY.
**4. on consent** (of a judicial action) taken because all parties agree to it, or at least none objects: *The injunction was entered on consent.*
—*v.* **5.** to give consent or manifest acquiescence: *The defendant consented to the entry of a preliminary injunction.*
—*adj.* **6.** describing action taken with the consent of those affected. See *consent decree* (under DECREE); *consent judgment* (under JUDGMENT); *consent order* (under ORDER); *consent search* (under SEARCH).

**consequential damages** *n.pl.* See under DAMAGES.

**conservator** *n.* the term used in some states for a court-appointed GUARDIAN for an incompetent adult. See also COMMITTEE.
—**conservatorship** *n.*

**consideration** *n.* **1.** that which is given or promised by a party to a CONTRACT in exchange for the other's promise. Unless something is given up by the promisee or some benefit is conferred on the promisor in exchange for the promise, the promise is merely GRATUITOUS and ordinarily will be unenforceable for *want of consideration* (see under WANT). See also FAILURE OF CONSIDERATION.
**2. nominal consideration** consideration recited in the contract but of no meaningful value, as in a contract to sell a parcel of land for one dollar. Although under traditional contract law courts do not pass judgment on the fairness of consideration, a court today might conclude that such a contract is unenforceable because of UNCONSCIONABILITY, or on the ground that the transaction is not a contract at all, but merely an unenforceable promise of a gift.
**3. past consideration** conduct in the past that is recited as "consideration" for a new promise; for example, "In consideration of the years of faithful

service that you have given me, I promise to leave you my house." In most situations, traditional contract law regarded such a promise as unenforceable because nothing was actually demanded or given in exchange for it, but in sympathetic cases modern courts sometimes find a way to enforce such promises despite the lack of real consideration.

**consign** *v.* to place goods into the hands of a carrier for delivery to another person (the **consignee**), or to place goods in the hands of a merchant (the **consignee**) for sale to others. In both cases, the original owner (the **consignor**) retains title to the goods until the ultimate delivery or sale occurs. Goods that have been consigned to a merchant and are awaiting sale are said to be "on consignment."
—**consignment** *n.*

**consolidate** *v.*, **consolidated, consolidating. 1.** to put two or more things together; to integrate two things of a similar or related nature. See, for example, *consolidated return* (under RETURN).
**2.** particularly, to combine two or more cases into one for administrative convenience. See also *consolidated appeal* (under APPEAL); *consolidated case* (under CASE[1]); *consolidated trial* (under TRIAL).
Cf. JOINDER; SEVER.
—**consolidation** *n.*

**Consolidated Omnibus Budget Reconciliation Act of 1985** *n.* See COBRA.

**consortium**[1] *n.* **1.** the companionship, affection, services, and sexual attention of a spouse. In some states, for some purposes, the concept has been extended to include the affection and companionship between parent and child. See also note at CIVIL UNION.
**2. loss of consortium** the loss of such companionship by reason of wrongful conduct of another. This is commonly an element of damages for which recovery is sought in a tort action, usually an action against someone who has negligently or intentionally injured or

killed one's spouse.
See also SERVICES.

**consortium**[2] *n., pl.* **consortia. 1.** a combination of financial institutions, businesses, investors, etc., for carrying into effect some financial operation requiring large resources of capital.
**2.** any association, group, or partnership of businesses, organizations, nations, etc., cooperating on a particular project or for a particular purpose.

**conspiracy** *n., pl.* **conspiracies.** an agreement among two or more persons (each referred to as a **conspirator** or CO-CONSPIRATOR) to do an unlawful act, or to achieve a lawful end by unlawful means; often described informally as a "partnership in crime." See also *seditious conspiracy* (under SEDITION); and see note at CO-CONSPIRATOR.
——**Note.** Conspiracy is a separate offense from the one it is formed to accomplish, and is a crime even if the contemplated acts are never performed. In most states, however, the agreement itself is not a crime until there has been some OVERT ACT by one of the conspirators in furtherance of the conspiracy.

**conspire** *v.*, **conspired, conspiring.** to participate in a CONSPIRACY.

**constitution** *n.* **1. a.** the fundamental law of a nation or state, providing a framework against which the validity of all other laws is measured; the system of fundamental principles according to which the nation or state is governed.
**b. Constitution** a particular constitution. Unless the context indicates otherwise, in American legal writing this always refers to the **Constitution of the United States** (see Appendices A and B).
**2.** a document embodying the constitution of a nation or state.
**3.** a set of fundamental governing rules for a corporation, association, or other organization.
**4. written constitution** a constitution consisting of a specific set of written principles originally drafted as a unit and embodied in a single instrument.

The United States has a written constitution.

**5. unwritten constitution** a body of fundamental legal and governing principles that evolved over time, finds its strength in generations of acceptance, and is expressed though royal decrees and concessions, statutes, case law, and hallowed tradition. Great Britain has an unwritten constitution.

**constitutional** *adj.* **1.** (of a law, policy, or action) in harmony with or not forbidden by a constitution, especially the Constitution of the United States. Cf. UNCONSTITUTIONAL.
**2.** pertaining or pursuant to a constitution, especially the Constitution of the United States.
**3. constitutional issue** (or **question**) an issue in a case that requires resort to the Constitution and cases interpreting it for resolution.
See also *constitutional right* (under RIGHT); *constitutional tort* (under TORT).
—**constitutionally** *adv.*

**constitutional court** *n.* See under COURT.

**constitutional law** *n.* **1.** a body or branch of law concerned with principles of constitutional governance generally, or a particular constitutional system.
**2.** in the United States, the branch of law concerned with the study, interpretation, and application of the Constitution of the United States.

**constitutionality** *n.* the quality or state of being CONSTITUTIONAL: *A case was instituted to test the constitutionality of the statute.*

**construction** *n.* **1.** the process of determining the meaning of a constitution, statute, or instrument and its legal effect in a particular situation, or the meaning and effect so determined. Often interchangeable with **interpretation,** although "construction" is the more common term with respect to constitutions, rules, and statutes **(statutory construction),** and "interpretation" is more commonly used with respect to private instruments such as contracts, wills, and deeds.
**2. liberal construction** construction of a statute or constitutional provision that considers the overall purposes for which it was enacted and interprets it in such a way as to further those purposes. This approach, also called **broad construction,** recognizes that words are always an imperfect tool and that not all possible circumstances to which a provision might apply can be anticipated and specifically addressed by the language used. As a general rule, statutes granting rights, benefits, and protections are construed liberally.
**3. strict construction** construction of a statute or constitutional provision that focuses on the specific words used and tends to reject application to circumstances not clearly within the ordinary meaning of those words. Also called **narrow construction.** Criminal statutes are usually construed strictly, on the ground that no one should be punished for conduct that the legislature has not clearly and specifically made a crime.
See also LEGISLATIVE HISTORY; LEGISLATIVE INTENT; ORIGINAL INTENT; PLAIN MEANING.
—**construe** *v.,* **construed, construing.**

**construction warranty** *n.* See under WARRANTY.

**constructive** *adj.* having the legal effect of; deemed by the law to exist or to have occurred even though that is not actually true. For example, a person who says "I'm giving you the contents of my safe; here's the key," would probably be held to have made "constructive delivery" of the contents of the safe (or to have "constructively delivered" them) by delivering the key, even though the contents have not actually been moved or put into the donee's hands. Thus the gift would be deemed complete, and the donor could not change her mind. See *inter vivos gift* (under GIFT). See also *constructive eviction* (under EVICTION); *constructive fraud* (under FRAUD); *constructive notice* (under NOTICE); *constructive service* (under SERVICE); *constructive trust* (under TRUST); *constructive trustee* (under

TRUSTEE). Cf. ACTUAL.
—**constructively** *adv.*

**construe** *v.,* **construed, construing.**
See under CONSTRUCTION.

**consul** *n.* **1.** an official appointed by the government of one country to look after its commercial interests and the welfare of its citizens in another country.
**2. consul general** a consular officer of the highest rank.
—**consular** *adj.*

**consul general** *n., pl.* **consuls general.** See under CONSUL.

**consularization** *n.* the act of a consul in authenticating a document by affixing her signature and seal. Consularization takes the place of *notarization* (see under NOTARIZE) for Americans abroad.
—**consularize** *v.,* **consularized, consularizing.**

**consultative privilege** *n.* Same as DELIBERATIVE PROCESS PRIVILEGE.

**consumer** *n.* an individual who purchases or leases goods, services, or real property primarily for personal, family, household, or other nonbusiness purposes. See also *consumer goods* (under GOODS); *consumer loan* (under LOAN).

**consumption tax** *n.* a tax paid by consumers of certain products or resources, such as electricity or oil, in proportion to the amount that they consume.

**contemnor** *n.* See under CONTEMPT.

**contemplation of death** *n.* See *gift in contemplation of death* (under GIFT).

**contempt** *n.* **1.** a judicial or legislative finding of willful disobedience of an order, or other willful conduct disrupting the procedures of a court **(contempt of court)** or legislature (e.g., **contempt of Congress**). Unless otherwise specified, "contempt" alone usually means contempt of court. The person or entity guilty of contempt is called a **contemnor.** See also CONTUMACIOUS; CONTUMACY.
**2. civil contempt** continuing contempt for which the court imposes a sanction that is to be lifted as soon as the contempt ends. The usual case is refusal to comply with a court order, for which

the court places a person in jail or imposes a daily fine with the understanding that the fine or jailing will end as soon as steps are taken to comply with the order.
**3. criminal contempt** contempt that is not continuing, for which a fixed sanction is imposed as a penalty. For example, in a courtroom proceeding a judge may impose an instant fine upon a lawyer who does something in front of the jury that the lawyer was told not to do, or even send a disruptive person directly to jail.

**content discrimination** *n.* a legal restriction on SPEECH that is based upon the subject matter of the speech. See also VIEWPOINT DISCRIMINATION.
——**Note.** In general, the First Amendment bars such discrimination. For example, the Supreme Court has held that a state cannot ban all picketing outside of schools except for labor picketing, because any restriction on expression must apply equally regardless of the subject matter of the expression. Speech that the Supreme Court has held to be outside the scope of First Amendment protection, however, may be legislated against. Examples include false advertising, fighting words, and obscenity.

**contingency** *n., pl.* **contingencies. 1.** a future event or circumstance that may or may not arise, upon the occurrence of which something else depends. See also CONTINGENT.
**2.** Short for **contingency fee,** also called **contingent fee.** An arrangement under which the amount of an attorney's fee in a civil case will depend upon the outcome of the case, usually being a percentage of the amount recovered: *The law firm took the case on contingency.*

**contingent** *adj.* uncertain; subject to future events. Said of something that will or will not occur, come into existence, or become definite, depending upon circumstances in the future. See *contingent annuity* (under ANNUITY);

*contingent estate* (under ESTATE[1]); *contingent interest* (under INTEREST[1]); *contingent liability* (under LIABILITY); *contingent fee* (under CONTINGENCY). Cf. VESTED.

**continuance** *n.* an order suspending or postponing a proceeding: *The defendant's new attorney moved for a 30-day continuance to allow her time to become familiar with the case.*

**continue** *v.,* **continued, continuing.** to grant or order a CONTINUANCE of: *The judge refused to continue the case, and instead ordered the parties to proceed as scheduled.*

**continuing injury** *n.* See under INJURY.

**continuing jurisdiction** *n.* See under JURISDICTION[1].

**continuing legal education (CLE)** training in legal topics intended to help lawyers keep up with changes in the law and in the practice of law after leaving law school. See also MANDATORY CONTINUING LEGAL EDUCATION.

**continuing objection** *n.* See under OBJECTION.

**continuing trespass** *n.* See under TRESPASS[1].

**contraband** *n.* illegal goods; goods that it is illegal to possess, sell, or transport; e.g., illegal drugs, smuggled goods.

**contract** *n.* **1.** broadly, any legally enforceable promise: *A bank's signature on a check that it has certified represents its contract to honor the check when it is presented for payment.*
**2.** in its usual sense, an agreement among two or more persons or entities (the parties to the contract; see PARTY) whereby at least one of them promises to do (or not to do) something in exchange for something done or promised by the others. Such a contract typically comes into existence when one party accepts (see ACCEPT) another's OFFER, provided that there is CONSIDERATION for the promises in the agreement. See also *breach of contract* (under BREACH); *option contract* (under OPTION); QUASI CONTRACT; SUBCONTRACT.

**3.** a document embodying such an agreement.
**4. adhesion contract** a preprinted contract that is not subject to negotiation, offered to a consumer on a "take it or leave it" basis; e.g., an automobile rental agreement or apartment lease. Also called **contract of adhesion.** If the terms are extremely oppressive, enforcement may be denied on the ground of UNCONSCIONABILITY.
**5. aleatory contract** (in civil law, as in Louisiana) a contract in which the performance of one or both parties, or the extent of performance, depends upon uncertain future events, as an insurance contract or an annuity.
**6. best efforts contract** a contract in which one party promises to use BEST EFFORTS to accomplish something, but does not promise that it will be accomplished. For example, a literary agent might promise to use best efforts to find a publisher for a book, but would not guarantee that a publisher will be found.
**7. bilateral contract** a contract in which promises are made on both sides. The consideration for each party's promise is the return promise made by the other. Cf. *unilateral contract.*
**8. contract under seal** an old form of contract in which the promise is embodied in a *sealed instrument* (see under SEAL[1]) delivered to the promisee. At common law such a promise was enforceable even if there was no consideration for it. In most states the role of the contract under seal has been modified or eliminated by statute. Also called **sealed contract** or, in earlier usage, **covenant under seal** or **covenant.** See also COVENANT.
**9. divisible contract** Same as *severable contract.*
**10. entire contract a.** a contract that is not susceptible of performance or enforcement in discrete pieces. A breach of any material term of such a contract would be regarded as a breach of the entire contract. Cf. *severable contract.* **b.**

Also called **entire contract of the parties** or **entire agreement of the parties.** Same as *completely integrated contract* (see under INTEGRATED CONTRACT).

**11. executed contract  a.** a contract in which nothing remains to be done by either party; for example, a contract of purchase and sale that is performed by exchanging goods for money immediately upon reaching agreement on the terms. Cf. *executory contract.* **b.** a signed contract.

**12. executory contract** a contract that remains to be performed in whole or in part; for example, a contract to build a house in the future. Cf. *executed contract.*

**13. express contract** a contract expressed in words, whether spoken **(oral contract)** or reduced to writing **(written contract).**

**14. illusory contract** a contract in which the only consideration on one side is an *illusory promise* (see discussion at PROMISE).

**15. implied contract  a.** Also called **contract implied in fact** or **implied-in-fact contract.** a contract manifested by conduct. For example, if you sit down in a barber's chair and allow your hair to be cut, it is understood that this amounts to an agreement to pay for the haircut, even though nothing is said about it. **b.** Also called **contract implied in law** or **implied-in-law contract.** a contract-like obligation imposed by law to do justice in a situation where there is no enforceable contract. For example, if a doctor provides necessary care to an unconscious accident victim, the law will "imply" an obligation to pay a reasonable amount for those services, even though the patient obviously never agreed to do so. See also QUASI CONTRACT.

**16. integrated contract** See INTEGRATED CONTRACT.

**17. output contract** a contract between a manufacturer or producer and a buyer, under which the former's entire output of a particular product during the term of the contract will be purchased by the latter. Cf. *requirements contract.*

**18. public contract** a contract under which a private individual or company is engaged to perform work on a public project such as building a school.

**19. procurement contract** a contract under which the government is to obtain goods or services from a private party.

**20. requirements contract** a contract between a buyer and seller under which the buyer's total requirements for a particular product during the term of the contract will be supplied exclusively by that seller. Cf. *output contract.*

**21. severable contract** a contract containing distinct components that can be performed or breached, enforced or invalidated, without affecting the rest of the contract. In effect, the contract can be treated as two or more separate contracts that happen to have been executed at the same time. For example, a contract for the sale of two automobiles with specific price and other terms for each automobile might be treated as severable. Also called **divisible contract**. Cf. *entire contract.*

**22. third-party beneficiary contract** a contract made for the purpose of conferring a benefit on someone other than the parties to the contract (the **third-party beneficiary**). For example, suppose A and B agree that A will plow B's field, in return for which B will permit C to grow his own crops on a portion of the field. If A plows the field but then B refuses to let C plant on it, C, as a third-party beneficiary, has an action against B for breach of the contract even though C was not a party to the contract. See also DONEE BENEFICIARY.

**23. unilateral contract** a contract in which there is a promise on only one side, the consideration for which is not a return promise but the doing of some act. For example, an offer of a reward for return of a lost dog is an offer of a unilateral contract: if someone who has seen the offer returns the dog, the offeror is contractually obligated to pay the reward. Cf. *bilateral contract.*

**24. yellow-dog contract** See YELLOW-DOG CONTRACT.

—*v.* **25.** to enter into a contract; make a

contractual promise.
—**contractual** *adj.*
—**contractually** *adv.*

**contractor** *n.* **1.** a party who contracts to provide goods or services, especially on a large scale.
**2. general contractor** a company that undertakes contractual responsibility for completion of a large project, especially a construction project, by hiring and coordinating the work of specialized *subcontractors* (see under SUBCONTRACT) for different facets of the project. Also called **prime contractor.**
**3. government contractor** a company, or occasionally an individual, hired by the government to furnish goods (such as airplanes or toilet seats for the military) or services (such as construction or consulting).
**4. independent contractor** an individual who contracts to provide services to others but, unlike an employee, retains significant autonomy in deciding how to carry out the work; e.g., a plumber, a management consultant, a freelance editor.

**contributing to the delinquency of a minor** *n.* the offense of causing or encouraging a minor to engage in illegal conduct, or engaging in conduct in a minor's presence that is likely to lead the minor into illegality or encourage disregard for the law.

**contribution** *n.* **1.** the principle that when one of several people liable for the same judgment or obligation is called upon to satisfy it, the others may be required to reimburse her ("make contribution") to the extent of their share of the total liability. The principle is often applied in tort cases, where it is called **contribution among joint tortfeasors.**
**2.** a payment or reimbursement under the principle of contribution, or the amount paid, or a claim or cause of action for such reimbursement.
See also CHARITABLE CONTRIBUTION.
—**contribute** *v.,* **contributed, contributing.**

**contributory negligence** *n.* See under NEGLIGENCE.

**control premium** *n.* See under PREMIUM.

**controlled substance** *n.* **1.** a drug whose addicting, intoxicating, or mood-altering qualities have led Congress and state legislatures to make its production, possession, importation, and distribution for all but very limited purposes a crime. Examples include narcotics, amphetamines, barbiturates, tranquilizers, hallucinogens, and marijuana. Controlled substances are listed on five schedules according to their perceived characteristics, and the schedules are subjected to different types and degrees of regulation. See also GATEWAY DRUG.
**2. Schedule I controlled substance** a drug with a high potential for abuse, no currently accepted medical use, and no accepted level of safety. Examples include heroin, methaqualone, LSD, peyote, and marijuana.
**3. Schedule II controlled substance** a drug with a high potential for abuse and whose abuse may lead to severe psychological or physical dependence, but which has a currently accepted medical use. Examples include opium, codeine, cocaine, methadone, amphetamine, and amobarbital.
**4. Schedule III controlled substance** a drug with a currently accepted medical use and a somewhat lower potential for abuse than in Schedule I or Schedule II, whose abuse may lead to moderate or low physical dependence or high psychological dependence. Examples include certain preparations containing limited dosages of stimulants, depressants, or narcotics, and anabolic steroids.
**5. Schedule IV controlled substance** a drug with a currently accepted medical use and a low potential for abuse relative to Schedule III, whose abuse may lead to limited physical or psychological dependence relative to Schedule III. Examples include barbital, fenfluramine, and phentermine.
**6. Schedule V controlled substance** a drug with a currently accepted medical use and an even lower potential for abuse than those in Schedule IV, whose

abuse may lead to even more limited physical or psychological dependence than those in Schedule IV. These are mostly medicines in which small quantities of narcotics are mixed with other active ingredients.
——**Note.** America's principal addictive and intoxicating recreational substances—tobacco and alcohol—are not included on any schedule.

**controlling authority** *n.* See under AUTHORITY.

**controversy** *n., pl.* **controversies.** See CASE OR CONTROVERSY.

**contumacious** *adj.* exhibiting behavior that justifies a finding of CONTEMPT: *The lawyer's conduct was contumacious. The lawyer was contumacious.*
—**contumaciously** *adv.*

**contumacy** *n.* disruptive or disrespectful behavior that would justify a finding of CONTEMPT.

**convenience and necessity** See CERTIFICATE OF CONVENIENCE AND NECESSITY.

**conventional war crime** *n. International Law.* any offense against internationally accepted laws and customs of war, including international treaties concerning war, particularly the Geneva Conventions of 1949. (See note at GENEVA CONVENTION.) Also called **war crime.**
——**Note.** Conventional war crimes constitute one of the three general categories of WAR CRIME in its broadest sense. In addition to the specific proscriptions of the Geneva Conventions, this category of offense against the law of nations condemns a very wide range of conduct in international armed conflict, and to some extent in armed conflict within a nation as well. Examples of such offenses include (a) employment of poison gas, expanding bullets, or other weapons calculated to cause unnecessary suffering; (b) wanton destruction of cities, towns, or villages, or devastation not justified by military necessity; (c) attack or bombardment of undefended towns, villages, dwellings, or buildings; (d) seizure, destruction, or willful damaging of historic monuments, works of art or science, hospitals, or institutions dedicated to religion, charity, education, art, or science; (e) plunder of public or private property; and (f) rape, forced prostitution, or other sexual violence.

**conversation** *n.* See CRIMINAL CONVERSATION.

**conversion** *n.* **1.** the tort of intentionally depriving another of the use or benefit of her personal property, as by taking it, seriously damaging it, or exercising control over it. One who does this is said to "convert (the property) to his own use."
**2.** the exchange of a *convertible security* (see under SECURITY²) for another security in accordance with the terms of the convertible security.
—**convert** *v.*
—**converter** *n.*

**convertible bond** *n.* See under BOND¹.

**convertible security** *n.* See under SECURITY².

**conveyance** *n.* **1.** a transfer of an interest in property, especially real estate, by means of a deed or other instrument other than a will.
**2.** the instrument by which a conveyance is accomplished.
**3. voluntary conveyance** a GRATUITOUS conveyance.
—**convey** *v.*
—**conveyable** *adj.*

**conveyancing** *n.* the branch of law practice consisting of examining titles, giving opinions as to their validity, and drawing of deeds, etc., for the conveyance of property from one person to another.
—**conveyancer** *n.*

**convict** *v.* **1.** to prove or officially declare someone GUILTY of an offense, especially in connection with a trial. See also AUTREFOIS CONVICT.
—*n.* **2.** a person convicted of an offense.
**3.** an individual serving a prison sentence.
—**convictable** *adj.*

**conviction** *n.* **1.** the act of convicting or

the state of being convicted.
**2.** a fixed or firm belief; the state of being convinced. See also ABIDING CONVICTION.

**cooperative** *n.* **1.** a jointly owned enterprise carrying out purchasing, distribution, management, or other activities on behalf of its members, not for profit but to achieve economies of scale and other benefits of combined rather than individual efforts and resources. A cooperative may be organized as an association **(cooperative association)** or a corporation **(cooperative corporation).** **2.** an apartment building owned by a cooperative corporation whose shareholders are the building's tenants, all of whom lease their apartments from the corporation.
Cf. CONDOMINIUM.

**cooperator** *n.* a participant in a COOPERATIVE; a member of a cooperative association or shareholder in a cooperative corporation.

**coparcenary** *n.* **1.** Also called **parcenary, coparceny.** co-ownership of property by two or more individuals who inherited it jointly under the laws of intestate succession. See discussion at IN COPARCENARY.
—*adj.* **2.** of or pertaining to *coparceners* (see under IN COPARCENARY).

**coparcener** *n.* See under IN COPARCENARY.

**copy** *n., pl.* **copies,** *v.,* **copied, copying.** —*n.* **1.** a transcript or reproduction of an original document, or one specimen of a document made in multiple originals. **2.** (in copyright law) a material object, other than a PHONORECORD, in which a WORK is fixed, and from which the work can be perceived, reproduced, or otherwise communicated, either directly or with the aid of a machine or device. —*v.* **3.** to make a copy of.
See also *certified copy* (under CERTIFY); CONFORMED COPY; COURTESY COPY; EXAMINED COPY.
——**False Friend.** In copyright law, even an original is a "copy." The copyright law protects only works "fixed in any tangible medium of expression"—not,

for example, an unrecorded improvisation, however creative. The copyright statute divides the universe of tangible media into two mutually exclusive categories: "copies" and "phonorecords." Since a handwritten musical composition, a sculpture, or an architectural work embodied in a building cannot be classified as a PHONORECORD, each of these—even one that has never been copied—is classified as a "copy."

**copyhold** *n. English Legal History.* **1.** an ancient type of ownership of land in England, evidenced by a copy of the manor roll establishing the title. **2.** an estate held under such ownership.
—**copyholder** *n.*

**copyright** *n., v.,* **copyrighted, copyrighting.** —*n.* **1.** the exclusive right, granted by federal statute to the creator of a written, musical, artistic, or similar work, to control the reproduction and exploitation of the work for a considerable period of time, usually the life of the author plus seventy years. It is not the ideas and facts in a work that are protected, but the way in which they are expressed.
—*v.* **2.** to take such steps as are necessary to secure or register a copyright.
See also ©; COPY; FAIR USE; PHONORECORD; WORK.
—**copyrightable** *adj.*
—**copyrighted** *adj.*

**coram nobis** *n. Latin.* (lit. "before us," "in our presence") a writ under which a court may review one of its own judgments for errors of fact and, if necessary, change the judgment in light of facts that were not and could not have been known when the judgment was rendered.

**core proceeding** *n.* an action concerning administration of an estate in bankruptcy or arising under the federal Bankruptcy Code. The bankruptcy courts have jurisdiction to hear and decide such actions. Cf. NON-CORE PROCEEDING.

**co-respondent** or **corespondent** *n.* **1.** in an action for divorce on the ground of adultery, the third party who is alleged to have participated in the adulterous act.

**2.** one of two or more RESPONDENTS named in a petition, writ, or the like.

——**History.** In England it was traditionally required that a petition for divorce on the ground of adultery name as a co-respondent the person with whom the respondent spouse allegedly committed the adulterous act. That requirement was finally abolished in 1991; now in England the naming of a co-respondent, who might then be required to appear in the case, is optional. Although the *word* "co-respondent" was adopted in the United States, the requirement of bringing that person into the action formally as a party—a RESPONDENT in the technical sense—was not widely adopted. Current law among the various states ranges from requiring that the co-respondent be named and served if possible to *forbidding* the identification of the alleged participant in the adultery unless identifying information is requested in order to rebut the charge.

——**Usage.** Newspapers usually omit the hyphen in *co-respondent* because it looks old fashioned, but in statutes, judicial opinions, and law reviews the overwhelming preference is to use the hyphen to avoid confusion with the word *correspondent.*

——**Pronunciation.** Whether or not the word is hyphenated in writing, it is always pronounced as if the hyphen were there, with a long vowel in *co* and *respondent* pronounced almost as a separate word. A *co-respondent* is not the same thing as a *correspondent.*

**corp.** *pl.,* **corps. 1.** Abbreviation for CORPORATION.

——*n.* **2.** Also, **corp** (without the period). *Informal.* corporation: *We advised him to incorporate as an S corp. and set up a nice pension plan for himself. The defendants are all Delaware corps.*

——**Pronunciation.** When this abbreviation is pronounced as a word or part of a corporate name ("Sub-S corp," "Acme Corp."), the final *p* is pronounced. Otherwise, it would sound as if one were saying "Acme Corps"—like "Marine Corps" or "the press corps." (See pronunciation note at JAG CORPS.) Similarly, in the plural (*corps.* or *corps*) both the *p* and the *s* are pronounced (like "corpse"). The word *corps* (as in "marine Corps") comes from French and utilizes the French pronunciation, in which both the *p* and the *s* are silent; by contrast, the abbreviations *corp.* and *corps.* (with or without the periods) come from the English word *corporation,* in which the *p* is pronounced.

**corporate** *adj.* **1.** pertaining to a corporation, to corporations generally, or even, in some broad contexts, to business matters generally.

**2. corporate law** broadly, the area or type of legal practice that deals with business organizations and transactions rather than personal legal matters; sometimes the term includes corporate LITIGATION, and sometimes it refers only to counseling and assistance with business matters rather than court-related work.

**3. corporate veil** the legal distinction between a corporation and its owners; the recognition of a corporation as a distinct legal entity for whose acts and debts its owners (the shareholders) are not personally responsible. In rare cases, a court may find that a corporation is essentially a sham or that the corporate form is being used for improper purposes, and will therefore disregard the corporate form **(pierce the corporate veil)** and hold the owner or owners (often a PARENT COMPANY) liable for its debts.

See also BODY CORPORATE; *corporate charter* (under CHARTER¹); *corporate income tax* (under INCOME TAX); *corporate seal* (under SEAL¹); *corporate security* (under SECURITY²).

——**corporately** *adv.*
——**corporateness** *n.*

**corporate governance** *n.* **1.** management and control of corporations, or of a specific corporation, by officers and directors on behalf of shareholders.

**2.** the principles, methods, theories, and philosophy of such governance.

**corporate opportunity doctrine** *n.*

the common law doctrine that an officer, employee, or agent of a corporation may not personally seize a business opportunity that otherwise might have been exploited by the corporation.

**corporation** *n.* **1.** a legally recognized entity formed by legislative act, or by individuals pursuant to general legislative authorization, with ownership ordinarily represented by shares of stock owned in varying quantities by anywhere from one to millions of stockholders. Corporations are typically characterized by LIMITED LIABILITY of stockholders, separation of ownership and management (in that the stockholders usually have no day-to-day role in management of the company, but merely vote once a year for directors), and treatment for most legal purposes as a distinct entity or "person" separate from its owners.
**2. business corporation** a corporation organized to carry out activities for profit. Also called **for-profit corporation; corporation for profit.** Cf. *nonprofit corporation.*
**3. C corporation** a corporation taxed directly on its income rather than through its shareholders; any corporation that is not an *S corporation.* Also called **subchapter C corporation.**
**4. close corporation** a corporation owned by a single shareholder or a small group of shareholders, who typically are all personally active in the business of the corporation or are related to each other, and ordinarily are not allowed to sell their shares to anyone else without approval of the group. Also called **closed corporation; closely held corporation; privately held corporation.** See also *private corporation.* Cf. *publicly held corporation.*
**5. domestic corporation a.** usually, a corporation incorporated in one's own state. **b.** sometimes (e.g., for federal income tax purposes), any corporation incorporated within the United States. Cf. *foreign corporation.*
**6. dummy corporation** a *shell corporation* established solely to shield its owners from personal liability or disclosure of their identities.

**7. foreign corporation a.** usually, a corporation incorporated in another state. For example, in a Maryland court or a discussion of Maryland law, a Delaware corporation would be referred to as a "foreign corporation." **b.** sometimes (e.g., for federal income tax purposes), a corporation or similar entity organized under the laws of another country. Cf. *domestic corporation.*
**8. municipal corporation** a city, town, village, or similar political unit that operates under a charter granted by the state legislature giving it the right of limited self-government and the power to enter into contracts, sue and be sued, and otherwise act as a legal entity.
**9. nonprofit corporation** a corporation organized for charitable, religious, educational, cultural, or similar purposes, and not to generate profits for the shareholders. Also called **not-for-profit corporation.** Cf. *business corporation.*
**10. nonstock corporation** a corporation that does not issue stock.
**11. parent corporation** Same as PARENT COMPANY.
**12. private corporation a.** a corporation established for nongovernmental purposes. Cf. *public corporation.* **b.** sometimes, a *close corporation.*
**13. professional corporation (P.C.)** a form of business organization allowed to individuals or groups practicing professions such as law or medicine, having some characteristics of corporations but not affording LIMITED LIABILITY to the members. In some states, called **professional association (P.A.).**
**14. public corporation a.** a corporation established by leglislative act to carry out specified governmental purposes. Cf. *private corporation.* **b.** sometimes, short for *publicly held corporation.*
**15. publicly held corporation** a corporation owned by a diverse group of shareholders, with stock freely traded among members of the public. See also *public corporation.* Cf. *close corporation.*
**16. S corporation** a small business corporation whose shareholders have elected, under Subchapter S of Chapter

1 of the Internal Revenue Code, to have the corporation's income treated as personal income to them and taxed as part of their personal income taxes, thus avoiding normal corporate income taxes. Also called **subchapter S corporation** or **Sub-S corporation,** with many variations on capitalization and hyphenation. Cf. *C corporation.*

**17. shell corporation** a corporation having no business or ongoing activity of its own, and sometimes lacking any substantial assets as well.

**18. sister corporations** corporations that are subsidiaries of the same parent corporation.

**19. subsidiary corporation** Same as SUBSIDIARY. See also *cooperative corporation* (under COOPERATIVE); CORP.; MUNICIPAL CORPORATION.

**corporeal hereditament** *n.* See under HEREDITAMENT.

**corpus** *n., pl.* **corpora, corpuses.** *Latin.* (lit. "body") **1.** the property of a trust; all of the assets under administration by a trustee pursuant to a particular trust instrument. See also PRINCIPAL; RES.

**2.** a principal or capital sum, as distinguished from interest or income.

**3.** any collection of things viewed as a unit.

**corpus delicti** *n. Latin.* (lit. "the body of the crime") the fact that a crime under discussion did occur—that there was in fact a crime. In general, American law does not allow a person to be convicted of a crime solely on the basis of his own confession, absent some independent evidence of the corpus delicti, that is, some evidence that the crime for which he claims responsibility actually happened.

——**False Friend.** In a murder case, the corpse of the victim is usually pretty good evidence that a crime did occur. And since "corpus" *sounds* like "corpse" (and in fact the two words are very distantly related), it is easy to understand how *corpus delicti* came to be popularly misunderstood as a fancy term for *corpse,* as in: *We have to get rid of the corpus delicti.* Perhaps to avoid this confusion, the English phrase

**body of the crime** is occasionally used instead of—or more often as a supplement to—the Latin. This phrase makes no sense in English, but at least it cannot so easily be confused with "corpse."

**Corpus Juris Civilis** *n. Latin.* (lit. "the body of the civil law") the body of ancient Roman law as compiled and codified under the emperor Justinian in the sixth century A.D. and given this collective name by scholars in the sixteenth or seventeenth century.

**corrective justice** *n.* Same as *retributive justice* (see under JUSTICE[1]).

**corroborate** *v.,* **corroborated, corroborating.** to provide support or confirmation from an independent source for testimony or other evidence already introduced; to back up independently.
—**corroboration** *n.*
—**corroborating, corroborative** *adj.*

**corruption of blood** *n.* disqualification from inheriting, retaining, or passing on to one's heirs any rank or title or any interest in land. Corruption of blood was an incident of ATTAINDER. Corruption of blood as a penalty for treason was prohibited in the United States by the Constitution, and was abolished by statute in England in 1870.

**cosinage** *n. Law French.* **1.** kinship; consanguinity; the state of being a blood relation.

**2. writ of cosinage** an ancient writ by which one who inherited land from a cousin or other somewhat remote blood relative could gain possession of the land from another person who had taken possession. See also note at MORT D'ANCESTOR.
Also spelled **cozenage** and in many other variations.

**cost and freight** See C. & F.

**cost basis** *n.* See under BASIS.

**cost, insurance, and freight** See C. I.F.

**costs** *n.pl.* **1.** Also called **court costs.** filing fees and certain other expenses necessarily incurred in pursuing or defending a civil case. The losing party is usually required to pay the winner's costs. Since "costs" does not include attorneys' fees, this is often a rather insignificant amount. See also BILL OF COSTS.

**2. costs to abide the event** a phrase appearing in appellate decisions indicating that a decision as to which party must pay the other's costs must await the outcome of further proceedings, usually a new trial.

**counsel** n., pl. **counsel. 1.** a lawyer or lawyers, particularly in the role of advisor to or representative of a particular client: *Upon the advice of counsel, he canceled the interview.*

**2.** a collective term for the lawyers representing parties in a case or present for a proceeding: *Copies of the scheduling order were sent to all counsel. Will counsel please approach the bench?*

**3. assigned counsel** counsel appointed by a court to represent a criminal defendant who cannot afford to hire a lawyer. See also RIGHT TO COUNSEL.

**4. counsel of record** Same as ATTORNEY OF RECORD.

**5. counsel pro hac vice** an attorney who, though not a member of the bar of a particular jurisdiction or a particular court, is given permission by the court to appear as counsel for a party in a specific case before the court. Also called **attorney pro hac vice.** See also note at PRO HAC VICE.

**6. general counsel** a company's chief legal officer.

**7. house counsel a.** a company's regular lawyer or law firm. **b.** Also called **in-house counsel.** a lawyer or lawyers who are employees of a company and do legal work only for that company.

**8. independent counsel** counsel hired or appointed to handle a matter because the lawyers who would normally do so have a CONFLICT OF INTEREST.

**9. lead counsel a.** among the lawyers or law firms representing various named plaintiffs in a class action, the one representing the *lead plaintiff* (see under PLAINTIFF) and primarily responsible for coordinating the litigation and representing the interests of the class as a whole. **b.** among several lawyers representing a party in a matter, the lawyer in charge.

**10. local counsel** an attorney admitted to practice in the court in which a case is pending, who assists an attorney not so admitted (usually from out of state) in representing a client in the proceeding. See also PRO HAC VICE.

**11. of counsel** See OF COUNSEL.

**12. outside counsel** any counsel performing services for a company other than *in-house counsel.*

**13. special counsel** counsel hired or appointed to assist in a matter because of special expertise, or to act as *independent counsel.*

**14. standby counsel** counsel appointed by a court to stand by and lend such assistance as she can to a criminal defendant who insists on representing himself, and to take over the representation if the defendant changes his mind. Occasionally referred to as **shadow counsel.**

**counselor** n. a lawyer.

**—Usage.** This use of this term is primarily confined to two contexts: (a) in letterheads, advertising, and the like, usually in the form **counselor at law** or the plural **counselors at law.** The British spelling **counsellor** is also seen. (b) as a form of oral address, especially in judicial proceedings: *Your objection is noted, counselor.* The usual plural in this context is COUNSEL rather than "counselors": *Will counsel please approach the bench?*

**count** n. each of several distinct claims or causes of action in a civil complaint, or charges in a criminal information or indictment. See also COMMON COUNTS.

**counterclaim** n. **1.** a CAUSE OF ACTION or *claim for relief* (see under CLAIM) asserted by a defendant against the plaintiff in a civil case. It is asserted in the ANSWER to the complaint.

**2. compulsory counterclaim** any claim that the defendant has against the plaintiff arising out of the same events that are the subject of the plaintiff's complaint. As a general rule, failure to assert such a counterclaim constitutes a waiver of it.

**3. permissive counterclaim** any other claim that the defendant has against the plaintiff, regardless of what it relates to. The defendant may assert such a claim as a counterclaim or hold it for a separate action, as she chooses.

**counterclaimant** *n.* one who asserts a counterclaim.

**counterfeit** *adj.* **1.** made in imitation so as to be passed off fraudulently or deceptively as genuine: *a counterfeit deed; a counterfeit twenty-dollar bill; a counterfeit trademark.*
—*n.* **2.** an imitation intended to be passed off fraudulently or deceptively as genuine; a forgery.
—*v.* **3.** to make a counterfeit of; forge.
—**counterfeiter** *n.*
—**counterfeitly** *adv.*

**counteroffer** *n.* a response to an OFFER of a contract that does not accept the offer as stated, but instead proposes different terms.

**countersign** *v.* to add a second SIGNATURE to a document to authenticate or reinforce the first.
——**Note.** Usually the individual countersigning an instrument is different from the first signer, as when a company checking account requires all checks to be signed by two officers. But sometimes an individual is requested or required to countersign something containing his own signature, so that the signatures can be compared.

**countersignature** *n.* the signature added to a document by one who countersigns.

**country** *n. English Legal History.* a jury chosen from the region; the neighborhood as represented by the jurors; a jury.
——**False Friend.** It is traditional in England to say that a criminal defendant who pleads not guilty and opts for a jury trial "puts himself upon the country," will be tried "by God and his country," or the like. This sounds like a statement of submission to the awesome power of the state, but the authentic meaning is quite the opposite. The word *country* in this context originally referred not to the nation, but just to the nearby countryside: To be tried by one's country was to be tried by one's neighbors, as distinguished from a judge who represented only the king. Thus trial "by the country" simply means trial by jury. See also GO TO THE COUNTRY, and see note at PER PAIS.

**course of business** *n.* See ORDINARY COURSE OF BUSINESS.

**course of dealing** *n.* a sequence of previous dealings between the parties to a particular transaction, to which courts will refer, in the event of a dispute about the latest transaction, as evidence of how the parties intended it to be carried out. Cf. COURSE OF PERFORMANCE; USAGE.

**course of employment** *n.* a series of activities normally engaged in by an employee while on the job, especially activities directly related to the task for which the employee was hired.

**course of performance** *n.* the carrying out of some recurring contractual obligation, such as the making of installment payments, in substantially the same way several times without objection from the other party to the contract. In the event of a dispute over a subsequent performance of that obligation, the previously established course of performance will normally be taken by the court as showing how the parties intended that step to be performed. Cf. COURSE OF DEALING USAGE.

**court** *n.* **1.** an institution of government whose function is to interpret and apply the law to specific cases within its jurisdiction. Within a judicial system, a court is referred to as a **lower court** or **higher court** in relation to others, as determined by the fact that decisions of the lower courts are subject to review by those above, and decisions of the higher courts are binding upon those below. In the basic three-tier judicial system of the United States and most states, the first level is primarily a trial court and the next two are primarily or exclusively appellate courts; the middle level is thus the lowest appellate court for most cases, but is usually referred to as the **intermediate appellate court.**

**2.** the judges, collectively, of a court.

**3.** the judge or panel of judges sitting on a particular case.

**4. Court a.** a particular court, especially the Supreme Court of the United States or the court in which a specific case is pending. **b.** a form of address commonly used in addressing or referring to the judge or panel of judges in a case: *May it please the Court... As the Court will recall...*

**5. appellate court** a court that hears appeals from decisions made in a *trial court.*

**6. Article I court** a specialized court that is quasi-judicial and quasi-administrative in nature, created by Congress as an extension of its legislative power under Article I of the Constitution rather than as an organ of the judicial branch of government under Article III. Examples include the Tax Court, bankruptcy courts, and territorial courts. Also called **legislative court.** See also *Article I judge* (under JUDGE).

**7. Article III court** a court established to exercise the judicial power of the United States as set forth in Article III the Constitution. The United States District Courts, Courts of Appeals, and Supreme Court are Article III courts. Also called **constitutional court.** See also *Article III judge* (under JUDGE).

**8. circuit court a.** in a state whose judicial system is divided geographically into circuits, a court whose jurisdiction is defined by a circuit. **b.** in the federal system, informally, the UNITED STATES COURT OF APPEALS for any of the geographically defined circuits. See also CIRCUIT.

**9. court a quo** the court from which a case is transferred or an appeal is taken. See also A QUO.

**10. court ad quem** the court to which a case is transferred or an appeal is taken. See also AD QUEM.

**11. court of general jurisdiction** a court with jurisdiction to hear any kind of case except one restricted to a specialized court. Cf. *court of limited jurisdiction.*

**12. court of last resort** a court whose decision is unappealable; the highest court to which a particular case can be appealed.

**13. court of law a.** formerly, a court for cases at law (see LAW, def. 4) as distinguished from proceedings in EQUITY. **b.** now, a rather formal way of referring to any court, especially a trial court.

**14. court of limited jurisdiction** a court with jurisdiction to hear only specific kinds of cases. See *limited jurisdiction* (under JURISDICTION[1]). Cf. *court of general jurisdiction.*

**15. court of record** a court that keeps a permanent record of its proceedings. In an earlier age, many routine legal matters were dispatched by local courts without written records; today virtually every court is a court of record.

**16. district court** a court whose geographic jurisdiction covers one *judicial district* (see under DISTRICT).

**17. trial court a.** a court whose normal business is to give cases their first full consideration and issue a judgment, holding a trial to determine the facts if necessary. **b.** the court in which the first judgment is issued in a particular case, with or without a trial: *The trial court dismissed the complaint for failure to state a claim, but the appellate court reversed and remanded the case for a trial.* Also called **court of first instance, court of original jurisdiction** (see *original jurisdiction* under JURISDICTION[1]).

See also CHANCERY; *court below* (under BELOW); *Court of Oyer and Terminer* (under OYER AND TERMINER); DRUG COURT; ECCLESIASTICAL COURT; FULL COURT; INFERIOR COURT; INTERNATIONAL COURT OF JUSTICE; INTERNATIONAL CRIMINAL COURT; JUVENILE COURT; KANGAROO COURT; MOOT COURT; *nisi prius court* (under NISI PRIUS); OUT OF COURT; PIEPOWDER COURT; STAR CHAMBER; SMALL CLAIMS

COURT; SUPERIOR COURT; SUPREME COURT; UNITED STATES COURT OF APPEALS; UNITED STATES DISTRICT COURT.

**court clerk** *n.* See under CLERK.

**court costs** *n.pl.* Same as COSTS.

**court day** *n.* Same as DIES JURIDICUS.

**court-martial** *n., pl.* **courts-martial** *v.*, **court-martialed,** **court-martialing.** —*n.* **1.** a military court; a court of military personnel convened to try a member of the military for an offense against military law. **2.** a trial or conviction in or by such a court. **3. general court-martial** the highest level of military trial court, presided over by a military judge and composed of at least five members (unless the defendant has chosen to be tried by the judge alone), with power to try any offense under the Uniform Code of Military Justice and impose any penalty not forbidden by that code, including death. **4. special court-martial** a military court composed of at least three members (unless the defendant has chosen to be tried by a military judge alone), with power to try any noncapital offense under the Uniform Code of Military Justice, but subject to various limitations as to the severity of the sentence that may be imposed, including a limit of six months for a sentence of confinement. **5. summary court-martial** the lowest level of military trial court, consisting of a single commissioned officer, with power to try relatively low-ranking military personnel who consent to be tried in such by such a court, and very limited sentencing power. For example, a sentence of confinement may not exceed one month. —*v.* **6.** to charge, try, or convict a person in a military court.

**court of chancery** *n.* See CHANCERY.

**Court of Common Pleas 1.** *English Legal History.* a court for the hearing of private civil suits—*common pleas* as distinguished from *pleas of the Crown* (see both under PLEA). **2.** in the United States, the name given to a variety of courts in different states, including some having criminal as well as civil jurisidiction and some having appellate rather than trial responsibility.

**court reporter** *n.* a person who makes a word-for-word record of what is said in a trial or similar proceeding, and if requested (and paid) by the litigants, produces a typed or printed transcript.

**court rules** *n.pl.* See under RULE.

**courtesy copy** *n.* an extra copy of a motion, brief, or other document being filed in a case, delivered directly to the judge's chambers "as a courtesy." Some judges find the extra copy so convenient that they require it; some find the extra paper such a nuisance that they forbid it.

**covenant** *n.* **1.** a legally enforceable contract or promise, especially a promise that a particular state of affairs will be maintained during the term of a contract or that certain actions will or will not be taken with respect to land. **2.** a WARRANTY, especially in connection with a transfer of land. **3.** Also called **covenant under seal.** historically, a contract or promise made in a *sealed instrument* (see under SEAL[1]). See also *contract under seal* (under CONTRACT). **4.** the common law FORM OF ACTION to recover damages for breach of a contract or promise made under seal, or the writ (in full, **writ of covenant**) by which the action was commenced. Cf. ASSUMPSIT. **5. covenant not to compete** a promise in an employment contract or contract for the sale of a business, that the employee or seller will not subsequently go into competition with the employer or buyer. Such covenants are enforceable only if limited in duration and geographic scope. **6. covenant not to sue** in an agreement settling a claim, dispute, or lawsuit, a promise not to pursue the matter in court. **7. covenant running with the land** a promise with respect to land that survives transfers of the land; it is binding

on and enforceable by subsequent owners. Also called **running covenant.**
**8. covenants** (or **warranties**) **of title**
See COVENANTS OF TITLE.
**9. restrictive covenant a.** a covenant
limiting the use or disposition that an
owner may make of land. A covenant
forbidding transfer of property to anyone of a particular race or ethnic group
**(racially restrictive covenant)** was formerly a tool for maintaining segregated
housing; such covenants are no longer
enforceable. **b.** Another term for *covenant not to compete.*

**covenant marriage** *n.* See under MAR-
RIAGE.

**covenantee** *n.* one to whom a covenant is made or who has a right to enforce it.

**covenantor** *n.* one who makes or is
bound by a covenant.

**covenants of title** *n.pl.* a set of covenants usually insisted upon by a buyer
of real estate as assurance that she will
receive good and unencumbered title to
the property, and included in a *warranty deed* (see under DEED) conveying
the property. Also called **covenants for
title** or **warranties of title,** and often
referred to in negotiations as the **usual
covenants,** these typically include most
or all of the following: **a. covenant of
seisin** a covenant that the grantor has
full ownership of the interest he purports to convey. Also called **covenant
of right to convey. b. covenant
against encumbrances** a covenant
that there is no undisclosed ENCUM-
BRANCE on the property, such as a
mortgage, tax lien, or easement. **c. covenant for further assurance** a promise that, if the need arises, the grantor
will make any further conveyance necessary to give the grantee the full title
intended to be conveyed by the deed.
**d. covenant of quiet enjoyment** or
**covenant of warranty** See under
QUIET ENJOYMENT.
—**Usage.** Note that none of these traditional "warranties of title" is ordinarily referred to as "the warranty of title";
rather, the various warranties collectively guarantee that the grantee will

get good title. The phrase "warranty of
title," in the singular, is usually used in
connection with sales of goods rather
than transfers of real property. See *warranty of title* (under WARRANTY).

**cover** *v.* **1.** (of a buyer of goods) to buy
substitute goods from another source
when a seller under contract to provide
certain goods fails to make delivery.
**2.** (of an insurer or insurance policy) to
protect a certain person or protect
against a certain risk: *My health insurance policy covers my children but does
not cover cosmetic surgery.*
—*n.* **3.** the purchase of substitute goods
elsewhere when a seller fails to deliver
as promised. If the reasonable cost of
"cover" exceeds the original contract
price, the buyer may recover the difference from the original seller as part of
the damages for breach of the contract.

**coverture** *n.* **1.** the legal condition or
status of a married woman under the
common law, which was that her legal
existence was substantially subsumed
in that of her husband. In particular,
with limited exceptions, she could not
make legally binding contracts or otherwise exercise any right or power with
respect to money or property, except
with the consent of her husband.
**2.** the inherent authority and presumed
protection of the husband over the wife
at common law.
**3. under coverture** in the condition
of being under the authority and protection of a husband at common law;
married.
See also FEME COVERT; *feme sole trader*
(under FEME SOLE); PARAPHERNALIA;
and see note at EJUSDEM GENERIS.
—**History.** It was not until the state-
by-state enactment of "Married
Women's Property Acts" in the second
half of the nineteenth and early twentieth centuries that women in most of
the United States acquired the right to
contract and to control their own property.

**cozenage** *n.* Same as COSINAGE.

**CPA** CERTIFIED PUBLIC ACCOUNTANT.

**craft union** *n.* See under UNION.

**cramming** *n.* a type of telecommunications fraud in which telephone services that a consumer has not intentionally ordered, such as voice mail, a personal 800 number, or paging, are added to the consumer's telephone bill, resulting in additional monthly charges, often with deceptive labels such as "Access Charges" or "Enhanced Services." These services are often tendered in misleading ways by a third party, as through a direct-mail sweepstakes entry that contains authorization for them in small print. Cf. SLAMMING.
—**cram** *v.*, **crammed, cramming.**
—**crammer** *n.*

**crave** *v.*, **craved, craving. 1.** to request earnestly; demand; pray for; move for: *Plaintiff craves judgment for the amount of the note.*
**2.** to long for; to desire greatly: *The parents crave the company of their children. The drug addict craved a fix.*
——**Usage.** Well into the twentieth century, this was a standard term in pleading and practice for any request addressed to the court.

**crave oyer** to request or demand that a document relied upon by an adversary be read in court or produced for inspection and copying. See note at OYER.

**credible** *adj.* believable; appearing to be true or honest: *credible testimony; credible evidence; a credible witness; a credible defense.*
—**credibility** *n.*
—**credibly** *adv.*

**credit** *n.* **1.** trust in the ability and intention of a person or entity to repay a loan or to pay for goods or services provided without immediate payment, or the quality of a person or entity that inspires such trust: *to extend credit to a purchaser; to make a purchase on credit.*
**2.** the amount of money loaned or made available, or of payments deferred or that a vendor is willing to defer, by reason of such credit: *We have used $1,500 of credit on our credit card and have $500 of credit left for additional purchases.*
**3.** a reduction in an amount owed, by

reason of a payment or correction or for some other reason. See also TAX CREDIT.
**4.** respect; deference. See also FULL FAITH AND CREDIT.
—*v.* **5.** to believe: *The jury credited the witness's testimony on the issue of self-defense.*

**creditor** *n.* **1.** a person to whom money is owed. Cf. DEBTOR.
**2. judgment creditor** a person who is owed money pursuant to a judgment entered in his favor in a civil case.
**3. secured creditor** a creditor who has been given security (see SECURITY[1]) to protect against loss in case the debtor fails to pay the debt in full.
**4. unsecured creditor** a creditor who has not been given security for the debt; a creditor who is not a *secured creditor.*

**crim. con.** *n.* Abbreviation, formerly used both orally and in writing, for CRIMINAL CONVERSATION: *It was widely rumored that he was guilty of crim. con., but no action was brought against him.*

**crime** *n.* **1.** an act or omission contrary to laws established for the welfare of the public at large, for which the law provides a punishment. Especially, an act or omission punishable by a sentence of incarceration; a FELONY or MISDEMEANOR. See also INFRACTION; OFFENSE; VIOLATION.
**2.** criminal activity collectively or generally.
**3. common law crime** an offense that was a crime at common law, before criminal laws were generally written into statutes. Most acts that were crimes at common law are also crimes under modern statutes. Because of the constitutional problem of vagueness (see VAGUE), it is doubtful that any common law crime not embodied in a statute could now be enforced.
**4. statutory crime a.** an act that was not a crime at common law, but has been made a crime by statute. **b.** broadly, any crime defined by statute, whether or not it was a crime at common law.

See also *anticipatory crime* (under IN-CHOATE CRIME); CRIME AGAINST HU-MANITY; CRIME AGAINST NATURE; CRIME AGAINST PEACE; CRIME OF PASSION; CRIME OF VIOLENCE; CONVENTIONAL WAR CRIME; HATE CRIME; HIGH CRIMES AND MISDEMEANORS; INCHOATE CRIME; STATUS CRIME; VICTIMLESS CRIME; WAR CRIME; WHITE-COLLAR CRIME.

**crime against humanity** *n. International Law.* inhumane conduct committed as part of a widespread or systematic attack directed against a civilian population, especially in connection with armed conflict between nations or within a nation.

——**Note.** Crimes against humanity constitute one of the three general categories of WAR CRIME. Conduct that may constitute a crime against humanity includes murder, extermination, enslavement, deportation, imprisonment, torture, rape, forced pregnancy or forced sterilization, APARTHEID, *enforced disappearance of persons* (see under DISAP-PEARANCE), and PERSECUTION on political, racial, religious, or similar grounds.

**crime against nature** *n.* **1.** Same as UNNATURAL ACT.
**2.** the crime of committing such an act. Also referred to in statutes as the **infamous crime against nature,** the **abominable and detestable crime against nature,** and the like. See also SODOMY.

**crime against peace** *n. International Law.* one of the three categories of WAR CRIME, encompassing any action that involves the planning, preparation, initiation, or waging of a WAR OF AGGRES-SION, or participation in a conspiracy for the accomplishment of such actions.

**crime of passion** *n.* a crime committed in the HEAT OF PASSION.

**crime of violence** *n.* under federal law, any offense that has as an element the use, attempted use, or threatened use of physical force against person or property, or any felony that by its nature poses a substantial risk that physical force might be used against person or property. Also called **violent crime.**

——**False Friend.** "Violent crime" is normally thought of as crime that causes or threatens physical harm to people, as in rape or armed robbery. Note that under this federal law providing for enhanced sentences for "violent" criminals, the crime need not involve any risk or threat to people at all. Any application of physical force to property, or substantial risk that physical force might used against property, is covered as well. Thus a pure property crime such as breaking the window of an empty car to steal the radio is classified as a "crime of violence."

**criminal** *adj.* **1.** constituting an offense or an element of an offense. See *criminal contempt* (under CONTEMPT); *criminal homicide* (under HOMICIDE); *criminal negligence* (under NEGLIGENCE); *criminal trespass* (under TRESPASS).
**2.** pertaining to crime, criminals, and punishment: *criminal case; criminal law.* See also *criminal action* (under AC-TION); *criminal liability* (under LIABIL-ITY); *criminal procedure* (under PROCE-DURE); *criminal prosecution* (under PROSECUTION); *criminal record* (under RECORD).
**3.** wrongful; offensive. See CRIMINAL CONVERSATION.
——*n.* **4.** a person who commits a crime.
**5. career criminal** a person who is repeatedly convicted of crimes, usually of the same general type.
—**criminally** *adv.*

**criminal complaint** *n.* see under COM-PLAINT.

**criminal conversation** *n.* the tort of engaging in sexual intercourse with another person's spouse. Formerly often referred to as CRIM. CON. for short.
——**False Friend.** Criminal conversation is not a crime, and it is most assuredly not about talking. The term *conversation* is used in the old sense of "sexual intercourse," and it is *criminal* in the sense of "unlawful, wrongful." Although the act complained of might technically also be punishable as a crime (see ADULTERY; FORNICATION), the phrase *criminal conversation* is used only when the act is viewed as the basis of an action for damages—originally

and specifically, an action by the husband of an adulterous wife against her paramour. Like many legal concepts having their origin in the concept of wife as chattel, this tort has been abolished in most states.

**criminal disenfranchisement** *n.* a state-law prohibition on voting by anyone who has been convicted of a felony, either while serving their sentence or for life. See also CIVIL DEATH.
—**Note.** Very large numbers of Americans in certain states are denied the vote because of past offenses for which they have completed their sentences. The criminal disenfranchisement laws in those states have been criticized on the ground that they discourage constructive participation in society by ex-offenders who have paid their penalty. Even more fundamentally, these laws, some of which were enacted after the Civil War for the express purpose of diluting black voting strength, are criticized for perpetuating and aggravating the discriminatory effect of a national legal system that studies have shown disproportionately arrests and imprisons blacks for certain crimes, notably drug offenses.

**criminal lawyer** *n.* a lawyer whose practice includes a substantial number of criminal cases.

**criminal profile** *n.* See under PROFILE.

**criminalist** *n.* a specialist in the collection and scientific analysis of physical evidence of crimes **(criminalistics).** Cf. CRIMINOLOGIST.

**criminality** *n.* the state or practice of being a criminal; criminal conduct.

**criminalize** *v.,* **criminalized, criminalizing. 1.** to make punishable as a crime; to make illegal. Cf. DECRIMINALIZE.
**2.** to make a criminal of: *Drug use has criminalized him.*
—**criminalization** *n.*

**criminally negligent homicide** *n.* See under HOMICIDE.

**criminologist** *n.* a person engaged in the sociological study of crime and

criminals **(criminology).** Cf. CRIMINALIST.

**critical legal studies (CLS)** *n.* **1.** a school of legal thought and scholarship that challenges conventional attitudes about the role of law in society, and analyzes traditional law as a political mechanism for maintaining and enforcing existing economic and power relationships.
**2. critical legal study** an analysis of a specific issue or a specific body of law or legal writing from the point of view of critical legal studies.

**critical race theory (CRT)** *n.* a school of legal thought and scholarship that analyzes the relationship of law and race and criticizes the role of law in perpetuating social and racial inequality.

**cross** *Informal.* —*n.* **1.** Short for *cross-examination* (see under EXAMINATION).
—*v.* **2.** Short for *cross-examine* (see under EXAMINE).

**cross-appeal** *n.* **1.** an appeal filed by the appellee in a case in which an appeal has already been filed, challenging the same judgment that is the subject of the first appeal but on a different ground. For example, a losing defendant might appeal a decision on the ground that the damage award was too high, then the plaintiff might cross-appeal on the ground that the damage award was too low.
—*v.* **2.** to file a cross-appeal.

**cross-claim** *n.* in a civil action against two or more defendants, a CLAIM or CAUSE OF ACTION asserted by one of the defendants against one or more of the other defendants. For example, in a tort case against several people alleged to have harmed the plaintiff jointly, the defendants often assert cross-claims against each other, each claiming a right of CONTRIBUTION from the others. In rare cases, a cross-claim might be asserted by one plaintiff against another in the same case.

**cross-complaint** *n.* the pleading in which one asserts a CROSS-CLAIM.

**cross-examination** *n.* See under EXAMINATION.

**cross-examine** *v.,* **cross-examined, cross-examining.** See under EXAMINE.

**cross-examiner** *n.* the person, usually a lawyer, who questions a witness on *cross-examination* (see under EXAMINATION) and also conducts any *recross-examination* (see under EXAMINATION). Cf. DIRECT EXAMINER.

**CRT** CRITICAL RACE THEORY.

**cruel and unusual punishment** *n.* punishment of a person convicted of a crime in a manner that fails to meet minimal contemporary standards of decency, or that is grossly disproportionate to the crime. The Eighth Amendment (see Appendix) forbids such punishments.

**cruelty** *n.* a traditional ground for divorce, consisting of a pattern of physical or psychological abuse by one spouse rendering married life intolerable for the other. The level of abuse that a married woman was formerly expected to tolerate from her husband is illustrated by the names given to this ground for divorce ("cruelty," "extreme cruelty," "cruel and inhuman treatment," and the like), and the fact that a single instance of cruelty was normally not considered sufficient to entitle one to a divorce.

**c.t.a.** See CUM TESTAMENTO ANNEXO.

**culpable** *adj.* blameworthy; meriting imposition of liability or punishment.
—**culpability** *n.*
—**culpably** *adv.*

**cum testamento annexo (c.t.a.)** *Latin.* with the will attached; with the will annexed. This phrase or its English equivalent **(with will annexed** or **with the will annexed)** arises in connection with the appointment by a court of an ADMINISTRATOR for the estate of a person who left a will but who did not designate an executor, or whose designated executor is unwilling or unable to serve. The will is annexed to the court's order appointing the administrator, which then becomes *letters of administration cum testamento annexo* or

*letters of administration de bonis non cum testamento annexo* (see both under LETTERS OF ADMINISTRATION).
—**Usage.** By extension, the phrase "cum testamento annexo" or its abbreviation or its English translation has come to be applied to the process of administration pursuant to such an order (*administration cum testamento annexo*) or the person appointed by such an order (see ADMINISTRATOR CUM TESTAMENTO ANNEXO; ADMINISTRATOR DE BONIS NON CUM TESTAMENTO ANNEXO).

**cumulative evidence** *n.* See under EVIDENCE.

**cumulative sentences** *n.pl.* See under SENTENCE.

**cumulative zoning** *n.* See under ZONING.

**curable defect** *n.* See under DEFECT[1].

**curative instruction** *n.* See under INSTRUCTION.

**curtesy** *n.* **1.** the life estate that, under the common law, a widower held in land that his wife owned at her death, provided that their marriage had produced a child. Cf. DOWER.
**2. curtesy consummate** the husband's interest in land after the wife's death.
**3. curtesy initiate** the interest that the husband acquired in the land upon the birth of the first child of the marriage.

**curtilage** *n.* the area around a dwelling to which the activity of home life extends, such as a yard and outbuildings, usually clearly demarcated and often fenced off. Cf. OPEN FIELD.
—**Note.** The curtilage is considered part of the home itself for purposes of SEARCH AND SEIZURE, and may not be searched without probable cause. However, the Supreme Court has held that law enforcement agents who circle over a house in a helicopter at minimum permissible flying altitude so as to peer behind the walls of the curtilage with the naked eye are not conducting a SEARCH, and therefore need not have a warrant or probable cause, because the homeowner does not have a reasonable

expectation of privacy from such observation. *Florida v. Riley,* 488 U.S. 445 (1989).

**custodial interrogation** *n.* See under INTERROGATION.

**custody** *n.* **1.** immediate possession and control over a thing, with responsibility for its care.
**2.** any significant restraint on a person's freedom of action imposed by law enforcement authorities.
**3.** Also called **child custody.** the right and responsibility of determining the residence, care, and education of a minor child.
**4. joint custody** an arrangement whereby divorced parents continue to share responsibility for raising their children.
**5. sole custody** custody of a child by one adult only. This is the most common arrangement for custody of a child following divorce of the parents.

**custom** *n.* **1.** Also called **customary law.** a traditional business practice of such ancient origin and universal application as to have acquired the status of a legal requirement.
**2.** Also called **custom and usage.** Same as USAGE.

**customs** *n.pl.* **1.** taxes imposed by the federal government on goods imported into or exported from the country. Also called **duties,** except that "duties" has a singular form (see DUTY) but "customs" does not.
**2.** the agency or procedure by which, or the place where, such taxes are collected.

**cy pres** *n. Law French.* (lit. "as near") the doctrine under which a court confronted with a deed or will whose terms cannot be carried out exactly may modify it so as to carry out the intent of the maker as nearly as possible, especially in the case of charitable bequests and trusts.

**cyber-** a prefix signifying that the term to which it is attached is being used in a context that involves computers or computer networks, especially the Internet.
——**Usage.** "Cyber" terms like those in

the entries that follow are very much in vogue in the popular media and are increasingly seen in serious legal writing; but they are just beginning to appear as terms of art in judicial decisions, statutes, and other formal legal contexts. Some may become established legal terms with reasonably settled definitions; others may remain popular nonlegal terms; others will no doubt fade from use. While this natural process of linguistic evolution plays itself out, careful legal writers should take pains to explain the intended scope of any such terms that they use.

**cyberalty** *n.* a term proposed by some legal writers for a hypothetical system of law that might govern conduct and legal relations on the Internet.
——**Note.** The term and the concept are taken by analogy from *admiralty* (see under MARITIME LAW) because of the similarities between cyberspace and the high seas—a region used by people of all nations but owned by no nation. See also LEX INFORMATICA.

**cyberattack** *n.* any destructive or disruptive electronic intrusion or attempted intrusion into computer systems that are important for national functioning.

**cybercop** *n.* **1.** a law enforcement officer specializing in computer crime; especially one who seeks evidence of criminal activity by surfing the Internet or infiltrating Internet chat groups in the persona of a consumer, a pedophile, a child, or the like.
**2.** a person employed by an on-line service provider to monitor the on-line activities of subscribers to the service—especially the conversations in chat rooms hosted by the service—to enforce the policies of the service and reduce the risk of its being used for an improper purpose.
**3.** a person who patrols the Internet on behalf of a governmental agency or a private interest group, or simply for personal satisfaction, seeking evidence of criminal or tortious conduct.

**cybercrime** *n.* Same as COMPUTER

CRIME.
—**cybercriminal** *n.*

**cyberfraud** *n.* Same as COMPUTER FRAUD.

**cyberlaundering** *n.* MONEY LAUNDERING carried out principally through electronic banking channels.

**cyberlaw** *n.* **1.** the broad area of law relating to computers, computer software and databases, and computer networks. **2.** especially, law relating to the Internet.

**cyberpiracy** *n.* Same as CYBERSQUATTING.
—**cyberpirate** *n.*

**cyberporn** *n.* pornography that is accessible on the Internet.

**cybersquatting** *n.* **1.** the act of registering and holding a desirable Internet domain name in the hope that another entity will pay to acquire the name for use in its own Internet address. **2.** especially, the act of registering, trafficking in, or using a domain name that is identical to, confusingly similar to, or dilutive of another's trademark, with a bad faith intent to profit thereby, as by obtaining a payment for release of the domain name to the trademark owner. The Anticybersquatting Consumer Protection Act, adopted by Congress in 1999, specifically gives the trademark owner a right of action in such a case, not only against the cybersquatter but also, if the cybersquatter cannot be found, IN REM against the offending domain name itself. Also called **cyberpiracy, domain name piracy, domain name grabbing.**
—**cybersquatter** *n.*
——**Note.** A domain name is the portion of an Internet address that is typically in the form "name.com," "name.org," or the like.

**cyberstalking** *n.* **1.** the use of computer communications, such as Internet chat rooms and e-mail, to seek out and develop an opportunity to meet a victim for an intended crime. **2.** the systematic or continued use of such communications to embarrass, intimidate, threaten, or harass a person, especially anonymously. When the chosen medium is e-mail, this is also called **e-mail harassment.**
—**cyberstalker** *n.*

**cyberterrorism** *n.* activities designed to damage, disrupt, or infiltrate computer systems and networks important to the safe and smooth functioning of a modern industrial nation, especially those that are essential for such functions as communications, energy distribution, air traffic control, the banking system, and national defense.
—**cyberterrorist** *n.*

**cybertort** *n.* a tort committed through the use of computers, especially over the Internet; for example, disseminating defamatory statements by e-mail or using the Internet to carry out a fraud.

# D

**D&O insurance** *n.* Same as DIRECTORS' AND OFFICERS' LIABILITY INSURANCE.

**D&O liability insurance** *n.* Same as DIRECTORS' AND OFFICERS' LIABILITY INSURANCE.

**damages** *n.pl.* **1.** a sum of money asked for by a plaintiff or awarded by a court in a civil action, to be paid by the defendant because of the wrong that gave rise to the suit. An action seeking an award of damages is called a **damage action.**
**2.** sometimes, the injuries for which the plaintiff seeks an award of damages.
**3. compensatory damages** damages awarded to compensate for the harm resulting from the defendant's wrong, including actual financial loss and intangible harm such as pain and suffering. These are the damages to which a plaintiff is normally entitled upon proving her case. Also called **actual damages**. For some purposes, compensatory damages are subdivided into **general damages,** which compensate for losses of a sort that would normally be expected to follow from the nature of the wrong, and **special damages** or **consequential damages,** which arise from the unique circumstances of the case.
**4. hedonic damages** damages for loss of enjoyment of life, usually as a result of the lasting effects of a personal injury suffered by the plaintiff. A few states also allow such damages to be awarded in wrongful death actions.
**5. incidental damages** under the Uniform Commercial Code, expenses reasonably incurred by a buyer or seller in dealing with a breach of the contract of sale by the other party; for example, the cost of storing, inspecting, or reshipping the goods involved in the contract. The party in breach is liable for those damages as well as the direct loss caused by the failure to deliver or accept or pay for the goods as promised.
**6. liquidated damages** damages for breach of contract in an amount stated in the contract, where the parties agreed at the time of contracting on a reasonable figure or formula for determination of the compensation to be paid in the event of a breach. Also called **stipulated damages.** Unlike the payment provided for in a *penalty clause* (see under PENALTY), agreements for payment of liquidated damages are normally enforceable.
**7. nominal damages** an award of a token amount, such as one dollar, indicating that the defendant did do the wrong alleged but that no significant measure of damages was established by the plaintiff. In certain kinds of DEFAMATION action, such an award can be made to vindicate the honor of the plaintiff.
**8. punitive damages** damages awarded in excess of actual damages in tort cases in which the defendant's conduct is deemed especially egregious. Punitive damages are awarded to punish the defendant, discourage repetition of such conduct, and set an example for others who might be tempted to engage in similar conduct. Also called **exemplary damages, vindictive damages.**
**9. speculative damages** claimed damages for injury or loss that may occur in the future but cannot be predicted or evaluated on any reasonable basis. Speculative damages are not allowed.
**10. treble damages** damages in an amount equal to three times the *actual damages,* awarded in cases under certain statutes specifically providing for such an award, notably the ANTITRUST laws and the RACKETEER INFLUENCED AND CORRUPT ORGANIZATIONS ACT.

**damnify** *v.*, **damnified, damnifying.** to damage; to cause injury or loss to. —**damnification** *n.*

**damnum** *n.*, *pl.* **damna.** *Latin.* loss; damage; injury; harm.

**damnum absque injuria** *n.*, *pl.* **damna absque injuria.** *n. Latin.* (lit. "loss without injustice") a loss or injury for which there is no legal remedy. Also, very rarely, called **damnum sine injuria.**
——**Note.** The law does not provide a remedy for every injury, even when it is caused by deliberate and avoidable acts of others. For example, suppose a property owner builds a house that he has every right to build, but in so doing obstructs his neighbor's view of the mountains. The neighbor has suffered loss, both in her enjoyment of life and in the value of her property. But she could not obtain a court order requiring that the builder of the house tear it down or compensate her for the reduction in her property value, because she did nothing legally wrong. Unfortunately for her, her loss is damnum absque injuria. See also *de minimis non curat lex* (under DE MINIMIS).

**damnum sine injuria** *n.*, *pl.* **damna sine injuria.** *Latin.* (lit. "loss without injustice") Same as DAMNUM ABSQUE INJURIA.

**dangerous propensity** or **dangerous propensities** *n.* potential for harm; tendency of a particular product, substance, person, animal, etc., to cause injury. In the case of dogs or other animals, also called **vicious propensity** or **vicious propensitites.** See also note at FERAE NATURAE.

**dangerous weapon** *n.* See under WEAPON.

**darrein presentment** *n. Law French.* (lit. "last presentation") **1.** an ancient writ—the **writ** (or **assize**) **of darrein presentment**—protecting the heir to a right of ADVOWSON from another who has tried to assert the right. The basis for the writ was that the claimant was the same person, or the heir of the person, who had last presented a candidate for a appointment to a certain church position, and therefore presumptively had the right to do so again when the position again became vacant.
**2.** Also called **assize of darrein presentment.** the cause of action or the legal proceeding founded upon such a writ.
See also *petty assize* (under ASSIZE) and accompanying note.

**date rape** *n.* See under RAPE.

**d/b/a** Abbreviation for "doing business as."
——**Usage.** This abbreviation is used, especially in case names, to identify the TRADE NAME under which an individual or entity operates in connection with the matters in suit: *Paul Jones v. James Smith, d/b/a Smith's Market.*

**d.b.n.** See DE BONIS NON.

**de bene esse** *adv. Latin.* (lit. "of well-being; as being good") **1.** provisionally; validly for present purposes but subject to objection or nullification if legally tested at a later date: *The judge allowed the attorney to ask questions about the document de bene esse, but when the attorney proved unable to authenticate the document, the testimony was stricken and the jury was instructed to disregard it.*
—*adj.* **2.** done de bene esse; provisional; done in anticipation of possible future need; subject to subsequent determination of correctness, validity, admissibility, or the like: *The de bene esse testimony was stricken from the record.*
See also *deposition de bene esse* (under DEPOSITION).
——**Usage.** This phrase is used almost exclusively in reference to procedures connected with a trial, especially depositions or other testimony.

**de bonis asportatis** *Latin.* for goods carried off; concerning goods carried away. See *trespass de bonis asportatis* (under TRESPASS²).

**de bonis non (d.b.n.)** *Latin.* a shortening of *de bonis non administratis* (lit. "of goods not administered"). This phrase is used in connection with the appointment of an ADMINISTRATOR to complete the administration of a decedent's estate when a previous administrator or executor ceases to serve before all the assets of the estate have been distributed: *Upon the death of the executor, Mr. Smith was appointed to handle the administration de bonis non.* See also ADMINISTRATOR DE BONIS NON; ADMINISTRATOR DE BONIS NON CUM TESTAMENTO ANNEXO; *letters of administration de bonis non* (under LETTERS OF ADMINISTRATION); *letters of administration de bonis non cum testamento annexo* (under LETTERS OF ADMINISTRATION).

**de clauso fracto** *Latin.* for broken CLOSE. See *trespass de clauso fracto* (under TRESPASS²).

**de ejectione firmae** *Latin.* (lit. "of ejectment of farm") the writ (in full, **writ de ejectione firmae**) for commencement of an action of *trespass de ejectione firmae* (see under TRESPASS²) in order to obtain damages for being wrongfully put out of land leased for a term of years before the expiration of the lease, or to be restored to the land. **—Note.** The term *farm* (Medieval Latin *firma*) used in the name of this ancient writ originally referred to the fixed ("firm") rent paid by a tenant for years, or to possession for a term of years at a fixed rent. Over time, the word came to refer to the land held under such a lease (which would invariably have been used for agricultural purposes), and ultimately to any land used for agriculture.

**de facto** *adj. Latin.* (lit. "arising from that which has been done") existing in fact, without regard to legal requirements or formalities; said of things that came into being without legal blessing, but that the law may choose to take cognizance of for practical reasons. See for example DE FACTO GOVERNMENT; DE FACTO SEGREGATION. Cf. DE JURE.

**de facto government** *n.* a government of a country that exists in reality even though it did not reach power in accordance with the country's laws; for example, a government that recently reached power through revolution or a coup. Cf. DE JURE GOVERNMENT.

**de facto segregation** *n.* SEGREGATION, particularly racial segregation, that is not legally required but exists for reasons of history, economics, and private discrimination. Cf. DE JURE SEGREGATION.

**de jure** *adj. Latin.* (lit. "arising from law") existing by reason of law; brought into existence and maintained in accordance with legal requirements and formalities. Sometimes the existence is more theoretical than real, as in the case of a DE JURE GOVERNMENT that has been ousted by war or revolution; sometimes it is all too real, as in the case of DE JURE SEGREGATION throughout much of American history. Cf. DE FACTO.

**de jure government** *n.* a government that ascended to power in a country through that country's established laws. Cf. DE FACTO GOVERNMENT.

**de jure segregation** *n.* legally enforced SEGREGATION, particularly racial segregation; for example, past segregation in South Africa under the doctrine of APARTHEID or in the United States under the doctrine of SEPARATE BUT EQUAL. Cf. DE FACTO SEGREGATION.

**de minimis** *adj. Latin.* (lit. "concerning trifles") insignificant; too small to merit attention: *The plaintiff suffered only de minimis damages. The chilling effect on speech, if any, is de minimis.* The phrase comes from the maxim **de minimis non curat lex** ("the law does not concern itself with trifles").

**de novo** *adj. Latin.* (lit. "anew") restarted from the beginning; begun all over again. See *de novo review* (under REVIEW); *de novo trial* (under TRIAL).

**dead-hand control** *n.* control of property through a RESTRAINT ON ALIENATION that is imposed in a grant of the property but lasts long after the grantor has died.

**dead man's statute** *n.* a state statute prohibiting anyone who has a claim against the estate of a decedent from supporting the claim through testimony about a personal transaction or conversation with the decedent. In some states the statute likewise bars testimony regarding personal transactions or conversations with an incompetent in support of a claim against the incompetent. The theory is that the testimony would be unfair because the decedent and the incompetent cannot give their side of the story.

**deadly weapon** *n.* See under WEAPON.

**dealer** *n.* a person who buys and resells things as a business. See also BROKER-DEALER.

**death** *n.* See BRAIN DEATH; CIVIL DEATH.

**death penalty** *n.* Same as CAPITAL PUNISHMENT.

**death qualification** *n.* the exclusion from a jury in a capital case of any jurors whose opposition to the death penalty would preclude them from voting for the death penalty under any circumstances. Also called **death-qualifying the jury.** See also *death-qualified jury* (under JURY).
——**History.** The Supreme Court has held that even in the GUILT PHASE of a capital case, when the question of a penalty is not at issue, the jury may be death-qualified. The Court found unpersuasive the studies indicating that death-qualified juries are more inclined to find defendants guilty than juries representing a broader cross-section of the community, but held that, even assuming death-qualified juries are somewhat more conviction-prone, states have a right to utilize a single death-qualified jury for every phase of a capital case. *Lockhart v. McCree,* 476 U.S. 162 (1986).

**death warrant** *n.* See under WARRANT[1].

**deathbed declaration** *n.* See under DECLARATION.

**debenture** *n.* a corporate debt obligation, usually a long-term bond or note, that is not secured or guaranteed, but depends solely upon the company's continued financial well-being for payment.

**debt** *n.* **1.** an unconditional obligation to pay a sum of money, either at present or in the future.
**2.** a common law FORM OF ACTION for recovery of a fixed sum of money, such as the amount of a loan, the agreed-upon price of a sale, or a rent due. See note at INDEBITATUS ASSUMPSIT.
**3. bad debt** a debt owed to a taxpayer that the taxpayer will be completely unable to collect. The taxpayer usually may deduct all or part of a bad debt for income tax purposes in the year in which the debt becomes worthless.
**4. secured debt** debt for which security (see SECURITY[1]) has been given to the creditor to protect against loss in the event that the debtor fails to pay the debt in full.
**5. scheduled debt** See SCHEDULED DEBT.
**6. unsecured debt** debt for which no security has been given; debt that is not a *secured debt.*

**debt security** *n.* See under SECURITY[2].

**debtor** *n.* **1.** a person who owes money. Cf. CREDITOR.
**2.** a person or entity that is the subject of a bankruptcy action.
**3. debtor in possession** a debtor in bankruptcy who is allowed to continue to control his business during REORGANIZATION.
**4. judgment debtor** a person who owes money pursuant to a judgment entered against him in a civil case.
**5. principal debtor** See under PRINCIPAL.

**decedent** *n.* a person who has died. See also *decedent's estate* (under ESTATE[2]).
——**Usage.** This is the term used in the law of trusts, wills, intestate succession, administration of estates, and the like; in a murder case or wrongful death action, "deceased" would be the more common term.

**deceit** *n.* **1.** the act or practice of deceiving; concealment or distortion of the truth for the purpose of misleading.
**2.** the tort of FRAUD.
——**deceitful** *adj.*

—**deceitfully** *adv.*
—**deceitfulness** *n.*

**deceive** *v.*, **deceived, deceiving.** to mislead by a false appearance or statement; delude.
—**deceivable** *adj.*
—**deceivability** *n.*

**decertify** *v.*, **decertified, decertifying.** to withdraw certification from; for example, to determine upon further consideration or on appeal that a group previously certified as a class for purposes of maintaining a class action may not proceed as a class after all: *The appellate court decertified the class.*
—**decertification** *n.*

**decide** *v.*, **decided, deciding. 1.** to reach or render a DECISION on: *The judge stated that he will decide the motion by the end of the week.*
**2.** to reach or render a decision: *The jury decided for the plaintiff in the amount of three million dollars.*
—**decidability** *n.*
—**decidable** *adj.*

**decision** *n.* **1.** the determination of a court, jury, or administrative tribunal on how a case should come out.
**2.** a judicial or administrative OPINION.
—**decisional** *adj.*

**decisional law** *n.* Same as CASE LAW.

**declarant** *n.* the person who makes a DECLARATION; particularly, in discussions of the *hearsay rule* (see under HEARSAY), the maker of an out-of-court statement whose admissibility is under discussion.

**declaration** *n.* **1.** an oral or written assertion; a statement.
**2.** a formal announcement: *Declaration of Independence; declaration of war.*
**3.** a word used in some jurisdictions for AFFIRMATION (def. 2).
**4.** an old word for the initial pleading in a case at law; now called a COMPLAINT.
**5. declaration against interest** a statement that is so strongly contrary to the interests of the declarant at the time it is made that a reasonable person in the declarant's position would not have made it unless he believed it to be true;

e.g., "I owe her $1,000," "I shouldn't have been driving so fast." Such statements are generally admissible under an exception to the *hearsay rule* (see under HEARSAY).
**6. declaration of trust** a document in which a property owner declares that she holds the property in trust for the benefit of someone else, thereby creating a TRUST with herself as trustee. Cf. DEED OF TRUST.
**7. declaration of war a.** a government's formal statement that it is in a STATE OF WAR with another nation or with opposing military forces within its own nation. See also note at WAR. **b.** a similar statement of military hostility by the leader of a revolutionary or breakaway group within a country, directed at the country's existing government. **c.** a statement or symbolic gesture of intent to confront a persistent problem and commitment to deal with it: *The President's speech announcing his new initiative on drugs was a declaration of war.*
**8. dying** (or **deathbed**) **declaration** a statement made in the belief that one is about to die, particularly about the circumstances of the impending death; e.g., "Joe shot me." Such statements are often admitted into evidence as an exception to the *hearsay rule* (see under HEARSAY), on the quaint assumption that no one would dare "go to his death with a lie upon his lips."
**9. spontaneous declaration** Same as EXCITED UTTERANCE.

**declaratory judgment** *n.* See under JUDGMENT.

**declare** *v.*, **declared, declaring.** to make a DECLARATION of: *to declare independence; declare war.*
—**declarable** *adj.*

**declared war** *n.* See under WAR.

**decree** *n.*, *v.*, **decreed, decreeing.** —*n.* **1.** a JUDGMENT. Before the MERGER OF LAW AND EQUITY, the final order disposing of a case was called a "judgment" at law but a "decree" in equity. Now "judgment" is the usual term for most cases, but "decree" is often used as a synonym and is the usual term in certain contexts: *bankruptcy decree, divorce decree.*

**2.** any judicial order.

**3. consent decree** a court order entered by agreement between a federal agency and a party accused of illegal conduct in the field regulated by the agency, resolving the case and typically including a promise by the party not to engage in certain activities in the future.

**4. decree absolute** a decree that, after starting out as a *decree nisi,* has become final.

**5. decree nisi** a tentative decree, issued at the behest of one party, which will become a *decree absolute* if the other party fails to appear and show cause why it should not. See also NISI.

**6. final decree** a decree issued at the conclusion of an action and disposing of the entire case.

**7. interlocutory decree** a preliminary or temporary decree issued in the course of a case; for example, a decree awarding temporary alimony and temporary custody in a divorce case, to remain in effect while the issues of alimony and child custody are being litigated.

—*v.* **8.** to ORDER or ADJUDGE.

**decretal** *adj.* **1.** of, pertaining to, containing, or contained in a decree or decrees. See, for example, *decretal child support* (under CHILD SUPPORT).

**2. decretal paragraph** a specific paragraph in a judgment or order that contains several paragraphs ordering distinct remedies: *The appellate court modified the judgment by deleting the second and eighth decretal paragraphs.*

**3. decretal portion** in a judgment or opinion that contain contains findings of fact or other explanatory or background information as well as the order of the court, the portion consisting of the order. Typically this is the final portion and is set off by such language as "It is therefore ordered, adjudged, and decreed that..."

Also, **decretory.**

**decriminalize** *v.,* decriminalized, decriminalizing. to repeal a criminal law or otherwise make conduct that previously was a crime no longer a crime. Cf. CRIMINALIZE.

—**decriminalization** *n.*

——**Usage.** DECRIMINALIZE is sometimes distinguished from LEGALIZE in that conduct that has been "legalized" might still be subject to extensive special regulation, whereas conduct that has been "decriminalized" would be regulated primarily by the general laws applicable to all conduct. For example, to "legalize" prostitution might mean to require prostitutes to have special licenses and practice in specific areas; to "decriminalize" prostitution might mean to remove the government from involvement with exchanges of money for sex except for enforcement of general rules regarding fraud, public decency, exploitation of minors, and the like.

**dedication** *n.* a gift or abandonment of an interest in land, in a copyrightable work, or in some other property, by the owner or creator to a governmental entity or to the public at large.

**deduct** *v.* to take or claim a DEDUCTION for on one's income taxes.

**deductible** *adj.* **1.** Also, **tax-deductible.** qualifying as a DEDUCTION for income tax purposes: *a deductible contribution to charity; a deductible trip to a business conference in Hawaii.*

—*n.* **2.** the amount for which the insured is liable on covered losses before the insurance company must begin paying under a policy: *a medical insurance policy with a $500 annual deductible.*

—**deductibility** *n.*

**deduction** *n.* **1.** a portion of income or an item of expense that a taxpayer may subtract from income for purposes of calculating income tax. Also called **tax deduction.** Cf. TAX CREDIT.

**2. itemized deduction** any of a number of specific types of expense that must be specifically listed on a tax return to be claimed as deductions; e.g., medical expenses, mortgage interest.

**3. standard deduction** a fixed amount that may be claimed as a deduction instead of claiming separate

itemized deductions.
See also CHARITABLE DEDUCTION.

**deed** n. 1. a formal instrument by which a living person or an entity conveys an interest in property, especially real property.
2. **quitclaim deed** a deed conveying to someone else whatever interest one has in a piece of real property, without any promise that the title one is purporting to convey is any good. Typically used for gifts of property.
3. **warranty deed** a deed conveying title to real property and containing *covenants of title* (see under COVENANT), making the grantor liable to the grantee for losses caused by undisclosed defects in the title.
—v. 4. to convey property by deed.

**deed of confirmation** n. See under CONFIRMATION.

**deed of trust** n. 1. an instrument by which the owner of certain property conveys it to another to be held in trust for the benefit of someone, thereby creating a TRUST with the person receiving the property as trustee. Cf. *declaration of trust* (under DECLARATION).
2. specifically, in some states, a deed conveying title to real property to a trustee to hold as security until the transferor repays a loan; similar to a MORTGAGE except that the mortgage is given directly to the creditor to hold. Also called **trust deed**.

**deem** v. to pronounce; to treat or declare something to be true or effective; especially, to treat or declare something to be different from what it is: *The legislature deemed the statute to take effect thirty days after approval by the governor. Tax returns postmarked by midnight on the day that they are due are deemed timely. Deposits made after the close of regular banking hours shall be deemed to have been made on the next banking day.*
——Usage. As illustrated by the last example, a common use of the word *deem* is to signal a LEGAL FICTION.

**deep pocket** n. *Informal.* **1.** an individual or entity with sufficient wealth to pay a potential judgment: *Although the*

tort *was committed by the employee, the suit names the employer as a defendant on the theory of respondeat superior in order to have a deep pocket.*
2. **deep pockets** sufficient wealth to pay a potential judgment: *We should have no trouble collecting the judgment if we win: The defendant's insurance company has deep pockets.*

**defalcate** v., **defalcated, defalcating.** to be guilty of defalcation.
—**defalcator** n.

**defalcation** n. 1. misuse, misappropriation, or loss of funds over which one has fiduciary responsibility as a trustee, a corporate or public official, or the like.
2. the sum taken or lost.

**defamation** n. the negligent, reckless, or intentional communication to a third person of a falsehood that is injurious to the reputation of a living individual, or of a corporation or other organization. Defamation is the basis for the torts of libel (see LIBEL[1]) and SLANDER. See also *actual malice* (under MALICE).
—**defamatory** *adj.*
—**defame** v., **defamed, defaming.**

**default** n. 1. failure to fulfill a legal obligation, such as performing a contract, paying a debt, or responding to a properly served summons.
—v. 2. to fail to perform a legal obligation.

**default judgment** n. See under JUDGMENT.

**defeasance** n. the termination or nullification of a fee interest in real property. See *fee simple defeasible* (under FEE[1]).

**defeasible** *adj.* 1. capable of being annulled or terminated.
2. of a fee interest in real property, subject to DEFEASANCE upon the occurrence of a future event. See *fee simple defeasible* (under FEE[1]).
—**defeasibility** n.
—**defeasibly** *adv.*

**defeasible fee** Same as *fee simple defeasible* (see under FEE[1]).

**defeat** *v.* to cause to be void or ineffective; to bar: *The original owner's title was defeated by adverse possession. The statute of frauds defeats the plaintiff's contract claim.*

**defect**[1] *n.* **1.** a deficiency, fault, or imperfection in a legal instrument, transaction, statute, proceeding, or the like; a circumstance or feature that is not in accord with legal requirements.
**2. curable defect** a defect that can be remedied; a minor defect that does not undermine the validity of the instrument, transaction, or the like, provided that the party responsible fixes it when it is objected to, or could have fixed it if it had been objected to in a timely way.
**3. fatal defect** a defect that renders an instrument, transaction, or the like invalid. See also FATAL.

**defect**[2] *n.* **1.** a flaw or characteristic that renders a product or property unreasonably dangerous or not fully functional.
**2. design defect** a defect in the way a product is designed making it unreasonably dangerous even if manufactured according to specifications.
**3. latent defect** a defect that is not discoverable by reasonable or normal inspection. Also called **hidden defect.** Cf. *patent defect.*
**4. manufacturing defect** a defect in a product arising from the process of manufacture or assembly rather than from the design.
**5. marketing defect** a deficiency in the instructions or warnings accompanying a product causing it to be unreasonably dangerous.
**6. patent defect** a defect that would be apparent to a buyer upon reasonable or normal inspection. Also called **apparent defect.** Cf. *latent defect.* ("Patent" in this phrase is an adjective; see note at PATENT.)

**defective** *adj.* having a defect; deficient; flawed. See, e.g., *defective title* (under TITLE).
—**defectively** *adv.*
—**defectiveness** *n.*

**defend** *v.* **1.** to contest a legal charge or claim: *The company will defend the case vigorously.*
**2.** to serve as an attorney for a defendant: *The attorney will defend the company vigorously.*
—**defendable** *adj.*

**defendant** *n.* **1.** the person against whom a lawsuit is brought. See also *third-party defendant* (under THIRD-PARTY ACTION).
**2.** a person against whom a criminal COMPLAINT or other charging instrument has been filed with a court in a criminal case.

**defendant in error** *n.* the APPELLEE in a case where the appeal is commenced by *writ of error* (see under WRIT).

**defender** *n.* **1.** one who defends something.
**2.** the defendant in a civil or criminal case.
**3.** the attorney for a defendant.
**4. appellate defender** in some states, a publicly employed attorney who represents indigent defendants in appeals of criminal cases.
**5. capital defender** in at least one state, a publicly employed attorney who represents indigent defendants in capital cases.
**6. public defender** a publicly employed attorney who represents indigent defendants in criminal cases. Also called **indigent defender, legal defender.** See also RIGHT TO COUNSEL.

**defense** *n.* **1.** the facts and legal theories relied upon, or the evidence and argument presented, in opposition to a civil claim or criminal charge. See also JOINT DEFENSE.
**2.** a legal justification for conduct that otherwise appears to be wrongful, or a legal principle that renders one immune from liability for wrongful conduct: *the defense of duress; the defense of statute of limitations.* See also TWINKIE DEFENSE.
**3.** the defendant and attorneys representing the defendant in a case.
**4. affirmative defense** a defense that, rather than simply showing that a claim or charge is untrue or arguing that it is legally insufficient, presents additional facts to defeat the claim or charge. For

example, the defense of RES JUDICATA in a civil case; the INSANITY DEFENSE in a criminal case; or the defense that one was acting in SELF-DEFENSE in a tort case or criminal case. In most situations the defendant who relies upon such a defense has the *burden of pleading* and *burden of proof* (see under BURDEN[1]) regarding the facts necessary to establish it.

**5. equitable defense** in a civil suit, a defense based upon principles that originated in courts of EQUITY; e.g., *fraud in the inducement* (see under FRAUD) or UNCLEAN HANDS.

**defensible** *adj.* capable of being defended against attack; capable of being defended or supported through argument: *a defensible legal position; a defensible interpretation of a contract.*
—**defensibility** *n.*
—**defensibly** *adv.*

**deferred annuity** *n.* See under ANNUITY.

**deferred compensation** *n.* compensation that is paid to an employee in a tax year subsequent to when it was earned, or that is paid in a way that postpones tax liability, as by contributing it to a pension plan.

**deficiency judgment** *n.* See under JUDGMENT.

**defined-benefit plan** *n.* See under PENSION PLAN.

**defined-contribution plan** *n.* See under PENSION PLAN.

**definite failure of issue** *n.* See under ISSUE[2].

**definite sentence** *n.* See under SENTENCE.

**defraud** *v.* to obtain money or property from (a person or entity) by FRAUD.
—**defrauder** *n.*

**degree** *n.* **1.** the GRADE of an offense.
**2.** Also called **academic degree.** a title conferred by a college or university as an indication of the completion of a course of study.
**3. honorary degree** a title conferred by a college or university in recognition of an individual's eminence and achievement in life. See LL.D.
**4. law degree** an academic degree awarded by a law school, especially the J.D. See also LL.M.; J.S.D.; S.J.D.

**degree of care** *n.* Same as STANDARD OF CARE.

**degree of consanguinity** *n.* any standardized measure of the closeness of a blood relationship for purposes of determining such things as which relatives will inherit an estate if a decedent leaves no will. See also CONSANGUINITY.

**degree of proof** *n.* Same as STANDARD OF PROOF.

**dehors** *prep. Law French.* outside; beyond the scope of: *facts dehors the record; evidence dehors the contract.*

**del credere** *Italian.* (lit. "of belief; of trust") a phrase used in connection with activities of agents, brokers, and the like who guarantee the solvency of the parties to whom goods are sold through their offices. See also *del credere agent* (under AGENT).

**delectus personae** *n. Latin.* (lit. "choice of the person") the right to choose close personal associates; particularly, the principle that a partnership can choose its own members.

**delegable** *adj.* capable of being delegated. See *delegable duty* (under DUTY[1]).

**delegate** *v.*, **delegated, delegating,** *n.*
—*v.* **1.** to commit a power, function, duty, or the like to another to exercise or perform as one's agent or deputy.
**2.** to transfer a power, function, duty, or the like to another.
**3.** to designate a person as one's agent or representative.
—*n.* **4.** a person designated to act for or represent another or others; particularly, one selected to speak and vote for a larger group or an entity: *The United States delegate to the United Nations.*
—**delegatee** *n.*
—**delegator** *n.*

**delegated power** *n.* See under POWER.

**delegation** *n.* **1.** the act of delegating or state of being delegated.

2. the body of delegates chosen to represent a political unit in an assembly.

**deliberate** *v.*, **deliberated, deliberating,** *adj.* —*v.* **1.** to weigh in the mind; consider carefully; analyze; reflect: *The jury deliberated for three hours.*
—*adj.* **2.** carefully considered; thought out.
**3.** intentional.
—**deliberation** *n.*

**deliberative process privilege** *n.* an *evidentiary privilege* (see under PRIVILEGE) permitting government agencies to refuse to disclose conversations, written communications, notes, and the like reflecting advisory opinions, recommendations, or deliberations comprising part of a process by which governmental decisions and policies are formulated. Also called **consultative privilege.**

**delict** *n. Civil Law.* a tort or offense for which damages may be recovered by the injured party.
—**delictual** *adj.*

**delinquency** *n.*, *pl.* **delinquencies. 1.** failure in or neglect of duty or obligation; dereliction; default: *delinquency in payment of dues.*
**2.** something, as a debt, that is past due or otherwise delinquent.
**3.** wrongful, illegal, or antisocial behavior, especially by a minor or by minors generally. See JUVENILE DELINQUENCY.

**delinquent** *adj.* **1.** (of an account, tax, debt, etc.) past due; overdue.
**2.** (of a person) failing in or neglectful of a duty or obligation.
—*n.* **3.** a person who is delinquent.
**4.** a JUVENILE DELINQUENT.
—**delinquently** *adv.*

**delivery** *n.*, *pl.* **deliveries.** the voluntary transfer of possession of property, or handing over of a piece of paper, with intent thereby to consummate a legal transaction. For example, a conveyance of land by DEED normally requires delivery of the deed. Delivery may be ACTUAL or CONSTRUCTIVE; see example at CONSTRUCTIVE. See also GIFT; *personal service* (under SERVICE).

**demand** *n.* **1.** a call for someone to perform a legal obligation.
**2.** a request for payment of a check or other instrument for the payment of money.
**3.** an assertion of legal right in a complaint or lawsuit.
**4. demand deposit** money deposited with a bank which can be withdrawn at any time. An ordinary checking or savings account is a demand deposit. Cf. *time deposit* (under TIME).
**5. demand for relief** Same as PRAYER FOR RELIEF.
**6. demand letter** a letter making a formal demand for payment of money owed, or for satisfaction of some other legal obligation. A demand letter is sent partly to lay the groundwork for a lawsuit, and partly in the hope that the recipient will perform as requested or work out a settlement so that a suit will not be necessary.
**7. demand loan** See under LOAN.
**8. due demand** demand that must be made before it can be said that a party has failed to perform a legal obligation. Usually this is made by means of a *demand letter.* For example, before suing to evict a tenant for nonpayment of rent, a landlord normally must make a formal demand for payment. Complaints seeking performance of a contract or remedy for breach typically recite that the defendant failed to perform "despite due demand," "due demand having been made," or the like.
**9. on demand** upon request; whenever requested. A negotiable instrument that does not specify a time for payment, such as a check, is **payable on demand,** and is referred to as a **demand instrument, demand note,** or the like. Cf. TIME.
—*v.* **10.** to make or issue a demand.
—**demandable** *adj.*

**demandant** *n.* one who makes a demand.

**demise** *n.*, *v.* **demised, demising.** —*n.*
**1.** the transfer of an estate in land, especially one for a limited time, particularly by lease or by will or intestacy.
**2.** the leasing of a ship by the owner

(the **demisor**) to another (the **demi-see**) upon terms whereby the owner completely relinquishes possession, command, and navigation of the vessel to the demisee for the duration of the contract; the granting of a *bareboat charter* (see under CHARTER²). See also OWNER PRO HAC VICE.
**3.** death, either literal or figurative: *A life estate terminates upon the demise of the holder. The Thirteenth Amendment signaled the demise of slavery in the United States.*
—*v.* **4.** to bring about a demise of real property, especially by renting out the property: *The tenant is required to maintain the demised premises.*
**5.** to lease out a vessel upon terms of a demise.
—**demisable** *adj.*

**demise charter** *n.* Same as *bareboat charter* (see under CHARTER²).

**demonstrative evidence** *n.* See under EVIDENCE.

**demur** *v.*, **demurred, demurring. 1.** to file a DEMURRER.
**2.** broadly, to raise any objection to a claim or procedure, especially on the ground that it is legally irrelevant or insufficient.
—**demurrable** *adj.*

**demurrant** *n.* one who demurs to a pleading or indictment.

**demurrer** *n.* a motion or pleading in response to a complaint or counterclaim, taking the position that the facts alleged, even if true, would not entitle the claimant to relief on any theory of law. In most American jurisdictions the demurrer has been replaced by the motion to dismiss for failure to state a claim (see discussion under CLAIM), but "demurrer" is sometimes used as an informal term for such a motion.
——**False Friend.** In law, a demurrer is not a person who demurs. (That's the DEMURRANT). The *-er* ending is a French infinitive ending indicating that a verb is being used as a noun. Thus a DEMURRER is not one who demurs but rather the act of demurring; a DISCLAIMER is not one who disclaims but the act of disclaiming; a WAIVER is not

one who waives but the act of waiving. The same principle accounts for DETAINER, IMPLEADER, INTERPLEADER, OUSTER, PLEADER², and other such words. See also note at TROVER. Although this pattern is particularly prominent in legal terminology because of the influence of Law French, it is not confined to the legal sphere: The English word *dinner* originated long ago as the French *dîner*—the act of dining.

**deny** *v.*, **denied, denying. 1.** to assert, in response to a complaint, counterclaim, or *request for admissions* (see under ADMISSION), that a particular allegation is untrue, or that the party responding lacks sufficient knowledge or information to form a belief as to its truth or falsity. All allegations not denied in one of these manners are deemed admitted and, absent special circumstances, can no longer be contested in the case.
**2.** (of a court) to refuse to grant a motion, petition, or other request for judicial action. Opposite of GRANT.
—**denial** *n.*

**deoxyribonucleic acid** *n.* See DNA.

**dépeçage** or **depecage** *n. French.* (lit. "carving up; dismemberment") a principle in CONFLICT OF LAWS, under which the problem of CHOICE OF LAW is dealt with on an issue-by-issue basis. If a court or jurisdiction accepts this approach, instead of applying the law of one state to the entire action the court might apply laws of different states to different aspects of the case, depending upon which state has the greatest interest or the closest connection with each separate issue.

**dependent** *n.* an individual who depends upon another for financial support. For income tax purposes, a taxpayer may claim an EXEMPTION for each dependent who meets certain tests, including receiving over half of his support from the taxpayer and either being a close relative of the taxpayer or living as a member of the taxpayer's household.

**depletion** *n.* **1.** reduction or exhaustion of a supply of something; especially,

the using up of a natural resource such as coal or oil, as through mining.
**2.** reduction in the value of land due to extraction of a natural resource.
—**depletable** *adj.*
—**deplete** *v.*, **depleted, depleting.**

**depletion allowance** *n.* an income tax deduction for businesses that sell natural resources such as minerals or oil, for the reduction in value of their property as the natural resources are extracted.

**deponent** *n.* a person who makes a written statement or gives testimony under oath or affirmation, especially the witness in a DEPOSITION.

**deport** *v.* to expel an ALIEN from a country. In the United States, DUE PROCESS requires that a person believed to be subject to deportation be allowed a hearing before an impartial tribunal before being deported. See also *deportable alien* (under ALIEN).
—**deportable** *adj.*
—**deportee** *n.*
—**deportation** *n.*

**depose** *v.*, **deposed, deposing. 1.** to give a sworn statement or testimony.
**2.** to say under oath or affirmation.
**3.** to ask questions of the deponent in a deposition; also referred to as "taking the deposition": *The lead attorney for the defense will depose the plaintiff.*

**deposit** *n.* See CERTIFICATE OF DEPOSIT; *demand deposit* (under DEMAND); *deposit account* (under ACCOUNT); *time deposit* (under TIME).

**deposition** *n.* **1.** a DISCOVERY procedure in which a witness testifies under oath in response to questions from the lawyer for one of the parties to a case. It is usually conducted much like a regular courtroom proceeding, complete with a court reporter and cross-examination by the opposing lawyer, but it normally takes place outside the courtroom and without a judge present. The purpose is partly to discover information and partly to have the testimony available on record in case the witness is no longer available when the trial is finally held.
**2.** the testimony, or the transcript of

the testimony, given at a deposition.
**3. deposition de bene esse** a deposition taken to preserve testimony for a trial, particularly the deposition of a witness who is likely to be unavailable at the time of the trial. Also called **de bene esse deposition.**
**4. deposition in aid of execution** a posttrial deposition of a party against whom a money judgment has been entered, for the purpose of identifying assets that could be seized to satisfy the judgment.

**depraved-heart murder** *n.* See under MURDER.

**depreciable** *adj.* capable of being depreciated for tax purposes.

**depreciate** *v.*, **depreciated, depreciating. 1.** (of property) to decline in value through normal wear and tear and obsolescence.
**2.** to claim a DEPRECIATION deduction on (property) for income tax purposes: *Because she uses her computer in her business she can depreciate it over five years.*

**depreciation** *n.* **1.** the gradual decline in the value of tangible property that occurs because of wear and tear and obsolescence.
**2.** a DEDUCTION allowed for income tax purposes because of depreciation in the value of property used in business or held for production of income. Ordinarily, a portion of the original cost of the property may be deducted each year for a number of years, until all or most of the original cost has been deducted.

**depth charge** *n.* Same as *Allen charge* (see under CHARGE).

**derelict** *adj.* **1.** abandoned: *a derelict ship.*
**2.** neglectful of duty; negligent in carrying out one's responsibilities.
—*n.* **3.** a vessel abandoned in open water by its crew without any hope or intention of returning.
**4.** anything that has been abandoned.
**5.** land left dry by the receding of a water line; land uncovered by RELICTION.

**dereliction** *n.* **1.** abandonment of something.

**2.** deliberate or conscious neglect in the carrying out one's responsibilities: *dereliction of duty.*
**3.** the state of being abandoned.
**4.** RELICTION.

**derivative action** *n.* See under ACTION.

**derivative work** *n.* See under WORK.

**derogation** *n.* limitation on the scope of something; partial repeal. Statutes on subjects that traditionally were governed by common law are said to be "in derogation of the common law."
—**derogate** *v.,* **derogated, derogating.**

**descend** *v.* **1.** (of property of a decedent, especially real property) to pass to one's heirs by INTESTATE SUCCESSION.
**2.** loosely, to pass by intestate succession or by will, especially if the person who takes by will is a child or other relative who would have received property by intestate succession if there had been no will.
—**descendibility** *n.*
—**descendible** *adj.*
—**descent** *n.*

**descendant** *n.* an offspring; any of one's children, grandchildren, great grandchildren, and so on.

**descent and distribution** *n.* **1.** the principles by which the property of a person who dies without a will is distributed. Also called **intestate succession.**
**2.** broadly, the principles by which property of a decedent is distributed, whether by intestate succession or by will.
See also DISTRIBUTION.

**desecrate** *v.,* **desecrated, desecrating.** to divest of sacred or hallowed character; to treat a sacred or hallowed object with disrespect.
—**desecration** *n.*
—**desecrator, desecrater** *n.*

**desecration of the flag** *n.* See FLAG DESECRATION.

**desegregate** *v.,* **desegregated, desegregating.** to eliminate segregation, especially racial segregation: *The club desegregated its facilities. The court ordered the schools to desegregate.*
—**desegregation** *n.*

**desertion** *n.* **1.** the breaking off of marital cohabitation, unprovoked by any wrongdoing by one's spouse, with the intent not to return and not to fulfill marital responsibilities. Desertion is one of the traditional grounds for divorce.
**2.** the military crime of abandoning one's post to avoid danger or of leaving one's unit with the intent of staying away permanently. Cf. ABSENCE WITHOUT LEAVE.

**design defect** *n.* See under DEFECT[2].

**destructible** *adj.* (of a legal interest or entity) susceptible of being extinguished or terminated by the occurrence of a future event or by operation of law.
—**destructibility** *n.*

**desuetude** *n.* the state of being no longer used or enforced.
——**Note.** Statutes that have not been enforced for a great many years, or that linger on the books even though the subject they address or the reason for their enactment no longer exists, are said to have "fallen into desuetude." Nevertheless, if they are on the books and have not been declared unconstitional or otherwise invalidated, they can be enforced. See, for example, notes at FORNICATION and SODOMY.

**detain** *v.* **1.** to keep a person in CUSTODY for a limited time for an official purpose: *detain for questioning.* See also PREVENTIVE DETENTION.
**2.** to retain possession of another's property.
—**detainable** *adj.*
—**detainee** *n.*

**detainer** *n.* **1.** a writ calling for continued detention of a person about to be released from custody, as when a prisoner is wanted for another crime.
**2.** Also called **unlawful detainer.** Wrongfully retaining possession of property of another, as by refusing to vacate an apartment upon expiration of

the lease.

**3.** any detention of person or property. See note at DEMURRER.

**detention** *n.* **1.** the act of detaining; especially the maintenance of a person in custody or confinement for a limited period, as while awaiting a court decision.
**2.** the state of being detained.
**3.** the withholding of what belongs to or is claimed by another.
See also PREVENTIVE DETENTION.

**determinate** *adj.* having defined limits; fixed; definite.

**determinate sentence** *n.* See under SENTENCE.

**determination** *n.* **1.** the decision of a court, an administrative agency or tribunal, an arbitration panel, or the like, either on an entire case or on some particular issue.
**2. determination letter** a letter from an administrative agency communicating its decision on a matter relating to the recipient of the letter; for example, a letter from the Internal Revenue Service to a corporation that had requested permission to change its tax year, or a letter from the Social Security Administration to an individual who had applied for disability benefits.
**3. final determination** the final decision of an administrative agency or arbitration panel with respect to a matter. Most administrative determinations can be reviewed in the courts; most determinations by arbitration panels are nonreviewable.

**determine** *v.*, **determined, determining. 1.** to reach a DECISION on: *to determine a case.* See also *hear and determine* (under HEAR).
**2.** to ascertain: *to determine the facts.*
**3.** (of an interest in real property) to terminate; come to an end; expire. See *fee simple determinable* (under FEE[1]).
—**determinability** *n.*
—**determinable** *adj.*

**detinue** *n.* a common law FORM OF ACTION for recovery of personal property from one who acquired possession of it lawfully but detains it without right,

and for damages for the detention. See also note at TROVER.

**detrimental reliance** *n.* See under RELIANCE.

**device** *n.* **1.** a plan or stratagem, especially for an evil or unlawful purpose: *The rules of the Securities and Exchange Commission prohibit the use of any device, scheme, or artifice to defraud in connection with the purchase or sale of any security.*
**2.** a mechanical or electrical contrivance; machine: *The company patented the device. Only those with a casino license are permitted to own a gambling device.* See also OBSCENE DEVICE.
**3.** Also called **medical device.** an apparatus intended to affect the structure or function of the body of humans or animals, or intended for use in the diagnosis, treatment, or prevention of disease in humans or animals. Such devices are subject to regulation to varying degrees by the federal Food and Drug Administration.
**4.** a graphic design: *A distinctive device may be registered as a trademark.*
**5.** a pattern of words or reasoning used for persuasive or emotional effect: *The defense attorney's repeated statement to the jury, "If it doesn't fit, you must acquit," was an effective rhetorical device.*

**devise** *v.*, **devised, devising,** *n.* —*v.* **1.** to dispose of real property by will. Cf. BEQUEATH, GRANT.
—*n.* **2.** a gift of real property by will, or the property interest so given. Cf. BEQUEST.
—**devisability** *n.*
—**devisable** *adj.*
——**Usage.** Although the very influential Uniform Probate Code uses *devise* in reference to personal as well as real property, that broader usage does not appear to have caught on among practicing lawyers generally.

**devisee** *n.* the recipient of a DEVISE. Cf. LEGATEE.

**devisor** *n.* one who makes a DEVISE.

**devolve** *v.*, **devolved, devolving.** to

pass from one person to another, especially BY OPERATION OF LAW: *Upon President Lincoln's death, the presidency devolved on Vice President Johnson. When the corporations merged, their debts devolved upon the successor corporation.* —**devolution** *n.*

**dictum** *n., pl.* **dicta.** *Latin.* (lit. "a remark") Short for OBITER DICTUM; a legal assertion in a court's opinion that is peripheral to its main argument and unnecessary to the actual HOLDING, or such assertions collectively. Because it may not have received the court's fullest consideration, dictum is regarded as less persuasive in a precedent than a fully considered holding. ——**Usage.** The term *dictum* is used to refer either to a single such assertion or to a number of them collectively; the plural *dicta* can properly be used only if two or more discrete passages are being referred to: *In support of its position, plaintiff cites only dictum. The defendant points to several dicta in older cases, but we find them unpersuasive.*

**dies** *n., pl.* **dies.** *Latin.* day; the day; a day. See also DE DIE IN DIEM; SINE DIE.

**dies a quo** *n., pl.* **dies a quibus.** *Latin.* (lit. "the day from which") the beginning date; the date from which a period of time is computed; the starting day for a transaction.

**dies ad quem** *n., pl.* **dies ad quos.** *Latin.* (lit. "the day to which") the ending date; the date through which a period of time is computed; the concluding day of a transaction.

**dies juridicus** *n., pl.* **dies juridici.** *Latin.* (lit. "juridical day") a day upon which the courts are open for regular business; a day upon which judicial business may be conducted. Rendered in English variously as **court day, judicial day,** or, in ancient usage in regard to certain courts, **law day.**

**dies non** or **dies non juridicus** *n., pl.* **dies non** or **dies non juridici.** *Latin.* (lit. "nonjuridical day"; "not a juridical day") a day upon which the courts are not open for regular business; a day upon which judicial business may not

normally be conducted. ——**Usage.** Although the short form "dies non" sounds like an informal shortening best suited to casual use, it is historically the more common form of this phrase even in formal legal usage.

**digest** *n.* **1.** a book or series of volumes in which HEADNOTES or other summaries of the holdings of cases are collected and arranged by subject matter for ease of reference by lawyers or others doing legal research. **2.** a summary of a case. —*v.* **3.** to create a summary of a case or a compilation of such summaries. —**digester** *n.*

**dilatory plea** *n.* a PLEA by a defendant in a civil action that attempts to delay or dispose of the case without reaching the merits; for example, a plea raising a defense based upon lack of jurisdiction or statute of limitations.

**diligence** *n.* serious and persistent attention and effort. In many contexts the law requires people to exercise diligence in regard to a matter in order to preserve their rights or avoid liability. —**diligent** *adj.*

**dilution** *n.* **1.** a lessening of the value of a company's stock resulting from the issuance of additional shares. **2.** Also called **vote dilution.** a reduction in the relative voting power of one group of citizens as compared to others, as through unfair reapportionment or CRIMINAL DISENFRANCHISEMENT. **3.** the lessening of the capacity of a trademark to identify and distinguish goods or services, as through use of the same or a similar mark by someone else in a manner that is likely to cause confusion. —**dilute** *v.,* **diluted, diluting.**

**diminished capacity** (or **responsibility**) *n.* mental retardation or other mental condition, sometimes including intoxication, that is not the kind or degree of impairment necessary to establish the INSANITY DEFENSE, but that calls into question whether a defendant could have had the necessary STATE OF

MIND to commit a particular crime. In some jurisdictions this may be considered as a factor reducing the degree of the crime for which a defendant may be convicted. See also note at TWINKIE DEFENSE.

**diplomatic immunity** *n.* See under IMMUNITY.

**direct¹** *adj.* **1.** proximate; straightforward; without intervening events. Often distinguished from "collateral"; for example, a **direct attack** on a judgment is one made in the same case, as by an appeal or motion for a new trial, and a **direct heir** is a direct descendent or ancestor (compare *collateral attack* and *collateral heir,* under COLLATERAL²). See also *direct examination* vs. *cross-examination* (under EXAMINATION); *direct evidence* vs. *circumstantial evidence* (under EVIDENCE).
—*n.* **2.** Short for *direct examination* (see under EXAMINATION).

**direct²** *v.* (of a judge or court) to instruct or order someone to do something; a gentle way of saying "order": *The jury is directed to disregard the answer. The plaintiff is directed to produce the documents requested by the defendant forthwith. Would Your Honor please direct the witness to answer the question?* In such contexts, "direct" is interchangeable with INSTRUCT. See also *directed verdict* (under VERDICT).
—**direction** *n.*

**direct examiner** *n.* the person, usually a lawyer, who questions a witness on *direct examination* (see under EXAMINATION) and also conducts any *redirect examination* (see under EXAMINATION). Cf. CROSS-EXAMINER.

**direct tax** *n. Constitutional Law.* a tax imposed at a flat rate per person or a tax on land. The Constitution prohibits the imposition of any federal tax of such a nature except in proportion to each state's population.
——**History.** In the Constitutional Convention of 1787, delegates from southern states were concerned that the new Congress, under the influence of small northern states that were densely settled but relatively slave-free, might try to raise revenue through property taxes measured by the acre (for land) or by the head (for slaves). It was felt that this would be unfair to taxpayers in the south, with its large tracts of land and its many slaves. To alleviate this concern, the Convention adopted a provision stating, "No Capitation, or other direct, tax shall be laid, unless in Proportion to the Census..."—for which purpose slaves were counted as only three-fifths of a person. Although the precise scope of the term *direct tax* was a mystery even to the delegates who adopted it (see note at FOUNDING FATHERS), the Supreme Court has generally held that it is limited to head taxes and taxes on land. When Congress first attempted to institute an income tax, however, the court decided that that, too, was a "direct tax," and struck it down because it was apportioned on a basis other than state population. To overcome this obstacle the Sixteenth Amendment was adopted, specifically authorizing a federal income tax.

**director** *n.* one of the persons elected by the stockholders of a corporation to manage its affairs. The directors together constitute the BOARD OF DIRECTORS. Cf. OFFICER.

**directors' and officers' liability insurance** *n.* insurance that indemnifies directors and officers of a corporation against liability for claims arising from the conduct of the business of the corporation. Also called **D&O insurance, D&O liability insurance.**

**disability** *n., pl.* **disabilities. 1.** for purposes of insurance, unemployment compensation, social security, and the like, a disease or injury that renders one unable to perform one's usual occupation, or a physical or mental condition making it impossible to engage in any substantial gainful employment. **2.** for purposes of the federal law against DISABILITY DISCRIMINATION, a physical or mental impairment that substantially limits one or more of the major life activities of an individual. **3.** Also called **legal disability.** Same as INCAPACITY.

See also CANONICAL DISABILITY; CIVIL DISABILITY.

**disability discrimination** *n.* discrimination against, or failure to provide reasonable accommodation for, people with disabilities or people who have been disabled or are perceived as being disabled, in such areas as employment, public accommodations, transportation, and communications. Such discrimination is prohibited by the federal Americans with Disabilities Act of 1990.

**disability insurance** *n.* insurance providing payments if the insured individual suffers a temporary or permanent DISABILITY.

**disallow** *v.* to reject; refuse permission for; rule adversely upon: *The judge disallowed the application for attorneys' fees.*
—**disallowable** *adj.*
—**disallowance** *n.*

**disappear** *v.* **1.** to vanish.
**2.** to cause (an individual) to vanish, especially by arresting or abducting the individual and then killing the individual and disposing of the body without any notice to the individual's relatives or acquaintances of what happened to the individual or whether the individual is dead or alive.
——**Usage.** "Disappearing" political enemies, or individuals regarded in any way as a threat, is a form of political terrorism particularly associated with right-wing regimes or groups in Central and South America, where the unusual transitive use of the verb originated. See also DISAPPEARANCE.

**disappearance** *n.* **1.** the act or an instance of vanishing.
**2.** the act or an instance of disappearing a person, or of being disappeared, as a form of political terrorism. See DISAPPEAR.
**3. enforced disappearance of persons** *International Law.* as defined in the 1998 agreement to establish the INTERNATIONAL CRIMINAL COURT, the arrest, detention, or abduction of persons by, or with the authorization, support, or acquiescence of, a state or a political organization, followed by a refusal to acknowledge that deprivation of freedom or to give information on the fate or whereabouts of those persons, with the intention of removing them from the protection of the law for a prolonged period of time. The enforced disappearance of persons, as so defined, is classified as a CRIME AGAINST HUMANITY within the jurisdiction of that court.

**disbar** *v.,* **disbarred, disbarring.** to take away an attorney's right to practice law, usually for criminal or unethical conduct.
—**disbarment** *n.*

**discharge** *v.,* **discharged, discharging,** *n.* —*v.* **1.** to satisfy or extinguish a debt or obligation: *He discharged the debt in three monthly installments.*
**2.** to release a person from a debt or obligation: *To settle the case they signed a release discharging the plaintiff from any further obligation under the contract.*
**3.** to perform or fulfill a duty or obligation: *The jurors discharged their duties in a responsible manner.*
**4.** to free; release; let go: *The judge discharged the jury with his thanks. The prisoner was discharged after serving her term.*
**5.** to terminate the employment of: *The company discharged the strikers.*
—*n.* **6.** the act of discharging or being discharged. See also WRONGFUL DISCHARGE.
**7. discharge in bankruptcy** the discharge of all or most of a bankrupt's remaining debts at the conclusion of a BANKRUPTCY proceeding.
—**dischargeable** *adj.*

**disciplinary proceeding** *n.* a proceeding, held by a state licensing agency or other body charged with regulating the conduct of professionals such as lawyers or accountants, to determine whether an individual is guilty of professional misconduct and what penalty should be imposed.

**disclaim** *v.* **1.** to renounce or disavow a right, interest, benefit, or claim.
**2.** to renounce or disavow a duty, responsibility, affiliation, or liability.

**disclaimant** *n.* one who disclaims something; the maker of a disclaimer.

**disclaimer** *n.* **1.** a statement, document, or assertion that disclaims; disavowal; denial.
**2.** the act of disclaiming.
See also note at DEMURRER.

**disclosure** *n.* See under DISCOVERY.

**discontinuance** *n.* DISMISSAL of a suit, especially *voluntary dismissal* (see under DISMISSAL), which is also called **voluntary discontinuance.**
—**discontinue** *v.,* **discontinued, discontinuing.**

**discovery** *n., pl.* **discoveries.** the set of procedures by which each side in a case may obtain pertinent information from the other. The most common discovery techniques are the DEPOSITION, *interrogatories* (see under INTERROGATORY), and PRODUCTION OF DOCUMENTS. Modern practice permits liberal discovery in order to prevent TRIAL BY AMBUSH. Discovery is primarily of use in the period leading up to the trial, and thus is often referred to as **pretrial discovery;** but in some situations it is also conducted during or even after a trial. In some jurisdictions discovery is usually referred to as **disclosure,** which is just the same thing from the point of view of the giver of the information rather than the receiver. Information, documents, or other things that may be obtained through discovery are said to be **discoverable.** See also FISHING EXPEDITION.

**discredit** *v.* to introduce evidence, by cross-examination or otherwise, casting doubt upon the believability of a witness or authenticity of a document.

**discretion** *n.* **1.** the power to exercise one's own judgment in a matter and choose among various options in dealing with it.
**2. absolute discretion** theoretically unlimited discretion, so that any choice among available options, however unreasonable it might appear, would be immune from challenge. For example, a will might give the executor "absolute discretion" to decide how certain property should be distributed among the testator's children. Even so, a court might set aside a distribution upon a showing that the decision was not made in good faith.
**3. judicial discretion** the power of a judge to make any reasonable ruling on matters with respect to which there is no single "right answer." A court's decision on such a matter may be reversed only for ABUSE OF DISCRETION.
**4. prosecutorial discretion** the discretion of prosecutors in choosing cases to prosecute and accepting or rejecting plea bargains. Not every violation of law can be prosecuted, and prosecutors have wide discretion in deciding which to pursue and which to drop, so long as their decisions are not discriminatory or vindictive.

**discretionary appeal** *n.* See under APPEAL.

**discriminate** *v.,* **discriminated, discriminating.** to engage in DISCRIMINATION.
—**discriminator** *n.*

**discrimination** *n.* **1.** treating some people differently from others for reasons that are extraneous to the matter at hand, especially because of some group membership or characteristic such as race, sex, religion, or national origin.
**2.** Also called **illegal discrimination.** discrimination in violation of a state or federal constitution, statute, or regulation.
**3. invidious discrimination** offensive and unfair discrimination, especially illegal discrimination on the basis of a SUSPECT CLASSIFICATION.
See also AFFIRMATIVE ACTION; AGE DISCRIMINATION; DISABILITY DISCRIMINATION; PREGNANCY DISCRIMINATION; RACIAL DISCRIMINATION; SEPARATE BUT EQUAL; SEX DISCRIMINATION; SEX-PLUS DISCRIMINATION.

**disenfranchise** *v.,* **disenfranchised, disenfranchising.** to deprive of the right to vote. See also CRIMINAL DISENFRANCHISEMENT; *vote dilution* (under DILUTION).
—**disenfranchisement** *n.*

**disfranchise** *n. v.*, **disfranchised, disfranchising.** Same as DISENFRANCHISE.
—**disfranchisement** *n.*

**dishonor** *v.* **1.** to fail or refuse to HONOR an instrument for the payment of money when presented for payment or acceptance.
—*n.* **2.** the act of dishonoring an instrument.

**disinherit** *v.* to exclude an heir from inheritance by writing a will that leaves all property to others.

**disinheritance** *n.* the act of disinheriting or the fact of being disinherited.

**disinterested** *adj.* lacking bias or interest (see INTEREST²) in a matter; impartial: *The judge and jurors in a case must be completely disinterested.* Cf. INTERESTED.
—**disinterestedness** *n.*
——**Usage.** There are two senses in which one can lack interest in a matter: One can lack a personal stake in the matter, or one can find it boring. Over the centuries, *disinterested* and *uninterested* have both been used in both senses, and they are still often used interchangeably today. Modern usage tends to favor *disinterested* in the sense of "impartial" and *uninterested* in the sense of "bored." The terms do overlap in both popular and legal usage, but in opposite ways: In popular speech, *uninterested* always means "bored" and *disinterested* often does also; in legal contexts, *disinterested* always means "impartial" and *uninterested* often does also.

**dismissal** *n.* **1.** an order or judgment in favor of a defendant, throwing a case out of court without a trial or without completing a trial.
**2.** the act of issuing such an order or judgment.
**3. dismissal with leave to replead** dismissal of a civil case because of some inadequacy in the complaint, with permission to file an amended complaint to try to cure the defect. Plaintiffs are normally given at least one chance to replead when their first complaint is inadequate.

**4. dismissal with prejudice** a dismissal barring the plaintiff or prosecution from ever reinstituting the case.
**5. dismissal without prejudice** a dismissal leaving the plaintiff or prosecutor free to try again later if circumstances change. For example, a dismissal for lack of personal jurisdiction would normally be without prejudice to the filing of a new case upon the same claims if jurisdiction can be obtained over the defendant.
**6. involuntary dismissal** dismissal upon motion of the defendant or upon the court's own motion, without the consent of the plaintiff.
**7. voluntary dismissal** dismissal at the request of the plaintiff, or with the plaintiff's consent.
—**dismiss** *v.*
—**dismissible** *adj.*

**disorderly conduct** *n.* a term used in some states for such minor offenses as public drunkenness, public fighting, making too much noise, urinating in public, or other conduct that is mildly dangerous or disturbing to the public. The particular conduct covered by the term must be clearly defined by statute; otherwise the statute making it an offense would be *void for vagueness* (see under VAGUE). Other terms sometimes used for the same general range of offenses include **breach of the peace** and **disturbing the peace.**

**disparagement** *n.* the tort of disseminating false and derogatory information about a person's property, products, or business such as to discourage others from doing business with the person or otherwise cause economic and personal injury. Also called **injurious falsehood.** See also FOOD DISPARAGEMENT; PRODUCT DISPARAGEMENT; SLANDER OF TITLE; TRADE LIBEL.
—**disparage** *v.*, **disparaged, disparaging.**
—**disparaging** *adj.*
—**disparagingly** *adv.*
——**Usage.** Although *disparagement* is akin to DEFAMATION in that both involve false derogatory statements, *defamation* involves statements about a

person, whereas the term *disparagement* is generally used in law to refer to statements about things.

**dispossess** *v.* to put someone out of possession of real property; for example, to evict a tenant. Cf. QUIT.
—**dispossession** *n.*
—**dispossessor** *n.*

**disseise** *v.*, **disseised, disseising.** to deprive a person of SEISIN; put the holder of a FREEHOLD estate out of possession, especially wrongfully or by force. Also, **disseize.**

**disseisee** or **disseizee** *n.* one who is disseised; one who is ousted from possession of his freehold.

**disseisin** or **disseizin** *n.* the act of disseising or the state of being disseised.

**disseisor** or **disseizor** *n.* one who disseises another; one who ousts the holder of a freehold from possession.

**disseize** *v.*, **disseized, disseizing.** Same as DISSEISE.

**dissent** *v.* **1.** to declare formally that one disagrees with a course of action being taken by a body of which one is a member, as when a stockholder dissents from a corporate action in order to pursue her APPRAISAL RIGHTS. **2.** specifically, of one or more members of a panel of judges, to put on record the fact that they voted against the decision of the majority. —*n.* **3.** the act of dissenting or the fact that one dissents. **4.** a *dissenting opinion* (see under OPINION).
—**dissenter** *n.*

**dissolve** *v.*, **dissolved, dissolving.** to terminate a legal relationship or bring the legal existence of an entity to an end: *dissolve a marriage; dissolve a partnership; dissolve a corporation.*
—**dissolution** *n.*

**distinguish** *v.* to recognize or point out differences between a previous case and a case currently under consideration that make it appropriate to reach a different result in the current case. A precedent that can be distinguished in this manner is said to be **distinguishable:** *The cases cited by the plaintiff are distinguishable in that they all involved fiduciary relationships rather than arm's-length contracts.*

**distrain** *v.* to seize a person's goods as security for an obligation, as when a landlord changes the locks on property upon which the rent has not been paid so that the lessee cannot remove the things inside until the rent has been paid, and if necessary they can be sold for back rent. Distraint is now regulated by statute in all or nearly all states.
—**distrainable** *adj.*
—**distrainee** *n.*
—**distrainor, distrainer** *n.*

**distraint** *n.* the act of distraining or the state of being distrained: *The landlord resorted to distraint. The tenant's property is under distraint.* Also called **distress.**

**distress** *n.* **1.** Same as DISTRAINT. **2.** See EMOTIONAL DISTRESS.

**distributee** *n.* **1.** a person entitled to share in the DISTRIBUTION of an intestate's estate or, more broadly, of any decedent's estate. **2.** generally, anyone who shares in any DISTRIBUTION of money or property.

**distribution** *n.* **1. a.** the parceling out of the property (especially the personal property) of a person who died without a will, to those entitled to it under the rules of INTESTATE SUCCESSION. **b.** more broadly, the parceling out of any decedent's estate, whether by the rules of intestate succession or under a will. See also ADMINISTER; ADMINISTRATOR; EXECUTOR. **2.** generally, any allocation and dispensing of money or property in which a number of people are entitled to share; e.g., a distribution of corporate profits to shareholders in the form of dividends, or the distribution of a bankrupt's assets to creditors. **3.** the total amount of money subject to such a distribution. **4.** Also called **distributive share.** the portion of an estate or other aggregate of property received by a particular DISTRIBUTEE.

—**distribute** *v.,* **distributed, distributing.**

**distributive justice** *n.* See under JUSTICE[1].

**district** *n.* **1.** generally, any geographic division established by a government for administrative convenience: *school district; election district.*
**2.** Also called **judicial district.** a geographic division established for purposes of organizing a court system. For federal judicial purposes, the United States is divided into over ninety such districts, with at least one for every state or other federal political subdivision, and from two to four in each of the larger states: *District of Delaware; District of Guam; Western District of Texas.*
See also UNITED STATES ATTORNEY; UNITED STATES DISTRICT COURT. Cf. CIRCUIT.

**district attorney** *n.* the public official responsible for managing the prosecution of criminal offenses under state law in a particular locality.

**district court** *n.* See under COURT.

**district judge** *n.* See under JUDGE.

**disturbing the peace** *n.* See under DISORDERLY CONDUCT.

**diversity case** *n.* See under CASE[1].

**diversity jurisdiction** *n.* See under JURISDICTION[1].

**diversity of citizenship** *n.* the situation that exists when a plaintiff and defendant in a federal case are citizens of different states. Often called **diversity** for short.
—**Note.** Diversity is one of the two major grounds upon which a federal court can exercise jurisdiction over a case. See *subject matter jurisdiction* and *diversity jurisdiction* (under JURISDICTION[1]).

**dividend** *n.* a portion of the earnings and profits of a corporation distributed to the shareholders in proportion to their holdings: *The company paid a year-end dividend of $1.25 per share.* See also EX DIVIDEND.

**divisible** *adj.* (of a legal obligation, interest, decree, etc.) susceptible of treatment as two or more independent parts, so that one part can be performed, enforced, modified, invalidated, or the like without affecting the others. See, e.g., *divisible divorce* (under DIVORCE); *divisible contract* (under CONTRACT). Cf. ENTIRE.

**divisible divorce** *n.* See under DIVORCE.

**divorce** *n., v.,* **divorced, divorcing.**
—*n.* **1.** Also called **absolute divorce.** the termination of a valid marriage other than by death. In the United States this can be accomplished only by obtaining a judgment (typically called a **divorce decree**) from a court in accordance with state law. The divorce decree typically includes provisions regarding division of property, custody of children, and alimony and child support. Cf. ANNULMENT; SEPARATION.
**2.** in older usage, the legal termination of cohabitation of a husband and wife without terminating the marriage, corresponding in modern law to a court-ordered *legal separation* (see under SEPARATION).
**3. divisible divorce** the doctrine that a divorce decree issued by the state where one spouse resides, in a case where the court did not have personal jurisdiction over the other spouse, may be binding upon the courts of the state where the other spouse resides insofar as it affects the parties' marital status, but not binding insofar as it purports to determine money and property issues, as by setting alimony or dividing property.
**4. divorce a mensa et thoro** *Latin.* (lit. "...from table and bed"). Also called **divorce from bed and board.** Same as DIVORCE (def. 2).
**5. divorce a vinculo matrimonii** *Latin.* (lit. "...from the bond of marriage"). Same as DIVORCE (def. 1).
**6. divorce mill** *Informal.* a state, municipality, or country where divorce is relatively easy to obtain, and where people from states with more restrictive divorce laws tend to go to obtain divorces. Resort to divorce mills, once a

prominent feature of the American cultural landscape, has become less common as divorce laws generally have become more liberal. Even so, the Supreme Court held in 1975 that an Iowa statute denying divorce to citizens of the state who had lived there less than a year was justified by, among other things, the state's possible interest in not becoming a divorce mill. *Sosna v. Iowa,* 419 U.S. 393 (1975). Cf. GRETNA GREEN.

**7. limited divorce** Same as DIVORCE (def. 2).

**8. mail-order divorce** a purported divorce obtained by mail from another country, especially Mexico. For a brief period this was a popular way for couples who lived in states with restrictive divorce laws to attempt to obtain divorces; the technique generally failed of its purpose, however, because American courts refused to recognize the divorces.

**9. migratory divorce** divorce obtained by a spouse or couple after moving to a state with less restrictive divorce laws in order to take advantage of those laws. If the party obtaining the divorce satisfies all jurisdictional, residency, and other requirements for a valid divorce in the state where it is obtained, the divorce must be given FULL FAITH AND CREDIT by other states.

**10. no-fault divorce** a divorce obtained without attributing blame to either party for the breakdown of the marriage. Traditionally, divorce was permitted only if one party proved wrongdoing by the other, such as ADULTERY, CRUELTY, or DESERTION. Now most divorces are granted without any showing of fault, and many states have completely abolished the concept of fault as a basis for divorce. See also BREAKDOWN OF THE MARRIAGE. Cf. *covenant marriage* (under MARRIAGE).

**11. uncontested divorce** a divorce obtained by one spouse without opposition by the other, or obtained by both spouses together.

—*v.* **12.** to obtain a divorce from one's spouse.

**13.** (of a judge or court) to grant a divorce to a married individual or couple.

**divorce agreement** *n.* an agreement between divorcing spouses regarding issues of property, child custody, and the like, typically incorporated into the divorce decree.

**divorce decree** *n.* See under DIVORCE.

**divorce settlement** *n.* **1.** a DIVORCE AGREEMENT, especially when viewed with a focus on its terms regarding money and property.
**2.** property or money received pursuant to such a settlement.
Cf. MARRIAGE SETTLEMENT.

**DNA** *n.* deoxyribonucleic acid, the macromolecule that contains the genetic information for any individual of any species of plant or animal.

**DNA fingerprint** *n.* Same as *DNA profile* (see under DNA PROFILING).

**DNA fingerprinting** *n.* Same as DNA PROFILING.

**DNA profiling** *n.* the use of chemical techniques to isolate portions of an individual's DNA (as from samples of blood, skin, hair, semen, or saliva) so as to identify a pattern **(DNA profile)** that has an extremely high likelihood of being unique to that individual. DNA profiles are used in linking suspects to evidence at crime scenes, determining whether separate crimes appear to have been committed by the same individual or different individuals, paternity testing, and the like. Also called **DNA fingerprinting, genetic profiling, genetic fingerprinting.** See also COMBINED DNA INDEX SYSTEM.

**docket** *n.* **1.** a chronological record of steps taken in a case—papers filed, orders entered, trial days held, etc. —maintained by a court clerk.
**2.** a complete list of cases pending in a court; a court's caseload.
**3.** a court CALENDAR.
—*v.* **4.** to record on a docket.
See also ROCKET DOCKET.

**Doctor of Juridical Science** *n.* See J.S.D. and S.J.D.

**Doctor of Jurisprudence** *n.* See J.S.D.

**Doctor of Laws** *n.* See LL.D.

**Doctor of the Science of Law** *n.* See J.S.D. and S.J.D.

**doctor-patient privilege** *n.* Same as PHYSICIAN-PATIENT PRIVILEGE.

**doctrine** *n.* a legal principle. The term sometimes connotes a firm rule, sometimes a general guideline to be applied flexibly and judiciously.

**document** *n.* anything upon which information is recorded; most often a writing (including telephone message slips, checks, grocery lists), but also, in some contexts, photographs, audio tapes, computer files, or any other form in which information can be preserved. See also ANCIENT DOCUMENT; PRODUCTION OF DOCUMENTS.

——**False Friend.** Although in most contexts, even in law, a *document* is simply a written instrument, in certain contexts the term extends far beyond this ordinary meaning. If one is required to produce all "documents" containing communications concerning an issue in a lawsuit, it would be a mistake to withhold a relevant telephone message tape on the theory that it is not a "document."

**document of title** *n.* **1.** a document, such as a BILL OF LADING or WAREHOUSE RECEIPT, issued by or addressed to a person or entity entrusted with goods for storage or shipment, identifying the goods and serving as evidence of the right of the person with the document to receive the goods or direct their delivery. **2. negotiable document of title** a document of title stating that the specified goods are to be delivered either to the order of a named person or simply to whoever presents the document. Title to the goods covered by such a document can be transferred from a seller to a buyer by indorsing and handing over the document. The buyer then presents the document to receive the goods. **3. nonnegotiable document of title** a document of title that provides for delivery of the goods covered by it only to a specific named person, who need not present the document to receive the goods.

**documentary evidence** *n.* See under EVIDENCE.

**doing business** *n.* (of a corporation) conducting regular activity within a particular state, of a nature sufficient to justify holding the corporation subject to suit in the state even on causes of action that are unrelated to any particular business transacted there. An out-of-state corporation found to be "doing business" in the state is deemed to be present in the state and subject to the jurisdiction of its courts for all purposes. Cf. TRANSACTION OF BUSINESS.

**doing business as** See D/B/A.

**doli capax** *adj. Latin.* (lit. "capable of deceit") capable of crime; of sufficient age and mental competence to form the intent necessary for a crime, and so to be held accountable for it. Also called **capax doli.** See note at DOLI INCAPAX.

**doli incapax** *adj. Latin.* (lit. "incapable of deceit") incapable of crime; lacking the mental capacity to formulate criminal intent, especially by reason of age.

——**History.** At common law, a child between the ages of seven and fourteen was presumed to be doli incapax, but could be held accountable for a crime if it was proved otherwise; a child under the age of seven was conclusively presumed to be doli incapax.

**domain** *n.* See EMINENT DOMAIN; PUBLIC DOMAIN.

**domain name grabbing** *n.* Same as CYBERSQUATTING.
—**domain name grabber** *n.*

**domain name piracy** *n.* Same as CYBERSQUATTING.
—**domain name pirate** *n.*

**domestic** *adj.* pertaining to the internal workings of the United States, a particular state, or a family. See, for example, *domestic corporation* (under CORPORATION); *domestic relations* (under FAMILY LAW).

**domestic partner** *n.* either of the two individuals forming a DOMESTIC PARTNERSHIP.

**domestic partnership** *n.* a committed relationship between two unmarried people, of the same or opposite sex, analogous to a marriage. Some municipalities and some private companies formally recognize such relationships, particularly for same-sex couples, granting them the same status and employment benefits as married couples. See also CIVIL UNION.

**domestic violence** *n.* violence against a person living in one's household, especially a member of one's immediate family.

**domicile** *n.* the place where one has one's permanent and primary home, or where a corporation has its headquarters or principal place of business; the place with which one is associated for taxing and voting purposes. One can have many residences, but only one domicile. One whose domicile is in a particular place is said to be **domiciled** there or to be a **domiciliary** of that place: *a person domiciled in Paris; an Idaho domiciliary.* See also RESIDENCE; RESIDENT.

**dominant estate** *n.* See under ESTATE³.

**dominant tenement** *n.* See under ESTATE³.

**domitae naturae** *adj. Latin.* (lit. "of a tamed nature; of a domesticated nature") (of an animal or animals) domesticated; of a kind customarily kept as a pet or work animal or raised for food; e.g., a dog, horse, or pig. Also, **mansuetae naturae.** See note at FERAE NATURAE.

**donee** *n.* **1.** the recipient of a gift.
**2.** the person designated to exercise a POWER OF APPOINTMENT.

**donee beneficiary** *n.* a *third-party beneficiary* (see under CONTRACT) who is to receive the promised performance as a gift from the person to whom the promise was made. Even though the donee beneficiary gave no consideration, he may enforce the contract because consideration was provided by the promisee.

**donor** *n.* **1.** a person who makes a gift.
**2.** one who confers a POWER OF APPOINTMENT.
**3.** the SETTLOR of a trust.

**Don't Ask, Don't Tell** the informal but universally used name for the policy of the United States military with regard to homosexuals in the military. Under this policy, individuals joining the military are not asked their sexual orientation; but once in the military, they are forbidden to engage in homosexual conduct either while on duty or while on leave, and if they are in fact homosexual or bisexual they are forbidden to say so. If a member of the military discloses such an orientation, the member will be discharged from the military unless the member can prove that he or she neither engages in homosexual conduct nor has a propensity making it likely that he or she will engage in such acts. Also called **Don't Ask, Don't Tell, Don't Pursue.**
——**History.** The name "Don't Ask, Don't Tell" was attached to this policy by Senator Sam Nunn, Chairman of the Senate Committee on Armed Services, when he first proposed the policy in 1993 as a compromise between the Clinton administration, which wanted to eliminate discrimination on the basis of sexual orientation in the military, and the military brass, which wanted to retain the previous policy of automatically discharging from the military any member found to be a homosexual. The Clinton administration sought some assurance that mere allegations that one or another member of the military was a homosexual would not be pursued in the absence of evidence of homosexual conduct, and gave the name "Don't Ask, Don't Tell, Don't Pursue" to the resulting compromise, which was adopted by the Department of Defense and later that year enacted into statutory law by Congress. Senator Nunn's shorter, catchier name for the policy, however, is the one usually used by courts and others referring to the policy.

**dormant partner** *n.* See under PARTNER.

**double-category    method** *n.*    a

method of calculating a taxpayer's *average basis* (see under BASIS) in shares of a mutual fund, in which the shares are first divided into two categories—LONG-TERM and SHORT-TERM—and the average basis is calculated separately for each category. Cf. SINGLE-CATEGORY METHOD.

**double indemnity** *n.* a clause in a life-insurance policy providing for payment of twice the face value of the policy in the event of accidental death. See also ACCIDENTAL DEATH BENEFIT.

**double jeopardy** *n.* being put in JEOP-ARDY twice for the same offense.
——**Note.** Double jeopardy is prohibited by the Fifth Amendment (see Appendix). Thus a defendant who has been acquitted may not be tried again in the hope of a conviction, a defendant who has been convicted may not be tried again to increase the punishment, and the government, seeing that a trial is going badly, may not ask for a mistrial in the hope of doing better with a new jury and a fresh start. On the other hand, a defendant may be retried if a conviction is overturned on appeal, if a mistrial is declared at the request of the defendant or because of a hung jury or other circumstance beyond the control of the prosecution, or if the same conduct also constitutes an offense in another jurisdiction. In addition, acquittal in a criminal trial does not protect the defendant from a subsequent civil suit for the very same conduct, since the standard of proof in the second action is lower.

**doubt** *n.* See BEYOND A REASONABLE DOUBT.

**dower** *n.* **1. a.** the common law right of a married woman, after the death of her husband, to retain for life one-third of the lands that her husband held in fee. **b.** the life estate held by a widow pursuant to that right. Cf. CURTESY. **2.** DOWRY.

**dowry** *n., pl.* **dowries.** the money, goods, or estate that a wife brings to her husband at marriage.

**draft** *n.* **1.** an instrument by which one person (the drawer) orders another (the drawee) to pay a specified sum of money to the order of someone else (the payee), or to the bearer. Also (but no longer commonly) called a **bill of exchange.** The most common form of draft is an ordinary check. See also DRAW (def. 2); NEGOTIABLE INSTRUMENT.
**2. time draft** a draft that is not payable until a specified time in the future.
**3. sight draft** a draft payable on demand.

**draw** *v.,* **drew, drawn, drawing. 1.** to prepare a legal instrument: *draw a contract; draw a will.*
**2.** to prepare and sign an instrument for the payment of money, especially a DRAFT. The person who draws a draft is called the **drawer,** the person ordered by the draft to pay money (often a bank) is the **drawee,** and the person designated to receive the money is the PAYEE; the draft is said to be drawn "on" the drawee and "to" or "payable to" the payee. Cf. MAKE.
**3.** to withdraw money from a fund or account.

**driving while black (DWB)** *n.* a popular name for the pseudo-offense that is commonly viewed as the real reason for many traffic stops of black drivers by police. By extension or analogy, disproportionate stops of Hispanic drivers in comparison to non-Hispanic whites have been attributed to the "offense" referred to as **driving while brown** or **driving while Mexican.** See also RACIAL PROFILING.

**driving while intoxicated (DWI)** the offense of driving a motor vehicle while intoxicated by alcohol or other drugs that impair driving ability. Also referred to in various jurisdictions as **driving under the influence (DUI), driving while impaired (DWI),** or **driving while ability impaired (DWAI),** and commonly known everywhere as **drunk driving.** In some jurisdictions several such terms are used to designate varying degrees of intoxication.

**droit moral** *n., pl.* **droits moraux.** *French.* (lit. "moral right") the usual name for a bundle of rights given to creative artists in some countries to prevent alteration of their works and otherwise retain considerable control over their works even after the works have been sold. A less expansive version of the droit moral was adopted by Congress in 1990 and is referred to as a statute protecting **moral rights.**

—**Usage.** By tradition, this bundle of rights is referred to collectively in the singular: *le droit moral.* Although the plural (*les droits moraux*) is now also seen, traditionalists still prefer the singular.

**drop gun** *n.* Same as THROW-DOWN GUN.

**drug** *n.* **1.** a substance intended to affect the structure or function of the body of humans or animals, or intended for use in the diagnosis, treatment, or prevention of disease in humans or animals. Such substances are subject to regulation by the federal Food and Drug Administration. **2.** a CONTROLLED SUBSTANCE. See also GATEWAY DRUG. **3. ethical drug a.** a drug that may be dispensed only upon a doctor's prescription. **b.** a drug targeted primarily to physicians and pharmacists rather than users. **4. generic drug** a drug containing the same active ingredient as one formerly protected by patent but on which the patent has expired, sold by competitors of the patentee either under their own brand name or under the drug's scientific name. **5. orphan drug** a drug for a disease or condition that is so rare in the United States that it is unlikely that the cost of developing and and making a drug available for that condition in the United States could be recovered from sales in the United States. Congress has enacted special tax and other incentives to encourage the development of such drugs. **6. over-the-counter drug** a drug that may be sold without a doctor's prescription. **7. pioneer drug** the first drug product containing a particular active ingredient that is approved by the Food and Drug Administration for a specified pharmaceutical use. **8. proprietary drug** a drug protected by patent, so that it may only be sold by the owner of the patent or under license from the owner.

**drug courier profile** *n.* See under PROFILE.

**drug court** *n.* a court established by state law for the purpose of dealing with low-level offenses that stem from drug use, with an emphasis on treatment for drug addiction and careful supervision and monitoring to guard against further drug use rather than punishment.

**drug-free zone** *n.* a region specified in criminal laws as one in which any offense involving a CONTROLLED SUBSTANCE carries enhanced penalties. Regions within a certain distance of a school are commonly designated as drug-free zones.

**drug paraphernalia** *n.* See under PARAPHERNALIA.

**drug profile** *n.* See under PROFILE.

**drunk driving** *n. Informal.* Same as DRIVING WHILE INTOXICATED.

**dry trust** *n.* Same as *passive trust* (see under TRUST).

**dual paternity** *n.* See under PATERNITY.

**duces tecum** *Latin.* (lit. "you will bring with you") See *subpoena duces tecum* (under SUBPOENA).

**due** *adj.* **1.** appropriate to the circumstances; such as is required to fulfill legal obligations or satisfy legal standards: *due care* (see under CARE); *due diligence; due demand* (see under DEMAND); *due delivery;* DUE PROCESS. **2.** owing; supposed to be paid or performed now; to be paid or performed at the time specified: *The rent is due. The account is past due. Payment is due upon delivery.*

**due process** *n.* **1.** fair administration of law in accordance with established procedures and with due regard for the fundamental rights and liberties of people in a free society. The concept is embodied in the Fifth and Fourteenth Amendments to the Constitution, which prohibit the federal government and state governments, respectively, from depriving any person "of life, LIBERTY, or PROPERTY, without due process of law." These provisions are interpreted as dealing primarily with the PROCEDURE by which law is administered (see *procedural due process*), but also as having some smaller and less well defined role in assessment of the SUBSTANCE of laws whose effect would be to deprive people of FUNDAMENTAL RIGHTS (see *substantive due process*). See also FUNDAMENTAL FAIRNESS.

**2. procedural due process** the concept that in administering a system of justice, and in taking any official action aimed at depriving a particular person of life, liberty, or property, the government must follow, and require individual litigants to follow, established and known rules, and that those rules must be fundamentally fair. At a minimum, the persons directly affected must be given NOTICE and an OPPORTUNITY TO BE HEARD; at the maximum, in criminal cases, a wide array of due process protections comes into play, from the MIRANDA RULE to proof BEYOND A REASONABLE DOUBT.

**3. substantive due process** the concept that there are some freedoms so fundamental that any law taking them away, absent a COMPELLING INTEREST, must be struck down as a deprivation of liberty without due process. Some such freedoms, notably the First Amendment freedoms of speech, press, religion, and assembly, are specified in the Constitution (see INCORPORATION DOCTRINE); others, including the RIGHT TO TRAVEL and the RIGHT OF PRIVACY in areas of marriage and childbearing, are regarded as inherent in the concept of LIBERTY. See also SCRUTINY.

**dues checkoff** *n.* See CHECKOFF.

**DUI** Abbreviation for *driving under the influence* (see under DRIVING WHILE INTOXICATED).

**dummy corporation** *n.* See under CORPORATION.

**dumping** *n.* **1.** the disposal or discharge of solid or liquid waste on land or at sea.
**2.** the export of goods by one country to another at unfairly low prices in the hope of obtaining some long-range competitive advantage. See also ANTIDUMPING and the terms *antidumping duty* and *antidumping law* under that entry.
**3.** the act of suddenly putting unusually large quantities of a product on the market at unusually low prices without regard to the effect on the market, or deliberately to disrupt the market and injure competitors.
**4.** the act of selling all or a substantial part of one's holdings of a security, typically because one expects the market price for the security to go down significantly. See also PUMP AND DUMP.
**—dump** *v.*

**durable power of attorney** *n.* See under POWER OF ATTORNEY.

**durable power of attorney for health care** *n.* Same as HEALTH CARE PROXY.

**duress** *n.* the use of force, or the threat of force or of other unlawful acts, to induce someone to do something that she otherwise would not do, such as sign an instrument or commit a crime. Also called **coercion.** See also ECONOMIC DURESS.
**——Note.** Conduct that is induced by duress that a person of reasonable firmness would not have been able to resist is usually relieved of its normal legal effect. For example, a will signed under duress may be void, a contract signed under duress is usually voidable, and duress can constitute a complete defense to a criminal charge. See also the maxim quoted at ACTUS (def. 1).

**duty¹** *n., pl.* **duties. 1.** a legal obligation, whether imposed by operation of law (e.g., the duty to pay one's taxes or to exercise due care so as to avoid unnecessary injury to others) or assumed voluntarily (e.g., the duty to perform a

contract or repay a debt). See also FI-
DUCIARY DUTY; JURY DUTY; OBLIGATION.

**2. delegable duty** a duty that can be
assigned to another person or entity to
perform, thereby relieving the original
holder of the duty of any responsibility
with respect to it.

**3. nondelegable duty** a duty from
which one cannot be relieved by assigning it to another. In many such
cases the original holder of such a duty
can arrange for another person or entity
to carry it out, but it remains the original holder's responsibility to make sure
that the obligation is fulfilled, and the
original holder remains liable if it is
not.

**duty²** *n., pl.* **duties.** a tax on imports or
exports.

**DWAI** Abbreviation for *driving while
ability impaired* (see under DRIVING
WHILE INTOXICATED).

**DWB** Abbreviation for DRIVING WHILE
BLACK or *driving while brown* (see under DRIVING WHILE BLACK).

**DWI** Abbreviation for *driving while intoxicated* or *driving while impaired*. See
DRIVING WHILE INTOXICATED.

**dying declaration** *n.* See under DEC-
LARATION.

**dynamite charge** *n.* Same as *Allen
charge* (see under CHARGE).

# E

**E&O insurance** *n.* Same as ERRORS AND OMISSIONS INSURANCE.

**earned income** *n.* See under INCOME.

**earnest money** *n.* a nonrefundable down payment made by a buyer at the time of entering into a contract of purchase, to compensate the seller if the buyer fails to go through with the transaction. It is a usual feature of real estate transactions.

**earwitness** *n.* a person who heard an event under discussion, such as a conversation or an accident; especially one who heard it but did not see it. Cf. EYE-WITNESS.

**easement** *n.* **1.** an interest in land belonging to another, consisting of a right to use it or control its use for some purpose, but not to take anything from it or possess it.
**2. affirmative easement** an easement allowing the holder of the easement to go on the land; for example, a right to use a path across the land.
**3. easement appurtenant** an easement in one piece of land specifically for the benefit of another; for example, a right to cross someone else's land in order to reach land of one's own that would otherwise be inaccessible **(easement of access).** Such an easement is deemed APPURTENANT to the benefited land, and upon any transfer of title to the benefited land passes automatically to the new owner. Also called **appurtenant easement.** See also *dominant estate* and *servient estate* (both under ESTATE³); *easement of access* (under ACCESS).
**4. easement in gross** an easement whose benefit is unrelated to specific other land; for example, an easement granted to a public utility company to run wires over or pipes under the property burdened with the easement.
**5. negative easement** an easement whose only effect is to limit the use that the owner of the burdened property can make of that land; for example, an easement in a neighbor's property prohibiting its owner from spoiling one's view by building above a certain height.
**6. public easement** an easement for the benefit of the public at large, such as a street across private land.
See also BURDEN². Cf. PROFIT (def. 2).

**eavesdropping** *n.* **1.** the act of listening in on conversations or activities of others without their knowledge. If done without any trespass and without electronic or other artificial assistance, this in itself normally has no legal consequences.
**2. electronic eavesdropping** eavesdropping by means of hidden microphones or other electronic aids. This is severely restricted by law; see WIRETAP. See also SURVEILLANCE.
—**eavesdrop** *v.,* **eavesdropped, eavesdropping.**
—**eavesdropper** *n.*

**EBT** EXAMINATION BEFORE TRIAL.

**ecclesiastical court** *n.* a court in a system of ECCLESIASTICAL LAW; especially any court in the rather elaborate judicial system of the Church of England, which historically had exclusive jurisdiction over marriage, divorce, and certain other matters, and still exists for dealing with internal church issues.

**ecclesiastical law** *n.* **1.** in English legal history, law pertaining to matters over which the church was given jurisdiction. This included matters relating to marriage, divorce, and wills, which were transferred to the jurisdiction of the civil courts in the nineteenth century.
**2.** church law, especially in the Church of England.

**economic duress** *n.* in contract law, exploitation of a party's financial straits by imposing unfair contract terms that the party has no reasonable choice but to accept. Also called **business compulsion.** See also DURESS.

—**Note.** Under modern contract principles, economic duress makes a contract voidable by the party that was the victim of the duress. It is often a close question, however, whether a contract is simply the fair result of hard bargaining and market conditions, or whether it results from the economic equivalent of holding a gun to someone's head.

**economic frustration** *n.* See FRUSTRATION.

**Ed IRA** *n.* See under IRA.

**education individual retirement account (education IRA, Ed IRA)** *n.* See under IRA.

**effective assistance of counsel** *n.* See under RIGHT TO COUNSEL.

**effective date** *n.* the date upon which a statute, treaty, or other legal instrument is scheduled to take effect.

**effective tax rate** *n.* See under TAX RATE.

**efficient cause** *n.* Same as PROXIMATE CAUSE.

**e.g.** (from Latin *exempli gratia,* lit. "for the sake of example") for example: *Several states have community property regimes for married couples; see, e.g., the laws of California and Louisiana.* See note at I.E.

**eggshell skull** *n.* **1.** literally, a thin skull; metaphorically, a particular sensitivity or susceptibility to injury that is not readily apparent. Also called **thin skull.**

**2. eggshell skull doctrine** the rule of tort law that one is liable for all damage proximately caused by one's negligent act even if, because of a particular weakness on the part of the injured person, the damage exceeds anything that could reasonably have been foreseen; the doctrine that a tortfeasor "takes his victim as he finds him." Also

called **eggshell skull rule, eggshell skull theory.**

——**History.** The origins of the hypothetical "eggshell skull" are usually traced to a discussion in an English case of an earlier American case involving injury to a woman who turned out to have been pregnant: "[N]o doubt the driver of the defendants' horses could not anticipate that she was in this condition. But what does that fact matter? If a man is negligently run over or otherwise negligently injured in his body, it is no answer to the sufferer's claim for damages that he would have suffered less injury or no injury at all, if he had not had an unusually thin skull or an unusually weak heart." *Dulieu v. White & Sons,* 2 K.B. 669 (1901). Generations of lawyers and judges have found the metaphor a convenient way to characterize the rule applicable to such cases, although the exact scope of the rule—particularly the extent to which it applies to psychological injury due to purely mental susceptibility—varies from state to state. See also note at AGGRAVATED.

**eigne** *adj. Law French.* (lit. "firstborn") **1.** firstborn; eldest. See also BASTARD EIGNE.
**2.** prior; superior: *eigne title.*
Cf. PUISNE.

**eject** *v.* **1.** to oust; evict; throw (a person) out.
**2.** especially, at common law, to drive the rightful occupant from land; to take over another's land wrongfully.

**ejectment** *n.* **1.** the act of ejecting a person wrongfully from possession of land.
**2.** the traditional name for an action to obtain possession of land from another person, such as a holdover tenant or a person claiming ownership of the land, by establishing paramount title to the property.
**3.** the common law FORM OF ACTION for recovery of land wrongfully occupied by another. The action grew out of earlier forms of action for trespass and originally allowed the rightful tenant only damages for the ejectment; by the

year 1500, the action also put the tenant back into possession of the land. Thereafter, through the process described in the note below, ejectment evolved into a general action for determining disputes over title to real property.

**4.** the writ (called in full **writ of ejectment**) by which such an action was commenced.

See also *trespass in ejectment* (under TRESPASS²).

——**History.** It is in the action of ejectment that the rigidity of the common law forms of action—and the use of legal fictions to circumvent that rigidity—achieved their highest expression. The action was originally available only to a tenant for a term of years. Other forms of action existed for holders of FREEHOLD estates who were ousted from their land, but there were disadvantages to those forms of action. Over the years, it came to be customary for freeholders to avail themselves of the procedural advantages of the action of ejectment by alleging that they had leased the land for a term of years to a tenant, one JOHN DOE, who had been been ejected by the present occupant of the land, and who therefore had a right to bring an action of ejectment, which the freeholder would graciously prosecute on his behalf. But this was not always enough, for the wrongful occupant might still prove that he never ejected anybody named Doe. So a further fiction arose, that a wayfarer, usually named RICHARD ROE, had happened by and casually gone onto the land and ejected Mr. Doe. Thus the fictitious Mr. Doe had a proper action in ejectment against the CASUAL EJECTOR—the fictitious Mr. Roe. And since Mr. Roe failed to appear to defend the action, the fact of ejectment was established by default. The current occupant of the land had a right to be notified of the action and to appear if he wanted to do so, but since there was no claim that *he* had ejected anyone, he could not contest the issue of ejectment of Mr. Doe. The only defense left to the

occupant of the land was that, regardless of anything that might have transpired among the plaintiff and Mr. Doe and Mr. Roe, he—the present occupant—was actually the person with title to the land. Since the "landlord" who was prosecuting the case *himself* claimed title to the land, issue was joined on the very question that the freeholder actually wanted resolved in the first place. So by styling the case as a suit by a fictitious tenant against a fictitious ejector, the freeholder could satisfy the requirements of the form of action and use the forum to prove his title to the land. If he succeeded, then his tenant "Doe" would be allowed to move back onto the land for the balance of his term of years. But as Mr. Doe was nowhere to be found, the freeholder himself would resume occupancy of the land. See also LEGAL FICTION.

**ejector** *n.* **1.** one who ejects another from possession of land.

**2. casual ejector** the fictitious ejector, typically named RICHARD ROE, in the common law action of ejectment. See note at EJECTMENT.

**ejusdem generis** *Latin.* (lit. "of the same kind") a principle of construction under which, unless there is evidence that another meaning was intended, catch-all words at the end of a list are construed as referring to items of the same kind as those specifically named.

——**Note.** For example, in a Wisconsin Supreme Court case decided in the days when married women were still under COVERTURE, a school teacher sued to have her salary paid to her, rather than to her husband, pursuant to a statute that said: "any married woman whose husband, either from drunkenness, profligacy or any other cause, shall neglect or refuse to provide for her support, or the support and education of her children, shall have the right in her own name to transact business, and to receive and collect her own earnings." The plaintiff showed at trial that her husband, a laborer, was a careless manager who had accumulated debts and proved himself unable to support his family. As characterized by the court, her attorney's argument was "that the words 'any other cause,' in the statute, are broad enough to embrace every case where, for any reason, the husband does not furnish his wife with food and raiment and all the necessaries of life." The court was appalled: "If this be so," it said, "then every poor and virtuous man who may be sick, or for any cause unable to work and provide his wife and minor children with necessaries, may be deprived entirely of their services, and of all control over them." To avoid the unimaginable conclusion that a woman should be allowed to use her income to support her family simply because her husband is unable to do so, the court held that "the words 'or from any other cause,' following 'drunkenness, profligacy,' must be limited to vices ejusdem generis.... Mere poverty, sickness, intellectual inferiority or physical inability of the husband, without being caused by vice, are not alone sufficient" to entitle the wife to receive her own earnings under the statute. *Edson v. Hayden*, 20 Wis. 682 (1866).

**elder abuse** *n.* physical or psychological mistreatment of an elderly person by the person's child or caretaker.

**elder law** *n.* the field or practice of law that is concerned with issues of particular concern to older people, including social security, Medicare, long-term care, and estate planning, and attempts to deal with such issues in an integrated way.

**elect** *v.* **1.** to make a choice in a situation where the law presents two or more permissible alternatives but allows only one to be selected: *The couple elected to file income tax returns separately rather than jointly. Since Congress does not allow immigrants to have dual citizenship, an immigrant must elect between becoming a United States citizen and retaining her original citizenship.*
**2.** to select a person to hold office by vote: *The shareholders elected the largest shareholder as chairman of the board of directors.*

**election** *n.* **1.** the act of making a legally or contractually required choice, or the choice made.
**2.** the process of voting for people to hold office, or the fact of having been chosen for office by vote.
**3. election of remedies** a plaintiff's choice among available remedies for the same wrong; e.g., between return of an item of property wrongfully taken and payment for the loss.
**4. election under the will** an election by a person named in a will either to be bound by all of the terms of a will or to give up all rights under the will and pursue independent claims to property in the estate. One cannot ordinarily take what one is given under a will and also assert claims to property that the will left to someone else.
**5. spouse's** (or **widow's** or **widower's**) **election** the election of a surviving spouse either to take the property left to her under the decedent's will or to take her ELECTIVE SHARE of the estate.

**elective** *adj.* **1.** pertaining to voting and elections.
**2.** selected or to be selected by election. —**electively** *adv.*

**elective share** the share of a decedent's estate to which the surviving spouse is entitled under state law when a married person dies and leaves a will. If the will leaves a different amount, the survivor may (but need not) choose to take the elective share instead of what the will provides. Also called **statutory share; spouse's elective** (or **statutory**) **share; widow's** (or **widower's**) **elective** (or **statutory**) **share.** See also *spouse's election* (under ELECTION); cf. *election under the will* (under ELECTION).

**elector** *n.* **1. a.** a qualified voter; one permitted to vote, or who does vote, in a particular election. **b.** in presidential elections in the United States, one of the individuals chosen by each state to cast that state's votes for President and Vice President. See also ELECTORAL COLLEGE.
**2.** one who makes an election.

**electoral** *adj.* **1.** pertaining to or composed of electors.
**2.** pertaining to elections and voting.
—**electorally** *adv.*

**electoral college** *n.* **1.** the group of ELECTORS chosen by a state to cast its votes for President and Vice President in a presidential election in the United States.
**2.** the entire group of electors chosen in such an election by all fifty states and the District of Columbia combined. It is those 538 individuals who elect the President and the Vice President in the United States.
——**Usage.** The term *electoral college* came into use in the nineteenth century. In its original sense, and the sense in which the term is still used in the United States Code, it refers to the group of presidential electors chosen by an individual state. That group is required by the Constitution to gather together within the state for the purpose of casting ballots for President and Vice President, and was conceived as a collegial body in which the merits of various possible candidates could be discussed and weighed. Under the winner-take-all system that has been adopted in all states, however, all of a state's electors are expected to vote for the candidate who received the most popular votes in that state in the national election; consequently there is nothing for the electors to discuss when they meet. Today, the phrase *electoral college* is usually employed to refer collectively to all of the presidential electors throughout the nation, although they never meet as a body or communicate with each other at all.

**electoral system** *n.* **1.** a system of holding elections.
**2.** the United States system of selecting a President and Vice President by vote of ELECTORS chosen by the states rather than through direct election by the people.

**electronic eavesdropping** *n.* See under EAVESDROPPING.

**electronic surveillance** *n.* See under SURVEILLANCE.

**element** *n.* a constituent part of something; especially, one of the components of a crime or cause of action that must be proved to sustain a charge or claim. For example, the usual elements of a claim for fraud are: (1) a false representation by the defendant, (2) knowledge by the defendant of the falsity, (3) intent by the defendant to induce some conduct by the plaintiff, (4) reasonable reliance by the plaintiff, and (5) resulting damage to the plaintiff.

**eloign** or **eloin** *v.* to remove to a distance; especially, to take beyond the jurisdiction of a court.
—**eloignment, eloinment** *n.*

**e-mail harassment** *n.* See under CYBERSTALKING.

**emancipation** *n.* **1.** the act of freeing from restraint, subservience, influence, or the like, or the state or fact of being freed.
**2.** the freeing of a slave or slaves; particularly, the freeing of all slaves in those portions of the Confederacy still in rebellion against the United States (but not in areas under Union control) by proclamation of President Lincoln on January 1, 1863 (the **Emancipation Proclamation**), and the subsequent extension of that liberty to millions of slaves in the rest of the nation by the Thirteenth Amendment (see Appendix).
**3.** the freeing of a minor from parental control (and of parents from their duties toward the child), giving the child the right to keep and control her own earnings and make decisions with regard to such matters as her own medical care. This may occur by agreement of parent and child, by order of a court upon petition of the child, or automatically upon marriage. A minor after emancipation is called an **emancipated minor.**
—**emancipate** *v.,* **emancipated, emancipating.**
—**emancipative** *adj.*
—**emancipator** *n.*

**embargo** *n., pl.* **embargoes,** *v.,* **embargoed, embargoing.** —*n.* **1.** Also called **hostile embargo.** an order of a government prohibiting the movement

of ships from another country into or out of its ports, as in anticipation of war.
**2.** Also called **trade embargo.** a country's prohibition of trade, or certain kinds of trade, between its own merchants and another country, or an agreement among several countries to restrict trade with another country, in order to exert political pressure on the other country.
—*v.* **3.** to impose an embargo on.

**embezzlement** *n.* the crime of converting to one's own use property of another that is lawfully within one's possession. The usual case involves the taking of money over which one exercises control in the course of one's job.
—**embezzle** *v.,* **embezzled, embezzling.**
—**embezzler** *n.*

**emblements** *n.pl.* the products or profits of land that has been planted; crops that will come to fruition within one growing season. At common law, a tenant who lost his tenancy after planting retained a right to the emblements: He could return and harvest the fruits of his labor.

**embracery** *n., pl.* **embraceries. 1.** an old word for the crime of improperly attempting to influence a jury, as by bribes or threats; now usually dealt with in statutes on bribery and obstruction of justice.
**2.** an act or instance of this crime.
—**embraceor, embracer** *n.*

**emend** *v.* **1.** to correct; remove errors from; make right.
**2.** especially, to correct a text.
Cf. AMEND.
—**emendable** *adj.*

**emendation** *n.* **1.** a correction, especially in a text.
**2.** the act of emending.
Cf. AMENDMENT.
—**emendatory** *adj.*

**eminent domain** *n.* the inherent power of a government to take private property for public purposes, e.g., to build a road or reservoir. See also TAKING; JUST COMPENSATION.

**emolument** *n.* anything received as compensation for services, especially by a public or corporate official.

**emotional distress** *n.* any highly unpleasant mental reaction, such as fright, horror, grief, shame, anger, or worry. Also referred to by many similar phrases, the most common of which are **emotional harm, mental anguish, mental distress,** and **mental suffering.** See also INTENTIONAL INFLICTION OF EMOTIONAL DISTRESS; NEGLIGENT INFLICTION OF EMOTIONAL DISTRESS.

**emotional harm** *n.* Same as EMOTIONAL DISTRESS.

**empanel** *v.,* **empaneled, empaneling** or (*esp. Brit.*) **empanelled, empanelling.** Same as IMPANEL.

**employee benefit plan** *n.* a program maintained by an employer or a group or association of employers, or by an employee organization such as a union, to provide health care, retirement, or other substantial nonsalary benefits to employees and their families and beneficiaries. For purposes of regulation by the EMPLOYEE RETIREMENT INCOME SECURITY ACT OF 1974, such plans fall into two categories: EMPLOYEE PENSION BENEFIT PLAN and EMPLOYEE WELFARE BENEFIT PLAN.

**employee pension benefit plan** *n.* an EMPLOYEE BENEFIT PLAN established to provide retirement income to employees, or which results in a deferral of income by employees for periods extending to or beyond the termination of the employment in which the income is earned. Also called **pension plan.** For more details, see PENSION PLAN.

**Employee Retirement Income Security Act of 1974 (ERISA)** *n.* the federal statute that regulates almost every private EMPLOYEE BENEFIT PLAN in the United States, setting standards for financial soundness, accountability to employees, and the like. (Plans for governmental employees and church employees are excluded from coverage.) The statute is usually referred to by its acronym, **ERISA.**

**employee stock option** *n.* See under STOCK OPTION.

**employee stock ownership plan (ESOP)** *n.* a program by which employees of a corporation can acquire stock in the company.

**employee welfare benefit plan** *n.* an EMPLOYEE BENEFIT PLAN established to provide benefits other than pension benefits, such as health care benefits; disability, death, unemployment, or vacation benefits; apprenticeship or other training programs; child care centers; scholarship funds; housing assistance; and legal services benefits. Also called **welfare plan.**

**employers' liability act** *n.* See under WORKERS' COMPENSATION.

**employers' liability insurance** *n.* See under WORKERS' COMPENSATION.

**employment** *n.* See SCOPE OF EMPLOYMENT.

**en banc** *Law French.* (lit. "as a bench") referring to consideration of a matter by all of the judges of a court together, as distinguished from a single judge or a panel. Some courts, including the Supreme Court, normally sit en banc; other courts, notably the United States Courts of Appeals, do so only in special situations. Also, **in banc, in bank.** See also PANEL; REARGUMENT.

**en ventre sa mere** or **en ventre sa mère,** *adj. Law French.* (lit. "in its mother's belly") unborn: *A child en ventre sa mere may inherit from the father if born alive after the father's death.*

**enabling** *adj.* **1.** (in reference to a statute) authorizing an official or agency to take the necessary steps to carry out a law or policy: *enabling clause; enabling legislation.* **2.** broadly, authorizing any particular conduct by anyone.

**enact** *v.* to pass into law; to make into a statute.
—**enactable** *adj.*

**enactment** *n.* **1.** the act of enacting. **2.** the state or fact of being enacted. **3.** something that is enacted; a statute.

**encouragement** *n.* conduct by a law enforcement officer creating an opportunity for a suspect to commit a crime and encouraging the suspect to do it. The fact that a crime was induced by such encouragement is not a defense in a subsequent prosecution for that crime. See also STING; cf. ENTRAPMENT.
—**encourage** *v.,* **encouraged, encouraging.**

**encroach** *v.* to trespass upon the property, domain, or rights of another, especially stealthily or by gradual advances: *The window sills of the house built on the lot line encroach two inches into the neighboring property.*
—**encroacher** *n.*
—**encroachment** *n.*

**encumber** *v.* **1.** to impose an encumbrance upon: *The borrower encumbered the house with a mortgage.* **2.** to be an encumbrance upon: *The mortgage encumbers the house.*

**encumbrance** *n.* any interest, right, or obligation with respect to property that reduces the value or completeness of the property owner's title; for example, a mortage, lease, easement, or covenant. See also *covenant against encumbrances* (under COVENANTS OF TITLE).

**encumbrancer** *n.* the owner or holder of an interest or claim that is an encumbrance upon property.

**endorse** *v.,* **endorsed, endorsing. 1.** to show support for or approval of: *to endorse a candidate; to endorse another court's interpretation of the law.* **2.** to write something on a document, as in the margin or on the back: *Instead of issuing a typed opinion regarding the motion, the judge endorsed her two-sentence decision on the notice of motion.* **3.** (in the law of negotiable instruments) to INDORSE.
—**endorsable** *adj.*
—**endorsee** *n.*
—**endorser** *n.*
——**Usage.** In reference to negotiable instruments, the spelling *indorse, indorsee, indorsement,* etc. has become standard in American (but not British)

legal writing, although *endorse* is acceptable and is still preferred in nonlegal writing.

**endorsement** *n.* **1.** the act of endorsing.
**2.** approval or support.
**3.** matter written on or added to a document.
**4.** a rider added to an insurance policy to modify or extend coverage in a particular way.
**5.** INDORSEMENT. See note at ENDORSE.

**enemy** *n., pl.* **enemies.** **1.** a nation or government with which another nation is at war; specifically, in the United States, a nation or government with which the United States is at war.
**2.** the military force of such a nation.
**3.** a citizen or subject of such a nation. Also called **enemy alien, alien enemy,** or **enemy subject.**
**4.** a nation or government allied with or actively supporting an enemy nation.
**5. public enemy** an enemy of the nation or the public at large, as distinguished from a personal enemy; specifically, **a.** an enemy nation. **b.** a criminal regarded as a particular menace, particularly one operating over a wide geographic area; a wanted criminal widely sought by the FBI and local police forces.
——**False Friend.** It would be natural to assume that if the law attaches the label "enemy" or "enemy alien" or "alien enemy" to an individual, then the individual must be dangerous or hostile to the United States. But the assumption would be misguided: The classification is not an expression of what is in a person's heart, nor a conclusion based upon the person's conduct; it is merely a statement of the individual's current citizenship status.

**enfeoff** *v.* to invest with a FIEF or fee (see FEE[1]).

**enfeoffment** *n.* **1.** the act of enfeoffing.
**2.** the deed or instrument by which a fee is conveyed.

**enforce** *v.,* **enforced, enforcing.** to compel compliance with a law, rule, or legal obligation, or with laws generally.

Specifically, **a.** to order or request compliance in a way that carries an implied or express threat of punishment or other bad consequences in the event of noncompliance: *The Judge enforced the contract by directing the defendant to perform as promised. The police enforced the anti-noise ordinance by asking the host of the party to turn down his stereo after midnight.* **b.** to seek to punish noncompliance or to require those who fail to fulfill civil legal obligations to pay damages: *The police enforce the traffic laws by giving out tickets; the courts enforce them through fines.* **c.** to take measures to carry out legal requirements or prevent violations: *The school board enforces building safety codes through a policy of regular inspections. The border police enforce immigration laws by patrolling the borders to discourage efforts to sneak into the United States.*
—**enforceability** *n.*
—**enforceable** *adj.*
—**enforcement** *n.*

**enforced disappearance of persons** *n.* See under DISAPPEARANCE.

**enfranchise** *v.,* **enfranchised, enfranchising.** **1.** to grant voting rights to. Cf. DISENFRANCHISE; CRIMINAL DISENFRANCHISEMENT.
**2.** to admit to full citizenship.
**3.** to set free; liberate, as from slavery.
—**enfranchisement** *n.*

**English-only law** *n.* a popular name for any of a variety of laws in a number of states, and of proposed federal laws, that designate English as the "official" language of the state or nation, require the use of English for various governmental purposes, and the like. Also called **official English law, official language law.**
——**Note.** These laws do not appear to have prevented lawyers and judges from using Latin locutions like CORPUS DELICTI, EX POST FACTO, IN LOCO PARENTIS, or FALSUS IN UNO, FALSUS IN OMNIBUS in official proceedings.

**English-only policy** *n.* an employer's policy prohibiting employees from speaking languages other than English while on the job. When such policies might be reasonable and when they might constitute illegal employment discrimination are matters of debate.

**engross** *v.* **1.** to put an instrument, such as a statute or a deed, into final form, originally by writing it out in a large clear hand on parchment.
**2.** to buy up large quantities of a commodity or contiguous tracts of land for resale. See also ENGROSSING.
—**engrosser** *n.*
—**engrossment** *n.*

**engrossed bill** *n.* the final form of a legislative bill as passed by one house of Congress, reflecting all changes agreed to during the process of debate and passage. The engrossed bill is prepared by a clerk and passed to the other chamber for consideration. Cf. ENROLLED BILL.

**engrossing** *n.* buying up such large quantities of a commodity as to corner the market and be able to resell the commodity at monopoly prices. This was a statutory crime in England until 1844. See also FORESTALLING THE MARKET; REGRATING.

**enjoin** *v.* to issue an INJUNCTION against; to forbid by court order: *The judge enjoined the sale of the land* (or *enjoined the parties from selling the land*).

**enjoy** *v.* to possess or exercise a right or interest; have the benefit of: *Judges enjoy absolute immunity from civil suit for judicial acts undertaken in their capacity as judge.* See also QUIET ENJOYMENT.
—**enjoyment** *n.*
——**False Friend.** In legal contexts, to "enjoy" something does not mean to take pleasure in it: *Americans enjoy the right of trial by jury in criminal cases.*

**enlarge** *v.,* **enlarged, enlarging. 1.** to expand: *The statute enlarged the rights of judgment creditors.*
**2.** especially, to extend a procedural time limit: *Defendant moved for an enlargement of the time to respond to the complaint.*
—**enlargement** *n.*

**enroll** *v.* to place upon a list or register; to record officially, as a deed or judgment.

**enrolled bill** *n.* the final copy of a bill as passed by both houses of Congress, printed on parchment. When the enrolled bill has been examined by officials of both houses for accuracy and signed by the presiding officers of both houses, it is sent to the President for signature or veto.

**entail** *v.* **1.** to convert into a FEE TAIL; to grant as a fee tail: *He entailed the estate to his first son in tail male. The property could not be transferred because it was entailed.*
—*n.* **2.** an entailed estate.
**3.** the rule of descent for a fee tail.
**4.** the act of entailing or state of being entailed.
—**entailable** *adj.*
—**entailer** *n.*
—**entailment** *n.*

**entente** *n.,* **ententes.** *French.* (lit. "understanding") *International Law.* **1.** an arrangement or understanding between two or more nations agreeing to follow a particular policy with regard to affairs of international concern.
**2.** a group of nations having such an understanding.

**enter** *v.* **1.** to go onto or into real property.
**2.** to place formally in the record, especially a court record, as by adding to the court file or making a notation in a docket, judgment book, or the like: *enter an appearance; enter an order; enter judgment for the defendant.*
See also ENTRY.

**enticement** *n.* **1.** Also called **enticement of a child.** the crime of luring a child into a secluded place for sexual purposes.
**2.** For the meaning in tort law, see under ABDUCTION.

**entire** *adj.* **1.** whole; complete.
**2.** of a piece; not separable into independent components.
Cf. DIVISIBLE; SEVERABLE.

**entire contract** *n.* See under CONTRACT.

**entirety** *n., pl.* **entireties. 1.** the whole, as distinguished from a part.
**2.** the state of being whole or complete, or something that is whole or complete.
**3.** the state of being indivisible, or something that is indivisible.
See also BY THE ENTIRETY. Cf. DIVISIBLE.

**entitlement** *n.* a legislatively created right or benefit, such as a driver's license or welfare benefits, which, once granted to a person, cannot be taken away without a fair hearing to make sure that the recipient is no longer entitled to the benefit.
——**Note.** Entitlements are sometimes regarded as PROPERTY and sometimes as a LIBERTY; either way, the Supreme Court holds that they cannot be taken away from an individual without *procedural due process* (see under DUE PROCESS).

**entrapment** *n.* the planning of a crime by law enforcement agents and their procuring of its commission by a person who had no predisposition to do it and would not have done so but for the trickery of the officers. Entrapment is a defense in a subsequent prosecution for the crime, but the police conduct must be extreme for the defense to succeed. See also STING; cf. ENCOURAGEMENT.
—**entrap** *v.,* **entrapped, entrapping.**
—**entrapper** *n.*

**entry** *n., pl.* **entries. 1.** the act of entering (see ENTER).
**2.** a notation entered in a record.

**enumerated power** *n.* See under POWER.

**environmental impact statement** *n.* a detailed analysis of the potential impact on the environment of a proposed project or of proposed legislation. Such statements are required under many circumstances by federal and state law. Also called **environmental impact report.**

**environmental law** *n.* the field of law that is concerned with the effect of laws on the natural environment and with the use of law to protect, restore, or improve the natural environment

through preservation of species, cleaning up of toxic waste sites, enhancement of air and water quality, and the like.

**eo die** *adv. Latin.* on that day: *The defendant borrowed the money in the morning and lost it at the race track eo die.*

**eo instante** *adv. Latin.* at that instant: *The deed was delivered at three o'clock, and the grantee became the owner eo instante; hence the fire that occurred at four o'clock was his loss alone.*

**eo nomine** *adv. Latin.* by that name; in that name: *Although the allegedly libelous article does not refer to Mr. Smith eo nomine, the description makes it clear that he is the one being accused of a crime.*

**equal protection** *n.* the principle that law should be even-handed in its application and that people should be free from irrational and invidious discrimination at the hands of the government. Under the Fourteenth Amendment (see Appendix), a state government may not "deny to any person within its jurisdiction the equal protection of the laws," and the DUE PROCESS clause of the Fifth Amendment has been interpreted as extending the principle of equal protection to the federal government as well. Thus any law or governmental practice having a discriminatory purpose or effect is subject to challenge in the courts to determine whether it meets constitutional standards. See also SCRUTINY; SEPARATE BUT EQUAL.

**equalization** *n.* **1.** the process of making equal or equitable.
**2.** Also called **tax equalization.** the process of distributing property tax assessments evenly and fairly among property owners in a region or among regions in a state.
**3. equalization board** Same as BOARD OF EQUALIZATION.
—**equalize** *v.,* **equalized, equalizing.**

**equitable** *adj.* **1.** pertaining to, enforceable under, or derived from principles of EQUITY as distinguished from LAW (def. 4). See, for example, *equitable action* (under ACTION); *equitable abstention* (under ABSTENTION); *equitable defense* (under DEFENSE); *equitable estoppel* (under ESTOPPEL); *equitable remedy* (under REMEDY); *equitable right* (under RIGHT).

**2.** in particular, describing property rights and interests deriving from something other than legal title, including the rights of a trust beneficiary with respect to the property held in trust. See, for example, *equitable estate* (under ESTATE[1]); *equitable owner* (under OWNER); *equitable interest* (under INTEREST[1]); *equitable title* (under TITLE).

**3.** fair; consistent with fundamental justice. See, for example, EQUITABLE DISTRIBUTION.

—**equitably** *adv.*

**equitable action** *n.* See under ACTION.

**equitable distribution** *n.* a method of dividing property in a divorce case, authorized by statute in most states, under which the court allocates property acquired by the couple during marriage according to what seems fair, without regard to whether *legal title* (see under TITLE) is in the name of the husband or the wife. The court takes into account a wide range of factors, such as the relative earning capacity of the parties and the role that each played in the family as an economic unit, including a homemaker's contribution to overall family welfare.

**equity** *n.*, *pl.* **equities** for 2. **1.** one of the two systems of justice that grew up side by side in England and together gave rise to the present-day system of justice in both England and the United States. Equity was a flexible system in which judges were able to fashion remedies for situations that did not fit within principles followed in the courts of LAW (def. 4); it was less concerned with technicalities and more concerned with reaching a fair result—"doing equity." Its most notable power was the power to issue INJUNCTIONS. See also MERGER OF LAW AND EQUITY.

**2.** a right or interest enforceable in equity.

**3.** Usually, **equities.** factors or considerations weighing in favor of one side or the other in connection with a request for equitable relief: *The equities favor the moving party.* See also BALANCING OF THE EQUITIES.

**4.** overall fairness; justice in a moral as well as legal sense.

**5.** the net value of an owner's interest in property; the market value of the property minus amounts still owed on debts secured by mortgages or liens on the property.

**6.** the *net assets* (see under ASSET) of an enterprise, representing the value of the owners' interest in the business.

**equity of redemption** *n.* a statutory right to avoid losing one's property through foreclosure of a mortgage by paying off the mortgage in full, with interest and costs, within a specified time after default.

**equity security** *n.* See under SECURITY[2].

**ergo** *conj., adv. Latin.* therefore.

**Erie doctrine** *n.* the doctrine that a federal court in a *diversity case* (see under CASE[1]) must apply the *substantive law* (see under SUBSTANCE) of the state in which it is located. Named after *Erie Railroad Co. v. Tompkins*, 304 U.S. 64 (1938).

**ERISA** *n.* EMPLOYEE RETIREMENT SECURITY INCOME ACT OF 1974.

**error** *n.* **1.** an incorrect ruling by a judge in a case, as determined by a higher court on appeal. In a nonjury trial, there can be error in the judge's findings of fact (see CLEARLY ERRONEOUS); however, the word is most often used in reference to rulings on matters of law, as in admitting or excluding certain evidence or giving certain instructions to the jury.

**2. harmless error** an error that did not affect the outcome of the case or prejudice a substantial right of a party. Reversal will not be granted on the basis of errors deemed to be harmless. See also note at FAIR TRIAL.

**3. plain error** an error so obviously prejudicial to substantial rights of a party that it amounts to an affront to the judicial system. Such an error will result in reversal even if the party adversely affected by it failed to object to it. Also called **fundamental error.**

**4. reversible error** an error that prejudiced the appellant in a way that could have affected the outcome of the trial. Such an error, if properly objected to when the ruling was made, requires modification or reversal of the judgment. Also called **prejudicial error, harmful error, fatal error.** See also WRIT OF ERROR; STANDARD OF REVIEW.

—**erroneous** *adj.*
—**erroneously** *adv.*
—**erroneousness** *n.*

**errors and omissions** or **(E&O) insurance** *n.* insurance that indemnifies the insured against liability for mistakes and oversights in the performance of work or conduct of a business.

**escheat** *n.* **1.** in feudal law, the reverting of an inheritable interest in land to the superior lord if the holder died without an heir.
**2.** in modern law, the reverting of property to the state (in England, to the Crown) if no claimant with a right to it can be found, especially upon the death of an owner who leaves no will and no known heirs.
**3.** property that has so reverted.
—*v.* **4.** to revert to by escheat.
**5.** to make an escheat of; confiscate as escheat.
—**escheatable** *adj.*

**escheator** *n.* a county or state officer charged with identifying properties subject to escheat and bringing actions to claim them for the state or the Crown.

**escrow** *n.* **1.** money or a deed or other instrument deposited with a third person for delivery to a given party upon the fulfillment of some condition. While in the keeping of the third party, the money or instrument is said to be **in escrow.**
—*v.* **2.** to place into escrow.

**escrow agent** *n.* the third party who holds funds that are in escrow. Also called **escrowee.**

**escrowee** *n.* Same as ESCROW AGENT.

**ESOP** *n.* EMPLOYEE STOCK OWNERSHIP PLAN.

**espionage** *n.* **1.** the gathering by one country of secret political or military information about another country; spying.
**2.** Also called **industrial espionage.** the gathering of secret information about a company or industry that could be used to harm it or compete with it, either by another company or by the government of another country.

**Esq.** Abbreviation of *Esquire,* a title often appended (usually in abbreviated form) to the names of American lawyers (instead of putting Mr. or Ms. in front of the name) in addressing letters or in certain other formal contexts.

**Esquire** *n.* See ESQ.

**esse** *v. Latin.* **1.** to be.
—*n.* **2.** being. See IN ESSE.

**essence** *n.* See OF THE ESSENCE.

**establishment of religion** *n.* governmental sponsorship of religion, including financial support for a religion or religions at public expense. This is prohibited by the **Establishment Clause** of the First Amendment to the Constitution. Under current Supreme Court doctrine, a government program having the effect of providing public financial support for religion does not violate the Establishment Clause if it is regarded as (1) having a secular purpose, (2) having a primary effect that neither aids nor inhibits religion, and (3) not involving "excessive entanglement" of government and religion. See also SEPARATION OF CHURCH AND STATE.

**estate**[1] *n.* **1.** an interest in real property which is or may become possessory; that is, it either confers upon the owner of the interest a current right to exclusive possession of the property for some period of time or embodies at least the possibility that the owner will have such a right in the future. An estate may be designated as JOINT, BY THE ENTIRETY, IN COMMON, IN COPARCENARY, or IN SEVERALTY, depending upon the ownership arrangement, and as either a **legal estate** or a **beneficial**

(or **equitable**) **estate,** depending upon whether it is viewed from the perspective of a *legal owner* or, in the case of property held in trust, a *beneficial owner* (see both phrases under OWNER). Because an estate is a form of property interest and a tenancy is a form of estate, the words "estate," "interest," and "tenancy" are interchangeable in many contexts. See INTEREST[1]; TENANCY.

**2. contingent estate** an estate that is not yet possessory, and in which the owner's right of exclusive possession in the future depends upon circumstances that are not certain to occur. For example, if A grants land "to B so long as the property is used for church purposes," then A retains a contingent estate in the land, called a POSSIBILITY OF REVERTER, because it is possible (but not certain) that the condition for continuation of B's estate will be violated and the land will revert to A's possession. Cf. *vested estate.*

**3. estate** (or **tenancy**) **in fee** Same as FEE[1].

**4. future estate** an estate which has not yet become possessory. For example, a grant of property "to A for life, then to B" gives B a future estate (called a REMAINDER), because B's right of possession will not arise until A dies. For types of future estate, see *executory interest* (under INTEREST[1]); POSSIBILITY OF REVERTER; REMAINDER; REVERSION. Cf. *possessory estate.*

**5. life estate** (or **tenancy**) an estate whose duration is measured by the life of some person or group of people (the MEASURING LIFE or lives); for example, the estates granted by the words "to A for life," "to B during the life of his mother," or "to C Church so long as any of its present parishioners remain alive." Also called **estate** (or **tenancy**) **for life** or, when the measuring life is not the grantee's own, **estate** (or **tenancy**) **pur autre vie** (*Law French.* lit. "for another life").

**6. particular estate** an estate of limited duration carved out of a larger estate. For example, in a grant of land "to A for one year, then to B for life, then

to C," the estates of A and B are particular estates.

**7. possessory estate** an estate whose owner has a current right to exclusive possession of the property, at least for a while. Also called **present estate** or **present possessory estate.** Cf. *future estate.* A possessory estate may be classified as either a **freehold estate** (same as FREEHOLD) or a **leasehold estate** (same as LEASEHOLD). For types of leasehold estate, see under TENANCY.

**8. vested estate** an estate that is either possessory or certain to become so in due course; the owner's right to eventual possession is not subject to a contingency. For example, if land has been granted "to A for life, then to B," both A's present estate (a *life estate*) and B's future estate (a REMAINDER) are vested estates: A's because it is already possessory, and B's because it will become possessory upon A's death, which is certain to occur. If B is no longer alive at that point, B's heirs or other successors will possess the property. Cf. *contingent estate.*

**estate**[2] *n.* **1.** an aggregate of money and property administered as a unit.

**2. bankruptcy estate** the total assets of a person or entity in bankruptcy. Also called **estate in bankruptcy.**

**3. decedent's estate** all money and property owned by a decedent at the time of death.

**4. residuary estate** in the case of a decedent who left a will, whatever is left of the decedent's estate after payment of debts and expenses and distribution of all bequests save the *residuary bequest* (see under BEQUEST). Also called the **residue** of the estate.

**estate**[3] *n.* **1.** a parcel of land.

**2. dominant estate** the parcel of land that benefits from an *easement appurtenant* (see under EASEMENT). Also called **dominant tenement.**

**3. servient estate** the parcel of land that is burdened by an easement appurtenant. Also called **servient tenement.**

**estate tax** *n.* a tax imposed on large estates left by decedents, based upon the value of the estate and required to be paid out of estate funds before the estate is distributed to heirs or takers under a will. Cf. INHERITANCE TAX.

**estimated tax** *n.* an advance on income taxes that must be paid approximately quarterly by taxpayers whose income is not subject to WITHHOLDING TAX, or whose withholding will not substantially cover their tax liability for the year.

**estop** *v.,* **estopped, estopping.** to hinder or prevent by ESTOPPEL. When the doctrine of estoppel bars a litigant from taking a position at trial contrary to a prior assertion, he is said to be "estopped to deny" or "estopped from denying" the truth of the assertion.

**estoppel** *n.* **1.** a bar or impediment preventing a litigant in certain situations from gaining advantage by asserting facts or claims inconsistent with facts previously established or with his own prior assertions or conduct.
**2. collateral estoppel** the doctrine that a person who has had a full and fair opportunity to litigate an issue of importance to a case and had the issue resolved against him may not relitigate the issue in a subsequent case against the same adversary but involving a different cause of action. Often the estoppel extends to subsequent cases against other adversaries as well. Also called **issue preclusion, estoppel by judgment, estoppel by verdict.** Collateral estoppel is distinguished from RES JUDICATA in that the former bars relitigation of a specific issue in a case whereas the latter bars reassertion of an entire claim or cause of action.
**3. direct estoppel** the doctrine that a person who has had a full and fair opportunity to litigate an issue of importance to a case and had the issue resolved against him may not relitigate the issue in a subsequent proceeding on the same cause of action.
**4. equitable estoppel** the doctrine that one who makes an assertion (or by conduct creates an impression) upon which another relies may not turn around and assert the opposite to gain advantage in subsequent litigation against the other person. Also called

**estoppel in pais,** because the estoppel arises from facts that occurred outside of court. (See IN PAIS.) The doctrines of LACHES and *apparent authority* (see under AUTHORITY[1]) are essentially special applications of equitable estoppel.
**5. estoppel by deed** estoppel to contradict in court representations that one has made in a deed, such as representations about ownership or condition of land.
**6. estoppel by record** estoppel to contradict the judgment of a court or an official record of a legislature (e.g., as to the terms of a statute).
**7. estoppel by silence** estoppel to rely in court upon an assertion that, if true, should have been made earlier, when the adverse party could have acted upon the information.
**8. file-wrapper estoppel** in patent law, estoppel that prevents the holder of a patent that is the subject of litigation from making claims about the scope of the patent that were expressly given up in the course of obtaining the patent. Also called **prosecution history estoppel.**
**9. promissory estoppel** the doctrine under which a promise that is not enforceable under traditional principles of contract law (for example, for lack of consideration) may nevertheless be enforced to the extent necessary to prevent injustice if the promisor should reasonably have expected that the promisee would take substantial action in reliance upon the promise, and the promisee did so.

**estrepement** *n.* **1.** in old law, damage to land in the hands of a tenant or in the hands of one whose title to the land is in dispute; WASTE.
**2.** a common law writ (in full, **writ of estrepement**) to prevent a party in possession from committing waste on an estate the title to which is claimed by another, pending the outcome of an action to determine who had title or following judgment in favor of the claimant but before the claimant was put in possession.

**et al.** *Latin.* Abbreviation for *et alius* ("and another") or *et alii* ("and others"); used primarily as a stand-in for the names of all parties except the first on each side of a case in the CAPTION on court papers and reports of decisions: *Samuel S. Smith et al. v. Jane J. Jones et al.* In citations to cases, even this is usually left out, and only the last name of the first party on each side is listed unless there is a special reason for indicating that there were others involved: *Smith v. Jones.*

**et alii** *Latin.* and others. See ET AL.

**et alius** *Latin.* and another. See ET AL.

**et seq.** *Latin.* Abbreviation for *et sequentia* ("and those following"); used in citations to include a number of pages or sections beyond the one listed: *appellant's brief at page* (or *pages*) *34 et seq.*

**et sequentia** *Latin.* and those following. See ET SEQ.

**et ux.** *Latin.* Abbreviation for *et uxor* ("and wife"); formerly used instead of the wife's name in case names and legal documents involving a husband and wife jointly: *Deed from Samuel S. Smith et ux. to John J. Jones.* The abbreviation is still frequently used in court papers and case reports in actions by or against a husband and wife, in the same way that ET AL. would be used if the parties on one side were not husband and wife. Cf. ET VIR.

**et uxor** *Latin.* and wife. See ET UX.

**et vir** *Latin.* and husband. The phrase is often used in court papers and case reports in actions by or against a wife and husband, in the same way that ET AL. would be used if the joint plaintiffs or joint defendants were not married, and the same way that ET UX. would be used if the husband instead of the wife were the first named party on their side. In modern practice, the wife's name is usually placed first if the action primarily involves her; for example, if the wife is suing over injuries that she suffered in an accident and the husband joins in the suit on a claim of loss of consortium.

**ethical** *adj.* **1.** in accordance with generally accepted standards of honesty and

fairness in the conduct of one's business or profession: *ethical behavior; an ethical businessperson.*
**2.** pertaining to ethics or morality generally: *an ethical issue; ethical considerations.*
—**ethically** *adv.*

**ethical drug** *n.* See under DRUG.

**ethical wall** *n.* See CHINESE WALL.

**ethics** *n.* **1.** (*used with a pl. v.*) standards of honesty and fairness in the conduct of a business or profession, often embodied in written rules adopted by professional associations.
**2.** (*used with a pl. v.*) moral principles generally.
**3.** (*used with a sing. v.*) the branch of philosophy that deals with values relating to human conduct, with respect to the rightness and wrongness of certain actions and to the goodness and badness of the motives and ends of such actions.

**ethnic cleansing** *n.* the elimination or attempted elimination of an unwanted ethnic group from a society or region, as through systematic terror campaigns, murders, or forced emigration.
——**History.** The term *ethnic cleansing* was coined during the Bosnian War (1992-1995), and the practice of ethnic cleansing in that war prompted the United Nations to create an INTERNATIONAL CRIMINAL TRIBUNAL to prosecute the individuals who directed and carried out the campaign.

**evade** *v.*, **evaded, evading.** to elude, escape from, or get around, especially by trickery or illegality.
—**evader** *n.*

**evasion** *n.* an act, instance, or practice of evading. See also TAX EVASION.
—**evasive** *adj.*
—**evasively** *adv.*
—**evasiveness** *n.*

**evict** *v.* to expel or exclude a person from one's property, either by legal proceedings or by personal action; especially, to remove a tenant from leased premises, as for nonpayment of rent.

—**evictable** *adj.*
—**evictee** *n.*

**eviction** *n.* **1.** the act of evicting or an instance of being evicted.
**2. actual eviction** physically excluding a tenant, as by changing the lock while the tenant is out.
**3. constructive eviction** conduct by a landlord rendering leased premises unfit for use and thus, as a practical matter, forcing the tenant out.

**evidence** *n., v.* **evidenced, evidencing.**
—*n.* **1.** information and things pertaining to the events that are the subject of an investigation or a case; especially, the testimony or objects (but not the questions or comments of the lawyers) offered at a trial or hearing for the judge or jury to consider in deciding the issues in a case.
**2. character evidence** evidence pertaining to the CHARACTER of a party or a witness.
**3. circumstantial evidence** evidence of a fact that makes the existence of another fact—one that actually must be decided in the case—more or less likely. Circumstantial evidence is not second-class evidence; it is as valid, as admissible, and as acceptable a basis for a verdict as *direct evidence.* Most evidence in most cases is circumstantial, and many kinds of issues, such as intent and good faith, depend upon a SUBJECTIVE TEST that cannot be satisfied in any other way. See also note at EYE-WITNESS.
**4. competent evidence** evidence that is ADMISSIBLE.
**5. cumulative evidence** additional evidence introduced to prove a fact for which there has already been considerable evidence, adding little to what has already been admitted. A trial judge has discretion to draw the line at a reasonable point and preclude further evidence on a particular issue, or of a particular type, on the ground that it is cumulative.
**6. demonstrative evidence** evidence that the jury can perceive directly instead of just being told about it by a witness, including documents and objects involved in the incident giving rise

to a case, lawyers' charts and diagrams admitted into evidence, courtroom demonstrations, site visits, and the demeanor of witnesses. Also called **autoptic evidence**.
**7. direct evidence** evidence purportedly showing the existence or nonexistence of a fact that must be decided in a case without the need for any application of reasoning or linking of related facts; sometimes a document or other *real evidence,* most often *eyewitness evidence.* See note at EYEWITNESS for discussion of reliability. Cf. *circumstantial evidence.*
**8. documentary evidence** *real evidence* in the form of a DOCUMENT.
**9. evidence in chief** evidence introduced as part of one's *case in chief* (see under CASE²).
**10. extrinsic evidence** evidence pertaining to a written instrument such as a deed, contract, or will, beyond what is contained in the writing itself. See also PAROL EVIDENCE.
**11. eyewitness evidence** evidence provided by a person who directly perceived the events under consideration. See also note at EYEWITNESS.
**12. hearsay evidence** See under HEARSAY.
**13. opinion evidence** testimony as to what a witness believes or concludes about a situation as distinguished from what the witness personally observed. Except for opinions on matters within common experience ("He sounded angry." "She acted drunk."), opinion evidence may be given only by an *expert witness* rather than a *fact witness* (see both under WITNESS).
**14. real evidence a.** broadly, any *demonstrative evidence.* **b.** specifically, a document or other object offered as having been involved in the events that are the subject of the case, such as a murder weapon, a ransom note, or a bloody glove.
**15. rebuttal evidence** evidence introduced for purposes of REBUTTAL.
—*v.* **16.** to be evidence of: *The letter evidenced her desire for a divorce.*
**17.** to support by evidence: *He evidenced his claim through the testimony of eyewitnesses.*

See also ALIUNDE; BEST EVIDENCE RULE; *burden of producing evidence* (under BURDEN[1]); CLEAR AND CONVINCING EVIDENCE; EXHIBIT; IN EVIDENCE; MATERIAL; PAROL EVIDENCE; PREPONDERANCE OF THE EVIDENCE; *prima facie evidence* (under PRIMA FACIE); RELEVANT; SCINTILLA OF EVIDENCE; SECRET EVIDENCE; STATE'S EVIDENCE; SUBSTANTIAL EVIDENCE; *weight of the evidence* (under WEIGHT); WITNESS.
—**evidentiary** *adj.*
—**evidential** *adj.*
—**evidentially** *adv.*

**evidentiary fact** *n.* See under FACT.

**ex**[1] *prep.* **1.** without; not including; without the right to have. See for example EX DIVIDEND; EX WARRANTS.
**2.** (in the delivery term of a contract of purchase and sale) from a specified place or thing; free of risk to the purchaser until the goods leave the specified place: *ex factory; ex warehouse.* See also EX SHIP.

**ex**[2] *prep. Latin.* from, out of; since, after; on account of, by reason of; according to, in accordance with; in regard to, with respect to; by, with, of.

**ex aequo et bono** *Latin.* according to what is equitable and good; an equitable standard as distinguished from a strict legal standard, often used in resolution of international disputes.

**ex contractu** *adj. Latin.* (lit. "arising from a contract") based upon a contract: *a right ex contractu; an action ex contractu.*

**ex delicto** *adj. Latin.* (lit. "arising from a wrong") based upon a breach of duty other than a contractual promise, as a tort or a crime: *an action ex delicto; a trust ex delicto.*

**ex dividend** *adj., adv.* without dividend.
——**Note.** Shares of stock are traded ex dividend when a forthcoming dividend will be paid to the seller because the buyer cannot become the record owner soon enough to qualify to receive the dividend. The price at which the stock trades normally drops when the stock goes ex dividend.

**ex hypothesi** *adv. Latin.* (lit. "by hypothesis") by hypothesis; according to what has been assumed; hypothetically.

**ex mero motu** *adv. Latin.* (lit. "out of mere impulse") on its own initiative; on its own motion (usually applied to action taken by a court): *Although neither side raised the issue, the court found that it lacked jurisdiction and dismissed the case ex mero motu.* See note at EX PROPRIO MOTU.

**ex necessitate** *adv. Latin.* out of necessity; necessarily.

**ex officio** *adv., adj. Latin.* (lit. "by virtue of office") by virtue or one's position or office; as an incident or duty of a particular office (used most often in regard to the holding of a second position by virtue of the first): *The Chief Justice serves ex officio as chief administrator of the court. The chair and vice-chair of the board are ex officio members (or members ex officio) of the executive committee.*

**ex parte** *adv., adj. Latin.* (lit. "from a side") by, for, or with one side of a case or dispute without notice to the other side: *an order granted ex parte; an ex parte application for emergency relief; an ex parte conversation between the judge and the plaintiff's attorney.* The situations in which ex parte proceedings are allowed are very limited. See, for example, *temporary restraining order* (under RESTRAINING ORDER). Cf. ON NOTICE.
——**Usage.** This phrase was formerly widely used, and in some states is still used, in the names of certain types of cases commenced by a direct application to the court by one party, as in a petition for a writ of habeas corpus. Such a proceeding initiated by John J. Jones might be named *Ex parte John J. Jones* or *John J. Jones, ex parte,* and would be cited *Ex parte Jones.*

**ex post facto** *adj., adv. Latin.* (lit. "from what is done afterward") **1.** after the fact: *an ex post facto rationalization; repairs made ex post facto.*
**2.** retroactive; retroactively.
**3. ex post facto law** a law

—especially a criminal law—that applies retroactively.

**—Note.** The Constitution prohibits the states and the federal government from passing any "ex post facto Law." This has been construed as barring any law that criminalizes conduct that was legal at the time it was done, or increases the penalty for a crime after it was committed. Laws affecting civil rights and duties can be made retroactive, however, as frequently occurs when tax laws are changed.

**ex proprio motu** *adv. Latin.* (lit. "out of its own impulse") on its own initiative; on its own motion (usually applied to action taken by a court).

**—Usage.** The phrases *ex proprio motu* and EX MERO MOTU are interchangeable; the choice between them is a matter of personal preference and local custom. For example, in Alabama decisions the former appears with great frequency and the latter is almost unheard of; in nearby Louisiana the situation is exactly the reverse. Nationwide, *ex mero motu* is the more common form, although in modern writing the English counterpart ON ITS OWN MOTION is many times more common than either of these Latin phrases. Of all the expressions indicating that a judge or court is acting on its own initiative rather than upon motion of a party, however, the most common of all, used more often than all the others combined, is the Latin SUA SPONTE.

**ex rel.** *Latin.* abbreviation for *ex relatione* ("on the proposal of"), appearing in the names of certain kinds of proceedings brought by a state or the United States on behalf of a private party (the RELATOR): *State of New York ex rel. Smith v. Jones* (Smith is the relator at whose request or for whose benefit the state instituted the action against Jones).

**—Note.** Some courts and lawyers use English equivalents such as "on behalf of," "for the use of," or, most commonly, **on the relation of.** All such phrases are usually shortened to "ex rel." in citations.

**ex relatione** *Latin.* (lit. "on the proposal of") See EX REL.

**ex ship** *adj., adv.* (in a contract for sale of goods) from the ship; i.e., with responsibility for the goods and risk of loss to pass from the seller to the buyer when the goods leave the ship.

**ex warrants** *adj., adv.* without warrants.

**—Note.** Stock is traded ex warrants when the seller or a previous owner has decided to keep warrants previously associated with each share of the stock. See WARRANT[2].

**examination** *n.* the questioning of a witness at a trial, hearing, or deposition. Examination of a witness begins with **direct examination,** also called **examination in chief,** by the side that called the witness, followed by **cross-examination** by the other side. Then each side in turn may ask follow-up questions, called **redirect examination** and **recross-examination** respectively, alternating back and forth until both sides run out of questions. Informally, these stages are called **direct, cross, redirect,** and **recross,** without the word "examination." Ordinarily, only subjects that were raised on direct may be inquired about on cross. Each redirect and recross is strictly limited to follow-up on the testimony in the immediately preceding examination, so these are quite brief. See also SCOPE OF EXAMINATION; BEYOND THE SCOPE; OPEN THE DOOR.

**examination before trial (EBT)** *n.* a pretrial DEPOSITION.

**examination in aid of execution** *n.* Same as *deposition in aid of execution* (see under DEPOSITION).

**examine** *v.,* **examined, examining. 1.** to ask questions of a witness at a trial, hearing, or deposition: *The lawyers for both sides examined the chauffeur at length.* **2. cross-examine** to conduct the cross-examination of a witness: *After Mr. Jones examined the chauffeur, Miss Smith cross-examined her.* Also, informally, **cross.**

**3. recross-examine** to conduct the re-cross-examination of a witness. Also, informally, **recross.**
—**examiner** *n.*
——**Usage.** Note a certain nonparallel-ism in vocabulary: Although one can *cross-examine* and *recross-examine* a witness, one cannot "direct examine" or "redirect examine."

**examined copy** *n.* a copy of a document that has been compared with the original and found to be accurate. See also CERTIFIED COPY.

**exceedingly persuasive justification** *n.* the level of justification needed to render constitutional a law or governmental action based on sex. See notes at HEIGHTENED SCRUTINY and SEPARATE BUT EQUAL.

**exception** *n.* **1.** a special situation excluded from coverage of an otherwise applicable rule, principle, contract, insurance policy, etc.; e.g., *hearsay exception* (see under HEARSAY).
**2.** a formal objection to a judge's overruling of an objection or denial of a motion at a trial, formerly required in order to preserve the issue for appeal. Modern rules of practice do away with the tedious and silly requirement of taking exception every time a trial judge makes an adverse ruling.

**excess insurance** *n.* supplemental insurance to cover a portion of potential loss in excess of the limits of other policies; essentially a policy with a large deductible. A company with large risks might have a basic insurance policy and several layers of excess insurance from different insurers, with coverage under each policy picking up where the previous one leaves off.

**excess parachute payment** *n.* See under PARACHUTE.

**excessive bail** *n.* See under BAIL[1].

**excessive verdict** *n.* See under VERDICT.

**excise** or **excise tax** *n.* **1.** a tax on products manufactured, sold, or used within the country; e.g., a gasoline tax, liquor tax, or tobacco tax.

**2.** a tax paid for the privilege of carrying on certain transactions or activities; e.g., a FRANCHISE TAX.
—**excisable** *adj.*

**excited utterance** *n.* a statement about a startling event or condition made in the excitement caused by the situation. Such utterances are usually admitted into evidence as an exception to the rule against HEARSAY on the theory that people cannot make up lies under such circumstances. (Of course, their perceptions may be distorted.) Also called **spontaneous declaration** (or **statement** or **exclamation**).

**excludable alien** *n.* Same as *inadmissible alien* (see under ALIEN).

**exclusion** *n.* **1.** the act of a judge in refusing to allow proffered evidence to be considered in a case. Cf. ADMISSION; RECEIVE. See also EXCLUSIONARY RULE.
**2.** the act of a judge in barring certain people, especially prospective witnesses in a case, from the courtroom during a trial. See also SEQUESTER.
**3.** the omission of a particular class of people, property, transactions, or events from coverage of a statute or of a contract or other instrument, or a provision expressly rejecting such coverage. In particular, **a.** the specification in an insurance policy of particular risks not covered by the policy. **b.** the specification in a tax law of particular kinds of income, property, or transactions that will not be subject to the tax; for example, the exclusion of most municipal bond interest from income subject to the federal income tax.
**4.** denial of permission for an alien to enter the country.
—**excludable** *adj.*
—**exclude** *v.*, excluded, excluding.
—**exclusionary, exclusive** *adj.*
—**exclusively** *adv.*

**exclusionary rule** *n.* the principle that the prosecution in a criminal case may not use evidence obtained in violation of the Constitution, particularly evidence derived from an illegal search and seizure in violation of the Fourth Amendment (see Appendix). In recent years the Supreme Court has created several exceptions to this rule, including the GOOD FAITH EXCEPTION and the INEVITABLE DISCOVERY EXCEPTION. See also FRUIT OF THE POISONOUS TREE.

**exclusionary zoning** *n.* See under ZONING.

**exclusive jurisdiction** *n.* See under JURISDICTION[1].

**exclusive zoning** *n.* See under ZONING.

**exculpate** *v.,* **exculpated, exculpating.** to clear from a charge of guilt or fault; free from blame; vindicate.
—**exculpable** *adj.*
—**exculpation** *n.*
—**exculpatory** *adj.*

**exculpatory no** *n.* a simple denial of guilt by one who is asked whether he has committed a particular criminal act; an answer of "no" to such a question, especially when asked by a federal official or agency in connection with any investigation or business of the federal government.
—**History.** For several decades prior to 1998, most federal courts held that a bare denial of wrongdoing could not form the basis of a prosecution for lying to a federal agency, especially where the question evoking the "exculpatory no" was asked in full knowledge of the true facts and for the sole purpose of generating an additional charge against the defendant. The Supreme Court overturned that line of cases in *Brogan v. United States,* 522 U.S. 398 (1998). Subsequent to the events involved in that case, however, Congress amended the federal FALSE STATEMENTS STATUTE so that only *material* false statements can now form the basis for a separate criminal charge under that statute.

**exculpatory statement** *n.* See under STATEMENT.

**excusable neglect** *n.* See under NEGLECT.

**excuse** *v.,* **excused, excusing,** *n.* —*v.* **1.** to regard with forgiveness or indulgence; pardon; overlook: *The law excuses homicide committed in self-defense.*

**2.** to release from an obligation or duty: *to excuse a debt; to be excused from jury duty.*
**3.** to release from a role in a court case: *The judge excused the juror with the sick child and substituted an alternate juror. After two days on the stand, the witness was finally excused. When the jury returned a verdict of not guilty, the defendant was excused.*
**4. excuse for cause** (in jury selection) to excuse a potential juror from serving in a case because of the possibility of bias: *The judge excused him for cause because his wife works for the corporation being sued.* See also *challenge for cause* (under CHALLENGE).
—*n.* **5.** an explanation offered as a reason for being excused; a ground or reason for excusing or being excused. See also ABUSE EXCUSE.
**6.** the act of excusing someone or something.
—**excusable** *adj.*
—**excusably** *adv.*

**execute** *v.,* **executed, executing. 1.** to sign a legal instrument such as a deed, will, or contract, and sometimes to take additional steps necessary to put the instrument into effect, such as delivering a deed or acknowledging a will.
**2.** to carry out an obligation fully; to complete performance.
**3.** to carry out a court order or judgment; especially, to seize and, if necessary, sell property of a *judgment debtor* (see under DEBTOR) to satisfy a money judgment. See also WRIT OF EXECUTION.
**4.** to put a person to death pursuant to a death sentence.
—**execution** *n.*

**executed** *adj.* **1.** complete; fully performed; leaving no uncertainty to be resolved. See, e.g., *executed contract* (under CONTRACT); *executed trust* (under TRUST). Cf. EXECUTORY.
**2.** signed; fully effective: *executed will; executed deed.*

**executive** *adj.* pertaining to the branch of government charged with implementing the law, headed at the state level by the governor of each state and at the national level by the President, and operating through executive departments and administrative agencies. See also SEPARATION OF POWERS.

**executive agreement** *n.* an agreement between the United States and one or more other countries, entered into by the President but not submitted to the Senate for ratification as a TREATY. Such agreements are sometimes negotiated pursuant to specific statutory authority, but even when they are not they are generally regarded as binding upon the United States so long as Congress does not specifically act to overrule them.

**executive clemency** *n.* Same as CLEMENCY.

**executive order** *n.* an order issued by the President or a state governor on a matter within the scope of executive authority, having the force of law. For example, the desegregation of America's armed forces after World War II came about not by any action of Congress or the courts, but by an executive order of President Truman.

**executive privilege** *n.* the right of the President, founded in the constitutional principle of SEPARATION OF POWERS, to refuse to disclose to the courts or Congress confidential communications within the executive branch. This is a *qualified privilege* (see under PRIVILEGE), so that a strong need for the information can outweigh the privilege when there is no strong need to keep the information secret.

**executive session** *n.* See under SESSION.

**executor** *n.* a person designated in a will to ADMINISTER the testator's estate in accordance with the terms of the will. The quaint term **executrix** is still often used to refer to an executor who is a woman. Cf. ADMINISTRATOR.

**executory** *adj.* not yet fully performed or fully resolved. See, e.g., *executory contract* (under CONTRACT); *executory trust* (under TRUST). See also *executory interest* (under INTEREST[1]). Cf. EXECUTED (def. 1).

**executrix** *n., pl.* **executrices.** a woman who is an EXECUTOR under a will.

**exemplar** *n.* a typical specimen or example, especially a sample of a criminal suspect's handwriting, voice, fingerprints, hair, or other identifying information taken under controlled conditions for analysis and subsequent use as evidence. The compelled production of such exemplars does not violate the constitutional ban on compulsory SELF-INCRIMINATION because an exemplar is not a statement or testimony by the suspect.

**exemplary damages** *n.* Same as *punitive damages* (see under DAMAGES).

**exempli gratia** See E.G.

**exempt** *v.* **1.** to free from an obligation or liability to which others are subject; to make an exception for a person or thing or a class of persons or things. —*adj.* **2.** exempted; excepted; subject to an EXEMPTION. See, e.g., *exempt property* (under EXEMPTION); TAX-EXEMPT.

**exemption** *n.* **1.** the relieving of a particular person or class of persons from a legal duty: *exemption of conscientious objectors from combat duty; exemption of an individual from jury duty on the ground of hardship.*
**2.** statutory protection of certain property of a debtor **(exempt property)** from attachment by creditors. See also HOMESTEAD EXEMPTION.
**3.** an income tax DEDUCTION, in an amount fixed by statute, for each taxpayer who is not claimed as a dependent on someone else's return and for each DEPENDENT claimed by the taxpayer.

**exhaust** *v.* **1.** to exploit to the fullest extent possible: *The defendant has exhausted his appeals and must now start serving her sentence.*
**2.** to use up completely: *When its funds were exhausted the charity ceased to operate.*
—**exhaustible** *adj.*
—**exhaustion** *n.*

**exhaustion of administrative remedies** *n.* the general rule that where the law provides an administrative procedure for dealing with a particular kind of matter, a person must pursue all possible avenues for redress within the administrative agency before resorting to the courts.

**exhaustion of state remedies** *n.* the general rule that a state prisoner who feels that he is being held in violation of the Constitution must pursue all possible avenues for redress in the state courts before seeking a writ of HABEAS CORPUS in federal court.

**exhibit** *n.* **1.** a document referred to in an affidavit, contract, or other instrument and attached to the instrument. Such exhibits are regarded as an intrinsic part of the instrument to which they are attached.
**2.** a document or object sought to be used as evidence at a trial. Each party's proposed exhibits are numbered or lettered sequentially ("marked") for ease of identification, and until they are admitted into evidence they are referred to as "Plaintiff's Exhibit C for identification," "Defendant's Exhibit 3 for identification," and the like. If the judge admits an exhibit into evidence, it is thereafter referred to as "Plaintiff's Exhibit C in evidence," "Defendant's Exhibit 3 in evidence," or the like.

**exigent circumstances** *n.* special circumstances under which law enforcement officers who have probable cause to conduct a search may do so without waiting to get a search warrant. These include, among others, any situation involving the search of an automobile on a roadway and any situation in which the police reasonably believe that the search is necessary to protect life or prevent serious injury. See also FRESH PURSUIT.

**exonerate** *v.*, **exonerated, exonerating. 1.** to clear of an accusation; free from guilt or blame; exculpate.
**2.** to relieve a person of an obligation or property of a burden; especially by shifting it to another person or other property.
—**exonerative** *adj.*

**exoneration** *n.* **1.** the act of exonerat-

ing or state of being exonerated.
**2.** the right of one who is secondarily liable for a debt to compel the one primarily liable to pay it or, having paid it, to obtain reimbursement from the one primarily liable; also the action or remedy by which this right is enforced.

**expectancy** *n., pl.* **expectancies.** a property interest that may or may not come into existence in the future; a hoped-for property right but not one that exists at present: *Her uncle has made a will leaving her the house; but he can always change his will, so all she has now is a mere expectancy.*

**expert** *n.* a person possessing the qualifications of education and experience to render advice to an attorney or party in a specialized field or to testify as an *expert witness* (see under WITNESS). See also BATTLE OF THE EXPERTS; *qualify as an expert* (under QUALIFY[1]).

**expertise** *n.* See SCOPE OF EXPERTISE.

**express** *adj.* explicit; set forth in words; oral or written. Opposite of IMPLIED. See *express assumpsit* (under ASSUMPSIT); *express authority* (under AUTHORITY[1]); *express contract* (under CONTRACT); *express repeal* (under REPEAL); *express trust* (under TRUST); *express waiver* (under WAIVER); and *express warranty* (under WARRANTY). For a somewhat broader use of the term, see def. b of *express warranty* (under WARRANTY).

**expropriation** *n.* a TAKING of private property by a government under the power of EMINENT DOMAIN.
—**expropriable** *adj.*
—**expropriate** *v.*, **expropriated, expropriating.**

**expunge** *v.*, **expunged, expunging. 1.** to erase; wipe out; remove; undo.
**2. expunge the record** to delete a conviction from an individual's official criminal record, as in certain cases involving a youthful offender or first-time offender.
—**expungement, expunction** *n.*

**extort** *v.* to obtain by EXTORTION.
—**extorter** *n.*
—**extortive** *adj.*

**extortion** *n.* the crime of obtaining money or property from a person by threat of harmful conduct in the future (e.g., killing, injuring, destroying property, disclosing embarrassing information) or threat of imminent harm falling short of the kinds of threatened harm necessary for ROBBERY (e.g., a threat to destroy property other than a home). See also KICKBACK (def. 2); BLACKMAIL.
—**extortionate** *adj.*
—**extortionately** *adv.*
—**extortionist, extortioner** *n.*

**extraditable** *adj.* **1.** capable of being extradited; subject to extradition: *an extraditable person.*
**2.** capable of incurring extradition: *an extraditable offense.*

**extradite** *v.,* **extradited, extraditing.**
**1.** to give up (a suspect) to another state or nation for prosecution.
**2.** to obtain the extradition of.

**extradition** *n.* **1.** the handing over by one state to another of a suspect wanted for criminal prosecution in the second state.
**2.** the handing over of a criminal suspect from one country to another. Cf. ASYLUM.
——**Note.** The Constitution requires the states of the United States to honor each other's requests for extradition if the suspect has been formally charged with a crime in the requesting state and was in that state at the time the crime was committed. The suspect may, however, be required to serve out a current sentence in the sending state before being handed over. Treaties between the United States and many other countries provide for mutual extradition between the countries involved.

**extrajudicial** *adj.* not part of court proceedings or not within the authority of a court.
—**extrajudicially** *adv.*

**extralegal** *adj.* beyond the province, authority, or regulation of the law: *extralegal activities; extralegal ethical norms.*
—**extralegally** *adv.*

**extraordinary care** *n.* See under CARE.

**extraordinary remedy** (or **relief**) *n.* See under REMEDY.

**extraordinary session** *n.* See under SESSION.

**extraordinary writ** *n.* See under WRIT.

**extraterritorial** *adj.* **1.** beyond local jurisdiction; pertaining to people, events, or things in other geographic areas: *Efforts to regulate the Internet raise issues of extraterritorial application of national laws.*
**2.** pertaining to persons or property having the privilege of EXTRATERRITORIALITY.
—**extraterritorially** *adv.*

**extraterritoriality** *n.* **1.** immunity from the jurisdiction of a nation, granted to foreign diplomatic officials, foreign warships on friendly visits to the nation's ports, etc. Persons and property having this privilege by international law or agreement are treated by the host country for legal purposes as if they were outside the country and so not subject to its laws.
**2.** the applicability or exercise of a sovereign's laws outside its territory.

**extrinsic evidence** *n.* See under EVIDENCE.

**eyewitness** *n.* **1.** a person who saw an event under discussion. Cf. EARWITNESS.
**2.** broadly, a person who directly perceived an event under discussion, whether by seeing, hearing, or otherwise.
See also *eyewitness evidence* (under EVIDENCE); *eyewitness identification* and *cross-racial identification* (both under IDENTIFICATION); *eyewitness testimony* (under TESTIMONY). Cf. *circumstantial evidence* (under EVIDENCE).
——**History.** Eyewitness evidence has been central to Anglo-American law since the earliest days, when jurors were chosen not for their impartiality but for their first-hand knowledge of the circumstances and events involved in a case. Jurors place great weight on eyewitness testimony, and prosecutors make great drama of having a witness

or victim identify the wrongdoer by pointing to the defendant in court. In the last few decades, however, scientific studies have shown that even the most conscientious and honest eyewitness accounts can be extremely unreliable; at the same time, forensic science has improved to the point where conclusions drawn from analysis of physical evidence from crime scenes and elsewhere can be extremely firm. As a result, many people who served many years in prison after being "positively identified" in a crime have been released because, through luck, evidence (often semen) was preserved and could be subjected to modern tests proving them innocent. In the courtroom, however, inherently unreliable eyewitness evidence still outweighs more reliable circumstantial or scientific evidence in the minds of many jurors.

# F

**face** *n*. **1.** the front of an instrument.

**2.** the obvious meaning of a statement or a writing; the explicit provisions of a writing: *The legislature's discriminatory purpose is clear from the face of the statute.*

**3.** the outward appearance as distinguished from the real significance: *Although the minimum height requirement for employees is facially neutral, in practice it discriminates against women.*

**4. on its face a.** obviously and without qualification: *unconstitutional* (or *invalid*) *on its face* (see under UNCONSTITUTIONAL). **b.** apparently; superficially: *The statement that one can buy bacon at a certain butcher shop, though innocent on its face, amounts to defamation when made in reference to a kosher butcher shop.*
—**facial** *adj.*
—**facially** *adv.*

**face amount** (or **value**) *n*. the sum shown on the face of an instrument; the principal amount of an obligation, not taking into account interest, deductions, or other adjustments: *The face amount of the mortgage is $60,000, but only $25,000 remains to be paid. The face value of the life insurance policy is $100,000, but with dividends it will pay $120,000.*

**fact** *n*. **1.** an event or circumstance; an aspect of reality. As distinguished from LAW, a matter ascertained by consideration of evidence; as distinguished from OPINION, a matter directly observed by a witness.

**2. evidentiary fact** a fact that is itself evidence of another fact at issue in a case; a fact providing a basis for determination of an *ultimate fact.*

**3. ultimate fact** one of the facts so basic to a claim, charge, or defense that their determination is the ultimate objective of a trial.

See also *fact witness* (under WITNESS); FINDING OF FACT; *implied in fact* (under IMPLIED); JURISDICTIONAL FACT; *stipulated fact* (under STIPULATION); *question of fact* and *mixed question of fact and law* (both under QUESTION²); TRIER OF FACT.

**fact-finder** or **fact finder** *n*. Same as FACTFINDER.

**fact finding** *n*. **1.** a FINDING OF FACT.
**2.** Same as FACTFINDING (def. 1).

**factfinder** *n*. Same as TRIER OF FACT. Also written **fact-finder** or **fact finder.**

**factfinding** or **fact-finding** *n*. **1.** Also, **fact finding.** the process of ascertaining facts.
—*adj*. **2.** pertaining to the process of ascertaining facts; having the ascertainment of facts as its purpose: *the factfinding process; a factfinding mission.*

**factor** *n*. **1.** a merchant who, instead of buying goods and reselling at a profit, receives goods on *consignment* (see under CONSIGN) and sells them for a commission.

**2.** a company that lends money to merchants or manufacturers, taking an assignment of their accounts receivable as security.

**factual** *adj*. **1.** of or pertaining to facts; concerning facts: *factual accuracy.*
**2.** based on or restricted to facts: *a factual report.*
—**factually** *adv.*

**factum** *n., pl.* **facta.** *Latin.* (lit. "a thing done") **1.** a person's act or deed; a thing done by a person; the doing of a thing, e.g., the making of an instrument. See also *fraud in the factum* (under FRAUD).
**2.** a written deed.
**3.** a fact.
**4.** a statement of facts.

**factum probandum** *n., pl.* **facta pro-banda.** *Latin.* (lit. "fact to be proved; fact that must be proved") an *ultimate fact* (see under FACT).

**factum probans** *n., pl.* **facta probantia.** *Latin.* (lit. "a proving fact") an *evidentiary fact* (see under FACT).

**fail** *v.* **1.** to be unsuccessful, inadequate, deficient.
**2.** (of a contract) to be unenforceable—for example, because the terms are too INDEFINITE, or a party lacked CAPACITY to contract, or the contract is against PUBLIC POLICY.
**3.** (of a gift or bequest) to be ineffective—for example, because the property no longer exists or the donee is deceased.
**4.** (of a corporation, company, or business) to become unable to meet or pay debts or business obligations; become insolvent or bankrupt.
—**failure** *n.*

**failure of consideration** *n.* a situation in which the CONSIDERATION agreed upon in a contract does not materialize or ceases to exist or becomes worthless. In some cases this renders the promise or the negotiable instrument given in exchange for that consideration unenforceable, or justifies other relief. The most common example of failure of consideration is simply the failure of a party to do whatever was promised in the contract. Cf. *want of consideration* (under WANT).

**failure of issue** *n.* See under ISSUE².

**failure to prosecute** *n.* in either a civil or criminal case, the failure of the plaintiff or prosecutor to pursue the case diligently once it has been commenced. Also called **want of prosecution.**
—**Note.** In extreme cases, a civil case may be dismissed for failure to prosecute; criminal cases will be so dismissed if there is a violation of the requirement of a *speedy trial* (see under TRIAL).

**faint pleader** *n.* a fraudulent or collusive manner of pleading. See PLEADER².
Also called **faint pleading.**

**fair¹** *adj.* **1.** free from bias or dishonesty.
**2.** balanced; equitable.
**3.** legitimately done; proper under the rules.
**4.** reasonable.
—**fairly** *adv.*

**fair²** *n.* a periodic, usually annual, gathering of buyers and sellers for the holding of a major market.
——**History.** Fairs in early England were events of considerable economic significance, typically held pursuant to a franchise granted to a town by statute or royal charter. The greater-than-ordinary confluence of people and intensity of economic commerce gave rise to a greater-than-ordinary volume of legal business, which it was best to handle on the spot according to rules adapted to the circumstances. See PIEPOWDER COURT.

**fair comment** *n.* the right to express one's opinion on matters of public interest, such as the conduct of a public official or the conduct of a private person in a matter affecting the community at large. As long as the comment is based upon an honest belief in the underlying facts and is not completely unreasonable, the person making it may not be held liable for DEFAMATION on account of it.

**fair hearing** *n.* **1.** a trial or other HEARING that comports with *procedural due process* (see under DUE PROCESS).
**2.** especially, such a hearing in an administrative proceeding.
——**Usage.** In a general sense, this phrase represents the kind of hearing that, under the Due Process Clauses of the Fifth and Fourteenth Amendments to the Constitution, an individual must be given before being deprived of life, liberty, or property by federal or state action. In criminal cases, the right is more specifically referred to as FAIR TRIAL; in administrative contexts the usual phrase is *fair hearing,* and the phrase is often used as the formal name for an administrative proceeding: *Your fair hearing is scheduled for 2:30 on Thursday.*

**fair housing** *n.* absence of discrimination in sale, rental, or management of residential property on the basis of race, color, religion, sex, disability, national origin, or pregnancy or the presence of children.
——**Note.** With certain exceptions, as for discrimination on the basis of religion by religious groups or exclusion of children from housing for the elderly, fair housing is mandated by federal law.

**fair market value** *n.* Same as MARKET VALUE.

**fair preponderance of the evidence** *n.* Same as PREPONDERANCE OF THE EVIDENCE.

**fair representation** *n.* union representation of employees in a bargaining unit in a manner that does not overlook the interests of any of them or discriminate unfairly among them.

**fair trial** *n.* a trial before an impartial tribunal that comports with constitutional and statutory standards of fairness, and in particular with *procedural due process* (see under DUE PROCESS).
——**Note.** It is often pointed out in appellate decisions that a party is entitled to a fair trial, but not a perfect trial. Perfection in human endeavors is an unattainable goal—a fact to which the law gives formal recognition in the doctrine of *harmless error* (see under ERROR).

**fair trial/free press** *n.* Also called **fair trial–free press, fair trial and free press.** Same as FREE PRESS/FAIR TRIAL.

**fair use** *n.* reasonable and limited use of a copyrighted work without permission of the owner, as in quoting a few lines from a book in a review of the book. Such use is not an infringement of the copyright.

**fairness** *n.* the quality or condition of being fair. See also FUNDAMENTAL FAIRNESS.

**faith** *n.* See GOOD FAITH; BAD FAITH; ABIDING FAITH.

**false** *adj.* **1.** untrue: e.g., FALSE STATEMENT.

**2.** misleading: e.g., FALSE ADVERTISING.
**3.** unlawful: e.g., FALSE IMPRISONMENT.
—**falsely** *adv.*
—**falseness** *n.*

**false advertising** *n.* advertising that is materially misleading about the nature, origin, or quality of a product or the training or skill of a provider of service. It is illegal. See also BAIT AND SWITCH.

**false arrest** *n.* See under FALSE IMPRISONMENT.

**false exculpatory statement** *n.* an *exculpatory statement* (see under STATEMENT) made by a criminal suspect and later shown to be untrue. See also EXCULPATORY NO.
——**Note.** When evidence is introduced in a criminal trial indicating that the defendant, upon being accused of a crime or informed that a crime had been committed, made a false exculpatory statement—for example, a statement that he was at a bar with friends at the time of the crime, when there is evidence indicating that the bar was closed that day—the jury will normally be instructed that if they find that the defendant did make a false exculpatory statement, they may regard that as evidence that the defendant is guilty of the crime. The theory is that an innocent person would ordinarily have no reason to lie. Of course, there are many reasons why an innocent person might lie. In effect, this instruction places the burden upon the defendant to show that there was a reason for this particular false statement other than a desire to conceal involvement in the crime charged.

**false impersonation** *n.* See IMPERSONATION.

**false imprisonment** *n.* the tort and crime of restricting a person to a particular area without legal justification, whether by means of physical restraints (as in a prison, a locked room, or a speeding automobile) or through force or threat of immediate harm to one's person or valuable property. Also called **false arrest,** especially when done by one falsely claiming to have law enforcement authority, or by a law enforcement officer who lacks probable cause or other legal grounds for detaining the arrestee.

**false personation** *n.* See IMPERSONATION.

**false pretenses** *n.* the crime of obtaining title to property, especially personal property, by means of false representations, as by swindling someone out of money or tricking someone into selling something.

—**Note.** Under traditional classification schemes, if only possession, rather than title, is obtained by trick, then the crime is not false pretenses but LARCENY. Under modern statutes, the two situations are often classified together as THEFT.

**false representation** *n.* Same as MISREPRESENTATION.

**false statement** *n.* **1.** an assertion that is not true, especially one made in words as distinguished from nonverbal conduct. See also STATEMENT.
**2.** any conduct or representation that violates a FALSE STATEMENTS STATUTE.

**false statements statute** *n.* **1.** any federal or state statute making it a crime to make false statements in dealings with government agencies or officials, either in general or in specific situations (as on a tax return or student loan application).
**2.** especially, the general federal statute, 18 U.S.C. § 1001, which makes it a crime in dealings with the federal government to (1) falsify or conceal a material fact, (2) make a materially false statement, or (3) make or use a document known to contain a materially false statement or entry.
Also called **false statement statute.** See also EXCULPATORY NO.

**false swearing** *n.* the crime of making a false statement under oath or affirmation, other than in the belief that what is being said is true. A broader and less serious offense than PERJURY.

**falsehood** *n.* an untrue statement.

**falsify** *v.*, **falsified, falsifying. 1.** to make false or incorrect, especially so as to deceive: *to falsify an income tax return.*
**2.** to represent falsely: *to falsify one's employment history on a job application.*
**3.** to show or prove to be false; disprove: *to falsify the prosecution's theory of the crime.*
—**falsifiable** *adj.*
—**falsifiability** *n.*
—**falsification** *n.*
—**falsifier** *n.*

**falsity** *n.*, **falsities. 1.** the quality or condition of being FALSE; incorrectness; untruthfulness; unlawfulness.
**2.** something false; a falsehood.

**falsus in uno, falsus in omnibus** *Latin.* (lit. "deceitful in one thing, deceitful in all things") the doctrine that a witness who is shown to have deliberately lied on a material issue in a case may be regarded by the jury as generally unworthy of belief, so that the jury may discount or disregard that witness's entire testimony.

**family** *n.*, *pl.* **families.** a group of people related by blood, marriage, or adoption, or in an analogous relationship linked by bonds of affection and commitment. The exact scope of the term varies with the context.

**family law** *n.* the area of law dealing with marriage, separation, and divorce; adoption, custody, and support of children; DOMESTIC PARTNERSHIP; and related matters. Also called **domestic relations.**

**faqih** *n.*, *pl.* **faqihs, fuqaha'.** *Islamic Law.* an Islamic religious lawyer.

**F.A.S.** free alongside. In an offer or contract for the sale of goods this means that the goods will be delivered by the seller, at the seller's expense and risk, to a specified vessel at a specified port.

**fast track** *n. Informal.* an expedited schedule: *Because of the need for a quick decision, the judge put the case on a fast track.* See also ROCKET DOCKET.

**fast-track** *adj. Informal.* **1.** Also, **fast track.** of or pertaining to expedited schedules or scheduling; expedited; streamlined.

—*v.* **2.** to subject to a fast-track schedule; to expedite; to push to a rapid conclusion.

**fatal** *adj.* causing invalidity; describing an error or defect that renders a transaction or interest void, an argument ineffective, a trial invalid, an instrument unenforceable, or the like: *The court held that the failure to obtain a search warrant was fatal to the search, and so excluded the evidence.*

**fatal defect** *n.* See under DEFECT[1].

**fatal error** *n.* Same as *reversible error* (see under ERROR).

**fatal variance** See under VARIANCE.

**fatwa** *n. Islamic Law.* an authoritative legal opinion; a decree.

**fault** *n.* wrongfulness; blameworthiness; broadly, the doing of anything that provides a basis for a suit or criminal action against oneself; narrowly, the element—often called STATE OF MIND or MENS REA—that makes an act a tort or crime. Cf. NO-FAULT DIVORCE; NO-FAULT INSURANCE; STRICT LIABILITY.

**f/b/o** Abbreviation for FOR THE BENEFIT OF.

**fealty** *n. Feudal Law.* **1.** fidelity of a tenant or vassal to a lord.
**2.** the obligation or oath of a tenant or vassal to be faithful to a lord.

**federal** *adj.* relating to the United States, and especially to the government and law of the United States, as distinguished from a state: *federal crime; federal income tax; federal government; federal judge.*

**federal case** *n.* See under CASE[1].

**Federal Circuit** *n.* See under CIRCUIT.

**federal common law** *n.* See under COMMON LAW.

**Federal Insurance Contributions Act (FICA)** *n.* See under SOCIAL SECURITY.

**federal law** *n.* law adopted or recognized by the government of the United States with respect to matters within its constitutional powers, uniformly applicable throughout the nation. It includes the Constitution; statutes adopted by Congress; executive orders of the President; regulations and rulings of federal agencies; treaties and executive agreements to which the United States is a party; international law, at least to the extent that the courts choose to recognize it and Congress has not acted to the contrary; judicial interpretations and rulings with respect to all of the foregoing matters; and *federal common law* (see under COMMON LAW).

**federal money** *n.* **1.** money received from the federal government as distinguished from other sources, as for a public health program or university research project.
**2.** in federal campaign finance law, same as HARD MONEY.

**federal question** *n.* an issue requiring the application or interpretation of FEDERAL LAW in a case. See also *federal question jurisdiction* (under JURISDICTION[1]).

**federal statute** *n.* See under STATUTE.

**federalism** *n.* **1.** a principle of government in which several states or countries are united as a single political entity with a common government while retaining a considerable degree of autonomy with respect to their internal affairs.
**2.** in particular, the governmental structure of the United States of America, in which each state is sovereign in matters left to the states by the United States Constitution, but all states are subordinate to the national government in matters delegated to that government by the Constitution. See also OUR FEDERALISM.

**fee**[1] *n.* **1. a.** Also called **estate** (or **tenancy**) **in fee, fee estate.** a possessory interest in real estate of potentially infinite duration. (See *possessory interest*, under INTEREST[1].) If not sold or given away during the owner's life or by will, and so long as no condition specified for its continued existence is violated, a fee descends automatically to the owner's heirs upon the owner's death, and then to their heirs, and so on indefinitely. The two basic categories of fee are the *fee simple* and the virtually extinct FEE TAIL. **b.** a territory held in fee; the parcel of land in which one has a fee estate.

**2. fee simple** a fee which is inheritable by any heir of the owner. Older forms of fee in which the property was permanently restricted to certain heirs, such as male descendants only, have been substantially abolished; hence for practical purposes almost every fee is now a fee simple, and the terms *fee* and *fee simple* are often used interchangeably. Cf. FEE TAIL.

**3. fee simple absolute** a fee simple that is not subject to any condition on its continuation in the hands of the present owner and his heirs so long as they do not transfer it to someone else. (Even a fee simple absolute, however, is subject to the state and federal governments' power of EMINENT DOMAIN.) Cf. *fee simple defeasible.*

**4. fee simple defeasible** a fee simple estate that is subject to termination (DEFEASANCE) upon the occurrence of some future event. Upon defeasance, the current owner loses the property and the fee vests in someone else. Also called **defeasible fee; conditional fee.** Cf. *fee simple absolute.*

**5. fee simple determinable** a defeasible fee which is to continue only so long as a certain state of affairs continues, or only until a certain event occurs. Such fees are most often created in gifts to charity, as when real estate is left by will to a university "so long as the property is used for educational purposes." If the deed or will creating such a fee specifies who should get the property if the fee is terminated, that person has an EXECUTORY INTEREST in the property; otherwise the transferor and his heirs retain a POSSIBILITY OF REVERTER. In either case, if the condition for continuation of the present fee is violated, the person next in line will automatically get the property in *fee simple absolute.*

**6. fee tail** See FEE TAIL.

——**Usage.** The term *fee* applies equally to ancient feudal estates and modern allodial estates (see FEUDALISM; ALLODIUM). This term came out on top in a

battle of linguistic evolution that included a considerable array of etymologically related terms, including FIEF, FEUD[1], FEOD, and the Latin FEUDUM and FEODUM, all of which mean the same thing but are confined to historical contexts in which they refer to a fee estate held of a feudal lord.

**fee[2]** *n.* **1.** compensation for services rendered by an *independent contractor* (see under CONTRACTOR), especially professional services by a lawyer, doctor, or the like. See also *contingency fee* (under CONTINGENCY); FINDER'S FEE.

**2.** a sum paid for a LICENSE or privilege, such as a fee paid to the government for a driver's license or for admission to a national park. See also *filing fee* (under FILE). Cf. TAX.

**fee tail** *n.* **1.** an obsolete form of fee estate (see FEE[1]) in which the property could descend only to "heirs of the body" of the holder; that is, to direct descendants (children, grandchildren, and so on) but not collateral heirs (siblings, cousins, nephews, nieces, and the like). If the line of permissible takers ran out (possibly after some generations), then unless the original grant creating the fee tail specified otherwise the estate reverted to the original grantor and his heirs in *fee simple* (see under FEE[1]). The fee tail no longer exists in its original form; where it is still recognized at all, it can be converted—or is automatically converted by statute—into a less restrictive form of estate.

**2.** Also called **fee tail general.** the usual form of fee tail, in which any direct descendant might take the property. A fee tail of this kind was created by a grant using the formula "to A and the heirs of his body."

**3. fee tail female** a fee tail with inheritance limited to direct female descendants, created by a grant "to A and the heirs female of his body." This kind of fee tail existed in theory as a complement to the *fee tail male,* but anyone who actually created such an estate would have been regarded as extremely eccentric.

**4. fee tail male** a fee tail limited to direct male descendants, created by a grant "to A and the heirs male of his body."

**5. fee tail special** an estate in fee limited to a particular class of direct descendants, as for example a man's descendants by a particular wife.

——**False Friend.** The *tail* in a *fee tail* has nothing to do with the tail on a dog or cat or the like, even in some metaphorical sense, such as the chain of direct descendants being in some way like a tail. The word comes from an old French word meaning "cut"; it signifies that the class of potential takers has been carved down—or to use another word from the same source, *tailored*—to the grantor's specifications.

**fellow servant** *n.* a co-worker employed by the same employer, especially one working at the same level as distinguished from a supervisor or subordinate. See note at MASTER AND SERVANT.

**fellow servant rule** *n.* the common law rule that an employer is not liable to an employee for injuries resulting from the negligence of a fellow employee on the job. Also called **fellow servant doctrine.**

——**History.** The fellow servant rule was an exception to the common law doctrine of RESPONDEAT SUPERIOR. Over the years the rule has been variously abrogated by statute, limited by judicial decision, and superseded by WORKERS' COMPENSATION laws, leaving it with little if any vitality today.

**felon** *n.* a person who commits a FELONY.

**felony** *n., pl.* **felonies.** a serious crime, usually defined as one punishable by death or by imprisonment for more than one year. Cf. MISDEMEANOR.

—**felonious** *adj.*
—**feloniously** *adv.*

**felony murder** or **felony-murder** *n.* the commission of a felony that is not itself a homicide but that accidentally or unexpectedly results in a death; for example, an act of arson that leads to

the death of a firefighter, or participation in a burglary during which another participant, contrary to the plan agreed upon, shoots a night watchman. Felony murder is punishable as MURDER. The Supreme Court has held, however, that the death penalty may not be imposed on a felony murderer who did not himself kill, attempt to kill, or intend that a killing take place or that lethal force be used in the underlying felony, unless he was a major participant in that felony and his actions reflected a reckless indifference to human life, as in the case of two individuals who supplied guns to a murderer for a prison break and then claimed that they were surprised when the guns were actually used to shoot people to death in the course of the escape. *Tison v. Arizona,* 481 U.S. 137 (1987).

—**felony murderer, felony-murderer** *n.*

——**History.** The concept of felony murder originated in the common law courts of England, and has been incorporated in one form or another into murder statutes throughout America. In its most extreme form it would hold a peripheral participant in a minor felony guilty of murder on account of a completely unforeseeable accidental death with which that participant had nothing to do. Most states limit the doctrine in various ways, as by applying it only to serious felonies and allowing a defendant to show as an *affirmative defense* (see under DEFENSE) that she was not involved in the killing and had no reason to believe that such a thing might occur. Nevertheless, the felony murder doctrine typically comes into play only when the defendant has not actually killed anyone and is not actually guilty of murder in any ordinary sense of the word. For that reason, the crime was abolished in England, where it was invented, in 1957. In the United States the trend in recent years has rather been to expand the crime. For example, although the original rationale for the doctrine was the protection of innocent parties caught up in a felony, it has now been used to convict one of two robbers of first degree murder because, when it turned out that their intended victim (an undercover police officer) had a gun, the other robber foolishly grabbed the officer and got himself shot to death. *People v. Dekens,* 182 Ill. 2d 247 (1998).

**feme covert** *n., pl.* **femes covert.** *Law French.* (lit. "a woman covered") at common law, a married woman; a woman under COVERTURE. Cf. FEME SOLE.

**feme sole** *n., pl.* **femes sole.** *Law French.* (lit. "a woman alone") **1.** at common law, an unmarried woman, including a widow or divorced woman. Unlike a FEME COVERT, an unmarried woman had the legal right to make decisions and enter into contracts and transactions involving her own property.
**2. feme sole trader** a married woman who was permitted to trade on her own account, and so with respect to her trading had the same legal rights as an unmarried woman. This was permitted by custom in London and perhaps elsewhere, and in the United States was recognized as a necessity for women deserted by their husbands.

**feminist legal theory** *n.* a body of legal thought and scholarship that analyzes law as it pertains to the political, economic, and social status of women and criticizes legal theories and institutions that wittingly or unwittingly perpetuate a historical male orientation in which women and women's concerns are subordinate. Also called **feminist jurisprudence.**

**fence** *n., v.* **fenced, fencing.** *Informal.*
—*n.* **1.** a person who receives or deals in stolen goods.
—*v.* **2.** to sell stolen goods to a fence.

**feod** *n.* See FEUD[1].

**feodary** *n., pl.* **feodaries.** See FEUDARY.

**feodatory** *n., pl.* **feodatories,** *adj.* See FEUDATORY.

**feodum** *n., pl.* **feoda.** *Latin.* See FEUDUM.

**feoff** *v.* to invest with a FIEF or FEE[1]; to ENFEOFF.

—**feoffee** *n.*
—**feoffor** *n.*

**feoffee to uses** *n.* a person to whom a fee interest in land was conveyed for the use of a third person. Cf. CESTUI QUE USE; see also STATUTE OF USES.

**feoffment** *n.* **1.** the action or fact of investing with a FIEF or FEE[1].
**2.** especially, the conveyance of land by LIVERY OF SEISIN; the ritual of livery of seisin.
**3.** the instrument or deed by which a fee is conveyed.

**ferae naturae** *adj. Latin.* (lit. "of a wild nature; of a wild character") **1.** (of an animal or animals) wild by nature; of a sort not normally domesticated.
—*n.pl.* **2.** wild animals; animals of a sort not normally domesticated.
——**Note.** Traditional common law rules regarding ownership of animals and liability for injuries caused by animals depend upon the classification of the animal as wild (animals ferae naturae) or domestic (animals DOMITAE NATURAE or MANSUETAE NATURAE). Under these rules, which have been modified to a greater or lesser extent by statute in many jurisdictions, ownership of an animal ferae naturae could be obtained only by bringing it under control, as by capturing or subduing it or penning it in, and was lost if the animal escaped. While in possession of such an animal, the owner was strictly liable for any injury it caused. Domestic animals, however, generally remained one's property even if they wandered off temporarily, and because they were presumed to be tame the owner was not ordinarily liable for injuries caused by them unless the owner had reason to know of a particular animal's VICIOUS PROPENSITY. See also ONE-BITE RULE.

**Feres doctrine** *n.* the doctrine that members of the military may not assert tort claims against the United States for injuries caused by negligence or other torts incurred in connection with their service in the military, but instead are relegated to the uniform statutory system of compensation for injuries or death of those in the armed services.

——**History.** The doctrine is named for *Feres v. United States,* 340 U.S. 135 (1950)—a set of consolidated tort cases including one brought by a soldier who, eight months after an abdominal operation in an army hospital, underwent further treatment in a civilian hospital, where surgeons discovered and removed from his stomach a towel, 30 inches long by 18 inches wide, marked "Medical Department U.S. Army." Somewhat remarkably, the trial judge did not treat this as a RES IPSA LOQUITUR case, and in fact declared the case to be "a difficult one on the facts as well as on the law." Any question as to the basis for liability was rendered moot, however, by the Supreme Court's holding that the soldier did not have any cause of action at all under the Federal Tort Claims Act.

**fertile-octogenarian rule** *n.* the conclusive presumption at common law, for purposes of applying the *rule against perpetuities* (see under PERPETUITY), that any person, regardless of sex, age, physical condition, or other circumstance, is fertile and might have additional children. Under this presumption, a will leaving certain land to an 80-year-old woman for her life, then to her surviving children jointly for their lives, and upon the death of the last surviving child to her grandchildren who are then alive, would violate the rule against perpetuities because of the theoretical possibility that she might have an additional child who would be born after the date of the gift and would outlive her other children by more than 21 years. The provision for ultimate vesting in the grandchildren, therefore, would be void. Also called **presumption of fertility.** See also UNBORN-WIDOW RULE.

——**Note.** The fertile-octogenarian rule has the advantage of certainty, which is the whole reason for the rule against perpetuities (see discussion at PERPETUITY): It avoids the unseemliness and uncertainty of a factfinding inquiry into the reproductive capacity of individuals named in a will, trust instrument, or the like. And modern technology and policy have in a sense caught up with the rule: Babies after menopause, reversal of sterilization, and social policies favoring adoption, among other things, have made it more difficult than ever to say with certainty that an individual will never have another child. But the rule has the disadvantage of ignoring reality and invalidating gifts that satisfy the spirit of the rule against perpetuities simply because a will or other instrument was inartfully drafted. To avoid these unfortunate consequences, some states have adopted the WAIT-AND-SEE APPROACH.

**feud**[1] *n.* **1.** an inheritable estate in land held of a feudal lord on condition of performing certain services. **2.** the geographic territory so held. Also, **feod.**

——**Usage.** The spelling *feod* appears only in historical works. See also note at FEE[1].

**feud**[2] *n.* **1.** a bitter dispute, especially one that extends over a considerable span of time: *a feud between labor and management.* **2.** a bitter, continuous hostility, as between two families or two nations, often lasting for many years or generations. —*v.* **3.** to engage in such a feud.

**feudal** *adj.* **1.** of, pertaining to, existing under, or having the characteristics of FEUDALISM. **2.** of, pertaining to, or in the nature of a FEUD[1] or FIEF. —**feudally** *adv.*

**feudal law** *n.* the regime of rights and responsibilities in the feudal system, particularly in relation to the holding and transfer of interests in land. See also FEUDALISM.

**feudalism** *n.* the political, social, and economic system that prevailed in Europe in the Middle Ages, including England for some centuries after the Norman Conquest, based upon the holding of lands by grant from an overlord and the owing of fealty and service to the lord in exchange. Also called **feudal system.** ——**History.** In the feudal system in

England the king was the ultimate lord of all the land in the realm; everyone else who set foot on land did so by virtue of a maze of rights and interests and duties parceled among the king's barons and those who held under them. This system was extended to the American colonies. Although feudalism is dead in the United States, and dead as a practical matter in England, its intricate system of dividing up and conveying and devising and inheriting interests in land is the backbone of Anglo-American property law. See also notes at ALLODIUM and MORT D'ANCESTOR.

**feudalistic** *adj.* characteristic of FEUDALISM.

**feudary** *n., pl.* **feudaries.** a person who holds lands by feudal tenure. Also, **feodary.**

**feudatory** *n., pl.* **feudatories,** *adj.* —*n.*
**1.** a person who holds lands by feudal tenure.
**2.** a FEUD[1] or FIEF.
—*adj.* **3.** (of a person) owing feudal allegiance to another; subject.
**4.** (of a feudal estate) held by feudal tenure.
**5.** (of a state, principality, etc.) under the overlordship of another sovereign or state.
Also, **feodatory.**

**feudum** *n., pl.* **feuda.** *Latin.* a FEUD[1]. Also, **feodum.** See also note at FEE[1].

**fi. fa.** abbreviation for FIERI FACIAS.

**FICA** See under SOCIAL SECURITY.

**fiction** *n.* **1.** Same as LEGAL FICTION.
**2.** any falsehood.
—**fictional** *adj.*
—**fictionally** *adv.*

**fictitious** *adj.* **1.** created, done, or assumed for the sake of concealment; not genuine; false.
**2.** of or pertaining to fiction, especially a LEGAL FICTION.
—**fictitiously** *adv.*
—**fictitiousness** *n.*

**fictitious name** *n.* a name assumed to conceal one's identity or used for a person whose identity is not yet known. See JOHN DOE.

**fictitious payee** *n.* a PAYEE named on a check or other instrument for the payment of money who either does not exist or is not intended by the maker or drawer of the instrument to have any interest in the instrument. Indorsement of such an instrument by anyone in the fictitious payee's name is effective to convey rights on the instrument to subsequent holders.

**fictitious person** *n.* **1.** a hypothetical person whose existence is assumed for purposes of a legal fiction, such as the fictitious tenant or the fictitious ejector in an action of ejectment (see note at EJECTMENT).
**2.** a nonexistent person utilized in connection with a fraud; for example, the "people" listed on a phony letterhead to make it look as if there is a real organization.
**3.** Same as *juridical person* (see under PERSON).

**fidelity bond** *n.* See under BOND[2].

**fidelity insurance** *n.* insurance against loss due to dishonest or unfaithful conduct by an employee. A fidelity insurance contract is also called a *fidelity bond* (see under BOND[2]).

**fides** *n. Latin.* faith. See also BONA FIDE[1]; BONA FIDES[1].

**fiduciary** *n., pl.* **fiduciaries,** *adj.* —*n.* **1.** a trustee or a person in a position analogous to that of a trustee, whereby another person or persons must rely upon the fiduciary to exercise special care, good faith, and loyalty in dealing with money and property. For example, an attorney is a fiduciary of her client, a corporate director is a fiduciary of the corporation, and each general partner in a business is a fiduciary of the other partners.
—*adj.* **2.** pertaining to a fiduciary or to relationships and matters requiring a high degree of trust and confidence.

**fiduciary bond** *n.* See under BOND[2].

**fiduciary duty** *n.* the duty of utmost good faith, loyalty, and care that the law imposes upon every FIDUCIARY in dealing with matters that are the subject of a FIDUCIARY RELATIONSHIP. See also *breach of fiduciary duty* (under BREACH); *utmost care* (under CARE); SELF-DEALING; and note at PUNCTILIO.

**fiduciary relationship** *n.* a legal relationship in which one party necessarily reposes special trust and confidence in the other, so that the other is held to be a FIDUCIARY of the first.

**fief** *n.* **1.** a FEUD[1]; an inheritable interest in land subject to feudal obligations to a lord.
**2.** Also, **fiefdom.** a territory held in fief.
See also note at FEE[1].

**fieri facias (fi. fa.)** *n. Latin.* (lit. "may you cause to be made") the common law writ for execution of a judgment. It directed the sheriff to make out of the goods and chattels of the defendant the sum of money for which the judgment was given.

**fieri facias de bonis testatoris** *n. Latin.* (lit. "may you cause to be made from the goods of the testator") the common law writ for execution of a judgment against the executor in a suit to recover a debt owed by the decedent. It directed the sheriff to make out of the property of the decedent the sum of money for which the judgment was given.

**FIFO** *n.* acronym for FIRST IN, FIRST OUT. Cf. LIFO.

**fighting words** *n.pl.* words spoken directly to a person that are of a sort likely to provoke violent retaliation. Such speech may be outlawed as a *breach of the peace* (see under BREACH). See also FREEDOM OF SPEECH; *hate speech* (under SPEECH).

**fikh** *n.* See FIQH.

**file** *v.,* **filed, filing,** *n.* —*v.* **1.** to commence an action by depositing a copy of the complaint, indictment, or other initial court paper with the court: *to file suit; file charges.*
**2.** to deposit a copy of each successive court paper with the court clerk for notation on the docket, for transmittal to

the judge if it is a matter requiring the judge's attention, and ultimately for placement in the court's official file on the case: *to file a motion for summary judgment.* See also COURTESY COPY.
**3.** to deposit any legal document with an appropriate governmental agency: *to file a tax return; file an application for a liquor license; file the registration statement for an issue of preferred stock.*
**4. file under seal** to file papers with a court in a sealed envelope to be opened only by the judge and not made available to the public, usually pursuant to a CONFIDENTIALITY STIPULATION.
**5. filing fee** a fee that must be paid to a court in order to commence an action in that court, or a fee required by any other government office upon the filing of certain kinds of papers. Cf. IN FORMA PAUPERIS.
—*n.* **6.** the complete set of documents pertaining to a matter kept by a court or other government or private office.
—**fileable** *adj.*

**file wrapper** *n. Patent Law.* the official record of proceedings in the United States Patent and Trademark Office upon an application for a patent. See also *file wrapper estoppel* (under ESTOPPEL).

**filiate** *v.,* **filiated, filiating.** to determine judicially the paternity of a child, especially one born out of wedlock. Also, **affiliate.**

**filiation** *n.* **1.** Also called **affiliation.** judicial determination of the paternity of a child, especially one born out of wedlock.
**2. filiation order** a court order determining that a particular man is the father of a particular child and so responsible for contributing to the child's support. Also called **affiliation order.**
**3. filiation proceeding** a judicial proceeding to determine paternity; a PATERNITY SUIT. Also called **affiliation proceeding.**

**fillius nullius** *n. Latin.* (lit. "son of no one") a child born out of wedlock, and thus, under the common law, not entitled to inherit. See note at ILLEGITIMACY.

**final** *adj.* **1.** (of a judgment, order, or the like) determining all issues presented in a case, so that, except in those rare cases where a judge or a tribunal can be persuaded to reconsider its action, no further litigation on the merits is possible save by way of appeal if that is available. Cf. INTERLOCUTORY. **2.** precluding further litigation; nonappealable: *Under the terms of the arbitration clause, the decision of the arbitrators is final.* —**finality** *n.*

**final appealable order** *n.* See under ORDER.

**final decree** *n.* See under DECREE.

**final determination** *n.* See under DETERMINATION.

**final judgment** *n.* See under JUDGMENT.

**final order** *n.* See under ORDER[1].

**financial statement** See under STATEMENT.

**find** *v.,* **found, finding. 1.** to make a determination of any kind in the course of a case: *The appellate court found the cases cited by the appellant unpersuasive. The jury found the defendant guilty. The hearing officer found for the claimant.* **2.** to discover or locate a person or thing. —**findable** *adj.*

**finder** *n.* **1.** a person or firm that locates and brings together individuals or companies for possible business transactions or relationships in return for a fee. **2.** one who discovers or locates anything. **3.** one who determines. See also FACT-FINDER; FINDER OF FACT.

**finder of fact** or **finder of the facts** *n.* Same as TRIER OF FACT.

**finder's fee** *n.* the fee earned by a FINDER (def. 1) for locating a business

opportunity or introducing a potential business partner.

**finding of fact** *n.* in a nonjury trial, a judge's decision on a purely factual issue (e.g., whether the light was red or green; whether the purchaser was acting in good faith). Cf. CONCLUSION OF LAW; see also FINDINGS OF FACT AND CONCLUSIONS OF LAW.

**finding of law** *n.* Same as CONCLUSION OF LAW.

**findings of fact and conclusions of law** *n.* the form in which a judge's decision is rendered in a civil suit tried without a jury in the federal courts and many state courts. This full statement of the factual and legal bases for the court's decision provides a clear record for appellate review. Also called, informally, **findings and conclusions.** See also FINDING OF FACT; CONCLUSION OF LAW.

**fine** *n., v.,* **fined, fining.** —*n.* **1.** a sum of money required to be paid as a civil or criminal PENALTY. —*v.* **2.** to impose a fine upon a person; to sentence a person to pay a fine.

**fine print** *n.* **1.** a set of clauses in a preprinted contract, such as an automobile rental agreement or a parking lot ticket stub, printed in small-sized type and typically including restrictions, qualifications, limitations of liability, and similar terms that are disadvantageous to the consumer. **2.** lengthy, detailed, and often disadvantageous contract terms in preprinted consumer contracts such as leases or insurance policies, regardless of the size of the print. ——**Usage.** Consumer laws now require much of the BOILERPLATE that used to be printed in minuscule type to be printed in more normal sized type. This has made contracts longer, but not necessarily more comprehensible to the average consumer. The terms that used to be in small-sized type are still referred to as the "fine print," and the conventional warning to "read the fine print before signing" is still generally ignored, since the terms in question, in addition to being often incomprehensible to the consumer, are usually standard throughout an industry and nonnegotiable anyway.

**fiqh** or **fikh** n. Islamic Law. Islamic jurisprudence; the system or process of determining the content of Islamic law (the shari'a). For the sources of used in making such determinations, see USUL AL-FIQH. See also note at SHARI'A.

**firm offer** n. See under OFFER.

**first impression** n. describing a legal issue not previously considered by the courts: question of first impression; matter of first impression. See also case of first impression (under CASE¹).

**first in, first out (FIFO)** n. an accounting convention that evaluates inventory and measures income from sales upon the assumption that the first items purchased are always the first sold, that is, every item sold is taken from the lot that has been in inventory the longest. Cf. LAST IN, FIRST OUT.

**first mortgage** n. See under MORTGAGE.

**first offender** n. See under OFFENDER.

**fishing expedition** n. Informal. a derogatory term applied to requests from an adversary for wide-ranging DISCOVERY. In general, the purpose of discovery is to obtain evidence, or information leading to evidence, pertaining to a known cause of action, not to "fish around" in the hope of stumbling upon a basis for maintaining a suit.

**fit** adj. **1.** (of goods) suitable; appropriate for the ordinary purposes for which goods of the kind are used, or for a particular purpose. See also warranty of fitness for a particular purpose (under WARRANTY). **2.** (of a parent) adequate; not so bad at parenting or dangerous to the children as to require that the parent's children be taken away. Cf. UNFIT.
—**fitness** n.

**fix** v. **1.** to set or determine a price or financial rate, especially with the intention that it remain unchanged until formal action is taken or agreement is reached to set a different price or rate, either legally (to fix the exchange rate for a currency) or illegally (to fix gasoline prices in a three-state region). See also PRICE FIXING. **2.** Informal. to exercise corrupt influence with respect to, as by bribery or coercion, so as to obtain a particular outcome: to fix a case; fix a game; fix a jury; fix a traffic ticket.
—n. **3.** Slang. a bribe or other corrupt arrangement intended to assure a particular outcome: Your bet on the game is safe: The fix is in. **4.** Slang. **a.** an injection of heroin or other narcotic. **b.** the narcotic or amount of narcotic injected.
—**fixable** adj.
—**fixed** adj.
—**fixer** n.

**fixed annuity** n. See under ANNUITY.

**fixed asset** n. See under ASSET.

**fixed-rate mortgage (FRM)** n. See under MORTGAGE.

**fixture** n. an article that is attached to real property in such a way that its removal would damage the property, such as a furnace or a built-in bookcase. Ordinarily such fixtures are regarded as part of the real property.

**flag burning** n. the burning of a flag, especially as a form of political protest.
——**History.** Flag burning, a form of political protest always sure to attract attention and ire, is the primary target of laws against FLAG DESECRATION. But the burning of flags per se has never been outlawed: If the purpose of the burning is to dispose of an old flag, it has always been legally acceptable. It is only when the flag is burned for some reason other than simply to destroy it—that is, when the burning has some symbolic significance—that legislatures and Congress have sought to make it a crime.

**flag desecration** n. a manifestation of disrespect for a flag, particularly the flag of the United States; especially, disrespectful physical action performed on, with, or with respect to the flag, as by mutilating, burning, or trampling upon it. Also called **desecration of the flag.** See also FLAG BURNING.

——**History.** The Supreme Court, in several narrowly decided and hotly debated cases from the 1960's to the 1990's, struck down laws against flag desecration, primarily on the ground that they inhibit *symbolic speech* (see under SPEECH). See also note at FLAG BURNING.

**flag of convenience** *n.* the flag of a country in which a merchant ship is registered solely in order to save on taxes and avoid the more stringent regulations imposed by other countries regarding such matters as safety, wages, environmental controls, and working conditions. The ship then sails under that flag whenever it is in service, even though it may have no real connection with the country. The fees received by such countries from the many ship registrations that they attract are a disincentive to the adoption of higher standards.

**flagrante delicto** *adv. Latin.* (lit. "as the wrongdoing rages on") in the very act of committing the offense or wrongful act: *The security camera filmed the bank robbers flagrante delicto.* See also note at IN FLAGRANTE DELICTO.

**flat tax** *n.* See under TAX.

**floating zone** *n.* See under ZONE.

**flotsam** *n.* **1.** the part of the wreckage of a ship and its cargo found floating on the water.
**2.** loosely, any material floating on water, including things deliberately jettisoned from a vessel.
Cf. DERELICT; JETSAM; LAGAN; WRECK.

**flout** *v.* **1.** to treat with disdain or contempt: *The defendant flouted the judge by refusing to stand.*
**2.** to ignore or disobey openly: *The demonstrators flouted the ordinance requiring a parade permit to march in the streets.*

**F.O.B.** free on board. In an offer or contract for the sale of goods this means that the goods will be delivered by the seller, at the seller's expense and risk, to the place named in the F.O.B. term. If a vessel or other vehicle is specified, the seller also assumes the expense and responsibility of getting the goods loaded onto the vehicle.

**FOIA** See FREEDOM OF INFORMATION ACT.

**follow** *v.* (of a court) to adhere to a PRECEDENT; to apply the principles articulated or used in a particular precedent to the case at hand.

**food disparagement** *n.* the tort of disseminating false information about the safety of a perishable food product to the injury of producers of the product. Also called **agricultural disparagement, food libel,** or, informally and disparagingly, **veggie libel.**

——**History.** Statutes providing a cause of action for food disparagement were enacted in the 1990's in at least thirteen states, in reaction to the difficulties faced by Washington State apple growers in their efforts to recover damages from CBS Television for losses they suffered when consumers stopped buying apples after a broadcast challenging the safety of a chemical called Alar used by apple growers. The statutes were intended to make such damages easier to recover than they were under the common law tort of TRADE LIBEL. The most famous use of the new statutes was an action by the Texas beef industry against television talk show celebrity Oprah Winfrey for remarks on her show; recovery under these statutes has proved difficult, however, and that action, like most others that have been tried, was unsuccessful.

**foolscap** *n.* a kind of writing paper traditionally used by lawyers for making notes and drafting; it usually consists of legal-size, lined, yellow sheets bound in tablet form. Also called **legal cap.** See also LEGAL PAD.

——**History.** The name *foolscap* is not gibe at lawyers, who are traditionally the best known users of this kind of paper. Rather, it derives from the watermark of a fool's cap that was placed on the paper by manufacturers some centuries ago.

**for cause** for a legally sufficient reason logically related to the action being taken, not for arbitrary, whimsical, or irrelevant reasons; for example, the firing of an employee because of inadequate performance would be a "termination for cause." See also *challenge for cause* (under CHALLENGE); *excuse for cause* (under EXCUSE).

**for-profit corporation** *n.* See under CORPORATION.

**for the benefit of 1.** words used to indicate that a person is acting, or is to act, as a trustee for a specified beneficiary: *The property is to be held by A for the benefit of B until B reaches the age of majority.*
**2.** words used to indicate that a person is acting on behalf of another: *the suit was brought by A, as guardian, for the benefit of B, an adjudicated incompetent.*
In both senses, often abbreviated **f/b/o** in instruments and pleadings.

**for the record** See under RECORD.

**for the use of 1.** words used to create or identify a trust for the benefit of a specified person: *The property was left in trust for the use of the testator's widow for her life.* See also USE (def. 2).
**2.** Also, **for the use and benefit of.** words used in the name of a case to indicate that a party to the suit is acting in a representative capacity. See USE (def. 1); see also note at EX REL.

**forbear** *v.,* **forbore, forborne, forbearing.** to deliberately refrain from enforcing a debt or other obligation for a period of time.
**—forbearance** *n.*
**—forbearer** *n.*

**force majeure** *n. French.* (lit. "superior force") an unforeseeable natural or human event beyond the control of the parties to a contract, rendering performance of a contract impossible. A "force majeure clause" in a contract relieves a party from the duty to perform if performance is rendered impossible by force majeure.

**forced heir** *n.* See under HEIR.

**forcible** *adj.* accomplished through force or threat of force.
**—forcibly** *adv.*

**forcible rape** *n.* See under RAPE.

**forcible sodomy** *n.* See under SODOMY.

**foreclosure** *n.* **1.** the termination of a property owner's rights in property that is subject to a mortgage or other *security interest* (see under INTEREST[1]) when the owner has failed to pay the debt secured by the property, so that the property can be sold to pay off the debt.
**2.** the entire procedure (normally a court action) by which foreclosure is accomplished, the property is sold (normally auctioned off), the proceeds are applied to the debt, and any money left over is refunded to the debtor.
**—foreclosable** *adj.*
**—foreclose** *v.,* **foreclosed, foreclosing.**

**foreign** *adj.* referring to another jurisdiction—sometimes another country (see *foreign commerce,* under COMMERCE), but often just another state (see *foreign corporation,* under CORPORATION).
**——False Friend.** The use of the word *foreign* to refer to a neighboring state sounds particularly odd to a nonlawyer, but in a federal system in which every state is a sovereign with its own separate legal system, any other jurisdiction, whether inside or outside the United States, is "foreign." In fact, in the Uniform Enforcement of Foreign Judgments Act, as adopted in most states, the definition of *foreign judgment* includes "any judgment, decree, or order of a court of the United States"—because in the United States even the federal courts are in some respects foreign to the legal system of any particular state. Because the word *foreign* includes fellow states, the phrase "foreign country"

is often used in order to avoid confusion when that is what is meant: *a foreign country judgment; a foreign country divorce.*

**forensic** *adj.* done, used, or practiced for law enforcement and courtroom purposes: *forensic analysis; forensic laboratory; forensic anthropolgy.*
—**forensically** *adv.*

**foreperson** *n., pl.* **forepersons.** a jury member selected either by lot or by vote of the jury to coordinate deliberations and render the jury's verdict in court.

**forestalling** *n.* **1.** in old law, obstructing the way; intercepting a person on the highway.
**2.** FORESTALLING THE MARKET.
—**forestall** *v.*
—**forestaller** *n.*

**forestalling the market** *n.* buying up commodities on their way to the market, with the intent of reselling them at a higher price. This was a statutory crime in England until 1844. See also ENGROSSING; REGRATING.

**forfeiture** *n.* the loss of a right, license, or property as a civil or criminal penalty; e.g., the loss of a fishing license as a penalty for taking fish that are too small or the loss of an automobile because it was used in a crime. See also ASSET FORFEITURE LAW.
—**forfeit** *v.*
—**forfeitability** *n.*
—**forfeitable** *adj.*

**forge** *v.,* **forged, forging.** to make a forgery of.
—**forgeable** *adj.*
—**forger** *n.*

**forgery** *n., pl.* **forgeries. 1.** the crime of making or altering a writing, recording, coin, or other document that is to be passed off as genuine and authorized when it is not, or of attempting to pass off such a document.
**2.** a writing, recording, coin, or other document produced by forgery.
See also *uttering a forged instrument* (under UTTER).

**form** *n.* **1.** the superficial appearance of a transaction as distinguished from the underlying reality. See example under SUBSTANCE.
**2.** Also called **legal form.** a model or preprinted document containing standard legal language for accomplishing a particular kind of transaction. Such forms can often be purchased in stationery and office supply stores.

**form of action** *n.* any of the dozen or so specific categories into which every action at law historically was required to fit. Each form of action had a special name, could be used only in certain types of cases, was commenced by a specific writ, had its own highly technical pleading rules, and provided only a specific kind of remedy.
——**History.** The rigidity of the common law forms of action was the main reason for the growth of EQUITY, and within the law courts themselves spawned a wealth of ingenious LEGAL FICTION. See note at EJECTMENT for a prime example. Under modern rules of civil procedure there is but one form of action—the civil action—and in it the plaintiff may request and obtain any relief that is warranted by the facts. The common law forms of action are still often referred to, however, because of their role in shaping English and American law over the centuries. The great English legal historian Frederic W. Maitland, in one of the most famous sentences in Anglo-American jurisprudence, put it this way at the outset of his *Lectures on the Forms of Action at Common Law,* which were compiled and published in 1909, three years after his death: "The forms of action we have buried, but they still rule us from their graves."

**forma pauperis** *n.* See IN FORMA PAUPERIS.

**formalism** *n.* a school of JURISPRUDENCE that views law as a formal set of rules and principles to be applied objectively and somewhat mechanically to the resolution of legal issues and disputes. Also called **conceptualism, legal conceptualism, legal formalism.** Cf. LEGAL REALISM.
—**formalist** *n., adj.*

—**formalistic** *adj.*
—**formalistically** *adv.*

**fornicate** *v.,* **fornicated, fornicating.** to engage in sexual intercourse while unmarried; to commit the crime of fornication.
—**fornicator** *n.*

**fornication** *n.* the crime of engaging in sexual intercourse while unmarried. Cf. ADULTERY.
——**Note.** This crime has been abolished in more than half the states. In the many states where fornication is still a crime, there are a lot of criminals; prosecution, however, is selective in the extreme. For example, a 1996 enforcement campaign in Gem County, Idaho, which generated worldwide publicity, was apparently targeted exclusively at pregnant teenage girls and their boyfriends—"to the relief of adults," as *The Times* of London noted in its story on July 9, 1996.

**forum** *n., pl.* **forums, fora. 1.** the tribunal or jurisdiction in which an action is pending or might be brought. See also *lex fori* (under LEX).
**2.** a gathering place; a place where people meet for discussion. See also PUBLIC FORUM.

**forum contractus** *n. Latin.* (lit. "the forum of the contract") **1.** the jurisdiction—usually the state or country—in which a contract was made. This is normally regarded as the location in which the offer was accepted.
**2.** a court of that jurisdiction.

**forum conveniens** *n. Latin.* (lit. "an appropriate forum") a suitable forum for a particular case, as distinguished from a FORUM NON CONVENIENS.
——**Usage.** The phrase *forum conveniens* arose well after the phrase *forum non conveniens* and is used only rarely, always in the context of discussions about the applicability of the doctrine of forum non conveniens to a particular case.

**forum domicilii** *n. Latin.* (lit. "the forum of residence") **1.** the jurisdiction in which a party is domiciled.
**2.** a court of that jurisdiction.

**forum non conveniens** *n. Latin.* (lit. "an inappropriate forum") **1.** the doctrine that a court in which an action has properly been filed may decline to exercise jurisdiction over it if the case has no significant relationship with that jurisdiction and would be more suitably litigated in another state or another country.
**2.** Also called **inconvenient forum.** an unsuitable forum for a case; a forum that may decline to exercise jurisdiction on the ground of forum non conveniens.

**forum rei gestae** *n. Latin.* (lit. "the forum of the thing done") **1.** the jurisdiction in which an act or transaction occurred.
**2.** a court of that jurisdiction.

**forum rei sitae** *n. Latin.* (lit. "the forum where the thing was situated") **1.** the jurisdiction in which the property or subject matter involved in a case is located.
**2.** a court of that jurisdiction.
Also called **forum rei.**

**forum selection clause** *n.* Same as CHOICE OF FORUM CLAUSE.

**forum shopping** *n.* the choosing of a forum where the judges or jurors are expected to be sympathetic to one's case; for example, the choice of a tobacco state for a suit by a tobacco company, of a nontobacco state for a suit against a tobacco company, or of a Bible Belt state for a pornography prosecution.

**foundation** *n.* **1.** evidence establishing the admissibility of an exhibit or other evidence. For example, in order to introduce testimony that the plaintiff made a certain out-of-court statement about the defendant, it would usually be necessary to "lay a foundation" by establishing that the witness was in a position to hear the statement, to know who was making it, and perhaps to know whom it referred to. See also AUTHENTICATE; CONNECT UP.
**2.** an institution established, usually by means of a large donation or legacy, to support research, the arts, or charitable activities.

**founder** *n.* **1.** one who establishes an institution or organization.
**2. founders** or **Founders**    Same as FOUNDING FATHERS.
——**Usage.** As between *founders* and *Founders,* the lowercase form is more common in phrases that include additional identifying information (*the founders of our nation*); the capitalized form is more common when the word stands on its own: *The Founders would never have imagined that a court might countenance such an outcome.* See also note at FOUNDING FATHERS.

**Founding Fathers** *n.pl.* men who were instrumental in the establishment of the United States; especially the delegates to the Constitutional Convention in Philadelphia in 1787. Sometimes, **founding fathers.**
——**Usage.** Discussions and decisions on constitutional issues typically include at least some reference to the writers and adopters of the Constitution or of the amendment in question, and competing assertions about what they intended, contemplated, envisioned, were trying to accomplish, hoped to guard against, would think if they were alive today, would be aghast to learn, and so on. This somewhat vaguely defined group (see ORIGINAL INTENT) is most commonly referred to (with or without the capital letters) as the *Framers,* the *Founders,* or the *Founding Fathers.* (See notes at FRAMER and FOUNDER regarding capitalization.) The phrase *Founding Fathers* now has a slightly archaic ring, both because it is rather flowery and because it so unashamedly highlights the fact that women were excluded from the American political process throughout the period that gave rise to the Constitution and most of its amendments. As it happens, however, this is by far the newest of these terms, having made its first appearance in a reported judicial opinion in 1935. The phrase made its way into Supreme Court usage in 1945, enjoyed a brief heyday in Supreme Court opinions in the 1970's and 1980's, and has been on the wane in that court since then. By contrast, the term *founders*

has been used in this sense in Supreme Court opinions since at least the mid-nineteenth century (originally in such phrases as "the founders of the Republic" and "the founders of our government"). And the term *framers* has been in use virtually from the beginning: the Supreme Court's first invocation of "the framers of the Constitution" occurred in *Hylton v. United States,* 3 U.S. 171 (1796). It is noteworthy that even then, less than nine years after that last *i* was dotted in the Constitution, the Supreme Court Justices—including William Paterson, who had personally played a major role in the Constitutional Convention as head of the New Jersey delegation—expressed uncertainty and disagreement about the exact scope of certain terms in the Constitution, notably the term DIRECT TAX. The fact that a Justice of the Supreme Court who was himself one of the Framers frankly admitted that he did not know just how far this important constitutional term might extend should cause to be received with caution any modern-day pronouncement as to how "the Founders" or "the Framers" or "the Founding Fathers" intended the words of the Constitution to be interpreted in the context of some unforeseen situation arising more than two centuries later.

**401(k) plan** *n.* See under RETIREMENT PLAN.

**403(b) plan** *n.* See under RETIREMENT PLAN.

**457 plan** or **457(b) plan** *n.* See under RETIREMENT PLAN.

**four corners** *n.pl.* the face of a contract, will, or other instrument; the contents of the writing taken as a whole.

**four unities** *n.pl.* See under UNITY.

**framer** *n.* **1.** one who participates in the writing of a statute or the like: *The framers of the rule could not have intended it to apply to this situation.*
**2. framers** or **Framers**    **a.** (in reference to the original text of the Constitution) participants in the Constitutional Convention in Philadelphia in 1787. **b.** (in reference to any amendment to the

Constitution) members of the Congress in which the amendment was adopted, particularly those closely associated with drafting or promoting the amendment.

—**Usage.** As between *framers* and *Framers,* the lowercase form is more common in phrases that include additional identifying information (*the framers of the Constitution; the amendment's framers*); the capitalized form is more common when the word stands on its own: *Under the theory of original intent, the job of a court in a constitutional case is to ascertain the intent of the Framers.* See also note at FOUNDING FATHERS.

**franchise** *n., v.,* **franchised, franchising.** —*n.* **1.** a right or license granted by a company (the **franchisor**) to an individual or group (the **franchisee**) to market its goods or services and use its trademark in a specific territory, usually pursuant to a detailed agreement requiring operation of the business in accordance with the franchisor's standards and setting forth the financial terms of the arrangement. **2.** a privilege granted by the government, such as the right to operate in the form of a corporation or to operate a bus company. **3.** the right to vote. —*v.* **4.** to grant a franchise to. **5.** to grant the voting rights to; ENFRANCHISE. —**franchisement** *n.*

**franchise tax** *n.* a tax imposed upon a corporation for the privilege of doing business in a state.

**frank¹** *adj. Legal History.* free. —**Usage.** This word appears in many ancient phrases relating to property interests, rights, and transactions.

**frank²** *n.* **1.** a signature or mark affixed to a letter or package to indicate that the sender has the privilege of sending mail free of charge. **2.** a letter or package carrying such a mark and delivered free of charge. **3.** Also called **franking privilege.** the privilege of sending official mail free of

charge, accorded to members of Congress and certain government officials. —*v.* **4.** to mark mail for delivery free of charge pursuant to a franking privilege; to send mail free of charge. **5.** to convey a person free of charge.

**fraud** *n.* **1.** Also called **actual fraud** or **fraud in fact.** the tort of obtaining money or property by means of a false portrayal of facts, either by words or by conduct. For a list of the elements of fraud, see ELEMENT. In criminal law, fraudulent conduct may be classified as larceny, forgery, theft, or other crimes depending upon the circumstances.

**2. constructive fraud** conduct viewed by a court as having the same effect as actual fraud though not involving any false representation of fact. This usually occurs when a FIDUCIARY abuses the trust and confidence of the person to whom she owes a fiduciary duty, profiting by keeping silent about matters that should have been disclosed to that person. (In a nonfiduciary relationship, as between an ordinary buyer and seller, there is no general duty to speak about things one is not asked about.) Also called **legal fraud** or **fraud in law.**

**3. fraud in the factum** a misrepresentation as to the fundamental nature of a contract, will, or other instrument being signed, as in a classic case in which a wife was told that a certain legal document was just a formality for tax purposes and it turned out to be a separation agreement. Such fraud renders an instrument VOID. Also called **fraud in the execution, fraud in the making.** See also FACTUM.

**4. fraud in the inducement** misrepresentation upon which a person relies in entering into a contract, not about the terms of the contract itself but about the subject of the contract or the surrounding circumstances, as when a seller turns back the odometer in a used car so as to misrepresent how much it has been driven. Such fraud renders the contract VOIDABLE. Also called **fraudulent inducement.**

**5. mail fraud** the federal crime of using the mails in connection with a scheme to defraud.

**6. wire fraud** the federal crime of using interstate telephone or telegraph wires in connection with a scheme to defraud.

See also SECURITIES FRAUD; TAX FRAUD.

**frauds, statute of** *n.* See STATUTE OF FRAUDS.

**fraudulent** *adj.* **1.** pertaining to or constituting FRAUD or an element of fraud. **2.** intentionally wrongful; dishonest; unfair.
—**fraudulence** *n.*
—**fraudulently** *adv.*

**fraudulent concealment** *n.* **1.** active concealment of a material fact, or failure to disclose a material fact when asked or when one is under a duty to speak.
**2.** especially, active concealment of facts that might lead a person to realize that she has a cause of action, as by painting over a crack in a poorly made structure or reporting false financial figures to conceal embezzlement. The statute of limitations on a cause of action will normally be tolled during the time that discovery of the potential claim is prevented by fraudulent concealment.

**fraudulent conveyance** *n.* a transfer of property by a debtor for less than its full value, in an effort to put it into friendly hands where it cannot be attached by creditors, or to favor one creditor over others. A court will usually set aside such a conveyance. Also called **fraudulent transfer.**

**fraudulent inducement** *n.* Same as *fraud in the inducement* (see under FRAUD).

**fraudulent transfer** *n.* Same as FRAUDULENT CONVEYANCE.

**free alongside** See F.A.S.

**free exercise of religion** *n.* the practice of one's religion and observance of its tenets without government interference—a right guaranteed by the **Free Exercise Clause** of the First Amendment to the Constitution. This right may be limited by laws of general applicability not targeted at religion, however; for example, in the 1980's and 1990's the Supreme Court upheld military regulations preventing Orthodox Jewish servicemen from wearing yarmulkes and criminal laws barring the sacramental use of peyote in Native American religious ritual.

**free on board** See F.O.B.

**free press** *n.* **1.** a body of book publishers, news media, etc., not controlled or restricted by government censorship. **2.** FREEDOM OF THE PRESS.

**free press/fair trial** *n.* the problem of balancing the constitutional guarantees of FREEDOM OF THE PRESS and FAIR TRIAL in situations where they appear to come into conflict, as when newspaper publicity about a case could make it difficult to obtain an impartial jury. Also called **free press–fair trial, free press and fair trial, fair trial/free press,** and the like.

**free speech** *n.* **1.** expression that is not controlled or restricted by government censorship. **2.** FREEDOM OF SPEECH.

**free trade** *n.* **1.** international trade free from protective duties and subject only to such tariffs as are needed for revenue. **2.** the system, principles, or maintenance of such trade.
—**free-trade** *adj.*

**freedom** *n.* absence of legal restraint; the RIGHT to do or not do something without governmental interference. The conventional term used to describe a number of constitutional rights, including those referred to in the next few entries.

**freedom of assembly** *n.* the right of people to gather peacefully for political or other purposes. This is guaranteed by the First Amendment (see Appendix), subject only to the government's right to impose reasonable restrictions on the TIME, PLACE, AND MANNER of such assembly. Cf. UNLAWFUL ASSEMBLY.

**freedom of association** *n.* the constitutional right to join with others for lawful purposes, derived primarily from a combination of First Amendment rights (assembly, religion, etc.).

**freedom of contract** *n.* the name given to a now discredited constitutional doctrine, which the Supreme Court followed from 1897 to 1937, holding that the government has only very limited power to regulate contractual relationships, especially in regard to conditions of employment. It is now accepted that federal and state governments have wide powers to dictate reasonable terms for employment relationships, consumer transactions, and other contracts, which no claim of "freedom of contract" can overcome.

**freedom of expression** *n.* a general term for FREEDOM OF SPEECH and FREEDOM OF THE PRESS; sometimes used broadly to include FREEDOM OF RELIGION also.

**Freedom of Information Act (FOIA)** *n.* a federal statute, widely imitated at the state level, requiring most government documents and records to be made available to the public on request and specifying procedures for requests and disclosure.

**freedom of religion** *n.* the freedom to hold and practice one's religious beliefs and freedom from government involvement in religious matters, guaranteed by the First Amendment clauses protecting FREE EXERCISE OF RELIGION and prohibiting ESTABLISHMENT OF RELIGION. See also SEPARATION OF CHURCH AND STATE.

**freedom of speech** *n.* the First Amendment right to express oneself. It covers any form or medium of SPEECH, not just speaking and writing, and generally prohibits the government from restricting expression on the basis of content or viewpoint. As interpreted by the Supreme Court, however, the degree of freedom depends upon the category of speech. It is greatest for speech conveying ideas about such matters as politics, art, religion, or science. It is lower for such categories as *commercial speech* and *indecent speech* (see under SPEECH). And some categories, most notably OBSCENITY, are completely unprotected—not regarded as "speech" at all within the meaning of the Constitution. See also TIME, PLACE, AND MANNER.

**—Note.** The terms "high-value speech" and "low-value speech" are often used to refer to categories of speech that have been given the highest level or less than the highest level of protection under judicial interpretations of the First Amendment. These terms are rare in judicial opinions, however; they are used primarily in academic discussions and writings to help impose a degree of order in a complex field.

**freedom of the press** *n.* the First Amendment right to publish books, newspapers, and magazines, and otherwise distribute and broadcast information, opinion, and expression, largely free from government censorship. See also PRIOR RESTRAINT.

**freehold** *n.* a possessory interest in real property amounting to an *estate in fee* or *life estate* (see under ESTATE¹). Also called **freehold estate** or **freehold interest.** Cf. LEASEHOLD.

**freeholder** *n.* **1.** one who possesses a FREEHOLD; a landowner.
**2.** (in some U.S. counties) a registered voter who owns local property and has been a local resident for a specified length of time.

**fresh pursuit** *n.* pursuit by a law enforcement officer of a suspected felon who is fleeing and may escape if the pursuit is abandoned. An officer in fresh pursuit may usually follow the suspect across jurisdictional lines to make the arrest, or pursue a suspect into a building and search for him there without a search warrant. Also called **hot pursuit.** See also EXIGENT CIRCUMSTANCES; HIGH-SPEED CHASE.

**friend of the court** *n.* Same as AMICUS CURIAE.

**frisk** *n.* See STOP AND FRISK.

**frivolous** *adj.* (of an action or procedural step) clearly having no basis in law or in any reasonable argument for

a change in the law: *a frivolous action; a frivolous motion; a frivolous appeal.* A court may SANCTION an attorney or party who takes frivolous action, as by requiring him to pay the attorneys' fees incurred by his adversary in opposing it.
—**frivolously** *adv.*
—**frivolousness** *n.*

**FRM** *n., pl.* **FRMs, FRM's.** *fixed-rate mortgage* (see under MORTGAGE).

**frolic of one's own** *n.* conduct by an employee outside the SCOPE OF EMPLOYMENT. The employer is not liable for the acts of an employee under such circumstances. The classic example is a company driver who, when sent to make a delivery, makes a detour to visit his mistress and causes an accident while on the detour. The company will not be liable for the damages because the employee was on "a frolic of his own." Cf. RESPONDENT SUPERIOR.

**fruit of the poisonous tree** *n.* evidence derived from information obtained through an illegal search or other illegal investigative technique. Such evidence is generally subject to the EXCLUSIONARY RULE to the same extent as the illegally obtained information that led to it.

**frustration** *n.* an unforeseen circumstance that destroys the purpose of a contract. Under the "doctrine of frustration," further performance of the contract is excused. For example, if an agreement is reached to rent a room overlooking a parade, and then the parade is unexpectedly cancelled, the would-be renter need not go through with the contract. Also called **commercial frustration, economic frustration.**

**full age** *n.* See under AGE.

**full court** *n.* all of the judges of a court sitting together in a case; a court EN BANC: *The panel assigned to hear the appeal affirmed the decision of the trial court, but upon reargument the full court reversed.*

**full faith and credit** *n.* obligatory deference given by the courts of one state of the United States to the laws and judicial proceedings of another. Cf. COMITY.
——**Note.** The Constitution requires the states to give full faith and credit to each other's laws and judgments; thus a judgment obtained in one state is generally enforceable in every other state, and may generally be attacked in another state only upon grounds that would have been allowed in the state where the judgment was rendered.

**full partner** *n.* See under PARTNER.

**full settlement** *n.* See under SETTLEMENT.

**full warranty** *n.* See under WARRANTY.

**fully integrated contract** *n.* See under INTEGRATED CONTRACT.

**fully paid stock** *n.* See under STOCK.

**fundamental error** *n.* See under ERROR.

**fundamental fairness** *n.* the kind and degree of objectivity and fair procedure in a legal proceeding necessary to satisfy the requirements of DUE PROCESS.
——**Usage.** The term *fundamental fairness* is used as an expression both of what results when due process is followed and of what is necessary to constitute due process. It is an expression of the concept of due process that captures what specific rules alone cannot: a subjective sense that courts and other legal institutions are treating people in a fundamentally civilized and just manner.

**fundamental right** *n.* any right expressly guaranteed by the Constitution, or deemed by the Supreme Court to be so basic to the concept of liberty as to be protected from government restriction (except to the extent necessary to serve a COMPELLING INTEREST) by the DUE PROCESS clause of the Fourteenth Amendment (see Appendix). Areas now deemed fundamental include voting and running for office, access to the courts, freedom of travel, freedom of association, and decision making in matters of marriage and procreation. See also RIGHT OF PRIVACY; *substantive* *due process* (under DUE PROCESS); STRICT SCRUTINY.

**fungible** *n.* (of goods or securities) interchangeable with another of the same kind; of such a nature that any unit is regarded within a trade as the equivalent of any like unit. For example, a commodity such as corn or sugar is fungible in that, so long as specified standards relating to quality and type are met, those who deal with the commodity regard one bushel or pound as the same as another.
—**fungibility** *n.*

**further assurance** *n.* See under COVENANTS OF TITLE.

**future estate** *n.* See under ESTATE[1].

**future interest** *n.* See under INTEREST[1].

**futuro** *n.* See IN FUTURO.

# G

**GAAP** *n.* GENERALLY ACCEPTED ACCOUNTING PRINCIPLES.

**GAAS** *n.* GENERALLY ACCEPTED AUDITING STANDARDS.

**gag order** *n.* a judge's order to parties and attorneys in a sensational case not to discuss the case publicly, issued in the hope of avoiding publicity regarded as damaging to the fairness and dignity of the proceedings. Cf. CONFIDENTIALITY STIPULATION.

**gage** *n., v.,* **gaged, gaging.** —*n.* **1.** anything given, taken, or pledged as security for payment of a debt or performance of an obligation.
—*v.* **2.** to give or pledge as security.
**3.** to stake or wager; to risk in a bet or an uncertain undertaking.

**gain** *n.* the profit on a sale or exchange of property; generally, the amount by which the value received in exchange for the property exceeds the owner's BASIS in the property. Ordinarily, the gain is subject to income tax. See also *capital gain* and *capital gains tax* (both under CAPITAL¹); REALIZE; RECOGNIZE. Cf. LOSS.

**gang profile** *n.* See under PROFILE.

**gaol** *n., v.* a British variant of JAIL.
—**Usage.** *Gaol* and *jail* are descended from two ancient varieties of French, the former from Norman French and the latter from Parisian French. In the United States, only *jail* survives; in England, *jail* is the prevailing form, although *gaol* is equally acceptable, and has a long tradition in statutory and official usage.
—**Pronunciation.** There is no variation in pronunciation: The original pronunciation of *gaol*—with a hard *g*—has been lost, and both spellings are now pronounced *jail.*

**gaol delivery** *n.* See JAIL DELIVERY.

**gaoler** *n.* a British variant of JAILER. See notes at GAOL.

**garnish** *v.* to serve a GARNISHMENT; to attach wages or other money or property owed to or held for a debtor, so that those assets can be redirected to the debtor's creditor.
—**garnishable** *adj.*

**garnishee** *n., v.,* **garnisheed, garnisheeing.** —*n.* **1.** a person or entity served with a GARNISHMENT; for example, the employer of a judgment debtor whose wages are being garnished.
—*v.* **2.** to GARNISH.

**garnishment** *n.* **1.** the ATTACHMENT of wages or other money or property owed to or held for a debtor, usually a judgment debtor, so that they can be used to satisfy the debtor's obligation. For example, the wages of a divorced parent who has failed to pay court-ordered child support may be subject to garnishment by the custodial parent to satisfy the child support obligation.
**2.** a judicial proceeding to effect such a garnishment.
**3.** the formal document which must be served on the employer or other person being garnished in order to effect a garnishment.

**garnishor** or **garnisher** *n.* the creditor for whose benefit a garnishment is effected.

**gateway drug** *n.* any mood-altering drug, such as a stimulant or tranquilizer, that does not cause physical dependence but is thought by some to tend to lead to the use of addictive drugs, such as heroin. The gateway-drug theory is often cited as a basis for the classification of marijuana as a CONTROLLED SUBSTANCE.

**gavelkind** *n.* an early system of land tenure in England before the Norman Conquest, under which a decedent's land was divided equally among his male children. After the Norman Conquest this system was largely supplanted by PRIMOGENITURE. Cf. BOROUGH-ENGLISH.

**Gemara** n. Jewish Law. **1.** the section of the TALMUD consisting essentially of commentary on the MISHNAH. **2.** the Talmud.
—**Gemaric** adj.
—**Gemarist** n.

**gender-based discrimination** n. Same as SEX DISCRIMINATION.

**gender discrimination** n. Same as SEX DISCRIMINATION.

**general** adj. describing the most usual, basic, comprehensive, or undifferentiated form or application of something, as distinguished from specialized forms, which are often characterized by such terms as "specific," "special," "limited," or "qualified." See general appearance (under APPEARANCE); general assumpsit (under ASSUMPSIT); general average (under AVERAGE); general bequest (under BEQUEST); general contractor (under CONTRACTOR); general counsel (under COUNSEL); general damages (under DAMAGES); general jurisdiction (under JURISDICTION¹); general partner (under PARTNER); general partnership (under PARTNERSHIP); general power of attorney (under POWER OF ATTORNEY); general release (under RELEASE); general verdict (under VERDICT).

**general court-martial** n. See under COURT-MARTIAL.

**general jail delivery** or **general gaol delivery** n. See under JAIL DELIVERY.

**general obligation bond** n. See under BOND¹.

**general public figure** n. See under PUBLIC FIGURE.

**general purpose public figure** n. See under PUBLIC FIGURE.

**generally accepted accounting principles (GAAP)** n.pl. standards, conventions, and rules for preparation of financial statements, established by various bodies in the accounting profession and government.
——**Usage.** The full phrase generally accepted accounting principles is used as plural; but it is often shortened to "GAAP" (pronounced "gap"), which is used as singular: GAAP requires that inventory be valued in a consistent manner from year to year.

**generally accepted auditing standards (GAAS)** n.pl. rules and principles established by the American Institute of Certified Public Accountants to be followed in audits of financial statements.
——**Usage.** The full phrase generally accepted auditing standards is used as plural; but it is often shortened to "GAAS" (pronounced "gas"), which is used as singular: GAAS requires auditors to perform tests to ascertain whether the inventory recorded on a company's balance sheet appears to exist in reality.

**generation-skipping transfer** n. Tax Law. a transfer of an interest in property to a person two or more generations below the transferor. In the case of recipients who are not lineal descendants of the transferor, any transfer to a person who is at least 37½ years younger than the transferor is deemed to be a generation-skipping transfer.

**generation-skipping transfer tax** n. a tax upon GENERATION-SKIPPING TRANSFERS, imposed by the Internal Revenue Code and by the tax laws of some states in order to prevent wealthy families from avoiding the gift and estate taxes that would normally be collected as their wealth is handed down from each generation to the next. Also called **generation-skipping tax.** See also GENERATION-SKIPPING TRUST.

**generation-skipping trust** n. a trust created, usually by will, in such a way that one's children will have the use and benefit (but not ownership) of certain property during their lives, and then ownership of the property will pass to their children.
——**History.** Formerly this device would

save a wealthy family one round of estate taxes because actual ownership of the property skipped over one generation. That tax loophole was plugged by the GENERATION-SKIPPING TRANSFER TAX, which is collected upon expiration of the beneficial interests of the first generation of children.

**generic** *adj.* **1.** applicable to all products or items in a general category; not distinctive. See for example GENERIC NAME. **2.** not owned or exclusively controlled by one person or company; unbranded; not PROPRIETARY. See for example *generic drug* (under DRUG). —*n.* **3.** a product sold without a brand name. **4.** a generic drug. —**genericness** *n.*

**generic drug** *n.* See under DRUG.

**generic name** *n.* **1.** the name for a general kind of product or service. Generic names may be used by anyone and cannot be registered as trademarks. For example, *cola* and *shuttle* are generic names: Distinctive names for specific brands of cola or specific air or bus shuttle services may be trademarked, but not the generic terms. The principle is that no one may have a monopoly on the use of ordinary English words. **2.** the scientific name or common name for a drug, as distinguished from any brand name under which the drug might be sold.

**genetic child** *n.* Same as *biological child* (see under BIOLOGICAL).

**genetic fingerprint** *n.* Same as *DNA profile* (see under DNA PROFILING).

**genetic fingerprinting** *n.* Same as DNA PROFILING.

**genetic mother** or **father** or **parent** *n.* Same as *biological mother* or *father* or *parent* (see under BIOLOGICAL).

**genetic redlining** *n.* the use of genetic information, such as predisposition to a serious disease, as a consideration in determining whether to offer a job, issue an insurance policy, or the like. Rapid technological advances in DNA analysis and information exchange have raised concerns about the potential for widespread use or misuse of genetic information for such purposes.

**Geneva Convention** *n.* any of a series of international agreements, first made in Geneva, Switzerland, in 1864, establishing rules for the humane treatment of prisoners of war; of the sick, the wounded, the shipwrecked, and the dead in battle; and of civilian populations in time of war. See also CONVENTIONAL WAR CRIME. ——**History.** Nearly all countries have agreed to some form of the Geneva Conventions, particularly a set of four very detailed and comprehensive conventions executed in Geneva on August 12, 1949, expanding and updating the principles in light of experience in World War II. Among the principal prohibitions of these conventions are willful killing, torture, or conduct causing great suffering or serious injury to persons protected by the conventions; wanton destruction or appropriation of property not justified by military necessity; compelling a prisoner of war or civilian to serve in the forces of a hostile power; depriving a prisoner of war or civilian of rights of fair trial; unlawfully deporting, transferring, or confining a civilian; and taking civilians as hostages. Many countries, however—including the United States—have not agreed to the protocols that were added in 1977, extending the requirement of humane treatment to combatants in guerilla wars against colonial domination and to combatants in civil wars once they have gained control of sufficient territory within a country to carry out military operations from that territory.

**genocide** *n.* *International Law.* the crime under international law of committing any of the following acts with intent to destroy, in whole or in part, a national, ethnic, racial, or religious group as such: (a) killing members of the group; (b) causing serious bodily or mental harm to members of the group; (c) deliberately inflicting on the group conditions of life calculated to bring about its physical destruction in whole or in part; (d) imposing measures intended to prevent births within the group; or (e) forcibly transferring children of the group to another group.

——**History.** One of the earliest acts of the United Nations after its founding in the wake of World War II was to affirm as a body that genocide is a crime under international law, and in 1948 the UN adopted a detailed convention on the subject, from which the definition above is taken. Genocide is considered a matter of international concern, not an internal matter, even if perpetrated by a government within its own territory.

**gens** *n., pl.* **gentes** *Latin.* a clan; a people. See also JUS GENTIUM.

**gentlemen's agreement** *n.* an agreement or understanding not intended by the parties to be enforced by legal action, but expected to be performed or adhered to solely as a matter of personal friendship or honor. Sometimes this is because the agreement is in fact illegal, as to fix prices or pay a bribe. Also called **gentleman's agreement.**

**geographic jurisdiction** *n.* Same as JURISDICTION².

**germane** *adj.* relevant; pertinent.
—**germanely** *adv.*
—**germaneness** *n.*
——**Note.** Legislative bodies typically have rules requiring that proposed amendments to a bill be germane to the subject matter of the bill, so that debate on the issues in the bill will not be sidetracked into unrelated issues. Cf. NONGERMANE AMENDMENT. The concept of germaneness, however, is sometimes interpreted very broadly.

**gerrymander** *n.* **1.** a voting district of seemingly illogical shape created in order to achieve a political purpose, such as diluting the votes of the opposing political party, protecting incumbents, or increasing the chance that a member of a racial or ethnic minority group will be elected to legislative office. The Supreme Court has been loath to upset gerrymanders created for the first two reasons, but has been strongly critical

of "bizarre" district lines drawn in an effort to increase minority representation in Congress.
—*v.* **2.** to create such a district; to draw irregular district lines for such purposes.

**gestational carrier** *n.* Same as GESTATIONAL SURROGATE.

**gestational mother** *n.* Same as BIRTH MOTHER.

**gestational surrogacy** *n.* See under SURROGACY.

**gestational surrogate** *n.* a woman who agrees to bear a child for a couple by having a fertilized egg or embryo provided by them implanted in her uterus. Also called **gestational carrier, surrogate carrier.** See also SURROGATE MOTHER.

**gestum** *n., pl.* **gesta.** *Latin.* (lit. "a thing done") *Roman Law.* **1.** a thing done; a transaction.
**2.** a thing done without words, as distinguished from ACTUM.

**get** *n., pl.* **gittin, gitim.** *Jewish Law.* **1.** a legal document, executed by a rabbi or jewish court of law, dissolving a marriage.
**2.** a divorce granted in accordance with Jewish law.

**gift** *n.* **1.** Also called **inter vivos gift** or **gift inter vivos. a.** a voluntary transfer of money or property, completed during one's lifetime, without expecting anything in return. For such a gift to be effective, the DONOR must understand and intend the consequences of the act, and the property must be delivered to and accepted by the DONEE. **b.** the property so transferred. See also DELIVERY; INTER VIVOS.
**2.** Also called **testamentary gift. a.** a transfer of property by will; a BEQUEST or DEVISE. **b.** property so transferred.
**3. class gift** a gift to a class whose membership may vary over time, as when a will leaves certain property to "my children" or "my brothers and sisters." In general the membership of the class is determined as of the date that the gift becomes effective rather than the date the instrument making the gift

was written.

**4. gift causa mortis** a conditional gift of personal property by a person who is ill or injured and expects to die. To be legally effective it must satisfy all the requirements of other inter vivos gifts, and in addition the donor must die of the illness or injury. If the donor recovers, the property must be returned. See also CAUSA MORTIS.

**5. gift in contemplation of death a.** a *gift causa mortis*. **b.** for tax purposes, a gift made within three years of death. Ordinarily the value of the gift is included in the donor's estate for estate tax purposes.

**gift over** *n., pl.* **gifts over.** a transfer of a future interest in property to one person in connection with the transfer of a present interest in the same property to someone else. For example, if property is granted "to A for life, then to B," the grant to B is a "gift over." The word *gift* is used even if the future interest being transferred was paid for.

**gift tax** *n.* a tax imposed by the federal government on very large gifts made during a person's lifetime. Payment of the tax is the obligation of the donor, not the recipients.

**give** *v.*, **gave, giving.** to make a GIFT.
—**givable, giveable** *adj.*

**global settlement** *n.* See under SETTLEMENT.

**gloss** *n.* **1.** an explanation or interpretation of a statute, constitutional provision, or judicial ruling, especially one that adds or makes explicit some qualification that is not expressly stated in the statute or ruling.
**2. judicial gloss a.** a court's gloss on a statutory or constitutional provision or prior court ruling, usually made in a discussion of its applicability or inapplicability to a particular case. **b.** the accumulated interpretations of a number of courts over a period of years; a judicial consensus on interpretation of a statutory or constitutional provision or a significant earlier ruling.

**go** *v.*, **went, gone, going.** to seek, submit, or have recourse for a decision, verdict, corroboration, defense, etc.; resort: *They went to court. The case will go to the jury by tomorrow afternoon. The President will go to Congress with his anticrime proposals.* See also GO TO THE COUNTRY.

**go forward** or **go forward with evidence** to introduce evidence on an issue in a case, thereby placing the issue before the factfinder. See also *burden of going forward* (under BURDEN[1]).

**go private** to cease to be a *publicly held corporation* and become a *closely held corporation* (see both under CORPORATION) through a transaction by which most shareholders are forced to accept money for their shares and the business is left in the hands of a few officers, directors, or major shareholders. Cf. GO PUBLIC.
—**going private** *n.*

**go public** (of a corporation) to issue shares to the general public for the first time, thereby becoming a *publicly held corporation* (see under CORPORATION) Cf. GO PRIVATE.
—**going public** *n.*

**go to** to bear upon; be relevant to the issue of: *That evidence is admissible because it goes to the witness's credibility. Point 3 of their brief goes to the constitutionality of the statute.*

**go to the country** English Legal History. **1.** to request a jury trial in a civil case.
**2.** to controvert a material fact in a preceding pleading, so as to preserve the issue for submission to the jury.
——**History.** In British common law pleading it was customary, even obligatory, in an answering pleading denying material allegations of the plaintiff, to conclude with the words "and of this he puts himself upon the country"—meaning the jury. See notes at COUNTRY and PER PAIS.

**going concern** *n.* an enterprise that is carrying on its normal business and is expected to continue indefinitely. Cf. WIND UP.

**golden handcuffs** *n.pl.* financial incentives provided to executives to discourage them from moving to other jobs; for example, a large low-interest loan that must be repaid in full upon leaving the company, or simply a huge salary.

**golden handshake** *n.* **1.** the giving of extremely generous severance compensation to a dismissed employee or executive, or the use of such compensation to induce an individual to leave a position.
**2.** the compensation so given.

**golden parachute** *n.* **1.** a term in an employment contract between a corporation and any of its high executives promising the executive very generous financial compensation in the event of a change in corporate control, such as a merger or takeover, in which the executive either is forced out or chooses to resign in the face of a reduction in status or benefits.
**2.** loosely, any very lucrative severance package for a corporate executive even if not connected with a change of corporate control, including a GOLDEN HANDSHAKE.
Cf. PLATINUM PARACHUTE; TIN PARACHUTE.
——**History.** Golden parachutes assure that, whatever might happen to ordinary employees who lose their positions as a result of a merger or takeover, the top executives will be amply rewarded. In 1984, in the wake of a well-publicized golden parachute award of $4 million to an executive who lost a costly takeover battle that he himself had started—an amount regarded in those days as a lot of money to make the shareholders pay somebody whose services are no longer needed or wanted—Congress attempted to rein in golden parachutes by amending the Internal Revenue Code. Under the new provision, any *excess parachute payment* (see under PARACHUTE) would be subject to a 20% tax (in addition to the usual income tax) and would not be deductible to the corporation making the payment. Far from curbing the practice, this resulted in the establishment of more and larger golden parachutes. Since the law penalized only "excess" parachute payments (payments beyond triple the executive's recent average annual pay), it was taken as a Congressional imprimatur on golden parachutes generally; the practice therefore spread to more corporations and to a broader range of executives within each corporation, with a promised payment of 299% of average salary becoming standard. And for the top executives in many corporations, the 20% tax on the "excess" portion of their more lucrative parachutes simply meant that the corporation had to promise a higher payment than ever, so that the executive would come out ahead even after taxes. The original rationale for golden parachutes was that corporate executives with a "security blanket" will not resist a takeover that might benefit shareholders out of fear of losing their jobs; some critics have argued that the parachutes have become so lucrative that they could make executives receptive to mergers and takeovers even if they are *not* in the interest of the shareholders.

**good** *adj.* generally, of a type approved or favored by law, or regarded as acceptable in the marketplace or by society at large. The specific legal significance of the word varies greatly from phrase to phrase.

**good behavior** *n.* **1.** (of federal judges) absence of corrupt or criminal conduct. See *Article III judge* (under JUDGE).
**2.** (of a prisoner serving a sentence) compliance with prison rules. Traditionally, prisoners who complied with rules and stayed out of trouble while serving their sentences would have their sentences considerably shortened through "time off for good behavior." Political trends in the latter part of the twentieth century substantially reduced the amount of time off that could be earned in this way for many prisoners.

**good cause** *n.* **1.** a legally sufficient reason or excuse, especially for taking or omitting some procedural step in a case. Cf. INSUFFICIENT CAUSE.

**2. for good cause shown** or **good cause having been shown** expressions often used by a court in issuing an order, indicating that the party seeking the order has made a sufficient showing of facts warranting its issuance.

**good faith** *n.* the quality of mind and heart possessed by a person who is acting with sincerity and honesty, and without intent to cheat or take unfair advantage of another. Cf. BAD FAITH.

**good faith exception** *n.* an exception to the EXCLUSIONARY RULE, whereby evidence found in an illegal search may be used against a defendant if the police made the search in good faith reliance upon a search warrant issued by a neutral magistrate, which turned out to be invalid through no fault of the police.

**good faith purchaser** *n.* a purchaser of property who acts in good faith in making the purchase and has no reason to suspect that someone else might have a right to the property. Unless the property was stolen, a good faith purchaser will ordinarily get to keep the purchased property even if it turns out that the seller did not have the right to sell it. Also called **good faith purchaser for value** or **bona fide purchaser (for value).** See also VALUE.

**good law** *n.* in accord with current law. The phrase is used mostly in discussing the status of past judicial decisions or statements of legal principle in light of subsequent evolution of the law: *The much-criticized rule that property owners owe a higher duty of care to business invitees than to social guests is still good law in most states; but in at least thirteen states it is no longer good law.* Cf. BAD LAW.

**good samaritan** *n.* a person who, without compensation or the expectation of compensation, renders emergency care, assistance, or advice to someone in distress. Also written **good Samaritan, Good Samaritan.**

**good samaritan law** *n.* **1.** a statute granting immunity to good samaritans, especially physicians or other health professionals who happen upon the scene of an emergency or happen to be present when an emergency occurs, for any alleged negligence in their efforts to render assistance to those in need. Typically such a law does not grant immunity for reckless or willful conduct. **2.** (in a few states and some foreign countries) a law requiring individuals at the scene of an emergency to render assistance to the extent that they can do so without danger to themselves or others.
Also called **good samaritan statute,** and written with various capitalizations.

**good title** *n.* Same as *marketable title* (see under TITLE).

**goods** *n.pl.* **1.** virtually any *tangible personal property* (see under PROPERTY); movable things. For purposes of Article 2 of the Uniform Commercial Code, which governs sales of goods, the term includes not only movable things but also the unborn young of animals and things that will have to be severed from land for transfer from the seller to the buyer, such as timber or growing crops, minerals (including oil and gas), or even a house that is to be moved. See also MONEY (def. 1). **2. consumer goods** goods used primarily for personal, family, or household purposes.
See also BILL OF GOODS.

**goods and chattels** *n.pl.* personal property of every kind; all of a person's property except real estate.

**goodwill** or **good will** *n.* **1.** friendly disposition; benevolence. **2.** the benefit to a business of customer loyalty, brand name recognition, reputation for quality and honesty, and the like. Wrongful conduct injurious to a company's goodwill may be the basis of an action for damages. **3.** the present value or a firm's anticipated profits in excess of the rate of return considered normal in the industry in which the firm operates. **4.** in the purchase of an existing business, the excess of the price paid over the net asset value of the company.

—**Usage.** The original phrase *good will* and the solid form *goodwill* have existed side by side for centuries. While the original is more conservative and always acceptable, the solid form is now more common, especially in technical senses (e.g., as an accounting term).

—**Pronunciation.** Even when the term is written as a single word, it is still typically pronounced as if two separate words, with stress on *will*.

**govern** *v.* **1.** to rule over or direct the affairs of by right of authority: *govern a nation; govern a corporation.*
**2.** to influence or direct a decision: *The interpretation of the contract is governed by the intent of the parties.*
**3.** to serve as the controlling law for: *The case is governed section 1207 of the statute. We are governed by a recent appellate decision on this very issue.*
—**governability** *n.*
—**governable** *adj.*

**governance** *n.* **1.** exercise of authority; control; management.
**2.** a method or system of government or management.
See also CORPORATE GOVERNANCE.

**government** *n.* **1.** the process of governing; direction of the affairs of a nation, community, or other political body; political administration.
**2.** a form or system of rule by which a nation, community, etc., is governed: *monarchical government; parliamentary government.*
**3.** the ruling authorities of a city, state, nation, or other political unit; the body of officials that makes and enforces the laws.
**4.** Often, **Government.** the prosecuting authority in a federal criminal case. Such cases are captioned "United States v. So-and-So," but in court and in court papers the prosecution is typically referred to as "the Government": *The Government argues that the search was reasonable.* Cf. STATE; PEOPLE.
**5. federal government** the national government of the United States.
**6. republican form of government** government by the people, through their elected representatives. According

to the Constitution, the federal government is required to guarantee that the states will maintain a republican form of government.
See also DE FACTO GOVERNMENT; DE JURE GOVERNMENT.
—**governmental** *adj.*
—**governmentally** *adv.*

**government contractor** *n.* See under CONTRACTOR.

**government in the sunshine** *n.* **1.** the practice or policy of making meetings of governmental bodies open to the public to the extent that this can be done without jeopardizing important governmental and individual interests.
**2. government in the sunshine law** or **government in the sunshine act** a statute implementing such a policy. The federal government and many states have enacted such statutes.

**government security** *n.* See under SECURITY[2].

**grade** *v.*, **graded, grading,** *n.* —*v.* **1.** to categorize offenses according to their degree of seriousness, setting more serious penalties for more serious crimes; for example, criminal homicide is typically graded into several levels, such as first degree murder, second degree murder, voluntary manslaughter, involuntary manslaughter, and criminally negligent homicide.
—*n.* **2.** Also called **degree.** the level of a particular offense in such a grading system.

**grand** *adj. Law French.* (lit. "large") large, major, greater. Used in certain phrases, usually in contrast to PETIT or PETTY. See for example *grand jury* (under JURY); *grand larceny* (under LARCENY); *grand theft* (under THEFT).

**grandfather** *v.* **1.** to exempt a person or entity from a new law: *Existing buildings were grandfathered by the new zoning law, so they can remain even if they are nonconforming.*
—*adj.* **2. grandfather clause** a clause in a statute that exempts a class of persons or entities established and operating under prior law from new requirements.

**grant** *v.* **1.** broadly, to transfer or bestow property or a right of any kind: *The inventor granted his patent to a university. The Fifth Amendment grants to all property owners the right of just compensation if the government takes their property.*
**2.** specifically, to convey an interest in real property.
**3.** to accede to a motion, petition, or other request for judicial action, by issuing the requested order or taking the requested action; opposite of DENY: *The judge granted our motion for a protective order.*
—*n.* **4.** the act of granting something.
**5.** the thing granted.
—**grantable** *adj.*

**grantee** *n.* a person or entity to which something is granted, especially an interest in real property.

**granting clause** *n.* The clause in a deed or lease in which an identified grantor affirmatively conveys specifically described property to an identifed grantee or grantees. It follows any recitals and is followed by the HABENDUM CLAUSE. See also PREMISES.

**grantor** *n.* **1.** a person or entity that grants something, particularly an interest in real property.
**2.** The SETTLOR of a trust. See also *grantor trust* (under TRUST).

**gratuitous** *adj.* **1.** given, said, or done without an obligation to do so and without receiving or expecting anything in return; without CONSIDERATION. See, for example, *gratuitous bailment* (under BAILMENT) and *gratuitous promise* (under PROMISE).
**2.** describing a party to a gratuitous transaction; for example, a *gratuitous bailee* (see under BAILMENT).
—**gratuitously** *adv.*
—**gratuitousness** *n.*

**gravamen** *n., pl.* **gravamina.** the fundamental or central allegation of an accusation; the essence or heart of a complaint or charge: *The gravamen of the complaint is defendants' alleged failure to disclose that their products contained lead acetate.*

—**Usage.** This word is extremely popular with lawyers and judges, but its meaning is not always fully understood. In the medieval Latin it meant "grievance"; in English it became even more focused, signifying the essential part of a grievance, the heart of the accusation, a succinct statement of what the person complained of actually did wrong. Lawyers who do not quite understand the term sometimes use it to mean the essence or gist of anything (*the gravamen of my argument; the gravamen of the court's opinion; the gravamen of the letter of recommendation*); more careful or better informed lawyers will use more appropriate terms in such contexts, such as *essence* or *gist* or *heart.*

**gray market** *n.* **1.** the MARKET existing in the United States for products produced for sale in other countries and imported into the United States without permission of the trademark owner; especially, the United States market for goods bearing United States trademarks but intended by the trademark owner only for sale in other countries.
—*adj.* **2.** describing or pertaining to goods or activities in the gray market.
—**Note.** Gray market goods, unlike those on the BLACK MARKET, are generally perfectly legal. But they are often made and sold more cheaply than the versions intended for sale in the United States, and may consequently be of lower quality. Trademark license agreements may forbid foreign licensees to export their version of a product to the United States, but such agreements are sometimes violated. In addition, third parties can often buy the non-United States version of a product in bulk and import it into the United States cheaply enough to make a profit selling it in competition with the higher priced American version, to the dismay of the trademark owner whose profits are affected.

**graymail** *n.* a means of preventing or attempting to prevent prosecution, as for espionage, by threatening to disclose government secrets during trial.
—**graymailer** *n.*

**Great Charter** *n.* the MAGNA CARTA.

**Great Writ** *n.* the writ of HABEAS CORPUS. Also called the **great writ of liberty.**

**green card** *n. Informal.* an identification card—formerly colored green —issued to foreign nationals who have been granted permanent resident status in the United States and thus have full employment rights in the country. See also *resident alien* (under ALIEN).

**greenmail** *n.* **1.** the practice buying a large block of a company's stock—thereby at least implicitly threatening to take over the company—and forcing or persuading the company to repurchase that block of stock at a premium to thwart the potential takeover. **2.** the money paid by the corporation to purchase the block of stock in such a situation.
**—greenmailer** *n.*

**Gretna Green** *n. Informal.* a name formerly given to towns in states with easily satisfied requirements for marriage (particularly the absence of a required waiting period) near the borders of states with more stringent requirements for marriage, to which impatient couples from the more restrictive states would go to get married.
**——History.** This term was taken from the name of a Scottish town close to the country's border with England, to which eloping couples from England went to take advantage of Scotland's more relaxed marriage laws until Parliament in 1856 declared that such marriages would not be recognized in England unless the parties had lived in Scotland for 21 days. In the United States, even a hasty out-of-state or out-of-country marriage is normally recognized in the couple's home state so long as it is valid in the place where it was performed and does not violate any strong public policy of the home state. Social changes, however—notably the growing acceptance of sex before marriage—have made Gretna Greens largely a thing of the past.

**grievance** *n.* **1.** in a unionized workplace, a formal complaint by an employee, the union, or the employer, alleging a violation of the *collective bargaining agreement* (see under COLLECTIVE BARGAINING) or complaining about working conditions. **2.** a similar internal complaint concerning some condition in a nonunionized workplace, school, prison, or other institution with formal procedures for dealing with such complaints. **3. grievance committee** a committee provided for by union contract or otherwise established to evaluate and attempt to remedy grievances. **4. grievance procedure** a formal procedure for dealing with grievances.

**gross** *adj.* **1.** (of a sum of money) total before taking account of deductions or adjustments: *gross income* (see under INCOME). See also *gross lease* (under LEASE). **2.** flagrant or extreme (as distinguished from SIMPLE or ORDINARY): *gross negligence* (see under NEGLIGENCE).

**ground lease** *n.* See under LEASE.

**group annuity** *n.* See under ANNUITY.

**group boycott** *n.* See under BOYCOTT.

**group insurance** *n.* See under INSURANCE.

**guarantee** *v.,* **guaranteed, guaranteeing,** *n.* **—v. 1.** to give a GUARANTY or become a SURETY; to act as a surety or GUARANTOR of someone else's obligation: *The bank would give me a loan only if my parents guaranteed it.* **2.** to assure: *The purpose of the program is to guarantee access to medical care.* **3.** *Informal.* to issue or stand behind a WARRANTY on a product. **—n. 4.** a guaranty or suretyship agreement. **5.** any assurance: *The Fifth Amendment guarantee of due process.* **6.** *Informal.* a nonlawyer's term for a warranty on a product.

**guaranteed bond** *n.* See under BOND[1].

**guaranteed security** *n.* See under SECURITY[2].

**guarantor** *n.* a person or entity that issues or is obligated under a GUAR-ANTY.

**guaranty** *n., pl.* **guaranties,** *v.,* **guar-antied, guarantying.** —*n.* **1.** in the strictest sense, a promise or contract to make someone whole if a third person fails to fulfill an obligation; that is, a promise by A to B that if C fails to pay a debt or perform some other obligation owed to B, then A will pay the debt or otherwise compensate B. **2.** any promise to answer for the debt, default, or miscarriage of another. In this broader sense, guaranty includes SURETYSHIP. Under the STATUTE OF FRAUDS, any such promise must be in writing and signed to be enforceable. **3.** in the broadest sense, any GUARAN-TEE. —*v.* **4.** to GUARANTEE anything.

**guardian** *n.* **1.** a person, especially one appointed by a court, with responsibility for the care of a child or an incompetent adult (the WARD) and legal control of the ward's affairs. Sometimes one person, such as a relative, is designated to take personal care of the ward, and another individual or a financial institution is designated to manage the ward's money and property; the former is then referred to as **guardian of the person** and the latter as **guardian of the property.** See also COMMITTEE; CONSERVATOR. **2. guardian ad litem** a person, usually a lawyer, appointed by the court to represent the interests of an infant or incompetent person or a class of such people in a case. Of course, in some cases opinions might vary as to what those interests really are. See also AD LITEM. **3. testamentary guardian** a guardian for a minor child, designated in the parent's will. —**guardianship** *n.*

**guest statute** *n.* See AUTOMOBILE GUEST STATUTE.

**guilt phase** *n.* The first phase of a capital case, in which the jury is to determine whether the defendant is guilty. Cf. PENALTY PHASE.

**guilty** *adj.* **1.** (of a criminal defendant) adjudged by a court to have committed an offense, either on the basis of a finding or verdict at trial, or because the defendant admitted or did not contest the charge. See also ADJUDGE; JUDG-MENT. Cf. NOT GUILTY; INNOCENT. **2.** designating a PLEA entered by a criminal defendant, admitting the charge. This is usually the result of a PLEA BAR-GAIN. Cf. NOLO CONTENDERE; NOT GUILTY. **3.** having committed a tort, a breach of contract, or an act damaging to one's position in a civil case: *guilty of breach of contract; guilty of contributory negligence.*

**gun control** *n.* legal restrictions on the manufacture, importation, distribution, or possession of guns. See also note at RIGHT TO BEAR ARMS.

# H

**habeas corpus** *n. Latin.* (lit. "have the body") **1.** an ancient English writ **(writ of habeas corpus)** commanding an official holding someone in custody to have the "body" (that is, the person) of the prisoner brought before the court so that the lawfulness of the imprisonment can be inquired into and the prisoner set free if not being held legally. The original Latin wording of the writ stated that the detainee was to be produced for the purpose of submitting to (*subjiciendum*) and receiving (*recipiendum*) whatever the court might decree in the case; thus the writ is more specifically named **habeas corpus ad subjiciendum** or **habeas corpus ad subjiciendum et recipiendum.** In both its ancient and modern forms (see defs. 2, 3) it is often referred to by such phrases as the **writ of liberty,** the **great writ of liberty,** or simply the **Great Writ.**
**2.** a modern procedure or writ for testing the legality of custody—usually of a criminal defendant or suspect, but sometimes of a child or of a civil detainee such as a person committed to a mental hospital.
**3.** particularly, the constitutionally guaranteed procedure by which the constitutionality of a state conviction and imprisonment can be tested in federal court **(federal habeas corpus).** Congressional action in recent years has substantially restricted the availability of federal habeas corpus.
**4.** any of a class of writs by which English courts commanded that persons under detention be produced in court for various purposes. The specific name of each such writ was derived from key language of the writ, as in the following examples.
**5. habeas corpus ad deliberandum et recipiendum** (lit. "...for the purpose of deliberating and receiving"), a writ commanding that a person already confined in one county be produced for trial in another county.
**6. habeas corpus ad faciendum et recipiendum** (lit. "...to do and receive"), a writ removing a civil case from a lower court, which has the defendant in custody, to a higher court for disposition of the case. It required delivery of the defendant with the cause of action, and so was also called **habeas corpus cum causa** (lit. "...with the cause").
**7. habeas corpus ad prosequendum** (lit. "...for prosecuting"), a writ directing production of a criminal defendant for trial.
**8. habeas corpus ad respondendum** (lit. "...to answer"), a writ directing that a person be produced from the custody of one court to answer a claim or charge in another court.
**9. habeas corpus ad satisfaciendum** (lit. "...to give satisfaction"), a writ directing that a person in the custody of one court be delivered to another court for execution of a civil judgment.
**10. habeas corpus ad testificandum** (lit. "...to testify"), a writ directing that a prisoner be delivered to a court to give evidence.

**habendum** *Latin.* to be had; to be possessed. See also note at HABENDUM CLAUSE.

**habendum clause** *n.* in a deed or lease, the clause that follows the GRANTING CLAUSE and specifies the nature and duration of the estate being granted (e.g., tenancy in common vs. joint tenancy, fee simple vs. life estate vs. term of years). In deeds written in Latin, the clause started with the words HABENDUM ET TENENDUM; in Law French, A AVER ET TENER; in English, TO HAVE AND TO HOLD, for example, "to have and to hold to himself and his heirs in fee simple absolute." Also called **habendum** or, rarely, **tenendum clause** or **tenendum.** See also note at TENENDUM CLAUSE. Cf. REDDENDUM CLAUSE.

——**Usage.** Historically, this clause was referred to simply as the *habendum.* The phrase *habendum clause* came into use in the mid-nineteeth century, and soon became the usual term, although the word *habendum* alone is still perfectly acceptable.

**habendum et tenendum** *Latin.* to be had and held. See HABENDUM CLAUSE; TENENDUM CLAUSE; and note at TO HAVE AND TO HOLD.

**habitable** *adj.* **1.** fit to live in; in compliance with building codes and free of dangers to health and safety. See also TENANTABLE.
**2. warranty of habitability** a landlord's WARRANTY, regarded by law in most states as inherent in every residential lease, that the premises are habitable and will be kept that way.
—**habitability** *n.*

**habitual criminal** *n.* Same as *habitual offender* (see under OFFENDER).

**habitual offender** *n.* See under OFFENDER.

**hacking** *n.* the use of one's programming skills to break into a computer or a computer network without authorization.
—**hack** *v.*
—**hacker** *n.*
——**Usage.** In computer circles, and among some legal writers and lawmakers, "hacking" refers to the actions of people whose primary motive is simply a sense of accomplishment, who might be described as more mischievous than malicious, more annoying than dangerous. But under the influence of popular media the term has generally been broadened to include more serious computer crimes in which data or software is stolen or corrupted.
——**History.** The Maryland Court of Appeals (the state's highest court) offers the following account of the origin of this expression: "The word 'hacker' has

become synonymous with a computer criminal, and typically refers to a person who breaks into computer networks. Originally, however, the term 'hacker' referred to members of The Tech Model Railroad Club of Massachusetts Institute of Technology (TMRC) and the term 'hack' referred to 'a project undertaken or a product built not solely to fulfill some constructive goal, but with some wild pleasure, taken in mere involvement.' The terms 'hack' and 'hacker' found their way into the computing world when the members of TMRC began work on the digital computers at Massachusetts Institute of Technology. The TMRC resents the application of the term 'hacker' to mean the committing of illegal acts, maintaining that words such as 'thieves,' 'password crackers,' or 'computer vandals' are better descriptions." *Briggs v. State,* 348 Md. 470 (1998) (citations omitted).

**haec verba** *n.* See IN HAEC VERBA.

**Haggadah** *n.* Same as AGGADAH.

**Halakhah** *n., pl.* **Halakhahs, Halakhoth, Halakhot, Halakhos.** *Jewish Law.* **1.** the entire body of Jewish law and tradition comprising the laws of the Bible, the oral law as transcribed in the legal portion of the TALMUD, and subsequent legal codes amending or modifying traditional precepts to conform to contemporary conditions.
**2.** a law or tradition established by the Halakhah.
Also spelled **Halakah, Halachah, Halacha,** and often uncapitalized.
—**Halakhic, Halakic, Halachic** *adj.*

**halal** *adj. Islamic Law.* **1.** lawful.
**2.** (of food, especially meat) lawful; slaughtered or prepared in the manner prescribed by Islamic law.
——*n.* **3.** that which is lawful; especially, lawful food.

**halfway house** *n.* a residence for individuals who have been in prison, providing a supervised and structured environment to help them adjust to outside life. Cf. WORK RELEASE.

**Hammurabi** See CODE OF HAMMURABI.

**Hanafi** *n. Islamic Law.* one of the four

principal schools of Islamic law, founded by Abu Hanifa (c.700–767). See note at SHARI'A.
—**Hanafite** n.

**Hanbali** n. Islamic Law. one of the four principal schools of Islamic law, founded by Ahmad ibn Hanbal (c.780–855). See note at SHARI'A.
—**Hanbalite** n.

**hand** n. **1.** Same as SIGNATURE.
**2. hand and seal** one's signature and seal (see SEAL¹) placed together on a document. See also note at SEAL¹.
—v. **3. hand down** to render a judicial opinion, ruling, sentence, etc. This phrase is used whether the decision is rendered orally or in writing, and whether rendered from the bench or from chambers. See also ISSUE⁴.
**4. hand up** to pass a document or exhibit up to the judge in court. This phrase is used whether the object is handed directly to the judge or simply given to a bailiff or clerk to hand up.

**handicap** n. Same as DISABILITY, which is generally the preferred term today.
—**handicapped** adj.

**hang¹** v., **hung, hanging.** (of a jury) to be unable to agree upon a decision; to be deadlocked: The jury hung and the judge declared a mistrial. See also hung jury (under JURY).

**hang²** v., **hanged, hanging. 1.** to suspend by the neck as a form of execution: The killer was sentenced to be hanged at dawn.
**2.** to be suspended from the neck: He'll hang for his crimes.
——**History.** Although the natural and intended consequence of hanging is normally death, in at least one particular circumstance another outcome was contemplated. The prescribed punishment for HIGH TREASON in early English law began with being hanged by the neck, cut down while still alive, and disemboweled. There was more, but the rest of the punishment, including the burning of the entrails and the carving up of the body, were probably of comparatively little consequence to the condemned criminal.

**hanging judge** n. **1.** historically, a

judge with a reputation for routinely sentencing defendants to be hanged, without necessarily having a great deal of evidence of guilt.
**2.** now, any judge with a reputation for harshness in sentencing, whether or not in capital cases.

**harass** v. to annoy a person, or engage in offensive conduct toward a person, in a manner that constitutes HARASSMENT.
—**harasser** n.
—**harassingly** adv.

**harassment** n. **1.** the crime of deliberately and repeatedly annoying or interfering with a person, as by telephoning repeatedly, sending anonymous messages, following, taunting, etc. See also INTENTIONAL INFLICTION OF MENTAL DISTRESS; STALKING; CYBERSTALKING.
**2.** annoying or offensive conduct in the workplace, directed toward an employee or group of employees because of their race, color, religion, sex, or national origin. Such harassment, when engaged in or tolerated by an employer, constitutes unlawful employment discrimination. See also HOSTILE WORKING ENVIRONMENT; SEXUAL HARASSMENT.

**hard labor** n. labor that a prisoner is compelled to perform as part of a sentence or as a disciplinary measure.
——**Note.** The Thirteenth Amendment, outlawing involuntary servitude in general, specifically allows it for punishment of a crime. But the Eighth Amendment, prohibiting cruel and unusual punishment, limits the nature of the labor that may be required of a prisoner. As a practical matter, therefore, the phrase hard labor in penal statutes providing for sentences of imprisonment "at hard labor" simply means "labor."

**hard money** n. a political contribution which satisfies certain limitations and disclosure requirements established by federal law, and therefore may be used in connection with the election campaign of a candidate for federal office, that is, for President or Vice President or for the Senate or House of Representatives. Also called **federal money,**

**regulated money.** See also POLITICAL ACTION COMMITTEE.

**——Note.** The laws and regulations governing federal election campaigns restrict both the amount of money that may be contributed to a campaign from any one source and the sources from which contributions may be accepted. In addition, reporting and disclosure must be made of most such contributions. Only contributions that meet these requirements—the so-called hard money contributions—may be used directly for campaign activities. Thus any contributions spent by or in coordination with a federal candidate or an authorized campaign committee for the candidate must be hard money (although a rich candidate may spend unlimited amounts of his own money). In addition, party advertisements explicitly electioneering for a federal candidate must be paid for with hard money even if they are not coordinated with the candidate, and a certain percentage (usually less than 40%) of money spent by state political parties on activities that benefit both state and federal candidates, such as get-out-the-vote drives, fund-raising, and general administrative expenses, must be funded by hard money. Because of the restrictions and disclosure requirements governing hard money, political parties now fund as much of their activity as possible with SOFT MONEY.

**hardships, balancing of** *n.* See BALANCING OF THE EQUITIES.

**harmful error** *n.* Same as *reversible error* (see under ERROR).

**harmless** *adj.* **1.** not harmful or prejudicial; inconsequential.
**2.** unharmed; safe from harm or prejudice.
**3. harmless error** See under ERROR.
**4. hold** (or **save**) **harmless a.** to release from liability or responsibility for loss or damage; to abandon any claim that one might have against someone. **b.** to indemnify; to promise to compensate someone for any loss that might be incurred by reason of claims asserted later by others.

**—harmlessly** *adv.*
**—harmlessness** *n.*

**hate crime** *n.* a crime motivated by ANIMUS or bias against a group identified by race, religion, sexual orientation, or other group characteristic, or a crime in which the victim is chosen because of perceived membership in such a group. States may impose extra penalties for such crimes. Also called **bias crime.**

**hate speech** *n.* See under SPEECH.

**have** *v.*, **had, having. 1.** to possess. See MONEY HAD AND RECEIVED; TO HAVE AND TO HOLD.
**2.** to cause to, as by command. See HABEAS CORPUS.

**have and hold** *v.* See TO HAVE AND TO HOLD.

**He Said, She Said** *Informal.* a phrase characterizing disputes or issues upon which there is little evidence other than the conflicting accounts of the participants, especially when the dispute is between a man and a woman and concerns their relationship, as in a divorce or date rape case. See also SWEARING CONTEST.

**head of household** *n.* an unmarried person (or married person living separately from his or her spouse and filing a separate tax return) who lives with and maintains a household for an unmarried child or a dependent relative. Under the Internal Revenue Code, such a person qualifies for special income tax rates.

**head tax** *n.* Same as POLL TAX.

**headnote** *n.* a capsule summary, usually in one sentence, of a legal point in a judicial opinion, inserted by an editor at the head of the published version of the opinion as an aid to legal research. Most published opinions are preceded by several headnotes. Cf. DIGEST; SYLLABUS.

**health** *n.* See BILL OF HEALTH.

**health care proxy** *n.* a document, provided for by statute in some states, authorizing another person to make medical decisions for the signer if the signer is unable to do so. Also called **durable**

**power of attorney for health care.** See also *durable power of attorney* (under POWER OF ATTORNEY); LIVING WILL; RIGHT TO DIE.

**hear** *v.*, **heard, hearing. 1.** (of a court or judge) **a.** to handle a case. **b.** to receive evidence and argument, usually orally and without a jury: *to hear a motion; hear an appeal; hear a case without a jury.* Cf. TRY (def. 1); *take on submission* (under SUBMIT). See also OPPORTUNITY TO BE HEARD.
**2. hear and determine** to hear and reach a decision on.
**3. hear and report** to hear and make a recommendation on. In the federal district courts, certain matters may be referred by a judge of the court to a magistrate judge to hear and determine or hear and report.
—**hearable** *adj.*

**hear ye** a phrase often called out (usually two or three times) at the opening of court proceedings, to get the undivided attention of everyone present and impress upon them the seriousness and importance of the proceedings about to commence. Means the same thing as the Law French OYEZ, which is still used in many courts. Cf. KNOW ALL MEN BY THESE PRESENTS.

**hearing** *n.* **1.** any factfinding proceeding at which testimony is taken, except a full-scale court trial; for example, a hearing by a court on a motion for a preliminary injunction, a trial before an administrative tribunal or arbitration panel, or a hearing before a legislative committee.
**2.** loosely, any proceeding at which legal matters are presented for consideration or decision, including full-scale court trials, appellate arguments, and even matters submitted entirely on papers.
**3. preliminary hearing** an early stage in a felony prosecution, in which the prosecutor must show a court that there is sufficient evidence to justify a trial. Also called **probable cause hearing, bindover hearing.**
**4. public hearing** a hearing held by an administrative agency at which the general public is invited to comment on proposed rules or actions of the agency. See also FAIR HEARING.

**hearing examiner** *n.* Same as ADMINISTRATIVE LAW JUDGE.

**hearing officer** *n.* Same as ADMINISTRATIVE LAW JUDGE.

**hearsay** *n.* **1.** (in a courtroom proceeding) any assertion, other than one made on the witness stand in that very proceeding, that is offered as evidence of the matter asserted; often loosely summarized as "an out-of-court declaration offered for its truth." For example, the statement "I saw my husband shoot Smith," made by a suspect's wife to police shortly after an incident, is hearsay if offered by the prosecution at the husband's trial to help prove that he is the person who shot Smith; but a testator's statement "I am Napoleon," if offered at the trial of a challenge to the will to show that the testator was of unsound mind, is *nonhearsay*, because it is not offered as evidence that the declarant truly was Napoleon. A hearsay assertion may be either oral or written, or even nonverbal (such as a nod of the head).
**2. hearsay evidence** any testimony or document offered in court that contains hearsay; for example, a police officer's testimony, "She told me she saw her husband shoot Smith," or a letter written by the defendant's wife containing the sentence, "I saw my husband shoot Smith."
**3. hearsay exception** any of the numerous exceptions to the *hearsay rule* under which hearsay evidence is deemed admissible, usually because the circumstances under which the hearsay assertion was made are thought to provide reasonable assurance of its reliability. See, for example, PRESENT SENSE IMPRESSION; EXCITED UTTERANCE; *dying declaration* and *declaration against interest* (under DECLARATION); *business record* and *public record* (under RECORD); *unavailable witness* (under WITNESS).
**4. hearsay rule** the American rule of evidence under which hearsay is generally deemed inadmissible because the assertion presented as "truth" is usually

not made under oath and is not subject to cross-examination under the scrutiny of the judge and jury.

**heart balm action** *n.* a generic name for any of the common law actions for the torts of ALIENATION OF AFFECTIONS, *breach of promise of marriage* (see under BREACH), CRIMINAL CONVERSATION, and SEDUCTION.

**heart balm statute** *n.* a state statute abolishing heart balm actions. Such statutes were widely adopted in the United States during the first half of the twentieth century. Sometimes (and more logically) called **anti-heart-balm statute.**

**heat of passion** *n.* extreme anger or other emotional disturbance provoked by circumstances that the law regards as sufficient to make a reasonable person lose control. Also called **sudden heat of passion, hot blood.** Killing in the heat of passion is generally regarded by the law as much less serious than killing "in cold blood."
——**Note.** The classic example is the man who discovers his wife in bed with another man, goes and gets his gun, and deliberately shoots them to death while still "in the heat of passion." (His, not theirs.) It is still the law in nearly all American jurisdictions that this is not murder, but merely *voluntary manslaughter* (see under MANSLAUGHTER).

**hedge** *v.,* **hedged, hedging.** to reduce the risk of loss in a transaction or investment that depends upon fluctuating market conditions, interest rates, or the like, by means of counterbalancing transactions or investments whose value would be affected by the same fluctuating conditions, but in the opposite direction.

**hedge fund** *n.* an investment vehicle, usually a limited partnership, in which a relatively small number of extremely large investors pool their assets for use in complex investment strategies intended to provide greater than usual returns while limiting risk. Because these investment vehicles are not available to the public, they have traditionally been relatively unregulated.
——**False Friend.** Despite the cautious and reassuring sound of the name, "hedge funds" can be very risky. This fact was brought home to the investment community in 1998, when Long-Term Capital Management L.P., a leading hedge fund whose founders and managers included two men who just the previous year had shared the Nobel prize in economics for their work in risk management, suffered losses so catastrophic that it required a government-orchestrated bailout of approximately $3.6 billion (provided by a consortium of banks and brokerage houses) to keep the fund out of bankruptcy.

**hedonic damages** *n.* See under DAMAGES.

**heightened scrutiny** *n.* a test of constitutionality applied by the Supreme Court to laws that are alleged to violate EQUAL PROTECTION because they treat people differently on the basis of a QUASI-SUSPECT CLASSIFICATION—usually sex. This test is stricter than the RATIONAL BASIS TEST but less demanding than STRICT SCRUTINY. A law or government action subject to heightened scrutiny will be upheld only if it is shown to be "substantially related" to the achievement of "important governmental objectives." Also called **intermediate scrutiny.**
——**History.** When laws discriminating on the basis of sex came under concerted attack in America in the 1970's, the Supreme Court was urged to subject them to the same strict scrutiny as laws based upon racial classifications, which can be sustained only upon a showing that the law is "necessary" to serve a "compelling governmental interest." It was argued that the same principles should apply because sex-based laws, like race-based laws, place people into separate classes for differential treatment on the basis of immutable characteristics over which they

have no control. In *Frontiero v. Richardson,* 411 U.S. 677 (1973)—a case argued by Ruth Bader Ginsburg, who twenty years later would return to sit on the other side of the bench—four members of the Court accepted the argument. The fifth vote needed to make sex a SUSPECT CLASSIFICATION was never found, however; instead, in *Craig v. Boren,* 429 U.S. 190 (1976), a majority was found for a new, intermediate-level test for classifications based on sex, which came to be called *heightened scrutiny.* In the 1980's, the Court extended this test to classifications based on legitimacy or illegitimacy. Over the years, in what appears to have developed into a concerted campaign by a Supreme Court majority to move "heightened scrutiny" toward the "strict scrutiny" end of the spectrum of constitutional tests (see SCRUTINY), the Court has increasingly emphasized that laws and governmental actions based on sex can survive constitutional scrutiny only upon a showing of "exceedingly persuasive justification." See also note at SEPARATE BUT EQUAL.

**heir** *n.* **1.** the person, or one of the people, to whom one's property passes by operation of law if one dies without leaving a will. Also called **legal heir, heir at law.** See also INTESTATE SUCCESSION. Cf. LEGATEE; DEVISEE.

**2. and his heirs** at common law, words that had to be included in any grant of real property to someone if the intent was to convey the property permanently—that is, to convey a *fee simple* (see under FEE[1]), so that the new owner could pass it on to his heirs or otherwise dispose of it. If the property was conveyed only to "John Smith," rather than to "John Smith and his heirs," Smith received only a *life estate* (see under ESTATE[1]), and upon his death the property reverted to the original owner or his successors. Although this rule has been abolished nearly everywhere, these traditional words are still found in many deeds. See also notes at WORDS OF LIMITATION and WORDS OF PURCHASE.

**3. apparent heir a.** same as *heir apparent.* **b.** loosely, one who appears to be an heir of a decedent.

**4. collateral heir** See under COLLATERAL[2].

**5. direct heir** See under DIRECT[1].

**6. forced heir** (especially in civil law) an heir who cannot be disinherited, or who cannot be disinherited except in limited circumstances.

**7. heir apparent** a person who is certain to become a particular individual's heir unless that individual outlives the person or leaves a will. Cf. *heir presumptive.*

**8. heir of the body** a lineal descendant, including descendants in generations yet unborn. Also called **bodily heir.** See also FEE TAIL.

**9. heir presumptive** a person who would be a particular individual's heir if that individual died immediately without leaving a will, but who could be displaced as an heir by the birth of a closer relative before the individual's death. Cf. *heir apparent.*

**10. heirs and assigns** everyone to whom one might leave, give, or sell property; a standard phrase covering anyone who might succeed to one's interest in a piece of property or rights in a matter. For example, a defendant who gives a plaintiff money to settle a case will normally receive in return a RELEASE against any further claims in the matter, executed by the plaintiff "for herself and her heirs and assigns"; this precludes anyone else from coming along and asserting a new claim as her successor. See also ASSIGN.

**11. presumptive heir a.** same as *heir presumptive.* **b.** in Louisiana law, an heir who has not yet accepted or renounced succession to the decedent's estate. **c.** loosely, one who appears to be an heir.

**12. pretermitted heir** a child, or sometimes a later-generation descendant who is an heir, who is omitted from mention in a will, usually because the will was made before the child was born. In most states a pretermitted heir—at least one who is a child of the testator—is entitled by statute to a share of the estate unless the will, or in

some states other evidence, shows that the decedent's failure to leave anything to that heir was intentional. Also called **pretermitted child**.
—**heirship** n.

**heir apparent** n., pl. **heirs apparent**. See under HEIR.

**heir presumptive** n., pl. **heirs presumptive**. See under HEIR.

**hereditament** n. **1.** something that can be inherited; inheritable property of any kind.
**2. corporeal hereditament** inheritable tangible property; especially, land.
**3. incorporeal hereditament** inheritable intangible property; especially, a right growing out of or relating to land, such as an easement or a right to receive rents.

**hidden defect** n. See under DEFECT².

**high crimes and misdemeanors** n.pl. the phrase used in the Constitution to denote misconduct by the President or another federal officer of sufficient gravity to warrant impeachment and removal from office.
——**Note.** Whenever impeachment is considered, arguments arise over just what kind of crime meets this test, or whether conduct within the scope of this phrase necessarily must be punishable as a crime at all (see MISDEMEANOR, def. 2). The Supreme Court has never had occasion to construe the phrase.

**high-speed chase** or **high-speed police chase** n. use of a motor vehicle by police to pursue a suspect at dangerously high speeds. Also called **high-speed pursuit** or **high-speed police pursuit** Cf. FRESH PURSUIT.
——**Note.** In 1998, the Supreme Court considered the case of a California police chase of a teenage motorcyclist and his passenger through a residential neighborhood at speeds reaching 100 miles per hour. When the motorcyclist tipped over while trying to negotiate a sharp turn, the officer slammed on his brakes and skidded into the 16-year-old passenger, propelling him 70 feet down the road and inflicting massive injuries from which he died on the scene. The

boy's family felt that he had been deprived of life by state action without due process of law, in violation of the Fourteenth Amendment to the Constitution. But the Court, without dissent, ruled to the contrary, holding that so far as the Constitution is concerned police officers are completely free to continue "causing death through deliberate or reckless indifference to life in a high-speed automobile chase aimed at apprehending a suspected offender." *County of Sacramento v. Lewis*, 523 U.S. 833 (1998).

**high treason** n. See under TREASON.

**high-value speech** n. See under SPEECH; see also discussion at FREEDOM OF SPEECH.

**higher court** n. See under COURT.

**highest and best use** n. See under USE.

**highest degree of care** n. See under CARE.

**hijacker profile** n. See under PROFILE.

**hindering prosecution** n. the crime of knowingly assisting a person who has committed a crime to avoid or hinder capture, prosecution, conviction, or punishment. Hindering prosecution is usually treated as an offense of a slightly lower grade than the crime whose prosecution is hindered. See also *accessory after the fact* (under ACCESSORY).

**His** (or **Her**) **Honor** n., pl. **Their Honors**. (a respectful form of reference for certain officials, especially a judge or mayor): *The attorneys met with His Honor in chambers to discuss the possibility of settlement*. The phrase is often written with only the word *Honor* capitalized, and occasionally, especially in older materials, with neither word capitalized.

**history** n. **1.** the sequence of proceedings in a case, or in the enactment of a statute. See also LEGISLATIVE HISTORY.
**2.** a series of repeated events, or occasionally a single event, that occurred in

the past: *a history of drug abuse; a history of disputes between the neighbors.*

**3.** any sequence of events occurring over time.

**4. prior history  a.** the proceedings leading up to a particular judicial decision; especially prior decisions in the case. In citations to decisions, prior history is sometimes included (often introduced by AFF'G or REV'G) if the earlier decision helps to clarify the point under discussion. **b.** Same as HISTORY (def. 2): *a prior history of drug abuse; a prior history of disputes between the neighbors.*

**5. subsequent history  a.** proceedings in a case that occurred after a particular decision was rendered; especially, decisions on appeal to higher courts or on remand to a lower court. In citations to decisions, the subsequent history is usually included; see, e.g., AFF'D; REV'D. **b.** any amendment or repeal of a statute, or hearings, debates, and the like related to such action, that occurred after the time that is relevant for a particular matter. In rare cases such subsequent legislative history is considered in determining how to interpret or apply the statute. **c.** any events occurring with respect to a matter after a particular time or event under discussion.

**hold** *v.*, **held, holding. 1.** to possess; especially, to possess lawfully: *The tenant holds the apartment under a three-year lease.* See also TO HAVE AND TO HOLD.

**2.** (of a judge, court, or judicial opinion) to state the court's conclusion in a case, or on a particular issue in a case, especially an issue of law (as distinguished from fact). See also HOLDING.

**3.** to detain: *The police held her for questioning.*

**4.** to engage in; preside over; carry on: *hold court; hold a session of Congress.*

**5.** to occupy a position: *hold office.*

**6. hold harmless**  See under HARMLESS.

**7. hold out**  to act in such a way as to create the impression—especially a false impression—that something or someone (often oneself) has certain qualities or status: *He held himself out*

as *a qualified lawyer.* Depending upon the circumstances, this may lead to criminal penalties, civil liability for FRAUD, or an application of the doctrine of ESTOPPEL.

**8. hold over**  to continue to occupy rented premises after the lease expires or the tenancy is legally terminated. The tenant who does this is commonly called a **holdover tenant.** See also *tenancy at sufferance* (under TENANCY).

**holder** *n.* **1.** one who possesses a right or a thing: *the holder of a future interest in land; the holder of the key to a safe deposit box.*

**2.** in the law of negotiable instruments, a person in possession of an instrument issued or indorsed to him or to his order, or a person in possession of a *bearer instrument* (see under BEARER).

**3. holder in due course**  a holder of a negotiable instrument who gives value for it (see *holder for value*) and takes it in an honest transaction in the normal course of the transferor's business or activities, without notice of any facts that might make it unenforceable. The right of a holder in due course to receive payment on an instrument is often stronger than that of an ordinary holder.

**4. holder for value**  a holder of a negotiable instrument who has not merely made a promise to the transferor to do something in exchange for the instrument, but has actually performed the agreed consideration, or has given a negotiable instrument or made an irrevocable commitment to a third person in exchange for the instrument, or has acquired a security interest in the instrument otherwise than by legal process, or has received the instrument in payment of or as security for an antecedent claim.

**holding** *n.* **1.** the ruling of a court in a case, or upon a particular issue in a case, especially an issue of law (as distinguished from fact). Cf. DICTUM.

**2.** Usually, **holdings.** legally owned property, especially stocks, bonds, or real estate.

**holding company** *n.* See under COMPANY.

**holding period** *n.* **1.** the period of time that a taxpayer keeps a piece of property before selling it.
**2.** the length of time that a taxpayer must keep a piece of property before selling it in order to qualify for special reduced tax rates on the gain realized on the sale.
See also *capital gains tax* (under CAPITAL[1]).

**holdover tenancy** *n.* Same as *tenancy at sufferance* (see under TENANCY).

**holdover tenant** *n.* See under HOLD.

**holograph** *n.* a document written entirely by hand by its author.
—**holographic** *adj.*

**holographic will** *n.* See under WILL.

**home** *n.* See TAX HOME.

**home equity conversion mortgage** *n.* See under MORTGAGE.

**home owner's warranty** *n.* Same as *construction warranty* (see under WARRANTY).

**home rule** *n.* the right of a city, town, or other local government to make its own laws on matters of local concern to the extent permitted by the state constitution or statutes.

**homestead** *n.* **1.** a dwelling and surrounding land occupied by the owner as a home.
**2. homestead exemption** the principle that property designated as one's homestead in accordance with a state statute (generally called the **homestead law, homestead exemption statute,** or the like) may not be seized by creditors to satisfy one's debts. The scope of such laws varies from state to state; under the most generous, a debtor can sometimes live quite luxuriously while leaving his creditors unpaid.

**homicide** *n.* **1.** an act or omission resulting in the death of another person.
**2.** Also called **criminal homicide.** The crime of causing of another's death through conduct that was intentional, knowing, reckless, or extremely negligent, without JUSTIFICATION. All states recognize several degrees of the crime

depending on the circumstances and the actor's STATE OF MIND. The major categories of homicide are usually called MURDER, MANSLAUGHTER, and *negligent homicide.*
**3. justifiable homicide** homicide committed under circumstances regarded by the law as justification for such an extreme act, the most common of which is SELF-DEFENSE. Justifiable homicide is not a crime.
**4. negligent homicide** the crime of causing another's death through *criminal negligence* (see under NEGLIGENCE); the lowest degree of criminal homicide. Called **criminally negligent homicide** in some states; in others, included in *involuntary manslaughter* (see under MANSLAUGHTER).
**5. vehicular homicide** a special category of homicide recognized in some states for dealing with homicides by careless and drunk drivers. Also called **homicide by automobile.**

**homologate** *v.,* **homologated, homologating.** *Civil Law.* **1.** to approve or confirm judicially.
**2.** to ratify.
—**homologation** *n.*

**homosexual marriage** *n.* See under MARRIAGE.

**Hon.** abbreviation for HONORABLE.

**honor** *v.* to pay, or to ACCEPT and pay, a check, note, or other instrument for the payment of money.

**Honor** *n.* (a respectful form of address or reference for certain officials, especially a judge or mayor.) See YOUR HONOR; HIS (OR HER) HONOR.

**Honorable (Hon.)** *adj.* (title of respect accorded to judges, mayors, and certain other officials.)
——**Usage.** This title is used with either the full name or an additional title, or both: *the Honorable Samuel S. Smith; the Honorable Samuel S. Smith, Judge; the Honorable Judge Smith.* When the abbreviation is used, the word *the* is omitted: *Hon. Samuel S. Smith, District Judge.* In the salutation of a letter (followed by a colon), older etiquette called for *Honorable Sir;* the feminine form would presumably be *Honorable*

*Madam.* Extreme formality and deference seldom hurts when addressing a judge, but the usual form of salutation today is simply *Dear Judge Smith.*

**honorary degree** *n.* See under DE-GREE.

**horizontal** *adj.* involving two or more entities performing the same or similar functions in an industry or business, especially competitors; functioning at the same level in a market structure.
**—horizontally** *adv.*
**——Note.** For example, two suppliers of the raw material for a product, or two companies providing the same or related services to consumers, are related to each other horizontally; hence a merger of such entities would be regarded as a "horizontal merger." Cf. VERTICAL.

**horizontal merger** *n.* See under MERGER.

**horizontal price fixing** *n.* See under PRICE FIXING.

**horizontal union** *n.* See under UNION.

**hornbook** *n.* **1.** a one-volume text or treatise organizing and summarizing a significant area of law, such as torts or corporation law. Cf. CASEBOOK; TREATISE.
**2. hornbook law** a legal principle regarded as so basic and well established as to require no citation to case authority: *"It is hornbook law that a principal is bound by the act of an agent within the scope of the agent's authority."*
Also called **black letter law.**

**hostile embargo** *n.* See under EMBARGO.

**hostile environment harassment** *n.* See under SEXUAL HARASSMENT.

**hostile witness** *n.* See under WITNESS.

**hostile working environment** *n.* working conditions in which an employee is subjected to HARASSMENT because of the employee's race, color, religion, sex, or national origin. The maintenance of such an environment constitutes unlawful employment discrimination. See also SEXUAL HARASSMENT.

**hot blood** *n.* Same as HEAT OF PASSION.

**hot pursuit** *n.* Same as FRESH PURSUIT.

**house counsel** *n.* See under COUNSEL.

**HR-10 plan** *n.* See under RETIREMENT PLAN.

**hue and cry** *n.sing. English Legal History.* **1.** the outcry or clamor that anyone coming upon a felony or a person sought as a felon was under a duty to raise, so that the felon could be chased down.
**2.** the pursuit of a felon with loud outcries or clamor to give an alarm.

**hui** *n. Hawaii Law.* a traditional form of cooperative association by which land is owned and shared.

**hung jury** *n.* See under JURY. See also HANG[1].

**husband-wife privilege** *n.* Same as MARITAL PRIVILEGE.

**hypnotically refreshed recollection** *n.* See under RECOLLECTION; see also RECOVERED MEMORY.

**hypothecate** *v.,* **hypothecated, hypothecating.** to pledge property (either tangible or intangible) as collateral to secure a debt, especially without giving up possession of the property.
**—hypothecation** *n.*
**—hypothecator** *n.*

**hypothetical** *adj.* **1.** assumed for purposes of discussion: *hypothetical facts; hypothetical case.*
**2.** based upon or relating to facts assumed for purposes of discussion; see, e.g., *hypothetical question* (under QUESTION[1]).
**—***n.* **3.** *Informal.* (used especially in law schools) short for hypothetical case or *hypothetical question* (see under QUESTION[1]).
**—hypothetically** *adv.*

# I

**ICC** INTERNATIONAL CRIMINAL COURT.

**ICJ** INTERNATIONAL COURT OF JUSTICE.

**id.** *Latin.* (abbreviation for *idem,* lit. "the same one; the same thing") the case, statute, treatise, or other writing just mentioned; a term used for all but the first of a series of citations to the same source. For example, three successive references to an appellant's brief (the first two to page 25 and the third to page 27) might read: "Appellant's Brief at 25," "Id.," "See id. at 27."

**id est** See I.E.

**identification** *n.* **1.** the act or an instance of identifying; the state of being identified.
**2.** something that identifies a person, animal, or thing; for example, a passport or dog tag.
**3. cross-racial identification** identification of a person of one racial group by a person of another racial group. Studies have established that the unreliability of eyewitness identification (see note at EYEWITNESS) is even greater in the case of cross-racial identification.
**4. eyewitness identification** identification of a particular individual as the person who was seen in some specific situation previously, as in the commission of a crime. See also note at EYEWITNESS.

**identify** *v.,* **identified, identifying. 1.** to recognize or establish as being a particular person or thing: *The victim identified his attacker in the lineup. The witness identified the document as a memo that she had received from her supervisor.*
**2.** to determine or specify the identity of a person or thing: *The police say that they have identified a suspect. The attorney refused to identify her client to the media.*
**3.** to serve as a means of identification: *The license plates identified the car as belonging to the defendant.*
**4.** in connection with a contract for the sale of goods, to designate particular goods as those to which the contract refers.

**Identi-Kit** *n. Trademark.* a brand name for a kit containing drawings of hairlines, eyes, noses, chins, etc., in a wide variety of shapes and sizes, used by law-enforcement agencies to construct a composite picture of a suspect from descriptions provided by witnesses.

**identity theft** *n.* **1.** the fraudulent use of another person's identification documents, or of identifying information about another person such as that person's credit card numbers, social security number, birthday, or mother's maiden name, in order to pose as the other person without that person's knowledge and consent. Most often, the object is to exploit the other person's creditworthiness to make purchases or engage in other financial transactions for which the other person will get the bills.
**2.** obtaining, possessing, or transferring identifying documents or information about another person for fraudulent purposes.

**i.e.** (from Latin *id est,* lit. "that is") that is; that is to say; in other words: *The statute permits a partial class action, i.e., a class action on some of the issues in the case.* Cf. E.G.
——**Usage.** In older writing the Latin phrases *id est* ("that is") and *exempli gratia* ("for example") were often spelled out in full, but today they are almost always abbreviated. Unfortunately, although *i.e.* and *e.g.* are no more alike than *to* and *of,* they are often confused, and lawyers appear to be as prone to confusion in this regard as anyone else. In legal contexts, however,

it is especially important to be clear about what one is saying. For example, in one case a tenant sought reimbursement of about $35,000 for repairing a roof, under a lease clause that said, "The Landlord is responsible for structural repairs only, i.e., air-conditioning, boiler, wiring and utility replacements and plumbing." The court rejected the argument that the roofing job should be regarded as a structural repair, saying: "the plaintiff's misunderstanding the term, 'i.e.,' or his belief that the document should have read 'e.g.' is immaterial. The unambiguous language here is, 'i.e.'.... Construed according to its ordinary meaning, the 'i.e.' language of paragraph five limited the landlord's responsibility to air-conditioning, boiler, wiring, utility replacements and plumbing." *Wolff v. Mitwalli,* 1995 Conn. Super. LEXIS 1480 (1995). The lesson for lawyers and nonlawyers alike is clear: If you aren't sure which abbreviation is which, write "that is" or "for example."

**ignoramus** *Latin.* (lit. "we do not know") the word formerly endorsed by a grand jury on a proposed bill of indictment to indicate that insufficient evidence had been shown to warrant putting the accused on trial; equivalent to a finding of *no bill* (see under BILL).
——**History.** This legal term signifying lack of knowledge (of information sufficient to hold an accused person for trial) was used as the name of the title character—an ignorant lawyer—in a 1615 play criticizing the legal profession; from there the term spread into general English as a word for an ignorant person generally.

**ijma'** *n. Islamic Law.* the consensus of believers, and especially of Muslim scholars in the past, as to the rightness of a belief or practice. Ijma' is one of the four generally accepted sources of Islamic law and jurisprudence (see USUL AL-FIQH).

**ijtihad** *n. Islamic Law.* original thinking; the use of independent thinking and reason to arrive at conclusions as to what is or is not lawful in a situation not clearly covered by the KORAN, the SUNNA, or IJMA'.

——**History.** In the first three centuries of Islam, ijtihad, in the form of personal opinion expressed by Muslim scholars and sometimes based on QIYAS (reasoning by analogy from situations addressed by the Koran or other authorities), was an accepted source of Islamic law. In the Sunni branch of Islam, however, it is generally held that no further independent or personal opinion was needed or permissible after about the third century (which ended in the ninth century A.D.): It is said that "the gates of ijtihad were closed." Qiyas remains, however, as one of the four accepted sources of Islamic jurisprudence (see USUL AL-FIQH), and from time to time reformers have argued that some broader use of ijtihad could be helpful in dealing with contemporary problems. In addition, the minority Shi'a branch of Islam has never accepted the principle that the doors to ijtihad are closed, and in Iran, an overwhelmingly Shi'ite nation, the powerful class of clerics known as mujtahids at least theoretically possess the authority to exercise such judgment.

**illegal** *adj.* contrary to law.
——**illegally** *adv.*
——**Usage.** This term is usually applied to conduct that is criminal or directly contrary to a specific statute or court order, or to a person engaged in such conduct. See, e.g., *illegal alien* (under ALIEN); *illegal discrimination* (under DISCRIMINATION). Cf. the more general term UNLAWFUL.

**illegality** *n., pl.* **illegalities. 1.** the condition or quality of being illegal.
**2.** an illegal act or practice.

**illegitimacy** *n.* **1.** the state or quality of being ILLEGITIMATE.
**2.** in particular, the state of being an illegitimate child, a child born out of wedlock.
——**History.** At common law the child born out of wedlock was regarded as *filius nullius*—son of no one. A BASTARD, as the term then was, having (by LEGAL FICTION) no father, could inherit nothing and could have no expectation of being supported. This status changed dramatically in the twentieth century

and remains in flux. For purposes of EQUAL PROTECTION analysis, laws treating people differently on the basis of their legitimacy or illegitimacy are now regarded by the Supreme Court as requiring HEIGHTENED SCRUTINY. In practice what this means is that it is very hard to predict whether such a law will be upheld or struck down. See also QUASI-SUSPECT CLASSIFICATION.

**illegitimate** adj., n., v., **illegitimated, illegitimating.** —adj. **1.** born out of wedlock; born of parents who are not married to each other.
**2.** not sanctioned by law or custom; improper; spurious.
—n. **3.** one who is illegitimate; a person born out of wedlock.
—v. **4.** to confer the status of an illegitimate child upon one seemingly legitimate, as by a husband's disavowal of paternity.
See also PRESUMPTION OF PATERNITY.
—**illegitimately** adv.
—**illegitimation** n.

**illegitimatize** v., **illegitimatized, illegitimatizing.** to ILLEGITIMATE.

**illicit** adj. **1.** not legally permitted or authorized; unlicensed; unlawful.
**2.** disapproved of or not permitted for moral or ethical reasons.
—**illicitly** adv.
—**illicitness** n.

**illusory** adj. seeming; deceptive; not real; not legally effective.

**illusory contract** n. See under CONTRACT.

**illusory promise** n. See under PROMISE.

**immaterial** adj. not MATERIAL. See, for example, immaterial breach (under BREACH); immaterial variance (under VARIANCE).
—**immateriality** n.
—**immaterially** adv.

**immateriality** n. **immaterialities. 1.** the state or character of being immaterial.
**2.** something that is immaterial.

**immediate annuity** n. See under ANNUITY.

**immigrant** n. a person who enters a country intending to reside there permanently.

**immigration** n. the entry of people into a country for the purpose of establishing permanent residence. The Supreme Court has interpreted the Constitution as conferring upon Congress virtually unlimited power to regulate immigration into the United States.
—**immigrate** v., **immigrated, immigrating.**

**immovable** adj. **1.** fixed in place; intended to be a permanent part of fixed property.
—n. **2.** Usually, **immovables.** Same as immovable property (see under PROPERTY).

**immune** adj. having immunity; exempt from a legal obligation or responsibility by reason of an immunity.

**immunity** n., pl. **immunities. 1.** exemption from a legal duty, responsibility, or liability.
**2.** especially, exemption from civil suit or criminal prosecution for allegedly wrongful acts, granted by law to certain classes of persons or by prosecutorial discretion to certain individuals, either by constitutional mandate or for reasons of public policy. In most cases the exemption is unqualified **(absolute immunity),** but sometimes it applies only if the wrongful acts were done in the good-faith (albeit erroneous) belief that they were legally justified **(qualified immunity).**
**3. diplomatic immunity** immunity from civil and criminal liability granted to foreign diplomats by the United States and most or all other countries.
**4. judicial immunity** immunity from tort liability for any official act of a judge within the scope of judicial functions.
**5. legislative immunity** constitutionally granted immunity from tort liability, and to a limited extent from criminal liability, for acts by members of Congress and their aides in carrying out legislative functions, including particularly the absolute right to speak freely in House and Senate debates without

fear of liability for defamation. State legislators generally enjoy similar immunity.

**6. official immunity** a general term for immunity of governmental officials of all sorts from liability for acts within the scope of their duties. Such immunity may be absolute or qualified, depending upon the official and the nature of the alleged wrong.

**7. sovereign immunity** the traditional immunity of the government itself from any suit at all—derived from the notion that "the king can do no wrong." The federal government and most states now have statutes permitting the assertion of most tort and contract claims against them. In addition, in certain kinds of cases sovereign immunity can be circumvented by seeking an injunction against a specific state officer rather than against the state itself.

**8. transactional immunity** immunity granted by a prosecutor to a witness, guaranteeing that the witness will not be prosecuted in connection with any event ("transaction") testified about. A witness who has been granted such immunity cannot refuse to testify on the basis of the Fifth Amendment privilege against SELF-INCRIMINATION. Cf. *use immunity.*

**9. use immunity** immunity granted by a prosecutor to a witness, guaranteeing that neither the witness's testimony nor any information derived from it will be used in any future prosecution against the witness. Although this does not preclude prosecution of the witness for involvement in the events testified about, any such case must be based entirely upon independently derived evidence. Therefore, like *transactional immunity,* use immunity makes it impossible for a witness to claim a Fifth Amendment privilege not to testify.

**immunize** *v.,* **immunized, immunizing.** to confer immunity upon; grant immunity to. Especially, to grant *transactional immunity* or *use immunity* (see both under IMMUNITY) to a witness in a criminal matter so as to obtain the witness's testimony.
—**immunization** *n.*

**impair** *v.* to diminsh; make worse; diminish the value of.
—**impairment** *n.*

**impanel** *v.,* **impaneled, impaneling** or (*esp. Brit.*) **impanelled, impanelling.** to select and seat the jury for a case. Also, **empanel.**

**impartial** *adj.* unbiased; objective; fair.
—**impartiality** *n.*
—**impartially** *adv.*

**impeachment** *n.* **1.** the instituting of formal misconduct charges against a government officer as a basis for removal from office. Under the Constitution, the House of Representatives has exclusive power to impeach federal officers, including the President, which it does by voting for ARTICLES OF IMPEACHMENT. A trial is then held in the Senate, and if convicted of an impeachable offense by the Senate, the officer may be removed from office. See also HIGH CRIMES AND MISDEMEANORS. **2.** the introduction of evidence calling into question the credibility of a witness; for example, a *prior inconsistent statement* (see under STATEMENT), evidence of interest (see INTEREST[2]) or bias; evidence that the witness has been convicted of crimes involving dishonesty; or simply evidence contradicting the witness's testimony. This is referred to as "impeaching the credibility of the witness," or simply "impeaching the witness." See also *hostile witness* and *interested witness* (both under WITNESS). Cf. REHABILITATION.
—**impeach** *v.*
—**impeachability** *n.*
—**impeachable** *adj.*

**impediment** *n.* a legal bar; especially a circumstance rendering one legally incapable of making a contract or entering into a legal relationship. For example, being underage is an impediment to marriage.

**impersonation** *n.* pretending to be someone else; passing or attempting to pass oneself off either as a specific other person (e.g., by voting in the name of another or using another's credit card) or as a person with authority or credentials that one personally

lacks (e.g., pretending to be a police officer or a doctor). When done for unlawful purposes, impersonation is a crime in itself; it is also a frequent component of many crimes and some torts. Also called **personation, false impersonation, false personation.**
—**impersonate** v., **impersonated, impersonating.**
—**impersonator** n.
——**Usage.** Although the addition of the word *false* can be used to distinguish unlawful from lawful impersonation (see FALSE, def. 3), most discussions of impersonation (also called *personation*) in legal contexts have to do with unlawful conduct, even if the adjective is omitted. Of the four listed terms meaning the same thing, *impersonation* is the most common and also the most likely to be used with a noncriminal meaning (e.g., an impersonation contest at a shopping mall). In criminal contexts, *false personation* is the second most common term; *personation* and *false impersonation*, though by no means rare, are less common.

**impertinent** adj. not pertinent to the case at hand. A court may order impertinent matter stricken from a pleading so that a party will not have to respond to allegations that have no place in the case.
—**impertinence, impertinency** n.
—**impertinently** adv.
——**False Friend.** Testimony can be impertinent without being rude, and rude without being impertinent: In law, the term *impertinent* is usually used in its earlier sense of "not pertinent" rather than in its usual modern sense of "presumptuous, rude, uncivil."

**implead** v., **impleaded, impleading.** to serve a complaint on a third party alleging that the third party should be held liable for all or part of any damages one is required to pay in a lawsuit; that is, to initiate a *third-party action* (see under THIRD PARTY): *The injured pedestrian sued the driver of the car, and the driver impleaded the auto mechanic, claiming that the accident was caused by the mechanic's poor* work on the car's brakes.
—**impleadable** adj.

**impleader** n. the act of impleading and the procedures for third-party actions. See note at DEMURRER.

**implied** adj. **1.** suggested by conduct or circumstances rather than explicitly stated; describing a right, interest, obligation, authority, or status recognized by law even though not put into words—and perhaps not even intended—by the parties involved; opposite of EXPRESS. See *implied assumpsit* (under ASSUMPSIT); *implied contract* (under CONTRACT); *implied repeal* (under REPEAL); *implied right of action* (under RIGHT OF ACTION).
**2.** Also, **implied in fact.** inferred from what a person has said or done; recognized by law because evidently reflecting a party's actual intent, even though nothing was specifically said about it. See *implied authority* (under AUTHORITY[1]); *implied waiver* (under WAIVER); and *contract implied in fact* (under CONTRACT).
**3.** Also, **implied in law.** imposed by law without regard to the intent of the parties; CONSTRUCTIVE. In essence, this means that in the eyes of the law, if the parties did not intend a certain result, they should have. See *implied warranty* (under WARRANTY); *contract implied in law* (under CONTRACT).
—**impliedly** adv.

**implied-in-fact contract** n. See under CONTRACT.

**implied-in-law contract** n. See under CONTRACT.

**imply** v., **implied, implying.** to impose an obligation or status, or declare it to exist, by operation of law: *The law implies duty of good faith in all contracts. The judge implied a contract to pay for life-saving medical treatment given while the defendant was unconscious, even though the defendant's intent was to commit suicide.*

**impossibility** n., pl. **impossibilities. 1.** inability to carry out a contract because of the occurrence of an unforeseen circumstance rendering performance in

accordance with the terms of the contract impossible. For example, a building to be rented might burn down, or a transaction to be completed might be made illegal, or the person whose services were contracted for might die. Under modern principles of contract law, further performance of the contract is usually excused in such cases (that is, the party whose performance became impossible will not have to pay damages for breach of contract), so long as this would not be unfair to the other party. Cf. IMPRACTICABILITY.
**2.** the condition of being impossible.
**3.** something that is impossible.

**impossible** adj. **1.** not possible; incapable of existing or being done.
**2.** not permitted by law: *It was impossible for the bank to turn over the funds because the bank had been served with a restraining order.*
Cf. IMPRACTICABLE.

**impost** n. a tax; especially a duty on goods imported from another country.

**impostor** n. a person who practices deception by posing as someone else or posing as something that he is not.

**impound** v. to take property into custody of a court or law enforcement agency for such purposes as testing, use as evidence, possible forfeiture, or holding pending a decision as to its proper disposition.
—**impoundable** adj.
—**impoundment** n.

**impracticability** n., pl. **impracticabilities. 1.** Also called **commercial impracticability.** practical inability to perform a contract because of an unforeseen circumstance that renders performance in accordance with its terms far more difficult and expensive than either party had reason to expect when the contract was entered into. Except in limited circumstances (notably contracts for the sale of goods), the law generally does not recognize impracticability as providing an excuse for nonperformance of a contract. Cf. IMPOSSIBILITY.
**2.** something that is impracticable, or a fact that renders something impracticable.

**impracticable** adj. not reasonably possible; not capable of being done without undue effort and expenditure; not economically feasible. Cf. IMPOSSIBLE.

**impress** v. **1.** to impose; especially, to impose a *constructive trust* (see under TRUST) upon property; that is, to deem or declare property in the hands of one person to be held, as a matter of equity, in trust for another: *The judge impressed a trust on the property obtained by fraud. Equity deems misdelivered property to be impressed with a trust for the benefit of the intended recipient.*
**2.** to force into military service, especially as a sailor. Britain's policy of impressing men seized from American ships into service in the British Navy was a cause of the War of 1812.
**3.** to seize for public or royal use.
—**impressment** n.

**impression** n. See FIRST IMPRESSION.

**imprison** v. **1.** to place or keep a person in jail or prison as punishment for a crime. Cf. DETAIN.
**2.** to confine; to restrict the movement of. See FALSE IMPRISONMENT.
—**imprisonable** adj.
—**imprisonment** n.

**improvement** n. a permanent change in real property that increases its value, prolongs its useful life, or adapts it to a new use, and is more than a repair or maintenance.
—**improve** v., **improved, improving.**

**improvident** adj. unwise, ill-considered, or based upon inadequate information. A term often used by courts in explaining a change of mind: *The injunction is vacated as improvidently granted.*
—**improvidently** adv.

**improvident exercise of discretion** n. Same as ABUSE OF DISCRETION.

**imputation** n. **1.** the act of imputing something to someone.
**2.** an allegation or accusation of fault or wrongdoing.

**impute** *v.*, **imputed, imputing.** to attribute or ascribe (a quality or characteristic to someone or something), especially by operation of law.
—**imputable** *adj.*

**imputed** *adj.* describing something attributed to a person by operation of law, often because of that person's relationship to a person more directly involved in a matter under consideration, as in the case of negligence of a driver imputed under the law of many states to the owner of the vehicle, or knowledge of an employee imputed to the employer. See also *imputed income* (under INCOME); *imputed interest* (under INTEREST³); *imputed knowledge* (under KNOWLEDGE); *imputed negligence* (under NEGLIGENCE).

**in absentia** *Latin.* (lit. "in absence") in (his, her, or their) absence; in the absence of the defendant(s): *The conspirators fled the country after being found guilty and were sentenced in absentia.*

**in bank** or **in banc** Same as EN BANC.

**in bar** See under BAR¹.

**in being** in existence; alive. See *life in being* (under PERPETUITY).

**in blank** describing an indorsement that does not specify a particular *indorsee* (see under INDORSE). See also *blank indorsement* (under INDORSEMENT).

**in bond** See under BOND².

**in camera** *Latin.* (lit. "in the chamber") (of judicial business or proceedings) in private; not in open court. Usually referring to something that takes place in CHAMBERS, in the ROBING ROOM, or in a courtroom from which spectators have been excluded: *The judge met with the lawyers in camera. The judge ordered that the disputed documents be submitted to her for in camera inspection.*

**in chief** principal; first in order; highest-ranking. See *case in chief* (under CASE²); *evidence in chief* (under EVIDENCE); *examination in chief* (under EXAMINATION).

**in common** signifying ownership of an interest in property by two or more people or entities with *undivided interests* (see under INTEREST¹) in the whole, responsibility for expenses and a right to profits from the property in proportion to their interests, and no RIGHT OF SURVIVORSHIP. For example, one co-owner might own a one-half undivided interest in an apartment building while two others each own a one-fourth interest; upon the death of one, that owner's interest would pass to her heirs or to a taker designated in her will, instead of vesting in the surviving co-owners as in the case of joint ownership or ownership by the entirety: *estate in common; ownership in common; tenancy in common; tenant in common.* See also *unity of possession* (under UNITY). See also IN COPARCENARY. Cf. BY THE ENTIRETY; JOINT; IN SEVERALTY; COMMUNITY PROPERTY.

**in contemplation of death** on account of impending death, or deemed by law to be so. See *gift in contemplation of death* (under GIFT).

**in coparcenary** signifying ownership of an interest in property by two or more individuals who inherited the property jointly under laws of intestacy. Each of the co-owners is called a **parcener** or, more frequently, **coparcener.** For modern-day purposes, an estate in coparcenary amounts to the same thing as an estate IN COMMON: Each coparcener has an undivided fractional interest in the property with no right of survivorship. Also called **in parcenary** or, rarely, **in coparceny.**
—**History.** In England, the PRIMOGENITURE that predominated as a system of inheritance assured that coparceners would almost always be women; for under that system an estate in coparcenary could only arise when, for lack of a male heir to take the entire estate, property fell to two or more daughters, sisters, or other female relatives of the decedent. In America, although the concept of descent and ownership in coparcenary found its way into many state statutes where it is still found today, it is treated as just a special case of ownership IN COMMON.

**in custodia legis** *Latin.* (lit. "in the

custody of the law") in the custody of the court; held by an officer of the court pursuant to a judicial order. Said of property that is kept under the control of a court pending the outcome of litigation over it.

**in equity 1.** under or pursuant to principles historically applicable in courts of EQUITY, as distinguished from courts of law (see LAW, def. 4); concerned with equity; before a court of equity. See also *action in equity* (under ACTION); *relief in equity* (under REMEDY); *suit in equity* (under SUIT). Cf. AT LAW; IN LAW.
**2.** in fairness; as a matter of justice as between two or more people without regard to specific legal principles.

**in escrow** See under ESCROW.

**in esse** *Latin.* in being; existing at the time under consideration. See example under IN POSSE.

**in evidence 1.** (of an EXHIBIT) admitted by the judge into evidence: *Exhibits 1 and 3 are in evidence; Exhibit 2 is not.*
**2.** describing a fact for which testimony or other evidence has been introduced that, if believed, establishes the fact: *That the defendant owned a gun is already in evidence.*

**in fact** in reality; in accordance with the actual intent of the parties or the actual evidence; not resulting solely from legal presumptions or fictions. See also ATTORNEY IN FACT; *contract implied in fact* (under CONTRACT); *implied in fact* (under IMPLIED). Cf. IN LAW.

**in flagrante delicto** *Latin.* (lit. "in flagrant wrongdoing") in the very act of committing the offense or wrongful act: *The night watchman discovered the burglars in flagrante delicto.*
——**Usage.** The Latin phrases FLAGRANTE DELICTO and *in flagrante delicto* are different grammatical constructions for saying the same thing. The latter is more like an English construction, and probably for that reason is more common. The Latin word *flagrante* (ablative of *flagrans*) originally meant "burning," and the continued popularity of this particular Latin expression may be due in part to the lack

of a common English word that so neatly combines the concepts of "in process, ongoing," "visible, obvious," and "in the heat of the moment; hotly engaged in the wrongful activity." This combination of meanings is especially fitting in the single most common application of the phrase, describing the circumstance in which an adulterous spouse is discovered with his or her paramour "in flagrante delicto."

**in force** (of a law or rule) in operation; legally effective.

**in forma pauperis** *Latin.* (lit. "in the character of a poor person") a method of proceeding in court under which filing fees and certain other requirements, such as the filing of multiple copies of printed briefs, are waived for indigent litigants. In certain situations indigent parties have a constitutional right to proceed in forma pauperis, but in most civil cases (including, ironically, petitions for bankruptcy) they do not.

**in futuro** *Latin.* in the future; taking effect at a future date. Cf. IN PRAESENTI.

**in haec verba** *Latin.* (lit. "in these words") using exactly the same words; verbatim: *The court's opinion sets forth the allegedly indecent material in haec verba.*

**in house 1.** (of a company's legal work) within or handled within an organization by lawyers and paralegals who are salaried employees of the company, rather than by an outside lawyer or law firm: *We saved money by drafting the brief in house.*
**2. in-house** designating such work or the lawyers who do it: *an in-house project; the in-house staff.*
See also *in-house counsel* (under COUNSEL).

**in kind 1.** (referring to a payment) made in goods or services rather than money. See also BARTER.
**2.** not the same, but of the same kind. For example, a neighbor who borrows a cup of sugar for baking will return it in kind—that is, will return a similar cup of sugar but not the same sugar that was borrowed.

**in law 1.** by reason of law; as a result of application of legal principles, assumptions, or fictions: *A child born in wedlock is usually deemed in law to be the legitimate child of the husband, even if the husband was away at sea when the child was conceived.* See also AS A MATTER OF LAW; BY OPERATION OF LAW; *implied in law* (under IMPLIED); *contract implied in law* (under CONTRACT). Cf. IN FACT.
**2.** (occasionally) Same as AT LAW: *The Constitution states that the judicial power of the United States "shall extend to all Cases, in Law and Equity, arising under this Constitution...."* Cf. IN EQUITY.

**in-law** *n.* a relative by marriage. Cf. INLAW.

**in limine** *Latin.* (lit. "at the threshold") at the outset; at the beginning of a case or proceeding. See also MOTION IN LIMINE.

**in loco parentis** *Latin.* (lit. "in the position of a parent") describing a person or institution that has assumed, at least for some purposes, the rights and responsibilities of a parent toward a child: *For the purpose of consenting to emergency treatment when the parents could not be located, the school acted in loco parentis.*

**in pais** *Law French.* (lit. "in the country; in the countryside") **1.** out of court; without judicial process.
**2.** without writing; by act or conduct rather than by written deed.

**in parcenary** Same as IN COPARCENARY.

**in pari delicto** *Latin.* (lit. "in equal fault") **1.** a defense sometimes available in a civil case, in which it is argued that the plaintiff should not be permitted to complain of wrongful conduct by the defendant because the plaintiff's conduct in the matter was equally wrongful; it applies particularly to situations in which the plaintiff and defendant were involved together in some unlawful activity.
**2.** describing participants in a crime whose roles make them guilty in the same degree: *The person who robbed*

the bank and the person who stood watch during the robbery are in pari delicto.

**in pari materia** *Latin.* (lit. "in regard to the same matter") referring to statutes, passages of a contract, clauses of an instrument, or the like that deal with the same matter. In general, writings that are in pari materia are to be construed to the extent possible as consistent with each other, each being interpreted in light of the other.

**in personam** *Latin.* (lit. "directed at the person") describing the fundamental nature of a legal proceeding as focused on a person or entity rather than a piece of property. For details, see *in personam action* (under ACTION); *in personam judgment* (under JUDGMENT); *in personam jurisdiction* (under JURISDICTION[1]). See also *actio in personam* (under ACTIO). Cf. IN REM, QUASI IN REM.

**in point** Same as ON POINT. See also *case in point* (under CASE[1]).

**in posse** *Latin.* (lit. "in potentiality") potential; not yet existing at the time under discussion. *The term "grandchildren" in the will was interpreted as meaning grandchildren in esse and in posse* (i.e., not only grandchildren existing at the time of the testator's death but also any future grandchildren). Cf. IN ESSE.

**in praesenti** *Latin.* in the present; effective immediately, Cf. IN FUTURO.

**in propria persona** *Latin.* (lit. "in one's own person") **1.** personally; in person.
**2.** especially, acting in a judicial proceeding in person rather than through counsel; PRO SE. Abbreviated **in pro. per.**

**in re** *Latin.* in the matter of. This introductory phrase appears in certain case names; it is also used in citations as a concise substitute for such introductory phrases as "petition of" and "application of." Thus a case captioned "Petition of John J. Smith for a Writ of Habeas Corpus" would most likely be cited as "In re Smith." See also IN THE MATTER OF.

**in rem** *Latin.* (lit. "directed at the thing") describing the fundamental character of a legal proceeding as focused on a piece of property (real or personal, tangible or intangible) or occasionally on a legal relationship (e.g., a marriage), rather than on a particular person or entity. For details, see *in rem action* (under ACTION); *in rem judgment* (under JUDGMENT); *in rem jurisdiction* (under JURISDICTION[1]). See also *actio in rem* (under ACTIO). Cf. IN PERSONAM, QUASI IN REM.

**in severalty** signifying ownership of an interest in property by one person or entity only, with no co-owners: *estate in severalty; ownership in severalty; tenancy in severalty; tenant in severalty.* Cf. JOINT; BY THE ENTIRETY; IN COMMON; IN COPARCENARY. See also COMMUNITY PROPERTY.

**in specie** *Latin.* (lit. "in kind") **1.** in kind; in original form: *Some of the decedent's personal belongings were distributed to the heirs in specie; the rest were sold and the proceeds distributed.*
**2.** of the kind or in the manner specified: *performance of the contract in specie.*
**3.** (of money) in coin.

**in statu quo** *Latin.* (lit. "in the position in which") **1.** in the state in which things are at present: *to leave the situation in statu quo.*
**2.** Also, **in statu quo ante** (with *ante*, "before"). in the state in which things were previously: *to put the situation in statu quo (ante).*
See also STATUS QUO.
——**Usage.** The best practice is to confine *in statu quo* to references to the current state of affairs, and use *in statu quo ante* when referring to the previous state of affairs.

**in suit** *adj.* involved in the suit; that is the subject of the suit: *The property in suit is located in the town of Springfield. The judge refused to allow the requested discovery because it did not pertain to the matters in suit.*

**in terrorem** *Latin.* (lit. "for the purpose of fear") as a threat or warning; done to instill caution or fear: *Supporters of the death penalty believe that it operates in terrorem to deter crime. The sign "Shoplifters will be prosecuted!" is posted for its in terrorem effect.*

**in terrorem clause** *n.* a clause in a will, legally enforceable in some states, that nullifies any bequest to a beneficiary who unsuccessfully contests the will. The purpose is to discourage will contests by those who receive less than they think fair under the will.

**in the matter of** an introductory phrase in certain case names, often shortened to **matter of** or IN RE in citations.

**in toto** *Latin.* (lit. "in the entirety") completely; in its entirety; as a whole: *The statute was repealed in toto.*

**in trust** See under TRUST.

**inadmissible** *adj.* (of evidence) not ADMISSIBLE.
—**inadmissibly** *adv.*
—**inadmissibility** *n.*

**inadmissible alien** *n.* See under ALIEN.

**inalienable** *adj.* **1.** not capable of being sold or given to another; nontransferable: *inalienable property; an inalienable interest.*
**2.** not capable of being taken away: *inalienable rights.*
See also note at UNALIENABLE.
—**inalienability** *n.*
—**inalienably** *adv.*

**inapposite** *adj.* (of a precedent or an analogous case) not pertinent; different from the case at hand in some respect that makes it inapplicable to the determination of the issue under consideration; *distinguishable* (see under DISTINGUISH).

**Inc.** Abbreviation for INCORPORATED in company names.

**incapacity** *n.* the absence of legal CAPACITY to perform an act; for example, if a party to a marriage is underage or already married, the marriage will be void on the ground of incapacity.

**incarcerate** *v.*, **incarcerated, incarcerating.** to imprison; confine.
—**incarceration** *n.*

**incest** *n.* the crime of having sexual intercourse, or living as husband and wife, with a close relative, such as a parent, child, or sibling. The exact list of prohibited relationships varies from state to state.
—**incestuous** *adj.*
—**incestuously** *adv.*
—**incestuousness** *n.*

**inchoate** *adj.* incipient; commenced but not yet completed or matured; unformed. See for example *inchoate lien* (under LIEN). Cf. INCHOATE CRIME.
—**inchoately** *adv.*
—**inchoateness** *n.*

**inchoate crime** *n.* a crime that is preliminary to another crime. The crimes so classified are ATTEMPT, CONSPIRACY, and SOLICITATION. Also called **inchoate offense; anticipatory crime; anticipatory offense.**
——**False Friend.** An "inchoate crime" is not inchoate in the usual sense of being unformed or unfinished: It is a completed crime and fully punishable. The term "inchoate" is applied, rather confusingly, only because the *ultimate* crime for which the anticipatory offense constituted a preliminary step need not have been completed.

**incident** *n.* **1.** something appertaining or attaching to something else; a feature, characteristic, or concomitant: *The use of the White House as a residence is an incident of office of the President of the United States.*
**2.** something that occurs in connection with something else but not as a necessary component or accompaniment: *An unfortunate incident of the battle was the accidental sinking of a friendly vessel.*
**3.** an occurrence or event: *The incident was reported to the police.*
—*adj.* **4.** pertaining; occurring in connection with: *the rules for a search incident to arrest.*

**incident of ownership** *n.* **1.** a right belonging to the owner of a particular type of property or property interest:

*The right to use common areas is an incident of ownership of a condominium unit.*
**2.** an indicium of ownership; especially, any right associated with ownership of a life insurance policy. The presence or absence of incidents of ownership are used as indicators in determining whether a decedent was the owner of a particular life insurance policy, the value of which must therefore be included in the decedent's estate for estate tax purposes. For example, if one retains the right to designate the beneficiary of a policy purportedly given to one's child, one has retained an important incident of ownership.

**incidental** *adj.* **1.** Same as INCIDENT (def. 4).
**2.** incurred or brought into being in connection with or in addition to something else: *incidental expenses.* See also *incidental beneficiary* (under BENEFICIARY); *incidental damages* (under DAMAGES).
—*n.* **3. incidentals** minor expenses; unitemized expenses associated with a trip, project, or the like.
—**incidentally** *adv.*
—**incidentalness** *n.*

**included offense** *n.* See LESSER INCLUDED OFFENSE.

**inclusionary zoning** *n.* See under ZONING.

**income** *n.* **1.** money received, or the value of property or services received.
**2. earned income** income derived from working for another **(wages)** or in one's own business **(self-employment income).** Cf. *unearned income.*
**3. gross income** total income potentially subject to income tax and required to be reported on an income tax return, before subtraction of any deductions.
**4. imputed income** a sum of money that a taxpayer is deemed for tax purposes to have received as taxable income from a transaction even though the transaction was structured or carried out in such a way that the amount in question did not actually flow to the taxpayer.

**5. net income** in a business, the excess of total income over expenses; profit.

**6. ordinary income** income subject to taxation at ordinary rates; that is, all income reportable on income tax returns except *capital gain* (see under CAPITAL[1]), which is subject to special lower tax rates.

**7. taxable income a.** any type of income subject to income tax; e.g., wages or alimony, but not gifts (usually) or child support. **b.** the portion of a taxpayer's income upon which income tax is based, consisting of *gross income* minus DEDUCTIONS.

**8. unearned income** income derived from investments and other sources other than employment or self-employment. Cf. *earned income.*

**9. unrelated business income** income received by a tax-exempt organization from business activities unrelated to the organization's religious, charitable, educational, or similar purpose. Unrelated business income is taxable.

**income in respect of a decedent** *n.* income earned by an individual who dies before the income is due to be paid, so that it actually goes to the individual's estate or heirs. For income tax purposes, such income is not included in the final tax return for the decedent, but is instead taxed to the actual recipient.

**income splitting** *n.* allocation of the total income of a couple or group in equal portions to each of its members for income tax purposes, so that the income is taxed at the lowest possible marginal rate. Partnership income is often split among the individual partners in this way, and the Internal Revenue Code treats the income of a married couple filing jointly this way. See note at MARRIAGE BONUS.

**income tax** a federal, state, or local tax on the annual INCOME of an individual or married couple **(personal income tax),** a corporation **(corporate income tax),** or a trust or estate. See also *capital gains tax* (under CAPITAL[1]); *flat tax* and *progressive tax* (under TAX); *marginal tax rate* and *effective tax rate* (under TAX RATE); MARRIAGE BONUS; MARRIAGE PENALTY; and note at DIRECT TAX.

**incompetent** *adj.* **1.** not competent (see COMPETENT[1] and COMPETENT[2]).
—*n.* **2.** an individual who is not mentally competent (see COMPETENT[1]): *a law protecting infants and incompetents.*
—**incompetence, incompetency** *n.*
—**incompetently** *adv.*

**inconsistent statement** *n.* See *prior inconsistent statement* (under STATEMENT).

**inconsistent verdict** *n.* See under VERDICT.

**incontestability clause** *n.* a clause in an insurance policy, especially a life insurance policy, providing that the insurance company may not contest the validity of the policy on the ground of fraud or mistake once the policy has been in force for a set period of time, such as two years. Such clauses are typically required by state law so that insurers cannot collect premiums indefinitely and then, when the time comes to pay under the policy, claim that the policy is invalid. Also called **noncontestability clause.**

**inconvenient forum** *n.* See under FORUM NON CONVENIENS.

**incorporate** *v.,* **incorporated, incorporating. 1.** to organize as a corporation; to attain the status of a corporation by going through the formalities required by state law.
**2.** to include as a part of: *Please incorporate these changes and additions into a revised draft of the legislation.*
**3. incorporate by reference** to include all or part of one writing in another, not by physically reproducing the first in the second but simply by referring to the first in the second. For example, an insurance policy on certain property might state that a particular appraiser's report is deemed to be a part of the policy and to establish the

value of the insured property, or a contract or statute might declare that certain words used shall have the same meanings they were given in a previous contract or another statute.
—**incorporation** n.

**incorporated** adj. **1.** formed as a corporation. This word (or its abbreviation, **Inc.**) in an entity's name indicates that the entity is a corporation; not all corporate names include this word, however.
**2.** combined in one body; included.

**incorporation doctrine** n. the principle by which most of the BILL OF RIGHTS, which originally operated only as a limitation on the power of the federal government, has been made binding upon state governments as well.
——**History.** The key to the process of incorporation is the Fourteenth Amendment to the Constitution, which was adopted after the Civil War and provided, for the first time, that no *state* may deprive any person of life, liberty, or property without DUE PROCESS of law. Over time, the Supreme Court decided that most of the protections in the Bill of Rights—including both procedural protections (such as the right to a jury trial in criminal cases) and substantive rights (such as the right to speak one's mind or practice one's religion)—are inherent in the concept of due process, and hence protected from state governmental interference by the due process clause of the Fourteenth Amendment. Thus almost the entire Bill of Rights was ultimately "incorporated" or "absorbed" into the Fourteenth Amendment.

**incorporeal hereditament** n. See under HEREDITAMENT.

**incriminate** v., **incriminated, incriminating.** to provide or serve as evidence or proof of involvement in a crime: *The witness incriminated his business partners. The DNA evidence incriminated the defendant.* See also SELF-INCRIMINATION.
—**incrimination** n.
—**incriminator** n.
—**incriminating, incriminatory** adj.

**indebitatus assumpsit** n. *Latin.* (lit. "being indebted, he undertook") **1.** a common law FORM OF ACTION employed for the collection of a debt.
**2.** a common law form of action for recovery on a contract implied in fact or in law; same as *general assumpsit* (see under ASSUMPSIT).
——**History.** The *indebitatus assumpsit* was but one form of action, a branch of ASSUMPSIT. It took on increasing functions as it evolved, however, ranging from recovery of fixed sums of money owed (supplanting the earlier but less flexible action of DEBT) to recovery for QUASI CONTRACT when there was no actual agreement at all. See also COMMON COUNTS.

**indecent** adj. offensive to generally accepted standards of propriety in matters relating to sex, bodily functions, and display of the human body.
—**indecency** n.
—**indecently** adv.

**indecent assault** n. See under ASSAULT.

**indecent exposure** n. the crime of exposing one's genitals under circumstances likely to cause alarm or offense.

**indecent speech** n. See under SPEECH.

**indefeasible** adj. not DEFEASIBLE.
—**indefeasibility** n.
—**indefeasibly** adv.

**indefinite** adj. **1.** not fixed or certain.
**2.** (of a contract) not sufficiently certain to be enforceable. If the material terms of a purported contract are so indefinite that a court cannot reasonably ascertain who is to do what, the contract "fails for indefiniteness." See also FAIL.
—**indefiniteness** n.

**indefinite failure of issue** n. See under ISSUE².

**indefinite sentence** n. See under SENTENCE.

**indemnifier** n. Same as INDEMNITOR.

**indemnify** v., **indemnified, indemnifying.** to compensate or reimburse a person for loss or liability, or agree to do so if a loss or liability arises in the

future.
—**indemnifiable** *adj.*

**indemnitee** *n.* one who is protected by a right of indemnity; the person indemnified.

**indemnitor** *n.* one who is obligated, by contract or by operation of law, to indemnify another; an individual or company that gives indemnity. Sometimes, less formally, **indemnifier.**

**indemnity** *n.*, *pl.* **indemnities. 1.** a right to receive compensation for a loss from someone other than a wrongdoer who caused the loss, or to receive reimbursement for a payment that one has had to make to someone else to compensate that other person for a loss.
**2.** a payment made, or the compensation or reimbursement received, pursuant to a right of indemnity.
——**Note.** A right of indemnity can arise in two ways: (a) by contract. An insurance policy is a contract by which the insurance company agrees (for consideration in the form of payment of premiums) to indemnify the insured against losses or liabilities specified in the policy. (b) by operation of law. In certain situations a person held liable for a tort is entitled to indemnity from another tortfeasor regarded as more directly at fault. For example, if the owner of a car is held liable under state law for injury caused by negligence of the driver, or an employer is held liable for the tort of an employee under the doctrine of RESPONDEAT SUPERIOR, the owner or employer is entitled to reimbursement from the driver or employee whose tortious conduct actually caused the injury.

**indemnity bond** *n.* See under BOND².

**indemnity insurance** *n.* insurance that protects the insured against injury or loss suffered by the insured directly, as distinguished from losses to others for which the insured might be held liable. For example, automobile collision insurance is a form of indemnity insurance that compensates the insured for damage to his own automobile in an accident. Cf. LIABILITY INSURANCE.

**indenture** *n.* **1.** an old term for a deed or written contract, especially one under seal (see SEAL¹).
**2.** Also called **trust indenture.** an instrument stating the terms and conditions governing an issue of bonds, setting forth the rights of bondholders and providing various measures for the protection of those rights, including appointment of a trustee to handle necessary transfers of money and to look out for the interests of bondholders.

**independent** *adj.* free, or at least relatively free, from control by others; autonomous. See *independent contractor* (under CONTRACTOR); *independent counsel* (under COUNSEL); *independent prosecutor* (under PROSECUTOR); *independent union* (under UNION).

**independent public accountant** *n.* Same as *public accountant* (see under ACCOUNTANT).

**indeterminate sentence** *n.* See under SENTENCE.

**indicium** *n.*, *pl.* **indicia.** an indicator; a clue which by itself might not justify a conclusion, but which may be persuasive when viewed together with other indicia pointing to the same conclusion.
——**Usage.** The term is often used in the plural, since it is only when several indicia are present that they are of much significance: *indicia of reliability; indicia of apparent authority.*

**indict** *v.* to issue an INDICTMENT against a person.
—**indictee** *n.*
—**indictor, indicter** *n.*

**indictable** *adj.* **1.** (of a person) liable to being indicted: *The person who solicited the murder is just as indictable as the person who pulled the trigger.*
**2.** (of conduct) making a person liable to indictment. See *indictable offense* (under OFFENSE).
—**indictability** *n.*
—**indictably** *adv.*

**indictment** *n.* **1.** the act of a *grand jury* (see under JURY) in formally charging a person with a crime, or the written instrument setting forth the charge. The written indictment is typically drawn up by the prosecutor, voted on by the grand jury after hearing evidence, endorsed with the words "a *true bill*" if approved by the jury (see under BILL), and then filed with the court, where it becomes the instrument upon which the rest of the case is based. See also BILL OF INDICTMENT. Cf. INFORMATION. **2. sealed indictment** an indictment that is ordered by the court to be kept secret until the defendant is arrested, and therefore sealed by the clerk to prevent any inadvertent disclosure.

**indigent defender** *n.* See under DEFENDER.

**indispensable party** *n.* See under PARTY.

**individual** *n.* **1.** a human being as distinguished from an entity such as a corporation; a *natural person* (see under PERSON).
—*adj.* **2.** involving only one individual or entity; not JOINT. See, e.g., *individual account* (under ACCOUNT); *individual return* (under RETURN). See also SEVERAL.
**3.** involving only the individual, and not the office or organization with with which the individual is associated. See, e.g., *individual capacity* (under CAPACITY).

**individual property** *n.* Same as SEPARATE PROPERTY.

**individual retirement account (IRA)** *n.* **1.** a trust or custodial account established with a financial institution for the purpose of holding and investing funds in connection with an INDIVIDUAL RETIREMENT ARRANGEMENT.
**2.** loosely, an individual retirement arrangement or INDIVIDUAL RETIREMENT ANNUITY.
——**Usage.** For practical purposes it is seldom necessary to distinguish between an *individual retirement account,* an *individual retirement annuity,* and an *individual retirement arrangement.* Unless there is a particular need to make a distinction, all three concepts are usually embodied in the phrase *individual retirement account*—or the conveniently ambiguous abbreviation *IRA.* For the various types of IRA, see IRA.

**individual retirement annuity (IRA)** *n.* an annuity contract issued by an insurance company and purchased by an individual in connection with an INDIVIDUAL RETIREMENT ARRANGEMENT. See also note at INDIVIDUAL RETIREMENT ACCOUNT.

**individual retirement arrangement (IRA)** *n.* a personal savings plan through which an individual, by following specific rules under the Internal Revenue Code, can obtain tax advantages by setting aside and investing money for retirement or for education expenses. For specific types of individual retirement arrangement, see IRA. See also note at INDIVIDUAL RETIREMENT ACCOUNT.

**indorse** *v.,* indorsed, indorsing. to sign one's name, sometimes with additional instructions or conditions, on the back of a NEGOTIABLE INSTRUMENT for the purpose of assigning the rights under it to someone else. The person whose name is signed is the **indorser;** the person (if any) named in the indorsement to receive the rights is the **indorsee.** Ordinarily the indorser will be liable to the indorsee or any subsequent holder of the instrument if the instrument is ultimately dishonored. See also NEGOTIATE; RECOURSE; and see note at ENDORSE.
—**indorsable** *adj.*

**indorsement** *n.* **1.** the act of indorsing an instrument, or the signature and accompanying writing indorsed on the instrument. See also ENDORSEMENT and note at ENDORSE.
**2. blank indorsement** an indorsement that does not name a specific person to receive rights under the instrument, usually consisting of a signature alone; for example, John Smith's signature (without more) on the back of a check made out to the order of John Smith. This turns the instrument into a *bearer instrument* (see under BEARER). Also called **indorsement in blank.** Cf. *special indorsement.*
**3. qualified indorsement** an indorsement that includes the words "without recourse." See RECOURSE for discussion.

**4. restrictive indorsement** an indorsement that limits or purports to limit the instrument in some way; for example, a signature with the phrase "for deposit," which forbids further negotiation except through banking channels.

**5. special indorsement** an indorsement that specifies the person to whose order it makes the instrument payable. This turns the instrument into an *order instrument* (see under ORDER²). Cf. *blank indorsement.*

**inducement** *n.* **1.** motivation; persuasion; the act of motivating or persuading. See also *fraud in the inducement* (under FRAUD).

**2.** in common law pleading, introductory matter setting forth facts necessary to an understanding of the core allegations upon which a claim is founded; especially, introductory matter in a complaint for libel or slander included to show the context in which the allegedly defamatory words must be understood. Cf. COLLOQUIUM; INNUENDO².

**industrial espionage** *n.* See under ESPIONAGE.

**industrial performance zoning** *n.* See under ZONING.

**industrial union** *n.* See under UNION.

**inevitable accident** *n.* Same as *unavoidable accident* (see under ACCIDENT).

**inevitable discovery exception** *n.* an exception to the EXCLUSIONARY RULE under which evidence obtained through an illegal search may be used against a defendant in a criminal case if the prosecution can show that it would have found the evidence sooner or later even without the illegal search.

**infamous** *adj.* **1.** suffering, characterized by, or associated with INFAMY.

**2.** (of a person) **a.** historically, especially in England, permanently disqualified from giving evidence in a court of law by reason of conviction of an offense regarded as particularly impugning one's integrity; suffering infamy. An infamous person was typically barred from any activity requiring public trust, such as holding public office or serving as a juror. **b.** having an extremely bad reputation.

**3.** (of a crime or punishment) involving infamy; having infamy as a consequence. See INFAMOUS CRIME; INFAMOUS PUNISHMENT; see also *infamous crime against nature* (under CRIME AGAINST NATURE).
—**infamously** *adv.*
—**infamousness** *n.*

**infamous crime** *n.* **1.** historically, especially in England, any of a class of crimes regarded as particularly dishonorable, and therefore disqualifying one convicted of the crime from thereafter giving evidence in a court of law or holding a position of public trust.

**2.** under the Fifth Amendment to the United States Constitution as now interpreted, any crime for which an INFAMOUS PUNISHMENT may be imposed. As currently understood, this includes any crime punishable by a prison sentence in excess of one year; this makes the term *infamous crime*, for most purposes, coextensive with the term FELONY.

——**History.** The Fifth Amendment prohibits the federal government from putting a person on trial "for a capital, or otherwise infamous crime" except with the approval of a grand jury. Until the late nineteenth century it was generally assumed that this required grand jury indictments only for crimes that traditionally would have disqualified a person as a witness under English law. The Supreme Court summarized these as cases of "treason, felony, forgery, and crimes injuriously affecting by falsehood and fraud the administration of justice, such as perjury, subornation of perjury, suppression of testimony by bribery, conspiring to accuse one of crime, or to procure the absence of a witness," though not "cases of private cheats, such as the obtaining of goods by false pretenses, or the uttering of counterfeit coin or forged securities." *Ex Parte Wilson,* 114 U.S. 417 (1885). In that decision, however, the Court concluded that the phrase *infamous* *crime* as used in the Fifth Amendment extends to a broader class of cases, determined not by the nature of the offense but by the nature of the possible punishment. See note at INFAMOUS PUNISHMENT.

**infamous punishment** *n.* an ignominious punishment; a punishment sufficiently severe so that, under traditional principles of English law as applicable to the government of the United States by virtue of the Fifth Amendment to the Constitution, no one may be put at risk of receiving such a punishment except upon indictment by a grand jury.

—**History.** The Fifth Amendment requires federal prosecutors to obtain the approval of a grand jury before trying anyone for an INFAMOUS CRIME. The Supreme Court in 1885 decided that the term "infamous crime" must be understood as referring to any crime for which an "infamous punishment" may be imposed. (See note at INFAMOUS CRIME.) The Court noted, however, that "[w]hat punishments shall be considered as infamous may be affected by the changes of public opinion from one age to another. In former times, being put in the stocks was not considered as necessarily infamous. And by the first Judiciary Act of the United States, whipping [so long as it did not exceed thirty stripes] was classed with moderate fines and short terms of imprisonment.... But at the present day either stocks or whipping might be thought an infamous punishment." *Ex Parte Wilson,* 114 U.S. 417 (1885). In that case and another decided the following year, the Court concluded that under then-contemporary standards any sentence involving hard labor or imprisonment in a penetentiary was an infamous punishment. Today this clause of the Fifth Amendment is implemented through Rule 7 of the Federal Rules of Criminal Procedure, under which federal crimes punishable by death, or by imprisonment for more than one year or at hard labor, may be prosecuted only be indictment (unless the defendant waives indictment in a noncapital case); this rule represents the current understanding of what constitutes an *infamous crime* or *infamous punishment.*

**infamy** *n., pl.* **infamies. 1.** loss of rights, especially the capacity to give testimony, as a consequence of conviction of an INFAMOUS CRIME.
**2.** extremely bad reputation, public reproach, or strong condemnation as the result of shameful, criminal, or outrageous conduct.
**3.** conduct or character deserving of such reproach.
**4.** an act or circumstance deserving of such reproach.

**infancy** *n., pl.* **infancies.** the state or period of being an INFANT; MINORITY: *Since the actress was 17 when she signed the $3.5 million movie contract, the contract was voidable on the ground of infancy.*

**infant** *n.* a person under the *age of majority* (see under AGE); a MINOR.
—**False Friend.** When a lawyer uses the term *infant* she is not necessarily thinking of a babe in arms: Although the legal period of "infancy" has now been reduced from twenty-one years to eighteen years, it is still perfectly reasonable for a lawyer to argue that a contract signed by a 200-pound high-school football star is void because the player is but an infant.

**inferior court** *n.* a court from which appeals may be taken to a higher court within the same judicial system. Especially, a court of *limited jurisdiction* (see under JURISDICTION¹) such as a probate court, family court, justice of the peace court, or municipal court, from which appeals are taken to the lowest court of *general jurisdiction* (see under JURISDICTION¹). Cf. SUPERIOR COURT.

**infeudation** *n.* **1.** investiture with a feud (see FEUD¹); ENFEOFFMENT.
**2.** a deed of enfeoffment.

**infliction of mental distress** *n.* See INTENTIONAL INFLICTION OF MENTAL DISTRESS.

**informant** *n.* **1.** an individual who provides incriminating evidence about someone else to law enforcement authorites, often in exchange for lenient treatment in connection with the informant's own criminal activity. Also called **informer.**

**2. jailhouse informant** an incarcerated individual who passes along to authorities incriminating information, such as a confession, received or claimed to have been received through conversation with another inmate in the jail or prison. Also called **jailhouse informer.**

**informant's privilege** *n.* an *evidentiary privilege* (see under PRIVILEGE) allowing the prosecution in a criminal case to keep secret the identity of an informant who provided leads in the case, unless the defendant can demonstrate a particular need for the information. Also called **informer's privilege.**

**information** *n.* a formal instrument charging a person with a crime, filed by a prosecutor instead of an INDICTMENT in cases where the law does not require involvement of a *grand jury* (see under JURY). In the federal courts this is allowed only for misdemeanors.

**information and belief** *n.* a basis for including facts in a pleading or in an affidavit, verification, or other sworn statement, even though one cannot claim personal knowledge of them. If one has received what one reasonably regards as reliable information, on the basis of which one believes a certain fact to be true, one can include that fact in the pleading or other writing, introduced by the phrase "On information and belief..." Cf. *personal knowledge* (under KNOWLEDGE).

**informed consent** *n.* See under CONSENT.

**informer** *n.* Same as INFORMANT.

**informer's privilege** *n.* Same as INFORMANT'S PRIVILEGE.

**infra** *adv. Latin.* (lit. "below") later in the same document. Opposite of SUPRA.

**infraction** *n.* **1.** the violation of a rule or law; especially a minor violation.
**2.** the name given in some states to an

offense below the level of MISDEMEANOR, punishable only by a fine or forfeiture and not classified as a crime: *a traffic infraction.*

**infringe** *v.,* **infringed, infringing.** to violate another's COPYRIGHT, PATENT, or TRADEMARK by copying or using the protected work, invention, or mark without permission from the owner. **—infringement** *n.*

**inherit** *v.* **1.** strictly, to receive property by INTESTATE SUCCESSION; to take as an HEIR.
**2.** broadly, to receive property from the estate of a decedent either by intestate succession or by will.

**inheritance** *n.* **1.** the act or fact of inheriting.
**2.** property that one has inherited: *an inheritance worth $150,000.*

**inheritance tax** *n.* a tax upon the recipient of money or property under a will or by intestate succession, based upon the value received. Cf. ESTATE TAX.

**initial public offering (IPO)** *n.* See under OFFERING.

**initiative** *n.* a lawmaking procedure, available in some states, that bypasses the state legislature. Under this procedure, if a certain number of citizens sign a petition calling for it, a proposed statute must be put to a vote at a general election, and becomes law if a majority of the voters vote for it. Cf. REFERENDUM.

**injunction** *n.* **1.** a court order directing a person to do or refrain from doing some act.
**2. mandatory injunction** an injunction requiring a person to do some affirmative act.
**3. permanent injunction** an injunction granted as part of the judgment at the end of a case, directing a party forever to refrain from certain conduct.
**4. preliminary injunction** an injunction granted shortly after the beginning of a case, to maintain the status quo while the case proceeds. A preliminary injunction will be issued only after a hearing.

**5. prohibitory injunction** an injunction prohibiting a person from taking certain action. This is the most common kind of injunction. Also called a RESTRAINING ORDER.

——**Note.** A typical sequence of events in an action for injunctive relief—say, a suit to prevent an owner from tearing down a landmark building—would be (1) a *temporary restraining order* (see under RESTRAINING ORDER) preventing the owner from beginning the wrecking process until a hearing can be held; (2) if the hearing convinces the judge that the plaintiff has a strong case, a *preliminary injunction* prohibiting the owner from tearing down the building until a trial can be held; and (3) if the trial persuades the judge that it would be illegal for the owner to tear down the building, a *permanent injunction* prohibiting the wrecking of the building.

**injurious falsehood** *n.* Same as DISPARAGEMENT.

**injury** *n., pl.* **injuries. 1.** any harm to an individual or entity through conduct regarded by the law as wrongful, including bodily injury, mental suffering, harm to reputation, property damage, financial loss, or deprivation of a legal right.
**2. bodily injury** physical harm to an individual's body. Also called **physical injury.**
**3. continuing injury** an injury that does not occur in a single event, but continues to occur even as an action is brought on account of it; for example, the maintenance of a public nuisance or the encroachment of another's building on one's land.
**4. irreparable injury** injury of a sort that cannot be suitably remedied by an award of damages, and for which a superior remedy exists in the form of equitable relief such as an INJUNCTION or SPECIFIC PERFORMANCE. In general, a party must show irreparable injury, or the prospect of irreparable injury, in order to obtain equitable relief.
**5. personal injury a.** narrowly, physical harm to an individual, as through disease, bodily injury, or death. **b.**

broadly, any harm or loss suffered by an individual as a result of a tort.

**inlaw** *v.* **1.** to restore legal rights to an OUTLAW; restore to the benefits and protection of the law; reverse a sentence of OUTLAWRY.
—*n.* **2.** one who is not an outlaw; one who either has never been outlawed or has been outlawed but then restored to legal rights.
——**False Friend.** This ancient legal term should not be confused with IN-LAW: Unlike an inlaw, an in-law may be an outlaw.

**inlawry** *n., pl.* **inlawries.** restitution of legal rights to one who had been outlawed; reversal of OUTLAWRY.

**innocent** *adj.* **1.** acting without knowledge of circumstances making an act or transaction legally defective or wrongful, and without reason to have such knowledge; acting in good faith. For example, a purchaser of property who has no reason to know that the seller had no right to sell it is an innocent purchaser; a person who wanders onto another's land while lost in the dark is an innocent trespasser.
**2.** done in good faith: *an innocent trespass.*
**3.** (in criminal cases) genuinely free from guilt, even if convicted of a crime and thus guilty in the eyes of the law: *Newly discovered evidence suggests that the prisoner is innocent of the crime for which he was convicted.*
—**innocence** *n.*
——**Usage.** "Innocent" is not used in law as a synonym for NOT GUILTY; a defendant cannot "plead innocent" or be "found innocent."

**innuendo**[1] *Latin.* (lit. "nodding to; signaling to") meaning; signifying; that is.
——**History.** When common law pleadings were written in Latin, this word was used to introduce explanatory interpolations; when they began to be written in English, the Latin word was sometimes retained: *The defendant stated: "He (innuendo the plaintiff) is a thief."* In later pleading, the word was translated into English: *"He (meaning the plaintiff)...."* The original use of the

Latin word, however, led directly to the term *innuendo* as now used in English. See INNUENDO² (def. 3).

**innuendo²** *n., pl.* **innuendos, innuendoes. 1.** in common law pleading, a parenthetical clause in a declaration, indictment, or other pleading containing an allegation that shows the meaning or significance of a preceding word or statement.

**2.** especially, in actions for libel or slander, matter inserted in a pleading to explain or make explicit the defamatory import of the words complained of. For example, the statement "Mr. Smith married Miss Jones yesterday" is not defamatory on its face, but if it has been alleged that the plaintiff, Mr. Smith, was already married to someone else on the day referred to (see INDUCEMENT and COLLOQUIUM), then the foundation has been laid for the innuendo: "Mr. Smith married Miss Jones yesterday" (meaning that the plaintiff is a bigamist)."

**3.** an indirect statement about a person, especially of a disparaging or derogatory nature; an intimation of wrongdoing, bad character, or the like.

**inquest** *n.* a name given to certain kinds of factfinding proceedings, including a proceeding in which the plaintiff in an action in which the defendant has failed to appear presents evidence to the court to establish the damages to be awarded in a default judgment. The traditional "coroner's inquest"—a hearing conducted by a coroner to inquire into the cause and circumstances of a suspicious death—has largely been supplanted by a combination of autopsy to determine the cause and police investigation to determine the circumstances.

**inquire** *v.,* **inquired, inquiring.** to ask questions; largely restricted to the formal phrase "You may inquire," sometimes said by a judge to a lawyer to grant permission for the lawyer to begin questioning a witness.

**inquiry notice** *n.* See under NOTICE.

**inquisitorial system** *n.* a method of adjudication in which judges play a prominent role in investigating facts

and questioning witnesses; used in CIVIL LAW countries. Cf. ADVERSARY SYSTEM; ACCUSATORIAL SYSTEM.

**insanity defense** *n.* an *affirmative defense* (see under DEFENSE) to a criminal charge, under which a defendant who proves that he was insane at the time of the crime is held not to be responsible for the crime. The verdict then is NOT GUILTY BY REASON OF INSANITY, and the usual consequence is incarceration in a mental institution. Most states (but not all) recognize some type of insanity defense, applying a variety of rules or tests as to what constitutes insanity, usually some form of the M'NAGHTEN RULE, the IRRESISTIBLE IMPULSE TEST, or the SUBSTANTIAL CAPACITY TEST.

**inside trader** *n.* Same as INSIDER TRADER.

**insider trader** *n.* a person who engages in INSIDER TRADING. Also called **inside trader.**

**insider trading** *n.* buying or selling stock in a publicly held corporation on the basis of "inside information"—that is, information that is known only to people inside the company (or outsiders who have been told privately) and has not yet been disclosed to the general public. Insider trading is illegal.

**insolvency** *n., pl.* **insolvencies. 1.** the condition of being INSOLVENT.
**2.** an act or instance of becoming or being insolvent.

**insolvency proceedings** *n.pl.* in the Uniform Commecial Code, any ASSIGNMENT FOR THE BENEFIT OF CREDITORS or other proceeding intended to liquidate or rehabilitate the estate of the person involved.

**insolvent** *adj.* **1.** usually, unable to pay one's debts in the ordinary course of business as they become due.
**2.** for some purposes, having liabilities exceeding assets. Opposite of SOLVENT. —**insolvency** *n.*

**installment** *n.* **1.** one of a series of payments, deliveries, or other steps required of a party by a contract, all of which together constitute the complete performance called for.

—*adj.* **2.** describing a contract calling for performance in installments, or referring to some aspect of such a transaction: *installment note* (see under NOTE[1]); *installment contract; installment loan.*

**installment sale** *n.* See under SALE.

**instant** *adj.* referring to that which is currently under consideration; at hand; current: *the instant case; the instant decision; the instant crime.*

**instanter** *adv.* immediately; forthwith; usually used in connection with a court order, and often suggesting that the limits of the judge's patience have been reached: *The Court will brook no further delay; the documents are to be produced instanter. So ordered.*

**instruct** *v.* **1.** Same as DIRECT[2].
**2.** to issue an INSTRUCTION or set of instructions to the jury: *The judge will instruct the jury tomorrow afternoon.*

**instruction** *n.* **1.** a judge's explanation and direction to a jury concerning a particular legal principle or duty of the jury: *The plaintiff objected to the court's instruction as to the inference that may be drawn from the plaintiff's failure to call his wife as a witness.*
**2. instructions** (*used with a pl. v.*) the comprehensive explanation of the applicable law and duties of the jury given by the judge to the jury at the end of a trial, just before the jury begins to deliberate. Also called the CHARGE to the jury.
**3. cautionary instruction** any warning, reminder, or admonishment to the jury; for example, not to commence deliberations until after all the evidence is in, or not to consider anything that a lawyer says as evidence.
**4. curative instruction** an instruction directing the jury to disregard certain inadmissible testimony, statements of counsel, or other potentially prejudicial events that occurred in their presence.

**instrument** *n.* **1.** a formal legal document, especially one that embodies legal rights or a legal interest (such as a stock certificate), or one that operates to cause legal consequences (such as a

deed or will). See also *sealed instrument* (under SEAL[1]); ACCUSATORY INSTRUMENT.
**2.** a NEGOTIABLE INSTRUMENT or NONNEGOTIABLE INSTRUMENT.

**insufficient cause** *n.* a legally insufficient reason for taking a particular action or seeking a particular court order. Cf. GOOD CAUSE.

**insurable interest** *n.* an interest in person or property justifying one in obtaining insurance on that person or that property. For example, since a company might suffer financially if its chief executive dies, the company has an "insurable interest" in the executive's life, which it may protect by purchasing a life insurance policy under which the company will be compensated if the executive dies.
—**Note.** The law prohibits people from taking out insurance on lives or property in which they have no insurable interest. Such a policy would amount to nothing more than a gambling contract, and moreover would put the policyholder in the unseemly position of hoping that harm will befall someone else so that the policyholder can obtain a windfall.

**insurable title** *n.* See under TITLE.

**insurance** *n.* **1.** a contractual arrangement whereby a company (the INSURER), in consideration for a payment or periodic payments of money (the PREMIUM), agrees to compensate its customer (the INSURED) in the event that the insured suffers some loss or injury (in the case of INDEMNITY INSURANCE) or liability (in the case of LIABILITY INSURANCE) of a kind specified in the written contract (the INSURANCE POLICY).
**2. group insurance** insurance covering an identified group of people, such as employees of a company or members of an association, upon terms agreed to between the insurance company and the employer, association, or the like.
**3. mutual insurance** insurance provided by a company that is owned solely by its policyholders in proportion

to the amount of insurance they have purchased from the company, rather than by stockholders. Since a mutual insurance company is not in business to make profits for stockholders, it can offer insurance at cost.

See also COINSURANCE; CASUALTY INSURANCE; DIRECTORS' AND OFFICERS' LIABILITY INSURANCE; DISABILITY INSURANCE; *employers' liability insurance* (under WORKERS' COMPENSATION); ERRORS AND OMMISSIONS INSURANCE; EXCESS INSURANCE; FIDELITY INSURANCE; NO-FAULT INSURANCE; LIFE INSURANCE; REINSURANCE; *term insurance* (under LIFE INSURANCE); TITLE INSURANCE; *unemployment insurance* (under UNEMPLOYMENT COMPENSATION); *workers' compensation insurance* (under WORKERS' COMPENSATION). Cf. SELF-INSURANCE.

**insurance adjuster** *n.* See ADJUSTER.

**insurance broker** *n.* See under BROKER.

**insurance policy** *n.* the written instrument embodying a contract of insurance. Also called **policy.**

**insure** *v.,* **insured, insuring.** to issue or procure an insurance policy on or for: *The homeowner insured the home against fire. The insurance company insures the home against fire.*
—**insurability** *n.*
—**insurable** *adj.*

**insured** *n., pl.* **insured, insureds.** an individual or entity protected from loss by a contract of insurance; one covered by an insurance policy.

**insurer** *n.* one who insures another against loss; a company that issues a contract of insurance.

**intangible** *adj.* **1.** incapable of being perceived by the sense of touch; not made of physical substance. See, e.g., *intangible asset* (under ASSET); *intangible property* (under PROPERTY).
—*n.* **2.** something intangible, especially an intangible asset.
—**intangibility, intangibleness** *n.*
—**intangibly** *adv.*

**integrated bar** *n.* See under BAR[2].

**integrated contract** *n.* **1.** a contract in which one or more terms have been expressed in final written form.
**2. completely integrated contract** a contract embodied in a writing or set of writings adopted by the parties as a complete and exclusive statement of all the terms of their agreement. Also called **fully integrated contract, entire contract, entire contract of the parties, entire agreement of the parties.**
**3. partially integrated contract** a contract in which some terms have been expressed in final written form and some have not.
——**Note.** A partially integrated contract may be supplemented by extrinsic evidence of additional terms, but only to the extent that they are not inconsistent with the written terms; a completely integrated contract may not be supplemented by additional terms within the scope of the agreement even if they are fully consistent with what has been written. See PAROL EVIDENCE RULE.

**integration** *n.* **1.** the act of bringing together or incorporating previously separate things into a unified whole.
**2.** the ending of social SEGREGATION, especially racial segregation.
**3.** in contract law, **a.** the act of putting the final agreement of the parties as to some or all terms of the contract into writing. **b.** the writing or set of writings so produced. See also *integrated contract* (under CONTRACT).
—**integrate** *v.,* **integrated, integrating.**
—**integrated** *adj.*

**integration clause** *n.* a clause in a written contract stating that the writing constitutes the entire agreement of the parties and supersedes all prior negotiations and agreements with respect to the subject matter of the contract. Also called **merger clause.**
——**Note.** The effect of the integration clause is to bar subsequent claims by either party that there were additional understandings beyond those found in the writing. See also INTEGRATED CONTRACT; MERGER; PAROL EVIDENCE RULE.

**intellectual property** *n.* See under PROPERTY.

**intent** *n.* **1.** broadly, a STATE OF MIND in which one either desires to achieve a certain result by one's conduct (even if that result is unlikely to occur) or knows that such a result is substantially certain to occur (even if that is not what is desired). This is the usual meaning of "intent" in tort law and the traditional meaning in criminal law. See, for example, *intentional tort* (under TORT); *intent to kill* (under MURDER).
**2.** narrowly, a conscious objective of causing a certain result. This is the usual meaning of the term under modern criminal codes, which classify KNOWLEDGE of likely results without an actual intent to achieve them as a separate state of mind. See also PURPOSELY.
**3.** Also called **intention.** the purpose or design underlying a statute, contract, will, or other instrument: LEGISLATIVE INTENT; *intent of the parties; the testator's intent.*
—**intentional** *adj.*
—**intentionally** *adv.*

**intentional infliction of emotional distress** *n.* the tort of intentionally or recklessly causing severe EMOTIONAL DISTRESS in a person by means of conduct of an extremely outrageous nature.
Also called **intentional infliction of severe emotional distress,** and referred to by many similar phrases using a variety of synonyms, the most common of which are listed in the entry for EMOTIONAL DISTRESS. Cf. NEGLIGENT INFLICTION OF EMOTIONAL DISTRESS.

**inter alia** *Latin.* among other things: *The contract provides, inter alia, that the parties will submit any dispute to binding arbitration.*

**inter pares** *Latin.* between or among equals.

**inter partes** *Latin.* between or among the parties; among two or more parties.

**inter se** or **inter sese** *Latin.* between themselves; among themselves.

**inter vivos** *Latin.* (lit. "between living persons; among the living") describing a transaction completed during one's lifetime, as distinguished from one occurring at death or effected by will or intestacy; for example, *inter vivos gift* (see under GIFT); *inter vivos trust* (see under TRUST). Cf. TESTAMENTARY.

**interest¹** *n.* **1.** a legally enforceable right with respect to real or personal property. An interest may be designated as either a **legal interest** or a **beneficial** (or **equitable**) **interest,** depending upon whether it is viewed from the perspective of the *legal owner* or, in the case of property held in trust, the *beneficial owner* (see both phrases under OWNER). See also ESTATE¹; TENANCY.
**2. contingent interest** an interest which may give the holder a right of possession, use, or enjoyment of the property at some time in the future, but only upon the occurrence of specific circumstances which are possible but not certain to arise; for example, a *contingent estate* (see under ESTATE¹). Cf. *vested interest.*
**3. executory interest** a *future estate* (see under ESTATE¹) which will become possessory only upon termination of a fee simple, and which is held by someone other than the person (or the successors of the person) who transferred the fee to its present owner. See also *fee simple determinable* (under FEE¹). Cf. POSSIBILITY OF REVERTER.
**4. future interest** an interest which does not confer a present right of possession, use, or enjoyment of property, but may do so in the future; for example, a REMAINDER or a POSSIBILITY OF REVERTER. Cf. *present interest.*
**5. possessory interest** a present right to possession of property, particularly real property.
**6. present interest a.** (in personal property) a present right to possession, use, or enjoyment of property. For example, the current beneficiary of a trust fund has a present interest in the fund. **b.** (in real property) Same as *possessory interest.* Present interests in real property may be classified as either a **freehold interest** (same as FREEHOLD) or a **leasehold interest** (same as LEASEHOLD).

**7. security interest** an interest in the property of another consisting of the right to sell that property in order to satisfy some obligation of the owner if the owner defaults; for example, the right of an automobile dealer or financer to take back a car and sell it to someone else if the buyer fails to keep up the payments. See also LIEN; MORTGAGE; PURCHASE MONEY SECURITY INTEREST.

**8. undivided interest** the rights of each of two or more co-owners of a single interest in property when, instead of dividing the property up physically, they all share the right to use the whole property. Also called **undivided fractional interest.**

**9. vested interest** a legally enforceable right to possession, use, or enjoyment of property which either exists at present or is certain to arise in the future; a present interest or a future interest that is not subject to any contingency. Cf. *contingent interest.* See also INSURABLE INTEREST; *successor in interest* (under SUCCESSOR).

**interest²** *n.* **1.** a financial or other direct legal stake in a matter, such that one's pocketbook or legal rights are directly affected. For example, a shareholder has an interest in a suit by or against the corporation; a child has an interest in a custody dispute between the parents. See also *real party in interest* (under PARTY).
**2.** broadly, any close personal stake in a matter; for example, one's interest in a suit against a friend, a relative, or a personal enemy. See also CONFLICT OF INTEREST.

**interest³** *n.* **1.** a sum paid or charged for the use of money or for the privilege of deferring a payment, expressed either as a dollar amount or as a percentage of the principal amount involved in the transaction.
**2. imputed interest** a sum of money treated for tax purposes as if it had been received by the taxpayer as interest for a loan, and thus as taxable income, even though no such interest payment was actually made.
**3. legal interest a.** the rate of interest

set by law for certain kinds of debts, such as an unpaid judgment. **b.** the maximum rate of interest that can be charged without violating laws against USURY.

**interested** *adj.* having an *interest* (see INTEREST²) in a matter; for example, *interested person* (see under PERSON); *interested witness* (see under WITNESS). Cf. DISINTERESTED.

**interlocutory** *adj.* interim; describing an order or other step occurring in the course of a case but not ending the case. See for example *interlocutory appeal* (under APPEAL); *interlocutory decree* (under DECREE); *interlocutory order* (under ORDER). Cf. FINAL.

**intermeddler** *n.* See OFFICIOUS INTERMEDDLER.

**intermediate appellate court** *n.* See under COURT.

**intermediate scrutiny** *n.* Same as HEIGHTENED SCRUTINY.

**internal law** *n.* the law of a state or nation exclusive of its CHOICE OF LAW rules; the substantive law that a state would apply to a case if all the parties and property and events in suit were located within that state. Cf. WHOLE LAW; see also RENVOI.

**Internal Revenue Code (I.R.C.)** *n.* the portion of the UNITED STATES CODE that contains all federal tax laws.

**Internal Revenue Service (I.R.S.)** *n.* the federal agency that administers most federal tax laws.

**International Court of Justice (ICJ)** *n.* the principal judicial organ of the United Nations, based in The Hague, Netherlands. It is authorized to render advisory legal opinions to the United Nations and to decide disputes between nations voluntarily submitted to it by the nations involved. With respect to most disputes between nations concerning the interpretation of a treaty, a question of international law, or an alleged breach of an international obligation, the United States and most other nations have agreed to compulsory jurisdiction of the court, so that no special agreement between such nations is needed for any one of them to submit such a dispute to the Court for resolution.

**International Criminal Court (ICC)** *n.* a permanent international court, to be established upon terms tentatively agreed to by nearly all of the countries of the world at a United Nations diplomatic conference in 1998, with jurisdiction to investigate and bring to justice individuals who commit the most serious crimes known to international law. It will have authority to try and punish individuals accused of conduct constituting a CRIME AGAINST HUMANITY, a WAR CRIME, or GENOCIDE, with the crime of AGGRESSION to be added to the list if agreement can be reached on the scope of that crime and of the court's jurisdiction with respect to it. (See note at AGGRESSION.) The court is to have jurisdiction in cases where (a) the conduct occurred in a state that either is already a party to the treaty establishing the court or accepts the jurisdiction of the court with respect to the crime in question, or (b) the person accused of the crime is a national of such a state.

——**History.** The roots of this court lie in unsuccessful efforts to establish an international tribunal in the wake of World War I. In 1948, with the Nuremberg and Tokyo war crimes tribunals as precedents, the United Nations established a commission to study the idea of a permanent court; but the project was promptly put into a deep freeze by the onset of the Cold War. With the end of the Cold War, serious consideration began again in 1992. After years of preparatory work, a five-week-long diplomatic conference, attended by delegations from nearly every nation and many international and nongovernmental organizations, was held in Rome in 1998, culminating with the adoption of a framework for the court on July 17, 1998. Various amendments reducing the power of the court had been adopted during the conference in an effort to gain the acceptance of the United States; but when, on the last day, the United States attempted to restrict the jurisdiction of the court even further, so that no national of any country could ever be tried before the court unless that country had accepted the court's jurisdiction, the nations present voted the American proposal down by 113 to 17 with 25 abstentions. The conference thereupon adopted the statute establishing the court by a vote of 120 to 7 with 21 absentions. At the request of the United States, that final vote was non-recorded—essentially a secret ballot—but the United States, Israel, and China put statements on the record explaining why they had voted against establishing the court: Israel objected to a specific provision treating the settlement of occupied territories as a war crime; the United States and China objected to the whole idea that soldiers or others accused of committing war crimes or crimes against humanity in a country that has agreed to let such accusations be resolved by an international court might be tried by that court without the consent of their own government. The agreement provides that the court will come into existence when sixty nations have ratified the agreement, but U.S. diplomatic pressure could slow down that process. By the end of the century, just six nations had ratified the agreement: Fiji, Ghana, Italy, San Marino, Senegal, and Trinidad and Tobago.

**international criminal tribunal** *n.* an ad hoc court established by the United Nations Security Council for the purpose of bringing to justice individuals who have committed serious violations of international humanitarian law, such as war crimes, crimes against humanity, and genocide, in connection with a particularly horrific war or internal conflict in a particular geographic region.

——**Note.** Two such tribunals were established in the 1990's, one for the territory of the former Yugoslavia (primarily because of the ETHNIC CLEANSING that took place there beginning in 1992) and one for Rwanda (because of the genocide that occurred there in 1994). For the UN's effort to create a permanent court with jurisdiction over such crimes wherever they occur, see INTERNATIONAL CRIMINAL COURT.

**international law** *n.* **1.** Also called **public international law** or the **law of nations.** a body of principles that are generally accepted among the nations of the world as governing their dealings with each other and each other's citizens or subjects. It is a combination of long-established custom and specific treaty obligations, depending for its vitality largely upon each nation's good will or desire for international acceptance. See also FEDERAL LAW.
**2. private international law** the branch of CONFLICT OF LAWS that deals with the application of potentially conflicting national laws to transactions, events, or litigation concerning two or more countries.

**interplead** *v.,* **interpleaded, interpleading. 1.** to plead against each other; said of competing claimants to property or money that has been deposited with court by the stakeholder in an action of INTERPLEADER.
**2.** to bring into court by filing an interpleader action; to name as a potential claimant: *The stakeholder deposited the disputed property with the court and interpleaded the three claimants.*

**interpleader** *n.* a type of action that may be commenced by a STAKEHOLDER in possession of property or funds known to belong to someone else but claimed by more than one other person, so that a court can determine which claimant should get the property. This procedure permits the stakeholder to deposit the property with the court and leave it to the competing claimants to plead their claims against each other (to INTERPLEAD), freeing the stakeholder both from the burden of litigating over the property and from the risk of turning it over to the wrong claimant.
——**False Friend.** See note at DEMURRER.

**interpretation** *n.* See under CONSTRUCTION.

**interrogation** *n.* **1.** the questioning of a criminal suspect by law enforcement authorities.
**2. custodial interrogation** the questioning of a suspect who has been arrested or otherwise deprived of his freedom of action in any significant way. This is the situation to which the MIRANDA RULE applies.
—**interrogate** *v.,* **interrogated, interrogating.**
—**interrogator** *n.*

**interrogatory** *n.,* *pl.* **interrogatories.** one of a set of written questions about the facts and contentions in a case **(interrogatories)** submitted to an adversary as part of the DISCOVERY process. Interrogatories are required to be answered in writing under oath. See also *special interrogatories* (under VERDICT).

**interstate commerce** *n.* See under COMMERCE.

**interstate compact** *n.* See under COMPACT.

**intervene** *v.,* **intervened, intervening.** to insert oneself as a party in a lawsuit that is already pending between other parties, in order to assert or protect some interest that one has in the subject matter of the case. Depending upon the extent of an intervenor's need to be involved and the extent to which intervention would contribute to or detract from efficient dispute resolution, intervention might or might not be allowed. See also *proper party* (under PARTY).
—**intervenor** *n.*
—**intervention** *n.*

**intervening cause** *n.* an action or event that alters the course of a chain of events leading to the injury or loss that is the subject of a tort case. If the intervening event was foreseeable it would not relieve a person who set the chain of events in motion from liability. Cf. SUPERVENING CAUSE.

**intestacy** *n.* the fact or state of being INTESTATE at death.

**intestate** *adj.* **1.** lacking a valid will, especially at the time of one's death: *to die intestate.*

—*n.* **2.** a person who dies without leaving a valid will.

**intestate succession** *n.* taking as an HEIR; succeeding to property of a decedent by operation of law, either because the decedent left no valid will or because the will did not effectively dispose of all of the decedent's property. Each state has laws dictating how such property is to be distributed among surviving relatives, generally referred to as laws of intestate succession or laws of DESCENT AND DISTRIBUTION.

**intra vires** *adj., adv. Latin.* (lit. "within the powers") within the scope of authority of the actor; not in excess of legal powers. Cf. ULTRA VIRES.

**invalid** *adj.* without legal force; legally ineffective or unenforceable; void. See also *invalid as applied* and *invalid on its face* (both under UNCONSTITUTIONAL).
—**invalidity** *n.*
—**invalidly** *adv.*

**invasion of privacy** *n.* the tort of unreasonable and highly offensive publicity about an individual or intrusion into an individual's private life and personal affairs. The contours of the tort vary from state to state, but in general it includes improper intrusions by such means as wiretapping, peeping, searching an individual's property and effects, or persistent telephoning; public disclosure of personal information about a private person without a legitimate news purpose; placing a person in a false public light (as by associating her with ideas or events with which she has no connection); and use of a person's name or image without consent for advertising or other commercial purposes.

**investigative privilege** *n.* an *evidentiary privilege* (see under PRIVILEGE) that protects the government from having to release documents or information whose disclosure might reveal law enforcement investigative techniques or sources in the absence of a showing of special need in a case. Also called **investigatory privilege, law enforcement investigative** (or **investigatory**)

**privilege, law enforcement evidentiary privilege.**

**investigatory privilege** *n.* Same as INVESTIGATIVE PRIVILEGE.

**investment adviser** *n.* a person in the business of advising as to the value of securities or the advisability of buying, selling, or investing in securities.
—**Usage.** Because the profession of investment adviser is defined and regulated by the federal Investment Advisers Act of 1940, this phrase almost always appears in legal writing with the *-er* spelling rather than the *-or* spelling of ADVISER.

**invidious** *adj.* offensive; unfair; hateful; offensively and unfairly discriminatory. See also *invidious discrimination* (under DISCRIMINATION).
—**invidiously** *adv.*
—**invidiousness** *n.*

**invidious discrimination** *n.* See under DISCRIMINATION.

**invitee** *n.* a person invited to enter real property to conduct business with the occupier or as a member of the general public invited for a public function.
—**Note.** In tort law, a property owner owes a higher degree of care to an invitee than to a mere LICENSEE. In most states an invited social guest is usually deemed to be a licensee rather than an invitee, on the theory that such a guest is like "one of the family" and thus is owed no special duty of care. See also note at LICENSEE.

**involuntary** *adj.* **1.** compelled by law, by duress, by necessity, or otherwise. See *involuntary bankruptcy* (under BANKRUPTCY); *involuntary confession* (under CONFESSION); *involuntary dismissal* (under DISMISSAL); *involuntary servitude* (under SERVITUDE). **2.** unintentional; accidental. For example, *involuntary manslaughter* (see under MANSLAUGHTER). Cf. VOLUNTARY.
—**involuntarily** *adv.*
—**involuntariness** *n.*

**involuntary public figure** *n.* See under PUBLIC FIGURE.

**IPO** *pl.*, **IPOs, IPO's.** *initial public offering* (see under OFFERING).

**IRA** *n.*, *pl.* **IRAs, IRA's. 1.** Abbreviation for INDIVIDUAL RETIREMENT ACCOUNT, INDIVIDUAL RETIREMENT ANNUITY, or INDIVIDUAL RETIREMENT ARRANGEMENT; in many contexts the abbreviation can be viewed as a convenient way of representing all three phrases at once.
**2. education IRA** a trust or custodial account created for the purpose of funding future expenses of higher education for a child. (See note.) Contributions to an education IRA are not tax deductible, but earnings from the amounts contributed are not taxed as they are earned, and to the extent that they are used for education expenses after the child reaches the age of 18 they are not taxed upon withdrawal either. Also called **education individual retirement account, Ed IRA.**
**3. Roth IRA** an IRA similar in most respects to a *traditional IRA*, except that the tax treatment is reversed: Contributions are not deductible when made, but the investment income is not taxed when earned and withdrawals after retirement are not taxable. Consequently the income received from the IRA, from investment of the amounts contributed and reinvestment of the proceeds over potentially an entire working lifetime, in most cases is never taxed at all.
**4. SEP-IRA** an IRA created in connection with a *simplified employee pension* (see under RETIREMENT PLAN) established by the individual's employer. Neither the employee contributions nor the employer contributions are taxed at the time they are made; funds withdrawn from the account after retirement are taxed at that time.
**5. SIMPLE IRA** an IRA created in connection with a *savings incentive match plan for employees* (see under RETIREMENT PLAN) established by the individual's employer. As with a *SEP-IRA*, contributions are deductible and withdrawals are taxable. But amounts that may be contributed each year, though more than in a *traditional IRA*, are less than in a SEP-IRA. Also called **simple retirement account** or **SRA.**
**6. traditional IRA** the original form of IRA, in which an individual may invest a certain amount of each year's earned income for retirement and not be taxed on it until then. So long as the amount invested does not exceed legal limits, it is deductible from income in the year invested, and the income it earns is free of tax until withdrawn. Withdrawals made after reaching retirement age are taxed as income at that time. Also called **regular IRA, ordinary IRA, original IRA.**
**——False Friend.** Despite its name, the "education individual retirement account"—to quote the full statutory language used by Congress—is not in the remotest sense a retirement account. Unlike all other IRA's, from which withdrawals ordinarily cannot be made without penalty before the individual reaches retirement age, the education IRA is required to be fully distributed within thirty days after the beneficiary's thirtieth birthday.

**irrebuttable presumption** *n.* See under PRESUMPTION.

**irreconcilable differences** *n.pl.* in some states, the phrase used to describe such severe disagreements and incompatibilities between a husband and wife as to cause an irretrievable BREAKDOWN OF THE MARRIAGE and so entitle the couple to a NO-FAULT DIVORCE.

**irrelevant** *adj.* not RELEVANT.

**irremediable breakdown of the marriage** *n.* See BREAKDOWN OF THE MARRIAGE.

**irreparable** *adj.* incapable of being rectified, remedied, or made good; especially, requiring something other than a payment of money to make good. See *irreparable injury* (under INJURY).
**—irreparability** *n.*
**—irreparably** *adv.*

**irreparable injury** *n.* See under INJURY.

**irresistible impulse test** *n.* the principle that an INSANITY DEFENSE may be established by evidence that the crime was committed under the influence of a mental disease that made it impossible for the defendant to control her behavior, even if she knew that what she was doing was wrong. This test, also called **uncontrollable impulse test,** is recognized in a few states as a supplement to the M'NAGHTEN RULE.

**irretrievable breakdown of the marriage** (or **of the marriage relationship**) *n.* See BREAKDOWN OF THE MARRIAGE.

**irrevocable** *adj.* not capable of being revoked, recalled, or nullified; final; unalterable.
—**irrevocability** *n.*
—**irrevocably** *adv.*

**irrevocable trust** *n.* See under TRUST.

**issuable** *adj.* **1.** capable of being issued; suitable to be issued; authorized to be issued.
**2.** disputable; litigable; going to the merits: *The answer states an issuable defense. For purposes of a motion to dismiss for failure to state a claim we assume the truth of all issuable allegations.*

**issue¹** *n.* **1.** a disputed proposition presented in a case; any material fact or legal principle upon which the two sides disagree. Same as QUESTION², although many standard legal phrases customarily employ only one or the other of the two words.
**2. constitutional issue** See under CONSTITUTIONAL.
**3. issue of fact** or **factual issue** See under QUESTION².
**4. issue of law** or **legal issue** See under QUESTION².
**5. issue preclusion** Same as *collateral estoppel* (under ESTOPPEL). Cf. *claim preclusion* (under RES JUDICATA).
**6. join issue** to file papers denying or contradicting an allegation in a case, thereby creating an issue for judicial determination. The point in a case where this occurs is called **joinder of issue.**

**issue²** *n.* **1.** descendants (children,

grandchildren, etc.); normally construed to include generations yet unborn, not just those descendants existing at a particular time.
**2. failure of issue** the absence of surviving issue. **a. definite failure of issue** the absence of surviving issue at the moment when property would have passed to them under the terms of a deed or will. This is the modern meaning of the phrase *failure of issue.* **b. indefinite failure of issue** the ultimate dying out of a person's line of descendants, which may (or may not) occur at an unknown time in the future. This older sense of the phrase *failure of issue* has been largely abandoned.

**issue³** *v.,* **issued, issuing,** *n.* —*v.* **1.** (of a corporation or other entity) to sell or put on the market a block of one's stock or other securities.
—*n.* **2.** an entire class or block of securities sold or offered for sale at the same time.
See also ISSUER.
—**issuance** *n.*

**issue⁴** *v.,* **issued, issuing. 1.** to formally announce an order, rule, decision, etc., either orally or in writing.
**2.** (of such an order, rule, etc.) to come forth; be announced: *The writ of mandamus issued from the Court of Appeals at 4:30 p.m.*
—**issuance** *n.*

**issue advertising** *n.* **1.** advertising by an individual or organization promoting a particular position on an issue of public policy, such as gun control or environmental policy.
**2.** more often, advertising in the form of an issue advertisement, but designed specifically to promote a candidate or group of candidates for office.
Also called **issue advocacy.**
—**issue advertisement** *n.*
—**Note.** By avoiding explicit electioneering language like "Vote for Smith" or "Support our candidates in the next election," the unions, corporations, political parties, political action committees, and other individuals and organizations that purchase such advertising seek to skirt regulation by the federal campaign financing laws. Specifically,

they take the position that since the advertisements do not use specific words endorsing a candidate, they may be paid for with SOFT MONEY rather than HARD MONEY. Although the law in this area is murky, campaign advertising in the guise of issue advertising, paid for by unregulated campaign money, grew under the pressure of electoral competition in the 1990's into an extremely prominent aspect of the American election process.

**issue advocacy** *n.* Same as ISSUE AD-VERTISING.

**issuer** *n.* the corporation or other entity that issued a particular security; the entity in which one is investing if one purchases a security.

**itemized deduction** *n.* See under DE-DUCTION.

**itemized deduction** *n.* See under DE-DUCTION.

# J

**J.** *pl.* **JJ.** abbreviation for Judge or Justice, always placed after the name: *The majority opinion was by White, J.; Brennan and Marshall, JJ., filed dissents.*

**jactitation** *n.* **1.** a false boast or claim, especially one that causes injury to another.
**2.** JACTITATION OF MARRIAGE.

**jactitation of marriage** *n.* **1.** a false boast or claim that one is married to another.
**2.** formerly, an action brought against the boaster by the individual falsely claimed to be the boaster's spouse, to enjoin the making of any such claim in the future.

**JAG** JUDGE ADVOCATE GENERAL.

**JAG Corps** *n., pl.* **JAG Corps.** JUDGE ADVOCATE GENERAL'S CORPS.

**jail** *n.* **1.** an institution, usually run by a county or municipality, for locking up offenders serving short sentences and accused people awaiting trial. Cf. PRISON.
—*v.* **2.** to confine to jail; to send to jail or keep in jail.
—**jailable** *adj.*

**jail delivery** or **gaol delivery** *n.* *Primarily Historical.* **1.** the removal from jail of an individual or a group of individuals who have been awaiting trial so that they can be tried and either released or convicted and sentenced.
**2.** the liberation of one or more individuals from jail or prison, as by legal process, by amnesty, or by force.
**3.** a court or session of court held for the purpose of trying criminal cases generally. Cf. OYER AND TERMINER.
**4. commission of gaol delivery** historically, a royal commission authorizing a judge or judges to hear cases of individuals in jail awaiting trial; especially, a commission for traveling judges to dispose of the cases of all those awaiting trial in the counties they visited (in which case it was a **commission of general gaol delivery**). In modern writing, especially in the United States, these may be written **commission of jail delivery** and **commission of general jail delivery.**
**5. general jail delivery** or **general gaol delivery** the clearing of a jail of all those awaiting trial by bringing them to trial.
——**False Friend.** *Jail delivery* in its usual legal sense is not at all the same thing as release from incarceration. The salutary purpose of jail delivery was to protect accused persons—some accused of relatively petty offenses and some perhaps even innocent—from languishing in jail awaiting trial. This important principle is embodied in the Sixth Amendment's guarantee of *speedy trial* (see under TRIAL). But from the point of view of those who were "delivered" from jail only to be tried, found guilty, and hanged, the phrase *jail delivery* must have had a bitterly ironic ring.
——**Usage.** On the history and usage of *jail* vs. *gaol,* see notes at GAOL.

**jailer** or **jailor** *n.* a jail-keeper; a person who is in charge of a jail or section of a jail.

**jailhouse informant** *n.* See under INFORMANT.

**jailhouse informer** *n.* See under INFORMANT.

**jailhouse lawyer** *n.* a prisoner who has acquired considerable knowledge of technical legal matters while serving time, usually primarily through working on his own case, and gives legal advice to fellow prisoners.

**Jane Doe** *n.* a fictitious name used to represent a woman in case names and in legal documents such as warrants and summonses, either to conceal the individual's identity, or because her real name is not known, or because it is not yet known whether such a person exists. See also JOHN DOE; JANE ROE.

**Jane Roe** *n.* a fictitious name used in case names and in legal documents in the same ways that JANE DOE is used, usually because the latter name has already been used to identify another individual in the same or a related proceeding. See also RICHARD ROE.

**J.D.** Abbreviation for **Juris Doctor** (*Latin,* lit. "Doctor of Law"), the lowest law degree; the degree granted to everyone who graduates from law school in the United States.
——**History.** This degree was formerly called Bachelor of Laws (see LL.B.), but the name was changed by law schools in the United States in the 1960's. Cf. LL.M.; J.S.D.; S.J.D.; LL.D.

**jeopardy** *n.* risk of punishment for an offense. A criminal defendant is put in jeopardy when the jury is sworn in or, in a nonjury trial, when the first witness is sworn in. See also DOUBLE JEOPARDY.

**jetsam** *n.* cargo, equipment, or other material deliberately thrown overboard from a vessel, especially to contend with a peril, as to prevent a fire from spreading or the vessel from sinking.
——**Usage.** Various legal authorities at various times have attempted to distinguish *jetsam* from FLOTSAM and LAGAN by restricting the use of this term either to jettisoned material that floated ashore or to jettisoned material that sank and was not attached to a buoy. In actual usage, however, the term simply refers to things deliberately jettisoned, regardless of what happens to them thereafter. See also JETTISON; WRECK.

**jettison** *v.* **1.** to throw overboard in order to lighten a vessel or aircraft or deal with an emergency.
**2.** to unburden oneself of; discard.
——*n.* **3.** the act of jettisoning.
**4.** the property jettisoned; JETSAM.
——**jettisonable** *adj.*

**Jim Crow** *n.* the practice and policy of racial segregation and discrimination that was characteristic of American public policy for most of the country's history.

**Jim Crow law** *n.* any law discriminating against black people, such as the laws embodied in the BLACK CODES.

**JJ.** See J.

**j.n.o.v.** See under JUDGMENT.

**John Doe** *n.* **1.** historically, the usual name given to the fictitious tenant and nominal plaintiff in a common law action of ejectment. See note at EJECTMENT. Cf. RICHARD ROE.
**2.** a fictitious name used, sometimes with slight variations, in case names and in legal documents such as warrants and summonses, either to conceal a person's identity, or because the person's real name is not known, or because it is not yet known whether such a person exists.
See also *John Doe summons* (under SUMMONS); *John Doe warrant* (under WARRANT¹); JANE DOE; RICHARD ROE.

**join** *v.* to bring an additional claim or party into a case. See also *join issue* (under ISSUE¹). Cf. SEVER.
——**joinable** *adj.*

**joinder** *n.* **1.** the joining together in one action of more than one plaintiff or defendant **(party joinder** or **joinder of parties)** or more than one claim or charge **(claim joinder** or **joinder of claims).** Modern practice generally encourages joinder in the interest of resolving all aspects of a complex dispute in a single trial.
**2. compulsory joinder** joinder of a *necessary party* or *indispensable party* (see under PARTY). Such a party must be joined in the action if possible; and if a party found by the judge to be indispensable cannot be joined, the action will be dismissed.
**3. permissive joinder** joinder of a *proper party* (see under PARTY). The court will allow, but not require, the joinder of such a party.
See also MISJOINDER; NONJOINDER. Cf. CONSOLIDATION; *joinder of issue* (under ISSUE¹); SEVER.

**joint** *adj.* **1.** collective; involving two or more people or entities acting or being dealt with together. See, for example, *joint account* (under ACCOUNT); *joint custody* (under CUSTODY); *joint liability* (under LIABILITY); *joint obligation* (under OBLIGATION); *joint owner* (under OWNER); *joint return* (under RETURN); *joint tortfeasor* (under TORTFEASOR); *joint will* (under WILL); *joint work* (under WORK). Cf. SEVERAL; JOINT AND SEVERAL.
**2.** referring to concurrent ownership of an interest in property by two or more people with equal *undivided interests* (see under INTEREST¹) in the whole, equal rights to possession and use of the property, and RIGHT OF SURVIVORSHIP: *joint estate; joint owner; joint ownership; joint tenancy; joint tenant.* See also *four unities* (under UNITY). Cf. BY THE ENTIRETY; IN COMMON; IN COPARCENARY; IN SEVERALTY; COMMUNITY PROPERTY.
—**jointly** *adv.*

**joint adventure** *n.* Same as JOINT VENTURE.

**joint adventurer** *n.* Same as *joint venturer* (see under JOINT VENTURE).

**joint and several** *adj.* susceptible of being treated legally either as JOINT or as SEVERAL—that is, as either collective or individual—at the option of the person initiating an action. See, e.g., *joint and several liability* (under LIABILITY); *joint and several obligation* (under OBLIGATION). Cf. JOINT; SEVERAL.
—**jointly and severally** *adv.*

**joint and survivor annuity** *n.* See under ANNUITY.

**joint annuity** *n.* See under ANNUITY.

**joint defense** *n.* a coordinated defense by two or more defendants in a case.
——**Note.** A joint defense strategy can be advantageous because it enables the defendants to pool resources and put up a united front. On the other hand, a defendant with a good argument that any liability or blame should fall solely on the other defendants might prefer to mount an independent defense.

**joint defense agreement** *n.* an agreement among two or more defendants in a case to mount a joint defense.
——**Note.** A joint defense agreement might include provisions on such matters as sharing expenses, dividing labor, postponing cross-claims, sharing information, and maintaining confidentiality.

**joint defense privilege** *n.* an extension of the ATTORNEY-CLIENT PRIVILEGE under which communications pursuant to a joint defense effort, either from a defendant to another defendant's attorney or from a defendant to the defendant's own attorney who then passes the information on to an attorney for another defendant, are protected from disclosure to the other side or in court. Also called **common interest rule, common defense rule.**

**joint life annuity** *n.* See under ANNUITY.

**joint stock company** (or **association**) *n.* See under COMPANY.

**joint venture** *n.* an arrangement between two or more people or entities to work together on a specific project. Joint ventures are usually entered into because each participant (**venturer** or **joint venturer**) possesses some necessary skill or resource that the other lacks. Also called **joint adventure.**

**journalist's privilege** *n.* Same as REPORTER'S PRIVILEGE.

**journalist's shield law** *n.* Same as REPORTER'S SHIELD LAW.

**J.S.D.** (from Latin *Juris Scientiae Doctor,* lit. "Doctor of the Science of Law") an abbreviation for the advanced law degree known variously as **Doctor of the Science of Law, Doctor of Juridical Science,** or **Doctor of Jurisprudence.** The J.S.D. is a Ph.D.–level degree held by very few lawyers; it is sought primarily by individuals who plan a career of legal scholarship and teaching, and even on law school faculties it is relatively rare. Requirements for the degree generally include a minimum of one year's study beyond the LL.M. or its equivalent, completion of a dissertation, and an oral examination on the topic of the dissertation. At some law schools the degree is called the S.J.D.

**judge** *n., v.,* **judged, judging.** —*n.* **1.** a public official whose function is to hear and decide legal disputes, preside over trials, and generally monitor the conduct of cases presented to a court or administrative body and move the cases toward a final settlement or decision.

**2. Judge** the title accorded to judges in many courts, including the United States District Courts and United States Courts of Appeals. Cf. JUSTICE².

**3. active judge** a judge who is not a *senior judge;* a judge responsible for a full share of the cases that come to a court.

**4. appellate judge** a judge who serves on an appellate court; one whose job primarily entails the hearing of cases on appeal.

**5. Article I judge** a judge of an *Article I court* (see under COURT). Unlike *Article III judges,* Article I judges do not have lifetime tenure.

**6. Article III judge** a judge of an *Article III court* (see under COURT). Under the Constitution, these judges serve "during good Behaviour"; that is, they are appointed for life to protect them from the need to curry political favor, and can only be impeached for corruption or similar misbehavior.

**7. associate judge a.** in some courts, a judge other than the chief judge of the court. **b. Associate Judge** the title accorded to such a judge.

**8. chief judge a.** the judge with leadership and administrative responsibility for a court. In some courts the chief judge is specifically selected for that position; in others the job falls automatically to the active judge with the most seniority. **b. Chief Judge** the title accorded to such a judge.

**9. circuit judge a.** historically, a judge who traveled from one town to another to hear cases. See also CIRCUIT. **b.** a judge of any court denominated a *circuit court* (see under COURT). **c.** a judge of a UNITED STATES COURT OF APPEALS. **d. Circuit Judge** the title accorded to such a judge. Cf. *Circuit Justice* (under

JUSTICE²).

**10. district judge a.** a judge of any court denominated a *district court* (see under COURT). **b.** a judge of a UNITED STATES DISTRICT COURT. **c. District Judge** the title accorded to such a judge.

**11. judge a quo** the judge from whose decision an appeal is taken. See also A QUO.

**12. presiding judge** or **president judge a.** the judge who sits in the middle and presides at a hearing or argument before a panel of several judges, usually the most senior of the active judges on the panel. **b.** in some courts, the *chief judge.* **c. Presiding Judge** or **President Judge** the title accorded to such a judge.

**13. senior judge a.** in some courts, including the United States District Courts and the United States Courts of Appeals, a judge who has reached the age of retirement but chooses to continue working as a judge. Senior judges are permitted to choose how heavy a caseload they will take responsibility for. **b.** in some courts, the judge with most seniority among those on the court. **c. Senior Judge** the title accorded to such a judge.

**14. trial judge a.** a judge in a court of first instance; a judge whose functions include presiding over trials. **b.** the judge who presides over the trial of a specific case, and ordinarily over all the pretrial and immediate posttrial procedures as well: *The trial judge denied the defendant's motion for judgment notwithstanding the verdict.*

—*v.* **15.** to carry out the functions of a judge: *to judge a case.*

**16.** to pass legal judgment upon; adjudge: *The court judged the book obscene.*

See also ADMINISTRATIVE LAW JUDGE; HANGING JUDGE; *puisne judge* (under PUISNE). Cf. MAGISTRATE; *magistrate judge* (under MAGISTRATE); JUSTICE.
—**judgeable** *adj.*
—**judgeship** *n.*

**judge advocate** *n., pl.* **judge advocates.** a United States military officer who is a lawyer and works in the military justice system. Specifically, an officer of the Judge Advocate General's Corps of the Army or the Navy, an officer of the Air Force or the Marine Corps who is designated as a judge advocate, or an officer of the Coast Guard who is designated as a law specialist.

——**Note.** Depending upon the circumstances and the individual's experience, a judge advocate may function either as a military judge or as counsel for the prosecution or the defense in a court-martial. Judge advocates also perform consultative functions with regard to proposed court-martial proceedings, review for error all court-martial proceedings resulting in a guilty verdict, and sometimes appear as counsel in civilian courts in cases involving the military.

**Judge Advocate General (JAG)** *n.*, *pl.* **Judge Advocates General.** the chief legal officer of a United States military service, acting both as chief legal adviser for the civilian and miltary authorities in charge of that service and as head of the military justice system for that service.

——**Note.** The Army, Navy, and Air Force each have a Judge Advocate General; in addition, the General Counsel of the Department of Transportation serves as Judge Advocate General of the Coast Guard except when the Coast Guard is operating as a service in the Navy (in time of war or otherwise at the President's direction). All four are appointed by the President with the advice and consent of the Senate.

**Judge Advocate General's Corps** *n., pl.* **Judge Advocate General's Corps.** the legal and judicial branch of the Army or Navy, headed by the Judge Advocate General for the Army or Navy. Abbreviated, and usually said as, **JAG Corps.**

——**Note.** Like the corresponding medical corps in each service, the Army JAG Corps is classified as a special branch of the Army and the Navy JAG Corps is classified as a staff corps of the Navy.

——**Pronunciation.** In the singular, *Corps* is pronounced like "core"; in the

plural it is pronounced like "cores." The *p* is silent in both cases. See also note at CORP.

**judge trial** *n.* Same as *bench trial* (see under TRIAL).

**judgement** *n.* (esp. British) a variant spelling of JUDGMENT.

——**Usage.** *Judgement*—with an *e*—is the original spelling of this word, and certainly the more logical one; but it is not the conventional spelling. *Judgment*—without an *e*—goes back at least to the seventeenth century, and is now the prevailing form. In the United States, *judgement* is regarded by many as a misspelling, or at best a Britishism; to use that spelling in a court paper is to invite quotation with a supercilious "[SIC]" by either the adversary or the court. In Britain that spelling is less stigmatized, but even there *judgment* is the standard form in legal contexts, and is the more common form in nonjudicial contexts even at their most British: *"Peter Bradley, the Labour MP at the heart of the row, called it further proof of Mr Hague's lack of judgment." The Guardian* (London), Apr. 3, 2000.

**judgment** *n.* **1.** a court's final decision in a case, or occasionally on a particular aspect of a case.
**2.** the formal document embodying such a judgment, usually written in very formal and formulaic language. Cf. OPINION.
**3. consent judgment** a judgment agreed to by the parties affected, usually implementing a settlement reached by negotiation.
**4. declaratory judgment** a judgment resolving a dispute about legal rights or status but not awarding any damages or specific relief. For example, two parties with conflicting claims to the same land might ask a court simply to declare which claim is valid.
**5. default judgment** a judgment against a party for failing to appear or to proceed with a case. Also called **judgment by default.**
**6. deficiency judgment** in a case in which property of a debtor was sold at a court-supervised auction to satisfy a debt but failed to bring in enough

money, a judgment against the debtor for the balance still owed.

**7. final judgment** a court's final decision in a case, disposing of the entire action.

**8. in personam judgment** or **judgment in personam** a judgment against a specific person or entity. If a money judgment against a party goes unpaid, any available property of that party may be seized to satisfy the judgment. Also called **personal judgment.** See also IN PERSONAM.

**9. in rem judgment** or **judgment in rem** a judgment determining the status or disposition of an item of property or a legal relationship. See also IN REM.

**10. judgment absolute** a judgment that, after starting out as a *judgment nisi,* has become final.

**11. judgment nisi** a tentative judgment, issued at the behest of one party, which will become a *judgment absolute* if the other party fails to appear and show cause why it should not. See also NISI.

**12. judgment notwithstanding the verdict** a judgment contrary to the jury's findings in a case, entered by the judge on the ground that the jury's verdict lacked evidentiary support or was contrary to law. Also called **judgment n.o.v.** or, informally, **j.n.o.v.,** from the Latin *non obstante veredicto* (lit. "notwithstanding the verdict").See also *verdict against the weight of the evidence* (under VERDICT). Cf. *judgment on the verdict.*

**13. judgment on the pleadings** judgment granted to one side or the other even before the parties have commenced pretrial discovery, because the pleadings themselves contain admissions that, as a matter of law, permit only one possible outcome.

**14. judgment on the verdict** judgment in accordance with the jury's findings. Cf. *judgment notwithstanding the verdict.*

**15. summary judgment** judgment entered without a full trial because the evidence (or lack of evidence) brought out in pretrial discovery makes it clear which side must prevail as a matter of law.

See also *judgment creditor* (under CREDITOR); *judgment debtor* (under DEBTOR); *judgment lien* (under LIEN); and see note at JUDGEMENT.

**judgment proof** describing a person or entity without assets that could be seized to satisfy a money judgment, making any such judgment worthless.

**judicial** *adj.* **1.** relating to a court or the courts: *the judicial branch of government.*
**2.** relating to a judge or judges: *judicial convention; judicial ethics.*
**3. judicial economy** efficiency in the management of judicial business; conservation of court resources: *The court consolidated the two related cases for trial in the interest of judicial economy.*
**4. judicial notice** acceptance of a fact by the judge in a case without requiring it to be proved. This is permitted when a fact is beyond reasonable dispute—either because it is generally known (the White House is located in Washington, D.C.) or because it is ascertainable from standard sources (on the night of the crime, the moon was 93% full).
See also *judicial bond* (under BOND[2]); *judicial day* (under DIES JURIDICUS); *judicial discretion* (under DISCRETION); *judicial gloss* (under GLOSS); *judicial immunity* (under IMMUNITY); *judicial legislation* (under LEGISLATION); *judicial review* (under REVIEW); *judicial sale* (under SALE).
**—judicially** *adv.*

**judiciary** *n., pl.* **judiciaries. 1.** the judicial branch of government; a system of courts.
**2.** judges collectively.

**jump bail** See under BAIL[1].

**junior** *adj.* Same as SUBORDINATE.

**junior partner** *n.* See under PARTNER.

**junk bond** *n.* See under BOND[1].

**junk science** *n. Informal.* purportedly scientific evidence sought to be presented to a jury by way of an expert witness but actually having no real foundation in existing scientific knowledge or reputable scientific theory.
**——Note.** The Supreme Court has held

that under the Federal Rules of Evidence it is the duty of the judge to make a preliminary assessment of the validity of the scientific reasoning and methodology before scientific evidence is presented to the jury. *Daubert v. Merrell Dow Pharmaceuticals, Inc.* 509 U.S. 579 (1993). The extent to which this procedure works to prevent cases from being decided on the basis of junk science is variable.

**jural** *adj.* **1.** pertaining to law; legal.
**2.** of or pertaining to rights and obligations.

**jurat** *n.* a certificate on an affidavit, by a notary public or other officer legally authorized to administer oaths, certifying that the affidavit was sworn to or affirmed in the officer's presence on a particular day.
——**Note.** The language of the jurat is a matter of custom and varies from place to place. A typical jurat reads: "Sworn to and subscribed before me this ____ day of [month], [year]," followed by the signature and seal of the officer.

**juridical** *adj.* pertaining to law or legal proceedings. See also *juridical person* (under PERSON).
—**juridically** *adv.*

**Juris Doctor** *n.* See J.D.

**jurisdiction**[1] *n.* **1.** the power and authority of a court or administrative tribunal to decide legal issues and disputes. The scope of a particular court's jurisdiction is determined by a combination of constitutional and statutory provisions.
**2. ancillary jurisdiction a.** broadly, the power of a court to decide issues incidental to a case properly within its jurisdiction, when those issues standing alone would have been beyond its jurisdiction. **b.** specifically, in a case that is properly before a federal court because the plaintiffs and defendants are from different states, the power to dispose at the same time of a related claim between two defendants, or occasionally two plaintiffs, from the same state. See also *diversity jurisdiction*; *supplemental jurisdiction*.
**3. appellate jurisdiction** jurisdiction to review orders and judgments of a lower tribunal. Cf. *original jurisdiction*.
**4. concurrent jurisdiction** jurisdiction of more than one court or agency with respect to the same type of case. For example, the state and federal courts have concurrent jurisdiction to enforce many federal laws. Cf. *exclusive jurisdiction*.
**5. continuing jurisdiction** jurisdiction over a case retained by the court even after final judgment has been rendered, for the purpose of dealing with any problems that arise in implementing the judgment.
**6. diversity jurisdiction** the jurisdiction of federal courts to entertain controversies between citizens of different states, or between a U.S. citizen and a foreign nation, citizen, or subject. See also CITIZEN; JURISDICTIONAL AMOUNT.
**7. exclusive jurisdiction** jurisdiction with respect to a type of case that may not be brought in any other tribunal. Specialized tribunals such as probate court or traffic court often have exclusive jurisdiction over cases within their specialty, and the federal courts have exclusive jurisdiction over cases in certain areas of federal law. Cf. *concurrent jurisdiction*.
**8. federal question jurisdiction** the jurisdiction of federal courts to decide cases arising under FEDERAL LAW.
**9. general jurisdiction** jurisdiction to hear any kind of case except one restricted to some specialized court. Cf. *limited jurisdiction*.
**10. in personam jurisdiction** or **jurisdiction in personam** jurisdiction to render a judgment that will be binding upon a particular person or entity. In a civil case, in personam jurisdiction exists over a party if that party either has appeared voluntarily in the case or has been properly served with a summons within the state or (in cases where *long-arm jurisdiction* applies) elsewhere. Also called **jurisdiction of** (or **over**) **the person.** See also *personal jurisdiction;* IN PERSONAM.
**11. in rem jurisdiction** or **jurisdiction in rem** jurisdiction to render a judgment with respect to property or a relationship located within the state in an

action concerning the property or relationship itself, such as an action to QUIET TITLE to land or to condemn contraband goods intercepted by federal agents at the border. See also *personal jurisdiction;* IN REM.

**12. jurisdiction of** (or **over**) **the case** jurisdiction to entertain a particular case; a court has jurisdiction over a case if it has both *subject matter jurisdiction* and *personal jurisdiction.*

**13. limited jurisdiction** jurisdiction to deal only with a particular category of cases; for example, the jurisdiction of a family court or a small claims court. Unlike some state courts, all federal courts are courts of limited jurisdiction, because they may hear only certain categories of cases specified in the Constitution and authorized by Congress. Also called **special jurisdiction.** Cf. *general jurisdiction.* See also *subject matter jurisdiction.*

**14. long-arm jurisdiction** jurisdiction to render a judgment binding upon a person or entity outside the state in a case arising out of conduct by that person or entity, either in person or through an agent, that either occurred within the state or occurred elsewhere and had an impact within the state. See also MINIMUM CONTACTS; TRANSACTION OF BUSINESS.

**15. original jurisdiction** jurisdiction to give a case its first hearing and issue a judgment. Every new case must be filed in a court or agency that has original jurisdiction with respect to such cases. Cf. *appellate jurisdiction.*

**16. pendent jurisdiction** in a case that is properly before a federal court because it arises under federal law, the power to dispose at the same time of related state-law claims. See also *federal question jurisdiction; supplemental jurisdiction.*

**17. personal jurisdiction** jurisdiction to render a binding decision with respect to a particular person or thing. Traditional analysis divides personal jurisdiction in civil cases into three categories: *in personam jurisdiction, in rem jurisdiction,* and *quasi in rem jurisdiction.* Cf. *subject matter jurisdiction.*

**18. quasi in rem jurisdiction** or **jurisdiction quasi in rem** jurisdiction to render judgment upon a claim against a person who has property within the state to the extent of the value of that property, even when the dispute in the case has nothing to do with the property. Traditionally this has been used as a device for initiating actions against people over whom *in personam jurisdiction* could not be obtained, but this would now generally be considered unconstitutional. See also *personal jurisdiction;* QUASI IN REM.

**19. subject matter jurisdiction** jurisdiction to hear and decide cases of a particular type. The two major categories of subject matter jurisdiction in the federal courts are *diversity jurisdiction* and *federal question jurisdiction.* Cf. *personal jurisdiction.*

**20. supplemental jurisdiction** the name now used in the federal courts for *ancillary jurisdiction* (def. 2a). The principal categories of supplemental jurisdiction are *ancillary jurisdiction* (def. b) and *pendent jurisdiction.*
—**jurisdictional** *adj.*
—**jurisdictionally** *adv.*

**jurisdiction²** *n.* the geographic area throughout which the authority of a court, legislative body, law enforcement agency, or other governmental unit extends.

**jurisdictional amount** *n.* the amount of money or the value of property that must be at stake in order for a case to be within the jurisdiction of a particular court. For example, Congress has decided that the federal courts should not be available to hear cases founded upon *diversity jurisdiction* (see under JURISDICTION¹) unless there is a lot of money at stake—currently more than $75,000. Diversity cases involving less than this jurisdictional amount must be brought in state court.

**jurisdictional fact** *n.* a fact relevant to the question of whether a court has jurisdiction over a person or a case, especially a fact tending to establish that the court does have jurisdiction.

**jurisprudence** *n.* **1.** the philosophy of

law; the consideration of broad questions relating to such matters as the sources, functions, and meaning of law. **2.** a body of judicial opinions: *the civil rights jurisprudence of the Supreme Court from 1954 to 1969.*
—**jurisprudential** *adj.*
—**jurisprudentially** *adv.*

**jurist** *n.* a person versed in the law, especially a judge or legal scholar.

**juristic** *adj.* of or pertaining to a jurist, jurisprudence, or the law.
—**juristically** *adv.*

**juristic person** *n.* See under PERSON.

**juror** *n.* **1.** a member of a jury.
**2.** loosely, a member of a jury array; a person who has appeared in response to a summons for jury duty.

**jury** *n., pl.* **juries. 1.** Also called **petit** (or **petty**) **jury.** a group of citizens called upon to hear the evidence at a trial, decide the facts, and render a verdict in accordance with the judge's instructions on the law. Traditionally this was a group of twelve men, often all white, required to reach a unanimous verdict. Under current interpretations of the Sixth and Seventh Amendments (see Appendix), people may not be excluded from a jury solely on the basis of race or sex; states may provide for six-member juries or nonunanimous verdicts in state criminal cases; and six-member juries may be used in civil cases in the federal courts. See also *jury trial* (under TRIAL); PETIT; PETTY. Cf. *grand jury.*
**2. death-qualified jury** in a capital case, a jury from which all potential jurors who would be unwilling to vote for the death penalty have been removed. See also note at DEATH QUALIFICATION.
**3. grand jury** a group of citizens summoned to hear evidence presented by a prosecutor and issue an INDICTMENT if they find sufficient evidence to warrant trying a particular person for a particular crime. The Fifth Amendment (see Appendix) requires such screening of

accusations by a grand jury before anyone can be prosecuted on a serious federal criminal charge. Federal grand juries are made up of 16 to 23 people, and it takes a vote of twelve to authorize an indictment. The constitutional requirement of indictment by grand jury has never been extended to state prosecutions; and since in practice grand juries seldom amount to more than a rubber stamp for prosecutors, they have been abolished, reduced in size, or given a reduced role in most states.
**4. hung jury** a jury unable to reach a verdict. This usually results, first, in an *Allen charge* (see under CHARGE), and if that fails, then a MISTRIAL.
**5. jury array** Same as VENIRE.
**6. jury panel** Also called **panel. a.** the jury in a particular case. **b.** sometimes, the entire VENIRE from which a jury is to be chosen. See also IMPANEL.
See also *jury trial* (under TRIAL); MOCK JURY; SHADOW JURY.

**jury consultant** *n.* an individual in the business of advising attorneys in major cases on techniques for obtaining a jury that is as likely as possible to be sympathetic to their client's position.
—**Note.** Jury consultants use sociological and psychological studies, and often perform their own surveys, to ascertain what demographic factors are likely to be associated with positive or negative attitudes toward issues or individuals involved in the case. They also set up and manage MOCK TRIAL and SHADOW JURY procedures, and sometimes conduct surveys on bias in the local jury pool to back up motions for CHANGE OF VENUE.

**jury duty** *n.* **1.** the obligation of a citizen to make himself or herself available periodically for possible service as a juror.
**2.** service as a juror or venire member.

**jury nullification** *n.* the power, and occasional practice, of a jury in a criminal case to ignore the judge's instructions on the law and acquit a defendant despite overwhelming evidence of guilt and absence of reasonable doubt.
—**Note.** Because of the constitutional

protection against DOUBLE JEOPARDY, the jury's acquittal must stand. Depending upon one's view of a particular case, jury nullification is either a gross injustice or the final safeguard of the citizenry against callous and overzealous prosecution.

**jus** *n., pl.* **jura.** *Latin.* right; law.

**jus cogens** *n. Latin.* (lit. "compelling law") *International Law.* a principle of international law so fundamental that nations may not withdraw from it or derogate it by treaty.

**jus gentium** *n. Latin.* (lit. "law of peoples") **1.** INTERNATIONAL LAW; the law of nations.
**2. jus gentium privatum** *private international law* (see under INTERNATIONAL LAW).
**3. jus gentium publicum** *public international law* (see under INTERNATIONAL LAW).

**jus tertii** *n. Latin.* (lit. "the right of a third [person]") the legal right of a third party; the right of a person who is not a party to a case with respect to the subject matter of the case.
——**Note.** Although the rights of third parties are often of concern in court cases, the specific phrase *jus tertii* is particularly associated with the common law action of EJECTMENT and disputes over title to land. In general, if a plaintiff seeks to remove a defendant from land upon a claim of superior title, it is not enough to show that the defendant does not have good title; it must be shown that the plaintiff does have good title. If in fact neither party has title—that is, the title actually resides in a third person—the defendant will win, because the plaintiff has no more right to be on the land than the defendant. It is said, therefore, that *jus tertii* is a defense in such an action: If the defendant can show that the right claimed by the plaintiff actually resides in a third person, the plaintiff will lose, even though the defendant has no right to be on the land.

**just compensation** *n.* the compensation that the Fifth Amendment (see Appendix) requires the state or federal government to pay to a property owner whose property is taken for *public use* (see under USE). In general, it is the MARKET VALUE of the property at the time of the taking, taking into account the *best and highest use* (see under USE) to which a private buyer could have put the property. See also TAKING; EMINENT DOMAIN.

**just war** *n.* the philosophical concept of a war that may be pursued by a nation without violating ethical norms or international law; a war conducted to defend a nation against AGGRESSION by another nation or to suppress serious violations of international law such as genocide or crimes against humanity, and not compromised by other motives such as hope for territorial or monetary gain. Cf. WAR OF AGGRESSION.

**justice¹** *n.* **1.** the ideal of fair and beneficent treatment of all people by each other and by their governments, which law in a democratic society attempts to serve.
**2.** the system of law and administration of law: *administration of justice;* OBSTRUCTION OF JUSTICE.
**3. commutative justice** justice in personal relationships; justice in relation to in business and personal dealings.
**4. distributive justice** justice in the apportionment of wealth and resources among people; justice in allocation of the benefits and burdens of life.
**5. retributive justice** justice in regard to punishment; particularly, a view of justice that stresses the importance and desirability of punishment of those deemed deserving of it. Also called **corrective justice.**

**justice²** *n.* **1. a.** a judge or magistrate in certain courts, particularly those designated "supreme" courts (most notably the Supreme Court of the United States) and inferior courts at the very lowest level (such as justice of the peace courts and police courts). **b. Justice** the title accorded to judges in those courts.
**2. associate justice a.** in some courts, including the Supreme Court of the United States, a judge other than the chief judge of the court. **b. Associate**

**Justice** the title accorded to associate justices in those courts.
**3. chief justice a.** in a court whose judges are referred to as justices, the justice with leadership and administrative responsibility for the court. **b. Chief Justice** the title accorded to the chief judge of such a court. See also CHIEF JUSTICE OF THE UNITED STATES.
**4. Circuit Justice** the title accorded to any justice of the United States Supreme Court when acting as the emergency appellate judge for a CIRCUIT of the United States judicial system. Each justice of the Supreme Court is responsible for handling emergency requests for injunctions, stays of execution, and the like arising in one or more of the federal judicial circuits when the UNITED STATES COURT OF APPEALS for that circuit has made its ruling in a matter and the only level of appeal left is to the Supreme Court. Until 1891, justices of the Supreme Court were required to travel regularly to their assigned circuit to handle regular cases; their title when performing those duties was also *Circuit Justice.*

**justiciable** *adj.* appropriate for adjudication; suitable for resolution by a court.
—**justiciability** *n.*
——**Note.** In general, to be justiciable a case must involve a genuine dispute over legal rights or interests, resolution of which will have some real effect beyond satisfying the litigants' curiosity. In addition, the issue involved must not be one that, under the Constitution, lies within the exclusive province of the legislative or executive branch of government. Cases that might be dismissed as nonjusticiable include a case seeking an ADVISORY OPINION, a *collusive suit* (see under SUIT), a case that is MOOT, and a case raising a *political question* (see under QUESTION[2]).

**justifiable homicide** *n.* See under HOMICIDE.

**justification** *n.* a legally sufficient excuse for having done something that otherwise would constitute a tort or a crime; for example, ENTRAPMENT, DURESS, or NECESSITY.

**juvenile** *adj.* **1.** youthful; immature; below the age of majority.
**2.** intended for or suitable for the young: *juvenile court; juvenile detention facility.*
—*n.* **3.** a youth; a minor.
**4.** especially, a person not yet old enough to be treated as an adult by the criminal justice system.
——**Note.** The ages and circumstances under which a young person in trouble with the law will be treated as a juvenile vary from state to state; typically, state statutes set one age below which a youngster must be treated as a juvenile and a higher age above which a person must be treated as an adult, with treatment between those ages depending upon the circumstances of the case.

**juvenile court** *n.* a special court established in some states to handle criminal matters in which the accused is treated as a juvenile, and sometimes also child protection proceedings.
——**Note.** As compared with criminal courts for adult offenders, the emphasis in juvenile courts is upon rehabilitation of youthful offenders rather than punishment.

**juvenile delinquency** *n.* **1.** antisocial and illegal conduct by minors generally.
**2.** the antisocial or illegal conduct of an individual juvenile delinquent.
**3.** the fact of being a juvenile delinquent.
Also called **delinquency.**

**juvenile delinquent** *n.* **1.** a *juvenile offender* (see under OFFENDER).
**2.** especially, a minor who persistently engages in antisocial or criminal conduct.
Also called **delinquent.**

**juvenile offender** *n.* See under OFFENDER.

# K

**kangaroo court** *n. Slang.* **1.** a mock court set up by criminals or vigilantes to reach a predetermined verdict of guilty.
**2.** a highly derogatory term for an actual judicial proceeding regarded as outrageously improper or manifestly unfair.
See also STAR CHAMBER.

**Keogh plan** *n.* See under RETIREMENT PLAN.

**kickback** *n.* **1.** a form of BRIBERY in which a company that is awarded a contract, or from which a purchase is made, turns over a portion of the money received to an official or employee of the other party to the transaction, as a reward for helping to bring about the transaction or as an incentive to exercise such influence in the future.
**2.** a form of EXTORTION in which an employer, supervisor, or union official demands a portion of a worker's rightful wages as a condition of continued employment.

**kidnapping** *n.* the crime of carrying off or isolating a person for the purpose of demanding money **(ransom)** for his release, using him as a hostage, harming or terrorizing him or others, or the like.
See also ABDUCTION; PARENTAL KIDNAPPING.
—**kidnap** *v.*, **kidnapped, kidnapping.**
—**kidnapper** *n.*
——**False Friend.** Despite the allusion to "kids," the victim may be either a child or an adult.

**kind** *n.* See IN KIND.

**King's Bench** *n.* an English court of general jurisdiction for both civil and criminal cases. The court goes back centuries and is the source of much of the common law still in effect in America today. When a queen is on the throne, the court is called **Queen's Bench.**

**kite** *v.*, **kited, kiting.** to write a check knowing that there are not yet sufficient funds in the account to cover it. Depending upon the circumstances, check kiting may be a crime, especially where such a check is deposited in another bank account to create a false balance which is then withdrawn.
—**kiter** *n.*

**kiyas** *n.* See QIYAS.

**knock and announce rule** *n.* the general rule that police officers must knock and announce themselves before breaking into a place to make an arrest or execute a search warrant.

**knock off** to make unlicensed copies of someone else's trademark or copyrighted design (for example, of clothing, fabric, watches, or furniture), usually for sale at a substantially lower price than the original. The copy is called a **knockoff.**

**know all men by these presents** an ancient but still quite common formulaic expression that may be placed at the beginning of a legal instrument, meaning essentially, "Let the world be put on notice by this instrument." See also PRESENTS.
——**Note.** The purpose of this introductory phrase is to impress upon both the person who signs the document and anyone who reads it the seriousness and legally binding nature of the instrument. It thus serves for legal writings much the same function that HEAR YE or OYEZ does for courtroom proceedings.

**knowledge** *n.* **1.** Also called **actual knowledge.** awareness of a fact. "Knowledge" that a certain result will follow from certain action means awareness that the result is practically

261

certain to occur. Knowledge is a crucial element in many tort cases and criminal cases, since assessment of culpability often depends upon what the people involved knew; for example, in a homicide case, the degree of guilt might depend in part on whether the defendant knew the gun was loaded. See also STATE OF MIND. Cf. *constructive knowledge; imputed knowledge.*

**2.** Also called **personal knowledge.** awareness of a fact gained from direct observation or experience, as distinguished from a belief based upon what others have said or upon a less-than-certain chain of reasoning from other information. In general, witnesses are allowed to testify only to matters within their personal knowledge, and statements in affidavits and pleadings, unless expressly made upon INFORMATION AND BELIEF, should be based upon personal knowledge. Cf. HEARSAY; OPINION; *opinion evidence* (under EVIDENCE).

**3. carnal knowledge** See CARNAL KNOWLEDGE.

**4. constructive knowledge** knowledge that the law attributes to a person regardless of whether that person has actual knowledge of the matter, usually because the circumstances are such that a failure to know a fact is regarded as inexcusable. For example, an individual who was personally served with a court order but failed to read it would be said to have constructive knowledge of its contents despite the lack of actual knowledge.

**5. imputed knowledge** in a relationship of principal and agent, employer and employee, or the like, the superior's constructive knowledge of facts of which the subordinate was made aware in the course of the subordinate's duties.

—**know** *v.,* **knew, known, knowing.**
—**knowing** *adj.*
—**knowingly** *adv.*

**Koran** or **Qur'an** *n. Islamic Law.* the sacred scripture of Islam, revered as the word of God as revealed to Muhammad. The Koran is the basic text from which Islamic law is derived—the first of the four USUL AL-FIQH.

# L

**labor organization** *n.* the term used in the National Labor Relations Act for a UNION. It is defined very broadly to include any group of employees whose purposes include dealing with employers with regard to grievances or terms and conditions of employment.

**labor union** *n.* Same as UNION.

**laches** *n.* unreasonable delay in pursuing a known right against someone.

——**Note.** Laches is an *equitable defense* (see under DEFENSE) that may be raised in a case in which the defendant's position has been prejudiced by the plaintiff's delay in taking legal action. In cases at law, a plaintiff ordinarily may wait until the last day before expiration of the STATUTE OF LIMITATIONS to sue; but if an injunction or other equitable relief is sought, the court may take laches into account. For example, a landowner may not sit back and watch a building being built knowing that it encroaches on his land, and then expect a sympathetic hearing in a suit to have the building torn down, although he might still be entitled to compensatory damages for the loss of a little piece of his land.

**lading** *n.* See BILL OF LADING.

**lagan** *n.* wreckage or jettisoned property lying under water at sea; especially goods to which a buoy has been attached as a marker in the hope that they can later be recovered. In older usage the term appears in many variant spellings, the most common of which is **ligan**. Cf. FLOTSAM; see also JETSAM; WRECK.

**lame duck** *n.* **1.** an elected official or group of officials, such as a legislator or president, continuing in office during the period between an election defeat and a successor's assumption of office. **2.** a president or other officeholder who is completing a term of office and chooses not to run or is ineligible to run for reelection.
—**lame-duck** *adj.*

**lame-duck session** *n.* See under SESSION.

**land** *n.* Same as *real property* (see under PROPERTY).

——**False Friend.** Although the term is sometimes used in the narrow sense of earth or soil, in law it is usually used as a shorthand for real property in general.

**landlord** *n.* the person who grants a LEASEHOLD interest in real property to a TENANT. See also LEASE.

**landmark case** See under CASE¹.

**lapse** *v.*, **lapsed, lapsing,** *n.* —*v.* **1.** to expire because of the passage of time or be extinguished by the happening of some event. For example, an OFFER of a contract will lapse if not accepted within the time specified in the offer (or within a reasonable time, if no time is specified); a BEQUEST or DEVISE will lapse if the taker named in the will dies before the testator (unless the bequest is saved by an ANTILAPSE STATUTE); a statute enacted with an expiration date will lapse if not renewed.
—*n.* **2.** such expiration or extinguishment.

**larceny** *n.* the crime of wrongfully taking possession of personal property from another with intent to convert it to one's own use. Often designated as **grand larceny** if the value of the property exceeds a certain amount, and **petit larceny** (or **petty larceny**) otherwise. See also ASPORTATION; ANIMUS FURANDI; GRAND; PETIT; PETTY; and notes at TRESPASSORY TAKING and LEGAL FICTION.
—**larcenist** *n.*
—**larcenous** *adj.*

—**larcenously** *adv.*

——**Note.** The term *larceny* has been abandoned in many modern criminal codes in favor of the broader concept of THEFT.

**last clear chance** *n.* a doctrine under which, as between two people whose negligence contributed to an accident, the one who clearly had the last opportunity to avoid the accident may be held liable for injuries to the other. Thus a person who negligently placed himself in a dangerous situation might nevertheless be able to recover in full from another who should have realized the danger and avoided the accident. In most states this principle has been abandoned in favor of the more flexible doctrine of *comparative negligence* (see under NEGLIGENCE).

**last in, first out (LIFO)** *n.* an accounting convention that evaluates inventory and measures income from sales upon the assumption that the last items purchased are always the first sold, that is, every item sold is taken from the lot most recently added to inventory. Cf. FIRST IN, FIRST OUT.

**last will and testament** *n.* a WILL. Sometimes called **last will.**

——**Usage.** The word "testament" adds nothing. In fact, the word "last" adds nothing; one can make a new "last will" every day. But like much archaic or redundant legal language, the traditional phrase "last will and testament" contributes an aura of seriousness and importance to the undertaking, which is not out of place when one is seriously contemplating one's own death. See also note at TO HAVE AND TO HOLD.

**latent** *adj.* not obvious; present but not such as would be discovered in an inspection made with reasonable care: *latent ambiguity; latent defect.* Allocation of liability for defects in products or property sometimes depends upon whether the problem was latent or PATENT.

—**latently** *adv.*

**latent defect** *n.* See under DEFECT².

**laugh test** *n.* a hypothetical test of whether an argument or position is sufficiently tenable to advance in a court case, negotiation, or the like. The test is: Can you say it without laughing?

——**Usage.** The so-called "laugh test" is the converse of the STRAIGHT-FACE TEST. The terms are used interchangeably. See note at STRAIGHT-FACE TEST for examples.

**launder** *v.* to disguise the true nature of proceeds of criminal activity by engaging in financial transactions, usually through other countries or through a number of intermediaries, designed to conceal the source and ownership of the funds. See also MONEY LAUNDERING; CYBERLAUNDERING.

—**launderer** *n.*

**law** *n.* **1.** the body of rules and principles for human behavior and the conduct of government in an organized community, state, or nation, created or recognized by custom or by government institutions and implemented or enforced by the government. **2.** a body of law relating to a subject: *constitutional law; the law of evidence.* **3.** a STATUTE. **4.** one of the two systems of justice—to some extent competing and to some extent complementary—that existed side by side in England prior to the MERGER OF LAW AND EQUITY. The law courts enforced criminal laws and granted awards of money damages for torts and breaches of contract. See also COMMON LAW (def. 3). Cf. EQUITY. **5.** the profession that deals with law and legal procedures: *the practice of law.* See also ADMINISTRATIVE LAW; AS A MATTER OF LAW; BAD LAW; BY OPERATION OF LAW; CASE LAW; CIVIL LAW; CONCLUSION OF LAW; CONFLICT OF LAWS; *corporate law* (under CORPORATE); *customary law* (under CUSTOM); ECCLESIASTICAL LAW; FEDERAL LAW; FEUDAL LAW; GOOD LAW; *implied in law* (under IMPLIED); INTERNAL LAW; INTERNATIONAL LAW; *maritime law* (under MARITIME); POSITIVE LAW; PRIVATE LAW; PROCEDURE; PUBLIC INTEREST LAW; PUBLIC LAW; *question of law* and *mixed question of fact and law* (both under

QUESTION²); SALIC LAW; SUBSTANCE; WHOLE LAW. Cf. CANON LAW; NATURAL LAW; PARLIAMENTARY LAW.

**law-abiding** *adj.* obedient to law.

**law and economics** *n.sing.* a school of legal thought that analyzes legal issues from the perspective of free market economic theory.

**law clerk** *n.* See under CLERK.

**law day** *n.* **1.** the due date for payment of a secured debt. Under old law, the property of a mortgagor who failed to repay the debt in full by the law day was immediately forfeited. The date is of less significance in modern law, under which failure to pay on time merely gives the mortgagee the right to commence foreclosure proceedings.
**2.** In ancient English law, the day upon which certain courts held open sessions.
**3. Law Day** (in the United States) May 1 of each year, a day set aside by act of Congress in 1961 as "a special day of celebration by the American people in appreciation of their liberties and the reaffirmation of their loyalty to the United States of America; of their rededication to the ideals of equality and justice under law in their relations with each other as well as with other nations; and for the cultivation of that respect for law that is so vital to the democratic way of life."

**law degree** *n.* See under DEGREE.

**law enforcement evidentiary privilege** *n.* Same as INVESTIGATIVE PRIVILEGE.

**law enforcement investigative privilege** *n.* Same as INVESTIGATIVE PRIVILEGE.

**law enforcement investigatory privilege** *n.* Same as INVESTIGATIVE PRIVILEGE.

**law merchant** *n.* The general body of law governing commercial transactions before such rules began to be codified in statutes.
——**History.** The law merchant grew out of the medieval LEX MERCATORIA and was also referred to by that name.

It was to some extent international in character, but was also incorporated into the English common law and thence into American common law. In the United States it is now largely supplanted by the UNIFORM COMMERCIAL CODE.
——**Pronunciation.** The word *merchant* in this phrase is an not a noun ("trader"), but an adjective ("pertaining to trade"). Therefore, instead of having stress only on the first word (as in *book merchant* or *fruit merchant*) the phrase is pronounced with equal or greater stress on the second word: LAW MER-chant.

**law of nations** *n.* Same as *public international law* (see under INTERNATIONAL LAW).

**law of the case** *n.* the principle that once an issue in a case has been decided by one judge or panel of judges, it will not be reconsidered if the case is transferred to a new judge or panel at the same level; except in special circumstances, the subsequent judges will adhere to the prior decision as the "law of the case" even if they disagree with it.

**law review** *n.* a journal for scholarly writing on legal topics. Most law schools publish one or more such periodicals, usually with the word "Review" or "Journal" in the title.

**law Salique** *n.* Same as SALIC LAW.

**law school** *n.* **1.** a school for the study of law and the training of lawyers. The basic curriculum normally consists of three years of study following graduation from college and leads to the degree of Juris Doctor (see J.D.).
**2. accredited law school** a law school certified by a recognized state or national body as meeting certain standards regarding qualifications of faculty, adequacy of facilities, completeness of curriculum, and the like.
——**Note.** In most states a would-be lawyer must have a degree from an accredited law school before taking the BAR EXAMINATION. The primary national accrediting body for law schools in the United States is the AMERICAN

BAR ASSOCIATION, although membership in the ASSOCIATION OF AMERICAN LAW SCHOOLS is also regarded as a form of accreditation. The latter organization is slightly more stringent in its requirements, but graduation from an ABA-accredited law school is sufficient to meet the formal educational prerequisites for taking the bar examination in all states. Cf. READ LAW.

**lawful** *adj.* **1.** authorized or permitted by law; in harmony with law: *lawful conduct; a lawful enterprise.* **2.** recognized or sanctioned by law: *lawful marriage; lawful money.* Cf. LEGAL.
—**lawfully** *adv.*
—**lawfulness** *n.*

**lawsuit** *n.* a SUIT.

**lawyer** *n.* a person whose profession is to advise or act for clients in legal matters; a person licensed by a state to practice law. Cf. JAILHOUSE LAWYER.

**lawyer-client privilege** *n.* Same as ATTORNEY-CLIENT PRIVILEGE.

**lay¹** *v.*, **laid, laying. 1.** to place, put, impose: *The attorney's opening statement will lay the case before the jury. The defendant laid the blame on her business partner. The Constitution gives Congress the power to lay and collect taxes.* **2.** to assert, allege, or describe; especially **a.** to state the venue that is believed to be proper for a case: *Paragraph 4 of the complaint lays venue in the Middle District of Tennessee.* **b.** to declare the amount of damages for which recovery is sought: *The plaintiffs laid damages at one million dollars.*
——**Usage.** Although the words *lie* (past tense: *lay*) and *lay* (past tense: *laid*) are often confused in popular speech, the distinction between them is generally maintained in legal usage, and especially in legal writing. In general, *lay* requires an object: If "place, put, impose," or the like can be substituted in a sentence, some form of LAY¹ is needed. But if the desired meaning is "recline, rest, exist, be situated," or the like, a form of LIE¹ is needed. For example: *The complaint lays venue* (or *Venue is laid*) *in this jurisdiction,* but

*Venue lies* (not *lays*) *in this jurisdiction.* Or in the past tense: *The jury laid the blame* (or *The blame was laid*) *on the parents,* but *The blame lay* (not *laid*) *with the parents.*

**lay²** *adj.* **1.** belonging to, pertaining to, or performed by the people or laity, as distinguished from the clergy. **2.** not belonging to, connected with, or proceeding from a profession, especially the law or medicine.

**layman** *n., pl.* **laymen.** See LAYPERSON.

**layperson** *n., pl.* **laypeople. 1.** a person who is not a member of the clergy; one of the laity. **2.** a person who is not a member of a given profession or possessed of expertise in a particular field, as law or medicine.
Also called **layman** or, in reference to a woman, occasionally **laywoman.**

**laywoman** *n., pl.* **laywomen.** See LAYPERSON.

**lead counsel** *n.* See under COUNSEL.

**lead plaintiff** *n.* See under PLAINTIFF.

**leadership PAC** *n.* See under POLITICAL ACTION COMMITTEE.

**leading case** *n.* See under CASE¹.

**leading question** *n.* See under QUESTION¹.

**lease** *n., v.* **leased, leasing.** —*n.* **1.** the grant of a LEASEHOLD interest in real property, usually in the form of a contract under which the person receiving possession of the property (the TENANT or **lessee**) agrees to pay rent to the grantor (the LANDLORD or **lessor**). **2.** a contract temporarily conveying the right to exclusive possession and use of tangible personal property from one person (the **lessor**) to another (the **lessee**). **3.** the instrument embodying such a grant or contract. **4. gross lease** a lease at a fixed rate of rent. Cf. *net lease; percentage lease.* **5. ground lease** a long-term lease (typically for 99 years) on the ground upon which a large commercial building sits or is to be built. **6. net lease** a lease under which the rent consists of a fixed minimum amount plus a variable sum to cover specified expenses of the landlord, such as taxes and maintenance.

**7. percentage lease** a lease of real property for commercial use in which the rent is based at least in part upon a percentage of the lessee's sales.

—*v.* **8.** to convey property rights by lease.

**9.** to take or hold by lease.

—**leasable** *adj.*

**leaseback** *n.* See *sale and leaseback* (under SALE).

**leasehold** *n.* a right to temporary possession of real property by agreement with the owner of the FREEHOLD or of a superior leasehold on the same property. Also called **leasehold estate; leasehold interest.** For types of leasehold, see TENANCY. See also ESTATE[1]; LANDLORD; TENANT; LEASE.

**leave** *n.* permission from a court to take some action. Also called **leave of court.** See also *dismissal with leave to replead* (under DISMISSAL).

**legacy** *n., pl.* **legacies.** Same as BEQUEST. See also LEGATEE.

**legal** *adj.* **1.** not against the law; not a crime: *Although it was legal to publish the defamatory statement, the publisher was ordered to pay damages for libel.*

**2.** satisfying requirements or formalities of the law; sufficient under the law: *legal consideration; legal demand.*

**3.** created, recognized, or imposed by law: LEGAL TENDER; *legal separation* (see under SEPARATION); *legal duty.*

**4.** pertaining generally to law or the practice of law: *legal theory; legal ethics.*

**5.** pertaining to law as distinguished from fact: *legal question.*

**6.** pertaining to, enforceable under, or derived from principles of LAW (def. 4) as distinguished from EQUITY: *legal title* (see under TITLE); *legal remedy* (see under REMEDY).

**7.** CONSTRUCTIVE: *legal fraud* (see under FRAUD).

See also *legal action* (under ACTION); *legal age* (under AGE); *legal capacity* (under CAPACITY); *legal cause* (under PROXIMATE CAUSE); *legal disability* (under DISABILITY); *legal estate* (under ESTATE[1]); *legal form* (under FORM); *legal heir* (under HEIR); *legal interest* (under INTEREST[1]); *legal interest* (under INTEREST[3]); *legal owner* (under OWNER); *legal person* (under PERSON); *legal right* (under RIGHT); and *legal relief* (under REMEDY).

**legal assistant** *n.* Same as PARALEGAL.

**legal cap** *n.* Same as FOOLSCAP. See also LEGAL PAD.

**legal conceptualism** *n.* Same as FORMALISM.

—**legal conceptualist** *n.*

**legal defender** *n.* See under DEFENDER.

**legal fiction** *n.* **1.** a court's assumption of a fact known to be untrue in order to fit a case into a category recognized by the law, so that relief can be granted and justice done. See note below.

**2.** any assumption contrary to fact that is made by the law for reasons of policy or practicality; for example, the PRESUMPTION OF PATERNITY or PRESUMPTION OF LEGITIMACY, the FERTILE-OCTOGENARIAN RULE, or the retroactive effect of an order made NUNC PRO TUNC. See also DEEM; and see note at ILLEGITIMACY.

Also called **fiction.**

——**History.** Legal fictions have been an important mechanism in the evolution of the common law. For example, LARCENY is traditionally defined as wrongfully taking property from another's possession; to cover situations in which a wrongdoer steals property that someone has accidentally left behind, the courts adopted the fiction that lost property is still in the "possession" of the person who lost it. See also CONSTRUCTIVE. For the ultimate use of legal fiction in the common law, see note at EJECTMENT.

**legal formalism** *n.* See FORMALISM.

—**legal formalist** *n.*

**legal pad** *n.* a tablet of legal-size, lined writing paper, traditionally yellow but now often white, used by lawyers for note-taking and legal drafting. Even in the computer age, it is a rare lawyer who does not have several legal pads with notes and drafts on different topics scattered about the lawyer's desk and office. See also the older and more colorful term FOOLSCAP.

**legal positivism** *n.* See POSITIVISM.
—**legal positivist** *n.*

**legal realism** *n.* a school of JURISPRUDENCE that emphasizes the propriety and the inevitability of taking political conditions and social considerations into account in interpreting and applying the law. Also called **realism.** Cf. FORMALISM.
—**legal realist** *n.*

**legal-size** or **legal-sized** *adj.* (of paper) 8½ × 14 inches.
——**Note.** The preparation of wills, leases, deeds, insurance policies, affidavits, briefs, and other legal documents on extra-long paper has been the a hallmark of the lawyer from time immemorial. And it has been a nuisance for file clerks for a good part of that time. Consequently, the use of legal-size paper for court filings has now been banned in the federal courts and in many states.

**legal tender** *n.* currency that may lawfully be used in payment of debts and may not be deemed inadequate by a creditor to whom it is tendered in the proper amount; the ordinary money of a country.

**legalize** *v.,* **legalized, legalizing.** to adopt legislation making conduct that formerly was unlawful lawful. See discussion under DECRIMINALIZE.
—**legalization** *n.*

**legatee** *n.* **1.** a recipient of a BEQUEST. Cf. DEVISEE.
**2. residuary legatee** a person designated by will to receive or share in the *residuary estate* (see under ESTATE²).

**legislation** *n.* **1.** the enactment of statutes by a LEGISLATURE.
**2.** a statute or body of statutes enacted or proposed.
**3. judicial legislation** a disparaging term for a court decision that interprets or applies the law in a way that the speaker disagrees with, suggesting that the court has usurped the function of the legislature. It is usually used in situations where the court has extended some right to a class of people. But if a court seriously misreads the will of the legislature and the people, the legislature can always pass a law overruling the court—even amending the Constitution if necessary.

**legislative** *adj.* **1.** pertaining to the making of law or having the function of making law: *legislative power; legislative proceedings.*
**2.** pertaining to a LEGISLATURE: *legislative hearings; legislative salaries.*
—**legislatively** *adv.*

**legislative court** *n.* See under COURT.

**legislative history** *n.* the process that a bill went through to become a law, often looked to by the courts as an aid in CONSTRUCTION of the statute that finally emerged. For example, if at some point a particular provision was removed from the bill, that may indicate the legislature's desire to limit the scope of the statute. Of course, it could also indicate the legislature's belief that other parts of the statute already cover that provision, so drawing conclusions from legislative history requires caution.

**legislative immunity** *n.* See under IMMUNITY.

**legislative intent** *n.* the purpose of a legislature in enacting a particular statute. In the case of federal legislation, also called **congressional intent.** Legislative intent is looked to by the courts for assistance in such matters as CONSTRUCTION of a statute, determination of whether a federal statute preempts local legislation (see PREEMPTION), and determination of whether a superficially neutral statute was enacted for a discriminatory purpose. Sometimes courts attempt to glean intent solely from the words of the statute (see PLAIN MEANING); often they resort to LEGISLATIVE HISTORY.

**legislature** *n.* a deliberative body elected and authorized to write laws; the lawmaking branch of government:

*state legislature; county legislature.* Congress is the national legislature. See also SEPARATION OF POWERS.

**legitimacy** *n.* **1.** the state or quality of being LEGITIMATE.
**2.** in particular, the state of being a legitimate child, a child born in wedlock. See note at ILLEGITIMACY; see also PRESUMPTION OF LEGITIMACY).

**legitimate** *adj., v.,* **legitimated, legitimating.** —*adj.* **1.** lawful; in accordance with established customs, rules, or procedures.
**2.** born in wedlock; born of legally married parents.
**3.** genuine; not spurious or unjustified: *a legitimate claim.*
—*v.* **4.** to make lawful or legal: *Parliament legitimated his accession to the throne.*
**5.** to confer the status of legitimacy upon a child born out of wedlock, as by subsequent marriage of the parents or acknowledgment of paternity by the father.
—**legitimately** *adv.*
—**legitimation** *n.*

**legitimize** *v.,* **legitimized, legitimizing.** to LEGITIMATE.
—**legitimization** *n.*

**lemon law** *n.* a statute that entitles the purchaser of a car that turns out to have substantial defects to return it for a refund or replacement.

**lèse-majesté** *n. French.* Same as LESE MAJESTY.

**lese majesty** *n.* **1.** *high treason* (see under TREASON).
**2.** the offense of speaking or acting in a way that violates the dignity of a ruler, especially royalty. This is not an offense in England, where ridiculing the royals is something of a national pastime; but it remains an offense in some countries.
Also spelled **lèse majesty, leze majesty.**

**lessee** *n.* See under LEASE (defs. 1 and 2).

**lesser included offense** *n.* an offense whose definition is included within the definition of a more serious crime, so

that one cannot commit the more serious offense without also committing the lesser.
—**Note.** For example, LARCENY is a lesser included offense of ROBBERY, and ATTEMPT to commit a crime is always a lesser included offense of the crime attempted. It is proper to charge a jury that if it fails to find that all the elements of the crime charged have been proved, it may nevertheless convict on a lesser included offense if the elements of the lesser offense were established.

**lessor** *n.* See under LEASE (defs. 1 and 2).

**let** *v.,* **let, letting. 1.** to LEASE real property to someone.
**2.** to award a contract for the performance of certain work, especially to one of several bidders for it.

**lethal weapon** *n.* See under WEAPON.

**letter of credit** *n.* a letter in which a bank or other person, at the request of a customer, promises a third person (the beneficiary) that it will honor demands by the beneficiary for payment of drafts drawn or sums owed by the customer upon satisfaction of specified conditions, such as presentation of documents proving that goods shipped to the customer have arrived and payment is due. The letter of credit facilitates long-distance commercial transactions by assuring the seller that payment will be made when the goods arrive while assuring the buyer that payment will not be made if the goods do not arrive.

**letter of intent** *n.* a letter confirming an *agreement to agree* (see under AGREEMENT). See also *memorandum of understanding* (under MEMORANDUM).

**letters** *n.pl.* a formal document; especially a document from the king, the government, a court, or a person in authority, granting a right, privilege, or authorization, or conveying an official order, request, or information.
—**False Friend.** Although *letters* is plural in form and used with a plural verb, in this technical sense the word refers to a single instrument or document. In Latin, the word *litera* meant a letter of

the alphabet, and its plural *literae* (letters collectively) was used to mean "a writing; a document." This Latin word—plural in form but singular in meaning—was translated literally (so to speak) into English.

**letters of administration** *n.pl.* **1.** a document issued by a court appointing someone as ADMINISTRATOR of a decedent's estate.
**2. letters of administration cum testamento annexo** or **letters of administration c.t.a.** a court order appointing an administrator for the estate of a person who left a will but did not designate an executor, and attaching a copy of the will. Also called **letters of administration with will annexed** or **letters of administration with the will annexed.** See also CUM TESTAMENTO ANNEXO.
**3. letters of administration de bonis non** or **letters of administration d.b.n.** a court order appointing a successor administrator to complete the administration of a decedent's estate when there is no will and the previous administrator has ceased to serve. See also DE BONIS NON.
**4. letters of administration de bonis non cum testamento annexo** or **letters of administration d.b.n.c.t.a.** a court order appointing an administrator to complete the administration of the estate of a person who left a will when the executor or a previous administrator ceases to serve. Also called **letters of administration de bonis non with will annexed** or **letters of administration de bonis non with the will annexed.**

**letters patent** *n.pl.* **1.** an official document issued to an individual but in the nature of a public record, formally evidencing a command or request, an agreement or contract, the grant of a right, property, or status, or the like.
**2.** in particular, a document formally evidencing the grant to an inventor of exclusive rights with respect to an invention for a period of years.
**——History.** The adjective PATENT in this context is taken directly from a Latin word meaning "lying open" as

distinguished from "closed; folded." A private communication from the king to an individual would be folded and sealed on the outside, whereas a communication of a more public nature, such as one officially conferring some right or status, would be left open, with the king's seal placed on the face of the document; in the latter case, the document was referred to as *letters patent.* (For the "letters" part of the phrase, see note at LETTERS.) Often "letters patent" were referred to for short as a "patent"; it was in this way that the word PATENT came to be used as a noun referring to the grant of exclusive rights to exploit an invention, or to the rights themselves.

**letters rogatory** *n.pl.* a formal written request by a court in one country to a court in another, asking the second court to take the testimony of a certain witness and transmit it to the first court for use in a case.

**letters testamentary** *n.pl.* a document issued by a court formally authorizing someone to act as EXECUTOR under a will.

**levy** *v.,* **levied, levying,** *n.* **—***v.* **1.** to impose a tax or fine: *The court levied a $500 fine for contempt.*
**2.** to collect or seize property in accordance with legal authority; especially, to attach or seize property of a judgment debtor in order to satisfy a judgment **(levy execution):** *The plaintiff levied on the defendant's car and bank account.*
**—***n.* **3.** the act of levying.
**—leviable** *adj.*

**lex** *n., pl.* **leges.** *Latin.* the law; a law: a term that shows up in countless Latin legal maxims and phrases, especially in older writing. See, for example, *de minimis no curat lex* (under DE MINIMIS).

**lex fori** *n. Latin.* (in conflict of laws) the law of the forum; that is, the law of the state in which a case is pending.

**lex informatica** *n. Pseudo-Latin.* a term suggested by some legal writers for a hypothetical body of legal principles to govern electronic exchanges of information, especially through the Internet.

**——Note.** The term and the concept are imitative of LEX MERCATORIA. It is suggested that users of today's transnational information superhighway are analogous to the merchants who traveled the roads from one kingdom or principality to another in the Middle Ages, and would similarly benefit from a distinct body of rules adapted to the nature of their activity and independent of local law. See also CYBERALTY.

**lex loci contractus** *n. Latin.* (in conflict of laws) the law of the place of the contract; that is, the law of the state or country where the agreement at issue in a contract case was entered into. Ordinarily, that is the state where the offer of a contract was accepted.

**lex loci delicti** *n. Latin.* (in conflict of laws) the law of the place of the wrong; that is, the law of the state or country where the conduct complained of in a tort case took place.

**lex mercatoria** *n. Latin.* (lit. "trading law") **1.** a body of rules and principles that evolved among itinerant traders in the Middle Ages to govern their dealings with each other. See also note at LEX INFORMATICA.
**2.** Same as LAW MERCHANT.

**lex Salica** *n. Latin.* SALIC LAW.

**leze majesty** *n.* Same as LESE MAJESTY.

**liability** *n., pl.* **liabilities. 1.** legal responsibility for a crime **(criminal liability)** or, more commonly, for a tort or breach of contract **(civil liability).**
**2.** the sum that one might be or has been ordered to pay in damages or fines because of such responsibility.
**3.** any debt or other financial obligation of a person or entity. Cf. ASSET.
**4. contingent liability** a specific financial obligation that may or may not arise or become payable, depending upon future events.
**5. joint and several liability** liability for damages caused by the combined action of two or more persons, or for an obligation undertaken by two or more persons, under circumstances in which the law permits the plaintiff to proceed either against the whole group

or against any member individually. Cf. *joint liability; several liability.*
**6. joint liability** liability of two or more persons as a group, as for a tort in which they all participated or for repayment of a loan made to them collectively. Cf. *several liability; joint and several liability.*
**7. liability over** liability to a person for all or part of what that person must pay to someone else. For example, if A and B jointly commit a tort against C, who recovers the full amount of her damages from B, then A is "liable over" to B for A's share of the damages that C collected from B. See also THIRD-PARTY ACTION.
**8. primary liability** liability of a person directly responsible for an obligation, in a situation where another person has *secondary liability.*
**9. secondary liability** liability that arises only if another person (the one with *primary liability*) defaults in an obligation. In a GUARANTY arrangement, the principal debtor is primarily liable and the guarantor is secondarily liable.
**10. several liability a.** liability of each individual member of a group for damages caused, or an obligation owed, by all of them together. **b.** liability of a member of a group for damages caused or an obligation undertaken by that member separately from the others. Cf. *joint liability; joint and several liability.*
**11. strict liability** civil or criminal liability imposed upon a person without regard to whether the person intentionally or knowingly did anything wrong or was in any way reckless or negligent. In tort law, also called **liability without fault.** Typical examples in tort law include PRODUCTS LIABILITY and liability for ABNORMALLY DANGEROUS ACTIVITY; in criminal law, *statutory rape* (see under RAPE) and speeding.
**12. vicarious liability** liability imposed by law upon one person for acts of another; for example, the liability of an employer, under the doctrine of RESPONDEAT SUPERIOR, for acts committed by an employee, or the liability of all partners in a law firm for malpractice committed by one of them.

See also LIMITED LIABILITY; PRODUCTS LIABILITY.

**liability insurance** insurance that protects the insured against liability to third persons. For example, automobile liability insurance covers (up to the maximum amounts specified in the policy) damages assessed against the insured for personal injuries or property damage suffered by others in an automobile accident for which the insured is held responsible. Cf. INDEMNITY INSURANCE.

**liable** *adj.* legally responsible; subject to liability. One is said to be "strictly liable," "jointly and severally liable," "vicariously liable," "secondarily liable," "liable over," etc., according to the nature of the LIABILITY.

**libel¹** *n., v.,* **libeled, libeling** or (*esp. Brit.*) **libelled, libelling. —***n.* **1.** the form of DEFAMATION in which the defamatory statement is communicated in writing or another medium having a degree of permanence, such as film. In some states, libel also includes defamatory statements broadcast on radio or television since, in their ability to reach a wide audience, such statements are more akin to the printed word than to back-fence gossip or even a public speech. Cf. SLANDER.
**2. libel per quod** libel in which the statement at issue is not defamatory on its face, but requires knowledge of extrinsic facts to appreciate its defamatory nature. In a few states, courts have held that a plaintiff cannot recover damages for libel per quod except upon proof of actual economic harm. See also PER QUOD.
**3. libel per se** libel in which the statement at issue is defamatory on its face. Plaintiffs may recover general damages for such a libel without proving specific pecuniary loss. The traditional common law rule, followed in most states, makes no distinction between libel per se and libel per quod, and permits recovery without proof of economic loss in all cases. See also PER SE.
—*v.* **4.** to publish a libel against a person.

See also *food libel* and *veggie libel* (under FOOD DISPARAGEMENT); TRADE LIBEL.
—**libeler** or (*esp. Brit.*) **libeller** *adj.*
—**libelous** or (*esp. Brit.*) **libellous** *adj.*
—**libelously** or (*esp. Brit.*) **libellously** *adv.*

**libel²** *n., v.,* **libeled, libeling** or (*esp. Brit.*) **libelled, libelling. —***n.* **1.** historically, the initial pleading in an admiralty or ecclesiastical court or case; corresponding to the complaint in modern practice. The plaintiff in such a case was called the **libelant** or (*esp. Brit.*) **libellant;** the defendant was called the **libelee** or (*esp. Brit.*) **libellee.**
—*v.* **2.** to bring an action against (a person, vessel, cargo, etc.) by means of a libel.
**3.** to allege or specify in a libel.
——**False Friend.** This terminology, still encountered in legal research, has nothing to do with defamation. To "libel" an individual or a company in these contexts is not to defame, but to sue.

**liberal construction** *n.* See under CONSTRUCTION.

**liberty** *n., pl.* **liberties.** freedom of action. As used in the constitutional provisions protecting people from deprivation of "liberty" without DUE PROCESS, the term is interpreted as including not only freedom from physical restraint (as by being put in jail or deported), but also, at least in a few basic areas, the broader freedom to control one's own life and engage in pursuits of one's choosing (as by traveling, pursuing an education, or deciding for oneself whether to bear a child). See also ENTITLEMENT; FUNDAMENTAL RIGHT; RIGHT OF PRIVACY; RIGHT TO TRAVEL; *substantive due process* (under DUE PROCESS).

**license** *n., v.,* **licensed, licensing. —***n.*
**1.** government permission for a person to do something otherwise forbidden, such as practice medicine, drive a car, keep a dog, or sell liquor.
**2.** a certificate evidencing such permission.
**3.** permission given by the owner of a

patent, copyright, or trademark for another to exploit it. Such licenses are usually embodied in detailed licensing agreements. See also SHRINK-WRAP LICENSE.

**4.** a right granted by the owner or tenant of real property for another to enter the property, which is revocable at will by the grantor; especially, express or implied permission to enter another's property for one's own purposes (e.g., to take a shortcut or solicit for charity or use the swimming pool) or as a social guest.

—*v.* **5.** to grant a license to or for: *to license a driver; license a car.*
See also LICENSEE; cf. INVITEE.
—**licensable** *adj.*

**licensee** *n.* **1.** a person to whom a LICENSE has been granted. Cf. INVITEE.
**2. naked licensee** a person permitted, but not invited, to be on another's land; one who enters land for his own purposes with the express or implied consent of the owner. (See LICENSE, def. 4.) Also called **bare licensee.**
——**Note.** The "naked licensee" has been described as "about the least favored in the law of men who are not actual wrong-doers," *Habina v. Twin City General Electric Co.,* 150 Mich. 41 (1907) (quoting Pollock on Torts), because he "has no right to demand that the land be made safe for his reception and must in general assume the risk of whatever he may encounter." *Yalowizer v. Husky Oil Co.,* 629 P.2d 465 (1981). See also notes at INVITEE and NAKED.

**licensor** *n.* a person who grants a LICENSE.

**licit** *adj.* legal; lawful; legitimate; permissible; sanctioned by moral or cultural norms.
—**licitly** *adv.*

**lie¹** *v.,* **lay, lain, lying. 1.** (of a cause of action or procedural right) to exist; to be sustainable: *The action lies in tort. Since the order was nonfinal, an appeal will not lie.*
**2.** to rest; to be situated: *Venue lies in the county where the defendant resides. The defect lies in the manufacture of the product, not in its design.*

——**Usage.** See discussion in note at LAY.

**lie²** *n., v.,* **lied, lying. —***n.* **1.** a false statement made with deliberate intent to deceive; an intentional untruth; a falsehood.
—*v.* **2.** to speak falsely with intent to deceive; to utter an untruth intentionally.
See also TESTILYING.
—**lier** *n.*

**lie detector** *n.* Same as POLYGRAPH.

**lien** *n.* **1.** a *security interest* (see under INTEREST¹) in property of a debtor or other obligor. Liens may arise either by agreement between the parties or, very often, by operation of law—especially in various commercial situations where they serve to ensure payment of a supplier of goods or services, as in the case of an *attorney's lien, mechanic's lien,* or *warehouser's lien.*
**2. attorney's lien** a lien on money, papers, and property of a client in the hands of an attorney, or a lien that an attorney may request from a court on a fund or judgment obtained for the client by the attorney's efforts, to secure payment of attorney's fees.
**3. inchoate lien** a lien that has not been perfected or is subject to some remaining uncertainty, as **a.** a lien agreed to by a debtor and creditor but not yet recorded in accordance with laws requiring filing of liens in a public office. **b.** a *judgment lien* that may be extinguished if the judgment is reversed.
**4. judgment lien** a lien that a judgment creditor may obtain on property of the judgment debtor, so that the property may be seized if the debtor fails to pay the judgment.
**5. mechanic's lien** the lien of one who works on, or supplies materials for use in, construction or repair of property (e.g., a house or automobile), imposed upon the property to secure payment for the work and materials.
**6. tax lien** a lien placed by the government on specific property to secure payment of back taxes on that property, or upon a taxpayer's property in general to secure payment of back income taxes.

**7. warehouser's** (or **warehouse-man's**) **lien** the right of a warehouser to refuse to return a customer's goods until the storage bill is paid, and if necessary to sell the goods for payment.

**lienee** *n.* a debtor or other obligor whose property is subject to a lien in favor of the creditor or obligee.

**lienholder** *n.* Same as LIENOR.

**lienor** *n.* one who holds a lien on property of another; a creditor or obligee in whose favor a lien is created. Also called **lienholder.**

**life annuity** *n.* See under ANNUITY.

**life estate** (or **tenancy**) *n.* See under ESTATE[1].

**life in being** *n., pl.* **lives in being.** See under PERPETUITY.

**life insurance** *n.* **1.** insurance under which the insurance company's undertaking is to pay out a specified sum of money upon the death of the insured person, either to the estate of the insured or to a beneficiary designated in the policy.
**2. straight life insurance** life insurance for which the annual premium never increases, and which remains in effect as long as the insured individual lives, provided that the premiums are paid. Also called **whole life insurance.**
**3. term life insurance** life insurance that remains in effect only for a specified period of time, after which the policy usually may be renewed for another term, but at a higher premium. Also called **term insurance.**

**lifer** *n. Slang.* **1.** a person in prison under a life sentence.
**2.** an alien who is kept in custody by the U.S. Immigration and Naturalization Service pending deportation—usually for a crime—but whose country of origin will not accept him. The result can be that an individual who committed a relatively minor offense, or at least an offense not punishable by anything like life imprisonment, is detained indefinitely, with no foreseeable possibility of release.

**LIFO** *n.* Acronym for LAST IN, FIRST OUT. Cf. FIFO.

**ligan** *n.* See LAGAN.

**like-kind exchange** *n.* an exchange of business or investment property of similar kinds, which is treated by the Internal Revenue Code as a tax-free exchange. See also BOOT.

**like-kind property** *n.* See under PROPERTY.

**limine** *n.* See IN LIMINE.

**limitation** *n.* See WORDS OF LIMITATION.

**limitation** (or **limitations**) **period** *n.* See under STATUTE OF LIMITATIONS.

**limitations** *n.pl.* See STATUTE OF LIMITATIONS.

**Limited (Ltd.)** *adj.* at the end of a company name, indicates that the company is a corporation. (Short for "limited company"—a reference to the LIMITED LIABILITY of the shareholders.)

**limited appearance** *n.* See under APPEARANCE.

**limited divorce** *n.* See under DIVORCE.

**limited jurisdiction** *n.* See under JURISDICTION[1].

**limited liability** *n.* **1.** the characteristic of corporations and certain other forms of organization that insulates investors from liability for debts or other obligations of the company, so that the most a shareholder can lose is the value of her shares.
**2.** a contractual arrangement by which one party agrees to a ceiling on the other's liability in case something goes wrong; for example, a commercial film processor usually accepts film only upon the customer's agreement that if the film is lost or destroyed, the processor's liability will be limited to the cost of a new roll of film.

**limited liability partnership** *n.* See under PARTNERSHIP.

**limited partner** *n.* See under PARTNER.

**limited partnership** *n.* See under PARTNERSHIP.

**limited public figure** *n.* See under PUBLIC FIGURE.

**limited purpose public figure** *n.* See under PUBLIC FIGURE.

**limited warranty** *n.* See under WARRANTY.

**line-item veto** *n.* See under VETO.

**lineup** *n.* a police procedure in which a number of individuals, including a criminal suspect, are displayed to a witness to see if the witness identifies the suspect as the perpetrator. Cf. SHOWUP. —**Note.** Unduly suggestive lineups, as when the suspect is the only individual resembling the witness's description, violate due process.

**liquid asset** *n.* See under ASSET.

**liquidate** *v.*, **liquidated, liquidating. 1.** to fix with certainty the amount of a debt or other liability, either because the obligation is certain by nature (e.g., a promissory note), or by agreement between the debtor and creditor or by judgment of a court. See also *liquidated damages* (under DAMAGES). **2.** to eliminate a debt or claim by paying or settling it. **3.** to sell assets for cash, especially other than in the ordinary course of business. **4.** to WIND UP an enterprise. —**liquidation** *n.*

**liquidating trust** *n.* See under TRUST.

**lis pendens** *n. Latin.* (lit. "a pending suit") the name of a notice that must be recorded in some jurisdictions to warn that certain real estate is the subject of pending litigation. A buyer of such property would be subject to the court's ultimate decision about the property.

**literary work** *n.* See under WORK.

**litigable** *adj.* **1.** susceptible of being made the subject of a lawsuit. **2.** capable of being argued or contended for in court; colorable; supportable. —**litigability** *n.*

**litigant** *n.* a party to a lawsuit. Cf. LITIGATOR.

**litigate** *v.*, **litigated, litigating. 1.** to make something the subject of a lawsuit or to contest an issue in a judicial proceeding: *My client will not hesitate to litigate her claim. Since the legality of the search and seizure was fully litigated in the pretrial hearing, the issue will not be reopened at the trial.* **2.** to perform all the tasks entailed in the pursuit of a court case—filing papers, taking discovery, making motions, questioning witnesses, arguing appeals, etc.: *The suit was litigated in the federal courts.*

**litigation** *n.* **1.** the process of litigating. **2.** a case or a set of cases discussed collectively. See also VEXATIOUS LITIGATION.

**litigation support** *n.* **1.** services provided to assist lawyers involved in litigation, such as document management and computerization of evidence, the making of graphical and other exhibits and visual aids, jury consulting, or the providing of expert testimony in specialized areas. **2.** the providing of such services. **3.** a category of computer software designed to provide such assistance, particularly with respect to creating and indexing document databases.

**litigator** *n.* a lawyer who specializes in litigation. Cf. LITIGANT.

**litigious** *adj.* readily or excessively inclined to litigate: *America is a litigious society.* —**litigiously** *adv.* —**litigiousness** *n.*

**livery of seisin** *n.* the ritual by which a freehold estate in land was formerly conveyed from one person to another in England. It consisted of the grantor and the grantee entering the property and the grantor handing the grantee a symbolic piece of the property such as a handful of turf, a twig, or a key to the door. See also SEISIN. —**History.** This ritual served a real purpose in centuries before writing was common: It emphasized to the participants the seriousness and finality of the transaction, and the public nature of the ritual assured that witnesses would be available to attest to it in the event of any future dispute over rights to the land. The ritual became less significant as people relied more and more on deeds, and any remaining need for the custom was ended by statute in 1845.

**living trust** *n.* Same as *inter vivos trust* (see under TRUST).

**living will** *n.* a formal instrument in which an individual states what medical measures he wants taken or withheld in the event of terminal illness or permanent unconsciousness. It will theoretically be followed if it is executed in conformity with state law, if those into whose hands the maker falls know about it and are sympathetic, and if the requests made are not contrary to public policy (see *physician-assisted suicide,* under SUICIDE); but the maker should also execute a HEALTH CARE PROXY so that somebody will have clear authority to insist that the living will be obeyed.

**LL.B.** (from Latin *Legum Baccalaureus,* "Bachelor of Laws") abbreviation for **Bachelor of Laws,** the traditional designation of the first law degree. See note under J.D.

**LL.D.** (from Latin *Legum Doctor,* "Doctor of Laws") abbreviation for **Doctor of Laws,** an honorary academic degree awarded for distinguished service or achievement, typically in a field connected with the humanities or public service. It does not signify that the recipient has any legal training or experience.

**LL.M.** (from Latin *Legum Magister,* "Master of Laws") abbreviation for **Master of Laws,** an advanced degree in law typically requiring one year of study beyond the basic law degree. Such degrees are most often sought by lawyers who plan to concentrate their practice in a specialized field such as taxation, or by lawyers from other countries who desire additional formal training in American or Anglo-American legal concepts and practices. Cf. J.D.

**L.L.P.** Abbreviation for *limited liability partnership* (see under PARTNERSHIP).

**loan** *n.* **1.** the act of lending; a grant of the temporary use of something.
**2.** something lent or furnished on condition of being returned, especially a sum of money lent at interest.
**3. bridge loan** a short-term loan to meet immediate financial needs while the borrower awaits other financing or funds that are expected.
**4. consumer loan** a loan made to an individual for personal, family, household, or other nonbusiness purposes.
**5. demand loan** a loan that is repayable on demand. Cf. *term loan.*
**6. mortgage loan** a loan for which repayment is secured by a MORTGAGE.
**7. nonrecourse loan** a secured loan made with the understanding that, in the event of default by the borrower, the lender may look for reimbursement only to the collateral (see COLLATERAL[1]) or to the GUARANTOR or SURETY, and not to the general assets of the borrower. Cf. *recourse loan.*
**8. participation loan** a loan in which two or more lenders each provide part of the money lent.
**9. recourse loan** a loan as to which, in the event of default, the lender may obtain a judgment against the borrower for the balance due and satisfy it from any assets of the borrower. Cf. *nonrecourse loan.*
**10. secured loan** a loan with respect to which the borrower has given security for repayment (see SECURITY[1]), especially in the form of a mortgage or other security interest in property of the borrower.
**11. term loan** a loan to be repayed after a specified period of time, or in installments over a specified period of time. Cf. *demand loan.*
—*v.* **12.** to make a loan of; lend.

**local** *adj.* **1.** referring to a jurisdiction smaller than a state, such as a city, county, town, or village: *a local ordinance; federal, state, and local taxes.*
**2.** sometimes, referring to a state and its subdivisions, as distinguished from the federal government: *In deciding the case, the federal court looked to local law.*
**3.** any small region: *local custom; the*

*local economy.*

—*n.* **4.** Short for *local union* (see under UNION).

**local counsel** *n.* See under COUNSEL.

**local rules** *n.pl.* See under RULE.

**lockout** *n.* the temporary closing of a business or refusal of an employer to allow employees to come to work, in order to pressure workers into accepting the employer's conditions. Cf. STRIKE[1].

**loco parentis** See IN LOCO PARENTIS.

**locus sigilli (L.S.)** *n.* See under SEAL.

**long-arm jurisdiction** See under JURISDICTION[1].

**long-term** *adj.* **1.** covering a relatively long period of time: *long-term lease; long-term loan.*
**2.** pertaining to property held for a sufficiently long period to qualify for favorable capital gains tax treatment upon disposition: *long-term property; long-term gain.*

**loss** *n.* **1.** in a sale or exchange of property, the amount by which the value received for the property falls short of the owner's BASIS in the property. See also *capital loss* (under CAPITAL[1]). Cf. GAIN.
**2.** any injury to person or property for which damages might be awarded in a civil action or payment obtained under an insurance contract.

**loss causation** *n.* See under CAUSATION.

**loss of consortium** *n.* See under CONSORTIUM.

**low-value speech** *n.* See under SPEECH; see also discussion at FREEDOM OF SPEECH.

**lower court** *n.* See under COURT.

**L.P.** Abbreviation for *limited partnership* (see under PARTNERSHIP).

**L.S.** See under SEAL[1].

**Ltd.** Abbreviation for LIMITED.

# M

**magistrate** *n.* **1.** broadly, any JUDGE.
**2.** specifically, a judge of an inferior court such as a police court, town court, or justice of the peace court, with limited jurisdiction to deal with minor offenses and sometimes some minor civil matters.
**3. Magistrate** the title accorded to some magistrates, though others have titles such as Justice of the Peace or Town Justice.
**4. magistrate judge** in federal district courts, an officer (formerly called a *magistrate*) authorized to carry out a wide range of judicial functions that otherwise would have to be performed by judges. See also *hear and determine* and *hear and report* (under HEAR). Cf. JUDGE; JUSTICE.

**Magna Carta** *n. Latin.* (lit. "great charter") a document executed by King John of England in 1215, recognizing certain rights of English subjects and establishing the principle that came to be known as DUE PROCESS, under which even the sovereign is required to follow the law in taking action against a subject.
——**Note.** The Magna Carta, often referred to as the **Great Charter,** is the source of many concepts embodied in the United States Constitution, and is still referred to in judicial opinions.
——**Pronunciation.** The term is sometimes spelled **Magna Charta,** but is always pronounced "magna karta."

**mail** *n.* See CERTIFICATE OF MAILING; *certified mail* (under CERTIFY); REGISTERED MAIL.

**mail fraud** *n.* See under FRAUD.

**mail-order divorce** *n.* See under DIVORCE.

**mailable** *n.* legally permitted to be transmitted by mail. Cf. NONMAILABLE.

**main brief** *n.* See under BRIEF.

**maintainor** *n.* a person guilty of the crime of MAINTENANCE.

**maintenance** *n.* **1.** Also called **separate maintenance.** money for basic living expenses paid to a spouse from which one is separated or divorced. See also ALIMONY.
**2.** the common law crime of giving financial or other support to assist a litigant in pursuing a case in which one has no legal, family, or other legitimate interest. See also BARRATRY; CHAMPERTY.

**majority** *n.* See under AGE.

**majority opinion** See under OPINION.

**make** *v.,* **made, making.** to execute an instrument: *make a contract; make a will; make a promissory note.* See also *fraud in the making* (under FRAUD).
—**maker** *n.*
——**Usage.** Although the term *make* can be applied to any instrument for the payment of money (e.g., *to make a check*), in strict usage one "makes" a note but "draws" a check or other draft. Hence the person who promises payment in a promissory note is the "maker" of the note, but the person who signs a check is the "drawer" of the check. See also DRAW.

**make a record** See under RECORD.

**make bail** See under BAIL¹.

**make book** See under BOOK.

**make law** or **make new law** to establish a new legal principle; specifically:
**a.** (of a judicial decision) to resolve a significant issue on which the courts in a particular jurisdiction have not previously spoken, or to enlarge upon or depart from precedent in a notable way.
**b.** (of a judge or court) to issue such a decision. **c.** (of a case) to result in such

a decision. **d.** (of an attorney or litigant) to bring such a case or argue successfully for such a decision. **e.** (of a legislative body) to adopt a statute.

**make whole** to compensate a person fully for injury or loss; to award or pay *compensatory damages* (see under DAMAGES).

**maker** n. **1.** one who executes an instrument: *the maker of the will.*
**2.** the person who promises payment in a promissory note. See also *accommodation maker* (under ACCOMMODATION PARTY).
Cf. *drawer* (under DRAW).

**mala fide** *adv. Latin.* in bad faith.

**mala fides** n. *Latin.* bad faith. See also note at BONA FIDES[1].

**malfeasance** n. the doing of an unlawful act; especially, misconduct by a public official, corporate officer, or other person in a position of trust. Cf. MISFEASANCE; NONFEASANCE.

**malice** n. **1.** (in criminal law) **a.** any of the mental states required for the different kinds of MURDER: intent to kill or knowledge that one's conduct is substantially certain to cause death, intent to do serious bodily injury, extreme indifference to human life, or willing participation in a felony. **b.** generally, criminal intent; a purpose to perform an act that is a crime.
**2.** (in tort law) improper purpose or lack of legally recognized justification. Such "malice" is often said to be an element of such torts as ABUSE OF PROCESS, DEFAMATION, DISPARAGEMENT, and MALICIOUS PROSECUTION.
**3.** spite or ill will. Occasionally courts or lawyers use "malice" in this ordinary (nonlegal) meaning. Since the legal and nonlegal meanings of the word are easily confused, the modern trend in law is to avoid the word altogether in defining torts and crimes. See STATE OF MIND.
**4. actual malice** (in defamation cases) knowledge that a statement one is publishing about a person is false, or *reckless disregard of truth or falsity* (see under RECKLESS DISREGARD). See notes below.

**5. malice aforethought a.** strictly, an intent to kill formulated in advance. See also PREMEDITATION. **b.** broadly, a term applied to any form of murder, whether premeditated or not and with or without intent to kill (see def. 1a above).
—**malicious** *adj.*
—**maliciously** *adv.*
—**maliciousness** n.
——**Note.** Because of the First Amendment's concern with promoting and protecting vigorous discussion of issues of public interest, the Supreme Court has held that a PUBLIC OFFICIAL or PUBLIC FIGURE cannot recover damages for libel or slander except upon proof that the defendant (usually a newspaper or other news medium) published the defamatory words with "actual malice"; mere carelessness or failure to investigate is not enough to make the publisher of the falsehoods liable. Moreover, although a PRIVATE FIGURE may recover damages for defamation upon a showing of negligence by the defendant rather than actual malice, if the false statement at issue relates to a matter of public concern then proof of actual malice is required for any award of presumed or punitive damages; in such a case, a plaintiff who cannot prove actual malice is limited to damages for actual demonstrated harm, including loss of business, harm to reputation, and mental anguish.
——**False Friend.** As used in the law of defamation, *actual malice* does not mean actual spite or ill will. A finding that a defamatory statement was published "with actual malice" is not a finding about the publisher's feelings toward the person the statement referred to; it is simply a finding that the publisher knew or suspected that the statement was false but, for whatever reason, published it anyway.

**malicious prosecution** n. the tort of initiating or continuing a criminal prosecution or civil case without probable cause and for an improper purpose. Cf. ABUSE OF PROCESS.

**Maliki** n. *Islamic Law.* one of the four principal schools of Islamic law,

founded by Malik ibn Anas (c.715–795). See note at SHARI'A.
—**Malikite** *n.*

**malpractice** *n.* negligence or other failure by a professional, such as a lawyer, doctor, or accountant, to live up to reasonable professional standards in the peformance of services for a client. The client may sue in tort to recover resulting damages.

**malum** *n., pl.* **mala,** *adj. Latin.* —*n.* **1.** a bad thing; an evil; a wrong.
—*adj.* **2.** bad; evil; wrong.

**malum in se** *n., pl.* **mala in se,** *adj. Latin.* (lit. "a wrong in itself") —*n.* **1.** an act that is made a crime because it is regarded as intrinsically wrong or evil, such as murder or larceny.
—*adj.* **2.** constituting such a crime; criminal because intrinsically wrong: *conduct malum in se; acts mala in se.*

**malum prohibitum** *n., pl.* **mala prohibita,** *adj. Latin.* (lit. "a prohibited wrong") —*n.* **1.** an act that is a crime, not because it is intrinsically evil, but because it is made a crime by law. For example, willfully failing to file a required income tax return is malum prohibitum.
—*adj.* **2.** constituting such a crime; wrong because prohibited by law: *an offense malum prohibitum; acts mala prohibita.*

**mandamus** *n., pl.* **mandamuses,** *v.,* **mandamused, mandamusing.** (from Latin, lit. "we command") —*n.* **1.** a writ (in full, **writ of mandamus**) by which a court directs a public or corporate body or officer, or a lower court or judge, to perform an official duty.
—*v.* **2.** to seek or obtain a writ of mandamus against: *The deputies mandamused the county commission to authorize an increase in their salaries to the level prescribed by state law.*
Cf. PROHIBITION.
——**Note.** Mandamus is a discretionary writ issued only in rare cases to remedy an injustice that otherwise might not be curable.

**mandate** *n., v.,* **mandated, mandating.** —*n.* **1.** an order from an appellate court to the lower court from which a

case was appealed, communicating the higher court's decision as to how the case should be dealt with.
**2.** loosely, any court order or legal requirement.
—*v.* **3.** to order or require; make mandatory.

**mandatory** *adj.* **1.** authoritatively ordered; obligatory; compulsory.
**2.** permitting no option; not to be disregarded or modified: *a mandatory clause.*

**mandatory bar** *n.* See under BAR[2].

**mandatory continuing legal education (MCLE)** *n.* CONTINUING LEGAL EDUCATION in those states where it is mandatory.
——**Note.** Most states require all practicing lawyers to spend a certain number of hours each year in continuing legal education, and a substantial industry has arisen to provide courses, conferences, seminars, and materials to enable lawyers to meet these requirements.

**mandatory injunction** *n.* See under INJUNCTION.

**mandatory presumption** *n.* See under PRESUMPTION.

**manipulation** *n.* See STOCK MANIPULATION.

**manslaughter** *n.* **1.** the crime of causing the death of another person under circumstances falling short of MURDER. Some states recognize different grades of manslaughter.
**2. involuntary manslaughter** causing death through RECKLESSNESS or, in some states, *criminal negligence* (see under NEGLIGENCE). In addition, some states include the unintentional causing of another's death while performing an unlawful act other than a felony, such as speeding or trespassing. (Cf. FELONY MURDER.) The most common occasion for involuntary manslaughter is reckless driving. See also *vehicular homicide* (under HOMICIDE).
**3. voluntary manslaughter** conduct that would be regarded as murder but for the fact that the killing, though not legally justified, occurred under extenuating circumstances. The most common

example is killing in the HEAT OF PAS-SION. See also *manslaughter by chance-medley* (under CHANCE-MEDLEY).

**mansuetae naturae** *adj. Latin.* (lit. "of a tame nature; of gentle disposition") Same as DOMITAE NATURAE. See also note at FERAE NATURAE.

**manufacturing defect** *n.* See under DEFECT[2].

**marginal tax rate** *n.* See under TAX RATE.

**mariner's will** *n.* See under WILL.

**marital communications privilege** *n.* See under MARITAL PRIVILEGE.

**marital community** *n.* See under COMMUNITY.

**marital confidences privilege** *n.* See under MARITAL PRIVILEGE.

**marital privilege** *n.* **1.** any *evidentiary privilege* (see under PRIVILEGE) whereby an individual is exempted or barred from giving evidence, or giving certain kinds of evidence, in a matter involving the individual's spouse or former spouse. Also called **husband-wife privilege, spousal privilege.** **2.** Specifically, **a.** a privilege not to testify against one's current spouse, or a privilege to prevent one's current spouse from testifying against oneself, especially in a criminal case. Also called **antimarital fact privilege, spouse's testimonial privilege. b.** a privilege not to disclose, and to prevent one's spouse or former spouse from disclosing, any confidential communication that passed between oneself and one's spouse during marriage. Also called **marital communications privilege, marital confidences privilege.**

**marital property** *n.* property acquired by a couple during marriage and subject to division upon divorce. Cf. SEPARATE PROPERTY. ——**Note.** Ordinarily, marital property includes any income or property obtained by either spouse during the marriage, except property received by one spouse as a gift or by will or inheritance. In community property states,

this is the same as COMMUNITY PROPERTY. In states with EQUITABLE DISTRIBUTION statutes, this is the property that is equitably divided between the spouses upon divorce.

**marital property agreement** *n.* an agreement between married people regarding ownership of property during marriage, division of property in the event of divorce, rights to portions of each other's estates, and the like. ——**Usage.** This term is used in reference to agreements entered into both before or during a marriage, but is often restricted to the latter, and thus used in distinction to PRENUPTIAL AGREEMENT.

**marital rape** *n.* See under RAPE.

**maritime** *adj.* **1.** pertaining to navigation and commerce by water, both at sea and on inland waters. **2.** Also, **admiralty.** pertaining to *maritime law* or its administration: *a maritime* (or *admiralty*) *case; maritime* (or *admiralty*) *jurisdiction.* **3. maritime law** the body of law governing maritime matters, including contracts relating to shipping by water, torts occurring at sea, property rights in vessels and freight, and the labor of ship and harbor workers. Maritime law is made and administered primarily by the federal government and the federal courts. Also called **admiralty law,** or just **admiralty.**

**mark** *n.* **1. a.** a distinctive word, phrase, logo, or design, or even a sound or smell or musical motif, used to identify products or services made, provided, or certified by a particular company or organization, or as a sign of membership in an organization. For particular categories of marks, see TRADEMARK; SERVICE MARK; CERTIFICATION MARK; COLLECTIVE MARK; and *collective membership mark* (under COLLECTIVE MARK). **b. registered mark** such a mark that has been registered in the United States Patent and Trademark Office. Unless the registrant's right to use the mark is successfully challenged within five years after registration, the registrant normally has the exclusive right to use the mark from then on. See also ®.

**2.** a design—usually an X—used as a signature by someone who is unable to write. See also entry for X.

**3. chairman's mark** in Congress, the version of a bill that the chairman of a committee brings to the committee for consideration.

—*v.* **4.** to place a letter or number on a document or other article used at a trial, hearing, or deposition, so that it can be referred to unambiguously in testimony and colloquy: *I hand you what has been marked as Plaintiff's Exhibit D for identification and I ask if you recognize it.* See also EXHIBIT.

**market** *n.* **1.** a place where people come together to buy and sell things, or a mechanism (such as a computer network or informal network of buyers, sellers, and agents) that puts people in touch with each other for that purpose: *stock market; real estate market.*

**2.** a geographic area where goods or services are sold: *the domestic market; the Los Angeles market.*

**3.** demand for goods or services, or a body of existing or potential buyers: *the market for personal computers.*

**4.** the level of prices prevailing in a market: *a rising market for shoes.*

—*v.* **5.** to sell or offer for sale in a market.

See also BLACK MARKET; GRAY MARKET.

**market manipulation** *n.* Same as STOCK MANIPULATION.

**market value** *n.* the price that a willing purchaser would pay and a willing seller would accept for a particular item in an ARM'S-LENGTH transaction in an open market, where both are acting with full information and neither is under particular pressure to buy or sell. Also called **fair market value.**

**marketable** *adj.* suitable for sale; readily salable.

**marketable security** *n.* See under SECURITY[2].

**marketable title** *n.* See under TITLE.

**marketing defect** *n.* See under DEFECT[2].

**marriage** *n.* **1.** the legal relationship of husband and wife, entered into in conformity with state law and carrying various rights and duties imposed by law. Many states, responding to fears of *same-sex marriage,* have amended their marriage statutes to restrict marriage explicitly to its traditional meaning of a union of one man and one woman. See also BIGAMY; CIVIL UNION; DOMESTIC PARTNERSHIP; POLYGAMY; RECIPROCAL BENEFICIARY.

**2.** a formal ceremony in which a marriage relationship is entered into.

**3. common law marriage** a marriage entered into without the usual ceremony; it is effected by an agreement to be married followed by living together as husband and wife. The common law recognized such do-it-yourself marriages if the parties had the legal capacity to marry, but this method of marrying is no longer permitted in most states. Mere cohabitation has never been sufficient to create a marriage: Even in a state where common law marriage is possible, simply living together, and even having children together, does not make a "common law husband" and "common law wife" of a couple in the absence of an explicit agreement to be married.

**4. covenant marriage** a form of marriage, made available in at least two states beginning with Louisiana in 1997, in which the spouses sign a formal statement agreeing that marriage is a life-long commitment and renounce the option—available to all other married couples domiciled in the state—of obtaining a relatively quick *no-fault divorce* (see under DIVORCE) should the occasion arise. See note below.

**5. same-sex marriage** a relationship analogous to a traditional marriage but not ordinarily accorded official legal status, in which two men or two women have pledged themselves to each other, usually before witnesses and with accompanying religious or secular ceremony. Also called **homosexual marriage.** See also CIVIL UNION; DOMESTIC PARTNERSHIP; RECIPROCAL BENEFICIARY.

—**Note.** The grounds for divorce that

are left to those who choose to enter into a *covenant marriage* in those states that provide it include the traditional fault grounds such as adultery, abandonment, and abuse; but they also include the fact of having living apart for two years and, in at least one state, the fact that "husband and wife both agree to a dissolution of marriage." It thus appears that the length of a life-long commitment has been set by statute in these states as two years, except when the parties agree to make it less.

**marriage bonus** *n.* **1.** the difference between a reduced income tax liability that is owed by a married couple filing a joint return and the greater amount they would owe if they were not married and filed as single individuals. **2.** Also called **singles' penalty.** the general principle or policy of United States tax law under which many married couples may choose to have their combined income taxed at lower rates than would apply if they were unmarried. Cf. MARRIAGE PENALTY. —**History.** The marriage bonus entered the tax system with the introduction of the joint income tax return in 1948, permitting married couples to lower their taxes through INCOME SPLITTING. Although the details of how the marriage bonus works and who benefits from it change with every major revision of the Internal Revenue Code, in general the greatest benefit goes to married couples in which one spouse is the primary earner. According to the Congressional Budget Office, slightly over 50 percent of the couples filing in 1996 benefited from a marriage bonus.

**marriage penalty** *n.* **1.** the difference between a greater income tax liability owed by a married couple filing a joint return and the lesser amount they would owe if they were able to file as single individuals. **2.** the general principle or policy of United States tax law under which married couples in which the two spouses have roughly equal incomes are taxed on their combined income at somewhat higher marginal rates than would apply if they were not married and each was taxed only on his or her own income. Cf. MARRIAGE BONUS. —**History.** The marriage penalty entered the tax system in 1969, as a by-product of a reform intended to ameliorate the inequity in tax treatment between married people and single people caused by the MARRIAGE BONUS. For most married couples, the effect of the change was to reduce the size of their marriage bonus; for a smaller number, the effect was to change a small bonus into a small penalty; thus the overall effect was to reduce the average difference between what married couples pay and what single people with the same income and expenses would pay. Although the exact working of the marriage penalty changes with every major revision of the tax law, it affects primarily couples with roughly equal earnings, and has always applied to fewer couples than the marriage bonus. According to the Congressional Budget Office, approximately 40 percent of couples incurred such penalties in 1996, while more than 50 percent received bonuses for being married.

**marriage settlement** *n.* **1.** (especially historical) **a.** the conveyance of property by deed to an intended spouse in contemplation of marriage. **b.** an agreement made in contemplation of marriage, pursuant to which such a transfer is made. **c.** the deed or written agreement. **d.** the property so transferred. **2.** any PRENUPTIAL AGREEMENT. **3.** Same as DIVORCE SETTLEMENT or SEPARATION SETTLEMENT. —**Usage.** Since the phrase *marriage settlement* has a long history of use in reference to agreements in contemplation of marriage, and other phrases such as *divorce settlement* and *separation agreement* are available to refer to dispositions of property when a marriage breaks up, to avoid confusion it is best to confine the phrase *marriage settlement* to its traditional realm of agreements and transfers at the outset of marriage, and to use phrases with the word "divorce" or "separation" when referring to agreements and transfers at the end of the marriage.

**marshal** *n.*, *v.*, **marshaled, marshaling** or (*esp. Brit.*) **marshalled, marshalling.** —*n.* **1.** a federal officer who serves summonses, executes writs, escorts criminal defendants between court and jail, and otherwise assists in the functioning of a federal court.
**2.** the name given to certain state or local law enforcement or other officials in various localities.
—*v.* **3.** to gather up the assets of a trust, estate, corporation, or the like and put them in order for distribution, especially in connection with administration pursuant to a trust instrument, a will, the laws of intestacy, a bankruptcy decree, or the like.

**martial law** *n.* government by the military, using military law and institutions in place of civilian. The Supreme Court has interpreted the Constitution as permitting martial law in the United States only in wartime and only if civilian courts are no longer able to function.

**Massachusetts trust** or **Massachusetts business trust** *n.* Same as *business trust* (see under TRUST).

**master** *n.* **1.** the traditional common law term for an employer (the employee being referred to as a SERVANT).
**2.** Also called **special master.** an individual appointed by a court to assist it in handling particular aspects of a case. See also REFEREE.

**master and servant** *n.* the traditional phrase for the area of common law concerned with the employment relationship and the rights and duties of employer and employee. This terminology is still in common use.
—**False Friend.** The terms *master* and *servant* do not import anything like the image one might have of a slavemaster or ship's captain, on the one hand, or an apprentice or domestic servant on the other. These are simply ancient terms that were well established in English law before the words *employer* and *employee* even entered the language. (The latter term, in fact, is a nineteenth century American coinage.)

In early times the relationship of master and servant was indeed personal and substantially a form of absolute rule; but the law that grew out of those relationships now applies, for example, to a corporation (the master) and its thirteen million dollar per year president and chief executive officer (the servant).

**Master of Laws** *n.* See LL.M.

**material** *n.* **1.** important; of consequence; potentially dispositive; such as a reasonably prudent person would take into account in making a decision. To say that something is "material" usually simply means that it matters: *material fact, issue, mistake, variance, representation, misrepresentation, omission,* etc.
**2.** essential; describing a component without which the whole will fail: *material allegation in a complaint; material element of a tort or crime; material term of a contract.*
**3.** logically related to a material fact or issue: *material evidence.*
—**materiality** *n.*
—**materially** *adv.*

**material breach** *n.* See under BREACH.

**material witness** *n.* See under WITNESS.

**matter of** See under IN THE MATTER OF.

**matter of law** *n.* See AS A MATTER OF LAW.

**mature** *adj.*, *v.*, **matured, maturing.**
—*adj.* **1.** due; presently payable or enforceable. Said of any right, claim, or obligation, but especially of bonds, notes, or other financial instruments.
—*v.* **2.** to become mature.

**maturity** *n.* **1.** the state of being mature.
**2.** the date upon which, or the time within which, a bond or negotiable instrument becomes due: *bonds with a maturity of 30 days.*

**maxim** *n.* a saying that expresses a general principle of law. See examples under DE MINIMIS and UNCLEAN HANDS.

**mayhem** *n.* the crime of maiming—that

is, disabling, dismembering, or disfiguring—a person, either intentionally or, in some states, by any conduct intended to cause serious injury.
——**History.** Mayhem was originally the crime of injuring or wounding a man in such a way that he lost the use of a member which would be useful in a fight. It was said, for example, that the cutting off of an ear or nose, or the breaking of "the hinder teeth," was not mayhem; presumably the front teeth could be useful in self-defense or combat and so fell into a different category. The crime was later extended by statute to include disabling or disfiguring generally. The modern trend is to include all such conduct in the general crime of assault and battery.

**MBE** Multistate Bar Examination.

**MCLE** mandatory continuing legal education.

**MDP** *pl.* **MDPs, MDP's.** multidisciplinary practice.

**means test** *n.* a requirement that people receiving a particular public benefit show that their income and assets are below a certain level.

**measuring life** *n.* **1.** the lifetime, or one of the lifetimes, determining the duration of a *life estate* (see under ESTATE[1]).
**2.** the lifetime of the person, or of the longest survivor of the group of persons, identified for purposes of applying the *rule against perpetuities* (see under PERPETUITY).

**mechanic's lien** *n.* See under LIEN.

**media ride-along** *n.* Same as RIDE-ALONG.

**mediation** *n.* a procedure in which a neutral outsider (a **mediator**) assists the parties to a dispute in reaching a settlement.
—**mediate** *v.,* **mediated, mediating.**
——**Note.** Mediation differs from ARBITRATION in that the purpose of mediation is to facilitate an agreement rather than to impose a decision on the parties. See also CONCILIATION.

**medical device** *n.* See under DEVICE.

**MEE** Multistate Essay Examination.

**meeting of the minds** *n.* a misleading phrase sometimes used to signify the making of a contract, derived from an earlier view that there is no contract unless the parties share the same understanding of the deal. The contemporary view is that people are entitled to rely upon the normal and reasonable meaning of each other's words and actions; thus a party can generally enforce a contract on certain terms if a reasonable person in her position would have understood it that way, even if the other party can show that he had something different in mind, or did not intend to enter into a contract at all.

**Megan's Law** a New Jersey statute, enacted in 1994, requiring registration by prior sex offenders whenever they take up residence in the state and prior to any subsequent change of address, and providing for official notification regarding their past records to the police, and sometimes to community groups and the general public, in the areas where they reside or intend to reside. The name has since been applied to similar legislation in other states providing various mechanisms by which law enforcement officials or private persons can monitor the whereabouts of prior sex offenders. See also COMMUNITY NOTIFICATION LAW.

**memorandum** *n., pl.* **memoranda. 1.** a brief written record or communication.
**2.** Also called **memorandum of law** or **memorandum of points and authorities.** terms used in some courts for BRIEF.
**3.** Also called **memorandum decision, memorandum order,** or **memorandum opinion.** a brief judicial decision, usually ranging in length from two words (e.g., "Motion denied.") to a long paragraph. When cited, such decisions are usually indicated by the abbreviation "mem."
**4. memorandum of understanding** a writing memorializing an *agreement to agree* (see under AGREEMENT).
See also LETTER OF INTENT.

**memorialize** v., **memorialized, memorializing.** to make a written record of; confirm in writing: *Their telephone agreement was memorialized in an exchange of letters.*
—**memorial** n.

**memory** n. See RECOLLECTION; RECOVERED MEMORY.

**mens rea** n. *Latin.* (lit. "guilty mind") the STATE OF MIND that makes the performance of a particular act a crime, or a crime of a particular degree; the element of fault that makes an otherwise innocent act or omission punishable. For example, a careful driver who hits a child who darts out from between parked cars may be guilty of no crime, whereas a driver who had time to avoid the child but carelessly failed to do so may be guilty of homicide. See also ACTUS REUS.

**mental anguish** n. Same as EMOTIONAL DISTRESS.

**mental distress** n. Same as EMOTIONAL DISTRESS.

**mental state** n. Same as STATE OF MIND.

**mental suffering** n. Same as EMOTIONAL DISTRESS.

**merchantable** adj. **1.** (of goods) fit for the ordinary purposes for which such goods are used, and of a quality that would be acceptable to merchants who regularly deal in goods of that kind. **2. warranty of merchantability** in a sale of goods by a merchant who regularly deals in goods of that kind, an implied WARRANTY that the goods are merchantable.
—**merchantability** n.

**merchantable title** n. Same as *marketable title* (see under TITLE).

**meretricious** adj. describing a relationship or contract having a sexual component unblessed by law, such as a living-together arrangement.
——**Note.** Because "meretricious" contracts are contrary to PUBLIC POLICY, plaintiffs seeking PALIMONY upon the breakup of a relationship must be careful not to allege that sex was any part of the consideration for the relationship.

**merger** n. **1.** the absorption of one entity, right, interest, claim, agreement, or other thing into another, so that the first ceases to have independent existence and is superseded by the second. **2.** especially, the absorption of one corporation or other business entity by another, which acquires the assets and assumes the liabilities of absorbed entity. **3. horizontal merger** a merger of entities that have similar businesses at the same level in the same industry; a merger of competitors or potential competitors. See note at HORIZONTAL. **4. vertical merger** a merger of entities that function at different levels in the same industry. See note at VERTICAL.
—**merge** v., **merged, merging.**
——**Note.** The broad concept of merger finds specific applications in many legal contexts. For example, one corporation may merge into another; a debt upon which a plaintiff has sued and won is merged into the judgment, so that the debt no longer exists as an obligation distinct from the debtor's obligation to pay the judgment; and a *merger clause* (see under INTEGRATION CLAUSE) in a contract provides that all prior negotiations and agreements between the parties are merged into the new contract, so that neither party can claim that the other has any obligation other than those expressed in the current contract.

**merger of law and equity** n. the blending of the two systems of justice that evolved side by side in England—LAW and EQUITY—into a single legal system.
——**History.** For centuries the systems of LAW and EQUITY dispensed different kinds of remedies in different kinds of cases from separate courts, using different procedures and even different basic vocabularies. In England this dual system was abolished by a series of acts in the 1870's. But it was not until 1937 that the federal courts in the United States adopted a unified procedure for law and equity cases, and provided that both legal and equitable relief can be sought in a single action. Although the

formal separation of law and equity is now largely a thing of the past, substantive and procedural distinctions between "legal" and "equitable" principles still pervade American law.

**meritorious** *adj.* successful or likely to succeed: *meritorious claim; meritorious defense.*
—**meritoriously** *adv.*
—**meritoriousness** *n.*

**merits** *n.pl.* the substance of a case, claim, controversy, or the like, as distinguished from procedural or technical aspects; the heart of a matter. A decision, judgment, opinion, trial, or the like is said to be **on the merits** if it disposes of or is based upon the actual claim or charge presented in a case.

**mesne profits** *n.pl.* **1.** the profits earned from land by one wrongfully occupying it during the period of wrongful possession.
**2.** the net rental value or the value of use and occupation of property during a period of wrongful occupation.
See also *trespass for mesne profits* (under TRESPASS²).

**method of accounting** *n.* Same as ACCOUNTING METHOD.

**midrash** *n.,* *pl.* **midrashim, midrashoth, midrashot, midrashos.** *Jewish Law.* **1.** an early Jewish interpretation of or commentary on a Biblical text, clarifying or expounding a point of law or developing or illustrating a moral principle.
**2. Midrash** a collection of such interpretations or commentaries, esp. those written in the first ten centuries A.D.
—**midrashic** *adj.*

**migratory divorce** *n.* See under DIVORCE.

**military law** *n.* the rules and procedures governing conduct in the armed forces. The Constitution gives Congress the power to enact such law for the American military, and it has done so in the UNIFORM CODE OF MILITARY JUSTICE.

**military will** *n.* See under WILL.

**militia** *n.* a military body with officers appointed by a state and members trained by the state.
——**Note.** The Constitution gives Congress the power to organize, arm, and discipline the militia, making it primarily an arm of the federal government. The principal unit of the militia is the National Guard. See also RIGHT TO BEAR ARMS.

**minimum contacts** *n.* activity sufficiently connecting a party located elsewhere to a state in whose courts a lawsuit is commenced to justify the exercise of jurisdiction over that party for purposes of that particular case. For example, an individual from another state who causes an automobile accident while visiting in the state, or a company based elsewhere that solicits mail order purchases and then sends a defective product into the state in response to such an order, would be found to have the minimum contacts necessary to be required to defend a suit in the state for injuries that occurred there as a result of their actions. See also *long-arm jurisdiction* (under JURISDICTION); TRANSACTION OF BUSINESS.

**ministerial** *adj.* done in accordance with specific instructions or requirements; carrying out a delegated task; nondiscretionary: *ministerial act; ministerial function.*
—**ministerially** *adv.*

**minitrial** *n.* a form of ALTERNATIVE DISPUTE RESOLUTION in which each side informally presents the essence of its case before a PRIVATE JUDGE or similar neutral party in order to facilitate settlement.

**minor** *n.* a person who has not yet reached the *age of majority* (see under AGE). See also *emancipated minor* (under EMANCIPATION).

**minority** *n.,* *pl.* **minorities. 1.** the state or period of being a MINOR.
**2.** Also called **minority group. a.** a group of people sharing a characteristic that distinguishes them from the majority; e.g., a racial or religious minority.
**b.** a group identified for protection by civil rights laws or the Constitution. In

this sense the term includes women even though they are a numerical majority.

**minority opinion** *n.* See under OPINION.

**Miranda rule** the rule that criminal suspects in police custody must be informed of certain basic constitutional rights before being questioned. In the 1966 case of *Miranda v. Arizona*, 384 U.S. 436, the Supreme Court held that before law enforcement personnel initiate any *custodial interrogation* (see under INTERROGATION) the suspect must be informed of his right to remain silent, his right to have a lawyer present, his right to have a lawyer appointed if he cannot afford one, and the fact that anything he says may be used against him. This information is referred to as the **Miranda warnings** or **Miranda warning.**

**Mirandize** *v.,* **Mirandized, Mirandizing.** to advise (a person) of his rights in accordance with the MIRANDA RULE.

**misbranding** *n.* placing a false or misleading label on a product.

**misdemeanant** *n.* a person who commits a MISDEMEANOR.

**misdemeanor** *n.* **1.** a crime less serious than a FELONY, usually one punishable by incarceration for up to one year. In some states misdemeanors include some offenses punishable only by a fine.
**2.** (especially historical) any crime, misdeed, misconduct, or misbehavior.
See also HIGH CRIMES AND MISDEMEANORS; INFRACTION; OFFENSE; VIOLATION.

**misfeasance** *n.* **1.** the negligent or otherwise improper performance of an otherwise permissible act. Cf. MALFEASANCE, NONFEASANCE.
**2.** broadly, any wrongful affirmative act.

**Mishnah** *n., pl.* **Mishnayoth, Mishnayot, Mishnayos, Mishnahs.** *Jewish Law.* **1.** the collection of oral laws compiled about A.D. 200 by Rabbi Judah ha-Nasi and forming the basic part of the TALMUD.

**2.** an article or section of this collection.
—**Mishnaic, Mishnic, Mishnical** *adj.*

**misjoinder** *n.* inappropriate JOINDER into a single action of unrelated parties, claims, or charges.

**misprision** *n.* **1.** failure by one not an accessory to prevent or notify the authorities of a crime.
**2.** a neglect or violation of official duty by one in office.
**3.** a contempt against the government, monarch, or courts, as SEDITION, LESE MAJESTY, or a *contempt of court* (see under CONTEMPT).
**4.** a mistake; misunderstanding.
**5.** historically, a misdemeanor; any crime less than a felony, especially one with no specific name of its own.

**misprision of felony** *n.* failure to report a known felony, in the absence of any agreement with or assistance to the felon. This was a misdemeanor under English common law, but absent some affirmative act to conceal the felony it is not normally a crime in the United States. Cf. *accessory after the fact* (under ACCESSORY); COMPOUNDING A CRIME; MISPRISION OF TREASON.

**misprision of treason** *n.* **1.** the crime of failing to report another's treasonous actions or intentions.
**2.** in the United States, the crime of one who owes allegiance to the United States and knows of the commission of any treason against the United States in failing to report the treason as soon as possible to the President, a state governor, or a federal or state judge.

**misrepresentation** *n.* **1.** a false or misleading REPRESENTATION, or words or conduct having the effect of preventing another's discovery of material facts. In this usual sense, misrepresentation is one element of the tort of FRAUD.
**2.** sometimes, another name for FRAUD.
—**misrepresent** *v.*

**mistake** *n.* an erroneous belief about a material fact **(mistake of fact)** or about the legal effect or significance of known facts **(mistake of law).** When a contract is entered into on the basis of mistake, it may be a misconception of one party only **(unilateral mistake)** or one shared and relied upon by both parties **(mutual mistake).** The legal effect or status of an act or transaction (e.g., a contract, a marriage, an alleged crime) may be altered if the parties were acting under the influence of mistake, depending upon such factors as the nature of the mistake, the reasonableness of the mistake, the mutuality of the mistake, and whether one party knew that the other was acting under a mistaken impression.

**mistrial** *n.* a trial that ends without a verdict, decision, or settlement. The most common cause of a mistrial is a *hung jury* (see under JURY), but sometimes a mistrial is precipitated by an error so serious that no instruction to the jury can cure it (such as seriously prejudicial remarks by a lawyer) or by circumstances such as the death of a juror or a natural disaster. The usual result is a new trial. See also DOUBLE JEOPARDY.

**mitigate** *v.,* **mitigated, mitigating.** to ameliorate; make less serious or severe. See also note at MITIGATION OF DAMAGES.
—**mitigable** *adj.*
—**mitigation** *n.*

**mitigating circumstance** *n.* a circumstance reducing or limiting (but not eliminating) the liability of a person for a crime or tort; e.g., DIMINISHED CAPACITY. Also called **mitigating factor.**

**mitigation of damages** *n.* the use of reasonable efforts by the victim of another's breach of contract to limit the adverse consequences of the breach.
——**Note.** As a general rule, the plaintiff in an action for breach of contract may not recover for any portion of the damages that could have been avoided by reasonable effort; this is often referred to as the "duty to mitigate damages" or just "duty to mitigate."

**mixed nuisance** *n.* See under NUISANCE.

**mixed question of fact and law** *n.* See under QUESTION[2].

**M'Naghten rule** (or **test**) *n.* the traditional test used in determining whether an INSANITY DEFENSE has been established, under which a defendant is not responsible for a crime if, because of a disease of the mind, he did not know the nature of his act or did not know that it was wrong. This is the test used in the federal courts and most other American jurisdictions, augmented in a few jurisdictions by the IRRESISTIBLE IMPULSE TEST.

**mock jury** *n.* the individuals who play the role of jurors in a MOCK TRIAL, and provide feedback to the other participants on how their conduct or their case came across from the point of view of a jury.

**mock trial** *n.* a pretend trial.
——**Usage.** A mock trial may be held as a MOOT COURT exercise to train students, but the term is used especially in reference to the procedure by which lawyers preparing for a real trial try out their case on a MOCK JURY hired to listen to the case and provide feedback that the lawyers can use in choosing and refining their strategies, determining what qualities to look for in selecting the real jurors, or even in deciding whether to settle the case.

**model law** (or **act** or **statute**) *n.* any proposed statute drafted by anyone and promoted for adoption by state legislatures. Two of the most successful such proposals, upon which statutes in a great many states have been based, are the American Bar Association's Model Business Corporation Act, which provides a general framework for regulating corporations, and the MODEL PENAL CODE. See also UNIFORM LAWS.

**Model Penal Code** *n.* a comprehensive model statute organizing, rationalizing, and unifying the basic areas of state criminal law.
——**History.** The Model Penal Code was drafted over a number of years by the AMERICAN LAW INSTITUTE and finally promulgated in 1962. It provides the underlying theoretical framework, the

overall approach, and a great deal of the exact language for the modern criminal codes that have been enacted in most states since then.

**moiety** *n., pl.* **moieties.** half; a one-half interest. Sometimes used to mean any portion or fractional interest.

**money** *n., pl.* **moneys, monies. 1.** a medium of exchange adopted by a government as a part of its currency; legal tender. Under the Uniform Commercial Code, however, rare or unusual coins used for numismatic purposes are classified as goods rather than money. **2.** assets viewed in terms of their value in money; especially assets with a fixed value readily convertible into money, such as a demand deposit: *money in the bank.* **3.** capital to be borrowed, loaned, or invested; capital dealt with as a commodity: *the money market.* **4. moneys** or **monies** funds; sums of money; a sum of money.
See also FEDERAL MONEY; HARD MONEY; NONFEDERAL MONEY; PURCHASE MONEY; PURCHASE MONEY SECURITY INTEREST; SOFT MONEY.

**money had and received** *n.* an action to compel payment of money received by another that should have gone to the plaintiff.

**money laundering** *n.* **1.** the crime of engaging in financial transactions designed to conceal the nature, source, ownership, or control of funds derived from criminal activity. **2.** the crime of transporting or transferring funds derived from criminal activity across United States borders in connection with a scheme to conceal their connection with crime.
See also CYBERLAUNDERING.
—**money launderer** *n.*

**money of account** *n.* a monetary denomination used in reckoning or record-keeping, especially one not issued as currency, as the United States mill.

**money order** *n.* an instrument similar to a check, which is purchased from a bank, post office, or other institution by a person wishing to make a payment or transfer money to another, naming the other as payee and entitling the payee to payment, by the issuer, of the sum specified in the instrument.

**monopolist** *n.* **1.** a company that has a monopoly with respect to a particular product or service. **2.** a company that is guilty of MONOPO-LIZATION.
—**monopolistic** *adj.*
—**monopolistically** *adv.*

**monopolization** *n.* the intentional acquisition or maintenance by a company or group of cooperating companies of MONOPOLY POWER in a relevant market for a product or service.
—**monopolize** *v.,* **monopolized, monopolizing.**
——**Note.** Monopolization, attempted monopolization, and conspiracy to monopolize are violations of the SHERMAN ANTITRUST ACT.

**monopoly** *n., pl.* **monopolies. 1.** exclusive control of a commodity or service in a particular market, or a control that makes possible the manipulation of prices. **2.** a company or group that has such control.
——**Note.** Simply having or being a monopoly is not a violation of ANTITRUST laws. Cf. MONOPOLIZATION.

**monopoly power** *n.* (in antitrust law) the power, concentrated in the hands of one company or group of cooperating companies, to control prices or exclude competition in a market for a type of product or service.

**month-to-month tenancy** *n.* See under TENANCY.

**moot** *adj.* **1.** (of a claim, issue, case, etc.) dead; no longer a real controversy with practical consequences for the parties. For example, a constitutional challenge to a law normally becomes moot if the law is repealed while the case is pending; a challenge to procedures in a pending criminal investigation or prosecution becomes moot if the suspect or defendant dies. See note below. **2.** hypothetical, of little practical value or meaning; purely academic: *Whether*

*the defendant would still have been convicted if he had testified is a moot question.*
**3.** open to discussion or debate; debatable; doubtful: *Whether the proposed legislation represents real reform is a moot point.*
—*v.* **4.** to make moot: *The parties' stipulation mooted the motion for a protective order.*
**5.** to present for discussion, or to discuss, argue, debate: *The issue of how best to reform the law was much mooted.*
—*n.* **6.** (especially in older British usage) a discussion or debate among lawyers or law students on a hypothetical legal issue.
—**mootness** *n.*
——**Note.** Cases that become moot before a final decision has been rendered are usually dismissed as no longer presenting a JUSTICIABLE controversy. But exceptions can be made in limited circumstances where dismissal would work an injustice, as when a party seeks to avoid judicial review by ending a challenged policy but might renew it after the case is dismissed, or a person challenging a criminal conviction has already served the full sentence but might suffer collateral injury in the future on account of the record of conviction, or the case is perceived as CAPABLE OF REPETITION, YET EVADING REVIEW (see note at that entry).

**moot court** *n.* a mock court proceeding in which law students or lawyers practice argument or trial techniques in hypothetical cases.

**moral certainty** *n.* **1.** the mental state of being firmly convinced of a fact on the basis of inference from other facts as distinguished from direct evidence or observation: *Circumstantial evidence is sufficient for conviction when it is so strong and cogent as to indicate the guilt of the defendant to a moral certainty.*
**2.** certainty resulting from MORAL EVIDENCE: *Despite the fingerprints on the gun, she expressed moral certainty that her husband could not have committed the murder.*

**3.** a sufficient degree of certainty so that one feels morally justified in acting upon it.
—**morally certain** *adj.*
——**Note.** The phrase *to a moral certainty* is often used in jury charges to explain the level of confidence needed for a finding of guilt BEYOND A REASONABLE DOUBT. Most commentators believe that the phrase does more to confuse than to enlighten. Perhaps the most serious problem with it is that it can be misconstrued as inviting the jurors to convict on the basis of individual moral beliefs rather than reasoned analysis of the evidence and dispassionate application of the law. See also note at ABIDING FAITH.

**moral evidence** *n.* **1.** an inference derived from general knowledge of human nature, or from knowledge or information about the nature of a particular person; for example, evidence of intent or motive inferred from conduct.
**2.** loosely, any evidence that is circumstantial or that, if accepted, does not establish a fact but merely increases the probability that it is true.

**moral rights** *n.pl.* See under DROIT MORAL.

**moral turpitude** *n.* dishonesty or immorality. Statutes providing special penalties or disadvantages (e.g., deportation or ineligibility for a professional license) for people convicted of a "crime involving moral turpitude," though notoriously vague, generally refer to more serious, intentional crimes as distinguished from less serious, technical crimes.

**mors** *n. Latin.* death. The word commonly appears in other forms; see for example ANTE MORTEM; *assissa de morte antecessoris* and *assissa mortis antecessoris* (under ASSISA); CAUSA MORTIS; POST MORTEM.

**mort d'ancestor** *n. Law French.* (lit. "death of an ancestor") **1.** an ancient writ—the **writ** (or **assize**) **of mort d'ancestor**—by which one who inherited a possessory interest in land from a parent, a sibling, or an aunt or uncle could gain possession of it from another person who had taken possession.

**2.** Also called **assize of mort d'ancestor.** the cause of action or the legal proceeding founded upon such a writ.

**—History.** The mort d'ancestor arose in the twelfth century as a mechanism for recovering possession of land inherited from a parent, and the principle was extended in the thirteenth century to land inherited directly from ancestors farther back in the line of direct descent (see AIEL; BESAIEL; TRESAIEL) or from other relatives (see COSINAGE). The provision of this remedy was a key step in the evolution of the English property system away from FEUDALISM. Since the person most likely to have possession of the deceased ancestor's land was the lord of the region, this writ helped establish the primacy of inheritance over lordship in rights to land. See also note at ASSIZE.

**mortgage** *n., v.,* **mortgaged, mortgaging. —***n.* **1.** a *security interest* (see under INTEREST¹) in real property. A mortgage is usually held for a considerable number of years to secure repayment, with interest, of a substantial debt of the owner of the property—often the debt incurred in borrowing the money to buy the property. The debtor whose property is subject to the mortgage is called the **mortgagor;** the creditor who holds the mortgage is the **mortgagee.**

**2.** the instrument evidencing a mortgage.

**3.** loosely, a *mortgage loan* (see under LOAN); that is, a loan secured by a mortgage: *The bank gave them a mortgage.*

**4. adjustable-rate mortgage (ARM)** a mortgage that provides for periodic changes in the interest rate, based on changing market conditions. Also called **variable-rate mortgage (VRM), flexible-rate mortgage.**

**5. balloon mortgage** a mortgage under which repayment is to be made in relatively small installments for term of

the loan, with one relatively large installment at the end. For example, payments during the term of the loan might cover interest only, with the entire principal to be repaid in a lump some at the end of the term.

**6. chattel mortgage** a security interest in personal property, analogous to a mortgage on real property.

**7. first mortgage** a mortgage on property that, at the time the mortgage is created, is not subject to any other mortgage.

**8. fixed-rate mortgage (FRM)** a mortgage with a fixed interest rate that remains unchanged throughout the life of the loan.

**9. purchase money mortgage** a mortgage on real estate purchased with borrowed money, taken by the lender to secure repayment of the loan used to make the purchase.

**10. reverse mortgage** a mortgage on a borrower's principal residence under which no repayment of principal or interest is required until the entire loan becomes due, which is usually only when the borrower moves, sells the home, or dies. Reverse mortgages, which often provide a line of credit or periodic payments to the borrower rather than a single lump-sum loan, are principally a mechanism for older people whose homes are fully paid for to benefit from the equity in the home without having to move out of it. Also called **home equity conversion mortgage.**

**11. reverse annuity mortgage (RAM)** a *reverse mortgage* under which the loan takes the form of periodic fixed payments to the borrower or is used to purchase an annuity that provides such payments.

**12. second mortgage** an additional mortgage on property that is already subject to a mortgage. If the debtor defaults and the property is sold in a FORECLOSURE proceeding, the debt to the first mortgagee is paid off first, and the second mortgagee is entitled to repayment only to the extent that there are proceeds left over.

**13. wraparound mortgage** or **wraparound mortgage** a *second mortgage*

that incorporates the first, which remains in effect but is assumed by the second lender. The borrower makes repayments only to the second lender, who uses part of each payment to pay off the first mortgage.
—*v.* **14.** to convey a mortgage interest in, or encumber with a mortgage: *mortgage the property to a bank; mortgage the property.*
—**mortgageability** *n.*
—**mortgageable** *adj.*

**motion** *n.* **1.** an application to a court for an order, made while a case is pending. Motions may be made orally or in writing, and ON NOTICE or EX PARTE, depending upon the circumstances. See also *motion papers* (under PAPERS); *on its own motion* (under SUA SPONTE).
**2. motion in limine** a motion filed at the outset of a case, or at least before a trial begins, in order to have an issue that is bound to arise in the case resolved in advance. See also IN LIMINE.

**movable** *adj.* **1.** not fixed in place; not intended to be a permanent part of fixed property.
—*n.* **2.** Usually, **movables.** Same as *movable property* (see under PROPERTY).

**movant** *n.* the party or lawyer who makes a motion.

**move** *v.*, **moved, moving.** to make a motion: *The attorney moved to strike the witness's answer. The defendant moved for judgment notwithstanding the verdict.*

**MPRE** MULTISTATE PROFESSIONAL RESPONSIBILITY EXAMINATION.

**MPT** MULTISTATE PERFORMANCE TEST.

**mulier** *n. Old English Law.* **1.** a woman or wife.
**2.** a legitimate child.

**mulier puisne** *n. Old English Law.* the legitimate son of parents whose first son was illegitimate. See also PUISNE. Cf. BASTARD EIGNE.

**multidisciplinary practice (MDP)** *n.*
**1.** a firm in which lawyers and other professionals, such as accountants and management consultants, offer clients a range of legal and other services, and share among themselves the combined profits from all services provided.
**2.** the nature of the business of such a firm.

**multijurisdictional practice** *n.* the practice of law in more than one jurisdiction.
——**History.** Traditionally, every state has had its own requirements for admission to the bar, and has allowed only those lawyers who have met those requirements and obtained a license from the state to give legal advice or represent clients in court within the state. In at least some cases the original motive was to assure that lawyers giving advice within a state would be qualified and at least minimally versed in the law of the state. In modern times, when most large transactions involve participants in more than one state and most lawyers in the country have passed the same set of examinations (see, e.g., MULTISTATE BAR EXAMINATION), it has been argued that the primary purpose served by laws barring out-of-state lawyers from serving clients within a state or appearing in local courts has been protection of the economic interests of local lawyers. With the commencement of the twenty-first century, the legal profession began serious discussion of lowering barriers to multijurisdictional practice. See also note at PRO HAC VICE.

**multiple access** *n.* See under ACCESS.

**multiple offender** *n.* See under OFFENDER.

**Multistate Bar Examination (MBE)** *n.* a multiple-choice examination developed by the NATIONAL CONFERENCE OF BAR EXAMINERS; included as one component of the BAR EXAMINATION in most jurisdictions and covering the fields of contracts, torts, constitutional law, criminal law, evidence, and real property.

**Multistate Essay Examination (MEE)** *n.* an essay examination developed by the NATIONAL CONFERENCE OF

BAR EXAMINERS; included as one component of the BAR EXAMINATION in participating jurisdictions, with the length and number of questions varying from jurisdiction to jurisdiction. Typically, the essays cover such topics as commercial paper, conflict of laws, corporations, family law, and federal civil procedure.

**Multistate Performance Test (MPT)** *n.* a test developed by the NATIONAL CONFERENCE OF BAR EXAMINERS that is included as a component of the BAR EXAMINATION in an increasing number of jurisdictions. The Multistate Performance Test is designed to test the practical skills of potential lawyers by providing them with research materials and asking them to indicate how they would use the materials to perform various tasks of the sort that would be required in real legal cases.

**Multistate Professional Responsibility Examination (MPRE)** *n.* a multiple-choice examination developed by the NATIONAL CONFERENCE OF BAR EXAMINERS; included as one component of the BAR EXAMINATION in most states, but given separately, often before graduation from law school. The MPRE tests candidates on their knowledge and understanding of the ethical standards of the legal profession.

**municipal** *adj.* relating to a MUNICIPALITY or to local governments in general.

**municipal bond** *n.* See under BOND[1].

**municipal corporation** *n.* See under CORPORATION.

**municipal security** *n.* See under SECURITY[2].

**municipality** *n., pl.* **municipalities.** a MUNICIPAL CORPORATION or other local governmental unit.

**murder** *n.* **1.** the most serious form of

*criminal homicide* (see under HOMICIDE). The exact scope of the crime varies from state to state, but always includes unjustified conduct resulting in a person's death and undertaken with **intent to kill**—that is, either a conscious purpose to kill or knowledge that death is substantially certain to result; depending upon the state, murder may also include one or more of the following: (1) causing death by unjustified conduct intended to cause serious bodily injury, (2) causing death by extremely negligent or reckless conduct that creates a very high risk of death or serious bodily injury to others or manifests extreme indifference to human life (often called **depraved-heart murder**), or (3) FELONY MURDER. Murder is usually divided into two or more degrees depending upon factors that vary from state to state.
—*v.* **2.** to commit murder; to kill by an act constituting murder.
See also MALICE; PREMEDITATION.

**mutiny** *n., pl.* **mutinies,** *v.,* **mutinied, mutinying.** —*n.* **1.** a concerted refusal by two or more members of the military or of the crew of a ship to obey officers or perform duties.
—*v.* **2.** to engage in mutiny.
—**mutinous** *adj.*
—**mutinously** *adv.*

**mutual fund** *n.* a company whose sole business is to invest in securities and return the profit to its own shareholders.

**mutual insurance** *n.* See under INSURANCE.

**mutual mistake** *n.* See under MISTAKE.

**mutual releases** *n.pl.* See under RELEASE.

**mutual will** *n.* See under WILL.

# N

**nail and mail** *n.* a form of *substituted service* of process (see under SERVICE) consisting of affixing the process to the door of the person to be served and sending a follow-up copy by mail.

**naked** *adj.* **1.** mere; simple; and nothing more. See, e.g., *naked licensee* (under LICENSEE); *naked trust* (same as *passive trust*, under TRUST).
**2.** without consideration or legal formality; lacking support, corroboration, authority, or the like. For example, "naked possession" is possession without ownership or authority; a "naked promise" is one unsupported by consideration.
Used interchangeably with **bare.**
——**False Friend.** This term sometimes serves—presumably unintentionally—to leaven an otherwise dry or even tragic case with a touch of amusing imagery: "As a general rule a mere naked licensee on railroad tracks assumes the risks incident to his position...." *Morser v. Southern Pacific Co.*, 124 Or. 384 (1927) (quoting a treatise).

**naked licensee** *n.* See under LICENSEE.

**naked trust** *n.* See under TRUST.

**name** *n.* See BRAND NAME; FICTITIOUS NAME; GENERIC NAME; TRADE NAME.

**named plaintiff** *n.* See under PLAINTIFF.

**Napoleonic Code** *n.* See CODE NAPOLÉON.

**narrow construction** *n.* See under CONSTRUCTION.

**national** *n.* **1.** a person who owes allegiance to a government and is entitled to its protection, but not necessarily to full citizenship status. All United States citizens are also nationals of the United States; however, persons born in American Samoa are United States nationals but not citizens. See also CITIZEN.

—*adj.* **2.** pertaining or belonging to the nation as a whole: *national affairs; a national park.*

**National Conference of Bar Examiners (NCBE)** *n.* a service organization that develops and provides standardized bar examinations to nearly every jurisdiction in the United States. See also MULTISTATE BAR EXAMINATION; MULTISTATE ESSAY EXAMINATION; MULTISTATE PERFORMANCE TEST; MULTISTATE PROFESSIONAL RESPONSIBILTY EXAMINATION.

**natural law** *n.* a hypothetical body of fundamental principles of ethics and government supposedly inherent in nature, usually regarded as being of divine origin. Although a belief in natural rights underlay the Declaration of Independence and certain Constitutional provisions, natural law itself is a philosophical and religious concept rather than a scientific or legal one. Cf. POSITIVE LAW; POSITIVISM.

**natural lawyer** *n.* a scholar or theorist of NATURAL LAW.

**natural person** *n.* See under PERSON.

**naturalize** *v.*, **naturalized, naturalizing.** to confer citizenship upon an individual who was not a citizen. See also CITIZEN.
—**naturalization** *n.*
——**Note.** Congress has virtually unlimited power to establish the criteria and procedures for naturalization; once naturalized, however, a naturalized citizen has the same status and rights as a citizen by birth in almost all respects, a notable exception being that, under the Constitution, only a natural born citizen may become President.

**NCBE** See NATIONAL CONFERENCE OF BAR EXAMINERS.

**ne bis in idem** *n. Latin.* (lit. "not twice

for the same thing") Same as NON BIS IN IDEM.

**necessaries** *n.pl.* basic goods and services needed by a child, dependent person, or family. Most or all states make both spouses liable for debts incurred by either one for necessaries for the children or family, though the range of goods and services covered usually depends upon the financial circumstances of the particular family; what is "necessary" for a rich family might be a luxury for a poor family.

**Necessary and Proper Clause** *n.* the clause of the Constitution that authorizes Congress to enact all laws "necessary and proper" to carry out the powers of the federal government under the Constitution. It is not limited to laws that are essential or indispensable; rather, it gives Congress discretion to adopt any convenient or appropriate means for accomplishing any constitutionally permissible objective.

**necessary party** *n.* See under PARTY.

**necessity** *n.* a circumstance leaving a person no reasonable choice but to do something that normally would be a tort or crime in order to avoid a greater evil. Where a person's conduct is reasonable under the circumstances, necessity (also called **choice of evils**) generally affords a defense to a tort action or criminal prosecution, especially if the harm avoided would have affected the public at large **(public necessity)** rather than only the individual interests of the person sued **(private necessity)**.

**neck-verse** *n. English Legal History.* a Biblical verse, usually the first verse of the Fifty-first Psalm, presented to persons claiming BENEFIT OF CLERGY to test whether they could read and so were entitled to be spared from hanging.
—**History.** The importance of memorizing the neck-verse, in case one was called upon to "read" it, did not escape notice in criminal circles.

**negative act** *n.* See under ACT.

**negative easement** *n.* See under EASEMENT.

**negative pregnant** *n.* a denial that leaves open the possibility that the proposition being denied may be partly or even substantially true.
—**Note.** An example of a negative pregnant statement might be, "Defendant denies that he recklessly drove the car onto the sidewalk, striking the plaintiff and injuring her." Such a denial is said to be "pregnant with an admission." (In the example, the defendant may be denying only that he was reckless, or only that the plaintiff was injured, or only that she was on the sidewalk when his car struck and injured her.) Under flexible modern pleading rules this might not have serious adverse consequences, but it is still bad form.

**neglect** *n.* **1.** failure to perform some act or fulfill some duty specifically required by law.
**2. child neglect** failure of a parent to support a child or to safeguard a child's health and well-being. Also called **parental neglect.**
**3. excusable neglect** a failure to perform some procedural step or court-ordered act in a case, for which there is an excuse that the law will recognize and the judge deems adequate.
**4. neglect of duty** failure of a public official or a member of the military to carry out official or military duties.
**5. willful neglect** intentional, knowing, or reckless failure to fulfill a legal duty, especially with respect to the care of a child.

**negligence** *n.* **1.** (in tort law) conduct involving an unreasonable risk of injury or loss to others; conduct that falls short of the degree of care that a *reasonable person* (see under REASONABLE) would have exercised in the same circumstances. Negligence is determined by an OBJECTIVE TEST: a person who considered a situation thoroughly and took what he genuinely regarded as a reasonable risk would nevertheless properly be found negligent if the jury concludes that a person of ordinary intelligence and prudence in that situation would not have done what the defendant did. Negligence is a tort; the wrongdoer is generally liable for any injury to person or property directly resulting from it. See also PROXIMATE CAUSE. Cf. *intentional tort* (under TORT); RECKLESSNESS.

**2.** Also called **criminal negligence.** (in criminal law) a gross deviation from the standard of care that a reasonable person would observe, under circumstances posing a substantial and unjustifiable risk of which the actor should have been aware. Except for relatively rare STRICT LIABILITY offenses, this is usually the minimum level of fault that will subject a person to criminal liability; *ordinary negligence* is normally insufficient. See also *negligent homicide* (under HOMICIDE); STATE OF MIND.

**3. comparative negligence** the modern doctrine that as between a plaintiff and a defendant in a tort case, and sometimes as among several defendants, fault (and liability for damages) should be allocated in proportion to each party's contribution to the injury or loss complained of. Cf. *contributory negligence.*

**4. contributory negligence a.** negligence by a plaintiff contributing to the injury or loss that is the subject of a tort case, as when a plaintiff sues over an automobile accident that was primarily caused by the defendant but was also partly caused or made worse by inattentiveness on the part of the plaintiff. **b.** the traditional doctrine that any contributory negligence by a plaintiff, however slight, bars the plaintiff from recovering in a negligence case. In most states this harsh common law doctrine has been superseded by some form of *comparative negligence.*

**5. gross negligence** highly unreasonable conduct; a term used primarily in civil contexts, sometimes interpreted as RECKLESSNESS but more often representing essentially the same degree of fault as *criminal negligence.* In most civil contexts it does not matter whether negligence is "gross" or "slight"; often the phrase "gross negligence" is used just for rhetorical effect.

**6. imputed negligence** negligence attributed to one person because of the negligent act of another with whom the first has a special relationship; for example, negligence attributed to an employer because of the negligent act of an employee. See also IMPUTED.

**7. ordinary** (or **simple**) **negligence** conduct falling short of the standard of *ordinary care* (see under CARE); negligence as described in def. 1 above.

**8. willful** (or **wanton**) **negligence** in theory, RECKLESSNESS. In practice, these concepts tend to shade into *gross negligence.*

—**negligent** *adj.*
—**negligently** *adv.*

**negligent homicide** *n.* See under HOMICIDE.

**negligent infliction of emotional distress** *n.* the causing of severe EMOTIONAL DISTRESS in another person through conduct that is negligent, but without recklessness or an intent to cause such distress. Also called **negligent infliction of severe emotional distress,** and referred to by many similar phrases using a variety of synonyms, the most common of which are listed in the entry for EMOTIONAL DISTRESS. Cf. INTENTIONAL INFLICTION OF EMOTIONAL DISTRESS.

—**History.** Under traditional tort rules, one normally could not recover damages for emotional distress resulting from another's negligence unless one had also suffered some physical injury as a result of the negligent act. For example, the mental distress resulting from being disfigured because of another's negligence would be compensible, but not the distress resulting from injury to one's child. The modern trend is to expand, rather cautiously, the circumstances under which negligent infliction of severe emotional distress will be regarded as a compensible tort. The most common circumstances in which recovery is allowed in the absence of bodily injury to the plaintiff are circumstances where the plaintiff directly observed the harm to another, particularly a family member (as when a parent sees a child struck by a negligently driven automobile), or when the plaintiff was herself within the ZONE OF

DANGER (as when a pedestrian suffers severe psychic trauma as a result of being narrowly missed by an automobile driven negligently and at high speed).

**negotiable** *adj.* (of an instrument evidencing certain rights) transferable by INDORSEMENT and delivery. The concept of negotiability applies particularly to three kinds of instruments: a DOCUMENT OF TITLE; a security evidenced by a certificate, such as a STOCK CERTIFICATE (see SECURITY[2] and BOND[1]); and a check or other "negotiable instrument" in the narrow sense of that phrase (see NEGOTIABLE INSTRUMENT, def. 2). In each case, if the instrument satisfies certain requirements specified in the UNIFORM COMMERCIAL CODE, then ownership of the instrument and the rights it represents may be transferred simply by indorsing it and delivering it to the transferee—and sometimes even the indorsement is unnecessary (see NEGOTIATE). See also *negotiable document of title* (under DOCUMENT OF TITLE); WORDS OF NEGOTIABILITY.
**—negotiability** *n.*

**negotiable instrument** *n.* **1.** broadly, any document that is NEGOTIABLE, including a negotiable document of title or a security.
**2.** specifically and usually, a financial instrument that (1) contains an unconditional promise or order to pay a specific sum of money, but (with certain exceptions) no other promise, order, power, or obligation; (2) is payable on demand or at a definite time; (3) is payable to order or to bearer; and (4) is signed by the issuer. If it is a promise it is usually called a note (see NOTE[1]); if it is an order it is a DRAFT, the most common example of which is an ordinary CHECK.
See also BEARER; DEMAND; ORDER[2]; TIME.

**negotiate** *v.*, **negotiated, negotiating.**
**1.** to transfer a check or other negotiable instrument or document in such a way that the transferee becomes a HOLDER. In the case of a *bearer instrument* (see under BEARER), this can be

done simply by handing over the instrument. In the case of an *order instrument* (see under ORDER[2]), it is done by indorsing the instrument (see INDORSE) and then delivering it. For example, a check may be negotiated by cashing it, depositing it, or signing it over to someone else. Negotiation transfers ownership of the instrument and the rights it represents to the person to whom the instrument is delivered.
**2.** to bargain or haggle: *to negotiate a contract.*
**—negotiation** *n.*

**net assets** *n.* See under ASSET.

**net income** *n.* See under INCOME.

**net lease** *n.* See under LEASE.

**newsman's privilege** *n.* Same as REPORTER'S PRIVILEGE.

**newsperson's privilege** *n.* Same as REPORTER'S PRIVILEGE.

**newsperson's shield law** *n.* Same as REPORTER'S SHIELD LAW.

**next friend** *n.* a person who files a lawsuit on behalf of a minor or incompetent who lacks legal capacity to sue or be sued, and stands in for that person as a party in the case.

**NGO** *pl.* **NGOs, NGO's.** NONGOVERNMENTAL ORGANIZATION.

**nisi** *adj. Latin.* (lit. "unless") tentative. A term still used in certain contexts in England and a few states to indicate that a judgment, order, or the like is not final but will become so—or as it is said, become ABSOLUTE—unless an adverse party appears and shows why it should not be made final. Examples include *decree nisi* (under DECREE); *judgment nisi* (under JUDGMENT); *rule nisi* (under RULE).

**nisi prius** *n. Latin.* (lit. "unless previously") a civil trial court; a court for trying civil cases before a jury: *The factual issues were determined at nisi prius. The nisi prius judge granted summary judgment.* Also called **nisi prius court.**
**—History.** This term originated in the words of an ancient writ commanding

that a jury be summoned to Westminster for the trial of a case on a certain date *unless previously* (*nisi prius*) the king's traveling judges reach the county where the action arose. By implication, this conferred on those judges the power to hold the trial when they held court in the county, and the courts that held such trials became known as *nisi prius courts.*

**no bill** *n.* See under BILL.

**no contest** *n.* Same as NOLO CONTENDERE.

**no-fault divorce** *n.* See under DIVORCE.

**no-fault insurance** *n.* a type of automobile insurance required in some states, under which compensation for minor personal injuries incurred in an accident is made by the insurance company covering the car in which the injured person was riding (or, in the case of pedestrian injuries, the car that struck the pedestrian), regardless of which driver involved in the accident was more at fault. The purpose of no-fault insurance laws is to spare everyone involved the time and expense of lawsuits to apportion blame for relatively minor accidents.

**no-par stock** *n.* Same as *stock without par value* (see under STOCK).

**nol. pros.** *n.* Abbreviation for NOLLE PROSEQUI.

**nol pros** or **nol-pros** *n., v.,* **nol prossed** or **nol-prossed, nol prossing** or **nol-prossing.** *Informal.* Same as NOLLE PROSEQUI.

**nolle** *n., v.* **nollied, nolleing.** *Informal.* Same as NOLLE PROSEQUI.

**nolle prosequi** *n., v.,* **nolle prosequied, nolle prosequiing.** (from Latin, lit. "to be unwilling to pursue") —*n.* **1.** the formal abandonment of a criminal charge by the prosecuting attorney, noted in the record. *Abbr.:* nol. pros. —*v.* **2.** to enter a nolle prosequi with respect to: *The Government nolle prosequied the indictment.* —**Usage.** In speaking, and often even

in writing, this phrase is often shortened to NOLLE or NOL PROS. —**Note.** A nolle prosequi frees a defendant from immediate prosecution but does not necessarily eliminate the risk of prosecution. If the nolle prosequi was entered before the trial began and the statute of limitations has not expired, the defendant can be reindicted on the same charge.

**nolo contendere** *n. Latin.* (lit. "I will not contest") a PLEA to a criminal charge, permitted in the federal courts and in many states (subject to the judge's consent), whereby the defendant states that he will not contest the charge. The result of such a plea is a conviction on the charge, and for sentencing purposes it is the same as a guilty plea. Unlike a guilty plea, however, it may not be used in a subsequent civil case as proof of guilt. Also called **non vult contendere** or **no contest.**

**nominal** *adj.* **1.** in name only; in form rather than in substance. For example, a nominal party is one (such as a NEXT FRIEND) named as a plaintiff or defendant only to satisfy technical requirements. **2.** symbolic, token: *nominal consideration* (see under CONSIDERATION); *nominal damages* (see under DAMAGES). —**nominally** *adv.*

**nominate** *v.,* **nominated, nominating.** to select or appoint as one's agent, representative, or designee: *The powers granted to my executor by this will are to be exercised by her or by such other person as she may nominate.* A person so selected is called a **nominee.** —**nomination** *n.*

**nominee trust** *n.* See under TRUST.

**non bis in idem** *n. Latin.* (lit. "not twice for the same thing") **1.** *Civil Law.* the doctrine that no one should be tried twice for the same offense; the civil law counterpart of the rule against DOUBLE JEOPARDY in Anglo-American law. **2.** *International Law.* the principle, applicable in an INTERNATIONAL CRIMINAL TRIBUNAL or the INTERNATIONAL CRIMINAL COURT, that no person tried in such a forum for an alleged crime under international law may be tried again for the same conduct in any other court, and that a person who was tried in a national court may not be tried again for the same conduct in an international tribunal *unless* the trial in the national court was for the purpose of shielding the person concerned from criminal responsibility, or was not conducted independently and impartially in accordance with international norms of due process and in an honest attempt to bring the person concerned to justice.

Also called **ne bis in idem.**

**non compos mentis** *adj. Latin.* (lit. "not in possession of the mind") insane; incompetent; not in full possession of one's mental faculties. Sometimes shortened to **non compos.**

**non obstante veredicto (n.o.v.)** *Latin.* (lit. "notwithstanding the verdict") See *judgment notwithstanding the verdict* (under JUDGMENT).

**non prosequitur** *n. Latin.* (lit. "he/she does not pursue") an older term for a judgment against a plaintiff who stops pursuing a case at some point after filing it. Shortened informally to **non pros.** Today this would usually take the form of a dismissal for FAILURE TO PROSECUTE or a *default judgment* (see under JUDGMENT).

**non vult contendere** *Latin.* (lit. "he/she will not contest") Same as NOLO CONTENDERE.

**nonage** *n.* the state of being under the *age of majority* or *legal age* (see both under AGE).

**nonassessable stock** *n.* Opposite of *assessable stock* (see under STOCK).

**nonconforming use** *n.* See under USE.

**noncontestability clause** *n.* Same as INCONTESTABILITY CLAUSE.

**non-core proceeding** or **noncore proceeding** *n.* an action that is related to a matter before a bankruptcy court but does not arise under the federal Bankruptcy Code or directly concern administration of the estate in bankruptcy. The bankruptcy courts do not have independent jurisdiction over such non-core proceedings, but for the sake of efficiency the federal district court to which a bankruptcy court is attached may refer such an action to the bankruptcy court handling the estate to which it relates, to hear and make recommended findings and conclusions. Also called **related proceeding.** Cf. CORE PROCEEDING.

——**Usage.** The hyphenated form is used in the relevant federal statute and rules, and thus is the usual spelling. Many courts, however—including the Supreme Court—drop the hyphen at least some of the time when they are not directly quoting the statute.

**nondelegable** *adj.* not capable of being delegated. See *nondelegable duty* (under DUTY[1]).

**nonfeasance** *n.* unjustified failure to perform a required act or carry out an official duty. Cf. MALFEASANCE; MISFEASANCE.

**nonfederal money** *n.* **1.** money received for a program or project, such as a public health program or university research project, from private or public sources other than the federal government.
**2.** in federal campaign finance law, same as SOFT MONEY.

**nongermane** *adj.* not relevant; not pertinent.

**nongermane amendment** *n.* a proposed amendment to a bill under consideration by a legislative body that is not pertinent to the subject matter of the bill. See note at GERMANE.

**nongovernmental organization (NGO)** *n.* a private, nonprofit, international organization concerned with global issues in such areas as human rights, the environment, economic development, arms control, food, health, science, and education.
——**Note.** Nongovernmental organizations do vast amounts of research and work around the globe, often augmenting what governments can do and often working to change what governments

do. They have come to wield substantial influence in international affairs, and their expertise and their views are taken into account in much of the work of the United Nations. For example, in addition to the 160 nations whose governments were represented (and allowed to vote) at the 1998 United Nations conference that established the framework for the INTERNATIONAL CRIMINAL COURT, the participants included (on a nonvoting basis) 14 specialized agencies and funds of the United Nations, 17 intergovernmental organizations, and 124 NGOs.

**nonjoinder** *n.* the failure of a party asserting a claim in a case to JOIN a *necessary party* or *indispensable party* (see under PARTY). See also JOINDER.

**nonjury trial** *n.* Same as *bench trial* (see under TRIAL).

**nonjusticiable** *adj.* not JUSTICIABLE. See note at that entry.
—**nonjusticiability** *n.*

**nonmailable** *adj.* not legally permitted to be transmitted by mail. A wide variety of dangerous or illegal plants, animals, objects, substances, and writings are nonmailable.

**nonnegotiable document of title** *n.* See under DOCUMENT OF TITLE.

**nonnegotiable instrument** *n.* an instrument that is substantially in the form of a NEGOTIABLE INSTRUMENT, but fails in some particular respect to meet the exact requirements for negotiability; for example, an unsigned check, or a note that says "I promise to pay to Mary Jones" instead of "I promise to pay *to the order of* Mary Jones" (see under ORDER²).

**nonpar stock** *n.* Same as *stock without par value* (see under STOCK).

**nonprivileged** *adj.* Same as UNPRIVILEGED.

**nonprivileged communication** *n.* Same as UNPRIVILEGED COMMUNICATION.

**nonprivileged speech** *n.* See under SPEECH.

**nonprofit** *adj.* (of an organization or institution) organized for purposes other than to make a profit, such as an educational, charitable, or cooperative organization; for example, a *nonprofit corporation* (see under CORPORATION).

**nonprotected speech** *n.* See under SPEECH.

**nonqualified** *adj.* **1.** not meeting legal requirements: opposite of QUALIFIED¹ (def. 2).
**2.** very rarely, not suited for a particular job; same as UNQUALIFIED (def. 1).
—**Usage.** It is best to confine this word to its usual sense of "not legally qualified," so as to preserve the convenient distinction between, for example, an *unqualified pilot* (one who lacks the necessary skill) and a *nonqualified pilot* (one who has not obtained the necessary or appropriate license or certification).

**nonrecourse** *adj.* lacking the right to proceed against a particular obligor personally in the event of nonpayment or default. See discussion at RECOURSE; see also *nonrecourse loan* (under LOAN).

**nonrefundable tax credit** *n.* See under TAX CREDIT.

**nonresident alien** *n.* See under ALIEN.

**nonresponsive** *adj.* Same as UNRESPONSIVE.
—**nonresponsively** *adv.*
—**nonresponsiveness** *n.*

**nonresponsive answer** *n.* Same as UNRESPONSIVE ANSWER.

**nonreviewable** *n.* not subject to judicial, appellate, or administrative REVIEW.
—**nonreviewability** *n.*
—**Usage.** *Nonreviewable* means the same thing as *unreviewable*, but is less commonly used. For the noun form, however, *nonreviewability* is more common than *unreviewability.*

**nonstock corporation** *n.* See under CORPORATION.

**nonsuit** *n.* **1.** an older term for DISMISSAL of a civil case.
—*v.* **2.** to issue a nonsuit against: *The judge nonsuited the plaintiff.*

**nonsupport** *n.* the crime of failing to provide needed financial support that one has the resources to provide to one's child, spouse, or other dependent where there is a duty to provide such support.

**not-for-profit corporation** *n.* See under CORPORATION.

**not found** Same as *no bill* (see under BILL).

**not guilty 1.** acquitted of a criminal charge; tried and not proved guilty. Cf. INNOCENT.
**2.** a PLEA by which a criminal defendant preserves the right to a trial to determine guilt.
Cf. GUILTY; NOLO CONTENDERE.

**not guilty by reason of insanity** deemed not legally responsible for a criminal act on the ground that the actor was insane at the time. See also INSANITY DEFENSE and specific tests listed there.

**not proven** not established at trial, but suspected to be true anyway: a verdict permitted by Scots criminal law. See SCOTCH VERDICT.

**notarial** *adj.* pertaining to or done by a NOTARY PUBLIC.

**notarize** *v.*, **notarized, notarizing.** to authenticate a document or attest to the performance of some other notarial act by affixing the signature and seal of a notary public.

**notary public** *n., pl.* **notaries public.** a person authorized by the government to administer oaths and affirmations, take acknowledgments, authenticate signatures, and tend to various other formalities relating to legal documents and transactions. Often shortened to **notary.**

**note¹** *n.* **1.** an instrument representing a promise to pay a sum of money, and often interest, to (or to the order of) the bearer or a named PAYEE. A note is a NEGOTIABLE INSTRUMENT if it meets the requirements listed under that entry. Also called **promissory note.** See also MAKE; *to the order of* (under ORDER²).
**2. accommodation note** a note

signed by at least two promisors, one of whom is signing solely as an ACCOMMODATION to another signer.
**3. cognovit note** a note in which the maker's promise to pay is coupled with a confession of judgment, so that the payee can automatically obtain a judgment against the maker if a payment is missed. See discussion under CONFESSION OF JUDGMENT. See also COGNOVIT.
**4. installment note** a note promising payments at fixed intervals over a period of time, or one of a set of notes each of which provides for one such payment.

**note²** *n.* an article on a legal topic, typically written by a law student and published in a law review, and usually quite comprehensive. Cf. *case note* (under ANNOTATION); COMMENT.

**notice** *n., v.*, **noticed, noticing. 1.** the act of conveying information of legal significance to a person, or, when such information is conveyed in writing, the document itself: *notice of deposition; notice of increase in rent.* See also ON NOTICE; SERVICE.
**2.** information of legal significance to a person that is known to, or at least available to, that person.
**3.** for purposes of satisfying DUE PROCESS, **a.** the publication of laws and regulations, so that no one will be charged with a crime for conduct that they had no way of knowing was illegal. **b.** formal warning of proposed action to be taken against a person (such as a criminal charge, a civil suit, or termination of welfare benefits), so as to advise the person of the nature of the charges, allegations, or proposed action and provide an OPPORTUNITY TO BE HEARD. In civil cases this is normally accomplished by service of a SUMMONS and COMPLAINT; in criminal cases, by ARRAIGNMENT.
**4. actual notice** notice actually received by, or information actually known to, a person.
**5. constructive notice** information that a person could have or should have known, or information conveyed in a way that was reasonably calculated

to give actual notice.

**6. inquiry notice** notice of facts sufficient to cause a reasonably prudent person to make further inquiry with regard to a matter if she wishes to safeguard her rights or avoid liability.

**7. judicial notice** See under JUDICIAL.

**8. notice by publication** publication of a notice in a newspaper in the hope of reaching persons affected by a matter who cannot otherwise be identified or located. Such notice is allowed or required in certain legal situations, but only as a last resort.

**9. notice pleading** See under PLEADING.

—*v.* **10.** to give formal legal notice of or to: *The judge noticed the hearing for Wednesday. Each of the defendants has been noticed for a deposition.*

**notorious** *adj.* open; well known; not concealed: *notorious possession; notorious cohabitation.* See also OPEN AND NOTORIOUS.

—**notoriously** *adv.*

—**notoriousness** *n.*

**n.o.v.** See *judgment notwithstanding the verdict* (under JUDGMENT).

**novation** *n.* the substitution of a new contract for an old one, extinguishing all rights and obligations under the old one, by agreement of all parties to both contracts. For example, the new contract might substitute new terms for the terms of the original contract, or substitute a new party for one of the original parties.

**novel disseisin** *n.* **1.** an ancient writ—the **writ** (or **assize**) **of novel disseisin**—by which one who had recently been thrown out of possession of land could regain possession.

**2.** Also called **assize of novel disseisin.** the cause of action or the legal proceeding founded upon such a writ.

See also *petty assize* (under ASSIZE) and accompanying note.

**NSF check** *n.* See under CHECK.

**nuisance** *n.* **1.** Also called **private nuisance.** the tort of engaging in conduct, or maintaining a condition on one's property, that substantially and unreasonably interferes with another's use and enjoyment of her own property; for example, activities that create unreasonable noise, vibrations, foul odors, or a health or fire hazard. See also ATTRACTIVE NUISANCE.

**2.** Also called **public nuisance.** conduct, especially in the use of one's own land, that unreasonably interferes with the health, safety, welfare, comfort, or rights of the public at large, or of a large number of people.

——**Note.** Examples of public nuisance include extending a building so that it encroaches on a public sidewalk; maintenance of an illegal establishment, such as a brothel or gambling house; violating zoning restrictions; or any kind of conduct that might constitute a private nuisance but is severe enough to interfere with more than a few immediate neighbors. Conduct amounting to a public nuisance is usually a crime, and may independently constitute a private nuisance with respect to certain individuals particularly affected, in which case it may be called a **mixed nuisance.**

**null** or **null and void** Same as VOID.

**nullification** *n.* **1.** an act or instance of nullifying.

**2.** the state of being nullified.

**3. nullification doctrine** the doctrine that individual states may determine for themselves whether a federal law or judicial decision is constitutional and declare it to be null and void within that state. The doctrine has been promoted from time to time and place to place in American history, but has been definitively rejected by the nation as a whole.

See also JURY NULLIFICATION.

**nullify** *v.*, **nullified, nullifying.** to make null; make VOID.

**nunc pro tunc** *Latin.* now for then; a phrase making an order retroactive to a certain date. For example, an order correcting an error in a previous order would normally be made "nunc pro tunc" to make it clear that the first order should be regarded as having said what was originally intended all along.

**nuncupative will** *n.* See under WILL.

# O

**oath** *n.* **1.** a solemn declaration that certain facts are true or that one will speak the truth, faithfully carry out one's official duties, uphold the law, or the like. The taking of an oath to tell the truth renders any dishonest statement punishable as FALSE SWEARING or PERJURY. See also SWEAR; UNDER OATH.
**2.** the words recited in giving or taking an oath.
**3. oath of office** the oath or affirmation of a person elected or appointed to public office, undertaking to support the Constitution and to perform the duties of the office faithfully.
——**Note.** In its traditional and strictest sense, an oath is an invocation of God, as distinguished from an AFFIRMATION, which lacks overt religious content. Broadly, an oath may take any suitably solemn form and need not refer to God; in this sense "oath" includes affirmations. See also OATH OR AFFIRMATION.

**oath or affirmation** a phrase used to avoid the religious issues that might be raised by the use of OATH alone: *The application must be accompanied by a statement made upon oath or affirmation.* See also SWEAR OR AFFIRM.
——**History.** The framers of the Constitution were sensitive to religious concerns about oaths and the need for the government they were creating to accommodate all views. Quakers had been persecuted in England and some colonies for their conscientious refusal to swear oaths; and in a bitter irony, after the Revolution they had been excluded from public office in the former Quaker colony of Pennsylvania by a requirement in the new state constitution that officers take an oath of loyalty to the constitution. The framers took care to make the new federal regime more tolerant: Instead of requiring a sworn oath of office, Article VI of the Constitution provides only that all state and federal legislators, judges, and executives "shall be bound by Oath or Affirmation, to support this Constitution." See also RELIGIOUS TEST and note at SWEAR OR AFFIRM.

**obiter dictum** *pl.* **obiter dicta.** *Latin.* (lit. "a thing said in passing") Same as DICTUM (see discussion there). Occasionally shortened instead to **obiter** (lit. "in passing," "by the way"): *Although the court's remark was obiter in the context of that case, we believe that it correctly states the rule applicable here.*

**objection** *n.* **1.** a formal statement or notice that one regards a claim or procedural step as impermissible or invalid; a request that a particular course of action not be permitted or pursued.
**2.** especially, such a statement or request in regard to a question asked, evidence sought to be admitted, or other conduct at a trial or hearing.
**3. continuing objection** a single objection applicable to all questions in a line of questioning. If an attorney regards an entire area of questioning as improper but the judge disagrees, then instead of requiring the attorney to object to each question in turn in order to preserve the issue for appeal, the judge may grant the attorney a "continuing objection" to the entire line of inquiry.
**4. speaking objection** an objection in a jury trial that contains more than the minimum necessary information for the judge to rule, often in an attempt to sway the jury. Some judges forbid lawyers to give any grounds for their objection unless specifically requested to do so, and some require lawyers to give their reasons by citing sections of a state evidence code or the federal rules of evidence by number, so that the jury will not understand what they are talking about.
——**object** *v.*

—**objectionable** *adj.*
—**objectionably** *adv.*
—**objector** *n.*
——**Note.** An objection to evidence or testimony is made by saying "Objection" or "I object" and, if necessary, adding just enough explanation to make clear what is being objected to and the legal grounds for the objection. For some types of questions likely to be objected to, see QUESTION[1] (defs. 2–5). The court's response to an objection is to SUSTAIN or OVERRULE it. If testimony and other evidence is not objected to at the time it is offered, it normally cannot be complained about on appeal.

**objective test** *n.* a legal test that does not depend upon what is in someone's mind, but on external criteria. For example, any legal principle that depends upon whether someone's conduct was REASONABLE involves an objective test, because what matters is not how the person involved viewed the situation, but how a reasonable person in that situation would have viewed it. Cf. SUBJECTIVE TEST.

**obligation** *n.* **1.** a legal requirement that one perform or refrain from performing some act, or the act that one is required to perform.
**2. joint and several obligation** a contractual obligation undertaken by two or more persons with the understanding that performance may be sought in court either from all of them collectively or from any one of them individually.
**3. joint obligation** a contractual obligation for which two or more persons have agreed to be liable as a group but not individually.

**obligee** *n.* a person or entity owed an obligation under a contract or negotiable instrument, especially an obligation to pay money.

**obligor** *n.* **1.** a person or entity owing an obligation under a contract or negotiable instrument, especially an obligation to pay money.
**2. principal obligor** See under PRINCI-

PAL.

**obscene device** *n.* (in the law of several states) a device designed or marketed as useful primarily for the stimulation of human genital organs.
——**Note.** Laws making the sale of sexual vibrators and other such "obscene devices" a criminal offense are not mere holdovers from the distant past; in the closing decades of the twentieth century several states enacted new obscenity laws with this prohibition, including one (Alabama) as recently as 1998. Constitutional challenges to these laws have produced wildly varying decisions: In some states the statutes have been held unconstitutional on the ground that they are not rationally related to any legitimate state interest (see RATIONAL BASIS TEST); in others they have been held merely to be unconstitutionally overbroad insofar as they prohibit distribution for "therapeutic" purposes; in still others they have been found to be wholly constitutional.

**obscenity** *n., pl.* **obscenities.** any form of expression, such as a book, painting, photograph, movie, or play, that deals with sex in a way that is regarded as so offensive as to be beyond the protection of the constitutional guarantee of FREEDOM OF SPEECH. Under the most recent of the Supreme Court's efforts to define obscenity, the term applies to material that appeals to PRURIENT INTEREST, depicts or describes sexual conduct in a way that is PATENTLY OFFENSIVE, and lacks "serious literary, artistic, political, or scientific value." *Miller v. California,* 413 U.S. 15 (1973). See also PORNOGRAPHY; PRIOR RESTRAINT; SPEECH.
—**obscene** *adj.*
—**obscenely** *adv.*

**obstruction of justice** *n.* the crime of attempting to impede or pervert the administration of justice, as by concealing or falsifying evidence, or by bribing, threatening, or otherwise attempting to influence witnesses, jurors, or court officials improperly. The term is sometimes extended to acts that impede police or other law enforcement activities as well. The exact terminology and classification scheme for such offenses varies from state to state.

**occupancy** *n. actual possession* (see under POSSESSION), or the act of taking actual possession, of real property. This does not require physical presence on the property at all times, but at the very least diligence in keeping others out except with one's own permission. Also called **occupation.**
—**occupy** *v.*, **occupied, occupying.**

**occupy the field** See under PREEMPTION.

**of age** having reached the *age of majority*, or *legal age* for a particular activity (see both under AGE). Cf. UNDERAGE.

**of counsel 1.** referring to a lawyer who assists the *attorney of record* (see under ATTORNEY) in a trial or appeal; a member of a legal team other than the leader.
**2.** a lawyer associated in some way with a law firm, but not as a member or employee; for example, one retained to assist in a particular matter, or a retired member of the firm who consults with it on specific matters when called upon.

**of record** See under RECORD.

**of the essence 1.** essential; said of contract terms whose exact performance is so central to the purposes of the contract that any failure by a party to adhere to them would be deemed a *material breach* (see under BREACH), justifying cancellation of the contract by the other party.
**2. time is of the essence** a phrase signifying that any failure to perform within the time specified in the contract will constitute a material breach, even if the delay is slight.

**off the record** See under RECORD.

**offender** *n.* **1.** a person who commits an OFFENSE.
**2. adult offender a.** an offender who was over the age of majority when the offense was committed. **b.** an offender who was under the age of majority when the offense was committed but who has since become an adult or who is treated as an adult.

**3. child offender a.** a *juvenile offender*. **b.** a person who commits an offense against a child.
**4. first offender a.** a person charged with or convicted of a particular offense for the first time. **b.** an offender who has not previously been convicted of any offense.
**5. habitual offender** a person previously convicted of several crimes, and thus subject to a more severe sentence for any subsequent crime. Also called **habitual criminal.** See also THREE STRIKES LAW.
**6. juvenile offender a.** an offender treated as a juvenile rather than as an adult by the criminal justice system. See JUVENILE (def. 4). **b.** an offender who is under the age of majority, or who was under the age of majority when the offense was committed. Also called **youthful offender.**
**7. multiple offender a.** a *repeat offender*. **b.** an offender charged with or convicted of several offenses at the same time.
**8. repeat offender a.** a person convicted more than once of the same kind of offense. Many laws and regulations provide more severe penalties for a second or third violation of the same law. **b.** a person convicted more than once of various kinds of crimes.
See also THREE STRIKES LAW.

**offense** *n.* **1.** any CRIME or other violation of law for which a penalty is prescribed.
**2. indictable offense** an offense that is ordinarily prosecutable only by INDICTMENT. In the federal system, all crimes for which a sentence of more than one year in prison may be imposed are indictable, although in noncapital cases the defendant may waive indictment. In states that have reduced or eliminated the role of the *grand jury* (see discussion under JURY), only more serious crimes are indictable, if any are.
**3. petty offense** a very minor offense, defined in some jurisdictions to include any misdemeanor for which the possible sentence does not exceed six months, in others as an offense below the level of misdemeanor for which no

jail sentence can be imposed.

See also *anticipatory offense* and *inchoate offense* (under INCHOATE CRIME); BAILABLE OFFENSE; LESSER INCLUDED OFFENSE.

**offer** *n.* **1.** a proposal to enter into a CONTRACT upon specified terms. A proposal is an offer if it is made in such a way that the person to whom it is made has only to ACCEPT it to bring the contract into existence. See also TENDER OFFER.

**2.** any PROFFER.

**3. firm offer**   an offer to buy or sell goods, made by a merchant in a signed writing that includes an assurance that the offer will be held open. Contrary to the usual rule that an offer may be withdrawn at any time before acceptance, an offer meeting these requirements is irrevocable for the period of time stated in the offer, or for a reasonable time if no specific time is stated.

—*v.* **4.** to make an offer.

**5.** to request admission of an exhibit into evidence: *"I offer this as Plaintiff's Exhibit 57."*

**offer of proof**   a brief statement by a lawyer to a judge, out of the hearing of the jury, of the testimony that a particular witness is expected to give in response to a particular question or line of questioning. A lawyer may request permission to make an offer of proof, also called a **proffer,** in response to a judge's initial ruling sustaining an objection to a question, both to try to persuade the judge that the testimony is admissible and to make a record for arguing on appeal that the judge was wrong to exclude it.

**offeree** *n.* a person to whom an offer is made.

**offering** *n.* **1.** the placing on sale of an issue of securities by a corporation or other entity. (See ISSUE[3].)

**2. initial public offering (IPO)**   a company's first offering of equity securities to the general public.

**3. private offering**   an offering of securities to a limited group of buyers, so that full public disclosure of the relevant financial information is not required. Also called **private placement.**

**4. public offering**   an offering of securities to the public at large.

**offering circular** *n.* a document providing relevant financial information regarding a private offering of securities, circulated only to the particular investors to whom the offering is made. Also called **offering statement.**

**offering statement** *n.* Same as OFFERING CIRCULAR.

**offeror** *n.* a person who makes an offer.

**officer** *n.* **1.** a person appointed or elected to a position of responsibility or authority in government or a private organization.

**2.** in a corporation, **a.** strictly, one of the handful of individuals selected by the board of directors to have overall responsibility for day-to-day management of the corporation's business. **b.** loosely, anyone in a management position to which an impressive title has been assigned, partly for their own satisfaction and partly to give them credibility in dealing with the public. A corporation may have thousands of such officers.

**officer of the court** *n.* any employee of a court or any lawyer involved in a matter before the court. The phrase is used to emphasize the responsibility of all such individuals to conduct themselves with utmost honesty and good faith in all matters involving the court.

**official** *n.* **1.** an individual appointed or elected to office or an employee holding a position of responsibility or authority in government or a private organization. See also PUBLIC OFFICIAL.

—*adj.* **2.** of or pertaining to an office or position of duty, trust, or authority: *official powers.*

**3.** authorized or issued authoritatively: an *official report.*

**4.** appointed or authorized to act in a designated capacity: *an official representative.*

—**officially** *adv.*

**official capacity** *n.* See under CAPAC-ITY.

**official English law** *n.* Same as ENG-LISH-ONLY LAW.

**official immunity** *n.* See under IMMU-NITY.

**official language law** *n.* Same as ENGLISH-ONLY LAW.

**officious intermeddler** *n.* a person who intrudes into the business of others without an invitation or a reasonable basis for believing that his involvement is needed. Even if the officious intermeddler's motives are good, he generally receives little sympathy from the law if, for example, he subsequently seeks payment for his services or compensation for an injury sustained.

**offset** *n., adj., v.,* **offset, offsetting.** —*n.* **1.** Same as *setoff* (see under SET OFF). —*adj.* **2.** of or pertaining to an offset: *the offset amount.* —*v.* **3.** to SET OFF.

**omission** *n.* a failure to do something that one should have done. An omission may be viewed as a type of act (see *act of omission,* under ACT), or as a failure to act (as in the phrase ACT OR OMISSION).

**omit** *v.,* **omitted, omitting. 1.** to forbear or fail to do (usually in a negative sense): *The plaintiff contributed to his own injuries by omitting to fasten his seatbelt.* **2.** to leave out: *The prospectus omitted material information about pending litigation against the company.* —**omissible** *adj.* —**omissive** *adj.*

**omnibus bill** *n.* a legislative bill in which, for convenience or for strategic reasons, a variety of related or unrelated proposals are combined into one bill to be voted up or down together. Cf. GERMANE.

**on all fours** a perfect fit. A phrase describing a PRECEDENT that is claimed to be so similar in its facts to the case at hand as to be legally indistinguishable: *The plaintiff contends that the decision in Smith v. Jones is on all fours, but the defendant argues that the case is distinguishable.*

**on bail** See under BAIL[1].

**on consent** See under CONSENT.

**on demand** See under DEMAND.

**on information and belief** (of an allegation or statement of fact) believed to be true on the basis of information other than personal knowledge. See discussion at INFORMATION AND BELIEF.

**on its face** See under FACE.

**on its (his, her, their) own motion** Same as SUA SPONTE. See also note at EX PROPRIO MOTU.

**on notice 1.** with advance notice; describing a procedural step taken after all concerned parties have been given sufficient notice, usually in writing, to allow them an opportunity to argue against the step: *The plaintiff moved on notice for summary judgment. The injunction was issued on notice. The judge ordered the defendant to submit a proposed order on three days' notice to the plaintiff.* Procedural rules dictate how many days' notice must normally be given for most steps in a case. **2.** having received sufficient information so that one should be aware of a certain fact: *The owner was on notice of the dog's dangerous disposition, because the dog had already bitten the letter carrier.*

**on or about** on approximately the date specified; a phrase often used to qualify a date when the exact date is not important, so as to avoid petty and irrelevant disputes over the accuracy of the date specified and allow for the possibility of a slight error.

**on papers** See under PAPERS.

**on point** referring to a precedent or authority regarded as particularly relevant or instructive with respect to an issue under discussion: *The remarks of Smythe, J., dissenting in Cox v. Swaine, are on point.* Also, **in point.** See also *case in point* (under CASE[1]).

**on the brief** listed on the brief as one

of the authors: *Jane Smith argued the appeal; with her on the brief were Samuel Baker and John Jones.*

**on the merits** See under MERITS.

**on the pleadings** on the basis of the pleadings in a case, without the need for additional evidence: *The case was decided on the pleadings.* See also *judgment on the pleadings* (under JUDGMENT).

**on the record** See under RECORD.

**on the relation of** Same as EX REL.

**one-bite rule** *n. Informal.* **1. a.** the common law rule that the owner of a dog is not liable for injuries caused by the dog unless the owner knew or had reason to know of the dog's propensity for viciousness. **b.** by analogy, any principle or proposed principle that would excuse a first offense or the first occurrence of a problem that might have been prevented if it had been foreseen.
**2.** any rule of law that allows a party only one chance to make a particular argument, invoke a particular procedure, pursue a particular remedy, or the like; often expressed in terms of allowing "only one bite of (or at) the apple."
——**Note.** The original one-bite rule, often expressed somewhat facetiously in the form of a maxim such as "Every dog is entitled to one bite," acquired this name because one bite would be sufficient to put a dog's owner on notice of its propensity for biting, and thus of the need to take whatever precautions are necessary to make sure that it does not happen again. But the rule does not require an actual bite to put the owner on notice; other evidence of dangerousness would suffice as well. In many states this ancient rule has been abrogated by statute or judicial decision, making owners responsible for any unprovoked attack by their pets upon people who are in a place where they have a right to be.

**one person, one vote** the principle that voting procedures and districts for elections to the House of Representatives and to state and local legislative bodies should be designed so that, as nearly as practicable, one person's vote will be worth as much as another's. See also GERRYMANDER; REAPPORTIONMENT.
——**History.** It was not until 1964 that the Supreme Court—by no means unanimously—decided that gross disparities in population among a state's congressional districts and state legislative voting districts (always giving rural voters many times the voting power of urban voters) were constitutionally impermissible. For many years thereafter the new constitutional principle was usually referred to as **one man, one vote;** but it is now usual to use the original phrase used by the Court itself: *one person, one vote. Gray v. Sanders,* 372 U.S. 368 (1963); *Wesberry v. Sanders,* 376 U.S. 1 (1964).

**onus**[1] *n., pl.* **onuses. 1.** burden of proof (from ONUS PROBANDI): *The party relying upon an affirmative defense usually has the onus on that issue.*
**2.** any heavy burden, task, or responsibility.
**3.** blame or responsibility.
—**onerous** *adj.*
—**onerously** *adv.*

**onus**[2] *n., pl.* **onera.** *Latin.* burden.

**onus probandi** *n. Latin.* (lit. "burden of proving") burden of proof.

**open** *v.* **1.** Also, **reopen.** to reconsider or permit further proceedings in a matter that once was regarded as closed: *open a judgment.*
**2.** to deliver an OPENING STATEMENT: *Ms. Smith will open for the prosecution.*
—*adj.* **3.** accessible to public view or knowledge; not private or concealed: *After the plea bargain was worked out in chambers, the judge took the guilty plea in open court.*
See also *open bidding* (under BID).
—**openly** *adv.*
—**openness** *n.*

**open account** *n.* See under ACCOUNT.

**open and notorious** *adj.* OPEN; NOTORIOUS; flagrant.

**open field** *n.* any land other than the immediate surroundings (the CURTILAGE) of a dwelling; any area that is open to the air and is not part of the curtilage of a dwelling. Under the **open fields doctrine,** police officers may enter and search such areas without probable cause.

——**Note.** The Supreme court has held that searches of such areas without probable cause are permissible under the Fourth Amendment even if the fields searched are private, secluded, have locked gates, and are posted with "No Trespassing" signs, because that is not enough to give rise to a reasonable expectation of privacy: "It is not generally true that fences or 'No Trespassing' signs effectively bar the public from viewing open fields in rural areas." *Oliver v. United States,* 466 U.S. 170 (1984). Where the areas in question were part of a securely walled-off factory complex from which the public was very effectively barred, the Court held that the warrantless search could be conducted from the air by means of high-resolution floor-mounted aerial cameras. In this case, it was said that the owner had no reasonable expectation of freedom from such warrantless government intrusion in part because "[t]he photographs at issue in this case are essentially like those commonly used in mapmaking. Any person with an airplane and an aerial camera could readily duplicate them." *Dow Chemical Co. v. United States,* 476 U.S. 227 (1986).

——**False Friend.** As the Supreme Court has remarked, "An open field need be neither 'open' nor a 'field' as those terms are used in common speech." *Oliver v. United States,* 466 U.S. 170 (1984). Dense forest or, as noted immediately above, the spaces between buildings in a securely enclosed factory complex, are "open fields" for purposes of Fourth Amendment analysis.

**open price term** *n.* a stated or unstated term in a contract for the sale of goods whereby the price to be paid is left for later determination.

——**Note.** Under the Uniform Commercial Code, a contract with no fixed price term will not fail for indefiniteness (see INDEFINITE); instead, in most cases the Code implies a reasonable price at the time of delivery.

**open session** *n.* See under SESSION.

**open shop** *n.* See under SHOP.

**open the door** to raise an issue at a trial or hearing by asking questions or submitting evidence about it, or sometimes just by commenting on the subject to the jury, thereby entitling the other side to introduce additional or contrary evidence or make adverse comment that otherwise would not have been allowed.

**opening statement** *n.* a lawyer's address to the judge or jury in advance of presenting evidence, to outline the case. Often described informally as a "road map of the case." Also called **opening.** Cf. SUMMATION.

**operation of law** *n.* the consequence or effect of legal principles as applicable to a particular set of facts. See BY OPERATION OF LAW.

**opinion** *n.* **1.** the beliefs, conclusions, and inferences one draws from observation of an incident or from scientific or other specialized knowledge and experience, as distinguished from a mere description of what one has observed. See also *opinion evidence* (under EVIDENCE); *expert witness* (under WITNESS). Cf. FACT.
**2.** Also called **opinion of counsel.** a formal document (sometimes in the form of a letter, called an **opinion letter**) setting forth an attorney's conclusions about the legality of a transaction or the legal aspects of a situation.
**3.** a court's explanation of how it reached a particular decision in a matter; its analysis and resolution of the legal issues involved in a motion or appeal. If the case was heard by a panel of judges (for example, the nine justices of the Supreme Court), there may be several opinions: Usually a majority of judges will agree upon both the result and most of the reasoning, which they give in a **majority opinion,** sometimes referred to as the **opinion for the court.** Judges who wish to add something to the majority opinion or express some disagreement with it may issue a

**separate opinion,** which is also referred to as a **concurring opinion** or **concurrence** if it reaches the same result as the majority opinion, and as a **minority opinion** or **dissenting opinion** or **dissent** if it advocates a different result. If no reasoning commands a majority of the court, the largest group that agrees upon the result reached may issue a **plurality opinion.** If all judges are in accord, they may issue a **unanimous opinion** or **opinion for a unanimous court.** Each of the foregoing opinions would normally be issued under the name of the judge who principally authored it, with a listing of other judges who have added their names to it. In cases not regarded as meriting elaborate discussion, a court may issue a short, unsigned opinion called a **per curiam opinion** or **opinion by the court,** or issue a decision with no opinion at all.

See also ADVISORY OPINION; *concurring in the result* or *concurring in the judgment* (under CONCUR); FINDINGS OF FACT AND CONCLUSIONS OF LAW; *memorandum opinion* (under MEMORANDUM); PER CURIAM; *reported opinion* (under REPORT); SLIP OPINION.

**opportunity** *n., pl.* **opportunities.** a chance, prospect, or possibility to do something that may be advantageous: *business opportunity; employment opportunity.* See also CORPORATE OPPORTUNITY DOCTRINE.

**opportunity to be heard** *n.* **1.** the DUE PROCESS right to present evidence and argument to a neutral decision maker in a fair proceeding when the government or a private person takes judicial or administrative action intended to affect one's legal rights. **2.** an opportunity often granted by a legislature or administrative agency, but not constitutionally required, for members of the public at large to comment formally on proposed legislation or administrative action at a public hearing or in writing.

**opt out** *v.* **1.** to withdraw from or choose not to participate in something. **2.** especially, in certain kinds of *class action* (see under ACTION), to withdraw from the CLASS; decline to be represented by those suing on behalf of the class.

**option** *n.* **1.** a contractual right, good for a specified length of time, to go through with a certain transaction on specified terms or to cancel it. **2.** Also called **option contract.** a contract that gives one such a right; for example, a contract under which A, in exchange for a certain payment to B, is given the right for 60 days to purchase ten tons of wheat from B at a specified price. The decision whether to go ahead with the purchase during that time is entirely A's, because A has paid for the privilege of keeping the choice open. See also STOCK OPTION.
—*v.* **3.** to grant or acquire an option on: *The author has optioned her novel to a studio for film adaptation.*
—**optionable** *adj.*

**optionee** *n.* a person who acquires or holds an option.

**oral** *adj.* spoken rather than written; see *oral argument* (under ARGUMENT); *oral contract* (under CONTRACT); *oral will* (under WILL). Cf. VERBAL.
—**orally** *adv.*

**order**[1] *n.* **1.** a ruling or direction of a court, administrative tribunal, or legislative or executive body or official. Willful violation of a court order directing a person to do or not to do something is punishable as CONTEMPT. **2. appealable order a.** a court order from which an immediate appeal can be taken. As a general rule in most jurisdictions, only a *final order,* such as an order granting a motion to dismiss the case, is immediately appealable. **b.** a court order that can be challenged in connection with an ultimate appeal of the entire case, but must be complied with in the meantime. For example, an order denying a motion to dismiss a case ordinarily cannot be appealed at once, but can be challenged on appeal if the case eventually goes to judgment and the judgment is appealed. See also *interlocutory appeal* (under APPEAL). **3. consent order** an order entered with the consent of all parties to a case.

**4. final order** a JUDGMENT or other order disposing of a case; an order that leaves nothing for the litigants to do except comply with the order or take an appeal. Also called **final appealable order.**

**5. interlocutory order** an order that concerns some matter connected with a case but does not end the case, such as an order granting or denying temporary alimony in a divorce case.

**6. order to show cause** a court order directing a party to appear and present reasons why a certain order, such as an injunction or an order of contempt, should not be issued. If the party to whom the order to show cause is directed fails to appear or appears but fails to make a sufficient showing, the threatened order will be issued. An order to show cause is usually an emergency measure, issued because there is reason to believe that a party is doing something or about to do something that routine court procedures would be too slow to deal with adequately. It is often issued EX PARTE, usually accompanied by a *temporary restraining order* (see under RESTRAINING ORDER), and almost always RETURNABLE on very short notice.

**7. unappealable order** an order that is not an *appealable order.*

—*v.* **8.** to issue an order; to direct that something be done or not done.

See also *confidentiality order* (under CONFIDENTIALITY STIPULATION); EXECUTIVE ORDER; INJUNCTION; PRECLUSION ORDER; PROTECTION ORDER; PROTECTIVE ORDER; SO ORDERED; *stipulation and order* (under STIPULATION).

—**orderable** *adj.*

**order²** *n.* **1.** a written direction to pay money. For example, a check is an order addressed to one's bank, directing it to pay out a certain sum of money from one's account. See also NEGOTIABLE INSTRUMENT, MONEY ORDER.

**2. to the order of** to the person named or a subsequent HOLDER. The use of these words is one way of signifying that a document or instrument is intended to be NEGOTIABLE. For example, an instrument that just says "pay to John Jones" may normally be enforced only by Jones, but if it says "pay to the order of John Jones," then Jones may sign it over to anyone else, making it payable to that person instead. Such an instrument is said to be **payable to order** and referred to as an **order instrument.** See also *order bill of lading* (under BILL OF LADING).

Cf. *bearer instrument* (under BEARER).

**ordinance** *n.* a municipal law; a law adopted by a city, town, county, or other local government with respect to a matter permitted by the state to be regulated at the local level.

**ordinary** *adj.* describing the normal, usual, or common, as against the unusual or exceptional. For example, compare *ordinary care* with *utmost care* (under CARE); *ordinary negligence* with *gross negligence* (under NEGLIGENCE); *ordinary income* (under INCOME) with *capital gain* (under CAPITAL¹).

—**ordinarily** *adv.*

—**ordinariness** *n.*

**ordinary course of business** *n.* the routine activities of one's business as distinguished from extraordinary events. For example, maintaining routine records as distinguished from writing a special report on a unique occurrence, or selling inventory piece by piece to different customers over time as distinguished from suddenly selling one's entire remaining stock of goods to a single purchaser at a discount.

**ordinary IRA** *n.* Same as *traditional IRA* (see under IRA).

**organic act** *n.* an act of Congress adopting an ORGANIC LAW: *National Park Service Organic Act; Organic Act of Guam.*

**organic law** *n.* **1.** the constitution, charter, statute, or similar body of law establishing a government or an organization and providing its legal foundation and structure; the fundamental law of an entity.

**2.** the fundamental law of a territory of the United States, analogous to a state constitution but enacted and imposed by Congress.

**organize** *v.*, **organized, organizing. 1.** to enlist or attempt to enlist into a labor union: *to organize workers.*
**2.** to enlist the employees of (a company) into a labor union; unionize: *to organize a factory.*

**organized crime** *n.* **1.** coordinated criminal activity conducted over a long span of time through a number of individuals and entities tied together in an organizational structure.
**2.** an organization through which such activity is carried out, or all such organizations and their members collectively.

**organized labor** *n.* **1.** all workers who are organized into labor unions.
**2.** these unions considered as a political force.

**original intent** *n.* a theory of constitutional interpretation under which it has been suggested that the meaning and proper application of constitutional provisions should be determined from the intent of the Constitution's framers. But at least a hundred people participated—to widely varying degrees—in the Constitutional Convention of 1787 and the first United States Congress (which put forth the Bill of Rights), and just about the only thing that can be said with certainty about how they would want their broad language applied in the unimaginable world of today is that they would disagree among themselves as much as constitutional scholars and Supreme Court Justices do today. See also note at FOUNDING FATHERS.

**original IRA** *n.* Same as *traditional IRA* (see under IRA).

**original jurisdiction** *n.* See under JURISDICTION[1].

**original work of authorship** *n.* See under WORK.

**original writ** *n.* See under WRIT.

**orphan drug** *n.* See under DRUG.

**Our Federalism** *n.* the principle of FEDERALISM as applied in the United States.
——**History.** This phrase was popularized by Justice Black in his opinion for the Supreme Court in *Younger v. Harris,* 401 U.S. 37 (1971), where the concept was invoked as one of the rationales for prohibiting federal courts from enjoining a state prosecution even when the state law under which the defendant is being prosecuted is very plainly unconstitutional. See *Younger abstention* (under ABSTENTION). The opinion described "Our Federalism" as embodying "the belief that the National Government will fare best if the States and their institutions are left free to perform their separate functions in their separate ways.... The concept does not mean blind deference to 'States' Rights' any more than it means centralization of control over every important issue in our National Government.... What the concept does represent is a system in which there is sensitivity to the legitimate interests of both State and National Governments...." Justice Black's eloquence—and his consistent highlighting of the phrase with both capital letters and quotation marks—elevated the phrase to talismanic significance, and it has been invoked by those on both sides of every major debate about allocation of federal and state power ever since.

**oust** *v.* **1.** to put out of possession of land; eject; evict.
**2.** to expel or remove from any place, position, or office.

**ouster** *n.* the act or result of ousting; dispossession; eviction; expulsion; removal. See also note at DEMURRER.

**out of court** *adv.* **1.** without litigation; without judicial involvement: *They threatened to sue us, but we settled out of court.*
**2.** not in the courtroom; not as part of formal judicial proceedings: *An attorney in a pending case must not speak to any of the jurors out of court.*
—*adj.* **3.** **out-of-court** taking place out of court: *out-of-court discussions; an out-of-court settlement.*

**out-of-court settlement** *n.* See under SETTLEMENT.

**out of order 1.** not in accordance with

rules of parliamentary or judicial procedure: *That motion is out of order. Your objection is out of order.*
**2.** inappropriate; unsuitable; disruptive; verging on contemptuous: *The witness's remarks are out of order and will be stricken from the record. Counselor, you are out of order; please sit down!*

**out on bail** See under BAIL¹.

**outlaw** *n.* **1.** originally, **a.** one who is put outside the protection of the law; for example, a person under a sentence of banishment, or a criminal who escaped after being sentenced to death. **b.** one who has been deprived of certain benefits of the law. See note at OUTLAWRY.
**2.** a lawless person or habitual criminal, especially one who is a fugitive from the law.
—*v.* **3.** to deprive of the benefits and protection of the law: *Those who participated in the treasonous conspiracy but evaded capture were outlawed.* Cf. INLAW.
**4.** to make unlawful or illegal; to prohibit by law: *The Eighteenth Amendment outlawed the manufacture, sale, or transportation of intoxicating beverages in the United States.*

**outlawry** *n., pl.* **outlawries. 1.** the act of declaring a person to be an OUTLAW; the process of putting someone outside the protection of the law or depriving a person of the benefits of the law.
**2.** the state of being outlawed.
**3.** disregard or defiance of the law.
——**History.** In earliest English history outlawry was tantamount to a death sentence; the outlaw could literally be hunted down like an animal and killed with impunity. In later times outlawry was more akin to declaration that a person was a fugitive who should be captured and brought in so that justice could be done. As the concept evolved, one could be outlawed for less and less serious reasons, such as failing to show up in response to a civil suit, with consequences that were correspondingly less severe, such as losing the right to invoke the law in support of one's own claims until one has responded to the

pending claim. Parliament abolished outlawry in civil cases in 1879.

**output contract** *n.* See under CONTRACT.

**outside** *prep.* not covered by; not governed by: *outside the statute.* Cf. WITHIN.

**outside counsel** *n.* See under COUNSEL.

**over** *adj.* occurring in succession; passing in turn from one person to another. See *action over* (under THIRD-PARTY ACTION); GIFT OVER; *liability over* (under LIABILITY).

**over-the-counter drug** *n.* See under DRUG.

**overbreadth** *n.* a constitutional doctrine applicable to laws that are intended to forbid certain impermissible conduct but are drafted so broadly that they also forbid a good deal of constitutionally protected conduct, such as a law that attempts to deal with violent picketing by prohibiting all picketing, even if it is peaceful.
—**overbroad** *adj.*
——**Note.** The Supreme Court will usually strike down an overbroad law in its entirety and leave it to the legislature to draft a narrower law.

**overreaching** *n.* taking advantage of trickery or superior knowledge or bargaining power to obtain a contract that is grossly unfair to the other party, especially in a consumer transaction. A contract resulting from such overreaching may be voided by a court on the ground of UNCONSCIONABILITY.
—**overreach** *v.*

**override** *v.,* **overrode, overridden, overriding,** *n.* —*v.* **1.** (of a legislature) to nullify a VETO by voting by a two-thirds majority for the vetoed bill, thereby making the bill law despite the disapproval of the executive.
—*n.* **2.** the act of overriding.

**overrule** *v.,* **overruled, overruling. 1.** (of a trial court) to rule unfavorably upon a motion or, especially, an objection raised at trial; to refuse to sustain an objection.

**2.** (of an appellate court) to nullify a legal principle announced or relied upon in a previous case by reaching a result inconsistent with it in a subsequent case; for example, a state supreme court, by issuing an opinion adopting the principle of comparative negligence, might overrule its prior cases holding that contributory negligence is a complete bar to recovery in a negligence case. Sometimes courts overrule a prior case expressly; on other occasions they do so SUB SILENTIO. Direct overruling of precedents is rather unusual, because it violates the principle of STARE DECISIS.

**overt act** *n.* an act in furtherance of a criminal purpose.

——**Note.** As an element in a prosecution for CONSPIRACY, the overt act need not itself be illegal, but it must constitute a step toward attainment of the unlawful objective. To convict a person of TREASON the Constitution requires "Testimony of two Witnesses to the same overt Act," and this has been construed as meaning an actual act of treason. Thus in the United States merely speaking out against government policy, without an intent to aid the enemy, is not treason.

**owner** *n.* **1.** a person or entity with a right to control and dispose of an interest in real or personal property, or for whose benefit such a right must be exercised.
**2. beneficial owner** a person for whose benefit another (the *legal owner*) holds property. Also called **equitable owner.**
**3. joint owner a.** one of the owners of equal undivided interests in property with right of survivorship, as described under JOINT (def. 2). **b.** informally, any co-owner; a person who shares ownership of something with another person upon any legally feasible terms.
**4. legal owner** a person with the actual legal right to control or dispose of an interest in property, either for his own benefit or as a trustee or constructive trustee for the benefit of another (the *beneficial owner* or *equitable owner*).
**5. record owner** the person whose name appears in a public record as the owner of land and thus as the person liable for property taxes, or in the records of a corporation as the owner of stock and thus as the person entitled to receive dividends and vote on corporate matters. Also called **owner of record.**

**owner pro hac vice** *n., pl.* **owners pro hac vice.** one who has control of a ship pursuant to a *bareboat charter* (see under CHARTER[2]) from the true owner of the vessel; charterer of a vessel under a bareboat charter; *demisee* (see under DEMISE). See also PRO HAC VICE.

**ownership** *n.* the status or rights of an owner regarding an interest in property. In addition to the types of ownership described under OWNER (*beneficial* or *equitable, joint,* etc.), ownership may be characterized as BY THE ENTIRETY, IN COMMON, IN COPARCENARY, or IN SEVERALTY, as appropriate.

**oyer** *n. Law French.* (lit. "to hear; hearing") **1.** in common law practice, the reading in court of a deed or other instrument referred to in the pleadings, or the making of a copy or transcript of it. **2.** the production of a document for inspection and copying.
**3.** short for OYER AND TERMINER.
——**History.** In traditional common law practice there was no right of DISCOVERY, but if a party's pleadings relied upon a deed or similar instrument, that party was required to make PROFERT of the instrument, whereupon the opposing party could CRAVE OYER so that the exact terms of the instrument could be known and made part of the record. This practice was abolished in England in 1852, but lingered in the United States, where vestiges of the practice can still be seen the occasional use of the term "oyer" to refer to document discovery. See also note at PROFERT.

**oyer and terminer** *n.* (from Law French *oyer et terminer,* lit. "to hear and determine") **1.** *English Legal History.* **a.** a special court or proceeding convened to inquire into charges of treason or felony in connection with a public disturbance or uprising. **b.** a court authorized to hear and determine criminal offenses generally.

**2. commission of oyer and terminer** the royal commission authorizing particular judges or other appointees to hold a court of oyer and terminer. Also called **writ of oyer and terminer.**

**3. Court of Oyer and Terminer** in some states of the United States, the name formerly given to courts of criminal jurisdiction.

**oyez** *interj. Law French.* hear ye. In many courts, this is called out (usually two or three times) at the opening of each session to impress upon those present the solemnity of the proceedings. Also spelled, especially in historical sources, **oyes.** See also HEAR YE; KNOW ALL MEN BY THESE PRESENTS.

——**Pronunciation.** *Oyez,* a form of the Anglo-French verb OYER, was originally pronounced "oh yets," but from at least the fifteenth century on has been pronounced "oh yes" or, less commonly, "oh yez." The pronunciation "oh yay," which is often heard today (even in the Supreme Court of the United States), is inauthentic: It represents an effort to apply modern French pronunciation to a word that is not modern French, but rather is from the distinct Norman French language that came into use in England after the Norman Conquest nearly ten centuries ago.

# P

**PAC** *pl.*, **PACs, PAC's.** POLITICAL ACTION COMMITTEE.

**paid check** *n.* See under CHECK.

**paid-up stock** *n.* See under STOCK.

**pain and suffering** *n.* physical and mental suffering caused by another's tortious conduct, as when one has suffered a personal injury or emotional loss. The compensatory damages awarded in a tort case may include a sum of money for the plaintiff's pain and suffering.

**pains and penalties** *n.pl.* See BILL OF PAINS AND PENALTIES.

**pais** *n. Law French.* **1.** the country; the countryside; the neighborhood. See IN PAIS.
**2.** the neighborhood as represented by those selected for a jury; a jury. See note at PER PAIS.

**palimony** *n.* an alimony-like financial provision upon the breakup of an unmarried couple who lived together. The courts in some states have expressed a willingness to make such awards in limited circumstances, but few if any separated lovers have actually received such an award. See also MERETRICIOUS.

**palming off** *n.* Same as PASSING OFF.

**pandering** *n.* Same as PROMOTING PROSTITUTION.

**panel** *n.* **1.** the set of judges hearing a case. For example, appeals in the United States Courts of Appeals are normally heard by a panel of three judges selected at random from among the several judges of the court. Cf. EN BANC.
**2.** Same as *jury panel* (see under JURY).

**paper** *n.* **1.** Same as COMMERCIAL PAPER. See also ACCOMMODATION PAPER; CHATTEL PAPER.
**2.** See PAPERS.

**papers** *n.pl.* **1.** the lawyer-generated documents in a case; for example, pleadings, affidavits, briefs. Occasionally a single such document is referred to as a **paper.**
**2. motion papers** the set of papers submitted to a court in support of or in opposition to a motion.
**3. on papers** the manner of submission of a matter to a court when no oral argument or testimony is offered or is allowed.
**4.** the personal or business documents of an individual or entity. See also *books and papers* (under BOOK).

**par value** *n.* **1.** the face value of a share of STOCK or of a bond (see BOND[1]).
**2. par value stock** Same as *stock with par value* (see under STOCK).
——**Note.** In the case of a bond or preferred stock, the par value is the basis upon which dividends and interest are calculated. In the case of common stock, par value used to represent the original selling price of the stock, but now is an arbitrary and largely meaningless figure, typically $1.00. Many states have eliminated the requirement that corporations assign a par value to stock.

**parachute** *n.* **1.** a term in an employment contract, especially that of an executive-level employee, providing for generous severance benefits in case the employee is demoted or forced out in a corporate merger or takeover. See GOLDEN PARACHUTE; PLATINUM PARACHUTE; TIN PARACHUTE.
**2. parachute payment a.** a payment pursuant to such an agreement. **b.** (in the Internal Revenue Code) any payment to a high-level corporate employee that is contingent on a change of

317

ownership or control of a corporation and is equal to at least three times the employee's average annual pay for the preceding five years, or for all years of employment if less than five.

**3. excess parachute payment** (in the Internal Revenue Code) the amount by which a parachute payment exceeds three times the employee's average annual pay. Excess parachute payments are subject to special tax treatment under provisions that were enacted to discourage corporations from providing exorbitant golden parachutes, but that failed to do so. See note at GOLDEN PARACHUTE.

**paralegal** n. a nonlawyer employed to assist a lawyer or lawyers by performing, subject to supervision by the lawyers, a variety of legal tasks requiring less than a full legal education. Also called **legal assistant.**

**paramount title** n. See under TITLE.

**paraphernalia** n. **1.** historically, the personal belongings of a wife, such as clothing and jewelry, over which the common law allowed her some control. See also COVERTURE.
**2.** Also called **drug paraphernalia.** equipment employed in manufacturing, using, or concealing a CONTROLLED SUBSTANCE.

**parcenary** n. Same as COPARCENARY.

**parcener** n. See under IN COPARCENARY.

**pardon** n. **1.** the release of a person from penalties for a past offense or alleged offense.
**2.** the document in which a pardon is declared.
**3. pardon board** Same as BOARD OF PARDONS.
—v. **4.** to grant a pardon to someone: *President Ford pardoned ex-President Nixon for all crimes that he may have committed as President.*
—**Note.** For federal offenses a pardon can be issued only by the President; for state offenses, usually only by the governor. A pardon may be granted before or after an arrest or conviction, and even after death. It bars any further prosecution or punishment, but it does

not remove a conviction from one's record. Cf. AMNESTY, COMMUTE, REPRIEVE. See also CLEMENCY.

**parens patriae** n. *Latin.* (lit. "parent of the country," originally a reference to the king or queen) a state government in its role as protector of the people, and especially of children and the mentally infirm.
—**Note.** The state as parens patriae may initiate certain civil actions to protect the interests of the state on behalf of all its people, or to protect people who lack the legal capacity to protect their own interests, as by taking children away from abusive parents or institutionalizing incompetents who pose a danger to themselves or others.

**parent company** n. a corporation that owns more than fifty percent of the voting stock of another corporation. Also called **parent corporation** or simply **parent.** Cf. SUBSIDIARY.

**parental access** n. See under ACCESS.

**parental kidnapping** n. the taking or secreting of a child by one parent in violation of the custody or visitation rights of the other parent.

**parental liability** n. liability of parents for damages caused by tortious conduct of their children, imposed to varying extents by statutes in some states.
—**Note.** Extensions of this concept to the criminal law, so that parents can be fined for offenses committed by their children, have been tried, but are of uncertain constitutionality.

**parental neglect** n. See under NEGLECT.

**pari delicto** See IN PARI DELICTO.

**pari materia** See IN PARI MATERIA.

**parliamentary law** n. the body of rules of procedure for meetings of organizations.
—**Note.** Parliamentary "law" is not part of federal or state law except in the peripheral sense that Congress and state legislatures necessarily adopt certain rules for the orderly conduct of their own debates and business.

**parol** n. *Law French.* (from Law French

*parol,* lit. "word; speech") **1.** something spoken; an oral declaration or communication. **2.** (historically) the oral pleadings in a case; pleadings as exchanged in cases centuries ago, before written pleadings became the norm. **3. a.** oral statements or communications concerning the subject of a written contract, deed, or other instrument. **b.** by extension, any extrinsic evidence relating to such an instrument; matter outside the writing itself; PAROL EVIDENCE: *Although parol cannot be introduced to vary the clear terms of a deed, where the deed recites as consideration a sum of money "and other consideration," the nature of the additional consideration may be shown by parol.* —*adj.* **4.** oral: *parol promise; parol agreement.* **5.** (historically) of a lease or other contract: merely written, as distinguished from sealed (see *contract under seal,* under CONTRACT). **6.** extrinsic; outside the four corners of a written instrument. See PAROL EVIDENCE.

**parol evidence** *n.* **1.** literally, either evidence of oral communications or evidence given orally.
**2.** in its customary use, any oral or written information about a written instrument such as a deed or will or written contract, or about the underlying transaction, apart from the language of the instrument itself; for example, prior correspondence in which a contract was negotiated.

**parol evidence rule** *n.* the rule of contract law that generally prohibits the use of extrinsic evidence, whether written or oral, to contradict contract terms that have been reduced to writing; in addition, if the writing was intended by the parties to embody their entire agreement, extrinsic evidence may not be used to add terms to it even if the added terms are entirely consistent with the writing.

**parole** *n., v.,* **paroled, paroling.** —*n.* **1.** release of a convicted criminal from jail or prison after serving part of a sentence, on the condition that he stay out of trouble with the law and comply with other requirements, such as meeting regularly with a parole officer. If parole conditions are violated, parole can be revoked and the parolee returned to confinement. Cf. PROBATION.
**2.** *Immigration Law.* **a.** the allowing of an alien who has arrived in the United States but whose application for legal admission is still under consideration to remain in the country temporarily without being kept in custody by the Immigration and Naturalization Service, or the release of an individual from INS custody pending determination of the individual's immigration status. **b. advance parole** a grant of parole made to an alien before the alien attempts to enter or reenter the country. Typically this mechanism is used to permit an alien who is already in the United States on parole to leave the country temporarily because of a family need and then reenter the country with no change of status.
—*v.* **3.** to release on parole.
**4.** to allow an alien to enter or remain in the United States without being kept in INS custody while awaiting a determination of immigrant status.
—**History.** The Immigration and Nationality Act gives the Attorney General—usually as represented by officials of the Immigration and Naturalization Service, a bureau of the Department of Justice—discretion to "parole into the United States" any alien applying for admission to the United States, but only "for urgent humanitarian reasons or significant public benefit" (except that refugees may be paroled only for "compelling reasons of public interest"). A noteworthy example of parole on humanitarian grounds, in which the Attorney General herself became directly involved, occurred in the case of Elián González, a five-year-old boy from Cuba who was found on Thanksgiving Day, 1999, floating in an inner tube off the Florida coast. He had been adrift for thirty-four hours after the boat in which his mother and her boyfriend had been attempting to smuggle him and several other people into the United States foundered. The mother and boyfriend having perished at sea, the child was paroled to the care of a

great-uncle in Miami while the politically charged question of his immigration status was considered. When the boy's father arrived from Cuba, with his wife and their baby, to claim the child, the Attorney General exercised her statutory discretion with respect to parole by ruling that the boy should be transferred to the custody of the father until the courts had finally ruled on the immigration question. The child's Miami relatives resisted turning him over to a parent seeking to take him back to Cuba, and supporters surrounded their house day and night in the hope of preventing authorities from enforcing the directive. In a controversial pre-dawn raid on April 22, 2000, the Immigration and Naturalization Service, armed with guns, tear gas, and a search warrant for the child, stormed the crowd and the house and took the child, then flew him to Washington to be with his father and step-family.
——**False Friend.** In the immigration context, *parole* does not necessarily mean release from custody; it only means release from the custody of the INS. An alien wanted for prosecution by a law enforcement agency in the United States may be "paroled" to the custody of that agency for prosecution.

**parole board** *n.* a public body responsible for passing upon applications for parole. Also called **board of parole, parole commission**.

**parson's writ of right** *n.* See UTRUM.

**partial** *adj.* **1.** biased; prejudiced in favor of one side over another in a dispute: *a partial witness; partial juror.*
**2.** incomplete; pertaining only to a part rather than the whole of a matter.
—**partiality** *n.*
—**partially** *adv.*

**partial breach** *n.* See under BREACH.

**partial renvoi** *n.* See under RENVOI.

**partial settlement** *n.* See under SETTLEMENT.

**partially integrated contract** *n.* See under INTEGRATED CONTRACT.

**particeps criminis** *n., pl.* **particies criminis.** *Latin.* (lit. "sharer of guilt;

participant in the crime") an ACCOMPLICE.

**participation loan** *n.* See under LOAN.

**particular average** *n.* See under AVERAGE.

**particular estate** *n.* See under ESTATE[1].

**particulars** *n.pl.* details; specifics. See also BILL OF PARTICULARS.

**partition** *v.* **1.** to divide property up among its co-owners, either physically or, more often, by selling it and dividing the proceeds.
—*n.* **2.** such a division, or a civil action seeking such a division by court order.

**partner** *n.* **1.** a member of a PARTNERSHIP. Cf. DOMESTIC PARTNER.
**2. general** (or **full**) **partner a.** a partner in a *general partnership* (see under PARTNERSHIP). **b.** one of the partners in a *limited partnership* (see under PARTNERSHIP) having responsibility for operation of the business and unlimited liability for its debts; a partner other than a *limited partner.* Unless otherwise specified, "partner" normally means general partner.
**3. junior partner** a low-ranking, usually relatively new, partner in a firm, whose influence in the management of the firm, and whose share of its profits, are still somewhat limited.
**4. limited partner** a partner in a *limited partnership* (see under PARTNERSHIP) who merely invests money in the enterprise; one who does not participate in its management or operation and whose liability is limited to the amount invested.
**5. secret partner** a partner whose involvement in a partnership is not publicly disclosed.
**6. senior partner** a high-ranking partner in a firm, usually one who has been a partner for many years and has considerable influence its management.
**7. silent partner** a partner who shares in the profits of a general partnership but does not participate actively in the management of its business. Also called **dormant partner.** Referred to in England as a **sleeping partner**—a term that might be misunderstood in America.

**partnership** *n.* **1.** an association of two or more people or entities to carry on a business for profit. Profits and losses are shared by the partners and taxed to them directly; the partnership as an entity does not pay income taxes. Cf. DO-MESTIC PARTNERSHIP.

**2. general partnership** an ordinary partnership, in which each partner is personally liable for the acts of every other partner in the conduct of the business and has unlimited personal liability for the debts of the partnership, and all partners have a voice in the management and conduct of the business. Unless otherwise specified, "partnership" means general partnership.

**3. limited liability partnership (L.L.P.)** a form of partnership in which individual partners are not subject to personal liability for claims against the partnership.

**4. limited partnership (L.P.)** a partnership consisting of one or more *general partners* and one or more *limited partners* (see under PARTNER).

**partnership of acquests** (or **aquets**) **and gains** *n.* See under ACQUEST and ACQUET.

**party** *n., pl.* **parties. 1.** a person or entity directly and officially involved in a transaction; especially, one of those bound by a contract or negotiable instrument.

**2.** a person or entity by or against whom a claim or charge is asserted in a case, especially one who has appeared or been served in the action.

**3. indispensable party** a person or entity whose rights are so bound up in a matter in suit that the case will not be allowed to proceed unless that person or entity is joined as a party. See also *compulsory joinder* (under JOIN-DER). Cf. *necessary party; proper party.*

**4. necessary party** a person or entity whose rights are sufficiently involved in an action to require joinder as a party if that is possible; but if it is not possible, the action will be allowed to proceed without that additional party. See also *compulsory joinder* (under JOINDER). Cf. *indispensable party; proper party.*

**5. party of the first part** in old drafting style, the first party named in a contract or other instrument, often the maker or drafter; subsequently named parties were identified as "party of the second part," "party of the third part," and so on. This terminology is no longer used, but shows up in old legal instruments, old judicial opinions, old movies, and old and new works of all kinds satirizing lawyers.

**6. proper party** a person or entity with a sufficient interest in a matter in suit to justify inclusion in the case, but whose absence would not hinder a just adjudication. A person bringing a case need not join every proper party in the action, although a proper party who is left out normally has a right to INTER-VENE. See also *permissive joinder* (under JOINDER). Cf. *indispensable party; necessary party.*

**7. real party in interest** the person or entity possessing the legal right sued upon, or having a direct *interest* in the outcome of a case (see INTEREST², def. 1). Under old procedural rules, actions sometimes had to be brought in the name of someone other than the real party in interest; modern rules eliminate such technicalities.

See also ACCOMMODATION PARTY; *accommodating party* and *accommodated party* (both under ACCOMMODATION PARTY); THIRD PARTY. Cf. *charter party* (under CHARTER²).

——**False Friend.** In nonlegal contexts, *necessary* means "essential; requisite; indispensable." But in the federal courts and most state courts, a "necessary party" is not necessarily indispensable. A potential party whose presence in a case is truly necessary for the case to proceed is referred to as "indispensable"; one whose presence is highly desirable, but who may be dispensed with if jurisdiction cannot be obtained or venue is improper, is confusingly referred to as "necessary."

**party joinder** *n.* See under JOINDER.

**passenger profile** *n.* See under PRO-FILE.

**passing off** *n.* marketing one thing as

if it were another; for example, a counterfeit as an original, another's product as one's own, or, particularly, one's own inferior product as if it were the superior product of a better-known company. Also called **palming off**.

**passion** n. See CRIME OF PASSION; HEAT OF PASSION.

**passive trust** n. See under TRUST.

**passport** n. a document issued by a national government to one of its citizens, subjects, or nationals, authorizing travel out of the country and requesting other countries to permit entry and grant legal protection to the person.

**past consideration** n. See under CONSIDERATION.

**past recollection recorded** n. See under RECOLLECTION.

**patency** n. the state of being patent; the state of being obvious or apparent.
——**Usage.** This is pronounced to rhyme with "latency." See note at PATENT.

**patent** n. **1.** the exclusive right to exploit an invention for a number of years, granted by the federal government to the inventor if the inventor applies for it and the invention qualifies (is PATENTABLE).
**2.** a formal document conferring rights, official status, or the like; short for LETTERS PATENT.
—v. **3.** to apply for and receive a patent on one's invention.
—adj. **4.** open; public rather than private; intended as a public record. (Used principally in the phrase LETTERS PATENT; see note at that entry.)
**5.** obvious; apparent at a glance or upon reasonable inspection: *patent defect; patent ambiguity.* Cf. LATENT.
—**patently** adv.
——**Pronunciation.** For the noun and the verb, the first syllable rhymes with *hat*. For the adjective and the adverb, the first syllable usually rhymes with *hate*. Thus the opposites *latent* and *patent*, and the opposites *latently* and *patently*, are rhyming pairs. In the phrase

"letters patent," however, the word *patent*, though an adjective, is usually pronounced like the noun.

**patent defect** n. See under DEFECT[2].

**patentable** adj. capable of being patented: *a patentable invention.*
—**patentability** n.

**patentee** n. the recipient of a patent; one granted rights, property, status, or the like by patent.
——**Usage.** This term includes the patenter of an invention, but also includes recipients of any other kind of patent (see PATENT, def. 2).

**patenter** n. one who patents an invention; the recipient of a patent on an invention.

**patently offensive** obviously offensive. For purposes of an OBSCENITY prosecution, a depiction of sexual conduct is patently offensive if the jury regards it as patently offensive, unless the highest court that hears the case subsequently decides that it is clearly not patently offensive.
——**Pronunciation.** See note at PATENT.
——**History.** In *Miller v. California,* 413 U.S. 15 (1973), the Supreme Court held that whether a work depicts or describes sexual conduct in a patently offensive way is to be determined by the jury on the basis of "contemporary community standards." A jury in Albany, Georgia, did just that, and concluded that the 1971 Hollywood film "Carnal Knowledge" was obscene. It convicted the manager of the local movie theater in which the film had been shown of distributing obscene materials. A majority of the Georgia Supreme Court, after viewing the film, concluded that "the evidence...amply supports the verdict of guilty." On appeal to the Supreme Court of the United States, the five justices who had agreed upon the *Miller* decision stated: "Our own viewing of the film satisfies us that 'Carnal Knowledge' could not be found under the Miller standards to depict sexual conduct in a patently offensive way." They stressed that the Miller test was aimed at "hard core" materials—a term they put in quotation

marks but did not undertake to define. *Jenkins v. Georgia,* 418 U.S. 153 (1974).

**paternity** *n.* **1.** the state of being a father; fatherhood.
**2.** especially, the state of being the biological father of a particular child.
**3. dual paternity** *Louisiana Law.* the concept, adopted by the state Supreme Court in 1989, that the child of a married woman and a man other than her husband can have two legally recognized fathers: Although the husband is the "legal father" for purposes of legitimacy and inheritance (unless he disavows the child within 180 days of birth), the biological father may also be recognized as having parental rights and responsibilities in regard to child support and certain other matters. The implementation of this principle is not free of difficulty, and other states have not rushed to embrace it.
See also PRESUMPTION OF PATERNITY.

**paternity suit** (or **action** or **proceeding**) *n.* an action to establish that a particular man is the father of a child born out of wedlock. The action may be brought, for example, by the mother, in order to obtain child support payments; by the state, in order to compel such payments; or by the putative father himself, in order to obtain parental rights.

**pawn** *n.* **1.** the deposit of goods as security for a loan or other obligation, especially an individual's deposit of personal possessions to secure a personal loan.
**2.** an item so deposited; the collateral for the loan.
**3.** the state of being deposited or held as security: *His television set is in pawn.*
—*v.* **4.** to make such a deposit: *She pawned her wedding ring.*

**pawnbroker** *n.* a person in the business of making loans secured by pawns of personal property.

**pay to play** *n.* the making of political contributions by lawyers and law firms to the campaigns of incumbent and prospective public officials upon the understanding that this is necessary if the lawyer or firm is to be considered eligible to bid on government contracts or be assigned to perform government legal services, such as services in connection with the issuance of municipal bonds.

**payable** *adj.* **1.** supposed to be paid; now due or to become due: *accounts payable; a check payable to the order of Jane Smith.* See also *payable on demand* (under DEMAND); *payable to bearer* (under BEARER); *payable to order* (under ORDER[2]).
—*n.* **2.** Same as ACCOUNT PAYABLE.

**payee** *n.* a person to whom, or to whose order, money is paid or is supposed to be paid; especially, the person so named in an instrument, such as the person or entity to which a check is made out. See also FICTITIOUS PAYEE.

**payment bond** *n.* See under BOND[2].

**payor** *n.* the person who makes, or is supposed to make, a payment; especially, the person or entity so designated in a negotiable instrument, such as the bank upon which a check or other draft is drawn **(payor bank).**

**payroll tax** *n.* any of several kinds of tax collected from employers on the basis of employee count or employee salaries. Some such taxes are paid by the employer in addition to the employees' salaries; others are paid by the employees through withholding from their salaries. See SOCIAL SECURITY TAX for an example.

**penal** *adj.* **1.** pertaining to a penalty or to penalties generally.
**2.** pertaining to crime and punishment.
—**penally** *adv.*

**penal bond** *n.* See under BOND[2].

**penalty** *n., pl.* **penalties. 1.** a punishment for a crime; e.g., the *death penalty* (see under CAPITAL PUNISHMENT).
**2.** a sum specified in a contract to be paid, beyond or instead of payment of damages, in the event of a breach, or agreed to as the price of being excused from an obligation.

**3.** a disadvantage or negative consequence attached to any action, condition, status, or the like. See, e.g., MARRIAGE PENALTY; *singles' penalty* (under MARRIAGE BONUS).

**4. civil penalty** a fine or forfeiture provided for by statute or regulation, not for commission of a crime but for failure to fulfill a legal obligation or adhere to regulations. Civil penalties are often imposed by administrative agencies. Examples: a percentage added to one's income tax bill as a penalty for failure to pay on time; removal of one's license to conduct a food business for persistent failure to maintain health standards.

**5. penalty clause** a contract clause requiring payment of a specific sum of money, unrelated to and usually greater than anticipated damages, as a penalty in the event of breach. As a general rule, such clauses are unenforceable. Cf. *liquidated damages* (under DAMAGES).

**6. prepayment penalty** in connection with a mortgage or other loan agreement, a penalty that the debtor must pay if the debt is repaid early. Prepayment penalties are often enforceable because they compensate the lender for loss of interest.

**penalty bond** *n.* Same as *penal bond* (see under BOND²).

**penalty phase** *n.* in a capital case in which the defendant was convicted of the crime in the GUILT PHASE of the case, the subsequent phase in which the evidence relating to mitigating and aggravating factors is taken and the decision is made whether or not to impose the death penalty. In some states that decision is made by the jury alone; in others by the judge alone; and in others by the judge with advice from the jury.

**pendent jurisdiction** *n.* See under JURISDICTION¹.

**pendente lite** *Latin.* (lit. "with a lawsuit pending") during litigation; while a case is in progress: *injunction pendente lite.*

**penetration** *n.* as an element in rape

and certain other sex crimes, the insertion of the penis, or sometimes a finger or a physical object, into the vulva, or sometimes the anus or another opening, of another person. See also RES IN RE.

**——Note.** More than mere physical touching is required to constitute penetration, but so little more that the usual expression for this element of a crime is "penetration, however slight." In one case, penetration by a finger was even found to have been accomplished through the victim's underwear and blue jeans. *United States v. Norman T.,* 129 F.3d 1099 (10th Cir. 1997).

**penitentiary** *n.* Same as PRISON.

**pension** *n.* **1.** regular payments to a retired worker or the survivors of a worker from a fund **(pension fund)** created by the worker's employer, union, or the like.

**2.** broadly, a fixed amount, other than wages, paid at regular intervals to a person or to the person's surviving dependents in consideration of past services, age, merit, poverty, injury or loss sustained, etc.

**3. vested pension** a pension to which an employee will become entitled upon retirement even if she quits or loses her job before then. Ordinarily an employee must stay with a particular employer for five to seven years for a pension associated with that position to become fully vested.

**pension plan** *n.* **1.** a program to provide pensions for retired employees.

**2.** an EMPLOYEE PENSION BENEFIT PLAN; that is, any program established by an employer or group of employers, or by an employee organization, to provide retirement income or deferred compensation for employees. The standards for most such plans are set by the EMPLOYEE RETIREMENT INCOME SECURITY ACT OF 1974 (ERISA).

**3. defined-benefit plan** a pension plan that promises a certain level of pension payments after retirement, usually determined on the basis of the employee's length of employment, salary, and age at retirement.

**4. defined-contribution plan** a pension plan under which the level of employer and employee contributions is fixed, but the level of benefits ultimately received may be higher or lower depending upon how successfully those contributions have been invested.

**5. qualified pension plan** a pension plan conforming to certain provisions of the Internal Revenue Code, making the employer's contributions tax deductible and deferring income tax for the employee until benefits are actually received, after retirement.
See also the specific types of pension plan listed under RETIREMENT PLAN.

**people** *n.pl.* **1.** human beings; especially, the inhabitants of a state or nation collectively.
**2. People** in many states, the name by which the state government and the prosecution are identified in criminal cases under state law: *The case of People v. Jones. The People called the county coroner as their first witness.* See also STATE. Cf. GOVERNMENT.

**per capita** *Latin.* (lit. "by the heads")
**1.** per person; divided equally among all the people in a defined group.
**2.** a principle for distributing a decedent's estate under which all takers of a particular portion of the estate, or at least all takers at the same generational level, receive equal shares without regard to what branch of the family they belong to. Cf. PER STIRPES.

**per curiam** *Latin.* by the court. See also *per curiam opinion* (under OPINION).

**per pais** *Law French.* (lit. "by the country") by jury.
——**History.** The earliest form of jury trial in England consisted of gathering men from the countryside in the neighborhood where the events at issue took place, to determine where the truth lay on the basis of their personal knowledge. Such cases were said to be tried "by the country," or in Law French, *per pais.* The nature of jury trials changed but the concept of trial by a jury selected from the vicinity endured, and for centuries a trial by jury was still sometimes referred to as "trial by the country" or "trial per pais." See also note at COUNTRY.

**per quod** *Latin.* (lit. "by which") whereby. Used in common law pleading to introduce a conclusion, and particularly to introduce the clause in a complaint setting forth the special damages that flowed from the wrongful act complained of, or as the name of that clause; now used primarily to identify certain kinds of actions in which special damages or other special facts must be pleaded and proved (as distinguished from PER SE actions). See *actionable per quod* (see under ACTIONABLE); *words actionable per quod* (under ACTIONABLE WORDS); *libel per quod* (see under LIBEL); *slander per quod* (under SLANDER).

**per se** *Latin.* (lit. "by itself") intrinsically; without more. Said of acts that constitute such strong evidence of wrongdoing that no further evidence is needed. For example, under the law forbidding UNREASONABLE RESTRAINT OF TRADE, price fixing is regarded as "unreasonable per se," and thus a "per se violation" of the law. See also *actionable per se* (under ACTIONABLE); *words actionable per se* (under ACTIONABLE WORDS); *libel per se* (under LIBEL[1]); *slander per se* (under SLANDER). Cf. PER QUOD.

**per stirpes** *Latin.* (lit. "by the stems"; "by the branches") describing a principle for distributing a decedent's estate under which the descendants of any person who would have received a share of the estate if he had still been alive at the time of the decedent's death divide up that person's share. Thus the portion left to each branch of the family is divided and subdivided only within that branch. Cf. PER CAPITA.

**percentage lease** *n.* See under LEASE.

**percentage of completion method** *n.* See under ACCOUNTING METHOD.

**peremptory challenge** *n.* See under CHALLENGE.

**perfect** *v.* to take all legal steps necessary to secure or put on record a claim,

right, or interest: *perfect a security interest; perfect title to land; perfect an appeal.*
—**perfectibility** *n.*
—**perfectible** *adj.*
—**perfection** *n.*

**perform** *v.* to carry out a legal duty; fulfill one's obligations, especially under a contract. See also SPECIFIC PERFORMANCE; SUBSTANTIAL PERFORMANCE.
—**performable** *adj.*
—**performance** *n.*

**performance bond** *n.* See under BOND².

**periodic tenancy** (or **estate**) *n.* See under TENANCY.

**perjury** *n., pl.* **perjuries. 1.** the crime of making a false statement under oath or affirmation on a material issue in a judicial or administrative proceeding, other than in the belief that what is being said is true. Cf. FALSE SWEARING.
**2.** an instance of committing perjury.
—**perjurer** *n.*
—**perjurious** *adj.*
—**perjuriously** *adv.*
—**perjuriousness** *n.*

**permanent injunction** *n.* See under INJUNCTION.

**permissive** *adj.* permitted but not required; opposite of compulsory or mandatory. See *permissive counterclaim* (under COUNTERCLAIM); *permissive joinder* (under JOINDER); *permissive presumption* (under PRESUMPTION).
—**permissively** *adv.*

**perp** *n. Police Slang.* short for PERPETRATOR.

**perp walk** *n. Police and Media Slang.* the arranged walking of a suspect or a convicted criminal past television and news photographers and reporters. See also RIDE-ALONG.
——**History.** The perp walk is a long tradition designed to provide material for the media, favorable publicity for law enforcement and government officials, and, some say, a moral lesson for the populace. Sometimes the walk is orchestrated to take advantage of the opportunity presented by a necessary move of the suspect or convict; sometimes a suspect is taken out for a walk solely to create a photo opportunity. Either way, one inevitable consequence is humiliation and injury to the reputation of suspects who turn out to be innocent of any crime, a fact that has led the practice to be challenged as unconstitutional. Another potential consequence became clear two days after the assassination of John F. Kennedy. His accused killer, Lee Harvey Oswald, was on a perp walk, held on each side by a law enforcement officer, when Jack Ruby emerged from the crowd of reporters and shot him to death.

**perpetrator** *n.* **1.** one who commits a crime: *The perpetrator was convicted after a two-month trial.*
**2.** one who commits a tort, fails to fulfill a contractual obligation, or does a harmful or evil act.
—**perpetrate** *v.,* **perpetrated, perpetrating.**
——**Usage.** The perpetrator of a crime is the person who did it. In discussions of police activity, the term is sometimes used more loosely or carelessly to refer to a suspect who has not yet been convicted, and who may actually turn out to be innocent.

**perpetuate** *v.,* **perpetuated, perpetuating.** to obtain and preserve testimony in a form suitable for later use at a trial, in case the witness becomes unavailable. See also DEPOSITION.

**perpetuity** *n., pl.* **perpetuities.** a *contingent interest* in real property (see under INTEREST¹) that might remain contingent for a length of time regarded by the law as excessive; that is, the contingency that would cause the interest to VEST might remain unresolved—not having occurred, but still possible—for a longer time than permitted by law. At common law, the maximum time limit (the **perpetuities period**) was the lifetime of someone identified in the instrument creating the interest and alive (or at least conceived) at the time the interest was created (a **life in being**), plus 21 years. This allowed, for example, a testator to leave his estate to his children for as long as they live, then finally "to such of my grandchildren as reach the age of 21." (In this example, if the testator's last living child died leaving a pregnant wife, that last grandchild's period of gestation would be added to the 21-year time limit.) Under the common law **rule against perpetuities,** any interest that might remain contingent longer than lives in being plus 21 years (plus a possible period of gestation) is regarded as just too uncertain, and is declared void. Some version of the rule against perpetuities exists in all or virtually all states, but the details vary from state to state. See also FERTILE-OCTOGENARIAN RULE; RESTRAINT ON ALIENATION; UNBORN-WIDOW RULE; WAIT-AND-SEE APPROACH.

**persecution** n. International Law. **1.** harassing, violent, or oppressive conduct directed toward an identifiable group on political, racial, national, ethnic, cultural, religious, gender-based, or other such grounds. **2.** deprivation of fundamental rights contrary to international law by reason of such group identity, especially pursuant to a government-sponsored or government-sanctioned campaign. See also CRIME AGAINST HUMANITY; ETHNIC CLEANSING. —**persecute** v., **persecuted, persecuting.** —**persecutor** n. —**persecutory** adj.

**person** n., pl. **persons. 1.** a human being **(natural person)** or an organization or entity **(juridical person, juristic person, artificial person, legal person,** or **fictitious person)**—such as a corporation—recognized by the law as capable of performing legal acts (such as entering into a contract) and having legal rights and responsibilities (such as the right to due process and liability for torts). **2.** the human body: injury to person and property. **3. interested person** a person with an interest (see INTEREST²) in a matter; particularly a person whose legal and financial rights will be directly affected by the outcome of a case or the disposition of a decedent's estate. Persons having such an interest will normally be allowed to INTERVENE in a case or otherwise assert their claims and rights in a matter if their interest is not already adequately represented. **4. protected person** an individual, especially an incompetent person, for whom a court has appointed a GUARDIAN or made some other order of protection. **5. reasonable person** See under REASONABLE. See also FICTITIOUS PERSON. —**Note.** The exact scope of the term person depends upon the context. In this dictionary, the phrase "person or entity" is often used to emphasize that a definition applies to juridical as well as natural persons, and the nonlegalistic plural "people" is sometimes used to indicate that a concept applies exclusively or primarily to natural persons rather than juridical persons. See also INDIVIDUAL.

**personal** adj. See personal bond (under BOND²); personal income tax (under INCOME TAX); personal injury (under INJURY); personal judgment (under JUDGMENT); personal jurisdiction (under JURISDICTION¹); personal knowledge (under KNOWLEDGE); personal property (under PROPERTY); personal service (under SERVICE); and release on personal recognizance (under RELEASE ON OWN RECOGNIZANCE).

**personal chattel** n. See under CHATTEL.

**personal representative** n. **1.** one who manages the legal and financial affairs of another who is incapable of doing so, and stands in for that person in lawsuits and other legal and financial transactions. **2.** Also called **personal representative of the estate** or **personal representative for the estate.** an EXECUTOR or ADMINISTRATOR.

**personalty** n. Same as personal property (see under PROPERTY).

**personam** n. See IN PERSONAM.

**personation** n. Same as IMPERSONATION.

—**personate** *v.*, **personated, person-
ating.**
—**personator** *n.*

**persuasion** *n.* See *burden of persuasion*
(under BURDEN[1]).

**persuasive authority** *n.* See under
AUTHORITY[2].

**petit** *adj. Law French.* (lit. "small")
small, minor, lesser. Used in various legal phrases, often in contrast to GRAND;
e.g., *petit jury* (see under JURY), *petit
larceny* (see under LARCENY), *petit theft*
(see under THEFT). See also *petit treason* (under TREASON).
—**Pronunciation.** *Petit* is pronounced,
and often written, "petty."

**petition** *n.* **1.** a formal request, addressed to a person or body in a position of authority, soliciting some benev-
olent exercise of power. The right to
present such petitions to the government is one of the rights guaranteed by
the First Amendment (see Appendix).
**2.** the name given to the initial pleading
in certain kinds of judicial or administrative proceedings, and to certain requests for special permission or relief
from appellate courts: *petition for a writ
of habeas corpus; petition in bankruptcy; petition for leave to appeal.*
—*v.* **3.** to present or file a petition: *to
petition the governor for a pardon; to
petition the legislature for a change in
the law; to petition for a writ of mandamus.*
—**petitioner** *n.*

**petty** *adj.* small, minor, lesser. See *petty
jury* (under JURY); *petty larceny* (under
LARCENY); *petty offense* (under OF-
FENSE); *petty theft* (under THEFT); *petty
treason* (under TREASON). Often rendered in the original French form PETIT,
especially in phrases where the term
used in contrast to the word GRAND (itself of French origin): *petit jury* vs.
*grand jury;* etc.

**phonorecord** *n. Copyright Law.* a material object in which sounds, other than
those accompanying a motion picture
or other audiovisual work, are fixed,
and from which the sounds can be perceived, reproduced, or otherwise communicated, either directly or with the
aid of a machine or device. See also
note at COPY.
——**False Friend.** This term illustrates
how, in law, technology often outpaces
terminology, and antiquated language
preserved in statutes or case law takes
on new meanings to keep up. When
this term found its way into a major revision of the copyright laws drafted in
the 1960's, the phonograph record was
the mass medium of sound recording.
Today we have tape casettes and compact disks, and tomorrow we may have
something different; but so far as the
copyright law is concerned they are all
classified as "phonorecords."

**physical injury** *n.* Same as *bodily injury* (see under INJURY).

**physician-assisted suicide** *n.* See under SUICIDE.

**physician-patient privilege** *n.* the
*evidentiary privilege* (see under PRIVI-
LEGE) by which a patient may prevent
disclosure of information that was communicated to a physician for the purpose of diagnosis and treatment. Also
called **doctor-patient privilege.**

**picket** *v.* **1.** to stand or parade in front
of a place of employment carrying
signs, in order to publicize a labor
grievance and discourage customers
and other employees from entering or
patronizing the establishment until the
dispute is resolved.
**2.** to engage in any similar demonstra-
tion in front of a government or private
building or site for the purpose of pub-
licizing a cause, protesting conduct, or
petitioning for action. Since picketing is
*speech plus* (see under SPEECH), it is
subject to greater regulation than pure
speech.
—*n.* **3.** an individual engaged in picketing.

**piepowder court** *n. English Legal History.* a court of special jurisdiction held
at fairs and markets for summary disposition of legal disputes and problems
arising among the merchants, buyers,
and general public present. Also called
**court of piepowders** or **court of piepowder,** and occurring in many variant
spellings.

——**History.** *Piepowder* is an Anglicized version of an early French phrase—itself occurring in many different spellings—meaning "dusty foot," hence "itinerant, wayfarer, vagabond" (modern French *pied-poudreux*). Itinerant merchants were called *piepowders*, and everybody else at a fair would have dusty feet as well; thus the name of the court that administered justice at such events. See also note at FAIR².

**pierce the corporate veil** See under CORPORATE.

**pioneer drug** *n.* See under DRUG.

**piracy** *n., pl.* **piracies. 1.** plundering, robbery, or other illegal violence on a ship, or the hijacking of a ship.
**2.** Also called **air piracy.** such conduct with respect to an airplane; particularly the hijacking of an airplane.
**3.** the unauthorized reproduction, imitation, or use of a copyrighted work, patented invention, or trademarked product; especially, unauthorized reproduction of copyrighted books, records, tapes, videotapes **(video piracy)**, and software **(software piracy)** on a large scale for commercial purposes.

**pirate** *n., v.,* **pirated, pirating. —***n.* **1.** a person who commits acts of PIRACY.
**—***v.* **2.** to take by piracy: *to pirate gold.*
**3.** to reproduce copyrighted or other legally protected matter without authorization for commercial profit: *to pirate movies on videotape.*
**—piratical** *adj.*
**—piratically** *adv.*

**pizza redlining** *n. Informal.* the practice of fast food restaurants, especially large chains of pizza restaurants, of demarking neighborhoods where they refuse to make deliveries, or where they will make curbside deliveries only, because of concerns for the safety of the delivery people. Some municipalities have tried to outlaw the practice. See also SERVICE REDLINING.

**place of abode** *n.* Same as ABODE¹.

**plagiarize** *v.,* **plagiarized, plagiarizing.** to present another's ideas, words, or other form of expression as if they were one's own.

**—plagiarism** *n.*
**—plagiarist** *n.*
——**Note.** Plagiarism may or may not be unlawful, depending upon whether it involves unauthorized use of copyrighted work and other factors, but in academic and scholarly contexts it is always unethical and may lead to disciplinary proceedings.

**plain error** *n.* See under ERROR.

**plain meaning** *n.* the apparent meaning of a statutory or constitutional provision as gleaned solely from the words of the provision itself, without consideration of other factors, such as the context in which the words were written and the objective the writers were trying to achieve. Cf. LEGISLATIVE INTENT.

**plain meaning rule** *n.* a theory of statutory and constitutional CONSTRUCTION that regards the PLAIN MEANING of a provision as dispositive and resort to LEGISLATIVE INTENT unnecessary or improper.
——**Note.** The plain meaning rule is regarded by most as too simplistic to be workable. It overlooks the fact that writing is an inherently inexact activity, that reasonable people can reach very different conclusions as to what a particular provision "plainly means," and that the "plain meaning" found by a judge is often as much a reflection of what the judge wants to find in the provision as of what the drafter put there.

**plain view doctrine** *n.* the principle that police who are lawfully in a place do not need a search warrant to seize evidence of crime that is in plain view; similarly, an officer may seize evidence obvious to the touch in the conduct of a lawful patdown for weapons.

**plaintiff** *n.* **1.** the person who starts a lawsuit by serving or filing a complaint.
**2. lead plaintiff a.** in a class action, the *named plaintiff* selected to take primary responsibility for conducting the litigation on behalf of the entire plaintiff class. See also *lead counsel* (under COUNSEL). **b.** in an action brought by several plaintiffs, the plaintiff named first in the caption.

**3. named plaintiff** in a class action, any of the plaintiffs named in the caption, as distinguished from the larger body of class members whose interests the named plaintiffs represent but who do not themselves participate as individual parties in the case.

**4. professional plaintiff** an individual who brings many lawsuits, especially one who buys small amounts of stock in many companies and then seeks to represent other shareholders in a class action whenever it turns out that the financial or other information made available by the company was materially misleading. The term "professional plaintiff" is almost always used disparagingly.

**5. third-party plaintiff** See under THIRD-PARTY ACTION.

**plaintiff in error** *n.* the APPELLANT in a case in which the appeal is commenced by *writ of error* (see under WRIT).

**plan of reorganization** *n.* See under BANKRUPTCY.

**platinum parachute** *n. Informal.* an especially lucrative GOLDEN PARACHUTE.

**plea** *n.* **1.** a criminal defendant's formal response to the charges: GUILTY, NOT GUILTY, or NOLO CONTENDERE. At ARRAIGNMENT, the usual plea is "not guilty," but this is often changed later, usually as the result of a PLEA BARGAIN. **2.** any of a considerable number of specific pleadings and motions that were used in civil cases prior to the adoption of modern rules of procedure, seldom referred to in modern cases. See also DILATORY PLEA. **3.** historically, a suit or action. **4. common pleas** *Legal History.* civil actions; private lawsuits as distinguished from criminal actions. See also COURT OF COMMON PLEAS. **5. pleas of the Crown** *English Legal History.* criminal proceedings, as distinguished from *common pleas.*

**plea bargain** *n.* a negotiated agreement between the prosecution and a criminal defendant whereby the prosecution grants some concessions in exchange for the defendant's plea of guilty to at least one charge. Typical concessions include dropping certain charges, especially the most serious ones, and agreeing to make a particular sentencing recommendation. Most criminal cases end in a plea bargain.

**plead** *v.,* **pleaded** or **pled; pleading.** to enter a PLEA or file a PLEADING, or to assert in a pleading: *He pleaded the defense of statute of limitations.* See also WELL-PLEADED COMPLAINT.
**—Usage.** "Pleaded" is the conventional past tense; "pled" was almost never seen in legal writing until the twentieth century, even though pleading lay at the heart of the common law system and virtually every written opinion made some mention of it. The twentieth century saw a steady rise in use of the word "pled" in America among nonlawyers, and this trend can be seen in American legal writing as well. Even so, at the end of the twentieth century "pleaded" was still the prevailing form being used in statutes, judicial opinions, and law reviews, and the wiser course for young lawyers who want to come across well to judges and other lawyers who have been around a while would be to use the traditional legal terminology. Those who must say "pled" should at least spell it that way; writing "plead" when "pled" is meant, as some do, is simply asking to be misread.

**plead the baby act** See under BABY ACT.

**pleader¹** *n.* **1.** one who pleads; one who enters a plea; one who files a pleading or pleadings. **2.** an advocate; one who argues another's cause.

**pleader²** *n.* in ancient usage, the practice or process of pleading. See note at DEMURRER. See also FAINT PLEADER.

**pleading** *n.* **1.** the formal document in which a party to a civil case sets out or responds to a claim or defense. Under modern rules, the principal pleadings are the COMPLAINT, the ANSWER, and if the answer contains counterclaims, a REPLY.

**2.** the art or practice of drafting such pleadings.

**3.** the act of asserting or filing a claim, defense, or plea.

**4. alternative pleading** the inclusion in a pleading of allegations or defenses based upon varying—or even conflicting—interpretations of the facts or the law. For example, "Defendant either negligently failed to see a red light or, in the alternative, saw the red light and deliberately ignored it"; "Defendant's conduct constitutes fraud, or alternatively a breach of contract." Such pleading was formerly disfavored, but under modern procedure is freely allowed.

**5. notice pleading** the modern philosophy that the function of pleadings is simply to give reasonable notice of the nature of one's claims or defenses, the details of which can be developed through DISCOVERY. This is in contrast to earlier practice, in which pleading was a highly technical exercise and cases could easily be lost because of minor pleading defects even if the facts supported the pleader.

See also *burden of pleading* (under BURDEN[1]); *faint pleading* (under FAINT PLEADER); *judgment on the pleadings* (under JUDGMENT); SHAM PLEADING.

**pledge** *n., v.,* **pledged, pledging.** —*n.* **1.** a deposit of personal property, or of documents (such as stock certificates) representing intangible property, with a lender or other person as security for a loan or other obligation.
—*v.* **2.** to make such a pledge.
—**pledgeable** *adv.*

**plenary** *adj., n., pl.* **plenaries.** —*adj.* **1.** full, complete, sufficient, unqualified: *plenary jurisdiction over a case; plenary trial.*
**2.** involving all members of a body: *a plenary session of the legislature.*
—*n.* **3.** a plenary session, meeting, or the like.

**plurality opinion** *n.* See under OPINION.

**pluries** *n.* **1.** a third writ or other process, to the same effect as the previous two, issued when the first two have

proved ineffective.
—*adj.* **2.** describing such a process; see for example *pluries summons* (under SUMMONS); *pluries writ* (under WRIT). Cf. ALIAS.
——**History.** The pluries gets its name from the original Latin wording of such writs, which included prominently the word *pluries* (lit. "often; many times").

**pocket part** *n.* a common form of supplement to a book of statutes or a treatise or other legal reference work, in which updated portions are tucked into a pocket in the back of the book.

**pocket veto** *n.* See under VETO.

**point** *n.* **1.** a proposition of fact or law.
**2.** a section of a brief devoted to argument in support of a particular point of significance in the case.
See also *case in point* (under CASE[1]); *memorandum of points and authorities* (under BRIEF); ON POINT.

**poisonous tree** *n.* See FRUIT OF THE POISONOUS TREE.

**police chase** or **police pursuit** *n.* See HIGH-SPEED CHASE; FRESH PURSUIT.

**police power** *n.* state legislative power; the inherent power of state governments, and of local governments to the extent delegated by the state, to enact laws safeguarding the health, safety, morals, convenience, and general welfare of people in the state, subject only to the constraints of the Constitution and the supremacy of federal law in matters within its purview.

**policy** *n., pl.* **policies.** **1.** action or procedure conforming to or considered with reference to prudence or expediency; a considered and consistent set of principles underlying the actions of an individual, company, government, etc. See also PUBLIC POLICY.
**2.** Same as INSURANCE POLICY. See also UMBRELLA POLICY.
**3.** a method of gambling in which bets are made on numbers to be drawn by lottery.

**political action committee (PAC)** *n.* **1.** an organization established to collect and distribute political contributions in order to assist candidates who favor the positions espoused by the organizers.

**2. leadership PAC** a political action committee run by a politician—usually a prominent officeholder, especially a United States Senator or Representative—who controls how the funds are spent.

——**Note.** Political action committees are important and influential in politics because, under the federal campaign financing law, individuals may make larger contributions to a PAC than to any individual candidate for federal office, and the PAC in turn may make larger contributions to each candidate it supports than any individual would be allowed to give. Politicians can therefore get more HARD MONEY through PACs than through individual contributors, and the PACs accordingly can have considerable influence over the politicians. Some PACs—notably leadership PACs—also raise large amounts of SOFT MONEY. Leadership PACs, especially those run by legislators who hold leadership positions in Congress, attract large contributions from corporations and industries that want to be sure their positions are given the most favorable possible consideration in Congress; the leaders who run the PACs, in turn, wield increased power because they can dole the funds out to colleagues and candidates who have demonstrated loyalty.

**political asylum** *n.* See under ASYLUM.

**political question** *n.* See under QUESTION[2].

**poll tax** *n.* a fixed tax imposed on everyone regardless of income. Also called **capitation, capitation tax, head tax**.

——**History.** After the Civil War, poll taxes were enacted in many states as a condition of being allowed to vote, making it difficult for the poor, and in particular the black populace, to vote. In 1964 this requirement was eliminated in elections for national office by the Twenty-fourth Amendment (see Appendix). Not until 1966—more than a hundred years after the end of the Civil War—did the Supreme Court, by a vote of 6–3, finally hold this blatant technique for reducing black political power

unconstitutional in state and local elections, on the ground that it denied impoverished voters equal protection of the laws. *Harper v. Virginia State Board of Election,* 383 U.S. 663 (1966).

——**False Friend.** The concept of a *poll tax* has nothing to do with *polls* or *polling.* Although poll taxes were implemented in the United States as a condition of voting, and so were in effect a tax on access to the polls, the occurrence of the the word *poll* in reference to both taxing and voting is just an etymological coincidence. The term *poll* originally meant "head." "Polling" is simply the process of counting heads, and a "poll tax" is a tax by the head (as opposed, for example, to a tax based upon income or property value or the amount of a sale).

**poll the jury** to require the jurors in a case in which a verdict has just been announced to declare in open court, usually one by one, whether that is, in fact, their verdict. This is done by the judge or a court officer if requested by a party.

**polygamy** *n.* the practice or condition of having more than one spouse—especially of a man having more than one wife—at a time.

—**polygamist** *n.*

—**polygamous** *adj.*

—**polygamously** *adv.*

——**Usage.** *Polygamy* is more a sociological term than a legal one; in law the practice is covered by the crime of BIGAMY.

——**History.** Although polygamy (in the narrow sense of a man having multiple wives) is permissible under Islamic law and was an original tenet of the major branch of Mormonism—a religion grown entirely on American soil—it has never received legal protection in the United States either under principles of FREEDOM OF RELIGION or as an aspect of the RIGHT OF PRIVACY. Indeed, settlers in the heavily Mormon region that is now Utah repeatedly sought statehood for almost fifty years, beginning in 1849, and were steadfastly rebuffed by Congress over the polygamy issue.

Only when the church finally re-nounced polygamy in 1890—and the territorial legislature enacted the new philosophy into law in 1892 by crimi-nalizing the practice—did Congress re-lent and allow Utah to become a state in 1896. Even then, Congress required that Utah include in its constitution a clause stating (more than a little ironi-cally, given that history) "That perfect toleration of religious sentiment shall be secured...; Provided, That polyga-mous or plural marriages are forever prohibited." See also *inadmissible alien* (under ALIEN).

**polygraph** *n.* a device for measuring certain involuntary bodily responses, such as blood pressure and perspira-tion, from which an opinion is drawn as to whether or not the person being tested is telling the truth. Also called, somewhat optimistically, a **lie detec-tor.**
——**Note.** The problem with the poly-graph is that while it may yield accu-rate opinions in many cases, it can make nervous or confused truth-tellers look like liars and amoral or self-deluding liars look like truth-tellers, and there is no way to know which results are accurate and which are not. Accordingly, polygraph results are ex-cluded from evidence under most circumstances in most jurisdictions, and federal law prohibits employers, except in very limited circumstances, from us-ing the device on employees and appli-cants for employment.

**pornography** *n.* **1.** broadly, any sexu-ally explicit material intended primarily to provide sexual entertainment and arousal to those who read or view it for that purpose.
**2.** narrowly, sexual material satisfying the constitutional test for OBSCENITY. In general, any commercial, and some-times noncommercial, involvement with such pornography is a crime.
**3. child pornography a.** any visual depiction of actual or simulated sexual conduct by an individual under the age of 18 or lascivious exhibition of the pu-bic area of such an individual. Courts have held that such material may be

banned even if it is not legally obscene and does not involve nudity. **b.** any vis-ual depiction that appears to be of a minor engaging in actual or simulated sexual conduct or lascivious exhibition of the pubic area, or that is advertised or presented in a manner that conveys the impression that it involves a minor engaging in such conduct, even if no minor is involved.
**4. virtual child pornography** comput-er-generated images that appear to be sexually explicit photographs of minors, but that are made by manipulating pho-tographs of adults or otherwise without the involvement of any actual individu-al under the age of 18.
—**pornographer** *n.*
—**pornographic** *adj.*
—**pornographically** *adv.*
——**History.** Federal anti-pornography legislation began with the COMSTOCK LAW, enacted in 1873. The first federal law specifically concerned with child pornography was not adopted until 1977, but Congress returned to the topic regularly thereafter, passing eight separate laws on the subject by the end of the century. The most notable changes in the child pornography laws occurred in 1984, when Congress raised the age threshold from 16 to 18 and eliminated the requirement that mate-rial be obscene to be illegal, and in 1996, when Congress eliminated the re-quirement that any actual minor be de-picted in the image or involved in its making. Although the primary target of the 1996 amendment was virtual child pornography, its immediate impact was on the Hollywood film of Vladimir No-bokov's *Lolita* then in production. In the process of filming, any scene in-volving nudity had been shot with a 19-year-old body double for the 15-year-old actress who was playing the ti-tle role; in light of the 1996 law, how-ever, a lawyer was brought into the ed-iting room to supervise the final cut, and the scenes with the body double were cut out for fear that they had been filmed convincingly enough to run afoul of the new provision banning vis-ual depictions of simulated sexual con-duct by anyone who *appears* to be a

minor. When the film was finally released, a national legal periodical heralded it with the headline "Coming Soon: 'Lolita,' the Lawyer's Cut." *National Law Journal*, Aug. 17, 1998, at A1.

**positive law** *n.* human-made law as distinguished from so-called NATURAL LAW; the actual rules of behavior and government enforced by a society.

**positivism** *n.* a school of JURISPRU-DENCE that stresses the distinction between POSITIVE LAW and ideal ethics or justice or NATURAL LAW, and analyzes legal decisions as justified or unjustified primarily within the framework of existing positive law. Also called **legal positivism.**
—**positivist** *n., adj.*
—**positivistic** *adj.*
—**positivistically** *adv.*

**posse** *n.* See IN POSSE; POSSE COMITA-TUS.

**posse comitatus** *n. Latin.* (lit. "force of the county") a group of people who may be called upon to assist law enforcement authorities in preserving the peace, making an arrest, or the like; or a group actually called upon and assembled for such a purpose. Also called a **posse.**
——**Note.** It is in the tradition of the posse comitatus that the National Guard may be called out for such purposes as enforcing school integration, quelling riots, or maintaining order after a natural disaster.

**possession** *n.* **1.** occupation or control of real property to the exclusion of others (save with permission of the possessor), or knowing dominion and control over personal property.
**2. actual possession** direct or immediate physical occupation or control of property. See also ADVERSE POSSESSION; OCCUPANCY.
**3. constructive possession** the power and intention of exercising control over property that is in the hands of someone else. For example, the owner of a house currently occupied by a lessee, or of furniture stored in a warehouse, has constructive possession of the house or furniture, while the tenant or the warehouser has actual possession. To sustain a charge of "criminal possession" of contraband, such as illegal drugs or stolen property, it is usually sufficient to show constructive possession.
—**possess** *v.*
—**possessor** *n.*
—**possessory** *adj.*

**possession is nine-tenths of the law** a somewhat overstated adage reflecting two realities: (1) that in disputes over real property, a person in possession can only be ousted by one with a superior right; a person with no right or a lesser right has no standing to complain, even if the present occupant's possession is wrongful; and (2) that because of the expense, uncertainty, and difficulty of obtaining and enforcing legal judgments, a person in possession of disputed property or a disputed sum of money has a strategic advantage over an adverse claimant. Sometimes, especially in England, the idiom is **possession is nine points of the law.** See also *paramount title* (under TITLE).

**possessory action** an action to recover or maintain possession of real or personal property; for example, an action to evict a holdover tenant or for RE-PLEVIN.

**possessory estate** *n.* See under ES-TATE[1].

**possessory interest** *n.* See under IN-TEREST[1].

**possibility of reverter** *n.* the *future estate* (see under ESTATE[1]) retained by the owner of a fee (see FEE[1]) in real property (or her heirs) when she transfers the entire fee to someone else but imposes a condition on its continued existence so that, upon violation of the condition, the fee will revert to the original owner or her heirs. See also *fee simple determinable* (under FEE[1]). Cf. *executory interest* (under INTEREST[1]); RE-VERSION.

**post bail** See under BAIL[1].

**pour-over trust** *n.* See under TRUST.

**power** *n.* **1.** legal authority to perform acts affecting legal rights and relationships, especially the authority of a legislative body to make laws on certain subjects (e.g., *commerce power,* under COMMERCE; POLICE POWER), the authority of other governmental bodies or officers to perform their respective duties (e.g., *executive power; judicial power*), or specific authority granted to a private person to take actions having legal consequences (e.g., POWER OF APPOINTMENT; POWER OF ATTORNEY). See also SEPARATION OF POWERS.
**2. delegated power a.** power granted by one person or body to another, to do something that the first could have done; especially, regulatory power conferred upon an administrative agency by Congress. **b.** Another name for *enumerated power.*
**3. enumerated power** a power conferred upon the federal government by the Constitution, such as the commerce power. The United States government is a "government of enumerated powers," having only those powers provided for in the Constitution.
**4. reserved power** a governmental power left to the states by the Constitution—that is, any governmental power that the Constitution neither grants to the federal government nor denies to state governments.

**power of appointment** *n.* the authority, granted by the owner of property (the DONOR of the power) to a person (the DONEE), to designate (APPOINT) the person or persons (the APPOINTEES) who are to receive the property upon the death of the donor, the death of the donee, or the termination of some intervening interest in the property.

**power of attorney** *n.* **1.** an instrument by which one individual (the PRINCIPAL) confers upon another (the *attorney in fact*; see under ATTORNEY) the power to perform specified acts or kinds of acts on behalf of the principal.
**2.** the power possessed by an attorney in fact by reason of such an instrument.
**3. durable power of attorney** a form of power of attorney allowed by statute, which remains effective if the principal

becomes incompetent to perform or consent to the acts delegated. At common law, the power of attorney was automatically revoked upon incapacity of the principal.
**4. durable power of attorney for health care** Same as HEALTH CARE PROXY.
**5. general power of attorney** a power of attorney granting wide power to perform any act of a specified kind or of a range of kinds, such as handling all business and financial matters for the principal.
**6. special power of attorney** a power of attorney to perform a certain act, such as signing a particular document or purchasing a particular parcel of land.

**practice** *n., v.,* **practiced, practicing.** —*n.* **1.** the procedural aspects of law; the presentation of matters to courts and the manner in which cases are handled: *civil practice; rules of practice; Supreme Court practice.*
**2.** the pursuit of a profession: *the practice of law; the practice of architecture.*
**3.** one's usual way of dealing with a particular kind of situation: *Her practice is to have her secretary open her mail. The practice in our industry is to ship by truck unless another method is specified.*
—*v.* **4.** to engage in a profession.

**praesenti** *n.* See IN PRAESENTI.

**prayer for relief** *n.* the portion at the end of a COMPLAINT in which the plaintiff states the damages or other remedy being sought in the action. Also called **demand for relief.**

**preamble** *n.* an introduction to a constitution, statute, contract, or other instrument, stating the reasons for enacting or writing it. It is usually not regarded as a part of the instrument, but is sometimes looked to for help in construing the instrument.

**precatory** *adj.* expressing or reflecting a hope, desire, or preference, but not a direction or command.

**precatory language** *n.* language in a trust instrument or will that indicates the maker's desire but is not legally binding; for example, "It is my hope that these funds will be used for educational purposes." Also called **precatory words.** Often it is difficult to know whether such language was intended to be mandatory or merely precatory. See also WISH.

**precedent** *n.* **1.** a judicial decision cited as authority by an attorney or court in a subsequent case involving similar or analogous facts and issues. Virtually all judicial decisions are based upon precedent, which is central to the doctrine of STARE DECISIS.
**2. binding precedent** Same as *binding authority* (see under AUTHORITY[2]).
—*adj.* **3.** preceding in time or rank; going before.
**4. condition precedent** See under CONDITION.
——**Pronunciation.** The noun is pronounced PRESSedent; the adjective (seen most often in the phrase *condition precedent*) is more appropriately preSEEdent—much like the word *preceding*, which means the same thing.

**preclude** *v.*, **precluded, precluding. 1.** to bar (a lawyer or litigant) from contesting certain issues, making certain arguments, or taking certain steps in a case: *The marital privilege precludes the defendant from questioning the wife about her confidential conversations with the husband.*
**2.** to prevent the presence, existence, or occurrence of; disallow; make impossible: *The insufficiency of the evidence precludes a conviction. The judge precluded the evidence of prior arrests.*
—**precludable** *adj.*
—**preclusive** *adj.*
—**preclusively** *adv.*

**preclusion** *n.* the act of precluding or the state of being precluded. See also *issue preclusion* (under ESTOPPEL).
——**Note.** Preclusion of evidence, issues, arguments, and the like can occur for many reasons. For example, evidence may be precluded by a rule of evidence such as the hearsay rule or by an evidentiary privilege, or an issue may already have been determined in another forum, or a party might have

failed to comply with discovery requirements and consequently be precluded from introducing evidence on the issue to which the discovery related.

**preclusion order** *n.* a court order precluding a party from introducing evidence or questioning witnesses on certain issues.

**predator** *n.* See SEXUAL PREDATOR.

**predatory pricing** *n.* selling goods or services at an unreasonably low price in the hope of driving competitors out of business and then raising the price. This is a violation of ANTITRUST laws.

**predecessor** *n.* one who previously possessed a right, interest, or duty now belonging to another (a SUCCESSOR). Also called **predecessor in interest.**

**preemption** *n.* **1.** the doctrine that a comprehensive federal regulatory scheme in a field of federal interest may be held to preclude any state regulation whatever in that field. In such a situation federal law is said to **occupy the field** and to **preempt** state law.
**2.** the enactment of a federal law that preempts state law, or the preemptive effect of a federal law.
See also SUPREMACY.

**preference** *n.* **1.** a payment or transfer of property or of an interest in property by an insolvent debtor to a creditor in such a way that the creditor gets more than its share of the debtor's property as compared with other creditors.
**2. voidable preference** a preference shortly before the debtor formally goes into bankruptcy, under circumstances permitting the bankruptcy court to recover whatever was given from the creditor who received it, so that it can be distributed fairly among all creditors.

**preferential shop** *n.* See under SHOP.

**preferred stock** *n.* See under STOCK.

**pregnancy discrimination** *n.* discrimination in employment on the basis of pregnancy, childbirth, or related medical conditions.
——**History.** After the Supreme Court held that discrimination on account of

pregnancy does not constitute discrimination against women, Congress in 1978 adopted a statute making it clear that pregnancy discrimination is to be regarded as a form of illegal sex discrimination.

**prejudicial effect** *n.* the tendency of a piece of evidence to inflame the jury unduly or to divert its attention to irrelevant matters. Relevant evidence in a case may be excluded if the judge concludes that its PROBATIVE VALUE is outweighed by its prejudicial effect.

**prejudicial error** *n.* See under ERROR.

**preliminary hearing** *n.* See under HEARING.

**preliminary injunction** *n.* See under INJUNCTION.

**premarital agreement** *n.* Same as PRENUPTIAL AGREEMENT.

**premeditation** *n.* contemplating something with a cool mind before doing it, if only briefly and on the spot. Premeditation is an element of the highest degree of MURDER in some states.
—**premeditated** *adj.*
—**premeditatedly** *adv.*

**premise** *n., v.,* **premised, premising.**
—*n.* **1.** a proposition supporting or helping to support a conclusion; an assumption or set of facts from which one or more conclusions are drawn through use of logic.
—*v.* **2.** to set forth beforehand, as by way of introduction or explanation.
**3.** to assume as a premise for a conclusion.

**premises** *n.pl.* **1.** statements previously made; that which has gone before; the foregoing.
**2.** in a deed or lease, everything going before the HABENDUM CLAUSE. The premises include any recitals, and in particular any recital of consideration or other facts motivating the transaction, and the GRANTING CLAUSE, in which the grantor, the grantee, and the property conveyed are identified.
**3.** all of the property described in the premises of a deed or bequest collectively, sometimes referred to later in the document for convenience simply as "the premises," "the said premises," or the like.
**4.** any building, usually with its grounds and associated outbuildings.
**5.** in equity pleading, the portion of the plaintiff's bill containing a complete narrative of the facts and circumstances on the basis of which the plaintiff seeks redress.

**premium** *n.* **1.** money paid to an insurance company for insurance coverage or for an annuity.
**2.** an extra amount paid or received for something because of some special or unusual circumstance.
**3.** the amount by which the market value of a bond exceeds its face value if the bond carries interest at a higher rate than the current rate for newly issued bonds.
**4. control premium** a premium paid for a substantial block of shares in a corporation, over the regular market price for smaller quantities of the stock, because the block is large enough to affect or determine who will control the corporation.

**prenup** *n. Slang.* Short for PRENUPTIAL AGREEMENT.

**prenuptial agreement** *n.* a contract between two people who are about to marry regarding their respective property and support rights upon termination of the marriage by divorce or death, and sometimes regarding property rights during the marriage as well. Such agreements are generally enforceable, and supersede otherwise applicable rules. Also called **antenuptial agreement** or **premarital agreement.** See also MARITAL PROPERTY AGREEMENT.

**prepack** *n. Slang.* Same as *prepackaged bankruptcy* (see under BANKRUPTCY).

**prepackaged bankruptcy** *n.* See under BANKRUPTCY.

**prepayment penalty** *n.* See under PENALTY.

**preponderance of the evidence** *n.* the lowest STANDARD OF PROOF; the degree of persuasion necessary to find for the plaintiff in most civil cases. It requires just enough evidence to persuade the jury that a fact is more likely to be true than not true. If the evidence is equally balanced, then the party with the *burden of persuasion* (see under BURDEN[1]) loses. Sometimes called **preponderance of the credible evidence** or **fair preponderance of the evidence.**

**prerogative writ** *n.* Same as *extraordinary writ* (see under WRIT).

**prescription** *n.* a method of obtaining an EASEMENT over real property belonging to someone else, such as the right to use a path across it, consisting of openly and consistently using it for a period of time set by statute, usually ten to twenty years. Acquisition of an easement by prescription is analogous to acquisition of title by ADVERSE POSSESSION.

**present estate** or **present possessory estate** *n.* Same as *possessory estate* (see under ESTATE[1]).

**present interest** *n.* See under INTEREST[1].

**present recollection refreshed** *n.* See under RECOLLECTION.

**present sense impression** *n.* a statement describing an event or situation, or the declarant's own physical condition or state of mind, made by a person while actually observing or experiencing the thing being described or immediately thereafter. Statements of present sense impression are commonly admitted into evidence as an exception to the rule against HEARSAY.

**presentence report** *n.* a background report on a convicted defendant, prepared by a probation department to assist the judge in deciding upon a sentence.

**presentment** *n.* **1.** the act of presenting an instrument for the payment of money, such as a check or promissory note, to the payor for acceptance or payment. **2.** a written statement of an offense prepared by a grand jury on its own initiative, as distinguished from an INDICTMENT requested by the prosecutor. **3.** the formal act of presenting a matter to a body or official for legal action.

**presents** *n.pl.* the present writings; the contents of this legal instrument. Now limited almost exclusively to the phrase KNOW ALL MEN BY THESE PRESENTS or some minor variation of it.

**president judge** *n.* See under JUDGE.

**presiding judge** *n.* See under JUDGE.

**press** *n.* See FREEDOM OF THE PRESS.

**press ride-along** *n.* Same as RIDE-ALONG.

**presumption** *n.* **1.** a legal assumption that if one fact or group of facts exists, then another fact must also exist, so that the second can sometimes be proved in a court case simply by introducing evidence of the first.
**2. conclusive presumption** a rule of law under which once one set of facts is established, the facts that normally follow from it must be found to be true, and no evidence to the contrary will be permitted; for example, the presumption that if a driver's blood alcohol content was above a certain level, then the driver was drunk. Also called **irrebuttable presumption.**
**3. mandatory presumption** a presumption that the factfinder in a criminal case must accept unless the defendant produces some evidence to rebut it.
**4. permissive presumption** a presumption that the factfinder in a criminal case may, but need not, accept in the absence of evidence to rebut it.
**5. rebuttable presumption** a presumption that can be defeated by introduction of sufficiently persuasive contrary evidence.
**6. violent presumption** See VIOLENT PRESUMPTION.
—**presume** *v.*, **presumed, presuming.**
—**presumed** *adj.*
—**presumptive** *adj.*
—**presumptively** *adv.*

**presumption of fertility** *n.* See FERTILE-OCTOGENARIAN RULE.

**presumption of innocence** *n.* the

principle that a criminal defendant need not introduce evidence of innocence to be found not guilty; rather, the prosecution must prove each element of the crime in order to convict.

**presumption of legitimacy** *n.* the presumption that a child born in wedlock is the legitimate child of the husband. Except for the focus on the child rather than the father, this is the same thing as the PRESUMPTION OF PATERNITY.

**presumption of paternity** *n.* the presumption that the husband of a woman who has a child is the father of the child.
——**History.** In older law, because the effect of illegitimizing a child was so serious, this presumption was usually conclusive. The mere fact, for example, that the husband had been away at war for several years would not alter the LEGAL FICTION that he had fathered the child. In recent times, the stigma and legal disability associated with illegitimacy have been mitigated (see note at ILLEGITIMACY), and the presumption has in some states been made rebuttable. See, e.g., *dual paternity* (under PATERNITY).

**presumptive heir** *n.* See under HEIR.

**preterlegal** *adj.* being beyond the scope or limits of law: *Whether the defendant's conduct was justified in the eyes of God is a preterlegal question.*

**pretermit** *v.,* **pretermitted, pretermitting. 1.** to let pass without notice; fail to mention: *The youngest child was pretermitted in the will.*
**2.** to disregard intentionally; decline to discuss: *The decision pretermits the statutory issue because the language of the contract is dispositive.*
—**pretermission** *n.*
—**pretermitted** *adj.*
—**pretermitter** *n.*

**pretermitted child** *n.* See *pretermitted heir* (under HEIR).

**pretermitted heir** *n.* See under HEIR.

**pretext** *n.* an ostensible reason advanced to conceal the actual reason for taking some action; usually, a proper reason advanced to explain conduct that was actually undertaken for an improper reason. See, e.g., *pretextual arrest* (under ARREST); *pretextual search* (under SEARCH).
—**pretextual** *adj.*

**pretrial conference** *n.* a conference among the judge and the lawyers for all parties in a case, convened by the judge at any time after the pleadings have been filed and before the trial, to discuss discovery issues, scheduling, and the general status of the case, and usually to discuss the possibility of settlement.

**pretrial detention** *n.* Same as PREVENTIVE DETENTION.

**pretrial discovery** *n.* See under DISCOVERY.

**pretrial order** *n.* an order issued by a judge just before a trial, usually reflecting things discussed or agreed upon at a final PRETRIAL CONFERENCE, setting forth ground rules for the trial.

**preventive detention** *n.* keeping a criminal defendant in jail before trial; not allowing release on bail. This is permitted in serious felony cases upon a finding that it is necessary to protect individuals or the community at large. Also called **pretrial detention.**

**price discrimination** *n.* selling goods or services at different prices to different customers. This can be a violation of ANTITRUST laws if done in such a way as to harm competitors and reduce competition.

**price fixing** *n.* the setting of prices at which goods or services are to be sold, by means of an agreement or understanding between competing sellers **(horizontal price fixing)** or an agreement or arrangement between the seller and the producer or wholesaler who provided the product in question **(vertical price fixing).** Price fixing is a violation of the SHERMAN ANTITRUST ACT. See also PER SE.

**priest-penitent privilege** *n.* Same as CLERGY-COMMUNICANT PRIVILEGE.

**prima facie** *Latin.* (lit. "at first appearance") **1.** so far as it appears; subject to further evidence; unless the contrary is shown: *The deed is in proper form, and so is prima facie valid.*
**2. prima facie case** (or **evidence** or **proof**) evidence sufficient to justify submitting a party's claim or affirmative defense to a jury, and to support a verdict in favor of that party on that issue, if the jury so finds; that is, evidence sufficient to satisfy a party's *burden of producing evidence* (see under BURDEN[1]).

**primary** *adj.* **1.** first or highest in rank, order, importance, time, right, etc.
**2.** original; not derived or subordinate; fundamental; basic.
—**primarily** *adv.*
—**primariness** *n.*

**primary authority** *n.* See under AUTHORITY.

**primary boycott** *n.* See under BOYCOTT.

**primary liability** *n.* See under LIABILITY.

**prime contractor** *n.* Same as *general contractor* (see under CONTRACTOR).

**primogeniture** *n.* the system of inheritance or succession by the firstborn, specifically the eldest son. Cf. BOROUGH-ENGLISH; GAVELKIND.
—**primogenitary** *adj.*

**primus inter pares** *Latin.* first among equals.
——**Usage.** Although this phrase finds varied applications, one repeated use of the phrase is to characterize the role of the chief judge of a court, and particularly the Chief Justice of the United States. In this context the masculine Latin form *primus* has always sufficed. When the occasion finally arises, the appropriate form of the phrase in reference to a female Chief Justice will be **prima inter pares.**

**principal** *n.* **1.** a person who authorizes another to act as her AGENT. If the agent does not disclose to those he deals with that he is acting on behalf of someone else, the principal is called an **undisclosed principal.** See also AGENCY.
**2.** Also called **principal debtor** or **principal obligor.** the person whose debt or other obligation is the subject of a SURETYSHIP contract or a GUARANTY. If the SURETY or GUARANTOR is required to pay or perform, that person normally has a right of reimbursement from the principal.
**3.** a direct participant in a crime; either an actual perpetrator or an aider and abettor who is present (personally or through an innocent agent) when the crime is committed.
**4.** a basic sum of money upon which interest or profit is calculated; e.g., the face amount of a bond (see BOND[1]).
**5.** the CORPUS of a trust, especially if the trust property consists almost entirely of money or securities.
—*adj.* **6.** primary; most important.

**prior art** *n.* See under ART.

**prior history** *n.* See under HISTORY.

**prior inconsistent statement** *n.* See under STATEMENT.

**prior restraint** *n.* a ban on publishing something. The First Amendment (see Appendix) has been construed as prohibiting most prior restraints, allowing publishers to publish even wrongful or potentially wrongful material (e.g., LIBEL[1]) if they are willing to take the risk of resulting liability or punishment. The primary exception to this rule is OBSCENITY, which may be censored in advance.

**priority** *n., pl.* **priorities. 1.** the right to satisfaction of one's claim against some property, such as the estate of a decedent or a bankrupt, ahead of someone else.
**2.** the order in which the law ranks claims to property.

**prison** *n.* a state or federal facility in which people convicted of serious crimes and given long sentences are incarcerated. Also called **penitentiary.** Cf. JAIL.

**privacy** *n.* freedom from unwarranted intrusion into one's personal life and from unwanted publicity or dissemination of personal information about oneself. Various types of privacy interest are protected from private interference by tort law (see INVASION OF PRIVACY) and from governmental interference by statutes and by the Constitution (see RIGHT OF PRIVACY).

**private** *adj.* **1.** pertaining or belonging to one person or a limited group of persons rather than to the government or the public at large: *private property.* Cf. PUBLIC.
**2.** pertaining to a person acting other than as a government official or the like: *private discrimination.*
**3.** kept away from the public at large: *private information; private conduct.*
See also *private attorney general* (under ATTORNEY GENERAL); *private capacity* (under CAPACITY); *private corporation* (under CORPORATION); *private international law* (under INTERNATIONAL LAW); *private necessity* (under NECESSITY); *private nuisance* (under NUISANCE); *private right of action* (under RIGHT OF ACTION); *private trust* (under TRUST); *private wrong* (under WRONG).

**private act** *n.* Same as PRIVATE LAW (def. 1).

**private bill** *n.* a legislative bill involving the private interests of a particular individual, entity, or local unit; a bill proposing a PRIVATE LAW.

**private figure** *n.* an individual who is not a PUBLIC OFFICIAL or PUBLIC FIGURE.
—**Note.** A private figure may sue for DEFAMATION and recover damages for actual harm resulting from the defamatory statements complained of without proving that they were made with *actual malice* (see under MALICE).

**private judge** *n.* the individual hired to act as the judge in a dispute to be resolved through PRIVATE JUDGING. Also called **rent-a-judge.**

**private judging** *n.* a form of ALTERNATIVE DISPUTE RESOLUTION in which a private individual is hired by the parties to decide the issues for them on the basis of a standardized or agreed-upon procedure for presention of the case. Also called **rent-a-judging.**

**private law** *n.* **1.** Also called **private act, private statute.** a statute directly affecting only one or a small number of individuals, entities, or localities; a statute providing specific relief or a specific benefit to named persons.
**2.** a branch of law dealing with the legal relationships of private individuals and companies, including tort law and contract law.
See also *private international law* (under INTERNATIONAL LAW). Cf. PUBLIC LAW.

**private offering** *n.* See under OFFERING.

**private placement** *n.* Same as *private offering* (see under OFFERING).

**private statute** *n.* Same as PRIVATE LAW (def. 1).

**privately held corporation** *n.* See under CORPORATION.

**privilege** *n.* **1.** in general, a special right or exemption that the law allows to a person or class of persons, or to people under certain circumstances, for reasons of public policy. Some privileges cannot be taken away under any circumstances **(absolute privilege);** others may be relied upon only if certain conditions are met, or may be defeated under certain circumstances **(qualified privilege** or **conditional privilege).**
**2.** in tort law, the right to take actions that are necessary and reasonable under the circumstances even if they injure the person, property, or reputation of another; for example, the right to use reasonable force in SELF-DEFENSE (constituting a defense to a claim of BATTERY), or the absolute privilege of legislators to speak freely in legislative debate or of persons involved in court cases to speak freely in court (rendering them immune from any claim of DEFAMATION based on words spoken in those circumstances).
**3. evidentiary privilege** an absolute or qualified right to withhold certain information or evidence in judicial proceedings, legislative investigations,

and the like. Also called **testimonial privilege,** especially in contexts where the focus is specifically on the withholding of testimony by a witness or prospective witness.

——**Note.** Some evidentiary privileges are founded in the Constitution; see, e.g., EXECUTIVE PRIVILEGE; PRIVILEGE AGAINST SELF-INCRIMINATION. Most, however, evolved as a matter of common law or, in more recent years, were enacted by statute. The public policy reason for such privileges is usually to protect confidential relationships, such as that between a lawyer and client or between a husband and wife, or to protect important public functions such as law enforcement investigations. The number, scope, and even names of such privileges vary from state to state; for examples, see ACCOUNTANT-CLIENT PRIVILEGE; ATTORNEY-CLIENT PRIVILEGE; CLERGY-COMMUNICANT PRIVILEGE; DELIBERATIVE PROCESS PRIVILEGE; INFORMANT'S PRIVILEGE; INVESTIGATIVE PRIVILEGE; JOINT DEFENSE PRIVILEGE; MARITAL PRIVILEGE; PHYSICIAN-PATIENT PRIVILEGE; PSYCHOTHERAPIST-PATIENT PRIVILEGE; REPORTER'S PRIVILEGE.

**privilege against self-incrimination** *n.* the right of an individual, guaranteed by the Fifth Amendment to the Constitution, to refuse to testify in any matter if the testimony might expose the individual to criminal penalties.

——**Note.** There is no privilege to withhold nontestimonial evidence such as skin or hair samples for DNA tests, breath for blood alcohol tests, voice or handwriting exemplars for comparison with other evidence, or one's entire person in a lineup. See also SELF-INCRIMINATION; *transactional immunity* and *use immunity* (under IMMUNITY).

**privileged** *adj.* entitled to, protected by, or exercising a PRIVILEGE.

**privileged communication** *n.* a communication that may be withheld from evidence because of an *evidentiary privilege* (see under PRIVILEGE).

**privileged speech** *n.* See under SPEECH.

**privileges and immunities** *n.* fundamental rights associated with state citizenship. The Constitution requires each state in the United States to accord citizens of other states the same privileges and immunities as its own citizens.

**privity** *n.* the relationship between two or more persons participating in, or having related interests in, a transaction, proceeding, or piece of property. For example, there is **privity of contract** between the parties to a contract; and the grantor and grantee, lessor and lessee, or co-owners of an estate in land are in **privity of estate.** Persons in privity with each other are called **privies;** each one is the other's **privy.**

**pro bono publico** *Latin.* for the public good. A phrase (usually shortened to **pro bono**) signifying that legal services are being provided without charge: *The firm is handling the matter pro bono. It is a pro bono case.*

**pro fine** *Latin.* for the fine. See *capias pro fine* (under CAPIAS).

**pro hac vice** *Latin.* (lit. "for this turn") for this case or occasion only; for a particular time or purpose. See also *admission pro hac vice* (under ADMISSION); *counsel pro hac vice* (under COUNSEL); OWNER PRO HAC VICE.

——**Usage.** This phrase is most often used in reference to a lawyer—usually from out of state—who is given special permission to represent a client in a particular court case in spite of the fact that the lawyer is not a member of the bar of that court or of the jurisdiction where the court is located. The attorney is said to "appear pro hac vice." When this is permitted, the court invariably requires that the party represented also retain *local counsel* (see under COUNSEL), so that there will be an attorney involved who is close by and familiar with the court's customs and rules. See also MULTIJURISICTIONAL PRACTICE.

**pro se** *Latin.* for himself or herself; relating to a party who acts as his or her own lawyer in a case: *The plaintiff is appearing pro se. This is a pro se case.*

**pro tanto** *Latin.* (lit. "for so much") to that extent; proportionately.

**probable cause** *n.* **1.** reasonable grounds, based on substantial evidence, for believing a fact to be true. Under the Fourth Amendment (see Appendix), a person cannot be arrested for a crime unless there is probable cause to believe she committed it, and one's person and property cannot be searched unless there is probable cause to believe that evidence of a crime will be found.
**2. probable cause hearing**  See under HEARING.

**probate** *n., v.* **probated, probating.** —*n.* **1.** a judicial proceeding in which a will is proved to be genuine and distribution of the estate is monitored. —*v.* **2.** to submit a will to probate; prove the authenticity of a will in a probate proceeding.

**probation** *n.* a sentence allowing a convicted criminal to remain free instead of going to jail or prison, or to go free after serving a brief period of confinement, provided that certain conditions are met, including staying out of trouble with the law and reporting regularly to a probation officer. If the conditions of probation are violated, probation can be revoked and the probationer sent to prison.

**probative** *adj.* tending to prove; affording proof or evidence.
—**probatively** *adv.*

**probative value** *n.* usefulness and persuasiveness of a piece of evidence in establishing a relevant fact. Cf. PREJUDICIAL EFFECT. See also WEIGHT.

**procedural** *adj.* of or pertaining to PROCEDURE.
—**procedurally** *adv.*

**procedural due process** *n.* See under DUE PROCESS.

**procedure** *n.* **1.** the methods used in investigating, presenting, managing, and deciding legal cases.
**2.** Also called **procedural law** or **adjective law.** The body of law that determines which of these methods will be allowed and governs how they will

be used: *appellate procedure; California procedure.* Cf. SUBSTANCE (def. 2).
**3. administrative procedure**  the body of law applicable to the procedures used by adminstrative agencies in carrying out all of their rulemaking, regulatory, and adjudicative functions.
**4. civil procedure**  the procedural aspects of a *civil action* (see under ACTION), including principles of jurisdiction, pleading, discovery, conduct of trials, and enforcement of judgments.
**5. criminal procedure**  the body of law—much of it based directly on the Constitution—governing all aspects of criminal law enforcement, including not only judicial proceedings but also police procedures and post-sentencing procedures such as probation, imprisonment, and parole.

**proceed** *v.* to take action in court; to file or pursue a case: *The tenants voted to proceed against the landlord.*

**proceeding** *n.* **1.** any matter handled by or filed with a court or administrative tribunal; a case or some aspect of a case.
**2. proceedings a.** the various steps in a case or some aspect of a case viewed collectively: *The proceedings lasted several years. The proceedings on appeal were even less amicable than those in the trial court.* **b.** a legal action: *She instituted proceedings for slander.* **c.** a formal record of the activities or transactions of an organization, committee, conference, convention, or the like, often as a title: *Proceedings of the Constitutional Convention of the Proposed State of Oklahoma.*
See also ADVERSARY PROCEEDING; CORE PROCEEDING; DISCIPLINARY PROCEEDING; NON-CORE PROCEEDING.

**process** *n.* **1.** a formal document through which a court obtains jurisdiction over a person or property, compels a person to appear in court or participate in a proceeding, or otherwise orders a person to do or not to do something; e.g., a SUMMONS, a writ of ATTACHMENT, or a SUBPOENA. See also *service of process* (under SERVICE); ABUSE OF PROCESS.
**2.** Same as PROCEDURE. The term

"process" in this sense is used almost exclusively in connection with the concept of DUE PROCESS.

**process server** *n.* **1.** an individual who is licensed or otherwise legally authorized to be in the business of serving process in court cases, or a public official whose duties include serving judicial process.
**2.** loosely, any individual who serves a summons or other judicial process.

**procurement contract** *n.* See under CONTRACT.

**procuring cause** *n.* **1.** the action of a real estate agent in bringing parties together or otherwise bringing about a transaction, thereby earning a commission.
**2.** PROXIMATE CAUSE.

**product** *n.* See *tying product* and *tied product* (under TYING ARRANGEMENT).

**product disparagement** *n.* the tort of making a false statement impugning the quality of another's product in order to harm that person's business. Product disparagement is a form of TRADE LIBEL. See also FOOD DISPARAGEMENT.

**production of documents** *n.* a DISCOVERY procedure in which a party is required, upon request from the other side, to produce potentially relevant DOCUMENTS for inspection and copying.

**products liability** *n.* **1.** the liability—usually strict liability—of manufacturers for damage caused by defects in their products. In cases dealing with a particular product, sometimes referred to as **product liability.**
**2.** the area of tort law dealing with such liability.
See also *strict liability* (under LIABILITY).

**profert** *n.* **1.** in common law pleading, an averment to the effect that the deed or similar instrument upon which the pleader relies is available for production and inspection in court. The term derives from the Latin phrases by which such a declaration was made: **profert in curia, profert in curiam,** or **profert ad curiam** (lit. "he produces in

court; he produces to the court").
**2.** production, to a court or to an adversary, of the document upon which a claim is based.
——**History.** The traditional rule in courts of law was that one could not obtain a judgment on a deed or certain other instruments unless one could produce the actual instrument to show that it existed and that its terms were as alleged; hence a pleader relying upon such a document was required to "make profert" so that the opposing party could inspect the document. (See OYER.) If the document had been lost or destroyed, the party relying upon it would have to seek relief in a court of equity, where the rules were less rigid. The requirement of profert was abolished in England in 1852 and gradually faded from use in the United States.
——**False Friend.** This term is sometimes erroneously used when PROFFER is meant. The word *profert* is out of place except in the narrow and largely historical senses discussed above.
——**Pronunciation.** *Profert* also differs from *proffer* in being pronounced with a long *o*, as in the word *prologue*.

**professional corporation (P.C.)** *n.* See under CORPORATION.

**professional plaintiff** *n.* See under PLAINTIFF.

**proffer** *v.* **1.** to present or put forth for acceptance; to offer. Said especially of evidence, explanation, or argument: *The court excluded the proffered testimony as cumulative. The jury apparently accepted the explanation proffered by the defendant.*
—*n.* **2.** the act of proffering, or the thing proffered.
**3.** an OFFER OF PROOF.
—**proferrer** *n.*

**profile** *n., v.* **profiled, profiling.** —*n.* **1.** a set of characteristics or qualities that identify a person or thing, or are believed to be sufficiently common among persons or things of a certain type to be helpful in identifying them: *the profile of a disease; the profile of a battered child.* See also *DNA profile* (under DNA PROFILING).

**2.** Also called **criminal profile. a.** a set of physical, social, and behavioral characteristics that the perpetrator of an unsolved crime is believed likely to possess or display, used to help focus the search for the perpetrator. Such profiles are drawn from a combination of evidence relating to the specific crime, awareness of the characteristics of others who have committed similar crimes, and psychological speculation. **b.** a set of characteristics believed to be typical of people who commit certain kinds of crimes, used to focus surveillance and security activities by law-enforcement officials or private companies.

**3. drug courier profile** a profile listing characteristics, such as behavior and dress, regarded as typical of individuals attempting to smuggle or transport illegal drugs. Also called **drug profile.**

**4. gang profile** a set of characteristics used in identifying possible members of street gangs, who are regarded as likely to be involved in various kinds of criminal activity.

**5. hijacker profile** a set of characteristics believed to be typical of individuals who hijack airplanes. Also called **terrorist profile.**

**6. passenger profile** any set of characteristics looked for in airline passengers who are embarking upon or disembarking from a flight, as evidence that they might be hijackers, drug couriers, or otherwise dangerous or involved in criminal activity.

—*v.* **7.** to draw up a list of characteristics for use as a profile.

—**profiler** *n.*

**profiling** *n.* **1.** the process of drawing up a set of characteristics for use as a profile, especially a *criminal profile* (see under PROFILE).

**2.** the use of a profile by law-enforcement officials, or private employees such as airline employees, in determining what individuals to stop, question, search, surveil, or otherwise subject to special scrutiny or procedures.

See also DNA PROFILING; RACIAL PROFILING.

**profit** *n.* **1.** financial gain from an investment, enterprise, or transaction. See also MESNE PROFITS; SHORT-SWING PROFITS.

**2.** Same as PROFIT A PRENDRE.

**profit a prendre** or **profit à prendre** *n., pl.* **profits a prendre** or **profits à prendre.** *Law French.* (lit. "benefit for the taking") **1.** an interest in land owned by another, consisting of a right to take something of value from it; e.g., mining rights, fishing rights, timber rights.

**2.** the thing that may be taken pursuant to such a right.

Cf. EASEMENT.

**profit a rendre** or **profit à rendre** *n., pl.* **profits a rendre** or **profits à rendre.** *Law French.* (lit. "benefit to be rendered") **1.** a rent or service to be rendered by a tenant to a landlord.

**2.** a PROFIT A PRENDRE viewed from the perspective of the estate or owner burdened by it.

**progressive tax** *n.* See under TAX.

**prohibition** *n.* **1.** a writ (in full, **writ of prohibition**) by which a court directs a lower court or public agency to cease all proceedings with respect to a particular matter on the ground that the matter is outside the scope of its jurisdiction. Cf. MANDAMUS.

**2.** a ban on manufacture, distribution, and consumption of alcoholic beverages.

**3. Prohibition Amendment** the Eighteenth Amendment to the United States Constitution, ratified in 1919 and repealed by the Twenty-First Amendment in 1933 (see Appendix).

**prohibitory injunction** *n.* See under INJUNCTION.

**promise** *n., v.,* **promised, promising.** —*n.* **1.** a commitment to perform, or refrain from performing, some act in the future. The person who makes a promise is the **promisor;** the person to whom it is made is the **promisee.**

**2. gratuitous promise** a promise for which nothing is given or promised in return; e.g., "When I die I will leave you my fortune." As many have learned the hard way, most such promises are unenforceable. See also CONSIDERATION.

**3. illusory promise** a statement that sounds like a promise but actually promises nothing; e.g., "For $25,000, I will give such assistance to your project as I deem appropriate for one year." Traditionally such promises, and "contracts" based upon them, were unenforceable; the modern trend is to read into them a duty to act in GOOD FAITH and enforce them.

—*v.* **4.** to make a promise.

**promissory** *adj.* containing, pertaining to, based upon, or in the nature of a promise.

—**promissorily** *adv.*

**promissory estoppel** *n.* See under ESTOPPEL.

**promissory note** *n.* Same as NOTE[1].

**promissory warranty** *n.* See under WARRANTY.

**promoter** *n.* **1.** a person involved in arranging a business transaction or launching a business venture. **2.** a person who sets up a corporation.

**promoting prostitution** *n.* the crime of inducing someone to become a prostitute, soliciting customers for a prostitute, or otherwise assisting in or benefiting from another's prostitution. Also called **pandering.**

**proof** *n.* **1.** the persuasive effect of evidence in the mind of a factfinder. **2.** the evidence submitted to establish a fact or support a position. **3.** the presentation of evidence. See also *burden of proof* (under BURDEN[1]); *prima facie proof* (under PRIMA FACIE); STANDARD OF PROOF.

**proof of service** *n.* proof that a summons or other process or court paper has been served upon the person who was to receive it, usually consisting either of an *affidavit of service* (see under AFFIDAVIT) or an acknowledgment of receipt of the paper written by the individual upon whom it was served. The latter form of proof of service is very common for motion papers, briefs, and the like exchanged by attorneys in the course of a case; it usually consists simply of the words "Copy received," along with the date and the name of the recipient, written or stamped by the recipient on the original paper that is to be filed with the court.

**proper party** *n.* See under PARTY.

**property** *n.* **1.** a thing, interest, or right that is capable of being owned and, usually, transferred. See also ENTITLEMENT.

**2. alien property** property owned by an ALIEN, especially by an *enemy alien* (see under ALIEN). During a war, alien property within the jurisdiction of the United States is subject to seizure to prevent it from being used to support the enemy's war effort.

**3. immovable property** *Civil Law.* fixed property, such as property intended to be a permanent part of a farm or homestead. The term generally corresponds to the Anglo-American concept of *real property,* but includes leasehold interests in land (which are traditionally classified as *personal property* in England and the United States) and can include such things as farming equipment that is viewed as an integral part of a farm. Also called **immovables.**

**4. intangible property** a property right in something that does not have physical existence, such as a copyright or trademark, a contract right or CHOSE IN ACTION, or an insurance policy or ownership interest in a corporation (although the documents representing such interests are tangible property).

**5. intellectual property** copyrights, patents, and other rights in creations of the mind; also, the creations themselves, such as a literary work, painting, or computer program.

**6. like-kind property** in an exchange of business or investment property by a taxpayer, property of such a similar nature to that being given or received in exchange that the transaction is regarded as a non-event for tax purposes. See also LIKE-KIND EXCHANGE.

**7. movable property** *Civil Law.* property that is not fixed in place or intended to be a permanent part of immovable property. The term generally corresponds to the Anglo-American concept of *personal property;* but see discussion of *immovable property* for exceptions. Also called **movables**.

**8. personal property** all property other than *real property;* movable things (including animals in captivity, trees that have been cut down, coal that has been mined) and all intangible property. For historical reasons, a LEASEHOLD interest is often classified as personal property as well, even though it is an interest in land. Also called **personalty.** See also CHATTEL.

**9. real property** an interest in land or things attached to it, including buildings or other structures and substantial vegetation. Also called **realty** or **real estate,** and very often referred to simply as LAND. See also FIXTURE.

**10. tangible property** physical property; property that can be touched.

See also COMMON LAW STATE; COMMUNITY PROPERTY; COMMUNITY PROPERTY STATE; MARITAL PROPERTY; SCHEDULED PROPERTY; SEPARATE PROPERTY.

**property tax** *n.* a state or local tax imposed annually on owners of real or personal property within the state or municipality, based upon the value of the property. See also *assessed value* (under ASSESS).

**proponent** *n.* one who offers or proposes something; in particular, one who offers or presents evidence in a case, or offers a will for PROBATE.

**propria persona** *n.* See IN PROPRIA PERSONA.

**proprietary** *adj.* **1.** pertaining to ownership: *proprietary rights; proprietary interest.*
**2.** owned by someone; describing something with respect to which a particular person or entity has the right to control use or access: *proprietary drug; proprietary information.*
Cf. GENERIC.

**proprietary drug** *n.* See under DRUG.

**proprietorship** *n.* See SOLE PROPRIETORSHIP.

**prosecute** *v.,* prosecuted, prosecuting. **1.** to pursue a civil or criminal action against someone: *The plaintiff prosecuted her case with vigor. The state prosecuted the young defendant as an adult.*
**2.** to follow up or carry forward something begun: *to prosecute an appeal; prosecute a war; prosecute an application for a patent.*
—**prosecutability** *n.*
—**prosecutable** *adj.*

**prosecution** *n.* **1.** the act of prosecuting: *The prosecution of the case went smoothly.*
**2.** the attorney or group of attorneys involved in prosecuting a criminal case, or the party they represent (e.g., the STATE or the PEOPLE): *The prosecution moved for a restraining order.*
**3.** Also called **criminal prosecution.** a criminal case.
**4. civil prosecution** the bringing of a civil case by a private party, particularly under the RACKETEER INFLUENCED AND CORRUPT ORGANIZATIONS ACT, to remedy what the party (often a business entity) believes to be illegal conduct (often by a competitor) that has resulted in damage to the plaintiff.

**prosecution history** *n.* the history of proceedings in the United State Patent and Trademark Office with regard to a particular application for a patent. See also *prosecution history estoppel* (under ESTOPPEL).

**prosecutor** *n.* **1.** a public official whose job it is to oversee the prosecution of criminal cases in a particular jurisdiction; for example, a county attorney, DISTRICT ATTORNEY, or UNITED STATES ATTORNEY.
**2.** an attorney prosecuting a particular criminal case.
**3. independent** (or **special**) **prosecutor** an outside person appointed to investigate and, if necessary, prosecute a case in which there has been an allegation of criminal conduct, when the prosecutor who would normally handle

it has a CONFLICT OF INTEREST. This occurs most commonly in cases of wrongdoing in high state or federal office.

**prosecutorial** *adj.* of or pertaining to a prosecutor or prosecution: *prosecutorial misconduct.*

**prosecutorial discretion** *n.* See under DISCRETION.

**prosecutory** *adj.* of, pertaining to, or concerned with prosecution: *prosecutory power.*

**prospectus** *n., pl.* **prospectuses.** a document prepared by the issuer of a security giving detailed information about the security and the issuer, including information bearing upon the riskiness of the security as an investment.
——**Note.** Federal regulations determine what information must be included in a prospectus, require it to be accurate, and require the prospectus to be provided to each prospective purchaser of a new security being offered to the public.

**prostitution** *n.* the crime of engaging in sexual intercourse or other sexual activity for hire. See also PROMOTING PROSTITUTION.

**protected person** *n.* See under PERSON.

**protected speech** *n.* See under SPEECH.

**protection** *n.* See ADEQUATE PROTECTION.

**protection order** *n.* a court order that one person keep away from another, to protect the other from harassment and threatened harm—a difficult kind of order to enforce, as attested by repeated reports of women murdered by present or former husbands or lovers who had been ordered to stay away. Also called **order of protection.**

**protective order** *n.* a court order prohibiting a party to a case from engaging in procedures that unnecessarily annoy, burden, or embarrass the adversary. Such orders are usually granted to limit DISCOVERY that exceeds the needs of a case.

**protest** *n.* a formal written statement objecting to some action of another, made to preserve one's rights, lay the groundwork for a suit, and avoid any contention that by not speaking up one in effect consented to the action. See also UNDER PROTEST.
—**protestable** *adj.*

**prove** *v.,* **proved** or **proven, proving.** to establish (a fact, claim, or charge) by the applicable STANDARD OF PROOF.
—**provability** *n.*
—**provable** *adj.*
—**provably** *adv.*

**provided** *conj.* on the condition or understanding (that). See note at PROVISO.

**provisional** *adj.* temporary; interim; conditional.
—**provisionality** *n.*
—**provisionally** *adj.*

**provisional remedy** (or **relief**) *n.* See under REMEDY.

**proviso** *n., pl.* **provisos. 1.** a clause in a statute, contract, or the like, stating a condition that must be satisfied for the preceding term to be effective, or specifying an exception.
**2.** the stipulation or condition contained in such a clause.
——**Usage.** Provisos are typically introduced by the phrase "provided that..." or "provided, however, that...": *This merger agreement will take effect on January 1, provided that the shareholders of each company approve the merger at their annual meetings.*

**proximate** *adj.* close to in time, space, or causal connection; especially, sufficiently close in the chain of causation to justify a finding of tort liability. See PROXIMATE CAUSE.
—**proximately** *adv.*
—**proximateness** *n.*

**proximate cause** *n.* in tort cases, wrongful conduct by a defendant leading to the injury complained of in a sufficiently direct way to justify holding the defendant liable for the plaintiff's damages. Also called **efficient cause, legal cause.**
——**Note.** To recover for a tort, it is not enough to show that the defendant did something wrong and that the plaintiff

suffered some injury; it must also be shown that the wrong was a proximate cause of the injury. In the words of the eminent British legal scholar Sir Frederick Pollock—made famous by Judge Benjamin Cardozo when he quoted them in a leading American case—"Proof of negligence in the air, so to speak, will not do." *Palsgraf v. Long Island Railroad Co.* 248 N.Y. 339 (1928).

**proxy** *n., pl.* **proxies. 1.** an instrument authorizing one person to act on behalf of another, especially by voting or otherwise participating in a meeting.
**2.** the authority given by such an instrument.
**3.** Also called **proxy holder.** The person to whom the instrument and the authority are given.

**prurient interest** *n.* an unacceptable interest in sex. The Supreme Court has said that, for purposes of its current test of OBSCENITY, material appeals to prurient interest if it has "a tendency to excite lustful thoughts," that is, "sexual responses over and beyond those that would be characterized as normal." *Brockett v. Spokane Arcades, Inc.,* 472 U.S. 491 (1985).
——**Note.** Whether a work appeals to prurient interest is a question for the trier of fact (usually a jury) to determine from the point of view of "the average person, applying contemporary community standards" to the work "taken as a whole." *Miller v. California,* 413 U.S. 15 (1973).

**pseudonymous work** *n.* See under WORK.

**psychotherapist-client privilege** *n.* Same as PSYCHOTHERAPIST-PATIENT PRIVILEGE.

**psychotherapist-patient privilege** *n.* an *evidentiary privilege* (see under PRIVILEGE) by which a patient may prevent disclosure of information communicated to a physician or psychologist for the purpose of diagnosis and treatment of a mental or emotional condition, including drug addiction. Also called **therapist-patient privilege,** **psychotherapist-client privilege, therapist-client privilege.**

**public** *adj.* **1.** pertaining, belonging, or available generally to the people of a municipality, a state, or the United States, or to the government on their behalf, rather than to a specific and limited group of persons: *public record* (see under RECORD); *public property; public office.*
**2.** occurring in a place open to the public or to public view: *public intoxication; public lewdness.*
—*n.* **3.** the people of a community, state, or nation, collectively.
Cf. PRIVATE.
—**publicly** *adv.*

**public access** *n.* See under ACCESS.

**public accommodation** *n.* a place offering services to the general public, such as a hotel, restaurant, gas station, or theater. Federal civil rights laws prohibit discrimination on the basis of race, color, religion, or national origin in places of public accommodation.

**public accountant** *n.* See under ACCOUNTANT.

**public act** *n.* Same as PUBLIC LAW (def. 1).

**public bill** *n.* a legislative bill involving the general interests of the people at large or of the entire state or nation; a bill proposing a PUBLIC LAW.

**public capacity** *n.* See under CAPACITY.

**public contract** *n.* See under CONTRACT.

**public convenience and necessity** See CERTIFICATE OF CONVENIENCE AND NECESSITY.

**public corporation** *n.* See under CORPORATION.

**public defender** *n.* See under DEFENDER.

**public domain** *n.* **1.** the status of a work or invention upon which the copyright or patent has expired, or which never was protected by a copyright or patent; such a work is said to be "in the public domain" and may be copied or used by anyone.

**2.** land owned by the government.

**public easement** *n.* See under EASE-MENT.

**public enemy** *n.* See under ENEMY.

**public figure** *n.* **1.** an individual who is not a PUBLIC OFFICIAL but who is nevertheless intimately involved in the resolution of important public questions or who, by reason of the individual's fame, shapes events in areas of concern to society at large. Because of the importance of the First Amendment right to publish facts and opinions on matters of public concern, and because such individuals have in most cases intentionally subjected themselves to public attention, the law makes it more difficult for public figures than for ordinary people to recover for INVASION OF PRIVACY or DEFAMATION. In particular, public figures may not sustain actions for defamation on account of false statements about matters relevant to their public activities unless they can prove that the statements were made with *actual malice* (see discussion under MALICE).

**2. all-purpose public figure** an individual of general fame or notoriety in the community and pervasive involvement in the affairs of society; one of such persuasive power and influence in the culture at large that any statement at all about the individual is protected by the rule that bars public figures from recovering for defamation except upon a showing of actual malice. For example, a celebrity who is active in a wide range of political issues might be found to be a public figure for all purposes. Also called **general purpose public figure, general public figure.**

**3. involuntary public figure** an individual who has become a public figure through no purposeful action of her own. Although much of the news every day is about individuals thrust into prominence by sheer accident or happenstance, the concept of "involuntary public figure" is limited to those who do nothing at all to promote their public role and nevertheless have attained such prominence on an issue as to be

subject to criticism under the actual-malice rule. The Supreme Court has stated that such cases might "hypothetically" exist, but lower courts almost invariably find either that a plaintiff has voluntarily assumed a public role or that the plaintiff is not a public figure at all.

**4. limited purpose public figure** an individual who voluntarily injects himself or is drawn into a particular public controversy and thereby becomes a public figure for a limited range of issues. The actual-malice rule applies to any statements relevant to those issues. In most cases where the actual-malice rule is applied, it is because the plaintiff is found to be a limited purpose public figure. Also called **limited public figure.**

**public forum** *n.* a public place of a sort where people traditionally gather to express views and exchange ideas, such as a park, street, or sidewalk, or which the government has opened to such uses, such as a school that is open after hours for community activities. The Supreme Court has held that the First Amendment (see Appendix) precludes the government from banning speech or assembly in such areas, although the time, place, and manner of such activities can be regulated so long as the regulations do not restrict the content of the speech.

**public hearing** *n.* See under HEARING.

**public interest law** *n.* an area of legal practice that emphasizes the handling of cases of importance to the public at large rather than just to the individual litigants, such as cases concerning civil rights, the environment, or the political process. A commonly used procedure in such a practice is the *class action* (see under ACTION).

**public international law** *n.* See under INTERNATIONAL LAW.

**public law** *n.* **1.** Also called **public act, public statute.** a law or statute of a general character that applies to the people of a whole state or nation.

**2.** a branch of law dealing with the legal relationships between the state and individuals and with the relations among governmental agencies, including constitutional law, criminal law, and administrative law.

See also *public international law* (under INTERNATIONAL LAW). Cf. PRIVATE LAW.

**public necessity** *n.* See under NECESSITY.

**public nuisance** *n.* See under NUISANCE.

**public offering** *n.* See under OFFERING.

**public official** *n.* **1.** an individual elected or appointed to public office at any level of government. **2.** any government employee holding a position of responsibility or authority at any level of government. ——**Note.** The Supreme Court has held that public officials who sue critics of their official conduct for defamation may not prevail except upon a showing that the false statement complained of was made with *actual malice* (see under MALICE). But in doing so the Court refused to lay down an inflexible rule as to what officials were covered by this principle, saying: "We have no occasion here to determine how far down into the lower ranks of government employees the 'public official' designation would extend for purposes of this rule." *New York Times Co. v. Sullivan,* 376 U.S. 254 (1964).

**public policy** *n.* a general concept of public good that colors judicial decisions in every field: *In interpreting statutes, extending the common law, and enforcing (or refusing to enforce) private instruments, courts strive to do so in ways that are in harmony with "public policy" as they perceive it.* The concept arises particularly in contract law, because for most purposes a contract that violates "public policy" is void. This includes contracts whose performance would be criminal or tortious, and occasionally other contracts that the courts regard as immoral, unconscionable, or otherwise unworthy of enforcement.

**public statute** *n.* Same as PUBLIC LAW (def. 1).

**public trial** *n.* See under TRIAL.

**public trust** *n.* Same as *charitable trust* (see under TRUST).

**public use** See under USE.

**public wrong** *n.* See under WRONG.

**publication** *n.* the act of publishing. See PUBLISH. See also *service by publication* (under SERVICE).

**publicly held corporation** *n.* See under CORPORATION.

**publicly traded stock** *n.* See under STOCK.

**publish** *v.* **1.** in a general sense, to make public or distribute to the general public: *The rules require notice of the proceeding to be published in a newspaper of general circulation in the county on three occasions at least a week apart.* See also *service by publication* (under SERVICE). **2.** for purposes of the copyright law, to distribute a work to the public in tangible form, as by sale, rental, gift, or lending, or to offer copies to a group of persons for further distribution, public performance, or public display. Public performance or display alone, without distribution of the physical embodiment of the work, does not constitute publication of the work. **3.** to communicate a defamatory statement to a person other than the subject of the statement. There is no cause of action for libel or slander if the defamatory statement has not been "published" to a third person. **4.** to declare formally to witnesses that a document one is signing is one's will. "Publishing" one's will to the witnesses who sign it is one of the formalities that the law usually requires in an effort to avoid disputes after a person is dead over whether a document is in fact her will. **5.** to display evidence to a jury or make it available, as by passing it among them. **6.** to pass an instrument, especially a forged instrument, or present it for payment; to UTTER.
—**publishable** *adj.*
—**publisher** *n.*

——**False Friend.** Note that in many legal contexts *publish* does not mean "to make generally available to the public," but merely to make known to a very select group of individuals, or even just to one individual. The private and confidential communication of a defamatory statement to one person, for example, constitutes "publication" of the statement for purposes of an action for libel or slander.

**puffing** *n.* **1.** conventional sales talk expressing a high opinion of a product but not intended to be taken too literally; for example, "It's a great little car. You won't find a better one. You can't beat the price. I'm sure you'll be completely satisfied." The law does not regard such talk as legally binding. Cf. WARRANTY.
**2.** fictitious bidding at an auction for the purpose of running up the price; bidding pursuant to a secret understanding with the seller that one will not actually have to purchase the item if one's bid turns out to be the last and highest.
—**puffer** *n.*

**puisne** *adj. Law French.* (lit. "subsequently born") **1.** younger; junior; more recent; subordinate; inferior in rank. See also MULIER PUISNE.
**2. puisne judge** in English law, an associate judge of certain courts; any judge other than the chief judge.
—*n.* **3.** a puisne judge.
—**puisneship** *n.*
——**Pronunciation.** *Puisne* is the word from which *puny* is derived; in fact, the latter is just a respelling of the former to reflect the English pronunciation. But even though the two words are pronounced the same, when one is brought before a puisne judge in England, puns and witticisms about His Lordship's stature or physical stength are not recommended.

**Pullman abstention** *n.* See under ABSTENTION.

**pump and dump** *n. Informal.* a type of securities fraud in which a group of people acquire at very low cost most of the stock of a marginal, failing, or virtually nonexistent company, then artifically "pump" up the price of the stock through any of a variety of means including BOILER ROOM SALES and talking up the company on the Internet, and finally sell ("dump") their holdings at the artificially inflated price.

**punctilio** *n., pl.* **punctilios** for 1. **1.** a fine point, particular, or detail.
**2.** strictness or exactness in the observance of proper conduct or prescribed procedure: *Courts must be concerned with just results, rather than compliance with procedural punctilio as an end in itself.*
——**History.** One of the most famous passages in American law is a statement of Benjamin Cardozo, writing as Chief Judge of the New York Court of Appeals, on the nature of fiduciary duty. It was a paragraph of unusually high rhetoric even for one of the great rhetoricians of American jurisprudence, and included these oft-quoted sentences: "A trustee is held to something stricter than the morals of the market place. Not honesty alone, but the punctilio of an honor the most sensitive, is then the standard of behavior." *Meinhard v. Salmon,* 249 N.Y. 458, 464 (1928).

**punctum temporis** *n., pl.* **puncta temporis.** *Latin.* (lit. "point of time") **1.** a precise moment, such as the moment from which the time for performing some legal action is calculated.
**2.** in a series of events, the key point at which legal relations change or legal consequences accrue; especially, the moment at which a TAKING is deemed to have occurred.
**3.** a span of time deemed too small to be significant, so that events occurring within that time may be regarded as simultaneous. For many purposes, the law treats a day as punctum temporis.

**punishment** *n.* See SENTENCE; CAPITAL PUNISHMENT.

**punitive damages** *n.pl.* See under DAMAGES.

**pur autre vie** See *estate* (or *tenancy*) *pur autre vie* (under ESTATE[1]).

**purchase** *n., v.,* **purchased, purchasing.** —*n.* **1.** in the most common usage, acquisition of rights or property of any kind, or an interest in property, by promising or giving something in exchange, usually money. See also GOOD FAITH PURCHASER; STRAW PURCHASE; STRAW PURCHASER.
**2.** as used in the UNIFORM COMMERCIAL CODE, the term also includes receipt of a negotiable instrument or a gift.
**3.** in its most general and traditional legal sense, "purchase" means any acquisition of an interest in property other than by INTESTATE SUCCESSION, and thus includes acquisition by gift or by will as well as by giving value. See also WORDS OF PURCHASE.
—*v.* **4.** to buy.
—**purchasability** *n.*
—**purchasable** *adj.*
—**purchaser** *n.*

**purchase money** *n.* the price to be paid for the purchase of something; money promised in payment.

**purchase money mortgage** *n.* See under MORTGAGE.

**purchase money security interest** *n.* a *security interest* (see under INTEREST[1]) in property—especially consumer goods—sold on credit or purchased with borrowed money, taken by the seller or lender as security for payment of the purchase price or repayment of the loan used to make the purchase.

**purge** *v.,* **purged, purging.** to remedy a CONTEMPT. For example, after a person has been jailed for refusing to testify in a case despite a court order to do so, she can change her mind and obey the order to testify; this is said to "purge the contempt" or "purge her of the contempt," and secures her release from jail.

**purposely** *adv.* with INTENT (def. 2).

**pursuit of happiness** *n.* a phrase from the Declaration of Independence, often erroneously thought to appear in the Constitution. The phrase is often used for rhetorical effect in legal arguments and occasionally appears in judicial opinions, but it has no specific or generally agreed-upon legal meaning.

**putative** *adj.* alleged; supposed; seeming: *putative father; putative marriage.*

# Q

**qiyas** or **kiyas** *n. Islamic Law.* analogy; reasoning by analogy; the judging of an act or belief by application of established principles governing some analogous act or belief. Qiyas, by which principles of the KORAN and the SUNNA were extended to situations not expressly addressed in the Koran and Sunna, is one of the four generally accepted sources of Islamic law and jurisprudence (see USUL AL-FIQH). See also IJTIHAD.

**quaere** *v. imperative. Latin.* (lit. "You must ask," "you should question") **1.** ask; question. **a.** (used to introduce a question, especially a hypothetical question): *Quaere: Should the manufacturer have anticipated that the user would ignore the safety warnings printed on the product?* **b.** (used to cast doubt on, or raise a question about, a proposition, especially a stated or suggested proposition of law): *Quaere the court's statement that a husband can never be guilty of raping his wife. Quaere whether the decision would have been the same if the husband and wife had been separated.*
—*n.* **2.** a query; a question.
——**Pronunciation.** Pronounced, and now often written, the same as the English word QUERY, which is derived from this Latin word.

**qualification¹** *n.* **1.** a necessary or desirable quality for one holding or aspiring to a particular position or status; in particular, a quality required by law for a person or organization to hold a certain status, power, or office. See also BONA FIDE OCCUPATIONAL QUALIFICATION; VOTER QUALIFICATION.
**2.** the act of taking the necessary steps to attain or become qualified for a position or status; especially, the taking of those steps required by law to acquire some legally recognized power or status.

**qualification²** *n.* **1.** a limitation or condition.
**2.** the act or process of limiting or imposing a condition.

**qualified¹** *adj.* **1.** having the qualities, accomplishments, etc., that fit a person for some function, office, or the like: *a qualified applicant for a job opening.* Opposite: UNQUALIFIED or, very rarely, NONQUALIFIED. See note at NONQUALIFIED.
**2.** having a certain legal status or entitled to certain legal benefits, such as special tax treatment, as a result of satisfying legal requirements, taking legally required actions, possessing legally prescribed characteristics, and the like. See *qualified pension plan* (under PENSION PLAN). Opposite: NONQUALIFIED.

**qualified²** *adj.* limited, conditional. See *qualified immunity* (under IMMUNITY); *qualified indorsement* (under INDORSEMENT); *qualified privilege* (under PRIVILEGE). Opposite: UNQUALIFIED.
—**qualifiedly** *adv.*

**qualify¹** *v.,* **qualified, qualifying. 1.** to be fitted or competent for something: *qualify for a job.*
**2.** to take the necessary steps to achieve some status; especially, to take the steps required by law to acquire some legally recognized power or status: *qualify as a licensed driver.*
**3.** to certify as possessing the necessary qualifications; certify as legally competent: *qualify bidders for a contract.*
**4. qualify as an executor** to post a bond or take such other steps as a state requires before a person designated in a will as an executor may begin managing and distributing the decedent's property.
**5. qualify as an expert** (or **expert**

354

**witness**) to demonstrate to the satisfaction of the court that one has sufficient training and experience to be permitted to express expert opinions on a particular issue in a trial. See also VOIR DIRE (def. 2).

**6. qualify for tax-exempt status** to file necessary documents and obtain certification from the Internal Revenue Service showing that a non-profit organization is not subject to taxation under the Internal Revenue Code.

**7. qualify to do business** (of a corporation) to register with the Secretary of State of a state other than the state of incorporation, so as to be authorized to do business in the new state.
—**qualifiable** *adj.*

**qualify**[2] *v.*, **qualified, qualifying.** to limit; place conditions on.
—**qualifiable** *adj.*

**quantum meruit** *n. Latin.* (lit. "so much as he deserved") **1.** a cause of action for the reasonable value of services rendered, or occasionally of goods or materials provided, under circumstances in which there was no enforceable contract to pay for them, or to pay a specific price for them, but it would be unfair to leave the plaintiff uncompensated.
**2.** the measure of recovery in such an action; that is, the reasonable value of the services or goods provided as found by the court.
See also COMMON COUNTS; QUASI CONTRACT; RESTITUTION; UNJUST ENRICHMENT.

**quantum valebant** *n. Latin.* (lit. "so much as they were worth") **1.** a cause of action for the reasonable value of goods sold or provided, under circumstances in which there was no enforceable contract to pay for them, or to pay a specific price for them, but the evidence shows that there was an intent to pay for them or the circumstances are such that it would be unfair to leave the plaintiff uncompensated.
**2.** the measure of recovery in such an action; that is, the reasonable value of the goods in question.
See also COMMON COUNTS.

**quantum valebat** *n. Latin.* (lit. "so much as it was worth") Same as QUANTUM VALEBANT, but applicable only to a single item. See also COMMON COUNTS.

**quare** *conj., adv. Latin.* whereby; wherefore; why.

**quare clausum fregit** *Latin.* whereby he broke the CLOSE. See also *trespass quare clausum fregit* (under TRESPASS[2]), where the fictional nature of this phrase is discussed.

**quash** *v.* to nullify a previously issued legal process or order, such as a summons, warrant, or injunction. See also SET ASIDE; VACATE.

**quasi** *Latin.* (lit. "as if," "a sort of") a word or prefix placed in front of a legal term to mean "resembling, but different from in some legally insignificant respect."

**quasi contract** *n.* **1.** a *contract implied in law* (see under CONTRACT).
**2.** a name for any claim for RESTITUTION, particularly a claim in QUANTUM MERUIT.
—**quasi-contractual** *adj.*

**quasi in rem** *Latin.* (lit. "as if directed at the thing") describing the fundamental character of a legal proceeding as being, in form, directed at a piece of property, but in substance, directed at the owner of the property. For details, see *quasi in rem action* (under ACTION); *quasi in rem jurisdiction* (under JURISDICTION[1]). Cf. IN PERSONAM; IN REM.

**quasi-suspect classification** *n.* a law's CLASSIFICATION of people into categories regarded by the Supreme Court as requiring HEIGHTENED SCRUTINY, but not STRICT SCRUTINY, under the EQUAL PROTECTION clause of the Fourteenth Amendment (see Appendix).
——**Note.** So far, the only classifications deemed to call for this level of SCRUTINY are those that discriminate on the basis of sex or ILLEGITIMACY. Cf. SUSPECT CLASSIFICATION. See also note at HEIGHTENED SCRUTINY.

**Queen's Bench** *n.* See under KING'S BENCH.

**query** *n., pl.* **queries,** *v.,* **queried, que-rying.** —*n.* **1.** a question.
—*v.* **2.** to raise a question.
**3.** to call into question.
See also QUAERE.

**question¹** *n.* **1.** something asked at a trial, hearing, or deposition, or in investigating an incident or crime. Cf. INTERROGATORY.
**2. argumentative question** a question, usually during cross-examination or examination of a hostile witness, in which the questioner improperly advances theories or arguments about the facts and testimony rather than simply eliciting factual testimony and reserving argument about it for the summation. Examples include questions that incorporate or inquire about inferences from the facts in evidence; questions that assume a fact not in evidence; questions designed to engage the witness in argument; and "questions" that are really statements about the evidence or commentary—often sarcastic—about the witness's previous answers.
**3. compound question** a combination of two or more questions into one; for example, "Did she speed through a red light?" instead of "Did she go through a red light? Was she speeding?" Compound questions can be confusing and misleading, and are therefore objectionable.
**4. hypothetical question a.** a question in which a witness is asked to assume certain facts and express an opinion based upon that assumption. This is permitted with expert witnesses if the assumed facts are related to the evidence in the case and the opinion sought is within the scope of the witness's expertise, but it is generally not allowed with fact witnesses. **b.** such a question as posed by a law professor to law students, to make them think about how slight changes in the facts of a case can alter the legal principles that apply and the legal conclusions that follow; referred to informally as a **hypothetical.** See also SOCRATIC METHOD.
**5. leading question** a question

phrased so as to suggest the desired answer. Except for routine preliminary questions intended to introduce a topic, this is generally forbidden in direct examination but allowed in cross-examination and in examining a *hostile witness* (see under WITNESS). Examples: "What color was the light?" is nonleading; "The light was red, wasn't it?" is leading. "Was the light red?" might be either, depending on the context.
**6. special questions** See under VERDICT.
—*v.* **7.** to ask questions of: *to question a witness; question a suspect.* Cf. the more specialized terms EXAMINE; INQUIRE; *interrogate* (under INTERROGATION).
**8.** to ask questions about; express doubt about: *to question the rationale for a decision; question the adequacy of the remedy.*
—**questionability** *n.*
—**questionable** *adj.*
—**questionably** *adv.*
—**questioning** *adj., n.*
—**questioningly** *adv.*

**question²** *n.* **1. Same as** ISSUE¹ (see discussion at ISSUE¹, def. 1).
**2. mixed question of fact and law** an issue in which facts and law are intertwined; for example, whether the defendant's conduct, as to which witnesses gave varying accounts, was "negligent" as that term is defined in law. In a jury case, such questions are typically submitted to the jury, but with careful instructions from the judge as to the law.
**3. political question** an issue that the courts will refuse to decide on the ground that it is of a type committed by the Constitution to the legislative or executive branch of government, rather than the judicial branch.
**4. question** (or **issue**) **of fact** a dispute over what circumstances and events have actually occurred or are likely to occur. In a jury trial, such questions are submitted to the jury for decision.
**5. question** (or **issue**) **of law** an issue concerning interpretation of law. These questions are decided by the

judge rather than the jury.

**6. questions presented** a formal section in an appellate brief or petition, stating the precise issues that the appellate court is being asked to consider. See also *constitutional question* (under CONSTITUTIONAL); FEDERAL QUESTION.

**qui tam** *n. Latin.* (lit. "who both") a civil action brought by a private citizen pursuant to a statute that defines certain conduct as illegal and authorizes private suits against violators to collect a penalty, which is to be divided between the plaintiff (also called the RELATOR) and the state. Thus the relator brings the action both for herself and for the state.

**Quia Emptores** *Latin.* (lit. "Because purchasers...") a statute of Edward I in 1290, prohibiting SUBINFEUDATION, and in its place granting tenants in fee the right to sell or transfer their interests in whole or in part. The purchaser of any part of such a fee, unlike one who acquired an interest by subinfeudation, held the acquired land directly of the seller's lord, and owed that lord a proportionate amount of the services previously owed by the seller. Also called **Quia Emptores Terrarum** ("Because purchasers of lands..."), **Statute Quia Emptores, Statute of Quia Emptores.** —**History.** Before Quia Emptores, every tenant in fee could become in his turn a lord, by granting the fee to another who would then hold of him and owe him feudal services. After the statute, a purchaser of any part of his fee would hold it not of the seller but of the seller's lord, and would owe to that lord a proportionate amount of the services previously owed by the seller. This fundamentally altered the nature of the feudal system and made alienability a feature of ownership in fee.

**quid pro quo** *n. Latin.* (lit. "What for what?") **1.** an informal expression, used more by nonlawyers than by lawyers, for CONSIDERATION in a contract. **2.** something demanded or expected, legally or illegally, in exchange for a favor, concession, or performance; for example, ransom demanded by a kidnapper in exchange for release of the victim, or a favorable vote expected from a corrupt legislator in exchange for a bribe. See also *quid pro quo harassment* (under SEXUAL HARASSMENT).

**quiet enjoyment** *n.* **1.** the use and possession of real property free from interference or dispossession by someone with a superior right to the property. **2. covenant** (or **warranty**) **of quiet enjoyment** the express or implied promise of a landlord or grantor of real property that no one with superior title will come along and put the lessee or grantee out of possession. Also called **covenant of warranty.**

**quiet title** *v.* to remove uncertainties about one's title to real property by bringing an action (called an "action to quiet title") against others who may have some claim to the property, challenging them to prove any claim they have or be forever barred from asserting any claim to the property. See also CLOUD ON TITLE.

**quit** *v.,* **quit** or **quitted, quitting. 1.** to remove oneself from (real property); vacate: *The the tenant was served with notice to quit the premises.* Cf. DISPOSSESS. **2.** to cease, release, give up, depart from generally: *She quit her job.* —**Usage.** The traditional past tense for the sense of vacating land is *quitted: He quitted the property at the end of the term.* This usage waned in the second half of the twentieth century, but it still occurs and is still perfectly acceptable.

**quitclaim** *n.* **1.** abandonment of a claim (for example, to land, or against another person), or a document given as evidence of such abandonment. —*v.* **2.** to abandon a claim. See also *quitclaim deed* (under DEED).

**quo warranto** *n. Latin.* (lit. "by what authority") **1.** a judicial proceeding brought by the state to determine whether a person or entity purporting to act in a public capacity has the legal authority to do so. **2.** a writ by which such a proceeding traditionally was commenced, directing the defendant to appear and produce evidence of his authority.

**quorum** *n.*, *pl.* **quorums.** the number of members of a legislative body or other group or organization required to be present to transact business legally.
—**Note.** Under the Constitution, a majority of the members of the Senate or House of Representatives constitutes a quorum.

**quota** *n.*, *pl.* **quotas. 1.** a share or proportional part of a total that is allocated to a particular district, state, person, group, institution, etc.
**2.** the number or percentage of persons of a specified kind permitted or sought to enroll in a college, join a club, immigrate to a country, etc.
**3.** a minimum, maximum, or target number or amount.

**quotient verdict** *n.* See under VER-DICT.

**Qur'an** *n.* See KORAN.

# R

® a symbol used to identify a name or design as a *registered mark* (see under MARK). Cf. SM; TM.

—**Note.** The registered mark symbol serves both as an assurance to consumers that the product or service with which the mark is associated is made or provided or approved by the company or organization identified with the mark, and as a warning to other companies or organizations that they may not use that mark.

**race** *n.* as used in the Constitution and civil rights laws, a term generally applicable to any grouping on the basis of race, ancestry, or ethnicity. As used in the Fifteenth Amendment (see Appendix), the term also includes national origin.

**racial animus** *n.* See under ANIMUS.

**racial discrimination** *n.* discrimination on the basis of racial or ethnic identification or ancestry. See also SEPARATE BUT EQUAL; STRICT SCRUTINY.

**racial profiling** *n.* the use of race or ethnicity as a factor in a *criminal profile* (see under PROFILE), or in determining to make a traffic stop or take other police action with respect to an individual, except in cases where a specific suspect has been described by race or ethnicity. See also DRIVING WHILE BLACK.

**racial segregation** *n.* See under SEGREGATION.

**racially restrictive covenant** *n.* See under COVENANT.

**Racketeer Influenced and Corrupt Organizations Act (RICO)** a federal statute enacted in 1970 and subsequently copied in many state statutes (informally called "Little Rico" statutes), designed to attack organized crime by providing special criminal penalties and civil liabilities for persons who engage in, or derive money from, repeated instances of certain types of crime.

—**Note.** RICO permits persons who are injured by conduct covered by the statute to sue the wrongdoers for *treble damages* (see under DAMAGES). This has provided an opportunity for many plaintiffs, with a little artful pleading, to turn what used to be routine tort claims for fraud into treble damage actions for "racketeering," much to the dismay of mainstream corporate defendants who chafe at being labeled "racketeers."

**raise** *v.,* **raised, raising. 1.** to invoke or bring into being: *to raise a defense; to raise the bar of statute of limitations; circumstances sufficient to raise a presumption of knowledge.*

**2.** to increase fraudulently the face amount of a financial instrument: *a raised check.*

**RAM** *n., pl.* **RAMs, RAM's.** *reverse annuity mortgage* (see under MORTGAGE).

**ransom** *n.* **1.** money paid to secure the release of a kidnapped person.

—*v.* **2.** to secure the release of a kidnapped person by paying ransom. See also KIDNAPPING.

**rape** *n., v.,* **raped, raping.** —*n.* **1.** at common law, unlawful carnal knowledge of a woman by force and without her consent. See note below.

**2.** in modern usage generally, the crime of forcing or causing a person to submit to sexual intercourse (whether vaginal, oral, or anal) against his or her will, or when consent is obtained by unfair and unlawful means (as by putting a drug in a drink), or under circumstances in which the person is incapable of giving legally valid consent (as with a person who is unconscious or UNDERAGE). The terminology for such offenses, and the exact range of conduct covered by each term used (such as "rape," "sexual assault," "sexual imposition," or "forcible sodomy") varies from state to state. See also PENETRATION.

**3. acquaintance rape** rape by someone known to the victim, such as a friend of the family or a former lover.

**4. date rape** rape by a person with whom the victim is on a date. Like *acquaintance rape*, this term was coined to draw attention to the fact that such rapes are more frequent than previously recognized, and traditionally prosecuted less consistently and with less vigor than rapes by strangers.

**5. forcible rape** rape effected through force or threat of force, or by rendering the victim incapable of resistance through administration of a drug.

**6. marital rape** rape by the victim's spouse. Also called **spousal rape.** See note below.

**7. statutory rape** the crime of having sexual intercourse with a person (or at least with a female) below the AGE OF CONSENT. In 1981 the Supreme Court held that statutory rape laws may constitutionally discriminate on the basis of sex, upholding the conviction of a 17½-year-old male for having sex with a 16½-year-old female under a statutory rape law that made sexual intercourse by an unmarried couple under the age of 18 a crime for the male but not for the female. *Michael M. v. Superior Court of Sonoma County,* 450 U.S. 464 (1981). See also *strict liability* (under LIABILITY).

—*v.* **8.** to commit a rape upon someone.

——**History.** The common law could not conceive of a situation in which sexual intercourse with one's wife could be unlawful; hence at common law the crime of rape could only be committed upon a woman other than one's wife. In the oft-cited words of renowned seventeenth century English jurist Sir Matthew Hale, "the husband cannot be guilty of a rape committed by himself upon his lawful wife, for by their mutual matrimonial consent and contract the wife hath given up herself in this kind unto her husband." This view prevailed in the United States until 1977,

when Oregon became the first state to make forced sex with one's spouse a crime. Within fifteen years thereafter, all states, either by legislation or by judicial decision, had eliminated marriage as an affirmative defense to a charge of forcible rape, although in some states the rules and penalties applicable to such charges are somewhat different from those that apply in cases of rape by a stranger. The modern view is that if one spouse finds the other's refusal to have sex intolerable, the remedy is not force, but divorce.

**rape shield law** *n.* a statute that limits or prohibits questioning or evidence about the sexual history of the victim in a rape case. Also called **rape victim shield law.**

**ratify** *v.,* **ratified, ratifying.** to manifest approval of a previous action by oneself or another so as to make it legally binding. Cf. AVOID.
—**ratification** *n.*
——**Note.** For example, treaties negotiated by the President must be ratified by the Senate; constitutional amendments adopted by Congress must be ratified by three-quarters of the states; a contract entered into by a party under legal age may be ratified by that party after reaching legal age; a contract entered into on behalf of a principal by an agent who lacked authority to do so may be ratified by the principal. In the contract situations, ratification may be either express (by announcing one's intent to adhere to the contract) or implied (by continuing to perform under the contract or by accepting benefits under it).

**ratio decidendi** *n., pl.* **rationes decidendi.** *Latin.* (lit. "reason for deciding") the rationale for a judicial decision; the rule or principle upon which the decision is based.

**rational basis test** *n.* the level of SCRUTINY applied to a law whose constitutionality is challenged as a violation of due process when no FUNDAMENTAL RIGHT is at stake, or as a violation of EQUAL PROTECTION when the challenged CLASSIFICATION is not one that the Supreme Court has recognized as meriting HEIGHTENED SCRUTINY or STRICT SCRUTINY. Under this test, a law will be upheld so long as it has a "rational basis" or is "rationally related" to a legitimate governmental purpose. Also called **rational relationship test.**

——**Note.** The Supreme Court has said that under this test "A statutory discrimination will not be set aside if any state of facts reasonably may be conceived to justify it." Findings of unconstitutionality under this test are extremely rare.

**re** *prep.* regarding; concerning: *Memo to Mr. Smith re year-end inventory.* See also IN RE.

**read law** to acquire legal training by self-education and apprenticeship to a lawyer rather than attendance at a law school.

——**History.** Although the nation's first law school—Harvard—was founded in 1817, reading law remained the primary path to becoming a lawyer in the United States until very much later. Cf. note at LAW SCHOOL.

**ready, willing, and able buyer** *n.* See under BUYER.

**real chattel** *n.* See under CHATTEL.

**real estate** *n.* Same as *real property* (see under PROPERTY).

**real estate broker** *n.* See under BROKER.

**real evidence** *n.* See under EVIDENCE.

**real party in interest** *n.* See under PARTY.

**real property** *n.* See under PROPERTY.

**realism** *n.* See LEGAL REALISM.
—**realist** *n., adj.*
—**realistic** *adj.*
—**realistically** *adv.*

**realize** *v.,* **realized, realizing.** to receive something of value from a transaction, especially from a sale or exchange of property. For income tax purposes, the amount realized includes the money received plus the market value of any property or services received. The amount by which this exceeds or falls

short of the taxpayer's BASIS in the property transferred is the realized gain or loss. See also RECOGNIZE.
—**realizable** *adj.*

**Realtor** *n.* **1.** *Service Mark.* a real estate agent who is a member of the National Association of Realtors.

**2. realtor** a real estate agent or broker; a person who deals in realty.

——**Usage.** The word *realtor* was coined in 1916 as a term to be used in connection with brokerage of real estate and related services by members of what was then called the National Association of Real Estate Boards. The term caught on only too well: In very short order it began to be used as a generic term for real estate agents—whether or not they belonged to the Association or met its standards. The Association registered the word as a COLLECTIVE MARK in 1948, but the tide of usage in a generic sense has proved impossible to stop.

**realty** *n.* Same as *real property* (under PROPERTY).

**reapportionment** *n.* **1.** the act of redistributing or changing the APPORTIONMENT of something.

**2.** Also called **redistricting.** an adjustment of *legislative apportionment* (see under APPORTIONMENT); the redistribution of representation and redrawing of legislative district lines after a CENSUS in order to comply with the rule of ONE PERSON, ONE VOTE.

**reargument** *n.* **1.** a second round of argument, or sometimes of briefing and argument, held by a court on a matter previously argued and submitted. Occasionally this is requested by the court because it wants further discussion of certain points before deciding a motion or appeal; more often (but still rarely) it is permitted at the request of the losing party after the matter has been decided, upon a showing that the court may have misunderstood or overlooked an important point. Also called **rehearing** or, when requested by the losing party after a decision has been rendered, **reconsideration.**

**2. reargument** (or **rehearing** or **reconsideration**) **en banc** reargument before all the judges of a court, of a matter previously heard and decided by a panel of some of them. This is occasionally permitted in matters of particular importance. See also EN BANC.

**reasonable** *adj.* **1.** appropriate in view of the circumstances; legally sufficient: *reasonable notice; reasonable search.* See also *reasonable care* (see under CARE); *reasonable reliance* (see under RELIANCE).
**2.** having a basis in fact or evidence; sensible; not arbitrary and capricious or purely speculative: *reasonable belief; reasonable exercise of discretion.* See also BEYOND A REASONABLE DOUBT.
**3. reasonable person** a person of ordinary intelligence and prudence. Traditionally referred to as a **reasonable man,** this is an imaginary person who sets the standard by which the defendant's conduct is evaluated in a negligence case: If a reasonable person would have done the same thing the defendant did in the same situation, then the defendant was not negligent. See also OBJECTIVE TEST.
**—reasonableness** *n.*
**—reasonably** *adv.*

**reasonable doubt** *n.* See BEYOND A REASONABLE DOUBT.

**rebut** *v.,* **rebutted, rebutting. 1.** to present evidence or argument to overcome or weaken the evidence or argument previously presented by an adversary.
**2.** to present evidence to overcome a *rebuttable presumption* (see under PRESUMPTION).
**—rebuttable** *adj.*

**rebuttal** *n.* **1.** broadly, the presentation of any evidence or argument in response to that of an adversary, or to overcome a PRESUMPTION.
**2.** specifically, a *rebuttal case* (see under CASE²).
**—adj. 3.** presented for purposes of rebuttal: *rebuttal case; rebuttal evidence; rebuttal witness.*

**recall** *v.* **1.** to vacate a previous order or judgment of the same court, especially because of a factual error.
**2.** to call a witness who previously testified in a case back to the stand for further testimony.
**3.** to remove an elected official from office before expiration of her term, by a special vote of the people.

**receivable** *adj.* **1.** (of evidence) Same as ADMISSIBLE.
**2.** owed to oneself by another: *accounts receivable.*
**—n. 3.** Same as ACCOUNT RECEIVABLE.

**receive** *v.,* **received, receiving.** to admit into evidence, especially in a non-jury case: *Exhibit 12 will be received.*

**receiver** *n.* a person appointed by a court to take over and manage property that is the subject of judicial proceedings—often the property or business of an insolvent debtor—and ultimately to dispose of it in accordance with the court's judgment.

**receivership** *n.* a proceeding in which a RECEIVER is appointed to preserve and distribute assets of an insolvent debtor.

**receiving stolen property** *n.* the crime of receiving, retaining, or disposing of property that one knows was stolen. It includes purchase, fencing, and receipt by gift.

**recess** *n.* **1.** a brief break in a trial or hearing: *a 15–minute recess.*
**2.** a lengthy period during which a court holds no sessions: *The Supreme Court is in recess from July through September.*
**—v. 3.** to take a recess: *We will recess for the weekend.*

**recidivist** *n.* a person who, after being convicted of a crime and serving a sentence or being released, commits the same kind of crime again.
**—recidivism** *n.*

**reciprocal beneficiary** *n.* in at least two states, one of two individuals who have entered into a formal, legally recognized relationship (called in Hawaii a **reciprocal beneficiary relationship** and in Vermont a **reciprocal beneficiaries relationship**) providing certain benefits of marriage, particularly in regard to rights of hospital visitation, health care decision-making, consent to the making of anatomical gifts, and the like.

——**Note.** The purpose of the concept of reciprocal beneficiary is to extend certain decision-making and emotional rights of spouses to individuals who are barred from marriage by closeness of relationship (for example, two siblings or a parent and an adult child), or by reason of being the same sex. In Vermont, the concept does not extend to the latter category because they can obtain the same rights by entering into a CIVIL UNION.

**reciprocal will** *n.* See under WILL.

**reciprocity** *n.* a relationship between two entities, as two universities or two states of the United States, in which each grants certain rights to the other entity or its people in exchange for equivalent rights for itself and its own people. For example, two states might agree to share certain kinds of information with each other, or to allow each other's lawyers to be admitted to their own bar without having to take a second bar examination.

**recital** *n.* a formal statement of fact or of a reason or purpose for taking certain action, typically appearing at the beginning of a contract or other instrument and introduced by the word "Whereas."

——**Note.** An instrument may have many recitals or none; they are not an operative part of an instrument, but may help in understanding and interpreting it.

**reckless disregard** *n.* **1.** concious disregard of the risks one's conduct poses to others; RECKLESSNESS.

**2. reckless disregard of truth or falsity** publication of a defamatory statement despite a high degree of awareness of its probable falsity, or at least serious doubts as to its truth. Also called **reckless disregard of the truth, reckless disregard for the truth.** See also *actual malice* (under MALICE).

**recklessness** *n.* conscious disregard of the safety or the rights of others. See also RECKLESS DISREGARD; STATE OF MIND.

—**reckless** *adj.*
—**recklessly** *adv.*

——**Note.** Sometimes the term "recklessness" is used as just another word for NEGLIGENCE, but usually it signifies a higher degree of culpability. To be negligent, it is enough that one fail to perceive a risk that a reasonably careful person would have perceived; to be reckless is to be aware of a significant risk to others and proceed anyway. But recklessness is a less culpable mental state than KNOWLEDGE, which is an awareness not just of a risk that something bad might happen, but of the near certainty that it will.

**recognition** *n.* **1.** the act of recognizing gain or loss for income tax purposes. See RECOGNIZE (def. 1).
**2.** *International Law.* an official act by which the government of one nation acknowledges the existence and legal authority of another nation or government.
**3.** Same as ASSIZE (def. 2).

**recognitor** *n.* a juror in an ASSIZE.

**recognizance** *n.* See RELEASE ON OWN RECOGNIZANCE.

**recognize** *v.*, **recognized, recognizing.**
**1.** to include, or be required to include, a gain or loss in one's income tax calculations. Usually a gain or loss is recognized in the year in which it is received (see REALIZE), but in special circumstances a gain may be realized in one year but not recognized until a later year, or perhaps never recognized at all.
**2.** *International Law.* (of a national government) to acknowledge the existence and legal authority of another nation or of a new government of such a nation; to grant RECOGNITION to.
—**recognizability** *n.*
—**recognizable** *adj.*

**recollection** *n.* **1.** memory; ability to remember; remembered facts.
**2. hypnotically refreshed recollection** facts supposedly brought forth from a witness's repressed or forgotten memory through hypnosis. Since hypnosis is as likely to create a memory as

to refresh it, testimony based upon such a procedure is normally inadmissible. See also note at RECOVERED MEMORY.

**3. past recollection recorded** a written record of an event, prepared or reviewed by a witness while the event was fresh in her mind. If the witness can no longer recall the details of the event by the time of the trial, but can recall writing or reviewing that record and for that reason can swear that it is true, then the contents of the writing may be admitted into evidence and read to the jury. Also called **recorded recollection.**

**4. present recollection refreshed** facts about an event that a witness at the trial cannot recall when first asked, but can recall when shown something that jogs her memory. Anything at all can be used to refresh a witness's memory, but the most common item is a writing containing the details she could not remember. If, after seeing the item as a refresher, the witness recalls the details, she can then testify to her recollection. The material used to jog her memory does not come into evidence. Also called **refreshed recollection.**

**reconsideration** *n.* See under REARGUMENT.

**reconsideration en banc** *n.* See under REARGUMENT.

**Reconstruction amendments** *n.pl.* Same as CIVIL WAR AMENDMENTS.

**record** *n.* **1.** generally, any writing or set of writings setting forth the facts of an event or series of events, made as the events happen or shortly thereafter and intended to be preserved as a reliable account for future reference. **2.** in a judicial or administrative action, **a.** the transcript of a deposition, trial, hearing, or argument. **b.** a full set of the papers, orders, and judgments filed, transcripts made, and evidence offered in a case. **c.** Also called **record on appeal.** those portions of the full record of a case that may be considered by the reviewing court in connection with an appeal. See also DEHORS. **3. books and records** See under

BOOK. **4. business record** a record made and kept in accordance with the normal practice of a business or organization, from information provided by an individual with personal knowledge of the event recorded. Such records are normally admissible into evidence under a *hearsay exception* (see under HEARSAY). **5. criminal record a.** an individual's history of arrests and convictions on one or more criminal charges. **b.** a written summary of such a history. **6. for the record** describing something said or done, especially in a case, not in the expectation that it will produce any immediate benefit, but in order to preserve a right or argument for the future. **7. make a record** to say or do something *for the record.* Failure to make a record on an issue may constitute an *implied waiver* (see under WAIVER). **8. of record** recorded; contained in a record: *attorney of record* (see under ATTORNEY); *owner of record* (see under OWNER). See also *court of record* (under COURT). **9. off the record** describing informal discussion that the court reporter in a proceeding is requested not to take down. **10. on the record** describing anything said in a proceeding that is taken down by the court reporter. **11. public record** any record, investigative report, or compilation of information or data created by a public office or agency pursuant to its legal authority or duties. Such records are usually admitted into evidence under a *hearsay exception* (see under HEARSAY). **12. spread upon the record** to include something in the record of a case; to make sure something is clear from the record. —*v.* **13.** to make a record of; especially, to file a deed, security agreement, or other instrument creating or transferring an interest in property with a county clerk or other designated public official so as to put the general public on notice of it.

See also TITLE RECORDING SYSTEM.

—**recordable** *adj.*
—**recordation** *n.*

**record owner** *n.* See under OWNER.

**recorded delivery** *n.* a service available for international mail that has substantially the same features as those provided within the United States by *certified mail* (see under CERTIFY).

**recorded recollection** *n.* Same as *past recollection recorded* (see under RECOLLECTION).

**recourse** *n.* **1.** resort or access to a person or thing for help, or the person or thing resorted to.
**2.** the right to receive payment on a negotiable instrument from the drawer or any previous indorser if the instrument is dishonored. For example, if A draws a check payable to the order of B, who indorses it to the order of C, and the check bounces when C deposits it, C ordinarily has a right of recourse against both A and B. A negotiable instrument confers no such liability upon a drawer or indorser who adds the words "without recourse" to her signature; the instrument is then a NONRECOURSE instrument and subsequent holders are said to take it **without recourse.**
**3.** the right to repayment of a loan from the borrower personally, out of any available assets she has.
See *recourse loan* and cf. *nonrecourse loan* (both under LOAN).

**recover** *v.* **1.** to obtain through litigation—usually by way of judgment, but sometimes through settlement; usually money or property, but sometimes other relief; usually compensation for what has been lost, but sometimes punitive damages: *Plaintiff A recovered $1,000 in a settlement; plaintiff B went to trial and recovered a judgment for $1,000 actual damages, $10,000 punitive damages, and injunctive relief.*
**2.** to find or get back: *The police recovered the murder weapon. The mugging victim recovered his wallet.*
**3.** to obtain an income tax benefit for all or part of one's BASIS in property. The most common ways of recovering

basis are through DEPRECIATION deductions and exclusion of the basis in computation of taxable income obtained through sale of an asset.
—**recoverable** *adj.*
—**recovery** *n.*

**recovered memory** *n.* memory of childhood abuse that is believed to have been "repressed" for many years and then "recovered," usually with the assistance of a therapist, in adulthood.
——**History.** Beginning in the 1980's, the courts encountered a wave of lawsuits by adult children against their parents for alleged physical abuse—usually systematic, long-term sexual abuse—believed to have occurred when they were children, but only recently remembered, usually as a result of therapy. The courts were generally receptive to these claims. But the theory that a victim's memory of such long-term abuse can be repressed for many years and then recovered under proper guidance, though passionately believed by many, has proved difficult to support through scientific evidence, and it has been noted that the techniques used by therapists to elicit such memories have much in common with *hypnotically refreshed recollection* (see under RECOLLECTION). Beginning in the 1990's, therefore, the trend in the courts has been to view such claims with somewhat greater caution than previously.

**recovery period** *n.* in tax law, the number of years over which the basis of an item of property may be recovered through annual depreciation deductions.

**recrimination** *n.* **1.** the making of a countercharge or counteraccusation.
**2.** a countercharge; counteraccusation.
**3.** retaliation.
**4.** in traditional divorce law, a charge by the defendant in a divorce action that the plaintiff is also guilty of conduct constituting a ground for divorce.
—**recriminate** *v.*, **recriminated, recriminating.**
—**recriminatory** *adj.*
——**Note.** Under traditional American law, still on the books in some states, recrimination is a defense to a divorce

action. In other words, if the marriage has so completely fallen apart that both spouses are engaging in conduct that would be a ground for divorce, such as cruelty or adultery, then either spouse can theoretically prevent the other from getting a divorce simply by pointing an accusing finger at the other. See also COLLUSION; CONNIVANCE.

**recross** *Informal.* —*n.* **1.** Short for *recross-examination* (see under EXAMINATION).
—*v.* **2.** Short for *recross-examine* (see under EXAMINE).

**recross-examination** *n.* See under EXAMINATION.

**recross-examine** *v.,* **recross-examined, recross-examining.** See under EXAMINE.

**recuse** *v.,* **recused, recusing.** to remove oneself from participation in a matter because of an actual or apparent CONFLICT OF INTEREST. Said especially of judges.
—**recusal** *n.*

**redact** *v.* to cover up or white out portions of a document; for example, to delete nondiscoverable information from a document being produced in DISCOVERY.
—**redactor** *n.*
——**False Friend.** In nonlegal usage, *redact* means "to revise; edit; put in literary form." As used by lawyers, the term has a much narrower sense, referring only to deletions.

**redaction** *n.* **1.** the act or an instance of redacting.
**2.** material deleted: *All of the redactions contain privileged information.*

**reddendum** *Latin.* to be given back. See also REDDENDUM CLAUSE.

**reddendum clause** *n.* the clause in a deed or lease requiring the grantee or lessee to pay rent or return something to the grantor out of the property granted, such as a royalty on minerals. Also called **reddendum.** In the traditional form of deed, the reddendum, if there is one, follows the HABENDUM CLAUSE. In feudal times, the service to be provided by the tenant to the lord

was specified either in a reddendum or in the same clause that identified the lord of whom the land was to be held (see discussion at TENENDUM CLAUSE).
——**Usage.** This clause is traditionally referred to as simply the *reddendum.* In the second half of the twentieth century the phrase *reddendum clause* largely displaced the single word; both forms, however, are now rare.

**redeem** *v.* **1.** to buy back or reacquire; especially, to reacquire property pledged as security for a loan by repaying the loan, or to extinguish a bond or other debt instrument by payment in accordance with its terms. See also *redeemable security* (under SECURITY²).
**2.** to turn in a bond or other certificate for cash or property in accordance with its terms.
—**redeemability** *n.*
—**redeemable** *adj.*
—**redemption** *n.*

**redirect** *n. Informal.* Short for *redirect examination* (see under EXAMINATION).

**redirect examination** *n.* See under EXAMINATION.

**redistricting** *v.* Same as REAPPORTIONMENT.
—**redistrict** *v.*

**redlining** *n.* **1.** refusal by a financial institution to make mortgage loans on property in certain geographic areas, especially inner-city neighborhoods. Redlining is an illegal discriminatory practice.
**2.** any analogous geographic differentiation or other screening device that a business might use: *taxi redlining; regulations to prevent redlining by cable television providers.*
See also GENETIC REDLINING; PIZZA REDLINING; SERVICE REDLINING.
—**redline** *v.* **redlined, redlining.**

**reentry** *n.* taking back possession of real property pursuant to a right reserved when possession was transferred to someone else, as in a lease.

**referee** *n.* a MASTER to whom a court refers a case for certain purposes, especially for the taking of testimony and reporting of proposed findings of fact.

**referendum** *n., pl.* **referendums** or **referenda. 1.** a procedure existing in most states by which certain proposed statutes or constitutional amendments may or must be put to a vote of the people before becoming effective. In some states, a statute adopted by the legislature must also be put to such a vote if a certain number of citizens sign a petition requesting it.
**2.** a measure put to such a vote.
**3.** the vote on such a measure.

**reform** *n.* **1.** a change or proposed change in the law regarded by its proponents as an improvement. Since people never propose changes that they regard as detrimental, all proposed change is called "reform" by its advocates.
—*v.* **2.** to bring about a reform of: *The bill reforms the rules of civil procedure.*
**3.** to effect a REFORMATION of: *Plaintiff asks the court to reform the contract.*

**reformation** *n.* **1.** judicially ordered interpretation or rewriting of a written instrument, usually a contract, which through fraud, mistake, or other circumstances failed to reflect the actual intent or agreement of the parties, so as to make it reflect what was originally intended or agreed upon.
**2.** a proceeding or decree by which reformation is accomplished.

**refresh** *v.* to jog memory. See also *refreshed recollection* or *present recollection refreshed* (under RECOLLECTION).

**refugee,** *n. International Law.* a person who has fled his country of nationality, or in some situations one who seeks to flee, because of persecution or a well-founded fear of persecution on account of race, religion, nationality, membership in a particular social group, or political opinion.

**refundable tax credit** *n.* See under TAX CREDIT.

**register** *n.* **1.** an official list, file, or record, such as a corporation's list of stockholders or a municipality's list of eligible voters.
**2.** the official who maintains such records.
—*v.* **3.** to cause to be listed in such a

record: *register a deed; register a child for school.*
**4.** to cause oneself to be listed in such a record: *register to vote.*
—**registrable** *adj.*
—**registration** *n.*

**registered certification mark** *n.* See under CERTIFICATION MARK.

**registered mail** *n.* a form of mail in which the item is numbered and individually tracked from the point of mailing to the destination. It is used for especially valuable or important mail. Cf. *certified mail* (under CERTIFY).

**registered mark** *n.* See under MARK.

**registered service mark** *n.* See under SERVICE MARK.

**registered trademark** *n.* See under TRADEMARK.

**registration statement** *n.* a statement containing detailed information about the issuer of a security and the security itself, which in most cases must be filed with the federal Securities and Exchange Commission before a security can be issued to the public.

**regrating** *n.* **1.** buying commodities at a market and reselling them at a profit in or near the same market. This was a statutory crime in England until 1844. See also ENGROSSING; FORESTALLING THE MARKET.
**2.** acting as a reseller; selling at retail.
—**regrate** *v.,* **regrated, regrating.**
—**regrater, regrator** *n.*

**regressive tax** *n.* See under TAX.

**regular** *adj.* **1.** normal, usual, customary.
**2.** in conformity, or apparently in conformity, with law, particularly with legal requirements as to form; not such as would arouse suspicion: *The check was regular on its face.*

**regular course of business** *n.* Same as ORDINARY COURSE OF BUSINESS.

**regular IRA** *n.* Same as *traditional IRA* (see under IRA).

**regular session** *n.* See under SESSION.

**regulated money** *n.* in federal campaign finance law, same as HARD MONEY.

**regulation** *n.* **1.** a directive adopted by an administrative agency, either for its own internal procedures or to govern public behavior in matters over which it has authority, and having the force of law: *income tax regulations; regulations of the city Department of Buildings.* See also RULE; RULEMAKING.
**2.** broadly, any rule or statute, or the act of controlling or attempting to control conduct by rules and laws.

**regulatory agency** *n.* an ADMINISTRATIVE AGENCY to which Congress or a legislature has delegated the power to adopt regulations governing public conduct; e.g., the federal Food and Drug Administration; a state Department of Motor Vehicles.

**regulatory taking** *n.* See under TAKING.

**rehabilitation** *n.* **1.** questioning of a witness or introduction of evidence designed to restore the credibility of a witness whose credibility has been attacked. Cf. IMPEACHMENT.
**2.** resolving an insolvent debtor's financial situation in bankruptcy court, especially through a *Chapter 13 bankruptcy* proceeding (see under BANKRUPTCY).
—**rehabilitate** *v.,* **rehabilitated, rehabilitating.**

**rehearing** *n.* See under REARGUMENT.

**reinsurance** *n.* insurance purchased by one insurance company from another, under which the second company agrees to cover all or part of a risk insured by the first company.

**related proceeding** *n.* Same as NON-CORE PROCEEDING.

**relation** *n.* See *on the relation of* (under EX REL.).

**relation back** *n.* the principle applied in various situations under which an act is deemed effective as of a date earlier than when it actually took place. For example, a new claim added in an amended complaint but arising from the same events that are the subject of the original complaint "relates back" to the date of the original complaint, so that expiration of the statute of limitations during the period between the two pleadings does not operate to bar the claim.

**relator** *n.* person at whose request, or for whose benefit, certain kinds of actions are brought. See also EX REL.; QUI TAM.

**release** *n., v.,* **released, releasing.** —*n.* **1.** the relieving of another person from an obligation or liability, or alleged obligation or liability, to oneself; the formal, permanent abandonment of a claim.
**2.** a formal document embodying such a release, given to the person being released. When a case is settled, it is usual for the parties to exchange **mutual releases** whereby each assures the other that no further claim will be asserted with respect to the matter being settled. Often a release given in connection with a settlement is a **general release,** which bars any claim by the releasor against the releasee in connection with anything that has happened "from the beginning of time to the date of this release."
—*v.* **3.** to give someone a release.

**release on own recognizance (ROR)** *n.* pretrial release of a criminal defendant upon his promise to appear in court as needed, without any requirement of bail. Also called **release on personal recognizance.**

**relevant** *adj.* tending to make the existence of a fact that is of consequence in a case more probable or less probable. Relevant evidence includes evidence bearing on the credibility of a witness. Evidence must be relevant to be admissible at a trial, but even relevant evidence may be excluded by the rules of evidence (see, for example, HEARSAY; *evidentiary privilege,* under PRIVILEGE) or as a matter of judicial discretion (see, for example, *cumulative evidence,* under EVIDENCE; PREJUDICIAL EFFECT).
—**relevance** *n.*
—**relevantly** *adv.*

**reliance** *n.* **1.** the taking of or failure to

take some action because of trust in what someone else has said or done. Reliance is an element of certain causes of action, such as FRAUD and PROMISSORY ESTOPPEL.

**2. detrimental reliance** reliance that results in a loss, an expenditure of time, effort, or money, or a change for the worse in one's legal position.

**3. reasonable reliance** conduct such as a reasonable person might have undertaken under the circumstances in light of another's words or actions. To support a claim for fraud or promissory estoppel, the plaintiff's reliance upon the defendant's false representation or promise must have been both reasonable and detrimental.

**relict** *n.* a surviving spouse; a widow or widower.

**reliction** *n.* an increase in land bordering upon water by the receding of the water line. Sometimes called **dereliction.**

**relief** *n.* **1.** the remedy or totality of remedies sought or awarded in a proceeding. See discussion and additional entries under REMEDY.

**2. affirmative relief a.** relief awarded to a plaintiff beyond payment of damages, especially relief that requires the defendant to perform some specific action. **b.** any relief granted to a defendant against a plaintiff beyond simple dismissal of the plaintiff's case.

**3. specific relief** any type of *equitable remedy* (see under REMEDY) that requires a party to take specified steps or that affects interests in specified property; for example, a judgment ordering *specific restitution* (see under RESTITUTION) or SPECIFIC PERFORMANCE.

**religion** See FREEDOM OF RELIGION.

**religious test** *n.* a requirement based on religion; especially, any requirement for public office that has the effect of excluding a class of people on the basis of religious belief or practice.

—**Note.** Article VI of the Constitution prohibits the imposition of a religious test for any office or position of public trust in the federal government. The Supreme Court has invalidated religious tests for state office—such as a Maryland requirement that notaries public swear that they believe in God (struck down in 1961) and a Tennessee ban on clergymen in the legislature (struck down in 1978)—as violations of the First Amendment. See also note at OATH OR AFFIRMATION.

**rem** See IN REM.

**remainder** *n.* **1.** the *future estate* (see under ESTATE[1]) created by a GIFT OVER of the balance of an estate in connection with a transfer of an estate of shorter duration. For example, if the owner of a fee estate grants the property "to A for life, then to B and his heirs," A receives a life estate and B a remainder. Cf. *particular estate* (under ESTATE[1]); REVERSION.

**2.** a right to receive trust property upon expiration of the trust. For example, a will might specify that certain assets are to be held in trust with the income to be used for the benefit of the testator's children until they reach the age of 21, and that when the last child reaches the age of 21 the trust is to terminate and the corpus is to be given to a particular charity. Under the will, the charity receives a remainder interest in the trust assets. See also *charitable remainder trust* (under TRUST).

**remainderman** *n., pl.* **remaindermen.** a person who holds a REMAINDER in real property; a grantee who will receive an estate after a particular estate carved out of it has expired. Cf. REVERSIONER.

**remand** *v.* **1.** to send a case back from an appellate court to the lower court from which it was appealed, for further proceedings in accordance with the appellate court's instructions.

**2.** to send a criminal defendant back into custody.

—*n.* **3.** the act of remanding or the state of being remanded. A case in a lower court after remand is said to be "on remand."

**remedy** *n., pl.* **remedies,** *v.,* **remedied, remedying.** —*n.* **1.** redress sought from or awarded by a court; any type of judgment that can be issued by a court in a civil action. See also RELIEF; and see note below regarding usage.

**2.** a right of action or a procedure for obtaining satisfaction of a claim or grievance: *If the car payments are not kept up, the lender has a remedy either in court or through repossession of the car.*

**3. adequate remedy at law** a *legal remedy* (almost always damages) that the law deems sufficient to compensate a plaintiff, making an *equitable remedy* (such as specific performance) unnecessary.

**4. equitable remedy** (or **relief**) relief of a type traditionally available only in courts of EQUITY, such as SPECIFIC PERFORMANCE, an INJUNCTION, or REFORMATION or a contract. Also called **relief in equity.** Cf. *legal remedy.*

**5. extraordinary remedy** (or **relief**) relief of a sort traditionally available only by *extraordinary writ* (see under WRIT).

**6. legal remedy** (or **relief**) a remedy of a type traditionally available in the law courts (rather than the equity courts), the most common of which is DAMAGES. Also called **remedy at law.** See LAW (def. 4). Cf. *equitable remedy.*

**7. provisional** (or **temporary**) **remedy** (or **relief**), an order issued during the course of an action to protect the interests of a party while the action proceeds; e.g., a *preliminary injunction* (see under INJUNCTION), temporary alimony, or appointment of a RECEIVER.

**—v. 8.** to redress; provide a remedy for.
**—remedial** *adj.*
**—remedially** *adv.*
**——Usage.** Before the MERGER OF LAW AND EQUITY, the conventional terminology was "a remedy at law" or "relief in equity." Now the terms "remedy" and "relief" are largely interchangeable, although the former is more often used in reference to damages and the latter in reference to other kinds of relief. In addition, one uses "a" or "the" with "remedy," but not with "relief."

**remission** *n.* See under RENVOI.

**remittitur** *n. Latin.* (lit. "it is given back") an order reducing the amount of damages awarded by a jury. If the plaintiff does not accept the reduced amount, the defendant will be granted a new trial. Cf. ADDITUR.

**remote cause** *n.* in tort law, an action or event that plays a role in bringing about an injury or loss, but is not a sufficiently direct cause to give rise to liability. Cf. PROXIMATE CAUSE.

**remove** *v.,* **removed, removing. 1.** to move or transfer a person or thing; change the location of: *remove a person from office; remove property from the state.*

**2.** to take away; eliminate: *remove a cloud on title.*

**3.** to transfer a case from one court to another; especially, to transfer a case, upon motion of the defendant, from a state court to a federal court of appropriate jurisdiction.
**—removability** *n.*
**—removable** *adj.*
**—removal** *n.*

**render** *v.* **1.** to issue or announce: *render a judgment; render a verdict.*

**2.** to give or perform: *render payment; render the performance called for by the contract.*
**—rendition** *n.*

**renew** *v.* **1.** to begin again: *renew a lease; renew a contract.*

**2.** to repeat or revive a request previously denied, in light of subsequent developments: *renew a motion; renew an objection.*
**—renewability** *n.*
**—renewable** *adj.*
**—renewal** *n.*

**renounce** *v.,* **renounced, renouncing. 1.** to give up a right, interest, or claim.

**2.** to abandon a criminal enterprise voluntarily and absolutely, before the crime is committed. In some jurisdictions renunciation is an affirmative defense to a criminal charge of ATTEMPT, SOLICITATION, or the like.
**—renounceable** *adj.*
**—renunciation** *n.*

**rent-a-judge** *n.* Same as PRIVATE JUDGE.

**rent-a-judging** *n.* Same as PRIVATE JUDGING.

**renvoi** *n.* **1.** in the field of CONFLICT OF LAWS, in a matter with respect to which the forum state (or nation) would apply the law of a second state, reference by the second state's law to the law of a third state **(transmission)** or, more often, back to the law of the forum state **(remission).**
**2. partial renvoi** reference back only to the INTERNAL LAW of the forum state, so that the forum ends up applying its own substantive law to the issue.
**3. whole renvoi** or **total renvoi** reference back to the WHOLE LAW of the forum state, which points back to the second state, so that the forum ends up applying the subtantive law of the second state to the issue (just as if it had never accepted renvoi in the first place).
—**Note.** The underlying goal of the renvoi principle is consistency in treatment of cases regardless of where they are brought: If State A's law points to State B, but State B would actually apply the law of another state (A or C), then State A should apply the same law State B would. But the simple fact is that different states have different laws and even different approaches to the problem of CHOICE OF LAW; therefore complete consistency is never possible. And the concept of renvoi, if carried to its ultimate conclusion, would often result in infinite circles in which State A looks to State B's law which looks to State A's law which looks to State B's law and so on. In recognition of these problems, most states in the United States simply do not accept the principle of renvoi at all: When their choice-of-law rules point to the law of another state, they simply look to the internal substantive law of that other state and apply it to the issue at hand.

**reopen** *v.* to permit further proceedings in a matter that had been concluded: *reopen a judgment; reopen the evidence; reopen a case.*

**reorganization** *n.* **1.** Also called **corporate reorganization.** any substantial restructuring of a corporation's financial structure.

**2.** Also called **bankruptcy reorganization.** the restructuring, and usually reduction, of a corporation's debt in a *Chapter 11 bankruptcy* proceeding (see under BANKRUPTCY).

**reorganization plan** *n.* See under BANKRUPTCY.

**repeal** *n.* the nullification of a statute, constitutional provision, or regulation by subsequent enactment. Usually the subsequent enactment explicitly states that the earlier is repealed **(express repeal),** but sometimes the earlier provision is regarded as null simply because the later enactment is inconsistent with it **(implied repeal).**

**repeat offender** *n.* See under OFFENDER.

**replevin** *n.* **1.** an action to recover possession of tangible personal property wrongfully taken or withheld by another.
**2.** a common law FORM OF ACTION for this purpose.
**3.** a writ (in full, the **writ of replevin**) requiring that property be turned over to the claimant pending the determination of such an action.
**4.** the return of property to a claimant, or the recovery of property by a claimant, preliminary to or as a result of such an action.
**5.** in ancient usage, the bailing of a person out of jail.
—*v.* **6.** to REPLEVY.

**replevy** *v.,* **replevied, replevying,** *n.,* *pl.* **replevies.** —*v.* **1.** to recover goods in connection with or as a result of an action of REPLEVIN.
**2.** in ancient usage, to release a person from jail by posting or granting bail.
—*n.* **3.** REPLEVIN (defs. 3–5).
—**repleviable, replevisable** *adj.*

**reply** *n.,* *pl.* **replies,** *v.,* **replied, replying.** —*n.* **1.** a plaintiff's PLEADING in response to a COUNTERCLAIM asserted by the defendant. A reply to a counterclaim is exactly like an ANSWER to a complaint.
**2.** generally, any response to an adversary's submission in opposition to one's own motion, argument, or appeal in a

case. See, for example, *reply brief* (under BRIEF).

—*v.* **3.** to make or serve a reply.

**report** *n.* **1.** a written account of something based upon the writer's observation, investigation, or analysis: *a master's report; a police report.*

**2.** an account of the proceedings or transcript of the decision in a court case, published for reference by lawyers and judges in subsequent cases: *The court in that case rejected a claim that bail was excessive, but the report does not mention the exact level at which bail had been set.*

**3. reports** a published compilation of opinions of a particular court, agency, or set of courts, usually in an unending succession of volumes. Sometimes called a **reporter.** A **reported opinion (case, decision,** etc.**)** is one that has thus been published. Cf. SLIP OPINION.

—*v.* **4.** to issue a report. See also *hear and report* (under HEAR).

**reporter** *n.* **1.** a person, sometimes a court official, who compiles and supervises publication of the decisions of a court or set of courts.

**2.** the *reports* (see under REPORT) so published.

**3.** a COURT REPORTER.

**reporter's privilege** *n.* an *evidentiary privilege* (see under PRIVILEGE) permitting a news reporter to refuse to disclose information obtained in the course of gathering news, including the identity of confidential news sources. Also called **journalist's privilege, newsman's privilege, newsperson's privilege.**

**reporter's shield law** *n.* a statute establishing a REPORTER'S PRIVILEGE. Also called **journalist's shield law, newsperson's shield law.**

**repossess** *v.* to take back property in which one has retained a security interest upon failure of the buyer to keep up with the payments.

—**repossessable** *adj.*

—**repossession** *n.*

—**repossessor** *n.*

**represent** *v.* **1.** to act on behalf of another or take over the position of another in a matter: *The lawyer represents the client. The executor represents the decedent.*

**2.** to assert as a fact, particularly in a context in which others might rely upon the assertion: *Counsel represented to the court that her client was on his way to the courthouse. The seller represented that the paint contained no lead.*

**representation** *n.* **1.** the act of representing or state of being represented: *The court remarked that the representation on both sides of the case had been very skillful.*

**2.** words or conduct amounting to an assertion of fact, particularly one that others might rely upon: *Certain representations in the prospectus were materially misleading.*

**3. false representation** Same as MISREPRESENTATION. See also FRAUD.

**reprieve** *n., v.,* **reprieved, reprieving.**

—*n.* **1.** the postponement of execution of a criminal sentence by executive order. The classic situation for a reprieve occurs when a person is about to be put to death for a capital crime; a reprieve does not necessarily mean that the prisoner will not be executed, but it does give her some extra time to make arguments. See also *stay of execution* (under STAY).

**2.** the document in which a reprieve is granted.

—*v.* **3.** to grant a reprieve to someone. Cf. COMMUTE; PARDON. See also CLEMENCY.

**republican form of government** *n.* See under GOVERNMENT.

**repudiation** *n.* **1.** refusal to carry out a duty, or denial that a duty exists. Repudiation may be rightful or wrongful, depending upon the circumstances.

**2.** especially, refusal to perform, or to continue performing, a contract. If a party repudiates a contract before any performance is due, that may be called *anticipatory repudiation* (see under BREACH).

—**repudiate** *v.,* **repudiated, repudiating.**

**request for admissions** *n.* See under ADMISSION.

**requests for instructions** *n.pl.* a party's list of proposed instructions for the jury, with citations to authority, usually submitted to the judge shortly before the end of the case. Also called **requests to charge.** See also INSTRUCTION.

**requirements contract** *n.* See under CONTRACT.

**res** *n., pl.* **res.** *Latin.* (lit. "thing," "matter," "property," "case") **1.** generally, a thing under discussion: *Whether property can be taxed by a state or seized by a sheriff depends upon the location of the res.*
**2.** the tangible or intangible property or relationship that is the subject of an IN REM or QUASI IN REM action.
**3.** the CORPUS of a trust; the property of a trust or estate.
See also FORUM REI GESTAE; FORUM REI SITAE.

**res adjudicata** *n. Latin.* (lit. "an adjudicated matter") Same as RES JUDICATA.

**res gestae** *n.pl. Latin.* (lit. "things done," "deeds," "exploits") an entire occurrence that is the subject of a legal action, including particularly the words spoken by participants and bystanders.
——**Note.** Under a traditional exception to the *hearsay rule* (see under HEARSAY), utterances that formed part of the "res gestae" were admitted into evidence on the theory that the jury is entitled to learn about the entire event in dispute, including words as well as actions. Modern rules of evidence shun the term as vague, and substitute such concepts as PRESENT SENSE IMPRESSION and EXCITED UTTERANCE.

**res in re** *n. Latin.* (lit. "a thing in a thing") sexual penetration; the element of PENETRATION that must be established in order to convict a person of rape or certain other sex crimes.
——**History.** This expression has been traced back at least to the classic writings of the English jurist Sir Edward Coke (1552–1634), and is still in occasional use. An unusual twist on the phrase appears in a case much celebrated among generations of law students, easily located (in the days before

many of the older case reports were put on microfiche) by the discoloration of the edges of the pages from the many hands that had turned them. In this 1915 decision, the Court of Appeals of Alabama affirmed a conviction upon an indictment charging that the defendant "against the order of nature, carnally knew a certain beast, to wit, a cow." The court began its notably thorough analysis of the evidentiary issues by stating this basic principle: "It must, as in rape, be shown that the res was in the re, but to no particular depth." *Tarrant v. State,* 12 Ala. App. 172, 67 So. 626 (1915).

**res ipsa loquitur** *n. Latin.* (lit. "the thing itself speaks," "the situation speaks for itself") the doctrine that the plaintiff in a negligence case need not show exactly how the defendant caused an accident if the accident was of a type that normally could not have occurred but for some negligence by the defendant. Such a case is said to be a **res ipsa loquitur case,** or **res ipsa case** for short. See also reference at *leading case* (under CASE[1]).
——**Note.** The classic res ipsa case is the sponge left in a patient's body after surgery: The patient can prevail in a malpractice case against the surgeon or the hospital even though the patient was unconscious and therefore cannot describe how the incident happened, because "the thing speaks for itself." But see note at FERES DOCTRINE.

**res judicata** *n. Latin.* (lit. "an adjudicated matter," "a decided case") the doctrine that prevents relitigation of a claim that has been fully considered and finally decided in the courts. If the losing party attempts to reassert such a claim in another action against the same defendant, the claim will be barred by the doctrine of res judicata.
Also called **claim preclusion, res adjudicata.** Cf. *collateral estoppel* (under ESTOPPEL).

**rescission** *n.* the cancellation of a contract and restoration of the parties to the positions they held before the contract was made. Rescission may be agreed to by the parties or sought in a

judicial action as an equitable remedy when a contract was entered into as a result of fraud, mutual mistake, or the like.
—**rescind** *v.*

**reserve** *v.*, **reserved, reserving,** *n.* —*v.*
**1.** to retain specified rights or interests in a transaction otherwise disposing of property or rights.
**2.** to set aside funds for a particular purpose or contingency.
**3.** to withhold for the time being; specifically, a judge or panel that does not rule from the bench upon a matter that has been argued is said to "reserve decision" or "reserve judgment."
—*n.* **4.** a fund set aside for a particular purpose or for future contingencies.

**reserved power** *n.* See under POWER.

**residence** *n.* **1.** in some contexts, same as DOMICILE.
**2.** usually, any place where one has a home, even if one's domicile is elsewhere.

**residency** *n.*, *pl.* **residencies. 1.** the act of residing or state of being a RESIDENT—that is, of having a residence or domicile within a jurisdiction.
**2. residency requirement a.** any legal requirement that a person have a residence or domicile within a particular state or local jurisdiction in order to vote, hold office, hold public employment, or receive public benefits in that jurisdiction. **b.** a state or municipal regulation that denies certain benefits or status, such as welfare or voting rights, to newcomers until they have resided within the jurisdiction for a specified length of time. Many such waiting periods have been struck down as unconstitutional infringements on the RIGHT TO TRAVEL. Also called **waiting period.**

**resident** *n.* one who has a RESIDENCE, or sometimes his DOMICILE, in a specified place: *a noted resident of Newport, Palm Beach, Aspen, and Monte Carlo, domiciled in Monaco.* See also *resident alien* (under ALIEN).

**residuary bequest** (or **legacy**) *n.* See under BEQUEST.

**residuary estate** *n.* See under ESTATE².

**residuary legatee** *n.* See under LEGATEE.

**residue** *n.* Same as *residuary estate* (see under ESTATE²).

**resolution** *n.* an expression of sentiment or opinion adopted by vote of a legislative body, not having the force of law.

**respondeat superior** *Latin.* (lit. "let the superior answer") the doctrine that an employer is liable for the torts of an employee acting within the SCOPE OF EMPLOYMENT, and in many situations a principal of any kind is liable for the torts of an agent arising from conduct within the agent's SCOPE OF AUTHORITY. See also *vicarious liability* (under LIABILITY); FELLOW SERVANT RULE.

**respondent** *n.* the name given in certain situations to the party who must respond to a procedural step in a case, such as a petition, motion, or appeal. In the case of an appeal, some courts use the term "respondent" and others APPELLEE.

**responsive** *adj.* **1.** describing papers, evidence, or argument offered in answer or opposition to something submitted by an adversary: *responsive pleading; responsive brief.*
**2.** responding without evasion to a question or questions; providing a clear answer; providing the information sought: *responsive witness; responsive testimony.*
**3.** responding readily and sympathetically to appeals, needs, efforts, etc.: *responsive government, responsive audience.*
—**responsively** *adv.*
—**responsiveness** *n.*

**responsive answer** *n.* a direct and clear answer to a question; an answer that provides the information requested rather than avoiding the question or adding unsolicited information. See discussion at UNRESPONSIVE ANSWER.

**Restatement of the Law** *n.* any of a series of very influential multi-volume works prepared over the decades by the AMERICAN LAW INSTITUTE, each undertaking to summarize and systematize a major area of United States law such as contracts, trusts, or foreign relations law.

**restitution** *n.* **1.** any remedy or order for the prevention of UNJUST ENRICH-MENT, usually involving the defendant's giving up some benefit that in justice should have gone to the plaintiff or paying for some benefit received from the plaintiff. It may also involve giving back some piece of property **(specific restitution)**, or other forms of relief tailored to the case at hand.
**2.** in criminal law, giving back ill-gotten gains or paying for property damage as part of one's sentence, as a condition of probation, or as part of a plea bargain. —**restitutionary** *adj.*

**restraining order** *n.* **1.** an INJUNCTION that prohibits someone from taking some action.
**2. temporary restraining order (TRO)** an injunction granted for a very short time, just to keep things as they are until a hearing can be held to determine whether it would be appropriate to issue a *preliminary injunction* (see under INJUNCTION). A TRO may be granted EX PARTE to avoid tipping off the person to whom it is directed and thus giving that person a chance to hurry up and do the act in question before being ordered not to. See also note at INJUNCTION.

**restraint of trade** *n.* See UNREASONA-BLE RESTRAINT OF TRADE.

**restraint on alienation** *n.* **1.** a provision in an instrument transferring land which forbids the taker from subsequently transferring the land to anyone else. Such provisions are usually unenforceable.
**2.** the practical effect of a transfer creating interests in land that may or may not vest for many years to come, making the future status of the land so uncertain that the property is unlikely to be marketable. A primary purpose of the *rule against perpetuities* (see under PERPETUITY) is to limit such de facto restraints on alienation.

**restricted stock** *n.* See under STOCK.

**restrictive covenant** *n.* See under COVENANT.

**restrictive indorsement** *n.* See under INDORSEMENT.

**resulting trust** *n.* See under TRUST.

**retainer** *n.* **1.** the act of contracting for someone's services—especially a lawyer's—or the fact of being so retained.
**2.** an initial fee paid to a lawyer upon being retained by a new client or for a new matter, usually viewed as a deposit on fees to be incurred.

**retirement plan** *n.* **1.** a PENSION PLAN or other arrangement by which money is set aside and invested during an individual's working years for use after retirement.
**2. 401(k) plan** a retirement plan established by an employer (other than a governmental employer) in accordance with § 401(k) of the Internal Revenue Code, under which both an employee and the employer may make tax-deductible contributions to an individual investment account, such as a mutual fund account, for the employee. The employee directs how the funds are invested, and the funds and proceeds ordinarily must remain in the account until the employee reaches retirement age. Thereafter, the employee becomes responsible for income tax on the funds and the proceeds as they are withdrawn. Also called **section 401(k) plan.** Such plans are fully subject to ERISA (the EMPLOYEE RETIREMENT IN-COME SECURITY ACT OF 1974).
**3. 403(b) plan** a retirement plan substantially similar to a 401(k) plan, but available only to charitable, religious, educational, and similar tax-exempt organizations, and to educational units of state and local governments. Some 403(b) plans, in which the funds come solely from the employee and the employer has little involvement with the plan, are exempt from ERISA. Also called **section 403(b) plan.**
**4. 457 plan** or **457(b) plan** a deferred compensation plan available only to state and local governmental employees and employees of tax-exempt organizations. It is similar in many respects to a

401(k) plan, but there is no possibility of employer contribution. Also called **section 457 plan** or **section 457(b) plan.**

**5. Keogh plan** a *qualified pension plan* (see under PENSION PLAN) for a self-employed individual, a sole proprietor, or a partnership. Also called **HR-10 plan.**

**6. savings incentive match plan for employees** a retirement plan with simplified procedures, available to employers with fewer than one hundred employees. Usually referred to as a **SIMPLE plan.** There are two types of SIMPLE plan: **a. SIMPLE 401(k) plan** a 401(k) plan for which certain of the usual requirements for such plans are relaxed. **b. SIMPLE IRA plan** a retirement plan under which an individual retirement account is established for each eligible employee, to which both the employer and employee contribute. See also *SIMPLE IRA* (under IRA).

**7. simplified employee pension (SEP)** a retirement plan in which individual retirement accounts are established for all eligible employees, to which contributions may be made both by the employer and by the employee. A SEP is governed by somewhat more stringent requirements than a SIMPLE IRA plan, but allows larger annual contributions. See also *SEP-IRA* (under IRA).

**retreat** *v.* to withdraw from a confrontation rather than fighting back.
——**Note.** In general, American law, in the spirit of the Wild West, holds that a person who is attacked need not retreat even if that can be done safely, but may stand his ground and use reasonable force in SELF-DEFENSE. Some jurisdictions make an exception for situations in which it appears that the only sufficient force to avoid death or serious bodily harm would be deadly force, requiring a person to withdraw (except from his own home or place of business) if it is clear that he can do so in complete safety, rather than use deadly force against the attacker. This is colloquially called a duty to "retreat to the wall."

**retrial** *n.* Same as *de novo trial* (see under TRIAL).

**retributive justice** *n.* See under JUSTICE[1].

**return** *v.* **1.** to submit to a court an account of action taken in a judicial matter, particularly action by an officer or official body: *The grand jury returned an indictment. The jury returned its verdict. The sheriff returned an affidavit of service of the writ of attachment.*
——*n.* **2.** the act of returning such an account, or the written document itself: *Return was made last week. The return of service was filed last week.* See also RETURN DATE.
**3.** Also called **tax return.** the document in which a taxpayer reports to the government on matters having tax consequences: *income tax return; estate tax return.*
**4. consolidated return** a tax return for a group of affiliated companies reporting as a unit for tax purposes.
**5. individual return** an income tax return filed by a person who is single, divorced, or legally separated pursuant to a judicial decree.
**6. joint return** an income tax return filed by a husband and wife together for the purpose of reporting and paying tax on their combined income.
**7. separate return** an income tax return filed by a married person for the purpose of reporting and paying tax only upon his or her own income.

**return date** *n.* the date upon which a return is due to be filed in court (see RETURN, defs. 1–2), a motion is to be argued or submitted, or a person is to appear or otherwise respond to a court order or PROCESS: *By stipulation, the return date for the motion was changed to a date after the Christmas holidays.* Also called **return day.** See also RETURNABLE.

**return day** *n.* Same as RETURN DATE.

**return of service** *n.* an account of the steps taken to serve a summons or other process or court paper, sworn to or affirmed by the individual who effected or attempted to effect the service and filed with the court.

——**Usage.** In most contexts, *return of service* means the same thing as *affidavit of service* (see under AFFIDAVIT): it is a sworn statement that service was accomplished, with details of how it was accomplished. But the term is also occasionally applied in cases where service could not be made, to returns that consist only of a sworn or affirmed description of the efforts that were made to find the person to be served and effect service.

**return receipt** *n.* See *certified mail* (under CERTIFY).

**returnable** *adj.* required to be submitted to the court or appropriately responded to (a term usually used in reference to the RETURN DATE): *The summons is returnable in twenty days. The order to show cause is returnable at 9:00 a.m. on Monday in Courtroom 3.*

**rev'd** REVERSED.
——**Usage.** The abbreviation is used in citations to indicate that the decision just cited was reversed on appeal in the decision whose citation follows immediately: *Reed v. Reed,* 93 Idaho 511 (1970), *rev'd,* 404 U.S. 71 (1971). Cf. AFF'D; REV'G.

**revenue bond** *n.* See under BOND[1].

**reverse** *v.,* **reversed, reversing.** (of an appellate court) to nullify the judgment of a lower court in a case on appeal because of some ERROR in the court below. Sometimes a reversal disposes of the entire case; in other situations it requires further proceedings on REMAND. Cf. AFFIRM[2].
—**reversal** *n.*
—**reversible** *adj.*

**reverse annuity mortgage (RAM)** *n.* See under MORTGAGE.

**reverse buy** *n.* See under STING.

**reverse mortgage** *n.* See under MORTGAGE.

**reverse sting** *n.* See under STING.

**reversed (rev'd)** overturned on appeal. See REV'D for usage.

**reversible error** *n.* See under ERROR.

**reversing (rev'g)** overturning on appeal. See REV'G for usage.

**reversion** *n.* **1.** the *future estate* (see under ESTATE[1]) retained by the owner of an estate in real property (or his heirs) when the owner transfers an estate of shorter duration carved out of the one he owns and does not dispose of the balance, as when the holder of a fee simple absolute conveys a life estate in the property, or a one-year tenant conveys the property to another for one week. Upon expiration of the particular estate, the right to possession of the property reverts to the grantor or his heirs. Cf. *particular estate* (under ESTATE[1]); POSSIBILITY OF REVERTER; REMAINDER. **2.** The return of land to the grantor or his heirs after the grant is over.
—**reversionary** *adj.*

**reversioner** *n.* a person who holds a REVERSION in real property; the grantor, or heirs of a deceased grantor, to whom property will revert upon expiration of a particular estate. Cf. REMAINDERMAN.

**reverter** *n.* See POSSIBILITY OF REVERTER.

**rev'g** REVERSING.
——**Usage.** The abbreviation is used in citations to indicate that the decision just cited is a reversal of the decision whose citation follows immediately: *Reed v. Reed,* 404 U.S. 71 (1971), *rev'g* 93 Idaho 511 (1970). Cf. AFF'G; REV'D.

**review** *n.* **1.** Also called **appellate review.** examination of the proceedings and decision in a court case by a higher court or, in an administrative matter, by a court or a higher authority or tribunal within the same agency, to determine if the result should be affirmed. **2. administrative review** review of an administrative decision, especially by a higher authority or tribunal within the agency itself. **3. de novo review** review in which the reviewing court or authority may completely disregard the findings of the original factfinder and draw its own conclusions from the evidence. See also DE NOVO. **4. judicial review** **a.** the power of the courts to declare laws unconstitutional. **b.** review by a court of an administrative decision.

—*v.* **5.** to examine for error; to conduct a review of.

See also SCOPE OF REVIEW; STANDARD OF REVIEW. Cf. LAW REVIEW.

—**reviewability** *n.*

—**reviewable** *adj.*

**revocable trust** *n.* See under TRUST.

**revoke** *v.,* **revoked, revoking. 1.** to nullify something one has done: *revoke a will; revoke an offer of contract.*
**2.** to take away a previously granted right or privilege by judicial or administrative action: *revoke a driver's license; revoke parole.*

—**revocability** *n.*

—**revocable** *adj.*

—**revocably** *adv.*

—**revocation** *n.*

**Richard Roe** *n.* **1.** historically, the usual name chosen for the fictitious CASUAL EJECTOR in the common law action of ejectment. See note at EJECTMENT. Cf. JOHN DOE.
**2.** a fictitious name used in case names and in legal documents in the same ways that JOHN DOE is used, usually because the latter name has already been used to identify another individual in the same or a related proceeding. See also JANE ROE.

**RICO** *n.* See RACKETEER INFLUENCED AND CORRUPT ORGANIZATIONS ACT.

**ride-along** *n.* a police activity or action, such as patrolling or making an arrest, in which a reporter, photographer, or television crew is permitted or invited to accompany the police so as to record the activity for news purposes or entertainment programming. Also called **media ride-along** or **press ride-along.**
—**Note.** This practice, which has become an especially popular form of mass entertainment, serves the same purposes as the PERP WALK, raises similar issues, and has come under similar legal attack. In 1999 the Supreme Court ruled that it is a violation of the constitutional prohibition on *unreasonable searches* (see under SEARCH) for police to bring members of the media or other

third parties into a home without permission during the execution of a warrant when the presence of the third parties in the home is not in aid of execution of the warrant.

**rider** *n.* a separate sheet of paper or set of pages containing one or more additions or amendments to a legal document such as a contract or an insurance policy, attached to and intended to be read as if integrated with the main document. See also CODICIL.

**rig** *v.,* **rigged, rigging.** to manipulate fraudulently: *to rig prices; rig the market.* See also BID RIGGING.

**right** *n.* **1.** a freedom, interest, power, protection, or immunity to which a person is entitled by reason of law, and for which one ordinarily may look to the government, and particularly the courts, for protection, enforcement, or, if a violation has already occurred, compensation or other remedy.
**2.** a term used by advocates to describe something that they believe should be a legally protected right, or that they claim as a right even if the law is otherwise.
**3. constitutional right** a right protected by a constitution; unless the context clearly indicates otherwise, the constitution referred to is that of the United States. See also FREEDOM; LIBERTY; FUNDAMENTAL RIGHT.
**4. equitable right** a right or interest of a *beneficial owner* of property (see under OWNER), or a right for the violation of which one would be entitled to *equitable relief* (see under REMEDY).
**5. legal right a.** broadly, any right protected by law; same as def. 1 above. **b.** in a narrow sense, a right or interest of a *legal owner* of property (see under OWNER), or a right for the violation of which one would be entitled to a *legal remedy* (see under REMEDY).
**6. vested right a.** a VESTED property interest. **b.** in constitutional law, a contract right that cannot be interfered with by a state, a property right that cannot be taken away by the government without just compensation, or an ENTITLEMENT.

See also BILL OF RIGHTS; CIVIL RIGHTS;

*moral rights* (under DROIT MORAL); VICTIMS' RIGHTS; WRIT OF RIGHT.

**right of action** *n.* **1.** a right to sue; a CAUSE OF ACTION or *claim for relief* (see under CLAIM).
**2. private right of action** a right to sue for damages caused by another's violation of a criminal or regulatory law. A statute outlawing certain conduct may expressly provide that persons injured by such conduct may sue the violator for damages. In the absence of language expressly creating such a right, under traditional principles of tort law an **implied right of action** nevertheless exists under a statute or regulation that was designed to protect people in certain situations from a certain kind of harm, if the defendant's violation in fact caused such harm.

**right of common** *n.* See COMMON.

**right of** (or **to**) **privacy 1.** in tort law, the complex of interests protected by the tort of INVASION OF PRIVACY.
**2.** under the federal Privacy Act and similar state statutes, the right to have personal information that is on file with the government kept confidential and used only for authorized purposes.
**3.** in constitutional law, **a.** the Fourth Amendment right to be free from unreasonable searches and seizures by the government, which the Supreme Court has held applicable in any area or situation in which the target would have a reasonable "expectation of privacy." **b.** the limited right to make decisions about marriage and procreation, including contraception and abortion, free from government interference, which the Supreme Court has found to be included in the concept of LIBERTY protected by the Fourteenth Amendment. The Court has been reluctant to expand this right to other areas of personal decision making and conduct; for example, under recent rulings the government still has the right to specify what sexual acts consenting adults may legally engage in in private.
See also *substantive due process* (under DUE PROCESS); and see note at SODOMY.

**right of survivorship** *n.* the characteristic of JOINT ownership of property (as distinguished from ownership IN COMMON) whereby, upon the death of any co-owner, that owner's interest passes automatically to the surviving owners, until finally the last survivor owns the entire property alone.

**right to bear arms** *n.* a popular phrase for the right referred to in the Second Amendment of the Constitution, which states: "A well regulated Militia, being necessary to the security of a free State, the right of the people to keep and bear Arms, shall not be infringed."
Also called **right to keep and bear arms.**
—**Note.** The Second Amendment applies only to the federal government, and so is not a hindrance to state or local GUN CONTROL legislation. Since Congress has never attempted to impose significant restrictions on gun ownership, the potential effect of the Second Amendment at the federal level remains a matter of debate. In the Supreme Court's one decision dealing directly with the Second Amendment, it upheld, by a vote of 8–0, a federal law regulating interstate transportation of sawed-off shotguns. The Court dwelt at length on the history and function of the MILITIA, and concluded that "[i]n the absence of any evidence tending to show that possession or use of a 'shotgun having a barrel of less than eighteen inches in length' at this time has some reasonable relationship to the preservation or efficiency of a well regulated militia, we cannot say that the Second Amendment guarantees the right to keep and bear such an instrument." *United States v. Miller,* 307 U.S. 174 (1939). Many argue, however, that a modern Supreme Court would, or at least should, construe the Second Amendment to afford individuals wide latitude to acquire, keep, and carry firearms.

**right to convey** *n.* See *covenant of right to convey* (under COVENANTS OF TITLE).

**right to counsel** *n.* the right of a criminal defendant to have a lawyer, guaranteed by the Sixth Amendment (see Appendix). It includes the right to have a lawyer present at any significant step of a criminal prosecution, including custodial questioning, plea bargaining, and lineups; the right to a lawyer at government expense if the defendant cannot afford one; and the right of a mentally competent defendant to represent himself. It also includes the right to a lawyer with some minimal level of professional competence, for which reason it is also called the **right to effective assistance of counsel.** The right does not extend to civil cases.

**right to die** *n.* a phrase of varying scope, referring at a minimum to the right of a competent adult to refuse medical care that would prolong life, which is generally recognized by law, and at a maximum to a purported right to *physician-assisted suicide* (see under SUICIDE), which is generally not recognized in the United States. The Supreme Court has yet to find any such right in the Constitution. See also HEALTH CARE PROXY; LIVING WILL.

**right to keep and bear arms** *n.* Same as RIGHT TO BEAR ARMS.

**right to travel** *n.* the constitutional right of Americans to travel freely from state to state and somewhat less freely to foreign countries. The right of interstate travel includes not only the right to go to another state, but also the right of a newcomer to a state to be treated equally with those already there. The right of foreign travel can be restricted to some extent on national security or foreign policy grounds. See also FUNDAMENTAL RIGHT; *residency requirement* (under RESIDENCY).

**right to work laws** *n.pl.* anti-union legislation enacted in many states, protecting the right of workers to gain and keep employment without joining or contributing to a union.

**ripe** *adj.* (of a case) ready for the next procedural step: *ripe for decision; ripe for review.* Under the doctrine of **ripeness,** a court may decline to entertain a

case that it feels is still speculative and has not "matured" into a real controversy, as when a plaintiff seeks to challenge the constitutionality of a law on the ground that it might be used against her when it has not yet been used in that way.

**risk** *n.* **1.** the potential injury or loss covered by an insurance policy.
**2.** any possibility of harm or loss.
See also ASSUMPTION OF RISK.

**risk of nonpersuasion** *n.* Same as *burden of persuasion* (see under BURDEN[1]).

**rob** *v.*, **robbed, robbing.** to commit robbery; to subject to a robbery.
—**robber** *n.*

**robbery** *n.* **1.** the crime of taking someone's money or other personal property from the victim's person or in the victim's presence by force or threat of imminent harm.
**2. armed robbery** robbery committed through the use of a dangerous weapon or, in some states, through the use of a replica or other object appearing to be a weapon or while armed with a weapon.
**3. unarmed robbery** robbery that is not armed robbery.
—**Note.** Robbery is essentially LARCENY with the added factor of personal danger. In general, the kinds of threat that suffice as an element of robbery are threat of imminent bodily harm to the victim or to another, or threat to destroy the victim's home (but not other property).

**robing room** *n.* a room just off a courtroom, where the judge can put on and take off the robe worn on the bench, meet with clerks or study papers during breaks in the proceedings, or meet with the lawyers out of public hearing and without the formality of a courtroom.

**rocket docket** *n. Informal.* **1.** the docket of the United States District Court for the Eastern District of Virginia and the case management policy in that court, which for decades has been noted for the speed with which it pushes cases on its docket to conclusion.

**2.** any similar policy adopted or proposed for other courts.

—**Note.** The phrase *rocket docket* arose among lawyers practicing in the federal courts in eastern Virginia to describe the uncompromising policy in that district of allowing minimal time for case preparation and brooking no delay. That district's policy was succinctly described by the Litigation Division of the United States Army Legal Services Agency in a discussion of certain aspects of litigation of federal cases involving civilians: "As the name [rocket docket] implies, nothing short of blood spilled by counsel in the presence of the trial judge will gain a continuance." 1996 Army Lawyer 47 (May 1996).

**Rooker-Feldman abstention** *n.* See under ABSTENTION.

**ROR** RELEASE ON OWN RECOGNIZANCE.

**Roth IRA** *n.* See under IRA.

**royalty** *n., pl.* **royalties. 1.** a sum paid to the creator of a copyrighted work or the inventor of a patented invention, or to the holder of a copyright or patent, for the right to exploit the creation. Such royalties are usually based on the number of units sold, such as copies of a book or units of machinery.
**2.** a sum paid to the owner of land for the privilege of extracting oil, gas, or minerals, based on the number of barrels, tons, or other units extracted.

**rule** *n., v.,* **ruled, ruling.** —*n.* **1.** any of a set of principles and directives formally adopted by or imposed upon a body for its own administration, the governance of its members, or the guidance of those dealing with it.
**2.** especially, a regulation governing procedures in the courts: *rules of civil procedure; rules of criminal procedure; rules of appellate procedure; rules of evidence.* In addition to such generally applicable bodies of law, every court has a set of its own rules **(court rules, rules of court,** or, especially in the federal district courts, **local rules)** detailing how matters in that court are to be presented and handled.
**3.** an administrative REGULATION.

**4.** a legal principle, especially one of common law; e.g., the *rule against perpetuities* (see under PERPETUITY).
**5.** an old word for a court order. **a. rule absolute** Same as *decree absolute* (see under DECREE). **b. rule nisi** Same as *decree nisi* (see under DECREE).
—*v.* **6.** to decide an issue in a case; to issue a RULING: *The court will rule on our motion after lunch.*

**rule against perpetuities** *n.* See under PERPETUITY.

**rule of five** *n.* the practice apparently followed by the Supreme Court of the United States of not granting a hearing on petitions for habeas corpus filed in that court unless a majority of the nine justices vote to do so. Cf. RULE OF FOUR.
—**History.** This apparent exception to the Supreme Court's traditional RULE OF FOUR came to the attention of Court-watchers when the Court, in denying the petition of Robert Lee Tarver challenging Alabama's use of the electric chair as CRUEL AND UNUSUAL PUNISHMENT, noted that four justices had voted in favor of setting the case down for oral argument. *In re Tarver,* No. 99-8044 (U.S. Feb. 22, 2000).

**rule of four** *n.* the unwritten rule traditionally followed by the Supreme Court of the United States of accepting cases for discretionary review whenever four of the nine justices vote to do so. Cf. RULE OF FIVE.

**rule of thumb** *n.* a rough but practical approximation; a general or approximate principle, procedure, or rule based on experience or practice, as opposed to a hard-and-fast rule or a scientific calculation or estimate.
—**History.** A persistent legend, which has been traced to late eighteenth century England, holds that the early common law permitted a man to beat his wife so long as he did not use a stick bigger around than his thumb. In the latter part of the twentieth century, a long-overdue explosion of interest in the legal status of women in America brought much-needed attention to the problem of battered women, which had

theretofore not been taken particularly seriously by the police and the courts. As a byproduct of this important movement for change, the old legend was revived and elaborated: It became the conventional wisdom—widely repeated in books, articles, and law reviews—that American law had acquired from the English a common law principle that a man is free to beat his wife so long as the stick is no bigger than his thumb, that this principle was known as the "rule of thumb," and that, in fact, this barbaric legal rule was the very source of that seemingly innocent everyday expression. In time, the accumulation of such claims provoked scholarly research into the matter, and the research demolished both the recent myth that the phrase "rule of thumb" has something to do with wife-beating and the more established myth that there ever was a common law rule, either in England or in the United States, about the size of the stick with which one could beat one's wife; see, e.g., 44 J. Legal Educ. 341 (1994). Indeed, it appears that as far back as the early seventeenth century it has been a matter of speculation and dispute whether the common law authorized wife-beating in any form—although it is undoubted that, prior to the women's rights activism of the late twentieth century, the legal system in general exhibited a disgraceful lack of concern about the practice. But the power of a good myth is great, and despite the results of such research, law reviews have continued, right through the twentieth century and beyond, publishing articles perpetuating one aspect or another of the "rule of thumb" legend.

**rulemaking** *n.* the enactment by an administrative agency of REGULATIONS governing conduct in those industries or areas of activity over which it has authority; the LEGISLATIVE function of an administrative agency.

**ruling** *n.* a judicial or administrative decision or order.

**running account** *n.* See under ACCOUNT.

**running covenant** *n.* See under COVENANT.

# S

**/s/** or **s/** signed; a symbol sometimes placed before the name of the signer of a document on a copy of the document, or put on the copy in place of the signer's name, to make it clear that the original (but not the copy) was actually signed by that person. For example, this symbol typically appears before the judge's name on the signature line of a CONFORMED COPY of an order signed by the judge.

**S corporation** *n.* See under CORPORATION.

**safe-conduct** or **safe conduct** *n.* **1.** a document authorizing safe passage through a region, especially in time of war. For example, a safe-conduct might be issued to an enemy soldier for the purpose of discussing a possible truce, or to a neutral ship so that it can make a particular voyage on the high seas without becoming a target.
**2.** Usually, **safe conduct. a.** the privilege of safe passage accorded by such a document. **b.** the act of conducting safely.

**safe harbor** *n.* in a statute or regulation governing some activity (usually a business activity) in broad terms, a provision setting forth specific steps that, if taken, will guarantee that one is in compliance with the law. The safe harbor is not the only way to comply, but if followed it eliminates all doubt about whether one is in compliance.

**said** *adj.* previously referred to; mentioned above; aforesaid: *The said John Smith there and then took said gun and shot said victim.*
**——Usage.** The use of *said* or *aforesaid* was once regarded as necessary in legal documents when referring to a person or thing previously mentioned in the document, so as to avoid uncertainty—or at least a claim of uncertainty—about which person or thing is being referred to. Though still common in formal documents such as wills and indictments, this classic mark of the lawyer is now generally recognized as superfluous: *Smith then shot the victim with the gun.*

**sailor's will** *n.* See under WILL.

**salable** or **saleable** *adj.* **1.** suitable for sale; MERCHANTABLE.
**2.** capable of being sold; sellable.
**3. salable value** or **saleable value** the price at which something can be sold; MARKET VALUE.
**—salability, saleability** *n.*

**sale** *n.* **1.** a transfer of title to property for money or its equivalent, or a contract for such a transfer. See also BILL OF SALE; BOILER ROOM SALES. Cf. BARTER.
**2. sales** income received from the sale of goods: *The company had sales of $350,000 last year.*
**3. conditional sale** a sale in which the buyer does not receive unencumbered title to the property until some condition is met, usually payment of the balance of the purchase price.
**4. installment sale** a sale in which the buyer obtains possession of the property immediately but the price is to be paid in installments, with the seller retaining a security interest in the property until the price has been paid in full.
**5. judicial sale** a sale of property ordered by a court, either to satisfy a debt of the owner or to effect a PARTITION of the property.
**6. sale and leaseback** a contract in which one party buys property from the other and simultaneously agrees to rent it back to the seller for a period of time; in effect, the buyer is lending money to

the seller and holding title to the property as security for repayment, which is made in the form of "rent."

**7. tax sale** a *judicial sale* of property to satisfy back taxes.

**8. wash sale** a sale, especially of stocks or bonds, entered into at about the same time as a purchase of the same thing, leaving the seller in the same position as if the transactions had never occurred. Tax law prohibits the taking of tax benefits from such a transaction, and the securities laws prohibit such transactions as a means of creating a false impression of market activity.

**sales tax** *n.* a tax imposed by many states and municipalities on purchasers of goods and services, consisting of a fixed percentage added to the selling price in each retail transaction. It is a *regressive tax* (see under TAX), since people with modest incomes must spend proportionately more of their income on taxable goods and services, and have proportionately less left over for investments that are not subject to sales tax, than people with high incomes.

**Salic law** *n.* **1.** a code of laws of the Salian Franks, dating from the sixth century and first written down in Latin; important as the purest example of pre-Christian Germanic law.

**2.** the particular provision of that law excluding females from the inheritance of land. This was later used as a rationale for excluding women from the French throne, in contradistinction to the English practice.

**3.** by extension, any law excluding females from inheritance or from royal succession.

Also called **law Salique, lex Salica.**

**salvage** *n., v.,* **salvaged, salvaging.** *Maritime Law.* —*n.* **1.** compensation that one who voluntarily comes to the aid of a vessel in peril, thereby saving the ship or its cargo, is entitled to receive from the shipowner or the owner of the cargo.

**2.** the act of saving a ship or cargo from peril.

**3.** the property so saved.

**4.** the process of locating a sunken vessel and recovering property from it for its value as treasure or scrap or for its historical value.

—*v.* **5.** to save from shipwreck or similar peril.

**6.** to remove from a sunken vessel.

—**salvageable** *adj.*

—**salvageability** *n.*

—**salvager** *n.*

**salvage value** *n.* **1.** in some methods of depreciation, the estimated value of property at the end of its useful life; the residual value of an asset after all depreciation has been taken.

**2.** the value of property that has been seriously damaged, as by a fire or flood; scrap value.

**salve** *v.,* **salved, salving.** *Maritime Law.* to save from loss or destruction; to salvage.

—**salvability** *n.*

—**salvable** *adj.*

—**salvor** *n.*

**same-sex marriage** *n.* See under MARRIAGE.

**sanction** *v.* **1.** occasionally, to manifest approval of something, either in advance or after the fact: *The court sanctioned the defendant's conduct* (i.e., approved of it).

**2.** usually, to punish someone or impose a punishment for something: *The court sanctioned the defendant's conduct* (i.e., imposed a penalty for it); *the court sanctioned the defendant* (i.e., punished her).

—*n.* **3.** permission or approval.

**4.** penalty or punishment.

**5.** Often, **sanctions.** punitive measures taken by one or more countries toward another to force it to comply with international law.

—**sanctionable** *adj.*

**sanitary** *adj.* dealing with conditions affecting health, especially with reference to cleanliness and precautions against disease, such as cleanliness of restaurants or disposal of garbage: *sanitary code; sanitary laws.*

**satisfaction** *n.* **1.** full performance of an obligation; especially, payment of a debt in full: *satisfaction of a mortgage;*

*satisfaction of a judgment.*
**2.** discharge of an obligation or undertaking by a performance or payment accepted in lieu of what was originally contemplated or agreed to: *satisfaction of a legacy by transfer of the property to the legatee prior to the testator's death.*
**3.** a document or notation by an obligee that an obligation, especially a judgment, has been satisfied.
**4.** fulfillment of a description, requirement, or set of requirements.
See also *accord and satisfaction* (under ACCORD).
—**satisfy** *v.*, **satisfied, satisfying.**

**satisfaction piece** *n.* a formal written acknowledgement that a debt or judgment has been satisfied.

**Saturday night special** *n.* a cheap handgun.

**sauf-conduit** *n., pl.* **sauf-conduits** *Law French and French.* Same as SAFE-CONDUCT.

**save harmless** See under HARMLESS.

**saving clause** or **savings clause** *n.* **1.** in a legislative enactment that modifies or repeals a previous statute, a clause that continues the previous law's effectiveness for certain purposes, such as for purposes of any lawsuit initiated prior to the effective date of the repeal.
**2.** in a statute that establishes a new cause of action, procedure, right, etc., a clause stating that rights and procedures under previously existing laws remain available, and are not repealed by the new statute.
**3.** Also called **separability clause** or **severability clause.** a clause in a statute or contract providing that if any part or a particular part of the statute or contract is found to be void or unenforceable, that part will be carved out and the balance enforced to the extent possible.

**savings incentive match plan for employees (SIMPLE plan)** *n.* See under RETIREMENT PLAN.

**scandalous matter** *n.* pejorative or offensive statements in a pleading that are not necessary to the pleading; especially, unnecessary matter tending to incriminate a person. Under the Federal Rules of Civil Procedure and similar state rules, the court may order that any "redundant, immaterial, impertinent, or scandalous matter" in a pleading be stricken.

**scène à faire** *n., pl.* **scènes à faire.** *French.* (lit. "a scene to do; a scene that must be done") **1.** in copyright law, a stock element in an otherwise creative work; an element that is standard in carrying out a particular theme, or is dictated by circumstances apart from the author's creativity.
**2. scènes à faire doctrine** the doctrine that elements that are standard for carrying out the particular theme of a work, and thus are not really the product of the author's creative effort, cannot be protected by copyright.
——**History.** This term was borrowed from French literary criticism, where it referred to the climactic scene of a play or opera, the inevitable culmination of the dramatic events leading up to it. In copyright law the term has traditionally been applied to any standard or stereotypical plot element or character, such as an automobile chase in a police drama or a sinister butler in a mystery story. The scènes à faire doctrine precludes copyright infringement claims based solely upon similarities in such plot elements. More recently, the doctrine has been applied in less dramatic contexts, to elements in computer software that are substantially dictated by external factors such as requirements of compatibility with operating systems and hardware, customary business practices of expected end users, and standard programming techniques. For example, an appellate court in one case held "a set of four-digit numeric instructions...to access the features of a piece of telecommunications hardware" to be scènes à faire. *Mitel, Inc. v. Iqtel, Inc.,* 124 F.3d 1366 (10th Cir. 1997).

**schedule** *n., v.,* **scheduled, scheduling.** —*n.* **1.** a written list or itemization, often appended to some other document.
—*v.* **2.** to place an item upon such a

list.
—**scheduled** *adj.*

**Schedule I controlled substance** *n.* See under CONTROLLED SUBSTANCE.

**Schedule II controlled substance** *n.* See under CONTROLLED SUBSTANCE.

**Schedule III controlled substance** *n.* See under CONTROLLED SUBSTANCE.

**Schedule IV controlled substance** *n.* See under CONTROLLED SUBSTANCE.

**Schedule V controlled substance** *n.* See under CONTROLLED SUBSTANCE.

**scheduled debt** *n.* a debt listed by a bankrupt on a schedule filed with the bankruptcy court showing all of the bankrupt's debts.

**scheduled property** *n.* **1.** property listed on a schedule attached to an insurance policy, identifying the items covered by the policy for loss or damage and stating their value.
**2.** property listed on a schedule filed by a debtor in bankruptcy, identifying the bankrupt's assets and their value.

**sci. fa.** Abbreviation for SCIRE FACIAS.

**scienter** *n.* (from Latin, lit. "knowingly") guilty knowledge; such knowledge of facts or circumstances as to render one criminally or civilly liable for one's actions or for another's injury or loss. Especially, **a.** in a fraud case, the element of intent to defraud, or knowledge of the falsity of one's representations. The term is used particularly in connection with SECURITIES FRAUD. **b.** in a suit against the owner or custodian of a dog or other animal that has caused injury, actual or constructive knowledge of the animal's vicious propensities. See also ONE-BITE RULE.

**scintilla** *n.* a minute particle; spark; trace.

**scintilla of evidence** *n.* any bit of material evidence, however small, that would tend to establish an issue in the minds of a juror. Cf. SUBSTANTIAL EVIDENCE.

**scintilla rule** *n.* any of various rules, adhered to to some extent in some jurisdictions, to the effect that a scintilla

of evidence is sufficient to defeat a motion for summary judgment or for a directed verdict, or to sustain a verdict on appeal.

**scire facias** *n. Latin.* (lit. "make (him) know") **1.** a common law writ (in full, **writ of scire facias**) to initiate an action regarding a matter of public record, as to revive a judgment upon which there had been no execution for a year and a day or to cancel a corporate charter.
**2.** the proceeding founded upon such a writ.
Formerly often abbreviated **sci. fa.**

**scofflaw** *n.* a person who flouts the law, especially by repeatedly ignoring citations or failing to pay fines for relatively minor offenses such as parking or sanitation violations.

**scope of authority** *n.* the range of an agent's duties or permitted activities on behalf of a principal. The principal is normally bound by and liable for the acts of an agent within the scope of the agent's *actual* or *apparent authority* (see under AUTHORITY[1]). Also called **scope of agency.** See also RESPONDEAT SUPERIOR.

**scope of employment** *n.* any job-related activity by an employee. The employer is normally liable for torts committed by an employee acting within the scope of employment, as when a company driver causes an accident while making a delivery. See also RESPONDEAT SUPERIOR. Cf. FROLIC OF ONE'S OWN.

**scope of examination** *n.* the range of subjects inquired into in the questioning of a witness at a hearing or trial. See also EXAMINATION; BEYOND THE SCOPE.

**scope of expertise** *n.* the area of an expert witness's specialized knowledge. An expert witness may not testify to opinions on matters beyond the scope of her expertise. See also *expert witness* (under WITNESS).

**scope of review** *n.* the extent of a court's power to review a decision of a lower court or of an administrative agency. Such power is usually limited by a combination of constitutional provisions, statutory provisions, judicial policy, and the court's own discretion. See also STANDARD OF REVIEW.

**Scotch verdict** *n.* a verdict of "not proven" permitted by Scots criminal law; it has the legal effect of an acquittal, but leaves the defendant under a cloud of suspicion.

**scrutiny** *n.* judicial consideration of the purposes and effects of an administrative regulation or a state or federal law or policy in order to determine whether it is valid, especially under the DUE PROCESS and EQUAL PROTECTION clauses of the Constitution. In constitutional challenges under those clauses, the Supreme Court has defined three levels of scrutiny, the choice of which depends upon the nature of the rights at stake or the CLASSIFICATION involved: RATIONAL BASIS TEST; HEIGHTENED SCRUTINY; STRICT SCRUTINY.

**seal¹** *n.* **1. a.** originally, an impression made in melted wax on a document such as a contract, deed, or will, containing the unique mark of the maker of the document and signifying the maker's intent to be bound by it. **b.** today, any mark on the paper intended to represent such a seal, most commonly the word "seal" or the letters **L.S.** (for the Latin **locus sigilli,** lit. "the place of the seal") placed next to the maker's signature. See also UNDER SEAL (def. 1). **2. corporate seal** an identifying design adopted by a corporation, embossed on legal documents executed by the corporation to authenticate them and to act as a seal. **3. sealed instrument** or **instrument under seal** an INSTRUMENT to which the seal of the maker has been affixed. See also *contract under seal* (under CONTRACT); *covenant under seal* (under COVENANT).
—*v.* **4.** to affix a seal to; to execute with a seal.
——**History.** In early common law, a sealed instrument became legally effective upon delivery to the person benefited by it; later it became usual to place one's signature on the document

before affixing the seal (see *hand and seal* under HAND), but the final act making the instrument effective was still delivery—hence the phrase **signed, sealed, and delivered**. The legal significance of the seal has been modified by statutes which vary from state to state, and in some states it no longer has any significance at all.

**seal²** *v.* to place or keep items or records relating to a matter in a sealed envelope, or otherwise shield them from public access. See also UNDER SEAL (def. 2); *file under seal* (under FILE); *sealed bid* and *sealed bidding* (under BID); *sealed indictment* (under INDICTMENT); SEALED VERDICT.
—**sealable** *adj.*

**sealed verdict** *n.* a verdict kept in a sealed envelope and kept secret—even from the judge in a case—until a suitable or proper time to announce it. For example, a verdict reached late at night might be sealed until court reconvenes the next day, or a verdict involving a defendant who has fled might be sealed until the fugitive is found and can be brought into court to hear it.

**search** *n.* **1.** inspection by law enforcement officials of a person's body, home, or any area that the person would reasonably be expected to regard as private, for weapons, contraband, or evidence of criminal activity. Under the Fourth Amendment (see Appendix), a search ordinarily may not be conducted without PROBABLE CAUSE.
**2. border search** a search of a person or property coming into the country. If not unduly intrusive, this is permitted without any reason to suspect wrongdoing; strip searches and body cavity searches require an objective basis for suspicion of smuggling, but less than probable cause.
**3. consent search** a search conducted with the consent of the subject, or of a person with control over the area searched. This is legal even in the absence of probable cause, and even if the consent was given only because the subject did not know and was not told that she had any choice in the matter, so long as the consent was not the

product of duress.

**4. pretextual search** a search whose real purpose is to find evidence of a crime for which there is no probable cause to conduct a search, but ostensibly conducted for some other purpose which would have been permissible. Also called **pretext search.**

**5. unreasonable search** a search conducted without probable cause and in the absence of other considerations that would make it constitutionally permissible, such as consent of the subject or protection of the nation's borders.

**6. warrantless search** a search conducted without a warrant (see WARRANT[1]). This is permissible under EXIGENT CIRCUMSTANCES requiring prompt action.

—*v.* **7.** to conduct a search.
See also CURTILAGE; EXCLUSIONARY RULE; OPEN FIELD; STOP AND FRISK.
—**searchable** *adj.*

**search and seizure** *n.* **1.** a SEARCH leading to a SEIZURE of property. Because searches and seizures are often linked in practice and are governed by the same body of law, they are often discussed jointly by use of this phrase.
**2. unreasonable search and seizure** an *unreasonable search* (see under SEARCH) leading to a seizure of property.

**search warrant** *n.* See under WARRANT[1].

**seasonable** *adj.* timely; within the time agreed upon; within a reasonable time.
—**seasonableness** *n.*
—**seasonably** *adv.*

**seaworthy** *adj.* (of a vessel) sufficient in materials, construction, equipment, officers, crew, and outfit to withstand normal perils associated with the trade or service in which the vessel is employed. A shipowner who obtains marine insurance is normally deemed to warrant that the ship is seaworthy.
—**seaworthiness** *n.*

**second-look doctrine** *n.* Same as the WAIT-AND-SEE APPROACH to the application of the rule against perpetuities.

**second mortgage** *n.* See under MORTGAGE.

**secondary** *adj.* subordinate; derivative; lesser; not of the first or highest rank or order. Cf. PRIMARY.
—**secondarily** *adv.*
—**secondariness** *n.*

**secondary authority** *n.* See under AUTHORITY.

**secondary boycott** *n.* See under BOYCOTT.

**secondary liability** *n.* See under LIABILITY.

**secondary meaning** *n. Trademark Law.* an association developed over time in the public's mind between a common or descriptive name, symbol, package design, or the like, and the source of a particular product or service.
——**Note.** A name, design, or the like that is not inherently distinctive is not protectable as a TRADEMARK unless it can be shown to have acquired a "secondary meaning"; that is, it has become distinctive in the sense that the public now associates it with a particular manufacturer's goods or a particular supplier's services, rather than just with any product or service of that type.

**secret evidence** *n.* evidence used against a party in a legal proceeding but not disclosed to that party so that it might be rebutted.
——**Note.** The Constitution protects United States citizens and *resident aliens* (see under ALIEN) from the use of secret evidence against them in legal proceedings. However, in the Anti-Terrorism and Effective Death Penalty Act of 1996 and the Illegal Immigration Reform and Immigrant Responsibility Act of 1996, Congress specifically authorized the use of secret evidence in proceedings to remove aliens who are suspected terrorists from the country.

**secret partner** *n.* See under PARTNER.

**secta** *n., pl.* **sectae.** *Latin.* **1.** a group of followers; group of witnesses. See note below.
**2.** suit.
——**History.** In very ancient practice, before written pleadings became the

norm, a plaintiff was required to produce two or more persons in court at the time of instituting a suit to back up his allegations; in medieval Latin, these witnesses were referred to as the plaintiff's *secta,* or "following." When written pleadings were introduced, it was standard form for the plaintiff to recite at the end of the allegations, in Latin, "...and thereupon he produces *secta*"—referring to his supporters brought along as witnesses. In time the requirement of bringing followers to court was discarded. But in medieval Latin the word *secta* could also mean "suit," and the traditional phrase continued to be used, being reinterpreted as a reference to the suit rather than to a group of witnesses. The ancient phrase survived the transition from Latin to English pleading, in such forms as "and thereupon he produceth suit," or in more modern times, "and thereupon he brings suit." In this way the phrase survived for centuries after the practice that gave rise to it became extinct. The word *secta* in the medieval sense of "suit" also appears in various Latin legal phrases and maxims that are no longer used, and survives in the phrase AD SECTAM.

**section** *n.* **1.** a subdivision of a statute or document, represented by the symbol § (or §§ for "sections"). Most statutes and codes are divided into sections.
**2.** a subdivision or special interest group within an organization: *American Bar Association Section of Legal Education and Admissions to the Bar.*
**3.** in much of the United States, a square parcel of land one mile on a side laid out by government survey, one of thirty-six numbered sections within a township. One section contains 640 acres.

**section 401(k) plan** *n.* See under RETIREMENT PLAN.

**section 403(b) plan** *n.* See under RETIREMENT PLAN.

**section 457 plan** or **section 457(b) plan** *n.* See under RETIREMENT PLAN.

**secure** *v.,* **secured, securing.** to provide assurance that a debt will be paid or that funds will be available to pay damages if an obligation is not performed, particularly by giving the obligee a lien, mortgage, or other *security interest* (see under INTEREST[1]) in property. Lawyers speak interchangeably of securing the obligee (see *secured creditor* under CREDITOR) or securing the obligation (see *secured debt* under DEBT). See also *secured loan* (under LOAN); *secured transaction* (under TRANSACTION). —**secured** *adj.*

**securities acts** *n.pl.* statutes regulating the issuance and marketing of stocks, bonds, and other securities (see SECURITY[2]) to the public. They seek to avoid the conditions that led to the stock market crash of 1929 by assuring that investors will have access to full and accurate information and will be treated fairly. The principal federal securities acts are the **Securities Act of 1933,** which regulates the initial distribution of a new security to the public, and the **Securities Exchange Act of 1934,** which regulates all subsequent trading of a security. See also BLUE SKY LAW.

**securities broker** *n.* See under BROKER.

**securities fraud** *n.* the tort and crime of knowingly making any materially misleading statement, or failing to disclose a material fact, in connection with the purchase or sale of a security.

**security[1]** *n.* **1.** something given or deposited to provide assurance of payment of a debt or fulfillment of an obligation; especially, a *security interest* (see under INTEREST[1]) in property.
**2. security deposit** money set aside and held as security; particularly, money paid by a tenant at the beginning of a lease and held by the landlord in case the tenant damages the property or leaves without paying rent.

**security[2]** *n., pl.* **securities. 1.** an ownership interest in an enterprise (the ISSUER) or a right to share in profits from it or a debt owed by it, deriving from an investment in the enterprise rather than from participation in it. Most commonly, a bond (see BOND[1]) or shares of

STOCK.

**2.** a certificate evidencing such an interest or right.

**3. convertible security** a security that can be exchanged for another kind of security from the same issuer upon specified conditions; e.g., a bond convertible into stock, or preferred stock convertible into common stock.

**4. corporate security** a security issued by a corporation.

**5. debt security** a bond or other security representing a right to receive a share of each payment of interest or principal made by an enterprise in connection with a particular debt owed by it.

**6. equity security** stock or another security representing an ownership interest in an enterprise, or carrying a right to acquire such an interest; e.g., a warrant (see WARRANT²).

**7. government security** a security issued by the federal government or a federal agency; sometimes, a security guaranteed by the federal government.

**8. guaranteed security** a security in which the issuer's obligation to make payments is guaranteed by an entity other than the issuer.

**9. marketable security** a security that can easily be sold if the present owner needs cash or no longer wants the security.

**10. municipal security** a security issued by, or sometimes guaranteed by, a state or local government or governmental agency.

**11. redeemable security** a security that the issuer has a right to buy back (or, in the case of a *debt security*, to pay off prior to maturity) upon specified conditions. Also called **callable security.**

**security interest** *n.* See under INTEREST¹.

**sedition** *n.* **1.** action or words that, while falling short of treason, tend to incite a people against a government or to undermine governmental authority by causing public commotions and discontent.

**2.** in the United States, the crime of inciting, assisting, or engaging in any rebellion or insurrection against the authority of the United States or its laws. Mere advocacy of rebellion, however, is protected by the First Amendment unless likely to lead to imminent lawless action.

**3.** Also called **seditious conspiracy.** in the United States, the crime committed by two or more persons who conspire to overthrow or destroy the government of the United States by force, to levy war against the United States, or to use force to oppose governmental authority, hinder the execution of any law, or seize United States property.

—**seditionist** *n.*
—**seditious** *adj.*
—**seditiously** *adv.*
—**seditiousness** *n.*

**seduction** *n.* inducing a person, especially an unmarried woman, to engage in sexual intercourse. The term includes both honest and dishonest means of persuasion, but usually not force. Depending upon various factors such as the age of the person seduced, her previous chastity, the means used, and the state where the conduct occurred, seduction may be a crime, a tort for which the seduced person may sue, a tort for which her father or mother may sue, or none of these.

—**seduce** *v.,* **seduced, seducing.**

**segregation** *n.* **1.** separation; especially, the policy, practice, or fact of separation of certain groups from the general body of society or from each other within society, as by the establishment or existence of separate public and private facilities such as schools and clubs, the existence of separate housing or residential neighborhoods, or the existence of prohibitions on intermarriage or other forms of social interaction.

**2.** Also called **racial segregation.** segregation on the basis of race; particularly the historical separation of blacks from whites in the United States.

See also DE FACTO SEGREGATION; DE JURE SEGREGATION.

—**segregate** *v.*, **segregated, segregating.**

—**segregated** *adj.*

**seise** *v.*, **seised, seising.** to invest with SEISIN; to put into possession of a freehold. Also, **seize.**

**seised** or **seized** *adj.* invested with seisin; having ownership (of a freehold estate): *His wife inherited all the lands of which he died seised.*

**seisin** or **seizin** *n.* possession of land in which one has a FREEHOLD interest; that is, actual occupancy of the land that one holds in fee simple, in fee tail, or for life. See also *covenant of seisin* (under COVENANTS OF TITLE); LIVERY OF SEISIN.

——**History.** Throughout most of the history of English land law, *seisin* was the quality that today we would generally think of as *ownership.* To have seisin one had to have at least a life interest in the property (a term of years, even if it was 999 years, was not sufficient), and one had to have gone onto the land (though occupancy by the owner's tenant could satisfy this requirement).

**seizure** *n.* **1.** (of a person) an ARREST.
**2.** (of property in criminal matters) the taking of possession, by law enforcement officials, of a weapon, contraband, or evidence of a crime, usually pursuant to a SEARCH. The government's right to make such seizures is limited by the Fourth Amendment (see Appendix); a seizure resulting from an *unreasonable search* (see under SEARCH) is unlawful. See also SEARCH AND SEIZURE; EXCLUSIONARY RULE.
**3.** (of property in civil cases) an ATTACHMENT or other procedure by which property is brought under the control of the court.

—**seizable** *adj.*

—**seize** *v.*, **seized, seizing.**

**selective** *adj.* **1.** characterized by selection of specific items or instances out of a set of possibilities.
**2.** making such a selection.

—**selectively** *adv.*

—**selectiveness** *n.*

**selective amnesia** *n. Informal.* disparaging characterization of the state of mind of a witness who appears to have a clear memory of events favorable to one side of a dispute, but claims to have only a vague memory or no memory of events favorable to the other side.

**selective conscientious objector** *n.* See under CONSCIENTIOUS OBJECTOR.

**selective enforcement** *n.* enforcement of the law in a discriminatory fashion, particularly in a way that unfairly or disproportionately targets members a particular race, religion, or other such group.

**selective prosecution** *n.* an abuse of *prosecutorial discretion* (see under DISCRETION) in which race, religion, or some other unjustifiable classification is used as a basis for the decision whether or not to prosecute a case.

**self-authenticating** *adj.* See under AUTHENTICATE.

**self-dealing** *n.* transactions by a trustee or other FIDUCIARY in which the fiduciary has a personal interest that might conflict with the interest of the party to whom she owes a fiduciary duty. Self-dealing usually constitutes a *breach of fiduciary duty* (see under BREACH).

**self-defense** *n.* the use of reasonable force against an aggressor by one who reasonably believes it necessary in order to avoid imminent bodily harm. Self-defense is a justification for conduct that would otherwise be a crime or tort. See also RETREAT.

**self-employment income** *n.* See under INCOME.

**self-employment tax** *n.* a tax on self-employed individuals requiring them to make a double contribution to the SOCIAL SECURITY system, paying both the employer's share and the employee's share. See also SOCIAL SECURITY TAX.

**self-executing** *adj.* (of a treaty, constitutional provision, statute, order, contract, or other legal instrument) effective without further action; requiring no implementing legislation or other action to become effective. For example, a statute that simply declares certain conduct to be unlawful would be self-executing, whereas a statute directing a particular agency to draw up regulations to govern a particular kind of business would not by itself regulate such businesses, but would depend upon the implementing regulations to be fully effective.

**self-help** *n.* the taking of action to remedy a wrong without calling upon the police or initiating legal proceedings. Some kinds of self-help are permitted by law, such as (usually) the repossession of an automobile whose buyer has fallen behind in installment payments.

**self-incrimination** *n.* the making of a statement that may expose the speaker to criminal penalties. Under the Fifth Amendment (see Appendix), the government may not require people to make such statements or penalize them for refusing to do so. See PRIVILEGE AGAINST SELF-INCRIMINATION; see also *transactional immunity* and *use immunity* (under IMMUNITY).
—**self-incriminating, self-incriminatory** *adj.*

**self-insurance** *n.* the setting aside of funds to cover certain potential risks or losses instead of purchasing insurance for those particular risks.
—**self-insured** *adj.*
—**self-insurer** *n.*

**sell** *v.*, **sold, selling.** to transfer title to property for money or its equivalent, or to make a contract for such a transfer.
—**sellable** *adj.*

**seller** *n.* **1.** a person who sells or contracts to sell goods or other property.
**2.** a potential seller.
**3.** for purposes of anti-fraud provisions of the federal securities laws, any person who proximately causes a sale of securities.

**semble** *Law French.* (lit. "similar; it seems") —*adj., adv.* **1.** similar; similarly; to the same effect. Used to introduce a citation, or parenthetically after a citation, to indicate that the cited case or passage supports the same general proposition as the immediately preceding citation, or supports the general proposition just stated, though perhaps in a different context and by way of analogy.
—*v.* **2.** (especially in older cases) it seems. Used in an opinion to introduce a legal proposition that is somewhat apart from or broader than the point being decided in the case. This signal, now seldom used, indicated that in the court's view the stated proposition was probably correct, but that it was not strictly a part of the court's holding: *Semble that, with the consent of the debtor, a part of a judgment might be assigned; in this case the question does not arise, however, because the whole of the judgment was assigned.*
—*n.* **3.** (especially in older cases) dictum; not a holding. Used in headnotes, or parenthetically after citations, to indicate that the proposition under discussion is stated by the court but not as part of its holding. Also used to refer to the statement itself: *The only authority for the position advanced by the plaintiff is a semble in the case of Smith v. Jones.*

**senior** *adj.* having priority among potential recipients of payment or benefits in the event that resources run short and a conflict arises among claimants with similar interests: *senior creditor; senior lien; senior security.* Opposite: JUNIOR; SUBORDINATE; SUBORDINATED.
—**seniority** *n.*

**senior judge** *n.* See under JUDGE.

**senior partner** *n.* See under PARTNER.

**seniority system** *n.* an employment policy, often required by union contract, under which workers who have worked for the same employer for longer periods are entitled to better benefits and more protection against firing than workers who have been there a shorter time. Although such policies perpetuate racial and other imbalances due to past discrimination in hiring, they are expressly permitted by most civil rights laws.

**sentence** *n.* **1.** a court's JUDGMENT imposing a penalty upon a person convicted of an offense, or the penalty imposed, such as imprisonment, a fine, community service, or death. See also CAPITAL PUNISHMENT.

**2. concurrent sentences** sentences on different charges to be served simultaneously. Concurrent sentences are often imposed so that if the defendant obtains a reversal of conviction on one or more counts, but less than all, it will not affect the length of time spent in prison.

**3. consecutive sentences** sentences on different charges to be served one after the other. Consecutive sentences may be imposed when a defendant's conduct constituted several distinct crimes, in order to maximize the total time of imprisonment. Also called **cumulative sentences.**

**4. determinate sentence** a sentence setting a definite term of incarceration. Also called **definite sentence.**

**5. indeterminate sentence** a sentence specifying minimum and maximum terms of imprisonment, with exact date of release between those limits to be determined by the parole board. Also called **indefinite sentence.**

**6. suspended sentence** a sentence that the defendant will not be required to serve unless she commits another crime or violates some other condition imposed by the court.

—**sentence** *v.,* **sentenced, sentencing.**
—**sentencer** *n.*

**sentencing guidelines** *n.pl.* a set of rules or standards for judges to follow in imposing sentences, depending upon various factors such as the nature of a crime, the presence or absence of aggravating factors, and the defendant's prior criminal record. The federal government and many states have established commissions to draw up such guidelines in order to increase uniformity in sentencing.

**SEP** *n., pl.* **SEPs, SEP's.** Abbreviation for *simplified employee pension* (see under RETIREMENT PLAN).

**SEP-IRA** *n.* See under IRA.

**separability clause** *n.* See under SAVING CLAUSE.

**separate but equal** *n.* the doctrine, formally adopted by the Supreme Court in 1896 in the infamous case of *Plessy v. Ferguson,* 163 U.S. 537, holding that legally mandated racial segregation does not violate the constitutional requirement of EQUAL PROTECTION so long as the law contemplates the provision of "separate but equal" facilities for people of color.

—**History.** In the celebrated case of *Brown v. Board of Education,* 347 U.S. 483 (1954), the Supreme Court finally recognized that racially separate educational facilities are not just demeaning but "inherently unequal," and took the first step away from the separate-but-equal doctrine by declaring racially segregated public schools unconstitutional. Shades of the doctrine persist, however, in the context of sex-segregated education: Almost a quarter century after *Brown* the Supreme Court affirmed a decision permitting the city of Philadelphia to maintain two separate high schools for academically gifted students—"Central High" for boys and "Girls High" for girls—upon a finding that "[t]he courses offered by the two schools are similar and of equal quality" and "[t]he academic facilities are comparable, with the exception of those in the scientific field where Central's are superior." *Vorchheimer v. School District of Philadelphia,* 532 F.2d 880 (3d Cir. 1976), *aff'd by an equally divided court,* 430 U.S. 703 (1977). On the Supreme Court brief for the losing side in that case was Ruth Bader Ginsburg, who nineteen years later wrote the majority opinion for the Court in a case holding that the state of Virginia's exclusion of women from the Virginia Military Institute was unconstitutional, and that the constitutional problem could not be cured by establishing a parallel but less prestigious and less well endowed institution for women. *United States v. Virginia,* 518 U.S. 515 (1996). Even in that case the Court left open the possibility that "separate but equal" public schools for males and females could pass constitutional muster; but by laying heavy emphasis on the requirement that any such scheme have an "exceedingly persuasive justification" (a phrase used nine times in the opinion), the Court made it clear that sex segregation in public education can no longer be justified simply by invoking the concept of "separate but equal."

**separate maintenance** *n.* See under MAINTENANCE.

**separate opinion** *n.* See under OPINION.

**separate property** *n.* **1.** property owned by one spouse separately from the other.
**2.** property that is not considered as MARITAL PROPERTY or COMMUNITY PROPERTY; for example, property that belonged to one of the spouses before they got married, property received by one spouse during the marriage as a gift or from a decedent by will or intestate succession, or property that the spouses have agreed to treat as separate property under a MARITAL PROPERTY AGREEMENT.
Also called **individual property.**

**separate property state** *n.* Same as COMMON LAW STATE.

**separate return** *n.* See under RETURN.

**separate trial** *n.* See under TRIAL.

**separation** *n.* **1.** the termination of cohabitation of a husband and wife, or the status of a husband and wife who are living apart, either preliminary to a divorce or instead of divorcing.
**2. legal separation** separation of spouses pursuant to a court order or, sometimes, pursuant to a SEPARATION AGREEMENT.

**separation agreement** *n.* a formal agreement between spouses stating that they will live apart and setting forth the terms of their separation.

**separation of church and state** *n.* the principle that government should not meddle in or involve itself with religion, as by dictating, discriminating among, or subsidizing religious beliefs or practices. The principle is embodied in the *Establishment Clause* and the *Free Exercise Clause* of the First Amendment to the Constitution. See discussion at ESTABLISHMENT OF RELIGION and FREE EXERCISE OF RELIGION. See also FREEDOM OF RELIGION; WALL OF SEPARATION BETWEEN CHURCH AND STATE.

**separation of powers** *n.* the theory that government should have three separate branches: a legislative branch to make laws, an executive branch to administer them, and a judicial branch to interpret them and resolve disputes arising under them. For the national government of the United States, the first three articles of the Constitution define the powers of each of these three branches in turn. In practice there is much overlap and interplay among the three branches.

**separation settlement** *n.* **1.** a SEPARATION AGREEMENT, especially one that provides for transfer or division of property.
**2.** property to which one obtains title pursuant to such an agreement.
Cf. MARRIAGE SETTLEMENT.

**sequester** *v.* to segregate, isolate, or set apart, especially by court order. To sequester property is to hold it aside pending a decision on its disposition; to sequester witnesses is to keep them from talking to each other or listening to testimony during a trial; to sequester a jury is to keep it in isolation during a trial or during deliberations so as to shield it from outside influence.
—**sequestrable** *adj.*
—**sequestration** *n.*

**sequestrate** *v.*, **sequestrated, sequestrating.** Same as SEQUESTER.

**sequestrator** *n.* **1.** the person designated by a court to hold sequestered property.
**2.** an official who executes a sequestration order.

**servant** *n.* an employee; a person hired to perform services for another (the MASTER) and subject to the other's control both as to what work is done and how it is done (in contrast to an INDEPENDENT CONTRACTOR, who has more autonomy). See also BORROWED SERV-ANT; FELLOW SERVANT; and see note at MASTER AND SERVANT.

**serve** *v.,* **served, serving.** to effect SERV-ICE of papers or process. See also PROC-ESS SERVER.
—**server** *n.*
——**Usage.** One can speak of serving either the person or the papers: *The marshal served the defendant with the summons. The marshal served the summons on* (or *upon*) *the defendant.*

**service** *n.* **1.** Also called **service of process.** the giving of formal notice of judicial proceedings or a judicial act to a person involved, by delivering a copy of the PROCESS to the person or following some other procedure prescribed by law.
**2.** the act of providing a copy of any paper filed with the court, such as a motion or affidavit, to the other parties or attorneys in the case. Normally a court will reject the paper if this has not been done. Cf. EX PARTE.
**3. personal service** hand delivery of a copy of the process directly to the intended recipient or to an agent authorized to accept process.
**4. service by publication** the printing of notice of an action in a newspaper in the hope that the person affected by it will see it. This is the least effective method of service, allowed only in certain situations and only as a last resort.
**5. sewer service** purported service of process by a process server who files a return falsely stating that he has effected service. The term derives from the idea of a process server throwing the papers down a sewer to save the trouble of locating and serving the individual who was to receive them. To make it difficult to file false affidavits of service, some statutes require that proof of service include a physical description of the individual to whom the papers were given.
**6. substituted service** any of several methods of service permitted in place of personal service under certain circumstances, such as service by mail. Also called **constructive service.**

See also *affidavit of service* (under AFFI-DAVIT); NAIL AND MAIL; PROOF OF SERV-ICE; RETURN OF SERVICE.

**service mark** *n.* **1.** a name, symbol, or other MARK used by a company to identify its services and distinguish them from the services of others. For example, the distinctive logo of a bank or a restaurant chain would be a service mark.
**2. registered service mark** a service mark that is a *registered mark* (see under MARK). See also ®; SM.

**service redlining** *n.* the practice of a business in refusing or failing to provice services to specific neighborhoods either out of safety concerns (as in the case of PIZZA REDLINING or taxi redlining) or because of economic considerations.

**services** *n.pl.* in older law, the labor of a wife or child contributing to the economic welfare of a man's household. The common law recognized a man's right to recover damages for the loss of such services from anyone who injured or enticed away his wife or child. Since the husband owed no services to his wife, she had no corresponding right of action. To the extent that loss of economic services of a family member is recognized as giving rise to a tort claim today, it applies without regard to the sex of the spouse or the parent. See also CONSORTIUM. Cf. THEFT OF SERVICES.

**servient estate** *n.* See under ESTATE³.

**servient tenement** *n.* See under ES-TATE³.

**servitude** *n.* **1.** Also called **involuntary servitude.** forced labor; working for another against one's will, whether for pay or not. This includes not only SLAV-ERY but also such schemes as requiring a person to work for one to whom he is indebted in order to work off the debt. It is outlawed by the Thirteenth Amendment (see Appendix), except as punishment for a crime. Public responsibilities such as jury duty and military service for draftees are not barred by the Thirteenth Amendment.
**2.** a right to use another's land for a

particular purpose, and the corresponding burden upon the land (see BURDEN²); an EASEMENT, LICENSE (def. 4), or PROFIT A PRENDRE.

**session** *n.* **1.** the period of time during which a legislature, court, council, or the like meets to transact business, typically spanning several months: *The annual session of the state legislature convenes on the first Monday after January 1 and usually ends in June.*
**2.** a single sitting of such a body: *Spectators must remain silent while the court is in session. The judge directed the parties to return by 1:00 for the afternoon session.*
**3. closed session** a private session of a legislature, court, or other body; a session that may be attended only by members of the body and others needed for the business at hand.
**4. executive session** a *closed session* of a legislature, committee, or other deliberative body.
**5. lame-duck session** a legislative session held during the period between a general election and the seating of newly elected members, so that some of the legislators participating in the session are LAME DUCKS.
**6. open session** a session that nonmembers or nonparticipants may attend and observe.
**7. regular session** a session commencing at a fixed time at regular intervals; for example, the annual session of a legislature.
**8. special session** a session held other than at the regular time, for a special purpose. For example, a legislature that has adjourned for the year might be called back into special session to consider emergency legislation. Also called **extraordinary session.**

**session laws** *n.pl.* the statutes enacted during a session of a legislature, published in the order and the exact form in which they are enacted, before they are codified (see CODIFY, def. 2).

**set aside** *v.,* **set aside, setting aside.** to nullify a judgment, verdict, or court order. See also QUASH; VACATE.

**set off** *v.,* **set off, setting off.** to balance two opposing claims against each other, eliminating the smaller and reducing the larger by that amount. The reduction is called a **setoff** or **offset:** *The landlord's claim against the tenant for $1,000 in property damage was set off against the tenant's claim for refund of the $3,000 security deposit, and the landlord was ordered to refund the remaining $2,000.*

**settle** *v.,* **settled, settling. 1.** to reach agreement resolving a dispute: *settle a case; settle a labor dispute.*
**2.** to pay in full: *settle a bill.*
**3.** to complete all the tasks of administration and distribution of a decedent's property: *settle an estate.*
**4.** to transfer title to property; especially (now mostly historical), to convey all or part of a family estate to one or more family members or to a prospective family member (see MARRIAGE SETTLEMENT): *settle the estate upon the eldest son; settle forty acres upon the bride and groom.*
**5.** to create a TRUST by placing money or property in the hands of a trustee for administration: *settle a trust.*
**6.** to submit to a court for approval and signing: *settle an order; settle a judgment.*
**7.** to take up residence in; to populate: *settle in a new location; settle a territory.*

**settlement** *n.* **1.** the act of settling something, or the state of being settled.
**2.** the terms upon which something is settled.
**3.** the instrument by which something is settled, as a deed or written agreement.
**4.** the final disposition of property or an estate.
**5.** the property settled upon a person.
**6. full settlement a.** the resolution of all issues between two parties in a case or dispute, usually including an exchange of *mutual releases* (see under RELEASE). **b.** payment of the full amount of a bill or other finanancial obligation, or of the entire amount not previously paid.

**7. global settlement** a settlement resolving all issues among all parties to a complex case or dispute.

**8. out-of-court settlement** or **settlement out of court** the settlement of a dispute before litigation is commenced, or of a case before it goes to trial, or of a case on trial before a verdict is rendered. See note below.

**9. partial settlement a.** a settlement of some but not all issues in a case or dispute, or a settlement among some but not all of the parties involved in a case or dispute. **b.** a payment of part of a bill or other financial obligation, if accepted by the obligee as partially satisfying the obligation.

See also DIVORCE SETTLEMENT; MARRIAGE SETTLEMENT; SEPARATION SETTLEMENT; VIATICAL SETTLEMENT.

—**Usage.** *Out-of-court settlement* is a term more often used by nonlawyers than by lawyers, often as just another term for *settlement* of a legal dispute. It is especially appropriate as applied to disputes that are resolved without instituting litigation, or at least to cases that are resolved before trial; but the phrase is also heard in situations where parties to a case that is on trial meet and settle the case before the trial is concluded, even if the meeting takes place in the courthouse. Thus what the media report as an "out-of-court settlement" may have been reached in the courthouse hallway, or restroom, or the judge's chambers—or even in the courtroom itself while the jury was out deliberating.

**settler** *n.* one who settles something (except in the sense of one who conveys property). See SETTLE (defs. 1–3, 6–7). Cf. SETTLOR.

**settlor** *n.* **1.** one who conveys property; the grantor in a settlement of property upon a person such as a family member or prospective spouse. See SETTLE (def. 4).
**2.** the person who creates a TRUST by transferring money or property to a TRUSTEE for administration.
Also called the GRANTOR, DONOR, or TRUSTOR. See SETTLE (def. 5). Cf. SETTLER.

**seven dirty words** *n.* a celebrated list of seven words featured in a monologue given by comedian George Carlin in the early 1970's, ruminating on the subject of "words…you couldn't say on the public airwaves."

—**History.** Carlin's linguistic and legal instincts were proved correct in 1978, when the Supreme Court upheld a finding by the Federal Communications Commission that a radio station's broadcast of a recording of his monologue during daytime hours violated federal law. Specifically, the broadcast was held to be INDECENT (though not OBSCENE) within the meaning of a federal statute making it a crime to utter "any obscene, indecent, or profane language by means of radio communication." The Court's decision did not turn on any particular words from Carlin's list (which had grown to ten by the end of the monologue), but dealt with the monologue taken as a whole, as broadcast at a time when children were likely to hear it. Although the decision is popularly thought to have been a ruling on specific words, it is better understood as an affirmation of the FCC's power to penalize broadcasters for indecent (as distinguished from obscene) broadcasts, as evaluated on a case-by-case basis. A transcript of the entire monologue is reprinted as an appendix to the Court's opinion: *Federal Communications Commission v. Pacifica Foundation,* 438 U.S. 726 (1978).

**seven years' absence** *n.* continuous and unexplained absence of an individual, with no communication or information about the person, for a period of seven years. This ordinarily suffices to give rise to a presumption that the person has died.

**sever** *v.* **1.** to split off a part of a case and make it a separate case, in order to avoid prejudice or for administrative convenience: *to sever a claim; sever a party; sever the case.* Cf. CONSOLIDATE; JOIN.
**2.** to divide or cut anything into parts, or split anything off from a greater whole: *to sever the bonds of matrimony; sever crops from the land; sever the oil*

rights from the mineral rights in a parcel of land.
—**severance** n.

**severability clause** n. See under SAVING CLAUSE.

**severable** adj. **1.** capable of being split into two or more parts to be treated differently: a severable case; severable statute; severable estate. See also severable contract (under CONTRACT); severability clause (under SAVING CLAUSE). Cf. ENTIRE.
**2.** capable of being split off from the rest: The case against the absconding defendant is severable; hence the prosecution can go forward against the remaining defendants. The unconstitutional section is severable from the rest of the statute.
—**severability** n.

**several** adj. separate; individual, independent of others in a group. See, e.g., several liability (under LIABILITY). Cf. JOINT JOINT AND SEVERAL.
—**severally** adv.

**severalty** n. the condition of being under individual ownership. See also IN SEVERALTY.

**sewer service** n. See under SERVICE.

**sex abuse** n. Same as SEXUAL ABUSE.

**sex discrimination** n. discrimination against women for not being men, or occasionally against men for not being women. Sex discrimination permeated American law at every level until the 1960's, when statutes and constitutional decisions limiting such discrimination began to appear. Also called **sex-based discrimination, gender discrimination, gender-based discrimination.** See also BONA FIDE OCCUPATIONAL QUALIFICATION; HEIGHTENED SCRUTINY; PREGNANCY DISCRIMINATION; SEPARATE BUT EQUAL; SEXUAL HARASSMENT; STATUTORY RAPE.

**sex-plus discrimination** n. discrimination based upon a combination of sex and other factors; for example, refusing to hire married women while hiring men without regard to marital status, or harassing young female employees but not older ones. For purposes of laws against employment discrimination, such conduct constitutes sex discrimination.

**sexual abuse** n. the crime of imposing sexual contact upon a person, especially upon a child. The term is usually applied to contact not amounting to RAPE, and is typically divided into degrees according to the nature and circumstances of the contact. Also called **carnal abuse, sex abuse.**

**sexual assault** n. See under ASSAULT.

**sexual harassment** n. a form of unlawful employment discrimination consisting of HARASSMENT of an employee or group of employees, usually women, because of their sex. This may take the form of requiring or seeking sexual favors as a condition of employment **(quid pro quo harassment)** or otherwise subjecting an employee to intimidation, ridicule, or insult because of her sex, whether or not the harassing conduct is sexual in nature **(hostile environment harassment).** See also HOSTILE WORKING ENVIRONMENT.

**sexual predator** n. a person with a history of sexual offenses against others, who is regarded as unlikely to be able to control the impulse to commit more such crimes in the future. Also called **sexually dangerous person.**

**shadow counsel** n. See standby counsel (under COUNSEL).

**shadow jury** n. a group of individuals hired by one side in a trial to observe the proceedings as if they were jurors and report their reactions as the trial goes along, so that the attorneys can adjust their strategies according to what plays well. The shadow jurors are selected to match the real jurors as closely as possible demographically, and the process is usually conducted under the aegis of a JURY CONSULTANT.

**Shafi'i** n. Islamic Law. one of the four principal schools of Islamic law, founded by al-Shafi'i (c.767–820). See

note at SHARI'A.
—**Shafi'ite** *n.*

**shall** *auxiliary v.* **1.** (expressing mandate, necessity, or compulsion, especially in statutory or judicial directives) must; is or are obliged, required, or condemned to: *The meetings of the council shall be public. Violators shall be imprisoned for ten to twenty years.*
**2.** (expressing determination, certainty, emphasis) is determined to; definitely will: *I shall return. We shall overcome.*
**3.** (expressing futurity) plan to, intend to, or expect to; will: *I shall be home in time for dinner.*
**4.** (in occasional contexts) should; ought; may; is supposed to.
——**Usage.** *Shall* is an overused term in statutes and legal instruments and a favorite bugbear of legal language reformers, who sometimes suggest that in order to avoid ambiguity legal drafters should never use the word except in its mandatory sense. Certain uses of the word in older statutes simply reflect ways of writing that were formerly common but have become outdated (*If he shall go... When they shall have arrived...*), and there is no reason for modern drafters to continue to use such archaisms. But the word *shall* is one of the oldest in the English language, and like most words it has acquired several meanings and uses; it is unrealistic to expect its use in law to be artificially restricted to a single meaning. The best course for drafters is simply to use the word in legal drafting just as they would in any other writing, and eschew it whenever it would strike the nonlegal ear as odd or artificial.

**sham** *n.* **1.** something that is not what it purports to be; a spurious imitation.
**2.** a person who is not what he purports to be.
—*adj.* **3.** pretended; counterfeit; feigned.

**sham pleading** *n.* a pleading that is obviously frivolous or palpably false.

**sham transaction** *n.* See under TRANS-ACTION.

**share** *n.* a partial right or interest allotted to one of several people who together have the whole right or interest; in particular, a unit of ownership of a CORPORATION or *joint stock company* (see under COMPANY)—that is, one of the equal fractional parts into which a class of STOCK of such an entity is divided. See also ELECTIVE SHARE.

**shareholder** *n.* Same as STOCKHOLDER.

**shareholder derivative action** *n.* See under ACTION.

**shari'a** or **shari'ah** *n.* Islamic law; the entire body of principles and rules of human conduct according to Islamic teaching.
——**Note.** In the predominant Sunni branch of Islam there are four basic schools or approaches to law: HANAFI, HANBALI, MALIKI, and SHAFI'I. These four distinct schools evolved within the first two centuries of Islam, each with its own emphasis among different sources and methods for determining and applying legal doctrine (see USUL AL-FIQH). Each is now the prevailing school of legal analysis and interpretation in one or more countries or geographic areas within the Muslim world.

**shell corporation** *n.* See under CORPORATION.

**Shepardize** *v.*, **Shepardized, Shepardizing.** *Trademark.* to look up a decision in SHEPARD'S or another citator, in order to check on the subsequent history of the case or find other cases referring to the decision.
—**Shepardizing, Shepardization** *n.*
——**Usage.** In a strict sense, to "Shepardize" a case or citation means to check it in a Shepard's citator. But there is no generic word meaning "to look up in a citator"; consequently, the word "Shepardize" is sometimes used loosely in that generic sense. In judicial decisions and law review articles, usage is about equally divided between capitalizing this word and writing it with a lowercase *s*.

**Shepard's** *n. Trademark.* The oldest and best known CITATOR for United States law.

**sheriff** *n.* the chief peace officer of a county, with responsibility for serving or carrying out judicial process, maintaining the county jail, and keeping the peace.
——**History.** Many common law writs were addressed to the sheriff and directed him to take specific action, such as bringing a prisoner to court, rounding up a jury, or seizing property of a debtor.

**Sherman Antitrust Act** *n.* the first federal ANTITRUST law. It prohibits MONOPOLIZATION, attempted monopolization, and any concerted action in UNREASONABLE RESTRAINT OF TRADE. Also called **Sherman Act.**

**shield law** *n.* a statute creating an *evidentiary privilege* (see under PRIVILEGE).
——**Usage.** This phrase is most commonly used to describe laws protecting victims in rape cases from unnecessary inquiry into their sexual history, or protecting reporters from having to disclose news sources. See RAPE SHIELD LAW; REPORTER'S SHIELD LAW.

**shift** *n.* See *burden shifting* (under BURDEN¹).

**shop** *n.* **1.** a business or place of employment, especially one in which the workers have a UNION.
**2. agency shop** a shop in which workers are required to pay union dues whether they join the union or not.
**3. closed shop** a shop in which one must be a union member to get a job, and must remain a member to keep it. Although federal labor law forbids closed shops, as a practical matter one cannot get work in some fields except through a union.
**4. open shop** a shop in which union and nonunion workers are treated equally.
**5. preferential shop** a shop in which union members are given preferential treatment over nonmembers.
**6. union shop** a shop in which nonunion workers may be hired but must then join and remain a member of a union.
See also RIGHT TO WORK LAWS.

**shoplifting** *n.* the crime of taking possession of merchandise in a store with the intention of keeping or using it without paying for it. Shoplifting is a form of LARCENY.

**short-swing profits** *n.pl.* profits realized by an officer, director, or ten-percent owner of a publicly traded corporation from any purchase and sale, or sale and purchase, of the corporation's stock within a six-month period. In general, under the federal securities laws, the corporation may claim such profits for itself, and if it fails to do so any shareholder may sue on behalf of the corporation to recover the profits. Occasionally called **short-swing profit.**

**short-term** *adj.* **1.** covering a relatively short period of time: *short-term lease; short-term loan.*
**2.** pertaining to property not held for a sufficiently long period to qualify for favorable capital gains tax treatment upon disposition: *short-term property; short-term gain.*

**show** *v.,* **showed, shown** or **showed, showing. 1.** to convince or try to convince a court of something by evidence and legal argument: *The plaintiff failed to show a need for an injunction; an injunction will issue only upon a showing that without it the applicant will suffer irreparable harm.*
**2. show cause** to present reasons why a court should issue, or refuse to issue, a particular order. See also *order to show cause* (under ORDER¹).
——**showing** *n.*

**show trial** *n.* **1.** (especially in a totalitarian state) a public trial, especially of a political offender, spy, or the like, often carefully orchestrated and with a predetermined outcome, conducted chiefly for political and propagandistic purposes, as to suppress further dissent against the government by making an example of the accused.
**2.** any criminal trial prosecuted with much publicity for political purposes, as to make an example of the accused or enhance the reputation or political career of the prosecutor or other officials associated with the prosecution.

**showup** *n.* the displaying of a criminal suspect singly to a witness for the purpose of identification, usually within a few hours after the crime; an inherently suggestive procedure that is nevertheless common. Cf. LINEUP.

**shrink-wrap license** *n.* a license to use copyrighted software that is printed or referred to on the sealed box or envelope in such a way that a potential user is advised that opening the container to get at the disk containing the software constitutes agreement to abide by the terms of the license. Typically these terms prohibit copying the software or installing it on more than one computer, and limit the liability of the manufacturer for any damage caused by the software.

**sic** *adv. Latin.* (lit. "thus; so") so in original. This word is used to indicate that something that might appear strange or incorrect in a quotation was that way in the original, and so is not an error by the person doing the quoting: *According to the teacher's note, "Johnnie needs to work on his speling [sic]."*
——**Usage.** This device should be employed sparingly. Although legal practice precludes changing or correcting quoted material without disclosing the change, unimportant errors can often be quoted without comment or dealt with less obtrusively (as by inserting a missing letter in brackets: *"spel[l]ing"*). When used, *sic* should be used with care and a sense of humility: It is extremely common to see *sic*'s that reveal, not a problem in the original writing, but ignorance or arrogance on the part of the quoter, as by treating historical or British spelling or usage as an error. Above all, one should avoid the common misstep of writing *sic* with a period at the end. It is not an abbreviation but a word, and incorrectly writing a word that one is using to call attention to someone else's error does not make a good impression.

**side bar** *n.* See under BAR³. See also SIDEBAR; SIDEBAR CONFERENCE.

**sidebar** *n.* **1.** short for SIDEBAR CONFERENCE: *The attorney requested a sidebar to explain his objection.*
—*adj.* **2.** taking place at the *side bar* (see under BAR³) or in a sidebar conference: *sidebar discussion; sidebar request; sidebar evidentiary ruling.*

**sidebar conference** *n.* in a jury trial, a brief courtroom conference among the judge and the lawyers, either on or off the record, conducted at or to the side of the bench so that the jury cannot hear it. Often shortened to **sidebar.** Also called **bench conference.**

**sight draft** *n.* See under DRAFT.

**sign** *v.* to affix a SIGNATURE to a document. See also COUNTERSIGN; SEAL¹.

**signatory** *n., pl.* **signatories. 1.** a person or entity whose SIGNATURE appears on a document.
**2.** a nation that has agreed to a treaty.

**signature** *n.* **1.** the name or mark of a person or entity placed on a document to authenticate it. It need not be written by hand, and it need not be placed there by the person named so long as it is authorized or adopted by that person. See also COUNTERSIGNATURE; HAND; SEAL¹; X.
**2. digital signature** an encrypted sequence embedded in a document that is transmitted electronically, serving to identify the sender and provide assurance that the document has not been altered.
**3. electronic signature a.** Same as *digital signature.* **b.** any line in a message transmitted electronically that purports to identify the sender; for example, the "from" line in an e-mail.

**signed, sealed, and delivered** See note at SEAL¹.

**silent partner** *n.* See under PARTNER.

**silver parachute** *n.* Same as TIN PARACHUTE.

**simple** *adj.* **1.** describing the basic form of something; lacking special or complicating features. See *fee simple* (under FEE¹).
**2.** (of a tort or crime) unaggravated; often used to describe the lowest grade of an offense: *simple negligence* (see under NEGLIGENCE); *simple assault.*

**SIMPLE 1.** Abbreviation for *savings incentive match plan for employees* (see under RETIREMENT PLAN).
—*adj.* **2.** connected with such a plan. See *SIMPLE plan, SIMPLE 401(k) plan,* and *SIMPLE IRA plan* (all under RETIREMENT PLAN); *SIMPLE IRA* (under IRA).
——**Usage.** Although the acronym "SIMPLE" ostensibly stands for a kind of retirement plan (namely, a "savings incentive match plan for employees"), it is never used as a noun: One does not "have a SIMPLE" or "make a contribution to a SIMPLE." The plan is actually referred to as a "SIMPLE plan," "SIMPLE retirement plan," "SIMPLE arrangement" or the like, as if the word "plan" did not already account for one-third of the letters in the acronym.

**simple retirement account (SRA)** *n.* Same as *SIMPLE IRA* (see under IRA).

**simplified employee pension (SEP)** *n.* See under RETIREMENT PLAN.

**simultaneous death** *n.* **1.** the death of two individuals under such circumstances that it cannot be determined that one died before the other, as when a husband and wife die in a common disaster.
**2.** in some states, the death of two individuals under circumstances where it cannot be proved that they died more than 120 hours apart.
——**False Friend.** Simultaneous death is a legal fiction created by the SIMULTANEOUS DEATH ACT. It does not necessarily mean that the evidence indicates that two individuals died simultaneously, but only that it cannot be determined which died first—or in states that have adopted the 120-hour rule, that it cannot be shown that they died at least five days apart, even if it is known that they did not die anywhere near simultaneously.

**simultaneous death act** *n.* a statute, adopted in some form in all or virtually all states, setting forth rules for distribution of property, life insurance proceeds, and the like, for people whose deaths are deemed to have occurred simultaneously (see SIMULTANEOUS DEATH).

——**Note.** Under such acts, jointly owned property is typically distributed as if each individual had owned a proportionate share outright; bequests and inheritance are treated as if the testator had outlived the intended recipient or the intestate had outlived the heir; and insurance policies in which one individual named the other as beneficiary are treated as if the insured had outlived the beneficiary.

**sin tax** *n. Informal.* a tax on a tobacco, liquor, gambling, or a similar product or activity that is not favored by the law but that is too popular or well established to ban.
——**Note.** Sin taxes serve the dual function of discouraging disfavored activity while raising substantial revenue from the many people who find the activity too appealing, or are too much addicted to it, to avoid it.

**sine** *prep. Latin.* without.

**sine die** *adv. Latin.* (lit. "without a day") indefinitely; without a set date for resumption; permanently. The term is used primarily in reference to the adjournment or termination of legislative or judicial proceedings: *The majority leader declared the legislative session a success and the legislature adjourned sine die.*

**sine prole (s.p.)** *adv., adj. Latin.* without issue; without descendants: *to die sine prole.* The abbreviation is used in genealogical charts.

**sine qua non** *adj., n., pl.* **sine qua nons** or, in Latin, **sine quibus non.** *Latin.* (lit. "without which not") —*adj.* **1.** indispensable; essential: *a condition sine qua non; the ingredient sine qua non.* See also CAUSA SINE QUA NON.
—*n.* **2.** an indispensable condition, element, or factor; an essential person or thing: *Detrimental reliance is one of the sine qua nons of a cause of action for fraud.*

**single-category method** *n.* a method of calculating a taxpayer's *average basis* (see under BASIS) in shares of a mutual fund, in which the average is taken over all shares of the fund owned by the taxpayer regardless of how long the taxpayer has owned them. Cf. DOUBLE-CATEGORY METHOD.

**singles' penalty** *n.* Same as MARRIAGE BONUS (def. 2).

**sinking fund** *n.* money or other assets set aside and accumulated to meet a future need, particularly the paying of a debt.

**sister** *n., pl.* **sisters, sistren,** *adj.* —*n.* **1.** a female fellow member of a trade union, sorority, profession, etc.
**2.** a term sometimes used to refer to a fellow judge who is a woman: *As stated by our sister, Judge Jones, in a recent opinion on this very point…* Cf. BROTHER.
—*adj.* **3.** fellow; designating a parallel jurisdiction, institution, etc., of the same rank: *sister court; sister circuit.*
——**Usage.** A few writers and speakers have used *sistren* as a parallel for *brethren* (the traditional term for fellow judges who are male)—usually either facetiously or in the belief that they are coining a word. But in fact *sistren* stood alongside *brethren, children,* and *oxen* as a standard plural form in Middle English and early Modern English. In the sixteenth and seventeenth centuries, *sisters* and *brothers* replaced *sistren* and *brethren* in ordinary usage, although the latter term was retained in references to fellow members of an all-male group such as an order of monks or a trade or profession—and in particular to fellow members of the bench and bar. Now that these professions have been opened to women, to the extent that the archaic plural *brethren* is retained for reasons of tradition it makes perfect sense to pair it with the corresponding feminine form and refer to fellow lawyers and judges as *brethren and sistren.*

**sister corporations** *n.pl.* See under CORPORATION.

**sister state** *n.* a state of the United States as viewed from the perspective of another state. See also FOREIGN.

**sistren** *n.pl.* a plural of SISTER. See note at that entry.

**sit** *v.,* **sat, sitting. 1.** (of a court or other official body) to hold a formal session for the conduct of business: *The Supreme Court normally sits from October to June.*
**2.** to preside over a particular case: *The appeal was decided by the Court of Appeals sitting en banc.*

**situate** *adj.* situated; located. A term found in descriptions of real property.

**situs** *n., pl.* **situses** or, in Latin, **situs.** *Latin.* (lit. "site") the place where a thing (tangible or intangible) is deemed to be located for legal purposes. For example, the situs of personal property for tax purposes is usually the domicile of the owner; for jurisdictional purposes, the situs of a debt is generally deemed to be wherever the debtor is at the moment.

**S.J.D.** (from Latin *Scientiae Juridicae Doctor,* lit. "Doctor of Juridical Science") an abbreviation for the advanced law degree known as **Doctor of Juridical Science** or **Doctor of the Science of Law.** The S.J.D. is a Ph.D.-level degree held by very few lawyers; it is sought primarily by individuals who plan a career of legal scholarship and teaching, and even on law school faculties it is relatively rare. Requirements for the degree generally include a minimum of one year's study beyond the LL.M. or its equivalent, completion of a dissertation, and an oral examination on the topic of the dissertation. At some law schools the degree is called the J.S.D.

**skip person** *n.* (in tax law) any individual who is two or more generations (that is, at least 37½ years) younger than the transferor in a GENERATION-SKIPPING TRANSFER, or a trust for the benefit of such individuals. See also GENERATION-SKIPPING TRANSFER TAX.
——**False Friend.** Note that a "skip person" is not a person skipped (e.g., the child skipped over in a gift from grandparent to grandchild), nor a person who skips (the grandparent who skips over a child by leaving property to a grandchild), nor even, necessarily, a

person (in the sense of a human being). It is the individual or trust that *receives* a generation-skipping transfer.

**skip tracing** or **skip-tracing** *n.* the business or activity of locating debtors who have moved or disappeared so that efforts can be made to collect the debts.
—**skip tracer, skip-tracer** *n.*

**slamming** *n.* a type of telecommunications fraud in which a long-distance telephone service provider unlawfully takes over service for another provider's customer who has not knowingly authorized the change. Stratagems employed to accomplish this include hiding authorization for the switch in small print on a contest entry form, and even switching customers who expressly declined an invitation to switch. Cf. CRAMMING.
—**slam** *v.*, **slammed, slamming.**
—**slammer** *n.*

**slander** *n.* **1.** the form of DEFAMATION in which the defamatory statement is communicated by spoken words or transitory gestures. Cf. LIBEL[1].
**2. slander per quod** slander other than *slander per se.* To recover damages for slander per quod, a plaintiff must prove that the words not only injured the plaintiff's reputation but also caused economic harm. See also PER QUOD.
**3. slander per se** slander in which the defamatory statement falsely imputes to the defamed person any of the following: commission of a crime; "loathsome disease" (usually a venereal or other communicable disease); conduct or characteristics incompatibile with the proper conduct of the person's lawful business, trade, profession, or office; or unchastity or sexual misconduct. By long tradition, the common law regards such statements as inherently damaging to reputation; consequently, recovery of general damages (such as compensation for emotional distress) is permitted without proof of injury to reputation or of specific pecuniary loss. See also PER SE.
—*v.* **4.** to utter a slander against a person; to defame orally.

—**slanderer** *n.*
—**slanderous** *adj.*
—**slanderously** *adv.*
—**slanderousness** *n.*

**slander of title** *n.* the tort of communicating to a third party a false statement that impugns or detracts from another person's title or other interest in property. Slander of title is a form of DISPARAGEMENT.
——**False Friend.** This tort was first recognized in cases involving spoken words impugning an individual's title to land; although it was never a form of SLANDER (spoken words impugning the character of a person), it was recognized as analogous, and so got its name. But the scope of the tort now extends much farther than the name implies: to written as well as oral statements, and to aspersions cast not just upon title to land but upon any legally recognized interest in property, whether real or personal and whether tangible or intangible.

**SLAPP** *n.*, **SLAPPs, SLAPP's,** *v.*, **SLAPPed, SLAPPing.** —*n.* **1.** Also called **SLAPP suit.** a civil complaint or counterclaim filed against a nongovernmental individual or group because of its communication to a government body, official, or the electorate on an issue of some public interest or concern; especially a suit of that type that is without merit and filed for an improper purpose.
—*v.* **2.** to bring a SLAPP suit against.
——**Note.** This term—an acronym for **Strategic Lawsuit Against Public Participation**—was coined in 1988 by two University of Denver professors who called attention to the use of such suits to intimidate, chill, or punish activists and divert their time and resources from their cause. For example, an individual or group opposing the granting of a permit to a company for a construction project might be SLAPPed with a suit for damages for defamation, interference with prospective business advantage, or the like. See also ANTI-SLAPP STATUTE.

**slavery** *n.* the ownership of one person by another, outlawed by the Thirteenth

Amendment (see Appendix). See also SERVITUDE. Cf. WHITE SLAVERY.

**sleeping partner** *n. Brit.* See under PARTNER.

**slip opinion** *n.* a judicial OPINION in the form in which it is first issued, typed or printed on slips of paper; cited as **slip op.** Cf. *reported opinion* (under REPORT).

**SM** an abbreviation indicating that the word, phrase, or design it accompanies is claimed as a SERVICE MARK, although it is not a *registered service mark* (see under SERVICE MARK).

**small claims court** *n.* a state or municipal court established to handle certain civil cases involving very small sums of money, using informal, streamlined procedures and often dispensing with lawyers.

**smuggling** *n.* the crime of importing or exporting prohibited matter, or importing or exporting permitted matter without paying a required DUTY.
—**smuggle** *v.,* **smuggled, smuggling.**
—**smuggler** *n.*

**so ordered** a formal expression often used by judges, both orally and in writing, to make it clear that a pronouncement is an official order of the court. See the example at INSTANTER.

**social security** *n.* a federal program designed to provide some continuing income to most workers after they retire or become disabled, and under some circumstances to their surviving spouse or children when they die. The program was established by the **Federal Insurance Contributions Act (FICA)** in 1935.

**social security tax** *n.* a payroll tax, paid one-half by the employee and one-half by the employer, to help fund the social security and Medicare programs; usually identified on pay stubs as "FICA" (see under SOCIAL SECURITY). It is a *regressive tax* (see under TAX), because it is paid only on *earned income* (see under INCOME) and not on income from investments, and also because most of it applies only to wages up to a certain maximum amount each year, so that employees with very high salaries (usually executives) pay the full tax only on a portion of their salary, whereas most ordinary workers pay it on their entire salary. In addition, individuals without a regular employer to pay the employer's share must pay double on whatever they earn, in the form of SELF-EMPLOYMENT TAX.

**Socratic method** *n.* a teaching method heavily used in law schools today, based upon the technique used by Socrates in ancient Greece, in which students are led to analyze legal issues and principles through a series of *hypothetical questions* (see under QUESTION[1]) from the teacher. See also CASE METHOD.

**sodomize** *v.,* **sodomized, sodomizing.** to perform an act of sodomy upon or with another person, especially by force or without that person's valid consent.
—**sodomist** *n.*

**sodomy** *n.* **1.** a term varying in meaning from state to state, but generally referring to any type of sex act regarded by a legislature as "unnatural" or "perverted." In the narrowest and most traditional sense, the term refers to anal sexual intercourse between men. In most legal contexts today the term includes, at a minimum, oral and anal intercourse between men, but it may extend to those or other acts between men and women (sometimes exempting married couples, sometimes not), or women and women, or people and animals. Also called **crime against nature, unnatural act.**
**2.** Also called **consensual sodomy.** an act of sodomy between consenting adults.
**3.** Also called **forcible sodomy.** an act of sodomy imposed upon a person by force or threat of force, or by rendering the victim incapable of resistance through administration of a drug.
——**History.** Sodomy is still a crime in many states, and as recently as 1986 the Supreme Court upheld a law providing for 20 years' imprisonment for either heterosexual or homosexual sodomy, as applied to a man who was found in bed with another man in his

own home by police who entered to serve an arrest warrant for public drinking. The court held that the Constitutional right of privacy (see RIGHT OF PRIVACY, def. 3b) does not include a right to engage in consensual homosexual acts in one's bedroom. *Bowers v. Hardwick*, 478 U.S. 186 (1986). Ironically, Georgia's own Supreme Court subsequently reached precisely the opposite conclusion, in the case of a man convicted of consensual sodomy (specifically, an act of cunnilingus) with his wife's 17-year-old niece. In an opinion by the Chief Justice for six of the seven members of the court, the court held that the due process clause of Georgia's own constitution—which is essentially identical to the clause upon which the federal right of privacy is based—guarantees Georgia citizens a right of privacy that bars the state from criminalizing "private, unforced, noncommercial acts of sexual intimacy between persons legally able to consent." *Powell v. State*, 270 Ga. 327 (1998).

**soft money** *n.* money raised and spent for political purposes, especially by state and national political parties, in ways that avoid regulation under the federal campaign financing laws. Also called **nonfederal money, unregulated money.** Cf. HARD MONEY.
—**Note.** Unlike money that is spent by candidates, parties, and political committees specifically to promote campaigns for federal office (see note at HARD MONEY), soft money—which is subject only to the patchwork of generally weak campaign finance laws in the various states—may for the most part be raised in unlimited amounts, from any source, with no disclosure requirements. Soft money may be used to support candidates for state office and to pay the bulk of general state party expenses (which benefit the party's candidates for federal office as much as its candidates for state office). Soft money has also been used to pay for so-called ISSUE ADVERTISING, which in the 1990's became a predominant form of political advertising in campaigns for federal office.

**software piracy** *n.* See under PIRACY.

**soldier's will** *n.* See under WILL.

**sole custody** *n.* See under CUSTODY.

**sole proprietorship** *n.* ownership of an unincorporated business by one individual, or the business so owned. For income tax purposes, the profits of such a business are taxed directly to the individual.

**solicitation** *n.* **1.** the crime of asking, advising, encouraging, or ordering another person to commit a crime, whether or not the offense solicited is then committed. This is usually punishable as a crime one degree lower in severity than the offense solicited.
**2.** the offense of offering to engage in sexual activity with a person for money or of attempting to entice a person to patronize a prostitute.

**solicitor** *n.* **1.** in England, a lawyer who gives legal advice and performs general legal services outside the courtroom, including preparing cases for a BARRISTER to present in court, but who normally does not appear in court personally except in certain lower courts.
**2.** in America, a title sometimes given to the chief legal officer of a municipality or governmental department: *county solicitor; town solicitor.*
—**solicitorship** *n.*

**Solicitor General** *n., pl.* **Solicitors General. 1.** the legal officer within the United States Department of Justice who oversees the representation of the United States in all cases in the Supreme Court to which the federal government or a federal agency is a party or has an interest.
**2.** a legal officer in some state governments, typically second in rank after the ATTORNEY GENERAL.

**solvent** *adj.* **1.** usually, able to pay one's debts in the ordinary course of business as they become due.
**2.** for some purposes, having assets greater than liabilities. Opposite of INSOLVENT.
—**solvency** *n.*

**sound** *adj.* **1.** (of body or mind) healthy, fit, normal.

**2. sound mind** or **sound and disposing mind and memory** the mental CAPACITY necessary to make a valid will; possession of a reasonable understanding of what property one has, what options for it one has, and what one is doing with it.

**sound in** (of a civil action) to have its basis in; to have as its fundamental nature: *To determine which statute of limitations applies, the court must decide whether the action sounds in tort or in contract.*

**source of law** *n.* **1.** a historical origin of a law or body of laws.
**2.** a philosophical basis for a law or body of laws.
**3.** the governmental institution responsible for creating a law or body of laws.
**4.** a code or other set of research materials from which the law can be ascertained.
——**Usage.** In all senses, the phrase is usually used in the plural: *sources of law.*

**sovereign** *n.* **1.** a king, queen, or similar supreme ruler.
**2.** the government of an independent state or nation; the supreme legal authority.
—*adj.* **3.** characteristic of a sovereign; having supreme authority; not answerable to others or subject to control from above or outside.

**sovereign immunity** *n.* See under IMMUNITY.

**sovereignty** *n.* **1.** the quality or state of being sovereign.
**2.** the power or authority of a sovereign; supreme and independent power or authority in government.

**s.p.** SINE PROLE.

**spam** *n., v.* **spammed, spamming.** —*n.*
**1.** unsolicited bulk e-mail, especially for commercial or fraudulent purposes: the electronic equivalent of junk mail.
—*v.* **2.** to send spam to a person.
See also ANTI-SPAM LAW.
—**spamming** *n.*
—**spammer** *n.*

**speaking objection** *n.* See under OBJECTION.

**special** *adj.* describing a form of something that is distinctive, particularized, limited, expanded, or otherwise worthy of separate consideration, often calling into play particular legal rules. Sometimes contrasted with GENERAL. See *special appearance* (under APPEARANCE); *special assumpsit* (under ASSUMPSIT); *special counsel* (under COUNSEL); *special damages* (under DAMAGES); *special indorsement* (under INDORSEMENT); *special jurisdiction* (under JURISDICTION¹); *special master* (under MASTER); *special power of attorney* (under POWER OF ATTORNEY); *special prosecutor* (under PROSECUTOR); *special verdict* (under VERDICT); *special questions* (or *interrogatories*) (under VERDICT).

**special circumstances** *n.* aggravating or mitigating circumstances affecting the degree of a crime or the severity of punishment; especially, aggravating circumstances that justify a prosecutor in seeking or a jury in imposing the death penalty for a murder, such as a defendant's infliction of torture on the victim or commission of multiple murders.

**special court-martial** *n.* See under COURT-MARTIAL.

**special session** *n.* See under SESSION.

**specie** *n.* **1.** coined money; coin.
**2.** See IN SPECIE.

**specific** *adj.* **1.** particular or special; not vague or general: *specific bequest* (or *legacy*) (see under BEQUEST).
**2.** as specified; in the manner or of the kind agreed to: SPECIFIC PERFORMANCE.
**3.** referring to a particular thing: *specific restitution* (see under RESTITUTION).
See also *specific relief* (under RELIEF).
—**specifically** *adv.*

**specific performance** *n.* an *equitable remedy* (see under REMEDY) in which a party is ordered to perform a contract according to its terms. The usual remedy for breach of contract is damages (a legal remedy), but in cases where money is not a satisfactory substitute for the thing contracted for, as in a contract for the sale of land or of a unique article such as a painting, the breaching party may be ordered to "perform specifically."

**specification** *n.* a detailed listing or description, such as a litigant's listing of the trial court's errors in appellate papers, the prosecution's listing of charges in a court-martial, or an inventor's detailing of an invention in a patent application.

**speculate** *v.,* **speculated, speculating.**
**1.** to guess; to reach conclusions not based on knowledge or evidence. Testimony based on speculation is ordinarily not admissible. See also *speculative damages* (under DAMAGES).
**2.** to make risky investments. The purpose of the SECURITIES ACTS is to make it possible for investors to know to what extent they are speculating.
**—speculation** *n.*
**—speculative** *adj.*

**speech** *n.* **1.** within the meaning of the First Amendment (see Appendix), any form of expression, including words (whether written or spoken), pictures or other visual devices, and expressive conduct. See also FREEDOM OF SPEECH.
**2. commercial speech** advertising or other speech promoting economic interests. Formerly regarded as constitutionally unprotected, commercial speech that is not false or misleading and does not promote illegal goods, services, or conduct is now given considerable protection under the First Amendment, though still not to the extent of noncommercial speech.
**3. hate speech** speech that grossly insults or demeans people because of a group characteristic such as race or religion. Such speech may not be censored or penalized by the government because of its group-related content, although FIGHTING WORDS may be outlawed.
**4. indecent speech** speech that does not amount to OBSCENITY, but uses vulgar words or deals with sex or bodily functions in a way that is regarded as PATENTLY OFFENSIVE. Unlike obscenity, speech that is merely indecent has been given considerable constitutional protection (for example, "dial-a-porn" services cannot be completely banned);

at the same time, some restrictions that would not be allowed for "decent" speech have been upheld, particularly in regard to broadcasting (see note at SEVEN DIRTY WORDS).
**5. protected speech** speech held by the courts to be within the scope of the First Amendment's guarantee of FREEDOM OF SPEECH.
**6. speech plus** speech accompanied by conduct deemed nonexpressive. Conduct is not immune from reasonable regulation merely because it is accompanied by speech.
**7. symbolic speech** expression other than through words. The expression may be political (waving a flag or burning a flag), artistic (painting or dance), or anything else. In general, symbolic speech is constitutionally protected to the same extent as verbal speech. See notes at FLAG DESECRATION and FLAG BURNING.

**speedy trial** *n.* See under TRIAL.

**spendthrift trust** *n.* See under TRUST.

**spoliation** *n.* **1.** the destruction or alteration of a will, negotiable instrument, or other instrument, especially by one who is not a party to the instrument.
**2.** the destruction or alteration of evidence, especially by one whose cause would be damaged by the evidence.
**3.** the act or an instance of plundering or despoiling.
**—spoliate** *v.,* **spoliated, spoliating.**
**—spoliator** *n.*

**spontaneous declaration** (or **statement** or **exclamation**). Same as EXCITED UTTERANCE.

**spot zoning** *n.* See under ZONING.

**spousal abuse** *n.* physical or psychological ABUSE of one spouse by the other, more often of the wife by the husband **(wife abuse.)** Traditionally viewed more as a ground for divorce than as a crime; now taken seriously as a crime. See also BATTERED PERSON SYNDROME; CRUELTY.

**spousal privilege** *n.* Same as MARITAL PRIVILEGE.

**spousal rape** *n.* Same as *marital rape* (see under RAPE).

**spousal support** *n.* Same as ALIMONY.

**spouse's election** *n.* See under ELECTION.

**spouse's elective** (or **statutory**) **share** Same as ELECTIVE SHARE.

**spouse's testimonial privilege** *n.* See under MARITAL PRIVILEGE.

**spread upon the record** See under RECORD.

**sprinkling trust** *n.* See under TRUST.

**squatter** *n.* a person who takes up residence on land or in a building, or remains in residence, without legal authority. Cf. CYBERSQUATTING.
—**squat** *v.,* **squatted, squatting.**
—**squatting** *n.*

**squeeze-out** *n.* any of a number of techniques permitted by law to force minority shareholders out of a corporation ("squeeze them out"). See also GO PRIVATE.

**SRA** *n., pl.* **SRAs, SRA's.** Abbreviation for *simple retirement account* (see under IRA).

**ss.** an abbreviation of uncertain origin and no particular meaning, customarily placed at the top of an affidavit or affirmation beside the statement of VENUE and followed by a colon, thus serving as a kind of introduction to the instrument.

**stakeholder** *n.* a person in possession of money or property to which she herself has no claim, but to which two or more others may have competing claims, so that the stakeholder cannot turn over the property to any claimant without the risk of being sued by one or more of the others. For the way out of this dilemma, see INTERPLEADER.

**stale** *adj.* rendered ineffective or unenforceable by the passage of time: *stale check; stale claim; stale offer.*

**stalking** *n.* **1.** the crime of following a person about in such a way as to instill fear of bodily harm. This is typically dealt with as a form of criminal HARASSMENT. It may also give rise to a tort action for ASSAULT or INTENTIONAL INFLICTION OF MENTAL DISTRESS.
**2.** secretly following a person about or lying in wait for the purpose of committing a crime. In most states this is punishable as an ATTEMPT to commit a crime.
See also CYBERSTALKING.
—**stalk** *v.*
—**stalker** *n.*

**stamp tax** *n.* a tax imposed upon a product (e.g., liquor or cigarettes) or a transaction (e.g., a transfer of land) by requiring someone to purchase a stamp and affix it to the product or instrument.

**stand** *n.* **1.** in a trial, the place where a witness sits while testifying; short for **witness stand.**
**2. take the stand** to go to the stand to testify.

**stand bail** See under BAIL¹.

**standard deduction** *n.* See under DEDUCTION.

**standard of care** *n.* the level or nature of conduct necessary to avoid liability for NEGLIGENCE, MALPRACTICE, or *breach of fiduciary duty* (see under BREACH). Also called **degree of care.** See details under CARE.

**standard of proof** *n.* the degree to which the TRIER OF FACT must be persuaded of a fact in order to find in favor of a party in a trial or hearing. Also called **degree of proof.** Depending upon the nature of the case or the issue, the standard may be proof by a PREPONDERANCE OF THE EVIDENCE, proof by CLEAR AND CONVINCING EVIDENCE, or proof BEYOND A REASONABLE DOUBT.

**standard of review** *n.* the test by which a court or administrative tribunal determines whether to uphold or reverse an administrative or judicial decision submitted to it for REVIEW.
——**Note.** The applicable standard depends upon many factors, including whether the issue being reviewed is one of fact or of law, and whether it was decided by a judge or by a jury. The usual test for upholding a jury verdict is whether there was evidence in

the case on the basis of which a reasonable jury, applying the proper STANDARD OF PROOF, could have arrived at that verdict. For other standards of review, see ABUSE OF DISCRETION; CLEARLY ERRONEOUS; *de novo review* (under REVIEW); SCINTILLA OF EVIDENCE; SUBSTANTIAL EVIDENCE RULE; and *harmless error, plain error,* and *reversible error* (all under ERROR).

**standby counsel** *n.* See under COUNSEL.

**standing** *n.* the right to have a court adjudicate a matter in which one is interested. To have standing to bring an action or otherwise raise an issue in court, one must have a legally cognizable interest in the matter (see INTEREST[1], def. 1).

**Star Chamber** *n.* **1.** an English court, finally abolished in 1641, whose unfettered powers, lack of procedural safeguards, and arbitrary punishments made it a symbol of much that our constitutional protections and rules of criminal procedure seek to guard against.
**2. star chamber proceeding** a phrase used to characterize a legal proceeding as grossly unfair to the defendant.
See also KANGAROO COURT.

**stare decisis** *Latin.* (lit. "to stand by the things decided; standing by things decided") the doctrine that legal principles established in previous judicial decisions will normally be followed in subsequent cases. This doctrine lends stability and fairness to the law; without it, each judge could make up a new rule for each case. But it also makes the law slow to react to social and scientific change. The evolution of common law depends upon judicious application of this doctrine.

**state** *n.* **1.** a nation or national government. See also ACT OF STATE.
**2.** one of the fifty states making up the United States, or the government of such a state. In many contexts, the word is used a little more broadly to include the District of Columbia.
**3. State** the government of a particular state. In many states, this is how

the government and the prosecution are identified in criminal cases under state law. See also PEOPLE. Cf. GOVERNMENT.

**state action** *n.* action taken by the government (especially a state government) or in which the government is intimately involved, as distinguished from purely private action. The constitutional guarantees of DUE PROCESS and EQUAL PROTECTION apply only to state action, not private action.

**state of mind** *n.* **1.** generally, the condition of mind or the element or degree of fault or blameworthiness that accompanies an act or omission.
**2.** particularly, the additional condition that is required in most crimes, beyond the mere fact that the defendant committed a certain act causing certain results, to make the act a particular crime; MENS REA.
**——History.** The common law used many overlapping and poorly defined terms to describe different states of mind; e.g., MALICE, WANTON, WILLFUL. Most states now have criminal codes that define most crimes in terms of four distinctly defined states of mind signifying successively greater levels of culpability: NEGLIGENCE, RECKLESSNESS, KNOWLEDGE, INTENT. See also STRICT LIABILITY.

**state of war** *n.* a condition of active military conflict between nations, whether or not either country has made a formal *declaration of war* (see under WAR).

**state statute** *n.* See under STATUTE.

**statement** *n.* **1.** an oral or written assertion, or sometimes nonverbal conduct intended as an assertion, such as nodding one's head or pointing. Often interchangeable with DECLARATION or REPRESENTATION, though in any particular context it is usually the case that one word is more common than the others.
**2.** Also called **financial statement.** a concise and systematic presentation of the financial status of a person or entity.
**3.** Also called **statement of account.** a

summary of the status of an ACCOUNT, showing the balance due and usually listing recent transactions.

**4. closing statement** See different meanings under CLOSING (def. 1) and SUMMATION.

**5. exculpatory statement** a statement that, if true, tends to exonerate a criminal suspect. For example, "I was at home watching TV with my wife"; "I bought the watch from a guy on the street." See also FALSE EXCULPATORY STATEMENT; EXCULPATORY NO.

**6. opening statement** Same as OPENING.

**7. prior inconsistent statement** an earlier statement by a witness which is inconsistent with the witness's testimony at a trial or hearing. It may be introduced as evidence, not for its truth (since that would violate the rule against HEARSAY), but to impeach the witness's credibility. See also *admissible for a limited purpose* (under ADMISSIBLE).

**8. spontaneous statement** Same as EXCITED UTTERANCE.

**9. statement of claim** a document, or portion of a document, formally setting forth the claim that one is making in a case.

**10. statement of the case** the portion of a brief summarizing the facts rather than arguing the law. Also called **statement of facts.**

**state's evidence** *n.* **1.** evidence voluntarily given by a participant or accomplice in a crime against others involved, usually in exchange for immunity or lenient treatment. A suspect or defendant who agrees to provide such evidence is said to **turn state's evidence.**
**2.** generally, any evidence offered by the prosecution in a state criminal case.

**states' rights** *n.* **1.** (used with a pl. v.) governmental powers of individual states of the United States, as distinguished from the power of the United States government to make law for the nation as a whole; the powers alluded to in the Tenth Amendment to the Constitution, which states, "The powers not delegated to the United States by the Constitution, nor prohibited to it by the States, are reserved to the States respectively, or to the People." Cf. SUPREMACY.
**2.** (used with a sing. v.) a slogan representing the concept that the individual states of the United States have, and rightfully should have, the exclusive right to regulate most affairs within their own borders.
**—states' righter** *n.*
**——History.** "States' rights" has been the slogan of resistance to the national government, particularly in regard to civil rights, virtually since the founding of the country. In the 1830's the phrase was used to support the concept that state legislatures could nullify federal tariffs and other federal laws. Before the Civil War it was used by opponents of those who argued for abolition of slavery and proponents of secession. In 1948 it was the rallying cry of the Dixiecrats—also called States' Rights Democrats—who bolted the Democratic party because of its civil rights platform, nominated Strom Thurmond of South Carolina for President, and carried four southern states in the general election. In the 1950's and 1960's it was the slogan of opponents of racial integration and federal civil rights legislation.

**status crime** *n.* a crime defined by what one is rather than what one does; for example, the "crime" of being a drug addict. The Supreme Court has held that punishing anyone for such a "crime" violates the Constitutional bar against cruel and unusual punishment.

**status quo** *n. Latin.* (lit. "the position in which") **1.** the existing state or condition: *to preserve the status quo.*
**2.** Also called **status quo ante** (with *ante,* "before"). the way things were previously: *to restore the status quo (ante).*
See also IN STATU QUO.
**——Usage.** The best practice is to use *status quo* to refer to the current or existing state of affairs, and *status quo ante* to refer to the previous state of affairs.

**statute** *n.* a written law; in the United

States, a law enacted by Congress **(federal statute)** or a state legislature **(state statute).** Often called an ACT or a LAW. See also BORROWING STATUTE; *private statute* (under PRIVATE LAW); *public statute* (under PUBLIC LAW). Cf. COMMON LAW; ORDINANCE; REGULATION; RULE.

**statute of frauds** *n.* a statute requiring certain kinds of contracts to be written, or at least to be memorialized in some writing signed by the party against which the contract is to be enforced. A contract of the specified type is said to be "within" the statute, and if it is adequately memorialized and signed it is said to "satisfy" the statute. The most common kinds of contracts covered by such statutes are agreements to be responsible for someone else's debt, contracts for the sale of land, contracts for the sale of goods above a certain price, and contracts requiring performance more than a year after the making of the contract.

**statute of limitations** *n.* a statute setting the length of time after an event within which a civil or criminal action arising from that event must be brought (the **limitation period, limitations period,** or **statutory period**). Cf. LACHES.

**Statute of Uses** *n.* a statute enacted by Parliament in 1535 declaring that henceforth any purported conveyance of a fee interest in land to one person for the use of another would have the effect of transferring the fee directly to the third person.
——**History.** Before the enactment of the Statute of Uses, various means were used to create beneficial interests in land that would be enforced in courts of equity but would spare the beneficiary the legal obligation of providing services to the feudal overlord. One technique was the BARGAIN AND SALE; another was the technique of transferring property to a FEOFFEE TO USES, who would hold the land solely for the benefit of a CESTUI QUE USE. The Statute of Uses changed the rules by vesting legal title to the land in the person who would be taking the profits from it

and imposing the feudal duties associated with the land directly on that person.

**Statute Quia Emptores** or **Statute of Quia Emptores** *n.* See QUIA EMPTORES.

**Statutes at Large** *n.pl.* (abbr. **Stat.**) the official compilation of acts and resolutions of Congress, treaties ratified, constitutional amendments proposed or ratified, and presidential proclamations issued, printed in chronological order for each session of Congress. Although this compilation reproduces federal statutes in the exact form in which Congress enacted them, the organization of the UNITED STATES CODE and the annotations added to it by private publishers make that the preferred version for legal research.

**statutory** *adj.* **1.** relating to statutes or a statute: *statutory construction* (see under CONSTRUCTION); *statutory period* (see under STATUTE OF LIMITATIONS). **2.** created by or pertaining to statutes rather than the common law: *statutory crime* (see under CRIME). **3.** existing by virtue of a statute, without regard to the intent of the parties involved or any agreement or lack of agreement among them: *statutory rape* (see under RAPE), *statutory share* (same as ELECTIVE SHARE).

**stay** *n.* **1.** the postponement or temporary suspension of a proceeding or of the legal effect of a statute or court order. **2. automatic stay** a stay imposed by statute, which takes effect automatically upon the occurrence of some event. **3. stay of execution a.** a stay preventing a person who has won a money judgment from immediately seizing the judgment debtor's assets, usually to allow the debtor time to appeal. **b.** an order that a prisoner sentenced to death not be put to death just yet. Such an order might be issued either by a court or by the governor of the state; in the latter case, it is commonly called a REPRIEVE. ——*v.* **4.** to order or cause a stay.

**steal** *v.*, **stole, stolen, stealing.** to obtain money or property by LARCENY or, more broadly, by larceny or other criminal means such as ROBBERY, EMBEZZLEMENT, or FALSE PRETENSES.
—**stealable** *adj.*

**step transaction** *n.* See under TRANSACTION.

**stepped-down basis** *n.* See under BASIS.

**stepped-up basis** *n.* See under BASIS.

**sting** *n., v.*, **stung, stinging.** —*n.* **1.** a CONFIDENCE GAME.
**2.** a law enforcement operation in which officers use deception to gain the confidence of criminals in order to catch them.
**3.** especially, an ostensibly illegal activity or operation employing undercover officers or agents to collect evidence of wrongdoing (as by offering to fence stolen goods) or induce criminals to commit crimes in the presence of the officers (as in a BUY AND BUST operation).
**4. reverse sting** a law enforcement operation in which undercover operatives offer illicit goods or services for sale, such as illegal drugs or child pornography, and then arrest those who accept the offer. Also called **reverse buy.**
**5. take-back sting** a law enforcement operation in which undercover operatives act as both the supplier and the buyer of drugs or other illicit goods. They induce a target individual to act as a middleman, and then arrest that individual for dealing in illicit merchandise. Also called **circular sting.**
—*v.* **6.** *Slang.* to cheat or take advantage of; to subject to a sting.
See also ENCOURAGEMENT; ENTRAPMENT.

**stipulation** *n.* **1.** a representation or condition spelled out in a contract.
**2.** an agreement between opposing lawyers with respect to some procedural step in a case, often altering normal time limits or other procedural requirements for mutual convenience or as a matter of courtesy. Typically such a stipulation will be submitted to the judge to be SO ORDERED, which turns it into a **stipulation and order.** See also CONFIDENTIALITY STIPULATION.
**3.** an agreement between the parties in a case with respect to a fact or a legal issue, so as to simplify the case by eliminating issues that cannot reasonably be disputed. A fact thus agreed upon is a **stipulated fact,** which must be accepted as true by the judge and jury. See also *stipulated damages* (under DAMAGES).
—**stipulable** *adj.*
—**stipulate** *v.*, **stipulated, stipulating.**

**stirpes** *n.pl.* See PER STIRPES.

**stock** *n.* **1.** a security (see SECURITY²) issued by a CORPORATION or *joint stock company* (see under COMPANY), representing an ownership interest in the issuer. An entity may issue several classes of stock conferring on their owners (called stockholders or shareholders) varying rights with respect to participation in control of the company (through voting for DIRECTORS and on certain company matters), participation in earnings (through DIVIDENDS declared by the directors), and participation in *net assets* (see under ASSET) upon liquidation of the company. The total stock of any class is divided into equal fractional parts (SHARES), varying quantities of which may be held by different owners, who have greater or lesser rights in proportion to the number of shares that they own.
**2. assessable stock** stock whose owners may be required to make additional financial contributions to the issuer if needed. Most stock carries no such obligation, and so is **nonassessable stock.**
**3. capital stock a.** broadly, any stock; the totality of a company's stock of all classes. **b.** narrowly, *common stock.*
**4. common stock** the lowest class of stock in a corporation. If the corporation has only one class of stock, it is common stock. In the event of liquidation, the common stockholders divide up anything that is left of the company after all obligations to creditors and preferred stockholders have been satisfied. Cf. *preferred stock.*
**5. paid-up stock** stock for which the

corporation has been paid in full. Also called **fully paid stock.**

**6. preferred stock** stock conferring preferential rights to dividends or to assets upon liquidation of the corporation, ahead of the rights of common stockholders. Cf. *common stock.*

**7. publicly traded stock** stock that is freely bought and sold among members of the general investing public; stock in a *publicly held corporation* (see under CORPORATION).

**8. restricted stock** stock that may not be transferred to a new owner except upon specified conditions. Stock in a *close corporation* (see under CORPORATION) is often restricted to prevent sale to an outsider who would not fit in with the small group of owners.

**9. stock with par value** a class of stock to which the issuer has assigned a PAR VALUE. Also called **par value stock.**

**10. stock without par value** a class of stock to which the issuer has not assigned a par value. Also called **no-par** (or **nonpar**) **stock.**

**stock association** *n.* Same as *joint stock company* (see under COMPANY).

**stock certificate** *n.* an instrument representing a specified number of shares of a specific class of stock in a particular company.

**stock manipulation** *n.* engaging in *wash sales* of stock (see under SALE) or other conduct in the stock market designed to create a false impression of widespread investor interest in a stock, usually in the hope of driving up the price. Also called **market manipulation.** This is a kind of *securities fraud* (see under FRAUD).

**stock option** *n.* **1.** a right to purchase or sell a specified number of shares of a particular stock at a specified price some time in the future.
**2.** Also called **employee stock option.** Such an option to purchase stock in a corporation, granted by the corporation to an employee as a form of compensation.

**stock warrant** *n.* Same as WARRANT[2].

**stockbroker** *n.* See under BROKER.

**stockholder** *n.* an owner of shares of STOCK. Also called **shareholder.**

**stockholder derivative action** *n.* See under ACTION.

**stop** *n., v.,* **stopped, stopping.** —*n.* **1.** momentary detention of a person by law enforcement officials, falling short of an ARREST, as at a highway checkpoint for drunk drivers or to question a person acting suspiciously.
**2. stop and frisk** a stop accompanied by a pat-down for weapons. This may be done upon grounds falling somewhat short of PROBABLE CAUSE for arrest or a full search, if the officer can articulate a sound basis for the procedure.
—*v.* **3.** to make a stop of a person.

**straight bankruptcy** *n.* See under BANKRUPTCY.

**straight bill of lading** *n.* See under BILL OF LADING.

**straight-face test** *n. Informal.* a hypothetical test of whether an argument or position is sufficiently tenable to advance in a court case, negotiation, or the like. The test is: Can you say it with a straight face? If not, it "doesn't pass the straight-face test" and had best not be advanced. See also LAUGH TEST.
——**Usage.** Although this rather facetious expression is occasionally used affirmatively (*Let's include that point in our brief; I think it passes the straight-face test.*), it is more commonly used negatively and derisively: *Your Honor, that argument doesn't even pass the straight-face test!*

**straight life insurance** *n.* See under LIFE INSURANCE.

**stranger** *n.* a person with no legally recognized right or interest in the transaction, proceeding, relationship, or other matter under discussion; an outsider.

**Strategic Lawsuit Against Public Participation** *n.* See SLAPP.

**straw buyer** *n.* See STRAW PURCHASER.

**straw purchase** *n.* a purchase made by a person purporting to act for herself but actually intending immediately to sell or transfer the thing purchased to someone else.

**straw purchaser** *n.* **1.** one who makes a STRAW PURCHASE of anything.
**2.** especially, an individual who buys a gun in order to turn it over to someone who would not be allowed to purchase it directly, such as an underage person or a person with a criminal record.
Also called **straw buyer.**

**street name** *n.* the name of a firm of stockbrokers acting as *record owner* (see under OWNER) of stock on behalf of one of the firm's customers. Holding stock in street name rather than in the names of individual stockholders facilitates the transfer of stock when it is bought and sold among customers of the various brokerage firms.

**strict construction** *n.* See under CONSTRUCTION.

**strict liability** *n.* See under LIABILITY.

**strict scrutiny** *n.* the standard by which the Supreme Court assesses the constitutionality of a law that limits a FUNDAMENTAL RIGHT (such as freedom of speech) or that treats people differently on the basis of a SUSPECT CLASSIFICATION (such as race). Under the strict scrutiny test, a law will be upheld only if it is found to serve a COMPELLING INTEREST of the government and to be "necessary" to the achievement of that interest.   See also SCRUTINY. Cf. HEIGHTENED SCRUTINY; RATIONAL BASIS TEST.

**strike¹** *n., v.,* **struck, striking. —***n.* **1.** a concerted stopping of work by employees in a company or industry, in support of a demand for higher wages or better conditions of employment, or in protest of some action of the employer. Cf. LOCKOUT.
**2. wildcat strike** a spontaneous strike not officially authorized by a union.
**—***v.* **3.** to engage in a strike.

**strike²** *v.,* **struck, striking.** to delete or nullify words spoken or written or papers submitted in a case. Stricken material is officially disregarded at trial, but normally remains in the record for

purposes of appellate review. See discussion at UNRESPONSIVE.

**strike suit** *n.* See under SUIT.

**sua sponte** *Latin.* of its (his, her, their) own accord. Said of action taken by a court without being asked to do so by a party. Often expressed in English as **on its (his, her, their) own motion,** although technically a court cannot make a motion to itself: *The court dismissed the action sua sponte* (or *on its own motion*) *for lack of jurisdiction.* See also note at EX PROPRIO MOTU.

**suability** *n.* See under SUE.

**suable** *adj.* See under SUE.

**sub judice** *Latin.* (lit., "under the judge") submitted to a judge or court (but not to a jury) and awaiting decision. See also SUBMIT.

**sub nomine (sub nom.)** *Latin.* under the name.
**—Usage.** The abbreviation *sub nom.* is used in case citations, and occasionally in other contexts, to avoid confusion when there has been a change of name or one party has been substituted for another in the course of a matter: *People v. Proctor,* 4 Cal. 4th 499 (1992), *aff'd sub nom. Tuilaepa v. California,* 512 U.S. 967 (1994).

**Sub-S corporation** *n.* See under CORPORATION.

**sub silentio** *Latin.* (lit. "under silence") implicitly; without saying so: *The court's holding overruled its prior decision sub silentio.*

**subchapter C corporation** *n.* See under CORPORATION.

**subchapter S corporation** *n.* See under CORPORATION.

**subcontract** *n.* a contract by which a party who has been engaged to carry out a large project engages someone else (a **subcontractor**) to do some of the work. See also *general contractor* (under CONTRACTOR).

**subinfeudation** *n.* **1.** the granting of a portion of an estate by a feudal tenant to a subtenant, who then owed to the tenant service similar to that owed by the tenant to lord.

**2.** the general process of creating tenures within tenures; the process by which feudal lands, interests, and duties became increasingly subdivided. See also QUIA EMPTORES.

**subject matter jurisdiction** See under JURISDICTION[1].

**subjective test** *n.* a legal standard that depends upon what is in someone's mind. For example, legal principles phrased in terms of INTENT, KNOWLEDGE, or GOOD FAITH involve a subjective test. Cf. OBJECTIVE TEST.

**sublease** *n., v.,* **subleased, subleasing.** —*n.* **1.** a LEASE granted by one who is already a lessee of the property. The grantor of a sublease on real property is called the **sublandlord** or **sublessor,** and the person to whom it is granted is the **subtenant** or **sublessee;** in the rare sublease of personal property, only the terms "sublessor" and "sublessee" would be appropriate. —*v.* **2.** to convey, receive, or hold by sublease.

**sublet** *v.,* **sublet, subletting,** *n.* —*v.* **1.** to SUBLEASE real property to or from someone. —*n.* **2.** a subleasing arrangement or relationship with respect to real property, or the property itself.

**submit** *v.,* **submitted, submitting. 1.** to place a matter formally and finally into the hands of the proper body for decision; for example, to submit a case to a jury, a motion to a judge, a dispute to an arbitration panel, or a referendum to the voters. See also SUB JUDICE. **2.** to present evidence and argument to a court solely in writing, without oral argument or testimony. See also *on papers* (under PAPERS). **3. take on submission** (of a judge or court) to receive or allow only written evidence and argument on a matter to be decided. Cf. HEAR. —**submission** *n.* —**submitted** *adj.*

**subordinate** or **subordinated** *adj.* lower in priority than a competing right, claim, or claimant. Also, **junior.**

Opposite of SENIOR. —**subordination** *n.*

**subornation of perjury** *n.* the crime of inducing a person to commit PERJURY. The person who commits this crime is said to **suborn** the witness or to **suborn perjury.**

**subpoena** *n., pl.* **subpoenas,** *v.,* **subpoenaed, subpoenaing.** —*n.* **1.** a PROCESS directing a witness to appear and give evidence in a court proceeding. **2. subpoena ad testificandum** a subpoena requiring the person served to appear and testify. See also AD TESTIFICANDUM. **3. subpoena duces tecum** a subpoena requiring the person served not only to testify but also to produce specified documents or other physical evidence. See also DUCES TECUM. —*v.* **4.** to serve a subpoena on a person.

**subrogate** *v.,* **subrogated, subrogating.** to substitute a new person for the original claimant with regard to a right or claim. For example, if A's car is damaged in an accident caused by B and A's insurance company pays the repair bill, then the insurance company may take A's place in suing B to recover those expenses; the insurance company is said to be "subrogated to" A's damage claim against B. The original claimant is called the **subrogor;** the substituted claimant is the **subrogee.** —**subrogation** *n.*

**subscribe** *v.,* **subscribed, subscribing. 1.** to sign a document, particularly a formal instrument such as a deed, will, or affidavit. **2.** to agree to contribute a certain amount of capital to a corporation in exchange for a certain amount of its stock, or to promise to contribute a certain sum to charity. —**subscription** *n.*

**subsequent** *adj.* See *condition subsequent* (under CONDITION).

**subsequent history** *n.* See under HISTORY.

**subsidiary** *n., pl.* **subsidiaries,** *adj.*

—*n.* **1.** a corporation more than 50 percent of whose voting stock is owned by another corporation. Also called **subsidiary corporation.** Cf. PARENT COMPANY.

**2. wholly owned subsidiary** a corporation all of whose voting stock is owned by another corporation.

—*adj.* **3.** of or pertaining to a subsidiary.

**substance** *n.* **1.** the real or underlying nature of a transaction, claim, law, or other matter, as distinguished from its FORM. For example, an exchange of valuable real estate for one dollar is a sale in form, but in substance a gift.
**2.** Also called **substantive law.** the entire body of law that establishes and defines those rights and duties that the legal system exists to protect and enforce; distinguished from PROCEDURE. For example, in an automobile accident, the questions of whether a driver was responsible and should pay damages or be fined or imprisoned are matters of substance, whereas the steps that must be gone through to determine responsibility and assess damages or a penalty are matters of procedure.
**3.** See CONTROLLED SUBSTANCE.
—**substantive** *adj.*
—**substantively** *adv.*

**substantial capacity test** *n.* the principle that a criminal defendant may establish an INSANITY DEFENSE by showing that as a result of mental disease or defect he lacked "substantial capacity" either to appreciate the wrongfulness of his conduct or to conform his conduct to the requirements of law. This test has been adopted in a significant minority of states.

**substantial evidence** *n.* more than a SCINTILLA OF EVIDENCE, but not necessarily very much more; evidence upon which a reasonable jury could find a fact to be true.

**substantial evidence rule** *n.* **1.** any rule that requires substantial evidence for something, as to overcome a motion for summary judgment or avoid a directed verdict, or holds substantial evidence sufficient for something, as to

uphold a verdict on appeal.
**2.** the standard usually used by courts in reviewing administrative determinations. It requires considerable deference to the agency, whose decision will be affirmed so long as there was more than a minimal amount of evidence to support it, even if the reviewing court believes that the preponderance of the evidence pointed to the opposite conclusion.

**substantial performance** *n.* performance of a party's obligations under a contract that complies with what was required in all but minor respects; performance in such a way that there has been no *material breach* (see under BREACH).

**substantive cite-check** *n.* See under CITE-CHECK.

**substantive due process** *n.* See under DUE PROCESS.

**substantive law** *n.* Same as SUBSTANCE (def. 2).

**substituted service** *n.* See under SERVICE.

**subtenancy** *n., pl.* **subtenancies. 1.** the leasehold or other estate held by a *subtenant* (see under SUBLEASE).
**2.** the state of being a subtenant.

**subtenant** *n.* See under SUBLEASE.

**succeed** *v.* to take over a right, interest, or duty of another; to take the place of another with respect to some matter: *When Company A was taken over by Company B, Company B succeeded to all the rights and obligations of Company A.*

**succession** *n.* **1.** broadly, any acquisition or taking over of another's right, interest, or duty.
**2.** narrowly, the acquisition of rights or property of another upon the other's death, especially by INTESTATE SUCCESSION.

**successor** *n.* one who succeeds to the right, interest, or duty of another (the PREDECESSOR). Also called **successor in interest.**

**sudden heat of passion** *n.* Same as HEAT OF PASSION.

**sue** *v.*, **sued, suing. 1.** to file a SUIT against; to institute legal proceedings: *The injured passenger sued the driver. Our client has threatened to sue.*
**2. sue out** to make application for or to apply for and obtain a writ or other special order from a court: *The plaintiff sued out a writ of attachment against the defendant.*
—**suability** *n.*
—**suable** *adj.*

**sufferance** *n.* See *tenancy at sufferance* (under TENANCY).

**suffrage** *n.* the right to vote.

**sui juris** *adj. Latin.* (lit. "of one's own right") possessing full legal capacity; legally entitled to manage one's own affairs. Cf. ALIENI JURIS.

**suicide** *n.* killing oneself. Attempted suicide is a crime in some states; aiding and abetting a suicide (making the death what is commonly referred to as an **assisted suicide** or, if a physician renders the assistance, a **physician-assisted suicide**) is a crime in virtually all states. See also LIVING WILL.

**suit** *n.* **1.** a *civil action* (see under ACTION) brought by one person or entity against another.
**2.** Also called **suit in equity.** historically, a proceeding brought in a court of EQUITY, as distinguished from an *action at law* (see under ACTION).
**3. collusive suit** an improper type of suit in which the parties pretend to be adverse in order to present a hypothetical question to the court or obtain a mutually desired outcome.
**4. strike suit** a disparaging term for a large-scale *class action* or *derivative action* (see under ACTION) that is viewed by the defendants as unfounded and intended solely to induce them to agree to a settlement (usually including payment of attorneys' fees to the plaintiff's attorneys) in order to avoid the expense of litigating the case on the merits.

**suitor** *n.* one who institutes a lawsuit; a plaintiff.

**sum certain** *n., pl.* **sums certain.** an exact amount of money; a sum of money that is stated or can be ascertained directly from the face of an instrument without reference to any other information.

**sum up** *v.*, **summed up, summing up.** to deliver a SUMMATION: *Mr. Smith will sum up the plaintiff's case, then Ms. Jones will sum up for the defense.*

**summary** *adj.* describing proceedings conducted in a simplified or abbreviated manner because the issues and circumstances do not require more extended or elaborate treatment; for example, *summary judgment* (see under JUDGMENT).
—**summarily** *adv.*

**summary court-martial** *n.* See under COURT-MARTIAL.

**summation** *n.* a lawyer's address to the judge or jury after all evidence has been presented, summarizing the case and attempting to convince them to find in favor of her client. Also called **argument, closing argument, closing statement,** or just **closing.** Cf. OPENING STATEMENT.

**summons** *n., pl.* **summonses,** *v.*, **summonsed, summonsing.** —*n.* **1.** a PROCESS directing a defendant to appear in court to answer a civil complaint or a criminal charge.
**2. alias summons** a subsequent summons issued to replace one that could not be served or otherwise failed; especially the first such replacement. See note at ALIAS.
**3. John Doe summons a.** a summons directed to a defendant whose name is not known, who is therefore identified by description rather than by name. Typically the party summonsed is identified in pleadings by a dummy name such as JOHN DOE or JANE DOE or RICHARD ROE until the party's actual name is ascertained. **b.** a direction by the Internal Revenue Service to a third party to surrender information concerning a taxpayer whose identity is currently unknown to the IRS. Such a summons may be served only with prior judicial approval.
**4. pluries summons** the third or subsequent summons in a series, each after

the first having been issued because the previous ones proved ineffective. See note at PLURIES.
—*v.* **5.** to serve with a summons.
—**summonsable** *adj.*

**sumptuary law** *n.* **1.** historically, a law regulating personal expenditures, especially for food or dress, to restrain extravagance.
**2.** a law regulating personal habits that offend the moral or religious beliefs of the community.

**Sunday closing law** *n.* a law forbidding certain otherwise legal activities on Sunday. See also BLUE LAW.

**Sunna** or **Sunnah** *n. Islamic Law.* the traditional part of Islamic law, as expressed and exemplified by the words and actions of Muhammad. The Sunna supplements the Koran and is second only to the Koran among the four sources of Islamic law (see USUL AL-FIQH).

**sunset law** *n.* a statute that expires automatically after a certain period of time.

**sunshine law** *n.* a statute requiring that official meetings of governmental agencies be open to the public.

**suo nomine** *Latin.* in his or her own name.

**Superior Court** *n.* the name given in some states to the lowest court of *general jurisdiction* (see under JURISDICTION[1]), and in a few states to the first level of appellate court. Cf. INFERIOR COURT.

**supersedeas** *Latin.* (lit. "You shall desist.") a stay of execution of a judgment to allow appellate review. See also *supersedeas bond* (under BOND[2]).

**superseding cause** *n.* in tort law, an action or event that intervenes so dramatically and unexpectedly in a chain of causation, and changes its course so significantly, that the law regards it as the PROXIMATE CAUSE of the injury or damage complained of. Cf. INTERVENING CAUSE.

**supervised visitation** *n.* See under VISITATION.

**supplemental jurisdiction** *n.* See under JURISDICTION[1].

**suppress** *v.* **1.** (of a court in a criminal case) to prohibit the prosecution from introducing evidence obtained in violation of the Constitution, such as evidence derived from an unlawful search and seizure or an involuntary confession. See also EXCLUSIONARY RULE; MIRANDA RULE.
**2.** (of a party in a civil or criminal case) to withhold evidence that should have been produced.
**3. suppression hearing** a hearing held in advance of a criminal trial to determine whether evidence objected to by the defendant should be suppressed.
—**suppression** *n.*

**supra** *adv. Latin.* (lit. "above") earlier in the same document. Used particularly in a second or later reference to an authority already cited in full: *In Doe v. Bolton, supra, the court found the law unconstitutional.* Opposite of INFRA.

**supremacy** *n.* the principle, set forth in the Constitution, that FEDERAL LAW is the "supreme Law of the Land," so that any conflicting state law is invalid.

**Supreme Court** *n.* **1.** Short for **Supreme Court of the United States.** The highest court in the federal judicial system, with final say in interpretation of FEDERAL LAW and jurisdiction to resolve controversies between states. Unless the context makes it clear that a state court is being referred to, in American legal writing the phrase "Supreme Court" always means the Supreme Court of the United States.
**2.** in most states, the highest court of the state, with final say in the interpretation of state law. In some states, the highest court has a different name or there may be more than one highest court handling different types of cases; in at least one state (New York) the Supreme Court is the lowest court of general jurisdiction, equivalent to what some states call the SUPERIOR COURT.
**3. supreme court** loosely, the highest court of any jurisdiction: *The final authority on interpretation of state law is the state's supreme court.*

**surety** *n.* a person who joins in a contract as a co-obligor in order to assure the obligee of an additional (usually more creditworthy) source for performance of the obligation. For example, when an automobile dealer insists that a young buyer get her father's signature on a car loan contract, the father becomes a surety; the daughter is called the **principal obligor** or **principal debtor,** or simply the **principal,** but the dealer (the **creditor** or **obligee**) may look to either the principal or the surety for payment.

**surety bond** *n.* See under BOND².

**suretyship** *n.* **1.** strictly, the three-way contract or relationship among a surety, a principal obligor, and their obligee. See discussion at SURETY.
**2.** broadly, any arrangement or undertaking by which one becomes answerable for the debt, default, or miscarriage of another, including a GUARANTY (def. 1). See also GUARANTY (def. 2).

**suretyship bond** *n.* See under BOND².

**surplusage** *n.* **1.** unnecessary or extraneous matter included in a pleading; matter that adds nothing material to the pleading.
**2.** redundant words in statute, instrument, or the like.

**surrebuttal** *n.* **1.** the presentation of evidence or argument in response to a REBUTTAL.
**2.** specifically, a *surrebuttal case* (see under CASE²).
—*adj.* **3.** presented in response to a rebuttal: *surrebuttal case; surrebuttal argument.*

**surreply brief** *n.* See under BRIEF.

**surrogacy** *n.* **1.** the process of acting as a SURROGATE MOTHER.
**2.** the arrangement between a couple and a woman serving as a surrogate mother for them.
**3. gestational surrogacy** surrogacy in which the embryo carried by the surrogate mother is produced through in vitro fertilization of an egg from the female partner in the couple for whom she is bearing the child and then implanted in the surrogate mother's uterus.
**4. traditional surrogacy** surrogacy in which the surrogate mother's own egg is used, and her pregnancy results from artificial insemination with semen from the male partner in the couple for whom she is bearing the child. It says something about the pace of social and technological change that courts and legal writers can apply the word "traditional" to such an arrangement.

**surrogate¹** *n.* **1.** a person appointed or undertaking to act for another; a substitute or deputy.
**2.** a SURROGATE MOTHER or GESTATIONAL SURROGATE.
—*adj.* **3.** regarded or acting as a surrogate.
**4.** involving or referring to the use of a surrogate mother to conceive or carry an embryo.

**surrogate²** *n.* **1.** in some states, the judge of a probate court or other court dealing with decedents' estates.
**2. Surrogate** the title given (instead of Judge or Justice) to such a judge.

**surrogate carrier** *n.* Same as GESTATIONAL SURROGATE.

**surrogate mother** *n.* a woman who bears a child for a couple when the wife is unable to do so, having agreed to relinquish parental rights to the couple upon the birth of the child. The child is usually conceived with the husband's sperm, either through artificial insemination of the surrogate mother or through in vitro fertilization of an egg from the wife, which is then implanted in the surrogate mother's uterus. See also BIRTH MOTHER.
—**Usage.** Sometimes the term *surrogate mother* is used in the more limited sense of one who becomes pregnant through insemination (and so is also the genetic mother of the child carried for the benefit of another couple), as distinguished from a GESTATIONAL SURROGATE (also called *gestational carrier* or *surrogate carrier*), whose pregancy results from implantation of a fertilized egg or embryo provided by the couple for whom she is to bear the child. See also the distinction between *traditional*

*surrogacy* and *gestational surrogacy* (under SURROGACY).

**surrogateship** *n.* the office or status of a surrogate; especially a judgeship in certain courts (see SURROGATE²).

**surveillance** *n.* **1.** covert monitoring of a person's movements and activities or of people and activities at a specific location, especially by law enforcement authorities; often includes EAVESDROPPING.
**2. electronic surveillance** the use of video cameras, radio transmitters, and other electronic devices in surveillance. See also *electronic eavesdropping* (under EAVESDROPPING); WIRETAP.

**survive** *v.,* **survived, surviving.** of a cause of action, to remain in existence ("alive") after the death of the plaintiff or defendant. At common law, most tort claims did not survive the death of either the injured party or the tortfeasor; most states have adopted "survival statutes" permitting most such actions to continue, with a representative of the decedent's estate substituted for the decedent as a party.
—**survival** *n.*

**survivorship** *n.* See RIGHT OF SURVIVORSHIP.

**survivorship annuity** *n.* See under ANNUITY.

**suspect classification** *n.* a law's CLASSIFICATION of people into categories regarded by the Supreme Court as requiring STRICT SCRUTINY under the EQUAL PROTECTION clause of the Constitution.
——**Note.** So far, the only classifications deemed to merit this highest level of SCRUTINY are those based on race, ethnicity, national origin, and ALIENAGE. Cf. QUASI-SUSPECT CLASSIFICATION. See also note at HEIGHTENED SCRUTINY.

**suspended sentence** *n.* See under SENTENCE.

**sustain** *v.* **1.** to rule favorably upon: *The court sustained the objection* (*the motion, the appeal*).
**2.** to satisfy: *The plaintiff sustained her burden of proof.*
**3.** to justify; to warrant: *The evidence sustained the verdict.*

—**sustainability** *n.*
—**sustainable** *adj.*

**swear** *v.,* **swore, sworn, swearing. 1.** to take an OATH or state under oath. Sworn statements are subject to the penalties for FALSE SWEARING and PERJURY.
**2.** (sometimes followed by *in*) to administer an oath to a person: *swear the witness; swear in the new Chief Justice.*
——**Usage.** In its narrow and traditional sense, "swearing" is an explicit or implicit invocation of God; in a more general sense, it is the making of any solemn promise or statement (backed up by the law of perjury), and so includes affirming (see AFFIRM¹). To avoid religious implications that are offensive both to some very religious and to some nonreligious people, in legal matters the word "affirm" may always be used instead of "swear." For example, the Constitution requires that the President of the United States take an oath or affirmation that begins: "I do solemnly swear (or affirm) that I will faithfully execute the Office of President...." See note at OATH OR AFFIRMATION; see also SWEAR OR AFFIRM.

**swear or affirm** a phrase used to avoid the religious issues raised by the use of SWEAR alone: *Do you swear or affirm that the testimony you give will be the truth, the whole truth, and nothing but the truth?* See also OATH OR AFFIRMATION, and see note at SWEAR.

**swearing contest** *n. Informal.* a situation in which the only evidence on an issue in a case is the conflicting testimony of opposing witnesses, each of whom swears (or affirms) that his version is correct and the opposing version is a lie. See also HE SAID, SHE SAID.

**sworn** *adj.* **1.** having taken an oath or made an affirmation; bound by an oath or affirmation: *a sworn witness; a duly elected and sworn official.*
**2.** given under oath or affirmation; made subject to the penalties for perjury and false swearing: *sworn statement; sworn testimony.*
See also SWEAR.

**syllabus** *n., pl.* **syllabuses, syllabi.** a

brief summary of the facts and holdings in a case, prepared or authorized by the court and printed at the top of the court's opinion for the convenience of readers, but not forming part of the official opinion. Cf. HEADNOTE.

**symbolic speech** *n.* See under SPEECH.

**synthesis** *n., pl.* **syntheses. 1.** the act of synthesizing.

**2.** the result of synthesizing several cases; the legal principle derived from them.

**synthesize** *v.,* **synthesized, synthesizing.** to derive a general legal principle from the decisions in a number of specific cases; to combine the holdings of several cases dealing with different fact patterns in the same general area of law into a statement that accounts for all of them.

# T

**tail** *n.* **1.** the limitation of an estate to a person and the heirs of his or her body, or some particular class of such heirs: *The estate was conveyed in tail.*
—*adj.* **2.** limited to a specified line of heirs; being in tail: *The interest conveyed was an estate tail.*
For details, see FEE TAIL.

**take** *v.,* **took, taken, taking. 1.** to seize; capture; arrest; appropriate: *take a fugitive; take property by eminent domain.*
**2.** to acquire property, as on the happening of an event: *Under the will, the widow takes a life estate in the family farm and the children take a remainder interest.*
**3.** to accept; undertake: *The lawyer took the case.*
**4.** to present: *take the dispute to court; take the issue to the jury.*
**5.** to carry forward; pursue: *take the case all the way to the Supreme Court; take an appeal.*
**6.** to assume the obligation of; be bound by: *take an oath; take a pledge.*
**7.** to proceed to handle in some manner: *take a matter under consideration.*
**8. take in** to transport to a police station: *take a suspect in for questioning.*
—**takable, takeable** *adj.*
—**taker** *n.*

**take-back sting** *n.* See under STING.

**take on submission** See under SUBMIT.

**take private 1.** (of a corporate executive or board of directors) to cause a corporation to GO PRIVATE.
**2.** (of a lawyer or law firm) to handle the legal work involved in carrying out such a course of action on behalf of a corporation.

**take public 1.** (of a corporate executive or board of directors) to cause a corporation to GO PUBLIC.

**2.** (of a lawyer or law firm) to handle the legal work involved in carrying out such a course of action on behalf of a corporation.

**take the stand** See under STAND.

**taking** *n.* **1.** the act of a state or federal government in depriving a property owner of the use of her property in order to serve a public purpose; an exercise of the power of EMINENT DOMAIN. This may occur through a formal proceeding to take title to the land and oust the owner, or by any law or government activity that substantially destroys the usefulness or economic value of the land or entails physical occupation of the land.
**2. regulatory taking** a statute or regulation that destroys the value of land and thus amounts to a taking.
See also TRESPASSORY TAKING.
—**Note.** When a taking occurs, the property owner whose land is affected has a constitutional right to JUST COMPENSATION.

**Talmud** *n. Jewish Law.* **1.** the collection of Jewish law and tradition consisting of the MISHNAH and the GEMARA.
**2.** the Gemara.
—**Talmudic** *adj.*

**tangible** *adj.* **1.** having physical existence; capable of being touched. See, e.g., *tangible asset* (under ASSET); *tangible property* (under PROPERTY).
—*n.* **2.** something tangible, especially a tangible asset.
—**tangibility, tangibleness** *n.*
—**tangibly** *adv.*

**tariff** *n.* **1.** an official list or table showing the duties or customs imposed by a government on imports or exports.
**2.** any duty or rate of duty in such a list or schedule.
**3.** any table of charges, as of a railroad,

telephone company, or public utility.
—*v.* **4.** to subject to a tariff.

**tarnish** *v.* to reduce the value of another's trademark by using it, or a confusingly similar mark, on products of inferior quality to those of the trademark owner.
—**tarnishment** *n.*

**tax** *n.* **1.** a sum of money required to be paid to the federal, state, or local government for the support of government activities and services to the public at large; distinguished from a fee (see FEE[2]) in that taxes are collected from a broad class of persons without regard to their use of a particular government service or exercise of a particular privilege.
**2. flat tax** a tax, particularly an INCOME TAX, set at a fixed percentage of the amount being taxed, so that those with low taxable incomes are taxed at the same rate as those with high taxable incomes. Most so-called "flat income tax" proposals, however, would not tax the first several thousand dollars of income, and in this respect would be progressive rather than flat. At the same time, some such proposals would tax only earned income (primarily wages), and make unearned income (interest, dividends, capital gains) entirely exempt from income taxes. Since the rich derive a much higher proportion of their income from investments than do people of ordinary means, this exemption would benefit high-income tax payers more than middle-income taxpayers, in this respect making the tax as a percentage of total income regressive rather than flat.
**3. progressive tax** a tax with rates that increase as the amount subject to the tax increases, so that taxpayers with more money pay proportionately higher taxes. The basic design of the federal income tax has traditionally been progressive, at least in theory, although over a 30-year period beginning in the 1960's the top marginal tax rate—the rate paid on the top portion of the taxable income of taxpayers with the very highest incomes—has been lowered repeatedly, from 91 percent to

less than 40 percent, making the system much "flatter" than was contemplated when the current Internal Revenue Code was adopted in 1954. See also TAX BRACKET; TAX RATE.
**4. regressive tax** a tax structured so that the effective tax rate decreases as income or value of the kind subject to the tax increases (e.g., the SOCIAL SECURITY TAX), or any other tax whose practical effect is to tax the poor more heavily in proportion to their incomes than the rich (e.g., the SALES TAX).
—*v.* **5.** to impose a tax on or by reason of: *to tax an individual or corporation; to tax income, imports, or property.*
**6.** to require the losing party to pay the winner's COSTS in a court case: *costs were taxed to the plaintiff.*
See also *ad valorem tax* (under AD VALOREM); ALTERNATIVE MINIMUM TAX; BETTERMENT TAX; *capital gains tax* (under CAPITAL[1]); CONSUMPTION TAX; DIRECT TAX; DUTY[2]; ESTATE TAX; ESTIMATED TAX; EXCISE; FRANCHISE TAX; *generation-skipping transfer tax* (under GENERATION-SKIPPING TRUST); GIFT TAX; IMPOST; INCOME TAX; INHERITANCE TAX; PAYROLL TAX; POLL TAX; PROPERTY TAX; SALES TAX; SELF-EMPLOYMENT TAX; SIN TAX; SOCIAL SECURITY TAX; STAMP TAX; USE TAX; VALUE ADDED TAX; WITHHOLDING TAX.

**tax avoidance** *n.* the structuring of transactions and choosing of options in filling out tax forms so as to minimize one's taxes by lawful means. Cf. TAX EVASION; TAX FRAUD.

**tax bracket** *n.* an income range to which a specific TAX RATE is applied for income tax purposes. In a progressive income tax structure (see *progressive tax,* under TAX), the portion of a taxpayer's taxable income that falls within the lowest bracket is taxed at the lowest rate, and the portions in higher brackets are taxed at successively higher rates. A taxpayer is said to be "in the X percent bracket" if the highest bracket into which her income reaches is taxed at the indicated rate; this does *not* mean that the taxpayer's entire taxable income is taxed at that rate. See also *marginal tax rate* and *effective tax rate* (under TAX RATE).

**tax credit** *n.* **1.** a reduction in a tax allowed to certain classes of taxpayers for reasons of public policy. A tax credit is a direct subtraction from the tax itself, in contrast to an income tax DEDUCTION, which only reduces the income upon which the tax is calculated and so has less impact on the actual tax bill.
**2. nonrefundable tax credit** a tax credit that can be used only to the extent that it does not exceed the tax that would be owed without it. For example, if the tax owed without the credit would be $400 and the credit is $600, the taxpayer can use only $400 of the credit, reducing the total tax owed to zero.
**3. refundable tax credit** a tax credit that can be used in its entirety even if it exceeds the tax that would be owed without it. For example, if the tax owed without the credit would be $400 and the credit is $600, the taxpayer is credited with the full $600 and consequently is entitled to a "refund" of $200.

**tax-deductible** *adj.* Same as DEDUCTIBLE (def. 1).
—**tax deductibility** *n.*

**tax deduction** *n.* Same as DEDUCTION.

**tax-deferred** *adj.* **1.** (of income) not taxable until a future time.
**2.** producing income that is not taxable until a future time: *A regular IRA is a tax-deferred investment.*
—**tax deferral** *n.*

**tax equalization** *n.* See under EQUALIZATION.

**tax evasion** *n.* the crime of contriving in any way not to pay the amount that one is legally obligated to pay in taxes. Cf. TAX AVOIDANCE.

**tax-exempt** *adj.* **1.** not required to pay taxes: *Qualified charitable organizations are tax exempt.* See also *qualify for tax-exempt status* (under QUALIFY[1]).
**2. a.** not taxable to the recipient or owner: *tax-exempt interest; tax-exempt property.* **b.** producing income that is

not taxable: *tax-exempt municipal bonds.*

**tax fraud** *n.* the crime of intentionally filing a false tax return or making other false statements under penalties of perjury to taxing authorities. Cf. TAX AVOIDANCE.

**tax-free** *adj. Informal.* Same as TAX-EXEMPT (def. 2).

**tax home** *n.* the city or general area where a taxpayer is deemed to be located for the purpose of determining whether the taxpayer may claim a federal income tax deduction for expenses incurred in traveling away from that area on business.
——**False Friend.** Usually the tax home is the taxpayer's main place of work, as distinguished from the place where she lives.

**tax lien** *n.* See under LIEN.

**tax rate** *n.* **1.** the percentage of taxable income or of the value of taxable property that must be paid as tax.
**2. effective tax rate** the actual percentage of one's taxable income that is owed as income taxes; in a progressive tax system, this is always lower than the *marginal tax rate* except for taxpayers in the lowest income bracket, because all taxable income below the taxpayer's top bracket is taxed at less than the marginal rate.
**3. marginal tax rate** in a progressive income tax system, the tax rate applicable to the portion of a taxpayer's income that exceeds the threshold for that taxpayer's top tax bracket. Cf. *effective tax rate.* See also *progressive tax* (under TAX); TAX BRACKET.

**tax return** *n.* See under RETURN.

**tax sale** *n.* See under SALE.

**tax shelter** *n.* an investment or other financial arrangement that serves to reduce taxes or to generate both income and offsetting deductions and credits so as to minimize tax on the income.

**taxable** *adj.* subject to being taxed: *taxable income* (see under INCOME); *taxable property; taxable gain; taxable costs.*

—**taxability** n.
—**taxably** adv.

**temporary remedy** (or **relief**) n. See under REMEDY.

**temporary restraining order (TRO)** n. See under RESTRAINING ORDER.

**tenancy** n., pl. **tenancies. 1.** broadly, any possessory estate in real property, including tenancy in fee and life tenancy. (See all three phrases under ESTATE[1].) A tenancy may be designated as BY THE ENTIRETY, IN COMMON, IN CO-PARCENARY, IN SEVERALTY, or JOINT, depending upon the ownership arrangement.
**2.** specifically, a LEASEHOLD or landlord-tenant relationship. See defs. 3, 5, and 6 for types of leasehold.
**3. periodic tenancy** (or **estate**) a tenancy which runs for successive fixed periods of time such as a month or a year, continuing indefinitely but terminable at will by either the landlord or the tenant upon reasonable notice at the end of any period. Also called **month-to-month tenancy, tenancy** (or **estate**) **from year to year,** or the like.
**4. tenancy** (or **estate**) **at sufferance** the interest of a person who wrongfully continues to occupy property after the right to possession has ended; this is not a real tenancy or estate because it is not a possessory interest. Also called **holdover tenancy.**
**5. tenancy** (or **estate**) **at will** a tenancy of indefinite duration terminable by either the landlord or the tenant upon reasonable notice at any time.
**6. tenancy** (or **estate**) **for years** tenancy for a specific length of time, not necessarily measured in years; for example, a one-week tenancy. Also called a **term of years.**

**tenant** n. a holder of a TENANCY; a person with a present right to possession of real property, especially the holder of a LEASEHOLD. A tenant is designated as a periodic tenant, tenant in common, tenant in fee, etc., according to the nature of the tenancy; see classifications under TENANCY and ESTATE[1]. See also

holdover tenant (under HOLD). Cf. LANDLORD.

**tenantable** adj. (of leased premises) in sufficiently good repair to be usable for the intended purpose. In the case of a residential lease, "tenantable" is the same thing as HABITABLE.

**tender** v. **1.** to offer something formally, in a way that makes it clear that the thing offered will be given, done, or effective immediately upon acceptance: to tender payment; to tender performance; to tender one's resignation.
—n. **2.** the act of tendering or the thing tendered. See also LEGAL TENDER.

**tender offer** n. a public offer to buy up a specified amount of stock in a particular corporation at a particular price if shares are tendered by the current stockholders on or before a particular date, made in an effort to take over control of the corporation.

**tender years** n. extreme youthfulness: a child of tender years.

**tenement** n. **1.** any property of a permanent nature, especially an interest in land. See also dominant tenement and servient tenement (both under ESTATE[3]).
**2.** a run-down or overcrowded apartment house in a poor section of a city.

**tenendum** Latin. to be held; to be possessed. See also HABENDUM ET TENENDUM; HABENDUM CLAUSE; TENENDUM CLAUSE; AND NOTE AT TO HAVE AND TO HOLD.

**tenendum clause** n. **1.** Same as HABENDUM CLAUSE.
**2.** in feudal times, the portion of a deed that specified the lord under whom the tenancy being conveyed was to be held—that is, whether the grantee would hold of the grantor or of the grantor's lord—and perhaps also the service to be rendered to the lord as a condition of holding the land.
Also called **tenendum.** Cf. REDDENDUM.
——**History.** The first printed treatise on English law, the fifteenth century Littleton on Tenures (written in Law French), drew a conceptual distinction between the habendum portion of a

deed (specifying the nature of the estate that the grantee would have) and the *tenendum* (specifying the lord of whom it would be held), and later writers—notably Sir Edward Coke in the seventeenth century—perpetuated the distinction. But it seems likely that in actual deeds these two functions were normally performed by a single clause introduced by a single phrase ("habendum et tenendum" or its equivalent in English or Law French), and that Littleton's distinction was a somewhat artificial assignment of different offices to two components of a single expression that had found its way into the conventional language of deeds for much less legalistic reasons. See note at TO HAVE AND TO HOLD.

**tener** *v. Law French.* (lit. "to hold; holding") See A AVER ET TENER.

**tenor** *n.* **1.** the exact words or terms of an instrument: *The defendant offered a compromise, but the plaintiff seeks to enforce the contract according to its tenor.*
**2.** the general meaning or course of thought in an informal communication: *The tenor of our conversation was that there is still ground for compromise.*

**term** *n.* **1.** a specific, finite period of time during which an agreement is operative or an interest remains good, or at the end of which an obligation matures: *the term of a lease; the term of a bond.*
**2.** (of a court) **a.** the period of time during which the court has sessions: *The October Term of the Supreme Court runs from October to June.* **b.** in some courts, a sitting of the court for a particular type of business: *trial term; appellate term.*
**3.** a portion of an instrument dealing with a certain matter, or the provision it makes for a particular matter: *The contract includes a cancellation term permitting either party to terminate the arrangement on 60 days' notice.*
**4.** a word or phrase. See also TERM OF ART.
—*adj.* **5.** lasting only for a specified term or maturing at a specified time: *term insurance; term loan.*

**term life insurance** or **term insurance** *n.* See under LIFE INSURANCE.

**term of art** *n.* a word or phrase having a special meaning in a particular field, different from or more precise than its customary meaning. Also called **word of art** or, when referring to a phrase, **words of art.**

**term of years** *n.* Same as *tenancy* (or *estate*) *for years* (see under TENANCY).

**terminus a quo** *n., pl.* **termini a quibus.** *Latin.* (lit. "boundary from which") the starting point, as of a private road or a period of time.

**terminus ad quem** *n., pl.* **termini ad quos.** *Latin.* (lit. "boundary to which") the ending point, as of a private road or a period of time.

**terms and conditions** *n.pl.* all of the provisions of a contract or other instrument; another way of saying "terms."

**terrorem** *n.* See IN TERROREM.

**terrorism** *n.* politically motivated violence or intimidation directed against a civilian population by a subgroup within the population, by an outside group, or by clandestine agents of another country. See also CYBERTERRORISM.
—**terrorist** *n., adj.*
—**terroristic** *adj.*

**terrorist profile** *n.* See under PROFILE.

**test case** *n.* See under CASE[1].

**testament** *n.* a WILL.
—**Usage.** In previous centuries, sometimes a technical distinction was drawn between "will" and "testament." In modern usage, "testament" is almost never used except in the phrase LAST WILL AND TESTAMENT.

**testamentary** *adj.* **1.** pertaining to a will or wills: *The will was declared void because the decedent lacked testamentary capacity.*
**2.** established or accomplished by will. See, e.g., *testamentary gift* (under GIFT); *testamentary guardian* (under GUARDIAN); *testamentary trust* (under TRUST).
Cf. INTER VIVOS.

**testator** *n.* a person, especially a man, who makes a will. When the maker of a will is a woman, it is still usual to refer to her by the old-fashioned word **testatrix.**

**testatrix** *n., pl.* **testatrices.** the traditional term for a woman who makes a will.

**testify** *v.,* **testified, testifying.** to give evidence under oath or affirmation at a trial, hearing, or deposition.

**testilying** *n.* the giving of false testimony by a police officer in a criminal case, particularly to bolster a case against a defendant believed to be guilty, as by falsifying the circumstances of a questionable search and seizure so as to avoid application of the EXCLUSIONARY RULE.
—**testilie** *v.,* **testilied, testilying.**
——**Usage.** This term originated as police jargon, but was introduced to a wider audience in 1994 when it was quoted in the report of a commission investigating police corruption in New York City, and is now commonly used by legal writers and the media.

**testimonial privilege** *n.* See under PRIVILEGE.

**testimony** *n., pl.* **testimonies. 1.** statements made under oath or affirmation by a witness at a trial, hearing, or deposition.
**2. eyewitness testimony** testimony given by a person who directly perceived the event that is the subject of the testimony. See also note at EYEWITNESS.
—**testimonial** *adj.*

**theft** *n.* **1.** a broad term for crimes involving the wrongful taking or keeping of money or property of another. The exact scope of the term varies from state to state, but it typically includes LARCENY, FALSE PRETENSES, EXTORTION, EMBEZZLEMENT, and RECEIVING STOLEN PROPERTY, but not ROBBERY, BURGLARY, or FORGERY. See also IDENTITY THEFT.
**2. grand theft** theft of property whose value exceeds a certain amount or of property of a type regarded as especially serious, such as an automobile, a gun, or a stop sign. Grand theft is a felony.
**3. petit** (or **petty**) **theft** theft of property whose value is below a certain amount. Petty theft, as a first offense and in the absence of aggravating circumstances, is a misdemeanor.

**theft of services** *n.* the crime of obtaining services of any kind (including professional services, labor, transportation, telecommunications service, restaurant service, lodging, or entertainment) by deception, threat, coercion, stealth, tampering, or use of false token or device.

**therapist-client privilege** *n.* Same as PSYCHOTHERAPIST-PATIENT PRIVILEGE.

**therapist-patient privilege** *n.* Same as PSYCHOTHERAPIST-PATIENT PRIVILEGE.

**Thibodaux abstention** *n.* See under ABSTENTION.

**thin skull** *n.* Same as EGGSHELL SKULL.

**thing in action** *n.* See under CHOSE.

**thing in possession** *n.* See under CHOSE.

**third party** *n.* a person who is not a party—or at least not initially or directly a party—to a transaction, proceeding, or other matter under discussion, but who may be affected by it: *The court considered the potential effect of its injunction on third parties.*

**third-party** *adj.* involving or pertaining to a third party, or to a THIRD-PARTY ACTION. See also *third-party beneficiary contract* and *third-party beneficiary* (under CONTRACT).

**third-party action** *n.* an action by which the defendant in a civil case files a complaint against a person who was not initially a party to the case, claiming a right of INDEMNITY or CONTRIBUTION from that third party in the event that the defendant is found liable to the plaintiff. The third-party action is an extension of the main action, and the issues in both actions are normally litigated together in one big case. The complaint against the third party is called a **third-party complaint,** the party filing it is referred to as the **third-party plaintiff,** and the party against whom the third-party action is brought is called the **third-party defendant.** A third-party action is also called an **action over:** *When the distributor was sued for selling a defective product, the distributor brought an action over against the manufacturer.* See also IMPLEAD.

**three strikes law** *n.* a law requiring an extremely severe sentence, such as twenty-five years to life imprisonment, for anyone convicted of a third serious crime; for example, a third violent crime or a third felony.  Also called **three-strikes-and-you're-out law.**

**through bill of lading** See under BILL OF LADING.

**throw-down gun** *n. Police Jargon.* an untraceable gun placed by police at the scene of an incident in which an police officer has shot an unarmed individual, in order to support a claim that the reason for the shooting was that the individual had a gun and posed a threat to the police.  Also called **drop gun, throw-down weapon, throw-down.**

**ticket** *n.* **1.** a piece of paper evidencing a contractual right to goods or services: *movie ticket; pawn ticket.*
**2.** a simple form of SUMMONS or CITATION issued for minor traffic and motor vehicle violations.

**tie** *v.,* **tied, tying.** to link one product or service to another in a TYING ARRANGEMENT.

**tie-in** *n.* Same as TYING ARRANGEMENT.

**tied product** *n.* See under TYING ARRANGEMENT.

**time** *adj.* **1.** lasting until, maturing on, or payable only on or after, a specific date in the future; not payable on demand: *time loan; time instrument.* See also *time draft* (under DRAFT). Cf. *payable on demand* (under DEMAND).
**2. time deposit**  money deposited with a bank which the depositor does not have the right to withdraw until a specific length of time has passed; for example, an account represented by an ordinary CERTIFICATE OF DEPOSIT. Cf.

*demand deposit* (under DEMAND).

**time-barred** *adj.* (of a legal action) incapable of being brought because barred by the STATUTE OF LIMITATIONS.

**time charter** *n.* See under CHARTER².

**time is of the essence** See under OF THE ESSENCE.

**time, place, and manner** a phrase describing the kinds of restrictions that a government may place on FREEDOM OF SPEECH and FREEDOM OF ASSEMBLY without violating the First Amendment. Restrictions may be placed on the time, place, and manner of speech and assembly if they are narrowly tailored to serve legitimate governmental interests and are not based on the content of the speech.
——**Note.** For example, to prevent chaos a city may prohibit marching in the streets without a parade permit, but the granting or denial of a permit may not depend upon the message the marchers seek to convey.

**timely** *adj.* in time; not too late: *A tax return filed by mail is regarded as timely if it is postmarked on or before the due date.*
—**timeliness** *n.*
—**timely** *adv.*

**tin parachute** *n.* a term in an employment contract between a corporation and an employee, usually in middle management, providing for substantial severance benefits in the event that the employee is terminated or demoted in connection with a merger or takeover of the corporation.  Also called **silver parachute.**
——**Note.** The tin parachute is an extension of the concept of GOLDEN PARACHUTE to employees below the highest executive level. In corporations that have them, they are typically provided only to fairly high-level employees. The benefits are substantial—and certainly far in excess of the UNEMPLOYMENT COMPENSATION that otherwise would be available—but are not as generous as a golden parachute. The rationale for creating tin parachutes is that the security they provide is an incentive for

covered employees to stay with the corporation in times of uncertainty.

**title** *n.* **1.** ownership of property, or of a *possessory interest* (see under INTEREST[1]) in property; the right to possess or control possession of property.
**2.** *Informal.* a document evidencing such ownership, such as a DEED or BILL OF SALE or, especially, a CERTIFICATE OF TITLE (defs. 1 and 2).
**3.** a portion of a statute or codification: *Employment discrimination is prohibited by Title VII of the Civil Rights Act of 1964.* See also UNITED STATES CODE.
**4. defective title** title that, because of a gap in records or for some other reason, is too uncertain to qualify as *marketable title.* Also called **bad title** or **unmarketable title.**
**5. equitable title a.** the ownership interest of a person who has a right to have title conveyed to her but to whom legal title has not yet been formally conveyed, especially a person who has entered into a specifically enforceable contract to purchase land but has not yet received the deed. **b.** the right of the beneficiary of a trust with respect to trust property of which the trustee is the legal owner. Cf. *legal title.*
**6. insurable title** title that a reputable insurance company would be willing to insure. Insurable title may contain minor defects that would make it unmarketable, but that are too remote to cause an insurance company to refuse to insure it. See also TITLE INSURANCE.
**7. legal title** actual title to property as recognized under traditional principles of law without consideration of equitable rights, including a seller's title in land as to which a deed has not yet been delivered to the buyer, and a trustee's title to property held in trust for the benefit of another. Cf. *equitable title;* EQUITABLE DISTRIBUTION.
**8. marketable title** title that is free of any reasonable risk of successful challenge by an outsider claiming *paramount title* to the same property. Also called **clear title, good title,** or **merchantable title.** If a person who has contracted to sell land proves unable to deliver marketable title, the purchaser

ordinarily may cancel the deal.
**9. paramount title** as between competing claims to possession of the same property, the superior claim. A person in possession of real property may be evicted only by one with paramount title; for example, although a holdover tenant has no right to possession of the premises, he cannot be evicted by an outsider who has no better right, but can be evicted by the landlord.
**10. Torrens title system** Same as TITLE REGISTRATION SYSTEM.
See also ABSTRACT OF TITLE; CHAIN OF TITLE; CLOUD ON TITLE; COLOR; COVENANTS OF TITLE; DOCUMENT OF TITLE; *try title* (under TRY); QUIET TITLE; *warranty of title* (under WARRANTY).

**title insurance** *n.* insurance purchased by a buyer of real estate to protect herself (or the bank that is taking a mortgage on the property) from loss due to previously unrecognized encumbrances on the property or competing claims to title. See also TITLE RECORDING SYSTEM.

**title recording system** *n.* the only mechanism made available by most state governments for keeping track of ownership of real estate. It consists of a public office in which copies of documents affecting title to land—such as deeds and mortgages—may be (but often are not) filed.
——**Note.** To attempt to determine the status of title to a parcel of land in a state using the title recording system, one must hire someone familiar with these records to do a TITLE SEARCH. But since the system is too haphazard to be reliable, anyone actually spending or lending money for the land in such a state must also purchase TITLE INSURANCE to be protected from loss due to unexpected claims or encumbrances upon the land. Cf. TITLE REGISTRATION SYSTEM.

**title registration system** *n.* an alternative to the TITLE RECORDING SYSTEM made available in a few states, under which title to land can be registered in a state or local government office and evidenced by an official certificate (see CERTIFICATE OF TITLE, def. 2), which is conclusive evidence of title for most purposes. Also called **Torrens title system.**

**title search** *n.* the process of searching through public records in an effort to assess the status of a claimed title to real property by tracing the CHAIN OF TITLE, noting mortgages or other encumbrances on the property, and the like. See also TITLE RECORDING SYSTEM.

**TM** an abbreviation indicating that the word, phrase, or design it accompanies is claimed as a TRADEMARK, although it is not a *registered trademark* (see under TRADEMARK). Cf. ®; SM.

**to have and to hold** to possess legally; have. See HABENDUM CLAUSE.

—**History.** The English language often places a higher value on rhythm, rhyme, and alliteration than on concision. Although the law is criticized for its verbosity—and not without justification—redundant expressions like *each and every, hale and hearty, hem and haw, part and parcel, safe and sound, wear and tear* are part of everyday speech, and the language would be poorer without the music they provide. In law, redundant expressions also serve additional purposes: as terms of art (*aid and abet*), as ritual (*Oyez, oyez, oyez!*), as emphasis (*null and void*). The ancient phrase *to have and to hold,* employed from time immemorial in conveying property, served all of these purposes—so well, in fact, that in 1549 it was incorporated into the marriage ceremony prescribed by *The Book of Common Prayer* for the Church of England, whose language has been closely followed in many churches ever since. Legal writers have at times sought to assign specific, distinct functions to the words "have" and "hold"; but early English equivalents of the phrase *have and hold* are attested from before the year 1000, and it is likely that the primary reason the phrase as a whole caught on in law is simply that it sounded good: Whether expressed in English or in Latin (HABENDUM ET TENENDUM) or Law French (A AVER ET TENER), it was one more flourish in the fundamentally important and always highly formalized act of transferring an interest in land. (See, e.g., *and his heirs* under HEIR; LIVERY OF SEISIN.) See also note at TENENDUM CLAUSE.

**to the order of** See under ORDER².

**toll** *v.* to suspend the running of the STATUTE OF LIMITATIONS under circumstances where the law recognizes that a plaintiff or prosecutor was prevented, through no fault of her own, from commencing an action. One speaks of circumstances that "toll the statute" or "toll the limitations period."

**Torah** *n. Jewish Law.* **1.** The first five books of the Old Testament, dealing particularly with law. **2.** the entire body of Jewish religious literature, law, and teaching as contained chiefly in the Old Testament and the TALMUD. **3.** law or instruction.

**Torrens title system** Same as TITLE REGISTRATION SYSTEM.

**tort** *n.* **1.** a wrongful act, other than a breach of contract, that results in injury to another's person, property, reputation, or some other legally protected right or interest, and for which the injured party is entitled to a remedy at law, usually in the form of damages. **2. constitutional tort** unconstitutional conduct by a public official causing injury to a private individual. The Supreme Court has held that under certain constitutional provisions—notably the Fourth Amendment ban on unreasonable searches and seizures—a person harmed by offical conduct in violation of her constitutional rights may sue the official for damages. **3. intentional tort** a tort committed by one who intends by his action to bring about a wrongful result or knows that that result is substantially certain to occur; e.g., BATTERY or TRESPASS. Cf. NEGLIGENCE; STRICT LIABILITY. —**tortious** *adj.* —**tortiously** *adv.*

**tortfeasor** *n.* **1.** a person or entity that commits a tort. **2. joint tortfeasor** one of a number of individuals or entities whose tortious conduct contributed to an injury.

**total breach** *n.* See under BREACH.

**total renvoi** *n.* See under RENVOI.

**toto** *n.* See IN TOTO.

**Totten trust** *n.* See under TRUST.

**trade dress** *n.* the packaging of a product or service; the shape and design of a product or its package, or the decor of the place where a service is rendered; for example, the distinctive shape of the bottle of a particular brand of perfume or soft drink. If the trade dress is distinctive and is used to identify and distinguish a particular product or service, it can be a TRADEMARK.

**trade embargo** *n.* See under EMBARGO.

**trade libel** *n.* the tort of communicating to a third party a false statement impugning the quality of another person's product, property, or business. Trade libel is a form of DISPARAGEMENT. See also FOOD DISPARAGEMENT; PRODUCT DISPARAGEMENT.
——**False Friend.** The conduct involved in this tort was first recognized as actionable in cases involving false written statements that impugned the quality of a trader's goods and thereby cut into his trade. Although it was not a form of LIBEL (written words directly impugning the character of an individual), it was recognized as analogous and so got its name. The scope of the tort now extends much farther than the name implies: to oral as well as written statements, and to economically damaging falsehoods about any kind of property (for example, the land upon which one's home is situated), not just about products in trade.

**trade name** *n.* a name used by an individual or entity to identify its business or vocation; for example, the name of a department store. Also called **commercial name.**
——**Note.** A trade name is not a TRADEMARK unless it is also used to identify and distinguish specific products or services. Nevertheless, a trade name is entitled to some common law protection in the region where it is used.

**trade regulation** *n.* the body of law that deals with government regulation of competitive business activities; it includes ANTITRUST law and laws dealing with unfair competition, false advertising, and the like.

**trade secret** *n.* confidential information used in a company's business, such as a secret formula or process or a database of client information, that gives the company an advantage over competitors and would be helpful to competitors if they learned of it. Trade secrets are valuable property of a company and courts are very protective of them.

**trade union** *n.* **1.** broadly, a labor UNION of any kind.
**2.** narrowly, a *craft union* (see under UNION).

**trade usage** *n.* See under USAGE.

**trademark** *n.* **1. a.** a name, symbol, or other MARK used by a company to identify its products and distinguish them from goods produced or sold by others. For example, the distinctive logo of a brand of athletic shoes or soft drink would be a trademark. See also BRAND NAME; TRADE DRESS; cf. TRADE NAME. **b.** broadly, any identifying MARK, including not only one identifying a particular company's goods (a trademark in the strict sense), but also a SERVICE MARK, CERTIFICATION MARK, or COLLECTIVE MARK.
**2. registered trademark** a *registered mark* (see under MARK), especially one that is a trademark in the narrow sense as distinguished from a service mark, certification mark, or collective mark. See also ®; TM.

**traditional IRA** *n.* See under IRA.

**traditional surrogacy** *n.* See under SURROGACY.

**transact** *v.* to carry on, conduct, or manage business, negotiations, or other activities, particularly involving matters of economic consequence.

**transact business** *v.* **1.** to engage in business activity.
**2.** (in civil procedure) to engage in corporate activity within a state of such a

nature as to constitute TRANSACTION OF BUSINESS for jurisdictional purposes.

**transaction** *n.* **1.** something that is transacted, especially a business agreement.

**2.** the act of transacting or the fact of being transacted.

**3.** an instance or process of transacting something.

**4.** *Civil Law.* an agreement between two or more persons to resolve their differences by mutual concessions so as to settle or stave off a lawsuit.

**5. sham transaction** a transaction entered into solely for tax purposes but having no real business or economic substance. A taxpayer is not entitled to tax benefits from such a transaction.

**6. secured transaction** any transaction which has as one of its elements the creation of a *security interest* (see under INTEREST[1]) in favor of one of the parties.

**7. step transaction** a single transaction carried out in a series of steps, each of which standing alone might have had particular tax consequences. For tax purposes, only the cumulative result of the several steps is considered; it is treated as a single transaction occurring all at once.

**8. transactions** the published records of the proceedings, as papers read, addresses delivered, or discussions, at the meetings of a learned society or the like.

**9. unsecured transaction** a transaction, particularly one creating a debtor-creditor relationship, in which no security interest is given to guarantee payment or performance; a transaction that is not a *secured transaction*.

—**transactional** *adj.*

—**transactionally** *adv.*

**transaction of business** *n.* any activity of a corporation within a particular state or having an impact within the state. Such transaction of business provides a sufficient basis for a court of that state to exercise jurisdiction over the corporation in a suit arising out of that specific activity, even if the corporation does not engage in regular activity in that state and thus is not generally subject to suit there. See also *long-arm jurisdiction* (under JURISDICTION); MINIMUM CONTACTS. Cf. DOING BUSINESS.

**transactional immunity** *n.* See under IMMUNITY.

**transmission** *n.* See under RENVOI.

**transport** *v.* to convey pursuant to a sentence of TRANSPORTATION: *a cargo of convicts being transported to Australia.*

**transportation** *n. English Legal History.* **1.** the sentence or punishment of being transported to a place out of the country.

**2.** the process of being transported pursuant to such a sentence.

—**Usage.** *Transportation* is usually distinguished from BANISHMENT or EXILE in that the criminal subject to the edict was not merely obliged to leave the country, but sentenced to be transported to a specific place, as to the American colonies or (later, and in considerable numbers) to a penal colony in Australia.

**travel** *n.* See RIGHT TO TRAVEL.

**treason** *n.* **1.** treacherous action in violation of a duty of allegiance, especially to a government or sovereign. Cf. SEDITION.

**2.** in the United States, the crime, committed by a citizen or other person who owes allegiance to the United States, of committing acts of war against the United States or intentionally giving aid and comfort to its enemies. See also OVERT ACT.

**3.** Also called **high treason.** in early English law, treason against the Crown. The crime encompassed a number of acts regarded as threatening to the king's authority or the royal succession, including plotting or imagining the king's death or that of his wife or heir apparent, violating the king's wife or eldest daughter or the wife of the heir apparent, making war against the king or aiding the king's enemies, or killing the king's chancellor or judges in the execution of their duties. See also note at HANG[2].

**4. petit** (or **petty**) **treason** in early English law, the murder of one (other than a royal) to whom one owed allegiance; most often, the murder of a master by his servant or of a husband by his wife. Parliament abolished the offense in 1828 and reclassified such crimes as simple murder.
—**treasonable, treasonous** adj.
—**treasonably, treasonously** adv.

**treatise** n. a book or, especially, a multivolume work, systematically and exhaustively discussing and analyzing an area of law, such as contracts, evidence, or federal procedure. Treatises are a major research tool for lawyers and are often cited as authority by judges. See also HORNBOOK.

**treaty** n., pl. **treaties.** a formal agreement between two or more nations on matters of international concern. Treaties of the United States are negotiated by the President and ratified by a two-thirds vote of the Senate. They are part of FEDERAL LAW and thus supersede any contrary state law and any prior federal statute; but Congress may negate or abrogate a treaty simply by refusing to enact any necessary implementing legislation or by enacting a subsequent statute inconsistent with the treaty. See also EXECUTIVE AGREEMENT.

**treble damages** n.pl. See under DAMAGES.

**tresaiel** n. Law French. **1.** great-great-grandfather.
**2. writ of tresaiel** an ancient writ by which a great-great-grandchild who inherited a possessory interest in land from a great-great-grandparent could gain possession of the land from another person who had taken possession. See also note at MORT D'ANCESTOR.
Also spelled **tresayle** and in many other variations.

**trespass¹** n. **1.** in the broadest sense, any unlawful conduct, especially any wrongful interference with the person or property of another.

**2.** Also called **trespass to land.** intentional or knowing conduct that directly results in invasion of land possessed by another, such as walking on it without permission, chopping down a tree onto it, tunneling under it, shooting a bullet over it, or staying on it after being asked to leave. Trespass in this usual sense of the word is a tort against the person entitled to exclusive possession of the land.
**3. continuing trespass** a trespass, usually to land, in the nature of a permanent or ongoing invasion; for example, a neighbor's building that due to mismeasurement extends two inches over the lot line, or whose roof hangs over the lot line.
**4. criminal trespass** the crime of entering or remaining upon another's land, structure, or vehicle after being notified (orally or by posting of signs or enclosure with fencing) to keep out or to leave.
**5. trespass to chattels** the tort of intentionally interfering with another's possession of goods, as by using, moving, or damaging the property. This tort, also called **trespass to goods,** is confined to relatively minor interference; serious interference with personal property is regarded as CONVERSION.
**6. trespass to person** any tort consisting of interference with person, such as assault, battery, or false imprisonment.
—v. **7.** to commit a trespass.
—**trespasser** n.
—**trespassory** adj.

**trespass²** n. **1.** the common law FORM OF ACTION to recover damages for wrongful interference with one's person or property. The action grew and branched out over the centuries, appearing in many varieties and subvarieties, the principal ones of which are listed in this entry. See also note below.
**2.** a modern tort action to recover damages for *trespass to land* (see under TRESPASS¹).
**3. trespass de bonis asportatis** Latin. (lit. "...for goods carried off") the common law form of action for damages for the wrongful taking of a

chattel out of the plaintiff's possession. The action lay even if the property was subsequently returned, for damages incurred in the interim. Often shortened to **trespass de bonis,** or rendered in English as **trespass for goods, trespass for goods taken and carried away,** or the like.

**4. trespass de ejectione firmae** *Latin.* (lit. "...for ejectment of farm") a common law form of action which lay for a tenant for a term of years who had been ousted from the land before expiration of the term, whether by the landlord or by anyone else. The action began as a special form of the *trespass quare clausum fregit* and ultimately evolved into the action of EJECTMENT. At the beginning it permitted the plaintiff only to recover damages for the wrongful eviction; as the action evolved, it became possible to recover the land itself. Also called **trespass in ejectment.** See also note at DE EJECTIONE FIRMAE.

**5. trespass for mesne profits** a common law form of action by which a tenant who had been wrongfully put out of land could recover the profits from the land for the period that the tenant was kept out of possession. The action lay against the person who had wrongfully been in possession, and was supplemental to the action of EJECTMENT. For example, if a landlord wrongfully evicted a tenant whose term had not expired and put a new tenant in his place, the evicted tenant could recover possession in an action of ejectment against the landlord, and recover his lost profits from the land in an action of trespass for mesne profits against the interim tenant.

**6. trespass in assault and battery** a common law form of action to recover damages for intentional injury to person.

**7. trespass on the case** a common law form of action that split off from *trespass vi et armis* (which was usually referred to simply as "trespass") beginning in the fourteenth century. The action of trespass on the case permitted recovery for injuries and losses that were indirect rather than direct, or that did not involve physical force or intrusion, or that resulted from negligence rather than intentional conduct. Also called **trespass on the special case, action on the case, action on the special case,** or simply **case:** *The parties disagreed on whether the action lay in trespass or in case.* All variants often appear with *upon* instead of *on:* **trespass upon the case,** etc.

**8. trespass quare clausum fregit** *Latin.* (lit. "...whereby he broke the close") the common law form of action to recover damages for *trespass to land* (see under TRESPASS[1]). Although the Latin words refer to the breaking of an enclosure around the land in question, both the breaking and the enclosure could be completely fictional; the essential element of the action was the physical invasion of another's land, even if just by stepping over an invisible line. If no actual damage was done, however, a plaintiff would be entitled only to nominal damages. Often shortened to **trespass quare clausum.** Also called **trespass de clauso fracto** ("...for broken close").

**9. trespass vi et armis** *Latin.* (lit. "...with force and arms") the original action of trespass: the general common law form of action to recover damages for direct physical interference with person or property. This title embraced the three basic categories of trespass, and the form of pleading varied accordingly: trespass to person (see *trespass in assault and battery*), to chattels (see *trespass de bonis asportatis*), and to land (see *trespass quare clausum fregit*).

——**History.** The history of the action of trespass is a case study in the expansion of legal remedies to meet the growing needs of a society. Maitland, in his *Lectures on the Forms of Action at Common Law* (see note at FORM OF ACTION) called trespass "that fertile mother of actions." The action of trespass took shape in the thirteenth century as a quasi-criminal procedure for dealing with violence that threatened the king's peace but did not rise to the level of a felony. Over time, the scope of that basic action was greatly expanded as the element of "force and arms" became a complete fiction: Although the phrase *vi et armis* still had to be pleaded, it was said that even the breaking of one blade of grass was sufficient to satisfy the requirement of force. The remedy became broader, too, as one branch of the action for damages for trespass to land evolved into an action for recovery of land by wrongfully evicted tenants and ultimately into a general action for resolving disputes as to ownership of real property. (See *trespass de ejectione firmae* in this entry, and see note at EJECTMENT.) Meanwhile, plaintiffs whose claims did not quite fit the original action of trespass (which required that the damage complained of result directly from intentional physical force, even if only the force involved in stepping on the grass) began to be allowed to bring actions on the special facts of their case. These actions "on the special case"—or simply "on the case"—over time created a line of precedent completely separate from trespass (though they were still formally called actions of "trespass on the case"). This line of development provided a remedy at law for defamation (formerly an ecclesiastical offense) and deceit. It spawned the action of trover, which evolved into a general action for determining ownership of personal property (see note at TROVER). It also spawned the action of ASSUMPSIT, which provided remedies for breach of contract in normal business settings where transactions are conducted without the formality of a seal, and in turn INDEBITATUS ASSUMPSIT, which extended the remedies to cases of quasi contract. And because intentional conduct was no longer required as a basis for recovery, this category of actions also gave rise to the entire area of negligence law.

**trespassory taking** *n.* the wrongful taking of personal property from the possession of another.

——**Note.** Trespassory taking is an essential element of the common law crime of LARCENY: If a person who converts another's property to her own use

was rightfully in possession of property at the time she decided to appropriate it—so that there was no trespassory taking—then her crime is not larceny but EMBEZZLEMENT.

**trial** *n.* **1.** the procedure by which evidence is presented in court under the supervision of a judge and the ultimate factual issues in a case are decided. **2. bench trial** a trial in which no jury is present and all factual issues are decided by the judge. Also called **nonjury trial, judge trial, trial to the court, trial by the court.**
**3. consolidated trial** a trial in which two or more separate cases, or certain issues in two or more separate cases, are tried together because they involve common issues of fact.
**4. de novo trial** a new trial, granted by the trial judge or ordered by an appellate court in a case because of some error or injustice in the first trial. Also called **trial de novo, retrial,** or simply a new trial. See also DE NOVO.
**5. jury trial** a trial in which the facts are determined by a JURY. Under the Sixth Amendment (see Appendix), state or federal criminal defendants facing potential sentences in excess of six months' imprisonment are entitled to demand a jury trial. The Seventh Amendment (see Appendix) gives litigants in the federal courts a right of jury trial in civil damage actions that would have been submitted to a jury in traditional common law courts; in the state courts, juries in civil actions are usually allowed by state law but are not required by the United States Constitution. Also called **trial by jury.**
**6. public trial** a trial open to observation by members of the public. The Sixth Amendment (see Appendix) gives state and federal criminal defendants the right to such a trial, and in 1980 the Supreme Court held that the First Amendment gives the press and public a general right to attend such proceedings. However, proceedings may be closed in rare cases in which a judge finds an overriding interest such as protection of a juvenile witness, and

cameras may be banned from the courtroom.

**7. separate trial a.** in criminal procedure, a trial of one or more defendants separately from others involved in the same incident, or of one or more counts against a defendant separately from other counts, in order to avoid prejudice to a defendant or to the prosecution. **b.** in civil procedure, a trial of one or more claims or issues in a case separately from others in order to avoid prejudice to a party or in the interest of judicial economy.

**8. speedy trial** a criminal trial commencing without unreasonable delay after arrest or indictment. The Sixth Amendment guarantees this right, and all jurisdictions have statutes or court rules setting standards for moving criminal cases to trial in a timely fashion.

See also FAIR TRIAL; FREE PRESS/FAIR TRIAL; MOCK TRIAL; SHOW TRIAL; *trial court* (under COURT).

**trial brief** *n.* See under BRIEF.

**trial by ambush** *n. Informal.* a disparaging term for trial procedures or strategies that involve withholding relevant information from the other side and then presenting it under circumstances in which the other side does not have a reasonable opportunity to investigate and rebut it. Modern procedural rules, especially those providing for DISCOVERY, seek to minimize opportunities for trial by ambush. Also called **trial by surprise.**

**trial judge** *n.* See under JUDGE.

**tribunal** *n.* any court or body established to decide disputes: *administrative tribunal; disciplinary tribunal; judicial tribunal.*

**trier of fact** or **trier of the facts** *n.* the person or group charged with deciding the factual issues in a proceeding; the jury in a jury trial or the judge in a nonjury trial. Also called **factfinder, finder of fact, finder of the facts.**

**TRO** See *temporary restraining order* (under RESTRAINING ORDER).

**trover** *n.* the common law FORM OF ACTION to recover damages for CONVERSION of personal property. Also called **trover and conversion.**

**——History.** The name of the action reflects its original function: *trover* is an ancient French word meaning "the act of finding," and the action originally lay only against a person who happened upon property belonging to another and kept it for his own use instead of giving it back to its owner. As the action evolved to cover a wider range of circumstances, the rigidity of the common law forms of action was such that it remained obligatory for the plaintiff to allege that he had been possessed of goods, that he lost them, and that the defendant found them and converted them to his use. The losing and finding, however, became a complete LEGAL FICTION; the only issue the courts allowed to be contested was the issue of conversion, and the action became the normal mechanism for trying title to moveable goods. For example, the defendant might be an innocent purchaser of property allegedly stolen from the plaintiff. Originally, the action permitted only a demand for money damages equal to the value of the converted property (cf. DETINUE, REPLEVIN); but by the mid-nineteenth century, at least in England, trover was expanded to permit return of the property itself, supplanting the action of detinue.

**true bill** *n.* See under BILL.

**trust** *n.* **1.** an arrangement in which one person (the TRUSTEE) holds money or other property for the benefit of another (the BENEFICIARY or CESTUI QUE TRUST), to whom the trustee owes a FIDUCIARY DUTY in regard to the safeguarding, management, and disposition of the trust property and income. See also SETTLOR; CORPUS; *breach of trust* (under BREACH).

**2.** broadly, any FIDUCIARY RELATIONSHIP.

**3.** a cartel or other monopolistic business arrangement or enterprise. This is the kind of trust for which the ANTITRUST laws were named.

**4. accumulation trust** a trust in which the principal and income are not to be paid out over time, but are to accumulate until the trust terminates.

**5. active trust** a trust in which the trustee has some duty to perform beyond merely holding title to the trust property. Cf. *passive trust*.

**6. blind trust** a trust in which assets of a public official are managed without disclosing to the official (who is the beneficiary) how they are invested; established to minimize CONFLICTS OF INTEREST.

**7. business trust** an unincorporated association serving the same general purposes as a business corporation and subject to the same taxes, but organized as a trust. Instead of shareholders it has beneficiaries, whose investments constitute the trust property and are usually represented by transferrable certificates. Also called **Massachusetts trust** or **Massachusetts business trust.**

**8. charitable remainder trust** a trust to be funded by the remainder of an estate after the expiration of a particular estate. For example, a will leaving an estate "in trust for my children for their lives, then in trust to support the public library" creates a private trust for the children and a charitable remainder trust for the library.

**9. charitable trust** a trust whose beneficiaries are charitable in nature or whose funds are to be used for the public good. Also called **public trust.** Cf. *private trust*.

**10. constructive trust** a trust that arises BY OPERATION OF LAW, without any intention by the parties to create a trust, when through fraud, duress, mistake, or the like, property, or legal title to property, falls into the hands of a person who has no right to it. Under principles of EQUITY, the person with the property is deemed to hold it in trust for the person who should have received it, with an obligation to turn it over in full and intact. See also IMPRESS.

**11. executed trust** a fully established trust; one to which all property being placed in trust has been conveyed, so that no further transactions are needed to make the trust fully operative. Cf. *executory trust*.

**12. executory trust** a trust that requires further transactions to establish fully; for example, a trust established to administer property that has not yet been conveyed to the trustee. Cf. *executed trust*.

**13. express trust** a trust established intentionally (unlike a *constructive trust*) and explicitly (unlike a *resulting trust*). It may be created orally, but usually is set up in a written TRUST INSTRUMENT, by which the person setting it up (the grantor or donor or settlor or trustor) transfers property to the trustee with instructions as to how and for whose benefit the property is to be managed and used.

**14. generation-skipping trust** See GENERATION-SKIPPING TRUST.

**15. grantor trust** a trust in which the grantor conveys property to a trustee to be held or managed for the grantor's own benefit (for example, a *blind trust*), or retains a reversionary interest in substantially the whole amount of the trust fund, or otherwise retains substantial control or ownership over the property in trust.

**16. in trust** subject to a trust: *He left $100,000 to his brother in trust for his brother's children, to be distributed to them when they reach the age of twenty-one.*

**17. inter vivos trust** a trust established and effective during the grantor's lifetime. Also called **living trust.** Cf. *testamentary trust*.

**18. irrevocable trust** a trust that cannot be revoked by the settlor. Cf. *revocable trust*.

**19. liquidating trust** a trust into which the assets of a business are placed for the purpose of winding up the business.

**20. nominee trust** a trust in which the beneficiaries are not named in the trust instrument; instead, the trustee or trustees are empowered to select ("nominate") the beneficiaries. This mechanism enables trustees to acquire and hold property for the benefit of undisclosed parties.

**21. passive trust**   a trust in which the trustee merely holds title to the trust property but the beneficaries actually control it, or the trustee simply transfers title to the beneficiaries. Also called **dry trust, naked trust.** Cf. *active trust.*

**22. pour-over** (or **pourover**) **trust**   a trust to be funded by assets "poured" into it from one or more identified sources, such as insurance proceeds or other assets that will become available at the grantor's death, or pension funds that become available at retirement.

**23. private trust**   a trust established to benefit private individuals rather than the public at large. Cf. *charitable trust.*

**24. resulting trust**   a trust inferred from a transaction or conduct of a sort that normally evidences an intent that property in the hands of one person be held for the benefit of another.

**25. revocable trust**   a trust that may be revoked by the settlor, who may then take back all property and income remaining in the trust. Cf. *irrevocable trust.*

**26. spendthrift trust**   a trust created to provide some income to the beneficiary while preventing both the beneficiary and the beneficiary's creditors from having access to the money or property held in trust except to the extent that the trustee doles it out.

**27. sprinkling trust**   a trust in which the trustee has discretion as to when and in what proportions to distribute portions of the principal or income among the beneficiaries.

**28. testamentary trust**   a trust established by will or taking effect only upon the grantor's death. Cf. *inter vivos trust.*

**29. Totten trust**   a bank account in which a beneficiary is named to receive any funds that happen to be left in the account if the account holder dies. Although the account is said to be "in trust for" the beneficiary, no trust arises so long as the account holder remains alive.

**30. voting trust**   an arrangement by which a number of shareholders in a corporation transfer their voting stock to a trustee for a period of time to hold and vote in accordance with an agreement among them, thereby concentrating their voting power and avoiding dissension.

**trust deed** *n.* Same as a DEED OF TRUST.

**trust indenture** *n.* See under INDENTURE.

**trust instrument** *n.* an instrument creating a TRUST, such as a *trust indenture* (see under INDENTURE), *declaration of trust* (see under DECLARATION), DEED OF TRUST, or will. The instrument must identify the trust property, the trustee, and the beneficiaries, and state the terms of the trust.

**trustee** *n.* **1.** the person who holds the property in a trust and administers it for the benefit of the beneficiaries.
**2.** very loosely, anyone with a FIDUCIARY DUTY to another.
**3. bankruptcy trustee**   a person appointed by a court to administer the property of a debtor. Also called **trustee in bankruptcy.**
**4. constructive trustee**   the person in possession of property subject to a *constructive trust* (see under TRUST).

**trustor** *n.* the creator or founder of a trust; the person who sets the terms and provides the property for a trust. See also SETTLOR (def. 2).

**try** *v.,* **tried, trying. 1.** (of a judge) to conduct the trial of a case, either with or without a jury.
**2.** (of a lawyer) **a.** to present or defend a case in court, through witnesses and other evidence. **b. try to the court** (or **to the judge**)   to try a case without a jury. **c. try to a jury**   to try a case with a jury.
**3. try title**   to test the validity of title to property in a judicial proceeding.

**turn state's evidence** See under STATE'S EVIDENCE.

**Twinkie defense** *n.* the popular name for the successful DIMINISHED CAPACITY defense utilized by the assassin of two San Francisco city officials in the 1970's.

——**History.** In 1978, Dan White, a former police officer, was a strongly anti-gay member of the San Francisco Board of Supervisors. He resigned from the Board on November 10, but at the urging of police supporters he changed his mind a few days later and asked the mayor, George Moscone, to exercise his power to fill vacancies by reappointing him to the board. Moscone was to announce his choice on November 27. White found out the night before that Moscone had chosen someone else, and understood that fellow-supervisor Harvey Milk, a leading figure in San Francisco's gay community, had lobbied against him. On the morning of the 27th, White entered City Hall through a basement window to avoid metal detectors, visited Mayor Moscone and Supervisor Milk in turn, felled each one with two to three bullets to the body, and finished each one off with two bullets to the head. At his trial in 1979, four psychiatrists and a psychologist, called as experts for the defense, testified to the rather obvious fact that White's judgment and capacity for rational deliberation had been impaired. They attributed this primarily to depression; one cited White's uncontrollable binging on sugar-laden junk food as evidence of depression, and suggested that the extra sugar could even have aggravated the condition. The press picked up on this dubious but rather incidental point and dubbed it the "Twinkie defense." The jury accepted the evidence of diminished capacity and convicted White of voluntary manslaughter rather than murder—a verdict that sparked riots in San Francisco and general outrage elsewhere. The "Twinkie defense" became for many a symbol of the creativity of lawyers in inventing excuses for criminal conduct and the credulousness of juries in accepting them. This contributed to a nationwide trend toward restriction or elimination of diminished-capacity and insanity defenses; in California itself, the legislature abolished the diminished capacity defense in 1981. White was then in Soledad prison serving his term of seven years and eight months. With good behavior, he was released after serving two thirds of his sentence. Despite his mental problems, during his entire time in prison he neither requested nor received any psychiatric help. On January 6, 1984, White was placed on parole for one year, during which he was required to stay well away from San Francisco. After his parole ended on January 6, 1985, White spent several months in Ireland and then, contrary to the advice of many, returned to his home in San Francisco. There, on October 10, he closed the garage door, ran a hose from the exhaust pipe of his car to a car window, stuffed the rest of the opening with towels, put the Irish ballad "The Town I Loved So Well" into the car's cassette player, turned on the engine, and died. He had never expressed remorse for the killings. The suicide notes he left did not mention them.

**tying arrangement** *n.* an arrangement whereby a business entity will sell one product (the **tying product**) only upon condition that the buyer also agree to purchase another product (the **tied product**) from the same company. Also, such an arrangement involving leases rather than sales, or services rather than physical products, or any combination of these. Also called **tie-in.** ——**Note.** As a general rule, tying arrangements are a violation of ANTITRUST laws.

**tying product** *n.* See under TYING ARRANGEMENT.

# U

**uberrima fides** *n. Latin.* (lit. "the most abundant honesty") utmost good faith—the quality required of a FIDUCIARY and, at least traditionally, of parties to insurance contracts.

**uberrimae fidei** *adj. Latin.* (lit. "of the most abundant honesty") of the utmost good faith; characterized by or requiring the utmost good faith.

**ultimate fact** *n.* See under FACT.

**ultimogeniture** *n.* Same as BOROUGH-ENGLISH.

**ultra vires** *adj., adv. Latin.* (lit. "beyond the powers") **1.** beyond the scope of authority of the actor; in excess of legal powers: *Any declaration of war by the President would be ultra vires, because under the Constitution the power to declare war resides in the Congress. The agent acted ultra vires in bidding more than the principal had authorized.* **2.** especially, of conduct by or on behalf of a corporation, beyond the powers of the corporation as set forth in the articles of incorporation or by law. Cf. INTRA VIRES.
——**Note.** Under traditional doctrine, an ultra vires contract or other ultra vires act of a corporation was sometimes treated as void. Modern articles of incorporation typically authorize the corporation to do "anything a natural person might do," making ultra vires corporate acts almost impossible so long as the corporation confines itself to lawful activities.

**ultrahazardous activity** *n.* Same as ABNORMALLY DANGEROUS ACTIVITY.

**umbrella policy** *n.* an insurance policy that supplements existing policies by providing additional coverage for the same risks.

**unalienable** *adj.* INALIENABLE.
—**unalienability** *n.*
—**unalienably** *adv.*
——**History.** Although the more common form of this word is *inalienable,* it is the *un-* form that was immortalized by Thomas Jefferson in the Declaration of Independence: "We hold these truths to be self-evident, that all men are created equal, that they are endowed by their Creator with certain unalienable Rights, that among these are Life, Liberty and the pursuit of Happiness."

**unanimous opinion** *n.* See under OPINION.

**unappealable** *adj.* not capable of being appealed. See *unappealable order* and compare *appealable order* (both under ORDER[1]).
—**unappealability** *n.*
—**unappealably** *adv.*

**unarmed robbery** *n.* See under ROBBERY.

**unavailable witness** *n.* See under WITNESS.

**unavoidable accident** *n.* See under ACCIDENT.

**unborn-widow rule** *n.* the presumption at common law, for purposes of applying the *rule against perpetuities* (see under PERPETUITY), that the "widow" of a living person named in a will or conveyance might turn out to be someone who was not yet born at the time the bequest or conveyance took effect. See also FERTILE-OCTOGENARIAN RULE.
——**Note.** Under this rule, a conveyance "to A for life, then to his widow for her life, then to A's surviving children," would violate the rule against perpetuities because before his death A might marry a woman born after the date of the conveyance, who in turn might outlive him by more than 21 years. The gift over to the children of A who survive his widow—all of whom might also have been born after the date of

the conveyance—would therefore be void. In many jurisdictions, this presumption can be overcome by evidence that the grantor's intent in referring to A's "widow" was to specify A's wife at the time of the conveyance; other jurisdictions have overcome the problem by adopting the WAIT-AND-SEE APPROACH.

**unclean hands** *n.* **1.** the quality of having acted unfairly in regard to the very matter with respect to which one is seeking relief in court. Cf. CLEAN HANDS.
**2.** the doctrine, derived from England's courts of EQUITY, that one who comes into court complaining of another's unfairness will be denied relief unless he himself acted fairly in the matter; expressed in such maxims as: "He who seeks equity must come into court with clean hands." Referred to equally as the **clean hands doctrine** and the **unclean hands doctrine.**
**3.** a defense often raised in response to claims for *equitable relief* (see under REMEDY), based upon the plaintiff's own improper and unjust conduct in the matter. Referred to as the **unclean hands defense** or somewhat less commonly as the **clean hands defense.** See also IN PARI DELICTO.

**unconditional** *adj.* not CONDITIONAL; absolute; not depending upon prior or subsequent conditions for effectiveness or validity.
—**unconditionality** *n.*
—**unconditionally** *adv.*

**unconscionability** *n.* the doctrine that a contract that is so unfair and one-sided as to "shock the conscience of the court" need not be enforced by the court. The doctrine is most often applied to consumer transactions in which the court believes that the consumer was taken advantage of. See also *adhesion contract* (under CONTRACT); BARGAINING POWER.
—**unconscionable** *adj.*
—**unconscionably** *adv.*

**unconstitutional** *adj.* **1.** in conflict with some provision of a constitution;

said particularly of state or federal statutes that violate the United States Constitution. Cf. CONSTITUTIONAL.
**2. unconstitutional** (or **invalid**) **as applied** unconstitutional in its impact upon a specific individual or class of individuals, but otherwise enforceable. For example, a public school dress code prohibiting the wearing of hats in class might be held unconstitutional as applied to children whose religions require head covering.
**3. unconstitutional** (or **invalid**) **on its face** unconstitutional in its entirety and hence not enforceable at all.
—**unconstitutionality** *n.*
—**unconstitutionally** *adv.*

**uncontested divorce** *n.* See under DIVORCE.

**uncontradicted** *adj.* (of testimony or other evidence) not contradicted or challenged by testimony or evidence to the contrary: *The jury may reject uncontradicted testimony if it finds that the witness is not credible.*

**uncontrollable impulse test** *n.* Same as IRRESISTIBLE IMPULSE TEST.

**uncontroverted** *adj.* Same as UNCONTRADICTED.

**uncorroborated** *adj.* not supported by evidence from an independent source: *The defendant was convicted on the basis of the uncorroborated testimony of a jailhouse informant.*

**undeclared war** *n.* See under WAR.

**under color of law** (of improper conduct by a state official) with the appearance of legal authority; in actual or purported performance of one's official duties. In some circumstances the phrase also applies to private conduct that is specifically authorized or approved by state law. Under the Civil Rights Act of 1871, anyone who has been deprived of federal civil rights under color of state law may sue the wrongdoer.

**under cover** *adv.* clandestinely; secretly; especially, of police work, in a manner that conceals the fact that the individuals involved are police officers: *The evidence was gathered by officers* *working under cover.* See also UNDER-COVER.

**under oath 1.** bound by an OATH; having taken an oath. Especially, of one who gives evidence in a case, sworn to tell the truth: *When the trial resumed after lunch, the judge reminded the witness that she was still under oath.*
**2.** done while bound by an oath, especially an oath to tell the truth: *The affidavit was signed under oath.*

**under protest** an expression signifying that in complying with some demand or performing some action one is not conceding that the action is legally required and reserves the right to contest the issue in court. A particularly common example is the payment of a tax bill under protest, in order to preserve the right to question its amount or validity while avoiding penalties for late payment should the tax be upheld.

**under seal** *adj., adv.* **1.** authenticated by the affixing of a wax or other seal. See SEAL¹); *contract under seal* (under CONTRACT); *covenant under seal* (under COVENANT); *instrument under seal* (under SEAL¹).
**2.** sealed to prevent public disclosure. See SEAL²; *file under seal* (under FILE).

**under the influence** affected by alcohol or other intoxicating drugs; especially, impaired in one's ability to drive because of alcohol or other drugs: *The driver was under the influence when he ran off the road.* See also *driving under the influence* (under DRIVING WHILE INTOXICATED).

**underage** *adj.* describing a person who has not yet reached the minimum age set by law for a specified activity, such as consumption of alcohol or engaging in sexual activity. See also *statutory rape* (under RAPE); AGE.

**undercover** *adj.* (of police work) **a.** done by posing as something other than a police officer: *an undercover investigation.* **b.** engaged in undercover work: *an undercover officer.* See also UNDER COVER.

**underlease** *n., v.* underleased, underleasing. —*n.* **1.** a SUBLEASE.

—*v.* **2.** to SUBLEASE.
——**Usage.** *Underlease* and related terms (*underlessee, undertenant, undertenancy*) mean the same thing as the corresponding terms *sublease, sublessee,* etc. The forms with *under-* are still often found in form leases, statutes, and other legal documents, but are outdated in ordinary usage.

**underlessee** *n.* Same as *sublessee* (see under SUBLEASE).

**undersigned** *n.* **1.** a term used in the body of a document to designate the person or persons whose signatures appear at the end. This expression is commonly used in preprinted form contracts to refer to anyone who might sign them.
—*adj.* **2.** of or pertaining to the undersigned.

**understanding** *n.* **1.** an agreement, particularly a somewhat informal or preliminary one. It may or may not be sufficiently definite to be enforceable as a contract. See also INDEFINITE; *memorandum of understanding* (under MEMORANDUM).
**2.** a party's interpretation of a contract term. If one party's understanding differs from another's, a court may have to interpret the contract.

**undertake** *v.,* **undertook, undertaken, undertaking. 1.** to promise, agree, or obligate oneself, especially contractually: *The insurance company undertook to compensate the insured for any covered loss.*
**2.** in older usage, **a.** to warrant or guarantee: *The seller undertakes that the goods are of merchantable quality.* **b.** to become a surety or guarantor of another's performance: *The bail bondsman undertakes for the defendant's appearance for trial.*

**undertaking** *n.* **1.** a bond (see BOND²), PLEDGE, or promise given to guarantee performance or indemnify another against loss.
**2.** any contractual or noncontractual promise.

**undertenancy** *n., pl.* **undertenancies.** Same as SUBTENANCY.

**undertenant** *n.* Same as *subtenant* (see under SUBLEASE).

**underwrite** *v.,* **underwrote, underwritten, underwriting. 1.** to provide insurance; to guarantee payment under an insurance policy: *to underwrite insurance; underwrite an insurance policy.*
**2.** to guarantee that an entire issue of securities will be sold, either by assisting in their sale to the public and agreeing to purchase any that remain unsold, or by buying up the entire issue for resale to the public: *to underwrite securities; underwrite an issue of securities.* But see *best efforts underwriting* (under BEST EFFORTS).
—**underwriter** *n.*
—**underwriting** *n.*

**undisclosed principal** *n.* See under PRINCIPAL.

**undivided interest** or **undivided fractional interest** *n.* See under IN-TEREST[1].

**undocumented alien** *n.* See under AL-IEN.

**undue** *adj.* **1.** unwarranted; excessive; inappropriate; unjustifiable; improper.
**2.** *Rare.* not owed or currently payable.
—**unduly** *adv.*

**undue influence** *n.* the use of a position of power or trust to induce a person to enter into a transaction that does not reflect his true wishes, or that he would not have entered into if given unbiased advice. This is a ground for rescinding or refusing to enforce wills, gifts, and contracts.

**unearned income** *n.* See under IN-COME.

**unemployment compensation** *n.* weekly payments made for a limited period of time to most workers who lose their jobs through no fault of their own, provided under a system of insurance **(unemployment insurance)** established by state law.

**unenforceable** *n.* **1.** legally invalid; not enforceable in the courts because contrary to law or public policy: *A racially restrictive covenant is unenforceable.*
**2.** not capable of being effectively enforced as a practical matter: *Despite massive law enforcement efforts, prohibition of alcohol ultimately proved to be unenforceable.*
—**unenforceability** *n.*
—**unenforceably** *adv.*

**unethical** *adj.* contrary to the generally accepted standards of honesty and fairness in the conduct of one's business or profession. **Unethical conduct,** also called **unprofessional conduct,** is not necessarily a crime, but is often the basis for a malpractice action or disciplinary proceeding.
—**unethically** *adv.*

**unfair competition** *n.* **1.** the use of product names, packaging, or other devices similar to those of a competitor so as to confuse the public about whose product they are buying.
**2.** Also called **unfair methods of competition.** any improper conduct by which a business might gain unfair advantage over competitors.
See also PASSING OFF.

**unfair labor practice** *n.* any of a long list of coercive, discriminatory, or otherwise improper activities of employers or unions prohibited by the National Labor Relations Act.

**unfair trade practice** *n.* **1.** a business practice that is fraudulent, deceptive, or otherwise unfair to consumers.
**2.** a business practice that is unfair to competitors; UNFAIR COMPETITION.

**unfit** *adj.* **1.** (of goods) unsuitable; not appropriate for the purposes for which they are sold.
**2.** (of a parent) so unsuited to the task of raising children, or so dangerous to the welfare of children in the parent's care, as to call for removal of any children from the parent's custody either temporarily or permanently.
Cf. FIT.
—**unfitness** *n.*

**unified bar** *n.* See under BAR[2].

**Uniform Code of Military Justice** *n.*

the federal statute establishing a comprehensive system of justice applicable to members of the armed forces in their military capacity, complete with its own courts and judicial procedures.

**Uniform Commercial Code (U.C.C.)** *n.* a lengthy statute, adopted in substantially the same form in every state except Louisiana, establishing a uniform basic body of law governing sales of goods, negotiable instruments, bank deposits and collections, and various other commercial instruments and transactions. See also UNIFORM LAWS.

**Uniform Laws** (or **Acts**) a set of model statutes on a wide range of subjects, approved by the National Conference of Commissioners on Uniform State Laws (made up of representatives appointed by the governors of all states) and recommended to state legislatures for adoption. The purpose of the Uniform Laws is to mitigate the legal uncertainty and confusion that inevitably arises when fifty states adopt different and often conflicting laws on the same subjects, particularly with regard to transactions involving people and property in different states. Many of the Uniform Laws have been widely adopted, most notably the UNIFORM COMMERCIAL CODE. See also CONFLICT OF LAWS; MODEL LAW.

**Uniform System of Citation** *n.* See BLUEBOOK.

**unilateral** *adj.* relating to or occurring on one side only; undertaken or done by or on behalf of one side or party only; not mutual.
**—unilaterally** *adv.*

**unilateral contract** *n.* See under CONTRACT.

**unilateral mistake** *n.* See under MISTAKE.

**unincorporated** *adj.* **1.** not chartered as a corporation; lacking the powers and immunities of a corporate enterprise: *an unincorporated business.*
**2.** not chartered as a self-governing village or city; lacking the tax, police, and other powers conferred by the state on incorporated towns: *an unincorporated*

*hamlet.*
**3.** not combined into a single body or unit; not made part of; not included: *Where certain provisions of a prior agreement are incorporated by reference in a later agreement, the unincorporated provisions may be looked to for assistance in interpreting the incorporated provisions.*

**unincorporated association** *n.* See under ASSOCIATION.

**unindictable** *adj.* not subject to INDICTMENT.

**unindicted co-conspirator** *n.* a person alleged to have been party to a criminal conspiracy, but that the prosecutor chooses not to indict for the crime even though one or more other conspirators are indicted. For example, one conspirator might have been allowed to plead guilty to a lesser offense in exchange for testifying against the others. Also, very rarely, called **unindicted conspirator.** See also note at CO-CONSPIRATOR.

**uninterested** *adj.* **1.** having no feeling of interest in a matter; bored.
**2.** lacking bias or interest (see INTEREST[2]) in a matter; impartial.
Cf. INTERESTED. See also note at DISINTERESTED.

**union** *n.* **1.** Also called **labor union.** an organization of workers formed for the purpose of bargaining collectively with employers over wages and working conditions. See also LABOR ORGANIZATION; TRADE UNION.
**2. craft union** a union composed only of people in the same trade or craft, regardless of the industry in which they work. Also called **horizontal union.** See also TRADE UNION. Cf. *industrial union.*
**3. independent union** a union of workers in a particular company, not affiliated with a larger union.
**4. industrial union** a union of workers in a particular industry, regardless of their individual trade or craft. Also called **vertical union.** Cf. *craft union.*
**5. local union** a local bargaining unit of a larger union.
**6. union certification** certification by

the National Labor Relations Board of a particular union as the exclusive collective bargaining agent for a particular group of employees, upon a vote of the employees.

**7. union shop**   See under SHOP.

**union, civil** *n.* See CIVIL UNION.

**United States Attorney** *n.* the chief lawyer for the United States government within a federal *judicial district* (see under DISTRICT). Each United States Attorney is appointed by the President and is responsible for prosecuting federal crimes and representing the United States in all civil litigation within her district. Lawyers on the staff of a United States Attorney, who usually do most of the actual courtroom work, have the title **Assistant United States Attorney (AUSA).** Cf. ATTORNEY GENERAL; SOLICITOR GENERAL.

**United States Code (U.S.C.)** the congressionally authorized codification of statutes enacted by Congress, organized into fifty broad subject areas, or "titles." See also ANNOTATED; STATUTES AT LARGE.

**United States Court of Appeals** *n.* one of the intermediate appellate courts in the federal judicial system, lying between the United States District Courts and the Supreme Court of the United States. There is one such court for each CIRCUIT in the federal system. Since very few cases are accepted for review by the Supreme Court, as a practical matter the Court of Appeals is the court of last resort for most federal litigants, and since the decisions of a Court of Appeals are binding upon all United States District Courts in its circuit, these decisions are extremely important in formulating federal law.

**United States District Court** *n.* the federal court of original jurisdiction for nearly all civil and criminal matters that can be brought in federal courts. There is one such court for each federal *judicial district* (see under DISTRICT), although each court has several judges and many have two or more courthouses located in different parts of the district.

**United States Supreme Court** *n.* an informal but generally accepted name for the *Supreme Court of the United States* (see under SUPREME COURT).

**unity** *n., pl.* **unities. 1.** the state or quality of being united or joined; the condition of two or more people or entities having a common interest, goal, point of view, government, etc.
**2.** in the law of real property, **a.** the agreement or coincidence of certain qualities of the estates held by two or more persons in the same land. **b.** the joining of separate estates into a single whole.
**3. four unities**   in traditional common law analysis, the four qualities shared by two or more co-holders of an estate in land that together characterize a JOINT tenancy as distinguished from a mere tenancy IN COMMON: *unity of interest, unity of possession, unity of time,* and *unity of title.* The four unities also characterize an estate BY THE ENTIRETY, although in that case they could be regarded under the common law simply as corollaries of a single overriding unity not present in ordinary joint tenancies: *unity of person.*
**4. unity of interest**   possession of exactly the same quantity and quality of interest in an estate by each of the holders. For example, unity of interest among three holders of an estate is present only if each has a one-third interest in the whole and each has the same kind of interest (e.g., fee simple or life estate).
**5. unity of person**   the common law concept of a married couple as a single person for many legal purposes, especially ownership of jointly acquired property. See also notes at BY THE ENTIRETY and CIVIL UNION.
**6. unity of possession**   the shared right of co-holders of an interest in land each to possess and enjoy the entire property. This is the only one of the *four unities* that must exist in a tenancy IN COMMON.
**7. unity of seisin**   ownership by the same person or group of persons of two parcels of land, one originally burdened by an easement or profit a prendre for

the benefit of the other. When both the benefited land and the burdened land come under common ownership, the easement or profit is extinguished.

**8. unity of time** the vesting of all holders' interests in an estate at the same time.

**9. unity of title** the acquisition of the interests of all the co-holders of an estate under the same deed or will.

**unjust enrichment** *n.* any situation in which a person receives a benefit that properly belongs to another or retains, without paying for it, a benefit that in justice should be paid for; for example, receiving delivery of goods intended for another, or refusing to pay a doctor who provided necessary emergency care while one was unconscious. See also RESTITUTION.

**unlawful** *adj.* contrary to, unauthorized by, or disapproved of by law.
—**unlawfully** *adv.*
—**unlawfulness** *n.*
——**Usage.** Conduct need not be criminal to be referred to as "unlawful"; the term is broad enough to include torts, or conduct (such as undue influence) that might lead a court to declare a transaction void. Cf. ILLEGAL.

**unlawful assembly** *n.* the offense of the coming together as a group of three or more people in public for the purpose of engaging in a riot or some other openly violent activity. Cf. FREEDOM OF ASSEMBLY.

**unlawful detainer** *n.* See under DETAINER.

**unlicensed** *adj.* **1.** not having a license: *unlicensed driver.*
**2.** done or undertaken without license or permission; unauthorized: *unlicensed practice of medicine; unlicensed use of copyrighted software; unlicensed entry onto private property.*

**unliquidated** *adj.* **1.** uncertain, disputed, or not yet determined as to amount: *unliquidated claim; unliquidated damages.*
**2.** not yet sold: *unliquidated assets; unliquidated inventory.*
Cf. LIQUIDATE.

**unmarketable title** *n.* Same as *defective title* (see under TITLE).

**unmeritorious** *adj.* unsuccessful or unlikely to succeed: *unmeritorious claim; unmeritorious defense.*
—**unmeritoriousness** *n.*

**unnatural act** *n.* oral or anal sex or sex with an animal—acts that the law traditionally regarded as so unspeakable that courts and legislatures literally would not speak their names, but instead condemned them under such names as "unnatural act" or "the detestable and abominable crime against nature." See also CRIME AGAINST NATURE; SODOMY.

**unprivileged** *adj.* not protected by PRIVILEGE. Also, **nonprivileged.**

**unprivileged communication** *n.* a commmunication that may not be withheld from evidence on the basis of any *evidentiary privilege* (see under PRIVILEGE). Also called **nonprivileged communication.**

**unprivileged speech** *n.* See under SPEECH.

**unprofessional conduct** *n.* Same as *unethical conduct* (see under UNETHICAL).

**unprotected speech** *n.* See under SPEECH.

**unqualified** *adj.* **1.** not suited to perform a function or hold a position: opposite of QUALIFIED¹ (def. 1). See note at NONQUALIFIED.
**2.** unlimited; unconditional; absolute: opposite of QUALIFIED².
—**unqualifiedly** *adv.*

**unreasonable** *adj.* significantly excessive, insufficient, or inappropriate in light of the circumstances; not such as would be expected of a *reasonable person* (see under REASONABLE) in the same circumstances.
—**unreasonableness** *n.*
—**unreasonably** *adv.*

**unreasonable restraint of trade** *n.* business conduct which tends to reduce competition in the marketplace, and whose adverse effect is not outweighed by some permissible business justification. Concerted action that unreasonably restrains trade, such as PRICE FIXING or a *group boycott* (see under BOYCOTT), is outlawed by the SHERMAN ANTITRUST ACT.

**unreasonable search** *n.* See under SEARCH.

**unreasonable search and seizure** *n.* See under SEARCH AND SEIZURE.

**unrecovered basis** *n.* See under BASIS.

**unregulated money** *n.* in federal campaign finance law, same as SOFT MONEY.

**unrelated business income** *n.* See under INCOME.

**unresponsive** *adj.* evasive; not answering the question or questions; not providing the information sought: *an unresponsive witness; unresponsive testimony.* Also, **nonresponsive.**
—**unresponsively** *adv.*
—**unresponsiveness** *n.*

**unresponsive answer** *n.* an evasive or unhelpful answer to a question; an answer that avoids the question, answers some other question, or includes commentary beyond what was asked for. Also called **nonresponsive answer.**
——**Note.** A lawyer who gets an unresponsive answer from a witness in court has several options. Depending upon strategic considerations, the lawyer might "move to strike" the answer or the unresponsive portion of the answer (see STRIKE[2]), request the judge to instruct the witness to answer the question, repeat the question, or simply move on. If the judge strikes an answer—often simply by saying "it is stricken"—the answer may not be regarded as evidence, and the judge will usually specifically instruct the jury to disregard it.

**unreviewable** *adj.* not subject to judicial, appellate, or administrative REVIEW. See also note at NONREVIEWABLE.
—**unreviewability** *n.*
—**unreviewably** *adv.*

**unseal** *v.* to remove from a sealed envelope; to disclose: *The prosecutor unsealed the indictments once the indicted individuals had been brought into custody.*
—**unsealable** *adj.*

**unsealed** *adj.* **1.** not possessing a seal: *an unsealed instrument.* Cf. SEAL[1].
**2.** not placed or kept in a sealed envelope for confidentiality: *unsealed bid.* Cf. SEAL[2].

**unseaworthy** *adj.* not SEAWORTHY.
—**unseaworthiness** *n.*

**unsecured** *n.* not protected by, characterized by, or involving a *security interest* (see under INTEREST[1]). See, e.g., *unsecured creditor* (under CREDITOR); *unsecured debt* (under DEBT); *unsecured transaction* (under TRANSACTION).

**unsworn** *adj.* not SWORN; not under oath or subject to penalties for perjury: *unsworn statement; unsworn witness.*

**untenantable** *adj.* not TENANTABLE.

**untimely** *adj.* **1.** not in time; coming or occurring too late: *The time limit for filing the petition is thirty days, but the court may accept an untimely petition upon a showing of good cause for the delay.*
**2.** occasionally, too early: *The complaint was untimely in that the cause of action had not yet accrued.*
—*adv.* **3.** in an untimely manner; too late or too early.
—**untimeliness** *n.*

**unwritten constitution** *n.* See under CONSTITUTION.

**uphold** *v.*, **upheld, upholding. 1.** to declare judicially to be valid, enforceable, or constitutional: *uphold a marriage; uphold a will; uphold a statute.*
**2.** to reaffirm judicially a prior holding: *On rehearing, the court upheld its earlier decision. Despite calls for reexamination, the court's latest decision upheld a long line of precedent.*
**3.** to support, defend, obey, or enforce: *uphold the law; uphold a principle.*

**usage** *n.* **1.** a practice or method of doing business that is followed with such consistency by people engaged in transactions of a certain type in a particular place, vocation, or trade that the law will normally presume, with respect to a particular transaction of that type, that the parties intended that practice to be followed. See also CUSTOM.

**2. usage of trade** a usage followed in a particular vocation or trade. Also called **trade usage.**
Cf. COURSE OF DEALING; COURSE OF PERFORMANCE.

**use** *n.* **1.** Also called **use and benefit.** benefit. For example, a case named *Smith for the use of Jones v. Lee* would be one brought for technical reasons by Smith although the person who would benefit from its success would be Jones. See also FOR THE USE OF (def. 2), and note at EX REL.
**2.** an old term for a *beneficial interest* (see under INTEREST[1]) in property, especially real property. See also CESTUI QUE USE; FEOFFEE TO USES; FOR THE USE OF (def. 1); STATUTE OF USES.
**3.** the manner in which land that has been zoned is or could be utilized.
**4. best use** the most lucrative use that could be made of a parcel of land as currently zoned. The assessed value of land for property tax purposes may be based upon this hypothetical use rather than the actual use. Also called **best and highest use** or **highest and best use.**
**5. conforming use** a use of land permitted by current zoning regulations.
**6. nonconforming use** a land use contrary to zoning regulations. Nonconforming uses typically exist because they were there before a zoning plan was adopted, and are usually permitted to continue for many years.
**7. public use** a use of land that benefits the public at large. Under the power of EMINENT DOMAIN, the state or federal government may take private property for any public use, provided that the owner is fairly compensated.

**use immunity** *n.* See under IMMUNITY.

**use tax** *n.* a state tax on the purchase price of goods purchased outside the state for use within the state from a vendor who does business in the state.

Also called **compensating use tax.**
—**Note.** Use taxes are imposed in an effort to make up revenue lost when consumers avoid local sales taxes by shopping out of state.

**usual covenants** *n.* See under COVENANTS OF TITLE.

**usufruct** *n. Civil Law.* the right of enjoying, for a period of time, all the advantages derivable from the use of something that belongs to another, as far as is compatible with the substance of the thing not being destroyed or injured.

**usufructuary** *n., pl.* **usufructuaries,** *adj.* —*n.* **1.** a person who has a usufruct; one who has a temporary right to the use and possession of another's property.
—*adj.* **2.** of, pertaining to, or of the nature of usufruct.

**usul al-fiqh** *n.pl. Islamic Law.* the sources of Islamic jurisprudence; the bodies of text and teaching from which the law is determined. See also FIQH; SHARI'A.
—**Note.** In the majority Sunni branch of Islam, four sources of law and legal thought are recognized: the KORAN, the SUNNA, IJMA', and QIYAS. See also IJTIHAD.

**usury** *n.* the crime of charging a higher rate of interest for a loan than is allowed by law.
—**usurer** *n.*
—**usurious** *adj.*
—**usuriously** *adv.*

**utmost care** *n.* See under CARE.

**utrum** *n. Latin.* (lit. "whether") **1.** an ancient writ, usually called the **assize utrum** or **assize of utrum,** by which a parson could obtain a judgment as to whether certain lands were privately owned or had been given as alms to God and the saints and thus were church property.
**2.** Also called **assize utrum.** the cause of action or the legal proceeding founded upon such a writ.
See also *petty assize* (under ASSIZE) and accompanying note.
—**History.** The utrum provided a

mechanism by which a parson could reclaim land improperly disposed of by a predecessor—a remedy analogous to that available to secular claimants through the WRIT OF RIGHT. For this reason, the utrum was also referred to informally as the **parson's writ of right**.

**utter** *v.* **1.** to put an instrument into circulation or offer it to someone as what it purports to be.

**2. uttering a forged instrument** the crime of passing a counterfeit or forged instrument or attempting to do so by offering it as if it were genuine.
—**utterer** *n.*
——**False Friend.** The usual nonlegal meaning of *utter* (to express; to make a sound) is simply another application of the core concept of the word: to issue, give out, put forth.

**ux.** Abbreviation for UXOR.

**uxor** *n., pl.* **uxores** *Latin.* wife. *Abbr.:* ux. See also ET UXOR; ET UX.

# V

**v.** Abbreviation for *versus*, meaning "against," in case names; usually read as a letter rather than a word: *Roe v. Wade* (pronounced "Roe vee Wade"). See also note at VERSUS.

**vacate** *v.*, **vacated, vacating.** to nullify a judgment or court order. This may be done by the court that issued the original judgment or order, or by a higher court on appeal. See also QUASH; SET ASIDE.

**vacatur** *n. Latin.* (lit. "Let it be made void.") **1.** a court order vacating a previous judgment or order.
**2.** Sometimes called **vacation.** the act of vacating a judgment or order.

**vague** *adj.* uncertain in meaning or scope. In a contract, a certain amount of vagueness is seldom a barrier to enforceability; the court will enforce the contract in accordance with whatever it finds to be the most reasonable interpretation. Cf. INDEFINITE. A criminal law that is excessively vague may be held unconstitutional **(void for vagueness)** on the ground that it is a violation of due process to convict a person of a crime for behavior that was not clearly defined as criminal.
**—vagueness** *n.*

**value** *n.*, *v.*, **valued, valuing.** —*n.* **1.** the monetary worth of something. See also *assessed value* (under ASSESS); MARKET VALUE; *salable value* (under SALABLE).
**2.** (in the law of sales and some other areas covered by the Uniform Commercial Code) that which is given in exchange for goods or rights. See note below.
—*v.* **3.** to calculate or estimate the monetary value of; assess; appraise.
——**Note.** As used in sense 2, *value* includes not only present consideration such as would traditionally support a contract, including a promise of future performance, but also past monetary consideration. For example, if a creditor makes a loan in one year and in the next year requests and receives a security interest in certain property of the debtor to secure repayment of the outstanding loan, then the creditor is deemed to have given value—the previous year's loan—for the security interest. (Cf. *past consideration* under CONSIDERATION). This is the sense of the word in the phrase *good faith purchaser for value* or *bona fide purchaser for value* (see GOOD FAITH PURCHASER). For the slightly different meaning in the law of negotiable instruments, see *holder for value* (under HOLDER).

**value-added tax (VAT)** *n.* a tax, used in many countries and sometimes proposed for the United States, levied upon the increase in value of a product at each stage of production or distribution. The tax at each stage is paid by the seller and added to the price paid by the buyer, having much the same effect as a SALES TAX.

**variable annuity** *n.* See under ANNUITY.

**variable-rate mortgage (VRM)** *n.* See under MORTGAGE.

**variance** *n.* **1.** in zoning law, permission to use property in a particular way that is not generally allowed in that zone, granted to an individual property owner to prevent undue hardship.
**2.** in procedure, a difference between what was originally alleged and what was actually shown at trial. This is seldom of much importance in civil cases.
**3. fatal variance** in criminal cases, so great a variance between what was charged and what was proved that the defendant was misled and deprived of a fair trial.
**4. immaterial variance** in criminal cases, an insignificant variance between

what was charged and what was proved; a variance that could not have prejudiced the defendant.

**VAT** VALUE-ADDED TAX.

**veggie libel** *n.* See FOOD DISPARAGEMENT.

**vehicular homicide** *n.* See under HOMICIDE.

**veil** *n.* See *corporate veil* (under CORPORATE).

**vel non** *Latin.* (lit. "or not") or the opposite; or the lack thereof: *The issue for decision is the adequacy, vel non, of notice.*

**vendee** *n.* a buyer.

**vendor** *n.* a seller.

**venire** *n.* a group of citizens called into court at the same time for jury duty, from which a jury or juries will be selected. Also called **array** or **jury array,** or sometimes **panel** or **jury panel.** See also *jury panel* (under JURY).

**venire member** or **veniremember** *n.* a member of a VENIRE.

**venireman** *n., pl.* **veniremen.** traditional term for a member of a venire; now more commonly referred to as VENIREPERSON or VENIRE MEMBER.

**venireperson** or **venire person** *n.* a member of a VENIRE.

**venture** *n., v.,* **ventured, venturing,** *adj.* —*n.* **1.** business enterprise or speculation in which something is risked in the hope of profit; a commercial or other speculation. See also JOINT VENTURE.
—*v.* **2.** to expose to hazard; risk: *The investors ventured $3,000,000 in the start-up company.*
—*adj.* **3.** of or pertaining to an investment or investments in new businesses: *venture capital; venture fund.*
—**venturer** *n.*

**venue** *n.* **1.** the county or judicial district where a case is maintained. When courts in more than one geographic area have jurisdiction to consider a case, rules of *venue* determine where the case should be filed. See also CHANGE OF VENUE; LAY (def. 2 and note).
**2.** in an affidavit or affirmation, the part that tells where the instrument was executed. See also SS.

**verbal** *adj.* **1.** in words; spoken or written; expressed in words rather than implied by conduct: *An offer of contract may be accepted either verbally or by conduct manifesting agreement, such as commencement of performance.* The word "verbal" is sometimes confused with ORAL.
**2. verbal act** words (written or spoken) having legal effect; for example, a written consent or an oral contract. A verbal act is not regarded as a mere assertion of fact, and so is not excluded from evidence as HEARSAY.

**verdict** *n.* **1.** the jury's decision in a case. Traditionally required to be unanimous, but now in many cases permitted by a vote of ten or eleven members of a twelve-member jury or five members of a six-member jury. Cf. JUDGMENT; FINDINGS OF FACT AND CONCLUSIONS OF LAW.
**2. chance verdict** one reached by flip of a coin or other process of chance. Obviously improper.
**3. compromise verdict** one arrived at as a compromise among conflicting views of jurors. Unless all jurors, after further deliberation, come to agree that the verdict is correct (i.e., consistent with the evidence and the judge's instructions), this is improper.
**4. directed verdict** one entered by the judge because, upon the evidence presented, the law permits only one outcome, so that there is nothing for the jury to decide.
**5. excessive verdict** one awarding damages grossly disproportionate to the plaintiff's injuries in light of the evidence and the nature of the case. A remedy for this is REMITTITUR.
**6. general verdict** one consisting of a single overall finding covering all issues; for example, "Guilty," "Not guilty," or "We find for the plaintiff in the amount of $60,000." Cf. *special verdict.*
**7. inconsistent verdict** one having two or more components that, under

the judge's instructions, are logically inconsistent. If this is noticed in time, the jury may be sent back to reconsider, with clarifying instructions.

**8. quotient verdict**  a type of *compromise verdict* in which the amount of damages is arrived at by averaging the amounts proposed by different jurors.

**9. Scotch verdict**  See SCOTCH VERDICT.

**10. sealed verdict**  See SEALED VERDICT.

**11. special verdict**  one in which the jurors are required to agree upon answers to a list of questions (called **special questions** or **special interrogatories**) about specific issues in the case. Used especially in complex civil cases. Cf. *general verdict.*

**12. verdict against the weight of the evidence**  one found by the judge to be so clearly contrary to the credible evidence that it would be unjust to let it stand. The usual remedy in such a situation is to set aside the verdict and order a new trial.

**verification** *n.* **1.** the act of verifying a document.

**2.** a statement affirming or swearing to the truth or authenticity of a document, written on the document itself or attached to it.

**verify** *v.,* **verified, verifying. 1.** to swear to or affirm the authenticity of a document, or the truth of the statements it contains.

**2. verified complaint**  a COMPLAINT to which a VERIFICATION has been affixed affirming or swearing to the truth of the facts alleged. (Other pleadings may likewise be verified.)

**3. verified copy**  Same as *certified copy* (see under CERTIFY).

—**verifiable** *adj.*

—**verifier** *n.*

**versus** *prep.* **1.** against. *Abbr.:* v.

**2.** as against; as compared to; in contrast with. *Abbr:* vs.

——**Usage.** The manner of writing case names in the captions of court papers is a matter of local custom: Depending upon the jurisdiction, the names of the adversaries may be separated by *v., vs., versus,* or *against.* In standard citation form, however, all these are rendered as *v.* (See also discussion at entry for v.) In contexts other than case names, *versus* is usually spelled out, but when abbreviated is almost invariably abbreviated *vs.: ordinary income versus capital gains; consecutive vs. concurrent sentencing.*

**vertical** *adj.* involving two or more sequentially related phases in the production and sale of a product; pertaining to different levels of the system of production and distribution in an industry.

—**vertically** *adv.*

——**Note.** For example, the supplier of raw materials, the manufacturer, the wholesaler, the retailer, and the customer for a product stand in a vertical relationship to each other; hence the merger of a supplier with a manufacturer or a manufacturer with a wholesaler would be regarded as a "vertical merger." Cf. HORIZONTAL.

**vertical merger** *n.* See under MERGER.

**vertical price fixing** *n.* See under PRICE FIXING.

**vertical union** *n.* See under UNION.

**vest** *v.* (of a power, right, or property interest) **1.** to come into being or become certain: *Your pension will vest when you have worked here for five years.*

**2.** to attach to or reside in someone (used with *in*): *Upon the death of the parents, title to the farm will vest in the children.*

**3.** to grant to or endow someone (used with *with*): *The deed vests the buyer with title to the property.*

**vested** *adj.* **1.** describing an interest in property that either confers a present right to possession, use, or enjoyment of the property or is certain to confer such a right in the future. See, for example, *vested estate* (under ESTATE[1]); *vested interest* (under INTEREST[1]); *vested pension* (under PENSION).

**2.** (of rights generally) protected by the Constitution from being arbitrarily taken away or nullified. See also *vested right* (under RIGHT).

**3. vested in interest**  (of property rights) not yet possessory, but certain to become so in the future.

**4. vested in possession** (of property rights) carrying a present right to possess and use the property.

**veto** *n., pl.* **vetoes,** *v.,* **vetoed, veto-ing. —***n.* **1.** the power or right vested in one branch of a government to cancel or postpone the decisions, enactments, etc., of another branch; especially, the right of a president, governor, or other chief executive to reject bills passed by the legislature, subject to the right of the legislature to OVERRIDE the veto. **2.** the exercise of this right. **3.** a nonconcurring vote by which one of the five permanent members of the United Nations Security Council can overrule the actions or decisions of the meeting on matters other than procedural. **4. line-item veto** the power possessed by some governors and mayors to veto portions of bills, especially specific items in budget and appropriations bills, without vetoing the entire bill. **5. pocket veto** a veto effected by simply not signing a bill that was enacted by a legislature shortly before it adjourned. **—***v.* **6.** to reject (a proposed bill or enactment) by exercising a veto. See also POCKET VETO.

**veto power** *n.* the right to exercise a veto.

**——Note.** The Constitution specifically gives the President the power to veto any bill of Congress within ten days of its enactment and return it to Congress for reconsideration.

**vexatious** *adj.* (of a legal proceeding or procedural step) instituted without sufficient grounds and serving only to annoy and harass; baseless and malicious. **—vexatiously** *adv.* **—vexatiousness** *n.* **——False Friend.** In litigation, *vexatious* is not the same thing as *vexing.* All litigation is vexing, and in many ways the more well-founded a claim, defense, or procedural step is, the more vexing it is. But conduct that has a firm basis in fact and law cannot be complained of on the ground of vexatiousness; only

conduct that is instituted for an improper purpose and without adequate legal justification is properly described as "vexatious" as well as a source of vexation.

**vexatious litigation** *n.* baseless LITIGATION commenced only to annoy and harass the defendant.

**vi et armis** *Latin.* with force and arms; by force and arms. See *trespass vi et armis* (under TRESPASS[2]), and see note at that entry for discussion of the fictional nature of the phrase.

**viatical settlement** *n.* an agreement or transaction for the sale of the beneficiary's rights under a life insurance policy, particularly a policy on the life of an individual who is terminally ill or suffering from a chronic or life-threatening illness or condition. The purchaser—ordinarily a company—typically pays a steeply discounted price and assumes the responsibility of paying the premiums; the sooner the insured individual dies, the greater the profit to the purchaser.

**——Note.** The viatical settlement business burst upon the American scene with three companies in 1989 and rapidly expanded into a multi-billion-dollar industry. In the typical viatical settlement transaction, a company buys the right to death benefits at a steeply discounted price and assumes the responsibility of paying the insurance premiums; many such companies now package the rights thus acquired and sell shares in them to investors. The quicker the insured individuals die, the greater the profit for the companies and the investors.

**viatical settlement provider** *n.* a company in the business of buying, at a discount, the rights to eventual payment of death benefits under insurance policies on the lives of individuals with chronic, life-threatening, or terminal illnesses or conditions. Also called **viatical settlement company.**

**viaticate** *v.,* **viaticated, viaticating.** to sell to a viatical settlement company the right to death benefits under a life insurance policy: *to viaticate the policy.*

**viator** *n.* the seller of a life insurance policy in a VIATICAL SETTLEMENT transaction. The viator is the person who owned the policy; most often this is the terminally ill individual, but sometimes it is another person, such as a spouse, who owned a policy on the life of that individual.

**vicarious** *adj.* performed, exercised, received, or suffered in place of another; taking the place of another person or thing; acting as a substitute.
—**vicariously** *adv.*
—**vicariousness** *n.*

**vicarious liability** *n.* See under LIABILITY.

**vicious propensity** or **vicious propensities** *n.* tendency of a dog or other animal to be dangerous to persons. Also called **dangerous propensity** or **dangerous propensities.** See note at FERAE NATURAE.

**victim impact statement** *n.* a report on the impact that a crime had on its victims, given to a judge for consideration in sentencing the convicted criminal. See also PRESENTENCE REPORT.

**victimless crime** *n.* conduct not in itself harmful to the person or property of anyone but consenting participants, but nevertheless defined as criminal; for example, gambling, drug use, or prostitution.

**victims' rights** *n.pl.* rights of individuals who have been the victim of a crime to be informed of various stages of the criminal justice process concerning the crime of which they were a victim and to present their views, as by addressing the judge before sentencing and the parole board at any parole hearing. Such rights are a relatively new concept enacted into law in some states.

**video piracy** *n.* See under PIRACY.

**video voyeur** *n.* an individual who surreptitiously videotapes others in ways that invade their privacy.

**video will** *n.* See under WILL.

**viewpoint discrimination** *n.* a legal restriction on SPEECH that is based upon the viewpoint expressed. See also CONTENT DISCRIMINATION.
——**Note.** Laws and governmental actions that allow certain expressions of opinion but prohibit contrary expressions of opinion under the same circumstances strike at the heart of the First Amendment, and are unconstitutional. For example, if a city allows parades or demonstrations in favor of racial, religious, and ethnic harmony, it cannot prohibit parades and demonstrations by the Ku Klux Klan.

**vindictive damages** *n.* See under DAMAGES.

**violation** *n.* **1.** a breach, infringement, or transgression of any rule, law, or duty.
**2.** the name given in some states to an offense below the level of MISDEMEANOR, punishable only by a fine or forfeiture and not classified as a crime: *a littering violation.*

**violent crime** *n.* Same as CRIME OF VIOLENCE. See also DOMESTIC VIOLENCE.

**violent presumption** *n.* **1.** a *conclusive presumption* (see under PRESUMPTION).
**2.** a very strong presumption or inference; an inference from the evidence that is conclusive on a point unless rebutted.
**3.** an invidious, unfair, or unwarranted presumption or assumption.
——**False Friend.** The "violence" in this phrase has never referred to physical violence. In its original sense, a "violent" presumption was simply an extremely forceful presumption, an inference that arises from evidence that is indirect but of such a nature that the conclusion necessarily follows, or at least must be assumed to follow in the absence of proof to the contrary. To indulge in such a presumption in a situation where it is not warranted, however, is to do violence in a different sense: It is to undermine or destroy the system of justice. These two concepts were easily conflated, and in time the phrase "violent presumption" came to be used primarily of assumptions that

are not just conclusive but also improper, unjust, and offensive. For example, in 1880 the Supreme Court condemned the practice of excluding blacks from a state's jury pool as the product of "a violent presumption... [that] the black race in Delaware were utterly disqualified, by want of intelligence, experience, or moral integrity, to sit on juries." *Neal v. Delaware,* 103 U.S. 370 (1880).

**vir** *n., pl.* **viri.** *Latin.* man; husband. See ET VIR.

**virtual child pornography** *n.* See under PORNOGRAPHY.

**vis** *n., pl.* **vires.** *Latin.* power; force; strength. See INTRA VIRES; ULTRA VIRES.

**visa** *n., pl.* **visas,** *v.,* **visaed, visaing.**
—*n.* **1.** written authorization to enter a country, issued to an individual from another country and normally stamped into the individual's passport. Typically a visa states when entry may be made, how long the individual may stay, and the permitted purpose for the visit. See also GREEN CARD.
—*v.* **2.** to give a visa to; approve a visa for.
**3.** to put a visa on (a passport).

**visitation** *n.* **1.** a visit or visits by a parent with a child who is in the custody of someone else, in a situation in which the parent has been deprived of custody, as through divorce or because of child neglect.
**2. visitation rights** authorization by court order for regular visitation, upon whatever terms the court decrees.
**3. supervised visitation** court-ordered visitation conditioned upon there being another adult present, in cases in which there is reason for concern regarding the safety of the child.
Cf. CONJUGAL VISIT.

**viva voce** *adv. Latin.* (lit. "by living voice") **1.** by voice; orally. Specifically, **a.** (of the giving of evidence or a statement) through oral testimony rather than in writing: *The witness was subpoenaed to give her statement viva voce.* **b.** (of voting) by voice rather than by ballot: *The Senate voted the amendment down viva voce.*
—*adj.* **2.** spoken; oral: *viva voce testimony; a viva voce vote.*

**void** *adj.* **1.** having no legal force or effect; not binding or enforceable because of a legal defect or for reasons of PUBLIC POLICY: *a void check, statute, contract, judgment, marriage,* etc. A transaction or instrument may be void from the outset **(void ab initio),** and thus never legally recognized at all, or it may become void at a later stage because of a change in circumstances. See also AB INITIO; *void for vagueness* (under VAGUE).
—*v.* **2.** to make or render void: *to void a check.*

**voidable** *adj.* describing a contract, instrument, transaction, or relationship that may be rendered VOID at the option of one party: *voidable contract; voidable marriage.* For example, a transaction entered into as a result of fraud would normally be voidable at the option of the defrauded party. See also AVOID; RATIFY.

**voidable preference** *n.* See under PREFERENCE.

**voir dire** *n., v.,* **voir dired, voir diring.** *Law French.* (lit. "to speak the truth")
—*n.* **1.** questioning of prospective jurors for possible sources of bias and for other information relevant to jury selection. See also CHALLENGE.
**2.** preliminary questioning of a trial witness, usually outside the presence of the jury, to determine competency to testify, admissibility of proposed testimony, qualification as an expert, and the like. See also *qualify as an expert* (under QUALIFY[1]).
**3.** anciently, an oath to tell the truth: *the oath of voir dire; sworn upon a voir dire.*
—*v.* **4.** to examine upon voir dire; conduct a voir dire examination of (a prospective juror or witness).
Occasionally spelled **voire dire.**
——**False Friend.** People familiar with the modern French verb *voir* (to see) and with the voir dire procedure itself (in which a witness or juror is scrutinized while answering questions) often assume that this phrase literally means

"to see to say; to see speaking." But the Old French word *voir* used in this phrase (also written in ancient sources as *voire* or *voier*) meant "truth, true, truly." It was descended from the Latin word *verum* (truth). The modern use of the phrase *voir dire* to refer to examination of a juror or witness is derived from its original use to refer to the oath administered to one being questioned: Originally, "examination upon voir dire" simply meant "examination upon oath to tell the truth."

**voluntary** *adj.* **1.** done without compulsion or obligation. See *voluntary bankruptcy* (under BANKRUPTCY); *voluntary commitment* (under COMMITMENT); *voluntary confession* (under CONFESSION); *voluntary discontinuance* (under DISCONTINUANCE); *voluntary dismissal* (under DISMISSAL).
**2.** done intentionally rather than accidentally or reflexively. See *voluntary manslaughter* (under MANSLAUGHTER);

*voluntary waste* (under WASTE).
**3.** gratuitous; without consideration. See *voluntary conveyance* (under CONVEYANCE).

**voluntary bar** *n.* See under BAR².

**vote dilution** *n.* See under DILUTION.

**voter qualification** *n.* a legal requirement for eligibility to vote in a public election, such as age or residence. Federal voting rights legislation has outlawed many such requirements, such as passing a literacy test, that tended to prevent disadvantaged minorities from voting. See also POLL TAX.

**voting trust** *n.* See under TRUST.

**voyage charter** *n.* See under CHARTER².

**VRM** *n., pl.* **VRMs, VRM's.** *variable-rate mortgage* (see under MORTGAGE).

**vs.** Abbreviation for VERSUS. See note at that entry.

# W

**wage earner's plan** *n.* See under BANKRUPTCY.

**wait-and-see approach** *n.* a modification of the common law *rule against perpetuities* (see under PERPETUITY), adopted in a few states, under which the validity of a contingent interest in property is determined according to when it actually vests rather than when it possibly could have vested. Also called **second-look doctrine.**
——**Note.** Under the wait-and-see approach to the rule against perpetuities, an interest that theoretically might not vest before the expiration of a life in being plus 21 years—which under the traditional rule would be declared void ab initio—will be held valid if it turns out that the interest actually vests within that period. For example, if the hypothetically fertile octogenarian in fact has no more children (see example at FERTILE-OCTOGENARIAN RULE), or the potential unborn widow fails to materialize (see example at UNBORN-WIDOW RULE), then the conveyances in those examples will be held valid under the wait-and-see approach. Under this approach to the rule against perpetuities, however, it can take many decades to resolve the question of whether a particular conveyance or bequest or a particular contingent interest in property is valid.

**wait and see zoning** *n.* See under ZONING.

**waiting period** *n.* See under RESIDENCY.

**waive** *v.,* **waived, waiving.** to abandon a right, privilege, or claim, intentionally and with knowledge of what one is giving up.
—**waivable** *adj.*

**waiver** *n.* **1.** the voluntary, intentional relinquishment of a right, privilege, or claim that one knows one has. See note at DEMURRER.
**2. express waiver** a waiver expressed in words.
**3. implied waiver** a waiver indicated by conduct. For mere conduct to be effective as a waiver, the circumstances must evidence the actor's awareness of her rights and intent to give them up.

**wall of separation between church and state** *n.* a metaphor for the constitutional principle of SEPARATION OF CHURCH AND STATE. Often shortened to **wall of separation.**
——**History.** This vivid phrase, like so many others that are central to American tradition, comes from the pen of Thomas Jefferson. Jefferson used the phrase in reference to the First Amendment in a letter to the Danbury (Connecticut) Baptist Association during his first term as President, in 1802.

**wall of silence** *n.* Same as BLUE WALL OF SILENCE.

**want** *n.* **1.** the absence of some necessary element or prerequisite: *The application for a search warrant was denied for want of probable cause. The fraud claim was dismissed for want of evidence of reliance.*
**2. want of consideration** the lack of CONSIDERATION for a promise, without which there is no enforceable contract: *The contract failed for want of consideration.* Cf. FAILURE OF CONSIDERATION.
**3. want of jurisdiction a.** a court's lack of *subject matter jurisdiction* (see under JURISDICTION[1]) over a particular case, making any decision it might render on the merits of the case void. **b.** a court's lack of *personal jurisdiction* (see under JURISDICTION[1]) over a party to a case, making any decision on the merits unenforceable as against that particular party unless the party appeared in the case without raising a

prompt jurisdictional objection.

**4. want of prosecution**  Same as FAIL-
URE TO PROSECUTE.

—*v.* **5.** to lack; need; desire.

**wanton** *adj.* an older term of somewhat
vague scope, generally describing conduct characterized by INTENT, KNOWL-
EDGE, or RECKLESSNESS rather than
mere negligence. (But see *wanton negligence,* under NEGLIGENCE.) The term is
often thrown in to add a note of moral
outrage to a description: *willful and
wanton; recklessly and wantonly.* See
also STATE OF MIND.

—**wantonly** *adv.*

—**wantonness** *n.*

**war** *n.* **1.** a conflict carried on by force
of arms, as between nations or between
parties within a nation.

**2. civil war  a.** a war between political
factions or regions within the same
country. **b. Civil War**  a particular civil
war. In the United States, unless stated
otherwise, this phrase always refers to
the war between the North and the
South, 1861–1865.

**3. declared war**  a war waged by a
nation or group that has made a *declaration of war* (see under DECLARATION).

**4. undeclared war**  a war waged in
the absence of a declaration of war.

See also JUST WAR; STATE OF WAR; WAR
OF AGGRESSION.

——**History.** Under the Constitution, the
power to declare war resides in the
Congress. But the Supreme Court has
consistently held, in effect, that declaring a war is not a prerequisite to going
to war. Consequently, the United States
has fought relatively few declared wars,
and such major conflicts as the Korean
War and the Vietnam War were undeclared wars.

**war crime** *n. International Law.* **1.** a
CONVENTIONAL WAR CRIME.

**2.** broadly, any offense against the law
of nations relating to the initiation or
waging of war, generally regarded as
encompassing three broad and overlapping categories: CONVENTIONAL WAR
CRIME; CRIME AGAINST HUMANITY; and
CRIME AGAINST PEACE.

**war of aggression** *n. International*
*Law.* a war initiated and pursued by a
nation in violation of the sovereignty,
territorial integrity, political independence, or other internationally recognized rights of another nation. A war of
aggression is a CRIME AGAINST PEACE.
See also AGGRESSION; cf. JUST WAR.

**ward** *n.* a person for whom a GUARDIAN
has been appointed.

—**wardship** *n.*

**ward of the court** *n. Informal.* any
minor or incompetent person involved
in legal proceedings. The common saying that "infants and incompetents are
wards of the court" signifies that judges
have a duty to make sure that the
interests of litigants who are unable to
look out for their own rights are adequately represented and well protected.

**warehouse** *n., v.* **warehoused, warehousing.** —*n.* **1.** a building for the storage of merchandise.

**2. bonded warehouse**  a government-
supervised warehouse in which merchandise may be kept until the im-
porter or manufacturer pays a tax and
the merchandise is released for sale.
Liquor and imported goods are sometimes stored in bonded warehouses.
Payment of the tax is secured by a
bond.

—*v.* **3.** to place or maintain in a warehouse.

**warehouse receipt** *n.* a receipt issued
by a warehouser identifying goods received for storage and evidencing the
right of the person with the receipt to
take possession of those goods. A warehouse receipt is a DOCUMENT OF TITLE.

**warehouseman** *n., pl.* **warehouse-
men.** a WAREHOUSER. See note at that
entry. See also *warehouseman's lien*
(under LIEN).

**warehouser** *n.* a person or entity engaged in the business of storing goods
for hire. See also *warehouser's lien* (under LIEN).

——**Usage.** Although the term *warehouser* appears in reported cases as
early as 1866, at the outset of the twenty-first century the more cumbersome
term *warehouseman* remains the usual
word in legal writing for one in the

business of warehousing—an odd linguistic artifact since the "warehouseman" is usually a company rather than an individual of either sex.

**warrant¹** *n.* **1.** a formal document, usually issued by a court, authorizing or directing an official to take a specific action.
**2. arrest warrant** a warrant directing or authorizing law enforcement officers to arrest an individual. It is issued upon a showing of PROBABLE CAUSE to believe that a crime has been committed and that the individual in question committed it. Also called **warrant of arrest.** Cf. SUMMONS CITATION.
**3. bench warrant** a warrant issued by a judge from the bench, directing that an individual be brought before the court, usually because the individual has failed to appear in response to a summons or subpoena or has violated a court order.
**4. death warrant** a warrant signed by the governor of a state directing the warden of a prison or another appropriate official to carry out a death sentence at a specific time on a specific day.
**5. John Doe warrant** a warrant for the arrest of a person whose name is not known, and who therefore is identified in the warrant by description rather than by name. Any description sufficient to identify the person to be arrested will suffice; for example, the defendant might be identified as the manager of a particular store or the wife of another defendant.
**6. search warrant** a warrant, issued upon a showing of probable cause to believe that items connected with a crime will be found in a particular place, authorizing law enforcement authorities to search for those items in that place and seize them if found.
**7. warrant of eviction** a warrant directing a sheriff to put a person wrongfully in possession of property (usually a holdover tenant) out of the property.

**warrant²** *n.* a certificate issued by a corporation entitling the holder to purchase a specified number of shares of a specified class of the company's stock

at a specified price, usually good until a specified date. Also called **stock warrant.** See also EX WARRANTS.

**warrant³** *v.* to issue or become bound by an express or implied warranty.
**—warrantor** *n.*

**warrantless** *adj.* performed without a warrant. See, e.g., *warrantless arrest* (under ARREST); *warrantless search* (under SEARCH).

**warranty** *n., pl.* **warranties. 1.** a legally binding representation made or implied in connection with a sale of goods, transfer of land, or other contract or financial transaction, ordinarily relating to the quality, integrity, or usefulness of the subject matter of the transaction (such as a product, a parcel of land, or a check); if the representation proves untrue, the person or company that made it (the **warrantor**) normally will be liable for any resulting loss or injury. Popularly called a GUARANTEE, though in legal usage that means something different. In some phrases, especially in real estate transactions, also called a COVENANT.
**2.** a representation made by the purchaser of an insurance policy, incorporated into the policy and relied upon by the insurance company in issuing the policy; if it proves untrue, the policy will be void.
**3. affirmative warranty** in an insurance policy, a policy owner's warranty of existing or past fact, such as that he is fifty-two years old and has never been treated for heart disease. Cf. *promissory warranty.*
**4. construction warranty** a warranty by the builder or seller of a new house that it is free from basic structural defects. Also called **home owner's warranty.**
**5. express warranty a.** a warranty expressed in words. **b.** in connection with a sale of goods, any words or conduct of the seller amounting to a representation about the quality or nature of the goods, such as the showing of a model or sample. Cf. *implied warranty;* PUFFING.
**6. full warranty** in the sale of a consumer product, a written warranty

meeting certain federal standards. To qualify as a full warranty, the warranty must include a promise to remedy any defect or malfunction that occurs within a specified period of time without charge, and to permit the consumer to choose between a replacement and a refund if the product cannot be fixed. Cf. *limited warranty.*

**7. implied warranty** a warranty imposed by law in connection with a particular transaction, because the law regards such a warranty as inherent in that type of transaction unless the circumstances clearly indicate or the parties explicitly agree otherwise. For example, if one buys a painting at a gallery, the gallery impliedly warrants that it is theirs to sell; therefore, if it turns out to be stolen and the rightful owner traces it and takes it back from the buyer, the buyer can sue the gallery to recover the value of the painting. Cf. *express warranty.*

**8. limited warranty** in the sale of a consumer product, any written warranty that falls short of the requirements for a *full warranty.* Under federal law, a limited warranty must be clearly labeled as such and must clearly state the scope of the warranty.

**9. promissory warranty** in an insurance policy, a policy owner's warranty that certain facts will continue to exist, or certain acts will or will not be done, during the term of the policy; for example, that she will not smoke. Cf. *affirmative warranty.*

**10. warranty of fitness for a particular purpose** the implied warranty of a seller of goods who has reason to know that the buyer needs the goods for a particular use and is relying upon the seller to furnish suitable goods, that the goods being furnished will in fact be suitable for that use.

**11. warranty of title** the implied warranty of a seller of goods that the title conveyed to the buyer will be good and unencumbered, and that its transfer is rightful. Cf. *warranties of title* (under COVENANTS OF TITLE).

See also *breach of warranty* (under BREACH); *warranty deed* (under DEED);

*warranty of habitability* (under HABITABLE); *warranty of merchantability* (under MERCHANTABLE); *warranty of quiet enjoyment* or *covenant of warranty* (both under QUIET ENJOYMENT). Cf. COVENANT; GUARANTEE; GUARANTY.

**wash** *n. Informal.* a transaction or set of related transactions leaving a party in substantially the same position as when he started. See also *wash sale* (under SALE).

**waste** *n.* **1.** substantial permanent change, beyond normal wear and tear, in the condition of real property while it is in possession of a tenant. A tenant who causes or permits waste is normally liable to the owner for damages.
**2. ameliorating waste** a substantial change that actually increases the value of the property. Normally this does not give rise to liability.
**3. commissive waste** waste caused by intentional conduct of the tenant. Also called **voluntary waste.**
**4. permissive waste** waste that the tenant negligently allows to occur, as by failing to provide routine maintenance.

**wasting** *adj.* of such a nature as to be used up or dissipated over time: oil and coal are *wasting assets;* a trust in which funds are used for trust purposes faster than they accrue is a *wasting trust.*

**weapon** *n.* **1.** anything designed or used to cause bodily injury.
**2. concealed weapon** a weapon carried in such a way as not to be obvious.
**3. deadly weapon** anything which, either by design or by the way it is wielded in a particular case, could cause death or serious injury. Also called **dangerous weapon; lethal weapon.**

**weight** *n.* **1.** Same as PROBATIVE VALUE.
**2.** of all the evidence on both sides of an issue, the more convincing body of evidence, as determined not by mere quantity but by its significance, coherence, and credibility.
See also *verdict against the weight of the evidence* (under VERDICT).

**welfare plan** *n.* Same as EMPLOYEE WELFARE BENEFIT PLAN.

**well-pleaded complaint** *n.* **1.** a complaint in a civil action that alleges all the elements of a claim for relief and, in courts of limited jurisdiction, facts showing that the court has jurisdiction over the case.
**2.** especially, in a case sought to be maintained in a federal court on the basis of the court's *federal question jurisdiction* (see under JURISDICTION), a complaint stating a claim that clearly arises under federal law.
**3. well-pleaded complaint rule** the principle applied in the federal courts that a case may not be brought into federal court on the basis of federal question jurisdiction unless a basis for such jurisdiction is shown in a well-pleaded complaint. In particular, the fact that the defendant relies upon federal law as a defense is not enough to sustain federal question jurisdiction, since it is the claim itself, not the defense, that must raise the federal question.
Also called **well-pleaded complaint doctrine.**

**whereas** *conj., n., pl.* **whereases.**
—*conj.* **1.** (used especially in a recitals) it being the case that; considering that. See also RECITAL.
**2.** while on the contrary: *One witness identified the defendant, whereas the others did not.*
—*n.* **3.** a qualifying or introductory statement, especially one having "whereas" as the first word: *the whereases in the contract.*

**whistleblower** *n.* **1.** an employee who reports dangerous or illegal conduct of an employer to authorities.
**2. whistleblower law** a statute protecting whistleblowers from retaliatory firing or other action by the employer.

**white-collar crime** *n. Informal.* any business or financial crime of a type typically engaged in by executives and professional people, often involving very large sums of money to which they have access in the course of their business. Punishments for such crimes

are sometimes thought to be disproportionately light when compared with those for nonviolent crimes, involving far less money, by people of lower social status.

**white slavery** *n.* until 1986, the statutory term for the federal crime of transporting a woman across state lines "for the purpose of prostitution or debauchery, or for any other immoral purpose."
—**History.** In 1986, the White-Slave Traffic Act was amended to sanitize it of sexist and racist terminology and make it as applicable to someone who takes a paid male companion on a trip as to one who takes a paid female companion.

**Whiteacre** *n.* See under BLACKACRE.

**whole** *adj.* See MAKE WHOLE.

**whole law** *n.* the law of a state or nation including its CHOICE OF LAW rules. Cf. INTERNAL LAW.
—**Note.** If the court in which an action is pending concludes that the applicable law is the law of another state and applies the *whole law* of that state, the result might be that the second state's choice-of-law rules point back to the first state or to a third state for the applicable law. See RENVOI.

**whole life insurance** *n.* Same as *straight life insurance* (see under LIFE INSURANCE).

**whole renvoi** *n.* See under RENVOI.

**wholly owned subsidiary** *n.* See under SUBSIDIARY.

**widow's** (or **widower's**) **election** *n.* See under ELECTION.

**widow's** (or **widower's**) **elective** (or **statutory**) **share** *n.* See under ELECTIVE SHARE.

**wife abuse** See under SPOUSAL ABUSE.

**wildcat strike** *n.* See under STRIKE[1].

**will** *n.* **1.** a person's declaration of how she wants her property to be distributed when she dies. Because the maker of a will (the TESTATOR or TESTATRIX) is never available to testify to its authenticity, the law normally requires considerable formality in the execution of a will. The requirements vary from state to state, and not following them exactly will ordinarily render the will invalid.

**2. holographic will** a will written out by hand, signed, and dated by the maker; recognized in a number of states as valid even if not witnessed like a normal will.

**3. joint will** the wills of two people, usually husband and wife, in a single document.

**4. military will** a will made by a member of the military while in military service, either orally or in writing but without the formalities normally required for valid execution of a will. The usual requirement of strict adherence to formalities of execution is often waived in the case of such a will. Also called **soldier's will, sailor's will, mariner's will.**

**5. mutual will** one of two or more wills executed simultaneously and containing reciprocal provisions, as when a husband and wife simultaneously execute separate wills in which each makes the other the principal legatee. Also called **reciprocal will.**

**6. nuncupative will** a will that is spoken, not written; allowed in a few states under special circumstances, notably when death is imminent. Also called **oral will.**

**7. video will** a will read or recited by the testator on videotape, sometimes augmented by explanations of the reasons for certain gifts (or nongifts) and expressions of sentiment for those left behind. Videotape cannot take the place of formalities required for a valid will, but can be a useful supplement.

**8. will contest** a challenge to the validity of a will.

See also CODICIL; *election under the will* (under ELECTION); TESTAMENT; LAST WILL AND TESTAMENT. Cf. AT WILL; LIVING WILL; INTESTATE SUCCESSION.

**willful** *adj.* describing wrongful conduct done with INTENT or KNOWLEDGE, and sometimes RECKLESSNESS: *willful violation of an injunction.* See, for example, *willful neglect* (under NEGLECT); *willful negligence* (under NEGLIGENCE). See also STATE OF MIND.

—**willfully** *adv.*
—**willfulness** *n.*

**wind up** *v.,* **wound up, winding up.** to bring the affairs of a corporation, partnership, estate, or other enterprise to an end by fulfilling or settling remaining business obligations, liquidating and distributing any remaining assets, and dissolving the organization. Cf. GOING CONCERN.

**wire fraud** *n.* See under FRAUD.

**wiretap** *n., v.,* **wiretapped, wiretapping.** —*n.* **1.** originally, the attachment of an extra wire to a telephone line to listen in on conversations. Now the term is used broadly and informally to cover any interception or recording of conversations or data transmissions by electronic or other artificial means without the consent of the participants. If done by a private individual, wiretapping is normally a crime, and may also give rise to a tort claim for INVASION OF PRIVACY. If done by law enforcement authorities, it normally requires a search warrant. In most states, however, one participant in a conversation may record it without the knowledge of the others.
—*v.* **2.** to install a wiretap or listen by means of one.
—**wiretapper** *n.*

**wish** *n., v.* an ambiguous word too often found in wills, sometimes construed as a directive and sometimes as a mere hope or suggestion. See also PRECATORY LANGUAGE.

**with all faults** AS IS.

**with prejudice** See under PREJUDICE.

**with will annexed** or **with the will annexed** Same as CUM TESTAMENTO ANNEXO.

**withholding tax** *n.* a sum of money required to be held back from an employee's wages, or in special circumstances from an investor's earnings, and sent directly to taxing authorities as an advance on the employee's or investor's taxes. Often simply called **withholding.**

**within** *prep.* covered by; governed by;

consistent with: *within the statute; within the usual meaning of the word; within the intent of the contract; within the language of Smith v. Jones.* Cf. OUTSIDE; DEHORS.

**without day** *adv.* indefinitely; without a set date for resumption; permanently: *The subcommittee voted to issue its final report as revised and adjourned without day.*

**without prejudice** See under PREJUDICE.

**without recourse** See under RECOURSE.

**witness** *n.* **1.** a person who has seen or heard something relevant to a case or an investigation. See also EYEWITNESS. **2.** a person who testifies in a legal or legislative proceeding. **3.** Also called **attesting witness.** a person who formally observes the execution of a document, especially a will, and signs it as evidence that it was duly executed. **4. alibi witness** a witness who testifies that the defendant was somewhere else at the time the crime was committed. **5. character witness** a witness called to testify about the CHARACTER of a party or of another witness. **6. complaining witness a.** the person who signs the COMPLAINT in a criminal case. **b.** the victim or other person who accuses another of wrongdoing in a criminal or disciplinary case; for example, the victim in a rape case or a person complaining of unethical conduct by a lawyer to a legal disciplinary body. **7. expert witness** a witness qualified by education or experience to testify about and render opinions on specialized subjects beyond the knowledge of average people. Unlike a *fact witness,* an expert witness need not have personal knowledge of the events or matters involved in the case. See also BATTLE OF THE EXPERTS; *qualify as an expert* (under QUALIFY¹). **8. fact witness** a witness called to testify about things she has personally

done or observed. Unlike an *expert witness,* a fact witness ordinarily may not express opinions. See also *opinion evidence* (under EVIDENCE). **9. hostile witness** a witness called by one side in a case but known to be friendly to the other side or found to be evasive in answering questions. If declared to be a hostile witness by the judge, such a witness may be asked leading questions even on direct examination and may be impeached even in states that normally do not allow impeachment of one's own witness. Also called **adverse witness.** **10. interested witness** a witness with an interest (see INTEREST²) in the case. That interest may be considered by the jury in assessing the witness's credibility. See also IMPEACHMENT. **11. material witness** a witness whose testimony is essential to one side or the other in a criminal case. Such a witness may be required to travel from one state to another to testify, and in some circumstances may even be held in custody to assure that she will appear to testify. **12. unavailable witness** a witness whose testimony cannot be obtained at a trial, for reasons ranging from outright refusal to answer questions while on the stand to being dead. In some circumstances, prior statements or testimony of such a witness may be admitted under a *hearsay exception* (see under HEARSAY). —*v.* **13.** to see or hear an event. **14.** to act as an attesting witness to the execution of a document: *to witness a will.*

**witness stand** *n.* Same as STAND.

**wobbler** *n. California Law.* an offense that is punishable either as a felony or as a misdemeanor. **—Usage.** Although this term is well established in California jurisprudence, it is usually enclosed in quotation marks, and sometimes preceded by "so-called": *The appellant was charged with a so-called "wobbler" offense.*

**word** (or **words**) **of art** *n.* Same as TERM OF ART.

**words actionable in themselves** *n.pl.* See under ACTIONABLE WORDS.

**words actionable per quod** *n.pl.* See under ACTIONABLE WORDS.

**words actionable per se** *n.pl.* See under ACTIONABLE WORDS.

**words of limitation** *n.pl.* in a transfer of real property by deed or will, the words identifying the nature and duration of the interest the taker is to have. Cf. WORDS OF PURCHASE.
——**Note.** For example, in a deed conveying property "to A for life," the words "for life" are words of limitation; they identify the interest given as a life estate. By centuries of tradition, the conventional language for transferring a fee simple takes the form "to A and his heirs"; in this phrase the words "and his heirs" are understood as *words of limitation:* they are not there to identify who is getting an interest in the property, but only to make it clear that the interest A is getting is of potentially infinite duration. See discussion at *and his heirs* (under HEIR), and note at WORDS OF PURCHASE.
——**False Friend.** As the example of "and his heirs" shows, *words of limitation* do not necessarily limit the estate being given: They are simply the words that identify the scope of the interest given, which may be unlimited.

**words of negotiability** *n.pl.* words used in an instrument to make it NEGOTIABLE, e.g. "to the order of" or "to bearer." See also NEGOTIABLE INSTRUMENT; NONNEGOTIABLE INSTRUMENT.

**words of purchase** *n.pl.* in a transfer of real property by deed or will, the words identifying the transferee. Cf. WORDS OF LIMITATION.
——**Note.** For example, in a conveyance "to A and his heirs," only the words "to A" are words of purchase, for it is not intended that the heirs have an interest in the property unless A chooses to leave it to them. See also note at WORDS OF LIMITATION.
——**False Friend.** "Words of purchase" do not signify that the transaction involves any payment or exchange of consideration. See PURCHASE (def. 3).

**work** *n. Copyright Law.* **1.** a product of creative effort, consisting of, e.g., sounds, images, or writing.
**2.** Also called **original work of authorship.** a creative work that was not copied from another's work, and that, when embodied in tangible form (see note at COPY) may be the subject of copyright protection. The principal categories of such works are literary, musical, dramatic, choreographic, graphic or sculptural, architectural, audiovisual (including motion pictures), and sound recordings.
**3. anonymous work** a work on which no natural person is identified as author. Cf. *pseudonymous work.*
**4. collective work** a work, such as an anthology or an issue of a periodical, in which a number of contributions, constituting separate and independent works in themselves, are assembled into a collective whole. A collective work is one type of COMPILATION.
**5. derivative work** a work based on one or more preexisting works, such as a translation, dramatization, adaptation, fictionalization, or abridgment. A work consisting of editorial revisions, annotations, or other modifications which, as a whole, represent an original work of authorship, is considered a derivative work.
**6. joint work** a work prepared by two or more authors with the intention that their contributions be merged into inseparable or interdependent parts of the whole.
**7. literary work** a work, other than a movie or other audiovisual work, expressed in words or numbers. See note below.
**8. pseudonymous work** a work on which the author is identified under a fictitious name. Cf. *anonymous work.*
**9. work made for hire** See WORK MADE FOR HIRE.
——**False Friend.** For copyright purposes, *literary work* should not be confused with *work of literature.* The term does not refer to intellectual content of a writing or recording, but merely to the fact that it is composed of words or numbers rather than, for example, music or design or architectural plans.

**work made for hire** *n.* any of a certain class of copyrightable works specified by statute, with respect to which the copyright is usually owned not by the creator of the work, but by the company that hired the creator to do the work. The principal categories of such works are those created by an employee whose job it is to produce such works (as in the case of a newspaper article by a staff reporter), and those created by an *independent contractor* (see under CONTRACTOR) who was specially hired to produce a compilation, a contribution to a larger work, or an adjunct to a work created by someone else, and who agreed in writing that the resulting work would be deemed a work made for hire. Often referred to informally as a **work for hire.** See also WORK.

**work product** *n.* **1.** Also called **attorney work product.** notes and other materials prepared by or for an attorney in preparing for litigation.
**2. work product doctrine** the principle that work product materials may not be demanded by the other side in pretrial DISCOVERY except upon a showing of special need, and that even then the attorney's analysis of the case need not be disclosed.

**work release** *n.* the release of a prisoner for a certain period of time each day to work at a job or participate in a training program. Cf. HALFWAY HOUSE.

**workers' compensation** *n.* payment to a worker as compensation for on-the-job injury. Most employees in America are covered by a state or federal law, often called a **workers' compensation act** or **employers' liability act,** requiring compensation for such injuries regardless of who was at fault, specifying the level of compensation for different types of injuries, and establishing a funding mechanism, such as an insurance program **(workers' compensation insurance** or **employers' liability insurance)** funded by employers.

**world** *n.* See ALL THE WORLD.

**World Court** *n.* Informal name for the INTERNATIONAL COURT OF JUSTICE.

**Worthier Title, Doctrine of** *n.* **1.** the common law rule of property law that one cannot give a REMAINDER to one's heirs. Under the common law Doctrine of Worthier Title, no longer enforced in most states, any conveyance or devise of an interest in property purporting to give a remainder to one's heirs was automatically treated as simply a retention of a REVERSION by the grantor, with no interest at all vesting in the heirs.
**2.** in many states, a rule of construction that favors interpreting any language in a deed, trust instrument, or the like that appears to create a remainder in the grantor's heirs as a retention of a reversion by the grantor.

**wraparound mortgage** or **wraparound mortgage** *n.* See under MORTGAGE.

**wreck** *n.* residue from a maritime incident or disaster thrown ashore by the action of the sea, such as jettisoned cargo or wreckage of a vessel.

**writ** *n.* **1.** any of a class of court orders that originated in early English law, each having a specific name and purpose, by which a court commands a certain official or body to carry out a certain action.
**2. alias writ** a writ replacing one that failed of its purpose; especially the first such replacement. Also called an **alias.** See note at ALIAS. Cf. *pluries writ.*
**3. alternative writ** a writ commanding that the person to whom it is directed do a specified thing or show cause to the court why he should not be compelled to do it.
**4. extraordinary writ** any of a special class of writs whose effect is in some way to interfere with or open to question the proceedings of a court or other body. Most of the writs that survive in America today are extraordinary writs. Also referred to by the older name **prerogative writ.**
**5. Great Writ** See HABEAS CORPUS.
**6. original writ** the writ by which a civil action was commenced. This was originally a writ issued in the king's

name, directing the sheriff of the county where the wrong allegedly occurred to command the person accused either to do justice to the complainant or to appear in court and answer the accusation.

**7. pluries writ** the third or subsequent writ in a series of writs of the same kind and to the same effect, each subsequent one having been issued because the previous ones proved ineffective. Also called a **pluries.** See note at PLURIES. Cf. *alias writ.*

——**Note.** The formal names of writs are always in the form "writ of..." (e.g., "writ of habeas corpus"), but the words "writ of" are often omitted. For specific writs other than those with separate entries below, see the entry for the specific name. The principal writs still in use in the United States include the writs of ATTACHMENT, CERTIORARI, CORAM NOBIS, HABEAS CORPUS, MANDAMUS, PROHIBITION, and QUO WARRANTO.

**writ of error** *n.* a writ issued by an appellate court to a lower court in cases that may be appealed as right, directing that the record of a case be sent up for review of alleged errors of law.

**writ of execution** *n.* a writ directed to a sheriff or similar officer directing the officer to seize property of a *judgment debtor* (see under DEBTOR) or take other action to enforce or satisfy a judgment of the court.

**writ of right** *n.* **1.** an ancient writ by which one claiming ownership of land as against the person currently in possession could assert his right to the land. See also *grand assize* (under ASSIZE) and accompanying note.
**2. parson's writ of right** See under UTRUM.

**written constitution** *n.* See under CONSTITUTION.

**written contract** *n.* See under CONTRACT.

**wrong** *n.* **1.** the violation of or failure to perform a legal duty, or the infringement of another's legal rights.
**2. private wrong** a wrong that injures

or interferes with the rights of a specific person or private entity, usually a basis for a tort or contract action.
**3. public wrong** a wrong that injures or interferes with the rights of the public at large, for which civil or criminal proceedings may be brought by the state or its agencies or the federal government.
—**wrongful** *adj.*
—**wrongfully** *adv.*
—**wrongfulness** *n.*

**wrongful abstraction** *n.* See under ABSTRACTION.

**wrongful birth** *n.* a relatively new kind of tort action, usually brought by the parents of a newborn infant on their own behalf or on behalf of the child, alleging that the child would not have been born but for the medical malpractice of the defendant, such as an unsuccessful sterilization or bad advice that led the parents to forgo abortion. The damages sought typically include the costs of raising the child, and particularly the extra costs of caring indefinitely for a severely disabled child. Also called **wrongful life.**

**wrongful death** *n.* a tort action brought by or on behalf of close relatives or beneficiaries of someone who has died, alleging that the death was caused by a wrongful act of the defendant, such as medical malpractice, reckless driving, or murder. The damages claimed include the loss of future income that the deceased would have earned over a normal lifespan. A few states also allow damages for the nonpecuniary value of the decedent's life; see *hedonic damages* (under DAMAGES).

**wrongful discharge** *n.* the firing of an employee for a reason not permitted by law or in violation of contract. Depending upon the circumstances, this may give rise to a tort or contract claim, a union grievance, or a civil rights claim. Also called **wrongful termination.**

**wrongful life** *n.* Same as WRONGFUL BIRTH.

**wrongful termination** *n.* Same as WRONGFUL DISCHARGE.

# XYZ

**X** *n.* a mark traditionally used as a SIG-NATURE by people who cannot write their names.

——**Note.** Typically, the person's name and the words "his mark" or "her mark" would be printed near the X, and one or more neutral individuals would sign as witnesses.

**X-rated** *adj.* a lay term popularly applied to sexually oriented or pornographic entertainment in any form. The label has no legal significance. Cf. OB-SCENE; INDECENT; PORNOGRAPHY.

**year-and-a-day rule** *n.* the common law rule, still followed in many states, that one cannot be found guilty of homicide if the victim lives for at least a year and a day after the act. Most states have abandoned the rule in light of modern medicine's ability to prolong dying in some cases for very long periods.

**yellow-dog contract** *n.* a contract between a worker and an employer in which, as a condition of employment, the worker agrees not to remain in or join a union. Yellow-dog contracts are illegal.

**Younger abstention** *n.* See under AB-STENTION.

**Your Honor** *n., pl.* **Your Honors.** (a respectful form of address for certain officials, especially a judge or mayor): *I object, Your Honor. We were notified of Your Honor's order this morning. Your Honors will find the pertinent testimony at page 312 of the record on appeal.* Sometimes written **your Honor;** occasionally, and especially in older materials, **your honor.**

——**Usage.** *Your Honor* takes a verb in the third person: *Our client will do as your Honor directs* (vs. "as you direct").

**youthful offender** *n.* See under OF-FENDER.

**zero-coupon bond** *n.* See under BOND[2].

**zone** *n., v.,* **zoned, zoning.** —*n.* **1.** an area or district within a city, town, or county designated for a particular use or uses under a ZONING plan. Cf. DRUG-FREE ZONE.
**2. combat zone** *Slang.* a zone in which sex-related businesses, such as topless bars and "X-rated" video stores, are concentrated. This was once viewed as a way to allow some such businesses to exist while limiting their spread. In recent years, zoning plans which require dispersion of such businesses, rather than concentration of them in one zone, have been more popular with municipal governments.
**3. floating zone** a zone definition included in a municipality's zoning law but not assigned a specific location on the map until some real estate developer proposes to put a particular tract of land to the specified use.
—*v.* **4.** to designate an area for particular uses under a zoning plan.

**zone of danger** *n.* a region or circumstance in which an individual would be physically endangered, or in reasonable fear of being physically injured, as a result of another's negligence. See note at NEGLIGENT INFLICTION OF EMOTIONAL DISTRESS.

**zone of employment** *n.* for purposes of WORKERS' COMPENSATION laws, an employee's workplace. Any accidental injury to a worker within the employee's zone of employment entitles the worker to compensation from the employer.

**zoning** *n.* **1.** the division of a locality into geographic zones, pursuant to a plan under which the kinds of uses to which the land may be put, and the kinds of structures that may be built, vary from zone to zone. See also ZONE.

**2. cumulative zoning** a zoning plan in which each successive zone definition merely adds to the list of permitted uses. Thus a zone might permit residential use only, or residential and trade use, or residential and trade and industrial use. Cf. *exclusive zoning.*

**3. exclusionary zoning** zoning that effectively keeps out low- and moderate-income families. For example, zoning in which all residential areas are restricted to single-family homes on large lots. Cf. *inclusionary zoning.*

**4. exclusive zoning** zoning in which each zone has its own distinct use; for example, residential only, trade only, or industrial only. Cf. *cumulative zoning.*

**5. inclusionary zoning** zoning that provides for a certain amount of low- and moderate-income housing. A few states have laws requiring that zoning plans be inclusionary. Cf. *exclusionary zoning.*

**6. industrial performance zoning** zoning in which the definition of permitted use depends upon the amount of noise, smoke, or other pollution generated, rather than upon general categorizations such as "industrial" vs. "nonindustrial." This allows nonpolluting industries to exist in zones where more polluting industries would be disruptive.

**7. spot zoning** the zoning of a single lot or small tract to allow a particular use that is not permitted in the surrounding area. Often attacked as political favoritism inconsistent with the general zoning plan.

**8. wait and see zoning** a zoning plan in which undeveloped areas are not designated for any use until a developer comes forward and proposes a particular use for a particular area.

—*adj.* **9.** pertaining to zoning: *zoning regulation.*

# Appendix A

## Guide to the Constitution

The Constitution of the United States of America was drafted by delegates from twelve of the thirteen original states over the summer of 1787 and signed on September 17, 1787. With ratification by a ninth state on June 21, 1788, the Constitution became binding upon the states that had ratified it. The process of transition to the new government did not begin, however, until the major states of New York and Virginia added their approval, by perilously thin margins, later that year. Government under the new Constitution officially commenced on March 4, 1789; Congress became functional on April 6; George Washington was inaugurated as the first President on April 30; and the Supreme Court became operative on February 2, 1790—the final step in establishing the new tripartite national government.

The Constitution is reproduced in full in Appendix B. This guide outlines the structure of the instrument and provides capsule descriptions of its provisions, including each of the amendments. Words and phrases in SMALL CAPITAL LETTERS refer to entries in the dictionary where more detailed information can be found; phrases in *italics* are discussed at entries indicated in small capitals.

The fundamental organizing principle of the new government was its division into three branches—LEGISLATIVE, EXECUTIVE, and JUDICIAL—each with its own distinct functions and *enumerated powers* (see under POWER). The basic text of the Constitution is devoted primarily to structural matters; its seven articles—though they contain no headings—deal with the following topics:

   I. Legislative Branch
  II. Executive Branch
 III. Judicial Branch
  IV. Relations among the States
   V. Mode of Amendment
  VI. Continuity and Supremacy of the Federal Government
 VII. Ratification

The Constitution thus assembled was a thing of austere, almost architectural, beauty; but it lacked a crucial pillar: There was no general declaration of the rights of the people. Some of the very freedoms for which the Revolution had been fought appeared to have been left unprotected. The framers (naively, in the view of many at the time) assumed that so long as they did not authorize the government to infringe individual rights, it could not do so. The absence of an explicit bill of rights nearly scuttled the Constitution; it was only with assurances from the Constitution's supporters that they would seek to have such a bill added that ratification in some key states became possible.

Pursuant to that promise, in 1789 the first Congress adopted and sent to the states for ratification a list of twelve proposed articles of amendment. By December 15, 1791, the third through twelfth of these had been ratified and were added to the Constitution as Amendments I through X—which have ever after been referred to as the BILL OF RIGHTS.[1] When Americans speak of "constitutional rights," they are often referring not to the original text of the Constitution, but to one or another of its amendments.

In the years since the adoption of the Bill of Rights, it is generally estimated that some ten thousand proposed amendments have been introduced in Congress. Of these, only twenty-one were approved by Congress and submitted to the states for ratification, and just sixteen were ratified—one of which, the Prohibition Amendment (Amend. XIX), was repealed fourteen years later.[2]

The Thirteenth, Fourteenth, and Fifteenth Amendments represent the nation's effort to embody in its fundamental law the principles of equality and human dignity that emerged from the Civil War, and are often referred to as the CIVIL WAR AMENDMENTS. In many respects, the Fourteenth Amendment has turned out to be

---

[1]Ratification of the second proposed amendment was completed over 200 years later in 1992, making it Amendment XXVII. The first proposed amendment was never ratified; it concerned the size of the House of Representatives for the first few decades under the Constitution and would have had no lasting significance.

[2]The unratified amendments include an early proposal to strip American citizenship from anyone who accepts a title of nobility or any money or present from a king or foreign power; an amendment to allow states to regulate child labor (which became unnecessary in 1941 when the Supreme Court overruled a prior decision and held child labor legislation constitutional); an amendment granting equal rights to women; and an amendment granting residents of the District of Columbia representation in Congress.

The remaining unratified amendment was adopted by a Northern-controlled Congress on March 2, 1861, with the assent of President-elect Abraham Lincoln, who was to be inaugurated two days later. Most southern states had already seceded; in an effort to win them back, Congress offered a constitutional amendment guaranteeing continued and perpetual protection for the institution of slavery. It read:

> No amendment shall be made to the Constitution which will authorize or give to Congress the power to abolish or interfere, within any State, with the domestic institutions thereof, including that of persons held to labor or service by the laws of said State.

The amendment was quickly ratified by Ohio, Maryland, and Illinois; but on April 12 Fort Sumter was fired upon, and the Civil War was on. If the South, instead of fighting, had accepted this amendment—which would have become the Thirteenth Amendment—American history would be very different. As matters turned out, the Thirteenth Amendment, ratified less than five years later, abolished slavery.

the most far-reaching of all additions to the Constitution after the Bill of Rights. The provisions of the Bill of Rights were originally intended only as limitations on the power of the federal government, and for most of the nation's history provided no protection against state laws that violated individual rights. It is only through the Fourteenth Amendment that the Supreme Court finally found a way to make most of the Bill of Rights applicable to state governments. (See note at INCORPO-RATION DOCTRINE.)

# Summary of the Original Constitution (ratified 1788)

## Preamble

Purposes of Constitution. The principal purpose was "to form a more perfect Union" in light of inadequacies of previous Articles of Confederation.

## Article I

§ 1. LEGISLATIVE power vested in Congress.

§ 2. House of Representatives apportioned by population and chosen by popular vote. Qualifications of members; terms; vacancies; organization. Decennial census to be held for purpose of apportionment (see note at CENSUS). House has sole power of IMPEACHMENT.

§ 3. Senate consists of two senators from each state, chosen by state legislature. (But now see Amend. XVII.) Qualifications of senators; vacancies; organization; Vice President to preside. Senate has sole power to try cases of IMPEACHMENT; punishment not to extend beyond removal and disqualification from office; Chief Justice to preside if President is on trial.

§ 4. Procedures for Congressional elections; Congress to meet at least once a year.

§ 5. Basic rules and procedures for each house of Congress.

§ 6. Compensation of members of Congress; PRIVILEGE from arrest while attending sessions and from claims of defamation for speech in sessions; proscription of certain conflicts of interest.

§ 7. Procedure for passing laws; revenue bills to originate in House of Representatives.

§ 8. *Enumerated powers* of Congress (see under POWER). These include power to levy taxes, borrow money, and coin money; power to regulate interstate and foreign COMMERCE, *naturalization* (see NATURALIZE), BANKRUPTCY, PATENT, and COPY-RIGHT; power to maintain a navy, raise armies, and make *declarations of war* (see under WAR); substantial power over the state MILITIA; complete power of government over the District of Columbia and federal property; and the power to make "all Laws which shall be necessary and proper" to carry out these or any other powers vested in the government by the Constitution (see NECESSARY AND PROPER CLAUSE).

§ 9. Limitations on Congressional power. Congress may not limit importation of slaves for at least twenty years (until 1808); suspend the privilege of HABEAS COR-PUS except in emergencies; pass any BILL OF ATTAINDER or ex post facto law (see note at EX POST FACTO); impose any DIRECT TAX except in proportion to population; tax exports; discriminate in regulation between ports of different states; spend money unless pursuant to an APPROPRIATION; or grant any title of nobility.

§ 10. Limitations on state power. States precluded from governmental activity in areas reserved to federal government, such as conduct of foreign policy; from enacting laws deemed inappropriate at any level, such as bills of attainder; and from engaging in certain activities save with the consent of Congress, such as entering into a COMPACT with another state.

## Article II

§ 1. EXECUTIVE power vested in President. Terms of office of President and Vice President; ELECTORAL SYSTEM established for choosing President and Vice President (see also ELECTORAL COLLEGE); qualifications of ELECTORS and time and manner of choosing them; qualifications of President; succession in case of death, disability, or removal; compensation; *oath of office* (see under OATH, and see note at SWEAR).

§ 2. Powers of the President. President as Commander in Chief of armed forces; power to grant PARDONS and REPRIEVES, and by implication to COMMUTE sentences, for federal crimes; power, with ADVICE AND CONSENT of Senate, to make treaties (see TREATY) and to appoint ambassadors, judges of the Supreme Court, and other officers; power to fill vacancies on a temporary basis when Senate is in recess.

§ 3. Additional powers and duties of President. President to report to Congress from time to time on the state of the Union, recommend legislation, call Congress into special session if necessary, receive foreign ambassadors and ministers, COMMISSION officers, and "take Care that the Laws be faithfully executed."

§ 4. Removal of President or other officers for treason, bribery, or other HIGH CRIMES AND MISDEMEANORS.

## Article III

§ 1. JUDICIAL power vested in SUPREME COURT and such INFERIOR COURTS as Congress may establish. Judges to hold office during GOOD BEHAVIOR, that is, for life unless they are guilty of misconduct (see *Article III judge,* under JUDGE). Compensation.

§ 2. JURISDICTION of federal courts specified. It includes *federal question jurisdiction* and *diversity jurisdiction,* jurisdiction over admiralty and maritime cases (see MARITIME), jurisdiction over cases affecting foreign diplomats accredited to the United States, and jurisdiction over controversies between two states and controversies to which the United States is a party. Jurisdiction also extended to controversies between a state and citizens of another state or between a state and a foreign nation or its citizens or subjects (now see Amend. XI). Supreme Court given *original jurisdiction* over cases affecting foreign diplomats and cases in which a state is a party, and *appellate jurisdiction* over other cases. (See all italicized terms under JURISDICTION[1]; see also *limited jurisdiction* at that entry.) Criminal trials (except for petty offenses) to be by jury.

§ 3. TREASON defined; high level of proof of treason required (see note at OVERT ACT); ATTAINDER limited as a penalty for treason by prohibiting any CORRUPTION OF BLOOD extending beyond the lifetime of the person attainted.

## Article IV

§ 1. States required to give FULL FAITH AND CREDIT to each other's laws, records, and proceedings.

§ 2. States required to grant each other's citizens the same PRIVILEGES AND IMMUNITIES that they grant their own citizens, and to honor each other's requests for extradition of persons charged with crime. (See note at EXTRADITION.) Fugitive slaves escaping from slave states to free states required to be returned to their owners.

§ 3. Congress has legislative power over territories, and may admit new states to the Union.

§ 4. Federal government to guarantee every state a REPUBLICAN FORM OF GOVERNMENT, to protect the states from invasion, and upon request to assist them in quelling domestic violence.

## Article V

Constitution may be amended by vote of two-thirds of both houses of Congress and ratification by three-fourths of the states. Alternatively, upon application by the legislatures of two-thirds of the states, Congress must call a convention for proposing amendments, which would likewise take effect upon ratification by three-fourths of the states. The second method has never been used.

## Article VI

Debts and contracts of the United States under the Articles of Confederation to be honored under the Constitution. Federal law to be supreme law of the land (see SUPREMACY; FEDERAL LAW). Federal and state legislators, judges, and executive officers to be bound by oath or affirmation to support the Constitution (see note at OATH OR AFFIRMATION). There shall be no RELIGIOUS TEST for federal office.

## Article VII

Ratification of the Constitution to be by convention in each state; ratification by nine of the thirteen states to be sufficient to establish the Constitution among the ratifying states.

# Summary of Amendments to the Constitution[3]

### Amendment I (1791)

guarantees FREEDOM OF RELIGION, FREEDOM OF SPEECH, FREEDOM OF THE PRESS, FREEDOM OF ASSEMBLY, and the right of PETITION.

### Amendment II (1791)

concerns the "right of the people to keep and bear arms" as an aspect of the maintenance of a well-regulated MILITIA. See note at RIGHT TO BEAR ARMS.

---

[3]The year that each amendment became part of the Constitution is given in parentheses.

### Amendment III (1791)

prohibits the housing of soldiers in private homes without the consent of the owner, except in time of war.

### Amendment IV (1791)

prohibits *unreasonable search and seizure* (see under SEARCH AND SEIZURE), and requires a showing of PROBABLE CAUSE for the issuance of any *search warrant* or *arrest warrant* (see both under WARRANT¹).

### Amendment V (1791)

requires INDICTMENT by a *grand jury* (see under JURY) before any person can be put on trial for a "capital, or otherwise infamous crime" except in military matters (see INFAMOUS CRIME, INFAMOUS PUNISHMENT, and notes at those entries); bans DOUBLE JEOPARDY and compulsory SELF-INCRIMINATION; prohibits the federal government from depriving any person of life, LIBERTY, or PROPERTY without DUE PROCESS of law; and prohibits the TAKING of private property for *public use* (see under USE) without JUST COMPENSATION.

### Amendment VI (1791)

guarantees criminal defendants the right to a speedy and public trial by an impartial jury (see *speedy trial, public trial,* and *jury trial* under TRIAL; see also JURY); also guarantees them the right to be informed of the charges, the right of CONFRONTATION of adverse witnesses, the right to use PROCESS to compel the attendance of witnesses for the defense, and the RIGHT TO COUNSEL.

### Amendment VII (1791)

preserves for litigants in civil damage actions in the federal courts the common law right of *jury trial* (see under TRIAL; see also JURY).

### Amendment VIII (1791)

prohibits criminal courts from requiring *excessive bail* (see under BAIL¹), imposing excessive fines, or inflicting CRUEL AND UNUSUAL PUNISHMENT.

### Amendment IX (1791)

states that the listing of specific rights in the Constitution is not to be interpreted as suggesting that other rights do not exist or are not equally deserving of protection.

### Amendment X (1791)

emphasizes that the federal government has only those powers delegated to it by the Constitution.

### Amendment XI (1795)

withdraws from the jurisdiction of the federal courts cases brought against a state by citizens of another state or by citizens or subjects of a foreign country; leaves intact federal jurisdiction over cases brought by a state against citizen of another state or country, and over controversies between a state and a foreign country.

## Amendment XII (1804)

revised the ELECTORAL SYSTEM to reduce the potential for deadlocks in elections for President and Vice President; established qualifications for Vice President, making them the same as those for President (Art. II, § 1).

## Amendment XIII (1865)

abolished SLAVERY and *involuntary servitude* (see under SERVITUDE), except as punishment for crime.

## Amendment XIV (1868)

§ 1. extended American citizenship to people of color by declaring that all persons born or naturalized in the United States and subject to United States jurisdiction are citizens of the United States and of the state where they reside. This amendment also prohibits the states from depriving any person of life, LIBERTY, or PROPERTY without DUE PROCESS of law, and guarantees all persons EQUAL PROTECTION of the laws. See also INCORPORATION DOCTRINE.

§ 2. revised method of apportionment of seats in the House of Representatives to count former slaves as whole people but reduce a state's representation proportionately to the extent that it keeps them from voting. (This was never enforced.)

§ 3. barred from federal and state office anyone who had actively supported the rebellion after holding an office requiring an oath to support the Constitution.

§ 4. prohibited the United States or any state from paying any debt incurred in aid of the rebellion or any claim for loss or emancipation of a slave.

§ 5. gave Congress power to enact legislation to enforce the amendment.

## Amendment XV (1870)

extended the vote to people of color by prohibiting the denial or abridgment of the right of citizens to vote on account of RACE, COLOR, or previous condition of SERVITUDE.

## Amendment XVI (1913)

empowered Congress to institute the federal INCOME TAX. See note at DIRECT TAX.

## Amendment XVII (1913)

changed the method of electing United States senators from election by state legislatures to direct election by the people.

## Amendment XVIII (1919)

the Prohibition Amendment: prohibited the manufacture, sale, or importation of alcoholic beverages in the United States. Repealed in 1933.

## Amendment XIX (1920)

the Woman Suffrage Amendment: extended the vote to women in all states by prohibiting the denial or abridgment of the right to vote on account of sex.

### Amendment XX (1933)

revised the starting dates for terms of office of the President, Vice President, and members of Congress, and made provision for various contingencies in presidential succession such as the death of a President-elect before taking office.

### Amendment XXI (1933)

repealed the Prohibition Amendment and gave the individual states the power to regulate the distribution and use of intoxicating liquors within their borders.

### Amendment XXII (1951)

prohibits any individual from being elected President more than twice, or more than once if the individual has also acted as President for more than two years of a term to which someone else was elected.

### Amendment XXIII (1961)

extended the right to vote in presidential elections to residents of the District of Columbia. The nation's capital still has no voting representation in Congress, even though the Constitution (Art. I, § 8) gives Congress ultimate legislative control over the District's affairs. A proposed constitutional amendment to allow citizens in the District of Columbia representation and voting rights on an equal footing with citizens of the 50 states was adopted by Congress in 1978, but failed when only sixteen of the necessary thirty-eight states voted to ratify it.

### Amendment XXIV (1964)

abolished the POLL TAX as a requirement for voting in primary and general elections for national office. (See note at POLL TAX.)

### Amendment XXV (1967)

provides a mechanism for filling vacancies in the office of Vice President, provides that the Vice President will serve as Acting President during periods of presidential disability, and specifies procedures for determining whether such a disability exists.

### Amendment XXVI (1971)

lowered the voting age to eighteen.

### Amendment XXVII (1992)

provides that no change voted by Congress in its own compensation may take effect until after the next biennial congressional election. This amendment was originally offered up to the states by Congress with the Bill of Rights in 1789, but most states at the time viewed it as too insignificant to add to the Constitution. Though still of scant practical significance, it became politically popular in the 1980's, and by 1992 enough states had ratified it to make it part of the Constitution.

# Appendix B

## Constitution of the United States of America

Authentic text of the Constitution with amendments to the year 2000. Formatting of article and section headings has been made consistent; otherwise the spelling, capitalization, and punctuation in the body of the Constitution conform to the engrossed copy signed by the framers on September 17, 1787. In citations to the Constitution, the separate paragraphs within a section—unnumbered in the original—are referred to as clauses; the numbers by which they are cited are given here in brackets. Passages shown in *light italic type* are affected by subsequent amendments as indicated in the footnotes. The year of ratification of each amendment is shown in parentheses at the full text of the amendment.

### [PREAMBLE]

**We the People** of the United States, in Order to form a more perfect Union, establish Justice, insure domestic Tranquility, provide for the common defence, promote the general Welfare, and secure the Blessings of Liberty to ourselves and our Posterity, do ordain and establish this Constitution for the United States of America.

### ARTICLE I

***Section 1.*** All legislative Powers herein granted shall be vested in a Congress of the United States, which shall consist of a Senate and House of Representatives.

***Section 2.*** [1] The House of Representatives shall be composed of Members chosen every second Year by the People of the several States, and the Electors in each State shall have the Qualifications requisite for Electors of the most numerous Branch of the State Legislature.

[2] No Person shall be a Representative who shall not have attained to the Age of twenty five Years, and been seven Years a Citizen of the United States, and who shall not, when elected, be an Inhabitant of that State in which he shall be chosen.

[3] Representatives *and direct Taxes*[1] shall be apportioned among the several States which may be included within this Union, according to their respective Numbers, *which shall be determined by adding to the whole Number of free Persons, including those bound to Service for a Term of Years, and excluding Indians not taxed, three fifths of all other Persons.*[2] The actual Enumeration shall be made within three Years after the first Meeting of the Congress of the United States, and within every subsequent Term of ten Years, in such Manner as they shall by Law direct. The number of Representatives shall not exceed one for every thirty Thousand, but each State shall have at Least one Representative; and until such enumeration shall be made, the State of New Hampshire shall be entitled to chuse three, Massachusetts eight, Rhode-Island and Providence Plantations one, Connecticut five, New-York six, New Jersey four, Pennsylvania eight, Delaware one, Maryland six, Virginia ten, North Carolina five, South Carolina five, and Georgia three.

[4] When vacancies happen in the Representation from any State, the Executive Authority thereof shall issue Writs of Election to fill such Vacancies.

[5] The House of Representatives shall chuse their Speaker and other Officers; and shall have the sole Power of Impeachment.

**Section 3.** [1] The Senate of the United States shall be composed of two Senators from each State, *chosen by the Legislature thereof*[3] for six Years; and each Senator shall have one Vote.

[2] Immediately after they shall be assembled in Consequence of the first Election, they shall be divided as equally as may be into three Classes. The Seats of the Senators of the first Class shall be vacated at the Expiration of the second Year, of the second Class at the Expiration of the fourth Year, and of the third Class at the Expiration of the sixth Year, so that one third may be chosen every second Year; *and if Vacancies happen by Resignation, or otherwise, during the Recess of the Legislature of any State, the Executive thereof may make temporary Appointments until the next Meeting of the Legislature, which shall then fill such Vacancies.*[4]

[3] No Person shall be a Senator who shall not have attained to the Age of thirty Years, and been nine Years a Citizen of the United States, and who shall not, when elected, be an Inhabitant of that State for which he shall be chosen.

[4] The Vice President of the United States shall be President of the Senate, but shall have no Vote, unless they be equally divided.

[5] The Senate shall chuse their other Officers, and also a President pro tempore, in the Absence of the Vice President, or when he shall exercise the Office of President of the United States.

---

[1]To the extent that an income tax is regarded as a "direct tax," this is superseded by Amendment XVI, which authorizes imposition of a federal income tax without apportionment among the states by population. (See note at DIRECT TAX in body of dictionary.)

[2]Superseded by Amend. XIII (abolishing category of non-free persons) and Amend. XIV, § 2 (establishing new basis for apportionment).

[3]Superseded by Amend. XVII, cl. 1 (direct election of senators).

[4]Superseded by Amend. XVII, cl. 2 (vacancies filled by special election or gubernatorial appointment).

[6] The Senate shall have the sole Power to try all Impeachments. When sitting for that Purpose, they shall be on Oath or Affirmation. When the President of the United States is tried, the Chief Justice shall preside: And no Person shall be convicted without the Concurrence of two thirds of the Members present.

[7] Judgment in Cases of Impeachment shall not extend further than to removal from Office, and disqualification to hold and enjoy any Office of honor, Trust or Profit under the United States: but the Party convicted shall nevertheless be liable and subject to Indictment, Trial, Judgment and Punishment, according to Law.

**Section 4.** [1] The Times, Places and Manner of holding Elections for Senators and Representatives, shall be prescribed in each State by the Legislature thereof; but the Congress may at any time by Law make or alter such Regulations, except as to the Places of chusing Senators.

[2] The Congress shall assemble at least once in every Year, and such Meeting shall *be on the first Monday in December,*[5] unless they shall by Law appoint a different Day.

**Section 5.** [1] Each House shall be the Judge of the Elections, Returns and Qualifications of its own Members, and a Majority of each shall constitute a Quorum to do Business; but a smaller Number may adjourn from day to day, and may be authorized to compel the Attendance of absent Members, in such Manner, and under such Penalties as each House may provide.

[2] Each House may determine the Rules of its Proceedings, punish its Members for disorderly Behaviour, and, with the Concurrence of two thirds, expel a Member.

[3] Each House shall keep a Journal of its Proceedings, and from time to time publish the same, excepting such Parts as may in their Judgment require Secrecy; and the Yeas and Nays of the Members of either House on any question shall, at the desire of one-fifth of those present, be entered on the journal.

[4] Neither House, during the Session of Congress, shall, without the Consent of the other, adjourn for more than three days, nor to any other Place than that in which the two Houses shall be sitting.

**Section 6.** [1] The Senators and Representatives shall receive a Compensation for their Services, to be ascertained by Law, and paid out of the Treasury of the United States. They shall in all Cases, except Treason, Felony and Breach of the Peace, be privileged from Arrest during their Attendance at the Session of their respective Houses, and in going to and returning from the same; and for any Speech or Debate in either House, they shall not be questioned in any other Place.

[2] No Senator or Representative shall, during the Time for which he was elected, be appointed to any civil Office under the Authority of the United States, which shall have been created, or the Emoluments whereof shall have been encreased during such time; and no Person holding any Office under the United States, shall be a Member of either House during his Continuance in Office.

---

[5]Superseded by Amend. XX, § 2 (annual meeting to begin on January 3).

*Section 7.* [1] All Bills for raising Revenue shall originate in the House of Representatives; but the Senate may propose or concur with Amendments as on other Bills.

[2] Every Bill which shall have passed the House of Representatives and the Senate, shall, before it becomes a Law, be presented to the President of the United States; If he approve he shall sign it, but if not he shall return it, with his Objections to that House in which it shall have originated, who shall enter the Objections at large on their Journal, and proceed to reconsider it. If after such Reconsideration two thirds of that House shall agree to pass the Bill, it shall be sent, together with the Objections, to the other House, by which it shall likewise be reconsidered, and if approved by two thirds of that House, it shall become a Law. But in all such Cases the Votes of both Houses shall be determined by yeas and Nays, and the Names of the Persons voting for and against the Bill shall be entered on the Journal of each House respectively. If any Bill shall not be returned by the President within ten Days (Sundays excepted) after it shall have been presented to him, the Same shall be a Law, in like Manner as if he had signed it, unless the Congress by their Adjournment prevent its Return, in which Case it shall not be a Law.

[3] Every Order, Resolution, or Vote to which the Concurrence of the Senate and House of Representatives may be necessary (except on a question of Adjournment) shall be presented to the President of the United States; and before the Same shall take Effect, shall be approved by him, or being disapproved by him, shall be repassed by two thirds of the Senate and House of Representatives, according to the Rules and Limitations prescribed in the Case of a Bill.

*Section 8.* [1] The Congress shall have Power To lay and collect Taxes, Duties, Imposts and Excises, to pay the Debts and provide for the common Defence and general Welfare of the United States; but all Duties, Imposts and Excises shall be uniform throughout the United States;

[2] To borrow Money on the credit of the United States;

[3] To regulate Commerce with foreign Nations, and among the several States, and with the Indian Tribes;

[4] To establish an uniform Rule of Naturalization, and uniform Laws on the subject of Bankruptcies throughout the United States;

[5] To coin Money, regulate the Value thereof, and of foreign Coin, and fix the Standard of Weights and Measures;

[6] To provide for the Punishment of counterfeiting the Securities and current Coin of the United States;

[7] To establish Post Offices and post Roads;

[8] To promote the Progress of Science and useful Arts, by securing for limited Times to Authors and Inventors the exclusive Right to their respective Writings and Discoveries;

[9] To constitute Tribunals inferior to the supreme Court;

[10] To define and punish Piracies and Felonies committed on the high Seas, and Offenses against the Law of Nations;

[11] To declare War, grant Letters of Marque and Reprisal, and make Rules concerning Captures on Land and Water;

[12] To raise and support Armies, but no Appropriation of Money to that Use shall be for a longer Term than two Years;

[13] To provide and maintain a Navy;

[14] To make Rules for the Government and Regulation of the land and naval Forces;

[15] To provide for calling forth the Militia to execute the Laws of the Union, suppress Insurrections and repel Invasions;

[16] To provide for organizing, arming, and disciplining, the Militia, and for governing such Part of them as may be employed in the Service of the United States, reserving to the States respectively, the Appointment of the Officers, and the Authority of training the Militia according to the discipline prescribed by Congress;

[17] To exercise exclusive Legislation in all Cases whatsoever, over such District (not exceeding ten Miles square) as may, by Cession of particular States, and the Acceptance of Congress, become the Seat of the Government of the United States, and to exercise like Authority over all Places purchased by the Consent of the Legislature of the State in which the Same shall be, for the Erection of Forts, Magazines, Arsenals, dock-Yards and other needful Buildings;— And

[18] To make all Laws which shall be necessary and proper for carrying into Execution the foregoing Powers, and all other Powers vested by this Constitution in the Government of the United States, or in any Department or Officer thereof.

**Section 9.** [1] The Migration or Importation of such Persons as any of the States now existing shall think proper to admit, shall not be prohibited by the Congress prior to the Year one thousand eight hundred and eight, but a Tax or duty may be imposed on such Importation, not exceeding ten dollars for each Person.

[2] The Privilege of the Writ of Habeas Corpus shall not be suspended, unless when in Cases of Rebellion or Invasion the public Safety may require it.

[3] No Bill of Attainder or ex post facto Law shall be passed.

[4] No Capitation, *or other direct,*[6] Tax shall be laid, unless in Proportion to the Census or Enumeration herein before directed to be taken.

[5] No Tax or Duty shall be laid on Articles exported from any State.

[6] No Preference shall be given by any Regulation of Commerce or Revenue to the Ports of one State over those of another: nor shall Vessels bound to, or from, one State, be obliged to enter, clear, or pay Duties in another.

[7] No Money shall be drawn from the Treasury, but in Consequence of Appropriations made by Law; and a regular Statement and Account of the Receipts and Expenditures of all public Money shall be published from time to time.

[8] No Title of Nobility shall be granted by the United States: And no Person holding any Office of Profit or Trust under them, shall, without the Consent of the

---

[6]As to income tax, superseded by Amend. XVI. (See note 1 above).

Congress, accept of any present, Emolument, Office, or Title, of any kind whatever, from any King, Prince, or foreign State.

**Section 10.** [1] No State shall enter into any Treaty, Alliance, or Confederation; grant Letters of Marque and Reprisal; coin Money; emit Bills of Credit; make any Thing but gold and silver Coin a Tender in Payment of Debts; pass any Bill of Attainder, ex post facto Law, or Law impairing the Obligation of Contracts, or grant any Title of Nobility.

[2] No State shall, without the Consent of the Congress, lay any Imposts or Duties on Imports or Exports, except what may be absolutely necessary for executing it's inspection Laws: and the net Produce of all Duties and Imposts, laid by any State on Imports or Exports, shall be for the Use of the Treasury of the United States; and all such Laws shall be subject to the Revision and Controul of the Congress.

[3] No State shall, without the Consent of Congress, lay any Duty of Tonnage, keep Troops, or Ships of War in time of Peace, enter into any Agreement or Compact with another State, or with a foreign Power, or engage in War, unless actually invaded, or in such imminent Danger as will not admit of delay.

## ARTICLE II

**Section 1.** [1] The executive Power shall be vested in a President of the United States of America. He shall hold his Office during the Term of four Years, and, together with the Vice President, chosen for the same Term, be elected, as follows

[2] Each *State*[7] shall appoint, in such Manner as the Legislature thereof may direct, a Number of Electors, equal to the whole Number of Senators and Representatives to which the State may be entitled in the Congress: but no Senator or Representative, or Person holding an Office of Trust or Profit under the United States, shall be appointed an Elector.

[3] *The Electors shall meet in their respective States, and vote by Ballot for two Persons, of whom one at least shall not be an Inhabitant of the same State with themselves. And they shall make a List of all the Persons voted for, and of the Number of Votes for each; which List they shall sign and certify, and transmit sealed to the Seat of the Government of the United States, directed to the President of the Senate. The President of the Senate shall, in the Presence of the Senate and House of Representatives, open all the Certificates, and the Votes shall then be counted. The Person having the greatest Number of Votes shall be the President, if such Number be a Majority of the whole Number of Electors appointed; and if there be more than one who have such Majority, and have an equal Number of Votes, then the House of Representatives shall immediately chuse by Ballot one of them for President; and if no Person have a Majority, then from the five highest on the List the said House shall in like Manner chuse the President. But in chusing the President, the Votes shall be taken by States, the Representation from each State having one Vote; A quo-*

---

[7]Expanded by Amend. XXIII (allowing District of Columbia to participate in elections for President and Vice President).

*rum for this Purpose shall consist of a Member or Members from two thirds of the States, and a Majority of all the States shall be necessary to a Choice. In every Case, after the Choice of the President, the Person having the greatest Number of Votes of the Electors shall be the Vice President. But if there should remain two or more who have equal Votes, the Senate shall chuse from them by Ballot the Vice President.*[8]

[4] The Congress may determine the Time of chusing the Electors, and the Day on which they shall give their Votes; which Day shall be the same throughout the United States.

[5] No Person except a natural born Citizen, or a Citizen of the United States, at the time of the Adoption of this Constitution, shall be eligible to the Office of the President; neither shall any person be eligible to that Office who shall not have attained to the Age of thirty five Years, and been fourteen Years a Resident within the United States.[9]

[6] *In Case of the Removal of the President from Office, or of his Death, Resignation, or Inability to discharge the Powers and Duties of the said Office, the Same shall devolve on the Vice President, and the Congress may by Law provide for the Case of Removal, Death, Resignation or Inability, both of the President and Vice President, declaring what Officer shall then act as President, and such Officer shall act accordingly, until the Disability be removed, or a President shall be elected.*[10]

[7] The President shall, at stated Times, receive for his Services, a Compensation, which shall neither be increased nor diminished during the Period for which he shall have been elected, and he shall not receive within that Period any other Emolument from the United States, or any of them.

[8] Before he enter on the Execution of his Office, he shall take the following Oath or Affirmation:— "I do solemnly swear (or affirm) that I will faithfully execute the Office of President of the United States, and will to the best of my Ability, preserve, protect and defend the Constitution of the United States."

**Section 2.** [1] The President shall be Commander in Chief of the Army and Navy of the United States, and of the Militia of the several States, when called into the actual Service of the United States; he may require the Opinion, in writing, of the principal Officer in each of the executive Departments, upon any Subject relating to the Duties of their respective Offices, and he shall have Power to grant Reprieves and Pardons for Offenses against the United States, except in Cases of Impeachment.

[2] He shall have Power, by and with the Advice and Consent of the Senate, to make Treaties, two thirds of the Senators present concur; and he shall nominate, and by and with the Advice and Consent of the Senate, shall appoint Ambassadors, other public Ministers and Consuls, Judges of the supreme Court, and all other Of-

---

[8]Replaced by Amend. XII (reworking the electoral system).

[9]A further restriction was added by Amend. XXII (disqualifying anyone who has twice been elected President, or who was elected once and also acted as President for more than two years of another's term).

[10]Superseded by Amend. XXV (comprehensive plan for death, disability, or resignation of President or vacancy in office of Vice President).

ficers of the United States, whose Appointments are not herein otherwise for, and which shall be established by Law: but the Congress may by Law vest the Appointment of such inferior Officers, as they think proper, in the President alone, in the Courts of Law, or in the Heads of Departments.

[3] The President shall have Power to fill up all Vacancies that may happen during the Recess of the Senate, by granting Commissions which shall expire at the End of their next Session.

*Section 3.* He shall from time to time give to the Congress Information of the State of the Union, and recommend to their Consideration such Measures as he shall judge necessary and expedient; he may, on extraordinary Occasions, convene both Houses, or either of them, and in Case of Disagreement between them, with Respect to the Time of Adjournment, he may adjourn them to such Time as he shall think proper; he shall receive Ambassadors and other public Ministers; he shall take Care that the Laws be faithfully executed, and shall Commission all the Officers of the United States.

*Section 4.* The President, Vice President and all civil Officers of the United States, shall be removed from Office on Impeachment for, and Conviction of, Treason, Bribery, or other high Crimes and Misdemeanors.

## ARTICLE III

*Section 1.* The judicial Power of the United States, shall be vested in one supreme Court, and in such inferior Courts as the Congress may from time to time ordain and establish. The Judges, both of the supreme and inferior Courts, shall hold their Offices during good Behaviour, and shall, at stated Times, receive for their Services, a Compensation, which shall not be diminished during their Continuance in Office.

*Section 2.* [1] The judicial Power shall extend to all Cases, in Law and Equity, arising under this Constitution, the Laws of the United States, and Treaties made, or which shall be made, under their Authority;— to all Cases affecting Ambassadors, other public Ministers and Consuls;— to all Cases of admiralty and maritime Jurisdiction;— to Controversies to which the United States shall be a Party;— to Controversies between two or more States;— *between a State and Citizens of another State;—*[11] between Citizens of different States;— between Citizens of the same State claiming Lands under Grants of different States, *and between a State, or the Citizens thereof, and foreign States, Citizens or Subjects.*[12]

[2] In all Cases affecting Ambassadors, other public Ministers and Consuls, and those in which a State shall be Party, the supreme Court shall have original Jurisdiction. In all the other Cases before mentioned, the supreme Court shall have ap-

---

[11]Partially repealed by Amend. XI (withdrawing federal jurisdiction from actions against a state by citizens of another state).

[12]Partially repealed by Amend. XI (withdrawing federal jurisdiction from actions against a state by citizens or subjects of foreign states).

pellate Jurisdiction, both as to Law and Fact, with such Exceptions, and under such Regulations as the Congress shall make.

[3] The Trial of all Crimes, except in Cases of Impeachment; shall be by Jury; and such Trial shall be held in the State where the said Crimes shall have been committed; but when not committed within any State, the Trial shall be at such Place or Places as the Congress may by Law have directed.

**Section 3.** [1] Treason against the United States, shall consist only in levying War against them, or in adhering to their Enemies, giving them Aid and Comfort. No Person shall be convicted of Treason unless on the Testimony of two Witnesses to the same overt Act, or on Confession in open Court.

[2] The Congress shall have Power to declare the Punishment of Treason, but no Attainder of Treason shall work Corruption of Blood, or Forfeiture except during the Life of the Person attainted.

## ARTICLE IV

**Section 1.** Full Faith and Credit shall be given in each State to the public Acts, Records, and judicial Proceedings of every other State; And the Congress may by general Laws prescribe the Manner in which such Acts, Records and Proceedings shall be proved, and the Effect thereof.

**Section 2.** [1] The Citizens of each State shall be entitled to all Privileges and Immunities of Citizens in the several States.

[2] A Person charged in any State with Treason, Felony, or other Crime, who shall flee from Justice, and be found in another State, shall on Demand of the executive Authority of the State from which he fled, be delivered up, to be removed to the State having Jurisdiction of the Crime.

[3] *No Person held to Service or Labour in one State, under the Laws thereof, escaping into another, shall, in Consequence of any Law or Regulation therein, be discharged from such Service or Labour, but shall be delivered up on Claim of the Party to whom such Service or Labour may be due.*[13]

**Section 3.** [1] New States may be admitted by the Congress into this Union; but no new State shall be formed or erected within the Jurisdiction of any other State; nor any State be formed by the Junction of two or more States, or Parts of States, without the Consent of the Legislatures of the States concerned as well as of the Congress.

[2] The Congress shall have Power to dispose of and make all needful Rules and Regulations respecting the Territory or other Property belonging to the United States; and nothing in this Constitution shall be so construed as to Prejudice any Claims of the United States, or of any particular State.

---

[13]Implicitly repealed by Amend. XIII (abolishing slavery).

***Section 4.*** The United States shall guarantee to every State in this Union a Republican Form of Government, and shall protect each of them against Invasion; and on Application of the Legislature, or of the Executive (when the Legislature cannot be convened) against domestic Violence.

## ARTICLE V

The Congress, whenever two thirds of both Houses shall deem it necessary, shall propose Amendments to this Constitution, or, on the Application of the Legislatures of two thirds of the several States, shall call a Convention for proposing Amendments, which, in either Case, shall be valid to all Intents and Purposes, as Part of this Constitution, when ratified by the Legislatures of three fourths of the several States, or by Conventions in three fourths thereof, as the one or the other Mode of Ratification may be proposed by the Congress; that no Amendment which may be made prior to the Year One thousand eight hundred and eight shall in any Manner affect the first and fourth Clauses in the Ninth Section of the first Article; and that no State, without its Consent, shall be deprived of its equal Suffrage in the Senate.

## ARTICLE VI

[1] All Debts contracted and Engagements entered into, before the Adoption of this Constitution, shall be as valid against the United States under this Constitution, as under the Confederation.

[2] This Constitution, and the Laws of the United States which shall be made in Pursuance thereof; and all Treaties made, or which shall be made, under the Authority of the United States, shall be the supreme Law of the Land; and the Judges in every State shall be bound thereby, any Thing in the Constitution or Laws of any State to the Contrary notwithstanding.

[3] The Senators and Representatives before mentioned, and the Members of the several State Legislatures, and all executive and judicial Officers, both of the United States and of the several States, shall be bound by Oath or Affirmation, to support this Constitution; but no religious Test shall ever be required as a Qualification to any Office or public Trust under the United States.

## ARTICLE VII

The Ratification of the Conventions of nine States, shall be sufficient for the Establishment of this Constitution between the States so ratifying the Same.

# Articles of Amendment[14]

## AMENDMENT I (1791)

Congress shall make no law respecting an establishment of religion, or prohibiting the free exercise thereof; or abridging the freedom of speech, or of the press; or the right of the people peaceably to assemble, and to petition the Government for a redress of grievances.

## AMENDMENT II (1791)

A well regulated Militia, being necessary to the security of a free State, the right of the people to keep and bear Arms, shall not be infringed.

## AMENDMENT III (1791)

No Soldier shall, in time of peace be quartered in any house, without the consent of the Owner, nor in time of war, but in a manner to be prescribed by law.

## AMENDMENT IV (1791)

The right of the people to be secure in their persons, houses, papers, and effects, against unreasonable searches and seizures, shall not be violated, and no Warrants shall issue, but upon probable cause, supported by Oath or affirmation, and particularly describing the place to be searched, and the persons or things to be seized.

## AMENDMENT V (1791)

No person shall be held to answer for a capital, or otherwise infamous crime, unless on a presentment or indictment of a Grand Jury, except in cases arising in the land or naval forces, or in the Militia, when in actual service in time of War or public danger; nor shall any person be subject for the same offence to be twice put in jeopardy of life or limb; nor shall be compelled in any criminal case to be a witness against himself, nor be deprived of life, liberty, or property, without due process of law; nor shall private property be taken for public use, without just compensation.

---

[14]By tradition dating from 1789, when Congress proposed the Bill of Rights as "ARTICLES in addition to, and Amendment of the Constitution of the United States of America," Congress captions proposed amendments to the Constitution "Article ___." But to avoid confusion, they are conventionally referred to as "Amendment ___," and that convention is followed here.

## AMENDMENT VI (1791)

In all criminal prosecutions, the accused shall enjoy the right to a speedy and public trial, by an impartial jury of the State and district wherein the crime shall have been committed, which district shall have been previously ascertained by law, and to be informed of the nature and cause of the accusation; to be confronted with the witnesses against him; to have compulsory process for obtaining witnesses in his favor, and to have the Assistance of Counsel for his defence.

## AMENDMENT VII (1791)

In suits at common law, where the value in controversy shall exceed twenty dollars, the right of trial by jury shall be preserved, and no fact tried by a jury, shall be otherwise re- examined in any Court of the United States, than according to the rules of the common law.

## AMENDMENT VIII (1791)

Excessive bail shall not be required, nor excessive fines imposed, nor cruel and unusual punishments inflicted.

## AMENDMENT IX (1791)

The enumeration in the Constitution, of certain rights, shall not be construed to deny or disparage others retained by the people.

## AMENDMENT X (1791)

The powers not delegated to the United States by the Constitution, nor prohibited by it to the States, are reserved to the States respectively, or to the people.

## AMENDMENT XI (1795)

The Judicial power of the United States shall not be construed to extend to any suit in law or equity, commenced or prosecuted against one of the United States by Citizens of another State, or by Citizens or Subjects of any Foreign State.

## AMENDMENT XII (1804)

The Electors shall meet in their respective states and vote by ballot for President and Vice-President, one of whom, at least, shall not be an inhabitant of the same state with themselves; they shall name in their ballots the person voted for as President, and in distinct ballots the person voted for as Vice-President, and they shall make distinct lists of all persons voted for as President, and of all persons voted for as Vice-President, and of the number of votes for each, which lists they shall sign and certify, and transmit sealed to the seat of the government of the United States, directed to the President of the Senate;— The President of the Senate shall, in the presence of the Senate and House of Representatives, open all the certificates and the votes shall then be counted;— The person having the greatest number of votes for President, shall be the President, if such number be a majority of the whole number of Electors appointed; and if no person have such majority, then from the persons having the highest numbers not exceeding three on the list of those voted for as President, the House of Representatives shall choose immediately, by ballot, the President. But in choosing the President, the votes shall be taken by states, the representation from each state having one vote; a quorum for this purpose shall consist of a member or members from two-thirds of the states, and a majority of all the states shall be necessary to a choice. *And if the House of Representatives shall not choose a President whenever the right of choice shall devolve upon them, before the fourth day of March next following, then the Vice-President shall act as President, as in the case of the death or other constitutional disability of the President.*—[15] The person having the greatest number of votes as Vice-President, shall be the Vice-President, if such number be a majority of the whole number of Electors appointed, and if no person have a majority, then from the two highest numbers on the list, the Senate shall choose the Vice-President; a quorum for the purpose shall consist of two-thirds of the whole number of Senators, and a majority of the whole number shall be necessary to a choice. But no person constitutionally ineligible to the office of President shall be eligible to that of Vice-President of the United States.

## AMENDMENT XIII (1865)

**Section 1.** Neither slavery nor involuntary servitude, except as a punishment for crime whereof the party shall have been duly convicted, shall exist within the United States, or any place subject to their jurisdiction.

**Section 2.** Congress shall have power to enforce this article by appropriate legislation.

## AMENDMENT XIV (1868)

**Section 1.** All persons born or naturalized in the United States and subject to the jurisdiction thereof, are citizens of the United States and of the State wherein they reside. No State shall make or enforce any law which shall abridge the privileges or immunities of citizens of the United States; nor shall any State deprive any person of life, liberty, or property, without due process of law; nor deny to any person within its jurisdiction the equal protection of the laws.

---

[15]Superseded by Amend. XX, § 1 (setting presidential term to begin on January 20) and § 3 (providing that if a President has not been selected or fails to qualify, then the Vice President elect will act as President only until a President has qualified).

**Section 2.** Representatives shall be apportioned among the several States according to their respective numbers, counting the whole number of persons in each State, excluding Indians not taxed. *But when the right to vote at any election for the choice of electors for President and Vice President of the United States, Representatives in Congress, the Executive and Judicial officers of a State, or the members of the Legislature thereof, is denied to any of the male inhabitants of such State, being twenty-one years of age, and citizens of the United States, or in any way abridged, except for participation in rebellion, or other crime, the basis of representation therein shall be reduced in the proportion which the number of such male citizens shall bear to the whole number of male citizens twenty-one years of age in such State.*[16]

**Section 3.** No person shall be a Senator or Representative in Congress, or elector of President and Vice President, or hold any office, civil or military, under the United States, or under any State, who, having previously taken an oath, as a member of Congress, or as an officer of the United States, or as a member of any State legislature, or as an executive or judicial officer of any State, to support the Constitution of the United States, shall have engaged in insurrection or rebellion against the same, or given aid or comfort to the enemies thereof. But Congress may by a vote of two-thirds of each House, remove such disability.

**Section 4.** The validity of the public debt of the United States, authorized by law, including debts incurred for payment of pensions and bounties for services in suppressing insurrection or rebellion, shall not be questioned. But neither the United States nor any State shall assume or pay any debt or obligation incurred in aid of insurrection or rebellion against the United States, or any claim for the loss or emancipation of any slave; but all such debts, obligations and claims shall be held illegal and void.

**Section 5.** The Congress shall have power to enforce, by appropriate legislation, the provisions of this article.

## AMENDMENT XV (1870)

**Section 1.** The right of citizens of the United States to vote shall not be denied or abridged by the United States or by any State on account of race, color, or previous condition of servitude.

**Section 2.** The Congress shall have power to enforce this article by appropriate legislation.

---

[16]Certain assumptions embodied in this provision were undermined by Amend. XV (prohibiting discrimination in voting rights on the basis of race), Amend. XIX (extending vote to women), Amend. XXIV (banning use of poll tax to inhibit voting in federal elections), and Amend. XXVI (reducing voting age to eighteen). The fundamental assumption, however—that in many states large numbers of black citizens would be systematically and effectively prevented from voting—remained true for a century.

## AMENDMENT XVI (1913)

The Congress shall have power to lay and collect taxes on incomes, from whatever source derived, without apportionment among the several States, and without regard to any census or enumeration.

## AMENDMENT XVII (1913)

[1] The Senate of the United States shall be composed of two Senators from each State, elected by the people thereof, for six years; and each Senator shall have one vote. The electors in each State shall have the qualifications requisite for electors of the most numerous branch of the State legislatures.

[2] When vacancies happen in the representation of any State in the Senate, the executive authority of such State shall issue writs of election to fill such vacancies: Provided, That the legislature of any State may empower the executive thereof to make temporary appointments until the people fill the vacancies by election as the legislature may direct.

[3] This amendment shall not be so construed as to affect the election or term of any Senator chosen before it becomes valid as part of the Constitution.

## AMENDMENT XVIII (1919)[17]

**Section 1.** *After one year from the ratification of this article the manufacture, sale, or transportation of intoxicating liquors within, the importation thereof into, or the exportation thereof from the United States and all territory subject to the jurisdiction thereof for beverage purposes is hereby prohibited.*

**Section 2.** *The Congress and the several States shall have concurrent power to enforce this article by appropriate legislation.*

**Section 3.** *This article shall be inoperative unless it shall have been ratified as an amendment to the Constitution by the legislatures of the several States, as provided in the Constitution, within seven years from the date of the submission hereof to the States by the Congress.*

## AMENDMENT XIX (1920)

[1] The right of citizens of the United States to vote shall not be denied or abridged by the United States or by any State on account of sex.

[2] Congress shall have power to enforce this article by appropriate legislation.

---

[17]Repealed by Amend. XXI, § 1.

## AMENDMENT XX (1933)

*Section 1.* The terms of the President and Vice President shall end at noon on the 20th day of January, and the terms of Senators and Representatives at noon on the 3d day of January, of the years in which such terms would have ended if this article had not been ratified; and the terms of their successors shall then begin.

*Section 2.* The Congress shall assemble at least once in every year, and such meeting shall begin at noon on the 3d day of January, unless they shall by law appoint a different day.

*Section 3.* If, at the time fixed for the beginning of the term of the President, the President elect shall have died, the Vice President elect shall become President. If a President shall not have been chosen before the time fixed for the beginning of his term, or if the President elect shall have failed to qualify, then the Vice President elect shall act as President until a President shall have qualified; and the Congress may by law provide for the case wherein neither a President elect nor a Vice President elect shall have qualified, declaring who shall then act as President, or the manner in which one who is to act shall be selected, and such person shall act accordingly until a President or Vice President shall have qualified.

*Section 4.* The Congress may by law provide for the case of the death of any of the persons from whom the House of Representatives may choose a President whenever the right of choice shall have devolved upon them, and for the case of the death of any of the persons from whom the Senate may choose a Vice President whenever the right of choice shall have devolved upon them.

*Section 5.* Sections 1 and 2 shall take effect on the 15th day of October following the ratification of this article.

*Section 6.* This article shall be inoperative unless it shall have been ratified as an amendment to the Constitution by the legislatures of three-fourths of the several States within seven years from the date of its submission.

## AMENDMENT XXI (1933)

*Section 1.* The eighteenth article of amendment to the Constitution of the United States is hereby repealed.

*Section 2.* The transportation or importation into any State, Territory, or possession of the United States for delivery or use therein of intoxicating liquor in violation of the laws thereof, is hereby prohibited.

*Section 3.* This article shall be inoperative unless it shall have been ratified an amendment to the Constitution by conventions in the several States, provided in the Constitution, within seven years from the date of the submission hereof to the States by the Congress.

## AMENDMENT XXII (1951)

*Section 1.* No person shall be elected to the office of the President more than twice, and no person who has held the office of President, or acted as President, for more than two years of a term to which some other person was elected President shall be elected to the office of the President more than once. But this Article shall not apply to any person holding the office of President when this Article was proposed by the Congress, and shall not prevent any person who may be holding the office of President, or acting as President, during the term within which this Article becomes operative from holding the office of President or acting as President during the remainder of such term.

*Section 2.* This article shall be inoperative unless it shall have been ratified as an amendment to the Constitution by the legislatures of three-fourths of the several States within seven years from the date of its submission to the States by the Congress.

## AMENDMENT XXIII (1961)

*Section 1.* [1] The District constituting the seat of Government of the United States shall appoint in such manner as the Congress may direct:

[2] A number of electors of President and Vice President equal to the whole number of Senators and Representatives in Congress to which the District would be entitled if it were a State, but in no event more than the least populous State; they shall be in addition to those appointed by the States, but they shall be considered, for the purposes of the election of President and Vice President, to be electors appointed by a State; and they shall meet in the District and perform such duties as provided by the twelfth article of amendment.

*Section 2.* The Congress shall have power to enforce this article by appropriate legislation.

## AMENDMENT XXIV (1964)

*Section 1.* The right of citizens of the United States to vote in any primary or other election for President or Vice President, for electors for President or Vice President, or for Senator or Representative in Congress, shall not be denied or abridged by the United States or any State by reason of failure to pay any poll tax or other tax.

*Section 2.* The Congress shall have power to enforce this article by appropriate legislation.

## AMENDMENT XXV (1967)

*Section 1.* In case of the removal of the President from office or of his death or resignation, the Vice President shall become President.

**Section 2.** Whenever there is a vacancy in the office of the Vice President, the President shall nominate a Vice President who shall take office upon confirmation by a majority vote of both Houses of Congress.

**Section 3.** Whenever the President transmits to the President pro tempore of the Senate and the Speaker of the House of Representatives his written declaration that he is unable to discharge the powers and duties of his office, and until he transmits to them a written declaration to the contrary, such powers and duties shall be discharged by the Vice President as Acting President.

**Section 4.** [1] Whenever the Vice President and a majority of either the principal officers of the executive departments or of such other body as Congress may by law provide, transmit to the President pro tempore of the Senate and the Speaker of the House of Representatives their written declaration that the President is unable to discharge the powers and duties of his office, the Vice President shall immediately assume the powers and duties of the office as Acting President.

[2] Thereafter, when the President transmits to the President pro tempore of the Senate and the Speaker of the House of Representatives his written declaration that no inability exists, he shall resume the powers and duties of his office unless the Vice President and a majority of either the principal officers of the executive department or of such other body as Congress may by law provide, transmit within four days to the President pro tempore of the Senate and the Speaker of the House of Representatives their written declaration that the President is unable to discharge the powers and duties of his office. Thereupon Congress shall decide the issue, assembling within forty-eight hours for that purpose if not in session. If the Congress, within twenty-one days after receipt of the latter written declaration, or, if Congress is not in session, within twenty-one days after Congress is required to assemble, determines by two-thirds vote of both Houses that the President is unable to discharge the powers and duties of his office, the Vice President shall continue to discharge the same as Acting President; otherwise, the President shall resume the powers and duties of his office.

## AMENDMENT XXVI (1971)

**Section 1.** The right of citizens of the United States, who are eighteen years of age or older, to vote shall not be denied or abridged by the United States or by any State on account of age.

**Section 2.** The Congress shall have power to enforce this article by appropriate legislation.

## AMENDMENT XXVII (1992)

No law, varying the compensation for the services of the Senators and Representatives, shall take effect, until an election of Representatives shall have intervened.

# Appendix C

## United States Government Agencies

This list shows the principal organizational units and selected subunits of the United States government, arranged hierarchically. Conventional abbreviations, informal names, and other information are given in parentheses following the organization names.

In cases where the officer heading a government body has a title of particular note, that title is given in italics and parentheses under the name of the body, unless it is obvious from the name of the organizational unit itself (as in, for example, the Office of the United States Trade Representative). In most other cases, the heads of government bodies are referred to simply as the Chairman, Director, Commissioner, or Administrator of the unit in question, except that high-level subdivisions of executive departments are usually headed by an Under Secretary or Assistant Secretary of the department.

Certain courts established by Congress under Article I of the Constitution are treated here as part of the judicial branch of government because they carry out an essentially judicial function, even though they technically do not exercise what the Constitution calls "the judicial Power of the United States" as do the courts established under Article III. (See *Article I court* and *Article III court* under COURT in the body of the dictionary.) Internet addresses are shown for major organizational units.

## LEGISLATIVE BRANCH

### The Congress of the United States

#### *The Senate*
*http://www.senate.gov/*
*(Head: Majority Leader. Presiding Officer: President of the Senate, a function of the Vice President of the United States)*

Committee on Agriculture, Nutrition, and Forestry

Committee on Appropriations

Committee on Armed Services

Committee on Banking, Housing, and Urban Affairs

Committee on the Budget

Committee on Commerce, Science, and Transportation

Committee on Energy and Natural Resources

Committee on Environment and Public Works

Committee on Finance

Committee on Foreign Relations

Committee on Governmental Affairs

Committee on Health, Education, Labor, and Pensions

Committee on Indian Affairs

Committee on the Judiciary

Committee on Rules and Administration

Committee on Small Business

Committee on Veterans' Affairs

Select Committee on Ethics

Select Committee on Intelligence

Special Committee on Aging

### The House of Representatives
*http://www.house.gov/*
*(Speaker)*

Committee on Agriculture

Committee on Appropriations

Committee on Armed Services

Committee on Banking and Financial Services

Committee on the Budget

Committee on Commerce

Committee on Education and the Workforce

Committee on Government Reform

Committee on House Administration

Committee on International Relations

Committee on the Judiciary

Committee on Resources

Committee on Rules

Committee on Science

Committee on Small Business

Committee on Standards of Official Conduct

Committee on Transportation and Infrastructure

Committee on Veterans' Affairs

Committee on Ways and Means

Permanent Select Committee on Intelligence

### Joint Committees

Joint Committee on the Library

Joint Committee on Printing

Joint Committee on Taxation

Joint Economic Committee (JEC)

## Legislative Branch Agencies

Architect of the Capitol

Congressional Budget Office (CBO)

General Accounting Office (GAO)
*(Comptroller General of the United States)*

Government Printing Office (GPO)
*http://www.gpo.gov/*
*(Public Printer)*
   Government Printing Office Style Board
   Superintendent of Documents
      Documents Sales Service
      Office of Electronic Information Dissemination

Library of Congress (LC)
*http://www.loc.gov/*
*(Librarian of Congress)*
   Congressional Research Service (CRS)
   United States Copyright Office
   Law Library
   Library Services

United States Botanic Garden

# JUDICIAL BRANCH

## Courts

The Supreme Court of the United States
*http://www.supremecourtus.gov*
*(Chief Justice of the United States)*

United States Courts of Appeals
   (One for each of twelve geographic regions: the First Circuit through the
   Eleventh Circuit plus the District of Columbia Circuit)

United States Court of Appeals for the Federal Circuit

United States District Courts
   (One for each of 91 geographic districts: from one to four in each state, plus
   one for the District of Columbia and one for Puerto Rico. Each such court
   includes a unit called the Bankruptcy Court for that district.)

Judicial Panel on Multidistrict Litigation

Territorial Courts
   (One District Court each for Guam, the Virgin Islands, and the Northern
   Mariana Islands)

United States Court of Federal Claims (Fed. Cl.)

United States Court of International Trade (Ct. Int'l Trade)

United States Tax Court (T.C.)

United States Court of Appeals for the Armed Forces (C.A.A.F.)

United States Court of Veterans Appeals (Vet. App.)

District of Columbia Court of Appeals

Superior Court of the District of Columbia

## Judicial Branch Agencies

Administrative Office of the United States Courts
*http://www.uscourts.gov/*

Federal Judicial Center (FJC)
*http://www.fjc.gov/*

United States Sentencing Commission (USSC)
*http://www.ussc.gov/*

# EXECUTIVE BRANCH

## The President of the United States

The Cabinet

## The Vice President of the United States

## Executive Office of the President
*http://www.whitehouse.gov/WH/EOP/html/EOP_org.html*

The White House Office

Office of the Vice President of the United States

Council of Economic Advisers (CEA)

Council on Environmental Quality (CEQ)

National Security Council (NSC)
*(The President of the United States)*

Office of Administration

Office of Management and Budget (OMB)

Office of National Drug Control Policy (ONDCP)

Office of Policy Development
   Domestic Policy Council
   National Economic Council

Office of Science and Technology Policy (OSTP)

Office of the United States Trade Representative (USTR)

## Executive Departments

### Department of Agriculture (USDA)
*http://www.usda.gov/*
*(Secretary of Agriculture)*

Farm and Foreign Agricultural Services mission
   Commodity Credit Corporation (CCC)
   Farm Service Agency (FSA)
   Foreign Agricultural Service (FAS)
   Risk Management Agency

Food, Nutrition, and Consumer Services (FNCS) mission
   Center for Nutrition Policy and Promotion (CNPP)
   Food and Nutrition Service (FNS)

Food Safety mission
   Food Safety and Inspection Service (FSIS)

Marketing and Regulatory Programs mission
   Agricultural Marketing Service (AMS)
   Animal and Plant Health Inspection Service (APHIS)
   Grain Inspection, Packers, and Stockyards Administration (GIPSA)

Natural Resources and Environment mission
   Forest Service
   Natural Resources Conservation Service (NRCS)

Research, Education, and Economics mission
  Agricultural Research Service (ARS)
  Cooperative State Research, Education, and Extension Service (CSREES)
  Economic Research Service (ERS)
  National Agricultural Statistics Service (NASS)

Rural Development mission
  Rural Business-Cooperative Service (RBS)
  Rural Housing Service (RHS)
  Rural Utilities Service (RUS)

Alternative Agricultural Research and Commercialization (AARC)
    Corporation

## Department of Commerce (DOC)
*http://www.doc.gov/*
*(Secretary of Commerce)*

Bureau of Export Administration (BXA)

Economic Development Administration (EDA)

Economics and Statistics Administration (ESA)

Bureau of the Census

Bureau of Economic Analysis (BEA)

International Trade Administration (ITA)

Minority Business Development Agency (MBDA)

National Oceanic and Atmospheric Administration (NOAA)
  National Marine Fisheries Service (NMFS)
  National Weather Service (NWS)

National Telecommunications and Information Administration (NTIA)

Patent and Trademark Office (PTO)
*(Commissioner of Patents and Trademarks)*

Technology Administration
  Office of Technology Policy (OTP)
  National Institute of Standards and Technology (NIST)
  National Technical Information Service (NTIS)

## Department of Defense (DoD)
*http://www.defenselink.mil/*
*(Secretary of Defense)*

Joint Chiefs of Staff (JCS)
*(Chairman of the Joint Chiefs of Staff)*

Department of the Air Force
*(Secretary of the Air Force)*

    United States Air Force (USAF)
    *(Chief of Staff of the Air Force)*

Department of the Army
*(Secretary of the Army)*

    United States Army (USA)
    *(Chief of Staff of the Army)*

Department of the Navy
*(Secretary of the Navy)*

    United States Marine Corps (USMC)
    *(Commandant of the Marine Corps)*

    United States Navy (USN)
    *(Chief of Naval Operations)*

    United States Coast Guard (USCG) (Normally a service in the Department of Transportation; operates as a service in the Navy in time of war or at the President's direction.)
    *(Commandant)*

Other Defense Agencies, Offices, and Activities
    Ballistic Missile Defense Organization (BMDO)
    Department of Defense Education Activity (DODEA)
    Defense Advanced Research Projects Agency (DARPA)
    Defense Intelligence Agency (DIA)
    Defense Prisoner of War/Missing Personnel Office (DPMO)
    Defense Security Assistance Agency
    Defense Special Weapons Agency (DSWA)
    Defense Technology Security Administration (DTSA)
    National Imagery and Mapping Agency (NIMA)
    National Security Agency/Central Security Service (NSA/CSS)
    Nuclear and Chemical and Biological (NCB) Defense Programs
    Office of Civilian Health and Medical Program of the Uniformed Services (OCHAMPUS)

### Department of Education (ED)
*http://www.ed.gov/*
*(Secretary of Education)*

    Office for Civil Rights (OCR)

    Office of Bilingual Education and Minority Languages Services (OBEMLA)

    Office of Educational Research and Improvement (OERI)

    Office of Elementary and Secondary Education (OESE)

    Office of Postsecondary Education (OPE)

    Office of Special Education and Rehabilitative Services (OSERS)

    Office of Vocational and Adult Education (OVAE)

## Department of Energy (DOE)
*http://www.doe.gov/*
*(Secretary of Energy)*

Energy Programs
Energy Information Administration
Office of Energy Efficiency and Renewable Energy
Office of Fossil Energy

Environmental Management Programs
Office of Civilian Radioactive Waste Management
Office of Environmental Management
Office of Fissile Materials Disposition

National Security Programs
Office of Defense Programs
Office of Nonproliferation and National Security

Science and Technology Programs
Office of Energy Research
Office of Nuclear Energy,Science, and Technology

Federal Energy Regulatory Commission (FERC)


## Department of Health and Human Services (HHS)
*http://www.dhhs.gov/*
*(Secretary of Health and Human Services)*

Administration for Children and Families (ACF)
Administration for Native Americans (ANA)
Administration on Children, Youth, and Families (ACYF)
Administration on Developmental Disabilities (ADD)
Office of Child Support Enforcement (CSE)
Office of Community Services
Office of Family Assistance (OFA)
Office of Refugee Resettlement (ORR)

Administration on Aging (AOA)

Agency for Health Care Policy and Research (AHCPR)

Agency for Toxic Substances and Disease Registry (ATSDR)

Centers for Disease Control and Prevention (CDC)
National Center for Chronic Disease Prevention and Health Promotion
(NCCDPHP)
National Center for Environmental Health (NCEH)
National Center for Health Statistics (NCHS)
National Center for HIV, STD, and TB Prevention (NCHSTP)
National Center for Infectious Diseases (NCID)

National Center for Injury Prevention and Control (NCIPC)
National Institute for Occupational Safety and Health (NIOSH)

Food and Drug Administration (FDA)

Health Care Financing Administration (HCFA)

Health Resources and Services Administration (HRSA)
Bureau of Health Professions (BHPr)
Bureau of Health Resources Development
Bureau of Primary Health Care (BPHC)
HIV/AIDS Bureau (HAB)
Maternal and Child Health Bureau (MCHB)

Indian Health Service (IHS)

Public Health Service (PHS)
Office of the Surgeon General
Agency for Health Care Policy and Research (AHCPR)
Bureau of Medical Services
Bureau of State Services
National Institutes of Health (NIH)
National Cancer Institute (NCI)
National Eye Institute (NEI)
National Heart, Lung, and Blood Institute (NHLBI)
National Human Genome Research Institute (NHGRI)
National Institute of Allergy and Infectious Diseases (NIAID)
National Institute of Arthritis and Musculoskeletal and Skin Diseases (NIAMS)
National Institute of Child Health and Human Development (NICHD)
National Institute of Dental Research (NIDR)
National Institute of Diabetes and Digestive and Kidney Diseases (NIDDK)
National Institute of Environmental Health Sciences (NIEHS)
National Institute of General Medical Sciences (NIGMS)
National Institute of Mental Health (NIMH)
National Institute of Neurological Disorders and Stroke (NINDS)
National Institute of Nursing Research
National Institute on Aging (NIA)
National Institute on Alcohol Abuse and Alcoholism (NIAAA)
National Institute on Deafness and Other Communication Disorders (NIDCD)
National Institute on Drug Abuse (NIDA)
Office of AIDS Research

Substance Abuse and Mental Health Services Administration (SAMHSA)
Center for Mental Health Services (CMHS)
Center for Substance Abuse Prevention (CSAP)
Center for Substance Abuse Treatment (CSAT)

### Department of Housing and Urban Development (HUD)
*http://www.hud.gov/*
*(Secretary of Housing and Urban Development)*

Office of Community Planning and Development

Office of Fair Housing and Equal Opportunity

Office of Federal Housing Enterprise Oversight

Office of Housing and Federal Housing Administration (FHA)
*(Federal Housing Commissioner)*

Office of Lead Hazard Control

Office of Policy Development and Research

Office of Public and Indian Housing

Government National Mortgage Association (GNMA or Ginnie Mae)

### Department of the Interior (DOI)
*http://doi.gov/*
*(Secretary of the Interior)*

Bureau of Indian Affairs (BIA)

Bureau of Land Management (BLM)

Bureau of Reclamation

Minerals Management Service (MMS)

National Park Service

Office of Insular Affairs

Office of Surface Mining Reclamation and Enforcement (OSM)

United States Fish and Wildlife Service

United States Geological Survey (USGS)

### Department of Justice (DOJ)
*http://www.usdoj.gov/*
*(Attorney General of the United States)*

Offices
  Asset Forfeiture Management Staff (AFMS)
  Community Relations Service
  Executive Office for United States Trustees
  Executive Office for United States Attorneys (EOUSA)
  Office of Information and Privacy
  Office of Intelligence Policy and Review
  Office of Legal Counsel
  Office of Professional Responsibility
  Office of the Pardon Attorney

Office of the Solicitor General
Office of Tribal Justice (OTJ)

Divisions
  Antitrust Division
  Civil Division
    Appellate Staff
    Commercial Litigation Branch
    Federal Programs Branch
    Office of Consumer Litigation
    Office of Immigration Litigation
    Torts Branch
  Civil Rights Division
    Appellate Section
    Coordination and Review Section
    Criminal Section
    Disability Rights Section
    Educational Opportunities Section
    Employment Litigation Section
    Housing and Civil Enforcement Section
    Office of Special Counsel for Immigration Related Unfair Employment
        Practices
    Special Litigation Section
    Voting Section
  Criminal Division
    Appellate Section
    Asset Forfeiture/Money Laundering Section
    Child Exploitation and Obscenity Section (CEOS)
    Computer Crime and Intellectual Property Section (CCIPS)
    Executive Office for the Organized Crime Drug Enforcement Task Force
        (Executive Office for OCDETF)
    Fraud Section
    Internal Security Section
    International Criminal Investigative Training Assistance Program
    Narcotic and Dangerous Drug Section (NDDS)
    Office of Enforcement Operations
    Office of International Affairs
    Office of Policy and Legislation (OPL)
    Office of Professional Development and Training
    Office of Special Investigations
    Organized Crime and Racketeering Section
    Public Integrity Section
    Terrorism and Violent Crime Section
  Environment and Natural Resources Division
    Appellate Section
    Environmental Crimes Section
    Environmental Defense Section
    Environmental Enforcement Section

General Litigation Section
Indian Resources Section
Land Acquisition Section
Policy, Legislation, and Special Litigation Section
Wildlife and Marine Resources Section
Tax Division

Bureaus
Bureau of Prisons
Drug Enforcement Administration (DEA)
Federal Bureau of Investigation (FBI)
Immigration and Naturalization Service (INS)
Office of Justice Programs (OJP)
Bureau of Justice Assistance (BJA)
Bureau of Justice Statistics (BJS)
Corrections Program Office (CPO)
Drug Court Program Office (DCPO)
National Institute of Justice (NIJ)
Office for Victims of Crime (OVC)
Office of Juvenile Justice and Delinquency Prevention (OJJDP)
Missing Children's Program
Violence Against Women Office (VAWO)
United States Marshals Service
United States National Central Bureau—International Criminal Police
Organization (USNCB or Interpol—Washington)

Boards
Executive Office for Immigration Review
Board of Immigration Appeals
Foreign Claims Settlement Commission of the United States
Office of Community Oriented Policing Services (COPS)
United States Parole Commission

### Department of Labor (DOL)
*http://www.dol.gov/*
*(Secretary of Labor)*

Office of the Deputy Secretary of Labor
Administrative Review Board
Benefits Review Board (BRB)
Board of Service Contract Appeals
Bureau of International Labor Affairs (ILAB)
Employees' Compensation Appeals Board (ECAB)
Wage Appeals Board
Women's Bureau (WB)

Bureau of Labor Statistics (BLS)

Employment and Training Administration (ETA)
Bureau of Apprenticeship and Training
Federal Unemployment Insurance Service

Office of Job Corps Programs
Office of Job Training Programs
Office of Regional Management
Office of Trade Adjustment Assistance
Office of Work-Based Learning
Office of Worker Retraining and Adjustment Programs
Senior Community Service Employment Program (SCSEP)
United States Employment Service (USES)

Employment Standards Administration (ESA)
Office of Federal Contract Compliance Programs (OFCCP)
Office of Labor-Management Standards (OLMS)
Office of Workers' Compensation Programs (OWCP)
Wage and Hour Division (WHD)

Mine Safety and Health Administration (MSHA)

Occupational Safety and Health Administration (OSHA)

Pension and Welfare Benefits Administration (PWBA)

Veterans' Employment and Training Service (VETS)

## Department of State (State)
*http://www.state.gov/*
*(Secretary of State)*

Bureau of Consular Affairs

Bureau of Democracy, Human Rights, and Labor

Bureau of Economic and Business Affairs

Bureau of Intelligence and Research

Bureau of International Communications and Information Policy

Bureau of International Narcotics and Law Enforcement Affairs

Bureau of International Organization Affairs

Bureau of Oceans and International Environmental and Scientific Affairs

Bureau of Political-Military Affairs

Bureau of Population, Refugees, and Migration

Foreign Service Institute

United States Mission to the United Nations
*(United States Representative to the United Nations)*

## Department of Transportation (DOT)
*http://www.dot.gov/*
*(Secretary of Transportation)*

Bureau of Transportation Statistics (BTS)

Federal Aviation Administration (FAA)

Federal Highway Administration (FHWA)

Federal Railroad Administration (FRA)

Federal Transit Administration (FTA)

Maritime Administration (MARAD)

National Highway Traffic Safety Administration (NHTSA)

Research and Special Programs Administration (RSPA)
Office of Emergency Transportation
Office of Hazardous Materials Safety
Office of Pipeline Safety
Transportation Safety Institute

Saint Lawrence Seaway Development Corporation (SLSDC)

Surface Transportation Board (STB)

United States Coast Guard (USCG) (Operates as a service in the Navy in time of war or at the President's direction.)
*(Commandant)*

### Department of the Treasury (Treasury)
*http://www.ustreas.gov/*
*(Secretary of the Treasury)*

Bureau of Alcohol, Tobacco, and Firearms (ATF)

Bureau of Engraving and Printing (BEP)

Bureau of the Public Debt (BPD)

Federal Law Enforcement Training Center (FLETC)

Financial Crimes Enforcement Network (FinCEN)

Financial Management Service (FMS)

Internal Revenue Service (IRS)

Office of the Comptroller of the Currency (OCC)

Office of the Treasurer of the United States

Office of Thrift Supervision (OTS)

United States Customs Service (USCS)

United States Mint (USM)

United States Secret Service (USSS)

### Department of Veterans Affairs (VA)
*http://www.va.gov/*
*(Secretary of Veterans Affairs)*

Board of Veterans' Appeals (BVA)

National Cemetery System (NCS)

Veterans Benefits Administration (VBA)

Veterans Health Administration

## Selected Independent Establishments, Government Corporations, and Interagency Programs

African Development Foundation

Central Intelligence Agency (CIA)
*(Director of Central Intelligence)*

Commodity Futures Trading Commission (CFTC)

Consumer Product Safety Commission (CPSC)

Corporation for National and Community Service
    AmeriCorps
        AmeriCorps*National Civilian Community Corps (AmeriCorps*NCCC)
        AmeriCorps*State and National
        AmeriCorps*VISTA (Volunteers in Service to America)
    Learn and Serve America
    National Senior Service Corps (Senior Corps)

Defense Nuclear Facilities Safety Board (DNFSB)

Environmental Protection Agency (EPA)
*http://www.epa.gov/*
    Air and Radiation
    Enforcement and Compliance Assurance
    International Activities
    Policy, Planning, and Evaluation
    Prevention, Pesticides, and Toxic Substances
    Research and Development
    Solid Waste and Emergency Response
    Water

Equal Employment Opportunity Commission (EEOC)
*http://www.eeoc.gov/*

Export-Import Bank of the United States (Ex-Im Bank)

Farm Credit Administration (FCA)

Federal Communications Commission (FCC)
*http://www.fcc.gov/*
    Cable Services Bureau
    Common Carrier Bureau
    Compliance and Information Bureau
    International Bureau
    Mass Media Bureau
    Office of Engineering and Technology
    Wireless Telecommunications Bureau

Federal Deposit Insurance Corporation (FDIC)

Federal Election Commission (FEC)

Federal Emergency Management Agency (FEMA)

Federal Housing Finance Board

Federal Labor Relations Authority (FLRA)

Federal Maritime Commission (FMC)

Federal Mediation and Conciliation Service (FMCS)

Federal Mine Safety and Health Review Commission

Federal Prison Industries (UNICOR)

Federal Reserve System (the Fed)
*http://www.federalreserve.gov/*
   Board of Governors of the Federal Reserve System (the Fed)
   Federal Reserve Banks
     (one in each of twelve geographic regions, with branch banks in 25
     additional cities)
   Consumer Advisory Council
   Federal Advisory Council
   Federal Open Market Committee
   Thrift Institutions Advisory Council

Federal Retirement Thrift Investment Board

Federal Trade Commission (FTC)
*http://www.ftc.gov/*
   Bureau of Competition
   Bureau of Consumer Protection
   Bureau of Economics

General Services Administration (GSA)

Inter-American Foundation

Merit Systems Protection Board (MSPB)

National Aeronautics and Space Administration (NASA)

National Archives and Records Administration (NARA)

National Capital Planning Commission (NCPC)

National Credit Union Administration (NCUA)

National Foundation on the Arts and the Humanities
   Institute of Museum and Library Services (IMLS)
   National Endowment for the Arts (NEA)
   National Endowment for the Humanities (NEH)

National Institute for Literacy

National Labor Relations Board (NLRB)

National Mediation Board (NMB)

National Railroad Passenger Corporation (Amtrak)

National Science Foundation (NSF)

National Transportation Safety Board (NTSB)

Nuclear Regulatory Commission (NRC)

Occupational Safety and Health Review Commission (OSHRC)

Office of Government Ethics (OGE)

Office of Personnel Management (OPM)

Office of Special Counsel (OSC)

Organized Crime Drug Enforcement Task Force (OCDETF)

Peace Corps

Pension Benefit Guaranty Corporation (PBGC)

Postal Rate Commission (PRC)

Railroad Retirement Board (RRB)

Securities and Exchange Commission (SEC)
*http://www.sec.gov/*
  Division of Corporation Finance
  Division of Enforcement
  Division of Investment Management
  Division of Market Regulation
  Office of Compliance Inspections and Examinations
  Office of Municipal Securities
  Office of Investor Education and Assistance

Selective Service System (SSS)

Small Business Administration (SBA)
*http://www.sba.gov/*
  Office of Advocacy
  Office of Business Initiatives
  Office of Financial Assistance
  Office of Government Contracting
  Office of International Trade
  Office of Minority Enterprise Development
  Office of Native American Affairs
  Office of Small Business Development Centers
  Office of Surety Guarantees
  Office of Technology
  Office of Veterans' Affairs (OVA)
  Office of Women's Business Ownership (OWBO)

Social Security Administration (SSA)

Tennessee Valley Authority (TVA)

Trade and Development Agency (TDA)

United States Arms Control and Disarmament Agency (ACDA)

United States Commission on Civil Rights (USCCR)

United States Information Agency (USIA)
   Bureau of Educational and Cultural Affairs
   Bureau of Information
   International Broadcasting Bureau

United States International Development Cooperation Agency (IDCA)
   Agency for International Development (USAID or AID)
   Overseas Private Investment Corporation (OPIC)

United States International Trade Commission (USITC)

United States Postal Service (USPS)

## Selected Quasi-Official and Private Agencies (established by Congress to fulfill a public purpose, but not officially part of the government)

Fannie Mae (the name under which the Federal National Mortgage Association does business)

Freddie Mac (the name under which the Federal Home Loan Mortgage Corporation does business)

Legal Services Corporation (LSC)
*http://www.lsc.gov/*

Sallie Mae (the name under which the Student Loan Marketing Association and affiliated companies do business)

Securities Investor Protection Corporation (SIPC)

Smithsonian Institution

State Justice Institute
*http://www.statejustice.org/*

United States Institute for Peace

# Appendix D

## International Organizations

This is a selected list of the principal multinational bodies through which governments and businesses of the world seek to cooperate on matters of international concern. First is the United Nations with its six principal organs and selected subsidiary bodies, its specialized agencies, and a selection of related organizations. Second is a listing of the principal organizational components of the European Union, and selected other consultative and specialized EU agencies. Third is a selection of other major international organizations, with emphasis on organizations in which the United States participates.

Many international bodies have official names in more than one language; the English forms are given here. Conventional abbreviations, short forms of names, and other information are given in parentheses following the organization names. Occasional abbreviations here or elsewhere that do not seem a good match for the names are usually derived from an earlier name for the organization or a non-English form of the name.

## UNITED NATIONS (U.N.)

*http://www.un.org/*

### General Assembly

#### *Main Committees*

Disarmament and International Security Committee (First Committee)

Economic and Financial Committee (Second Committee)

Social, Humanitarian and Cultural Committee (Third Committee)

Special Political and Decolonization Committee (Fourth Committee)

Administrative and Budgetary Committee (Fifth Committee)

Legal Committee (Sixth Committee)

### *Other Bodies of the General Assembly*

Advisory Board on Disarmament Matters

Advisory Committee of the United Nations Programme of Assistance in the Teaching, Study, Dissemination and Wider Appreciation of International Law

Committee on Contributions

Committee on Relations with the Host Country

Committee on the Peaceful Uses of Outer Space (COPUOS)

Conference on Disarmament (CD)

High-Level Open-Ended Working Group on the Financial Situation of the United Nations

Informal Open-Ended Working Group on an Agenda for Peace

International Civil Service Commission (ICSC)

International Criminal Court Preparatory Commission

International Law Commission (ILC)

Special Committee on Peace-keeping Operations

United Nations Commission on International Trade Law (UNCITRAL)

United Nations Disarmament Commission (UNDC)

United Nations Scientific Committee on the Effects of Atomic Radiation (UNSCEAR)

## Security Council

### *Committees*

Committee on Admission of New Members

Military Staff Committee

### *Peacekeeping and Security Operations*

United Nations Iraq-Kuwait Observation Mission (UNIKOM)

United Nations Military Observer Group in India and Pakistan (UNMOGIP)

United Nations Mission in Bosnia and Herzegovina (UNMIBH)

United Nations Disengagement Observer Force [in the Golan Heights] (UNDOF)

United Nations Interim Administration Mission in Kosovo (UNMIK)

United Nations Interim Force in Lebanon (UNIFIL)

United Nations Iraq-Kuwait Observation Mission (UNIKOM)

United Nations Military Observer Group in India and Pakistan (UNMOGIP)

United Nations Mission for the Referendum in Western Sahara (MINURSO)

United Nations Mission in Bosnia and Herzegovina (UNMIBH)

United Nations Mission in Sierra Leone (UNAMSIL)

United Nations Mission of Observers in Prevlaka (UNMOP)

United Nations Mission of Observers in Tajikistan (UNMOT)

United Nations Monitoring, Verification and Inspection Commission [for Iraq] (UNMOVIC)

United Nations Observer Mission in Georgia (UNOMIG)

United Nations Organization Mission in the Democratic Republic of the Congo (MONUC)

United Nations Peacekeeping Force in Cyprus (UNFICYP)

United Nations Transitional Administration in East Timor (UNTAET)

United Nations Truce Supervision Organization [in the Middle East] (UNTSO)

### *Special Tribunals for the Prosecution of Persons Responsible for Genocide and Other Serious Violations of International Humanitarian Law*

International Criminal Tribunal for Rwanda (ICTR)

International Criminal Tribunal for the Former Yugoslavia (ICTY)

## Economic and Social Council (ECOSOC)

Commission for Social Development (CSD)

Commission on Crime Prevention and Criminal Justice

Commission on Human Rights (CHR)

Commission on Human Settlements (Habitat)

Commission on Narcotic Drugs (CND)

Commission on Population and Development

Commission on Science and Technology for Development

Commission on Sustainable Development (CSD)

Commission on the Status of Women (CSW)

Committee on Economic, Social and Cultural Rights

Committee on Non-Governmental Organizations

Inter-Agency Committee on Women

Statistical Commission

**Trusteeship Council** (Inactive—no territories left under United Nations trusteeship)

**International Court of Justice (I.C.J.)**
*http://www.icj-cij.org/*

**Secretariat**

Executive Office of the Secretary-General

Administrative Committee on Coordination (ACC)

Department for Development Support and Management Services

Department for Economic and Social Information and Policy Analysis

Department for Policy Coordination and Sustainable Development

Department of Humanitarian Affairs

Department of Peace-keeping Operations

Department of Political Affairs

Office of Legal Affairs

**Specialized Agencies of the United Nations** (United States a member of each except for the two noted)

Food and Agriculture Organization (FAO)

International Civil Aviation Organization (ICAO)

International Fund for Agricultural Development (IFAD)

International Labour Organization (ILO)

International Maritime Organization (IMO)

International Monetary Fund (IMF)

International Telecommunication Union (ITU)

United Nations Educational, Scientific and Cultural Organization (UNESCO) (United States not a member)

United Nations Industrial Development Organization (UNIDO) (United States no longer a member)

Universal Postal Union (UPU)

World Bank Group
International Bank for Reconstruction and Development (IBRD or World Bank)
International Centre for Settlement of Investment Disputes (ICSID)
International Development Association (IDA)
International Finance Corporation (IFC)
Multilateral Investment Guarantee Agency (MIGA)

World Health Organization (WHO)

World Intellectual Property Organization (WIPO)

World Meteorological Organization (WMO)

## Other United Nations–Related Organizations (United States a member or participant in almost all)

Commission on the Limits of the Continental Shelf

Committee Against Torture (CAT)

Committee on the Elimination of Discrimination Against Women (CEDAW)

Committee on the Elimination of Racial Discrimination (CERD)

Committee on the Rights of the Child

Convention on Biological Diversity (CBD)

Convention on International Trade in Endangered Species of Wild Fauna and Flora (CITES)

Convention on the Conservation of Migratory Species of Wild Animals (CMS or Bonn Convention)

Global Environment Facility (GEF)

Human Rights Committee

Intergovernmental Panel on Climate Change (IPCC)

International Atomic Energy Agency (IAEA)

International Consultative Group on Food Irradiation (ICGFI)

International Narcotics Control Board (INCB)

International Research and Training Institute for the Advancement of Women (ISTRAW)

International Seabed Authority

International Trade Centre UNCTAD/WTO (ITC)

International Tribunal on the Law of the Sea

International Union for the Protection of New Varieties of Plants (UPOV)

Office of the United Nations High Commissioner for Human Rights

Office of the United Nations High Commissioner for Refugees (UNHCR)

Ozone Secretariat

United Nations Capital Development Fund (UNCDF)

United Nations Children's Fund (UNICEF)

United Nations Conference on Trade and Development (UNCTAD)

United Nations Development Fund for Women (UNIFEM)

United Nations Development Programme (UNDP)

United Nations Environment Programme (UNEP)

United Nations Framework Convention on Climate Change (UNFCCC)

United Nations Institute for Disarmament Research (UNIDIR)

United Nations Institute for Training and Research (UNITAR)

United Nations International Drug Control Programme (UNDCP)

United Nations Interregional Crime and Justice Research Institute (UNICRI)

United Nations Population Fund (UNFPA)

United Nations Research Institute for Social Development (UNRISD)

United Nations Volunteers (UNV)

World Food Programme (WFP)

World Tourism Organization (WTO)

World Trade Organization (WTO); successor to the General Agreement on
    Tariffs and Trade (GATT)


# THE EUROPEAN UNION (EU)

*http://www.europa.eu.int/*

## Original Organizations (traditionally referred to collectively as the European Community or the European Communities (EC))

European Coal and Steel Community (ECSC)

European Economic Community (EEC or Common Market), now officially
    named the European Community (EC)

European Atomic Energy Community (Euratom)

## Principal Legislative, Judicial, Policy Making, and Financial Bodies

Council of the European Union

Court of Justice

European Commission

European Council

European Court of Auditors

European Investment Bank (EIB)

European Parliament

## Other Consultative and Functional Bodies

Committee of the Regions

Economic and Social Committee

European Agency for Safety and Health at Work

European Agency for the Evaluation of Medicinal Products (EMEA)

European Environment Agency (EEA)

European Foundation for the Improvement of Living and Working Conditions

European Monetary Institute (EMI)

European Monitoring Centre for Drugs and Drug Addiction

Office for Harmonization in the Internal Market (Trade Marks and Designs) (OHIM)

## OTHER INTERNATIONAL ORGANIZATIONS

(* means United States is a member or participant.)

*African Development Bank Group

*Arctic Council

*Asian Development Bank (ADB)

*Asia-Pacific Economic Cooperation (APEC)

Association of Caribbean States (ACS)

Association of South East Asian Nations (ASEAN)

Benelux Economic Union

Black Sea Economic Cooperation (BSEC)

Caribbean Community and Common Market (CARICOM)

Central African Customs and Economic Union (UDEAC)

Central American Common Market (CACM)

Central European Initiative (CEI)

*Colombo Plan for Cooperative Economic and Social Development in Asia and the Pacific

The Commonwealth (formerly the British Commonwealth)

Commonwealth of Independent States (CIS)

Council of Europe

*Customs Co-operation Council (CCC); official name of the World Customs Organization (WCO)

*European Bank for Reconstruction and Development (EBRD)

European Commission of Human Rights
*http://www.dhcommhr.coe.fr*

European Court of Human Rights
*http://www.echr.coe.int/*

European Economic Area (EEA)

European Free Trade Association (EFTA)

European Organization for Nuclear Research (CERN)

European Space Agency (ESA)

*Fund for the Protection of the World Cultural and Natural Heritage

*Group of Seven (G-7)

*Group of Eight (G-8)

*Group of Ten (G-10)

*Hague Conference on Private International Law

*Inter-American Defense Board

*Inter-American Development Bank (IDB)

*International Bureau of Weights and Measures

*International Chamber of Commerce (ICC)

*International Council for the Exploration of the Seas (ICES)

*International Criminal Police Organization (ICPO or Interpol)

*International Energy Agency (IEA)

*International Institute for the Unification of Private Law

*International Mobile Satellite Organization (Inmarsat)

*International Organization for Legal Metrology

*International Organization for Migration

*International Telecommunications Satellite Organization (Intelsat)

*International Union for Conservation of Nature and Natural Resources (IUCN or World Conservation Union)

*International Whaling Commission

*Interparliamentary Union

Latin American Economic System (LAES)

Latin American Integration Association (LAIA)

League of Arab States (Arab League)

Nonaligned Movement (NAM)

Nordic Council

*North American Free Trade Agreement (NAFTA)

*North Atlantic Cooperation Council

*North Atlantic Treaty Organization (NATO)

*Organization for Economic Cooperation and Development (OECD)

*Organization for Security and Co-operation in Europe (OSCE)

*Organization for the Prevention of Chemical Weapons

Organization of African Unity (OAU)

*Organization of American States (OAS)

Organization of Arab Petroleum Exporting Countries (OAPEC)

Organization of the Islamic Conference (OIC)

Organization of the Petroleum Exporting Countries (OPEC)

*Pan American Health organization (PAHO)

*Partnership for Peace

*Permanent Court of Arbitration

South Asian Association for Regional Cooperation (SAARC)

*South Pacific Commission (SPC)

Southern African Development Community (SADC)

Western European Union (WEU)

*World Customs Organization (WCO) (working name of the Customs Co-operation Council (CCC))

# Appendix E

## Legal Metasites on the World Wide Web

A mass of legal information is available through the Internet. The sites listed here are gateways to that information. Most provide links to scores of specialized legal sites, usually categorized by type (law firms, government sites, case law, etc.) or subject area (family law, comparative law, etc.). Many provide facilities for searching databases of statutes, judicial opinions, government documents, and the like.

No one metasite, however comprehensive or specialized, can keep up with the explosion of legal information on the Internet. For general research, it is advisable to go through several gateways. This list highlights noteworthy features of certain sites, but those sites usually have other features as well, and similar features can be found on other sites.

As with all other information on the World Wide Web, legal information found there must be viewed with caution: Web sites can be biased or selective for commercial or ideological reasons, and they are sometimes simply wrong. Beyond the normal hazards of Internet research, the law itself is constantly changing; legal information on the Web cannot always be completely up-to-date. Finally, materials on the Web are not always as complete, accurate, or clearly formatted as the print versions; it is still often the case that the most reliable source for a statute, decision, or other legal document is the appropriate volume in a law library.

### General Sites with Primary Focus on U.S. Law

Cornell Law School: *Legal Information Institute*
*http://www.law.cornell.edu/*
Combines capsule descriptions of areas of law with links to basic sources.

FindLaw
*http://www.findlaw.com/*

Georgia State University College of Law: *Meta-Index for U.S. Legal Research*
*http://gsulaw.gsu.edu/metaindex/*
Search engines for many legal databases conveniently organized.

Hieros Gamos
*http://www.hg.org/*

Internet Legal Resource Guide
*http://www.ilrg.com/*
Includes large "Academia" category for information of special interest to law and pre-law students.

Katsuey's Legal Gateway
*http://www.katsuey.com/*

MegaLaw.com
*http://www.megalaw.com/*

Open Directory Project: *Law*
*http://www.dmoz.org/Society/Law/*

Rominger Legal
*http://www.romingerlegal.com/*

# U.S. Government Sites[1]

Government Printing Office: *GPO Access*
*http://www.access.gpo.gov/su_docs/*
Keyword searching of many government documents, including a large and varied collection under the heading "Core Documents of U.S. Democracy."

Library of Congress

### Law Library of Congress: *Guide to Law Online*
*http://lcweb2.loc.gov/glin/worldlaw.html*
Links to primary and secondary legal materials for virtually all nations of the world.

### THOMAS
*http://thomas.loc.gov/*
Search engine for information about current and recent federal legislation.

National Archives and Records Administration
*http://www.nara.gov/*
Links to text of certain legislative and executive materials including Presidential documents; links to Web sites for Presidential libraries; photographic images of the Declaration of Independence and the Constitution.

---

[1]See also sites in Appendix C (*United States Government Agencies*).

**The White House**
*http://www.whitehouse.gov/*
Well-organized links to specific government information and services on the
Internet, and to government Web sites generally, under the headings "Commonly
Requested Federal Services" and "Interactive Citizens Handbook."

## Sites Emphasizing International and Non-U.S. Law[2]

**American Law Sources On-line (ALSO)**
*http://www.lawsource.com/*
Links to materials on the law of Canada, the United States, and Mexico.

**American Society of International Law: *ASIL Guide to Electronic Resources for
International Law***
*http://www.asil.org/resource/Home.htm*

**University of California at Berkeley Library: *European Union Internet Resources***
*http://www.lib.berkeley.edu/GSSI/eu.html*

**University of Toronto Law Library: *Legal Resources***
*http://www.law-lib.utoronto.ca/resources/intro.htm*
Comprehensive links to Canadian law sites.

**The University of Western Australia Faculty of Law: *Public International Law***
*http://www.law.ecel.uwa.edu.au/intlaw/*

**Washburn University School of Law: *Foreign and International Law Web***
*http://www.washlaw.edu/forint/*

**York University Law Library**

*http://info.library.yorku.ca/depts/law/linksuk.htm*
Links for the law of the United Kingdom.

*http://info.library.yorku.ca/depts/law/linksForeign.htm*
Links for international and non-U.K. law.

## Specialized Sites

**Canon Law Homepage**
*http://canonlaw.anglican.org/Section15.htm*
Links to materials on both Anglican and Roman Catholic canon law, plus
extensive list of "Links to Cognate Subjects."

---

[2]See also sites in Appendix D (*International Agencies*).

## Courts.net
*http://www.courts.net/*
Links to official Web sites of federal, state, and local courts in the United States.

## University of Pittsburgh School of Law: *Jurist*
*http://www.jurist.law.pitt.edu/*
Site focusing on legal scholarship and teaching; includes links to sites maintained by individual professors on particular topics.

## Law Library Research Xchange
*http://www.llrx.com/*
Site focusing on electronic legal research and related subjects; frequent reviews and links to useful sites for legal research. Includes list of "meta links" at *http://www.llrx.com/sources.html.*

## Villanova University School of Law: *State Court Locator*
*http://vls.law.vill.edu/Locator/statecourt/*
Links to home pages and opinions of state judiciaries.